In Mortal Hands

IN MORTAL HANDS

A CAUTIONARY HISTORY OF THE NUCLEAR AGE

STEPHANIE COOKE

Dearest —
With very best
wishes
Stephanie Cooke

BLOOMSBURY

NEW YORK · BERLIN · LONDON

Published by Bloomsbury USA, New York

All papers used by Bloomsbury USA are natural, recyclable products made from
wood grown in well-managed forests. The manufacturing processes conform to the
environmental regulations of the country of origin.

LIBRARY OF CONGRESS CATALOGING-IN-PUBLICATION DATA

Cooke, Stephanie.
In mortal hands : a cautionary history of the nuclear age /
Stephanie Cooke.—1st U.S. ed.
p. cm.
Includes bibliographical references and index.
ISBN-13: 978-1-59691-617-3 (hardcover)
ISBN-10: 1-59691-617-6 (hardcover)
1. World politics—20th century.   2. World politics—21st century.
3. Nuclear energy—Political aspects.   4. Nuclear weapons—Political aspects.
5. Nuclear terrorism—Prevention.   I. Title.
D445.C7355 2009
909.82'5—dc22
2008039388

First published by Bloomsbury USA in 2009
This paperback edition published in 2010

Paperback ISBN: 978-1-60819-041-6

1 3 5 7 9 10 8 6 4 2

Designed by Rachel Reiss
Typeset by Westchester Book Group
Printed in the United States of America by Worldcolor Fairfield

For James, my son

Contents

Foreword to the Paperback Edition

MY LIBRARY CONTAINS ONE BOOKSHELF dedicated to the history of nuclear bombs, and one to the history of nuclear power. Yet aside from the classic writings of Walt Patterson and Margaret Gowing, scarcely a book on either shelf addresses the other topic more than in passing—as if the nuclear power industry's anxiety to separate these intertwined subjects had somehow infected their chroniclers.

The 1946 Acheson-Lilienthal report, drafted under J. Robert Oppenheimer's guidance, concluded that "the development of atomic energy for peaceful purposes and the development of atomic energy for bombs are in much of their course interchangeable and interdependent," so only a global authority controlling all nuclear materials, starting at the uranium mines, could block the spread of bombs. This proved infeasible. Evolving technology and commerce have since nearly eliminated the report's distinction between "safe" and "dangerous" activities. But the report's prediction that national rivalries, subnational instabilities, and human frailties would prove stronger than policing and treaties has turned out to be true. By 2010, the overlapping and mutually reinforcing evolution of government-driven nuclear bombs and business-driven nuclear power had created a world with

- threats of nuclear bomb capabilities' spreading (both to new countries and to substate actors) that are now formally considered just as grave as the threat of great-power conflicts;

- nine known nuclear weapons states, several of which have been major clandestine arms exporters;
- a perpetual shadowy battle by intelligence services to keep tens of thousands of nuclear bombs, and materials to make far more, from reaching the terrorist groups that seek them, or, if terrorists do get their hands on the bombs, to prevent their use;
- existential threats to the stability of nuclear-armed Pakistan, which appears to have proliferated to Iraq, Iran, Libya, Syria, North Korea, and perhaps others, yet now wants help with its ostensibly civilian nuclear program;
- major obstacles to stopping volatile Iran's bomb program;
- perhaps forty non-weapons states with the technical capability to make bombs—some, including at least two major industrial countries, within months;
- accelerating collapse—often spurred by intertwined commercial and national interests—of the weak international systems meant to inhibit the spread of bombs;
- a world nuclear watchdog—tasked with both nuclear safeguards *and* promotion—so schizophrenic that Sigvard Eklund, its head for twenty years, turned out to have helped lead and conceal a clandestine nuclear weapons program in his own country;
- rapidly spreading interest among developing countries in obtaining nuclear technologies, often with thinly disguised military motives;
- concealment by clever propaganda, led by major firms and governments, of nuclear power's continued economic collapse in all market economies; and
- a stew of venality, dishonesty, secrecy, bureaucracy, carelessness, and ignorance masking these developments in a dense fog of disinformation.

The root cause of this suicidal spiral is the interaction of mortally dangerous technologies with inherent human frailties. To get through the nuclear age alive, we must understand, confront, and overcome this challenge. Stephanie Cooke summarizes: "The entire nuclear endeavor was fertile ground for human fallibility, wishful thinking, deception, and plain naïveté. The temptations proved too irresistible, and the dangers too large, for mere mortals to control." Her masterly, sweeping, lucid book reunifies the sundered halves of the world's nuclear history, leaving almost no significant gaps (other than nuclear naval propulsion). Only by seeing the nuclear era as an integrated whole can we grasp

> the relationship between the military and civilian sides, and the fact that one sprang from the other, more for political reasons than because nuclear electricity was necessarily the best way forward. This in turn encouraged fanciful thinking about risks and costs and created a situation in which safeguards against proliferation were essential, yet never adequate to the task.

Understanding this—especially nuclear power's troubled history and unpromising future—must inform today's choice between, as Bernard Baruch said in 1946, the quick and the dead.

If combining nuclear technology with human nature creates peril, which of these two parts can change? Millennia of experience teach us that the perfection of human beings is a long and arduous quest, so nuclear weapons may well kill us long before we've become perfect enough to manage them safely. That's why some of the sagest voices in security and diplomacy across the political spectrum now call for the abolition of nuclear weapons. Realization is spreading that neither America's $5.5 trillion nuclear weapons effort nor any other has brought or can bring security. In 2009, President Obama, echoing President Reagan, declared in Prague that the U.S. would "take concrete steps towards a world without nuclear weapons"—steps lately crafted in the Nuclear Posture Review and a new U.S./Russian arms reduction agreement. Meanwhile, nuclear power's marketplace collapse, faster and surer than progress in arms control, holds the promise that vibrant competitors can more effectively, cheaply, and promptly meet energy needs and solve the oil and climate problems.

But this is not currently the prevalent policy. "Nuclear weapons," notes Ms. Cooke, "have not made the world safer; nor has nuclear energy weaned us from oil. Yet we are pouring significantly more money, brainpower, and resources into both." But policy *can* change if both policymakers and citizens become informed and insistent. It is hardly an exaggeration, therefore, to say that this book's insights are vital for human survival.

Serious students of global affairs have known since the 1970s that climate change and nuclear proliferation are the two biggest threats to

human survival, so energy policy must avoid both. Instead, by choice or
ineptitude, it's often *driving* both, or, at best, trading off one for the
other even though neither risk is necessary or economic. In fact, as I
noted in *Foreign Policy* on January 21, 2010, "The problems of [nuclear]
proliferation, climate change, and oil dependence share both a nuclear
non-solution that confounds U.S. policy goals and a non-nuclear solution that achieves them."* All three issues seem difficult only because
of the incorrect assumption that their solutions will be costly. Actually, the solutions are not costly but *profitable*, even if we assume that
all "external" costs, those paid in taxes or risks rather than at the meter
or fuel pump, are zero—a conservatively low estimate.

Climate protection, for example, is generally profitable because saving fuel costs less than buying fuel. Discussing profits, jobs, and competitive advantage rather than cost, burden, and sacrifice sweetens the
politics. Major firms have made profits of billions of dollars by substi-
tuting efficiency for fuel, cutting energy per dollar of output by 6 to 16
percent a year. China sustained for a quarter century, briefly lost, and
has now resumed 5 percent annual cuts in energy intensity, and when
the U.S. paid attention to oil in 1977–85, it cut oil intensity by 5.2 percent a year—yet refraining from adding to climate chaos requires low-
ering global energy intensity by just 3 to 4 percent a year. Moreover,
most of the projected economic growth is in China and India, making
energy efficiency easier because both are still building their infrastructure, and building it correctly now is far easier than fixing it later.

Carbon emissions come about two-fifths each from burning coal,
chiefly in power plants, and from burning oil. Both coal and oil can be
entirely and even profitably displaced by more efficient use and benign, secure, reliable alternative supplies. (The U.S., for example, can
profitably displace the coal-fired half of its electricity more cheaply
than operating existing power plants; indeed, there are enough energy-
efficiency and renewable options available to replace existing coal
plants more than 22 times over before any new coal-fired plant would
be economically competitive—all without nuclear power.) In 2011,
Rocky Mountain Institute will publish *Reinventing Fire*, a detailed
roadmap of this journey beyond fossil fuels. The oil solution has al-

---

*www.rmi.org/rmi/Library/2010-03_ForeignPolicyProliferationOilClimate
Pattern, expanded at www.rmi.org/rmi/Library/2010-02_ProliferationOilClim
atePattern.

ready been published (in 2004)* and implementation appears to be ahead of schedule. U.S. gasoline demand peaked in 2007; the oil demand of industrialized countries in 2005; and Deutsche Bank forecasts that world oil use will peak in 2016, and by 2030 fall to 8 percent less than in 2009. In short, oil is becoming uncompetitive even at low prices before it becomes unavailable even at high prices.

Today's "nuclear renaissance" is meant not to displace oil (which rarely makes electricity nowadays) but to displace *coal* and thus protect the climate. But observed market prices and deployment rates tell the opposite story. New nuclear power would displace coal, but is so costly and slow that it would save about 2 to 20 times less carbon per dollar and about 20 to 40 times less carbon per year than buying cheaper, faster competitors instead. These competitors are (a) efficient use, (b) renewable power sources, and (c) cogenerating electricity together with useful heating or cooling in factories and buildings. The climate problem needs judicious, not indiscriminate, investments to get the most solution per dollar and per year. The nuclear industry is keen that you not understand this choice and that the press ignore it.[†]

Nuclear expansion not only reduces and retards climate protection, but the assumption of many policymakers that it's real, necessary, and economical also makes nonproliferation impossible. Fortunately, all these assumptions are demonstrably wrong. The variability of wind and solar power has been overcome at trivial extra cost, even at very large scale, by properly diversifying, forecasting, and integrating them with the grid; electricity storage breakthroughs are not needed. The prices of such renewable power sources—often led by China—continue to plummet while nuclear capital costs soar. Nuclear construction struggles to offset reactor retirements (global net nuclear capacity fell in both 2008 and 2009), and totaled only about 4.4 percent of all global generating capacity under construction in 2007. Of the 57 nuclear units listed by the International Atomic Energy Agency as "under construction" at the time of this writing, 12 have been so listed for over twenty years, 36 have no official start-up date, half are late, 42 are in four centrally planned and nontransparent systems (China with 40 percent, followed by Russia, India, and South Korea), and 100 percent were bought by central planners, generally

*www.oilendgame.com.
[†]www.rmi.org/rmi/Library/E09-01_NuclearPowerClimateFixOrFolly.

from the public purse. None were free-market transactions properly compared with or competed against alternatives.

In 2010, press reports claimed U.S. nuclear power had officially revived as President Obama announced an $8.3 billion federal loan guarantee for twin reactors in Georgia from an $18.5 billion fund, and his budget sought to triple that fund to $54.5 billion. Those reports are premature. His announcement—a bid for Republican votes on energy and climate bills—was only provisional, because the plant must first be licensed (its design has yet to be approved), two agencies and members of Congress strongly disagree about default risk and hence the fee the utility is legally required to pay in order to cover it, and the builders haven't yet provided the required 20 percent equity. In August 2005, the next half dozen U.S. nuclear reactors, assuming that any would actually be built, were offered new subsidies (on top of old ones) rivaling or exceeding their forecast construction costs. For the next three years, nuclear power also enjoyed the most robust political support and capital markets in history. Yet none of the thirty-three proposed plants received a penny of equity investment from the private capital market—because there's no business case. In the several years needed to license the Georgia plant, or any other plants offered loan guarantees, the competitive disadvantage will widen even further (new nuclear is already thrice the cost of new firmed windpower). This may become obvious even to the plant owners, whose shareholders won't want to take even a quarter of the risk imposed on taxpayers.

In short, the United States, like many other countries, was hit by a tsunami of nuclear socialism, oddly promoted by arch-foes of socialism in other spheres. Massive federal bailouts may seem to work at first: If you defibrillate a corpse, it will jump—but it won't revive. All the fundamental economic trends disfavor nuclear power. So, paradoxically, does the fervent support of political leaders, because historically that support has tended to harm nuclear power by degrading safety culture, suppressing concerns, and hence encouraging accidents (many near misses quietly continue worldwide*). Governments will be the last to know, but the global marketplace has already rejected nuclear power. French president Nicolas Sarkozy, the world's top nuclear salesman, decried the "scandal" of the "ostracism of nuclear en-

---

*www.greens-efa.org/cms/topics/dokbin/181/181995.residual_risk@en.pdf.

ergy by international financing,"* but Citigroup's latest analysis explains why in its title: "New Nuclear—The Economics Say No."†

"Micropower"—cogeneration plus renewables, excluding big hydro dams—delivered in 2008 some 91 percent of the world's new electricity and 17 percent of the world's total electricity (vs. nuclear power's approximate 13 percent share of total electricity, heading for 10 percent or less by 2030). In 2008, renewables got more global investment than fossil-fueled generation; renewables (excluding big hydro) added 40 billion watts and received $100 billion of private capital, while nuclear received and added zero. New policy or polity can't reverse the collapse of the nuclear market: even France's uniquely single-minded 1970–2000 nuclear program suffered 3.5-fold escalation in real capital cost per kilowatt and nearly doubled construction duration.‡

"New" kinds of reactors (many even more proliferative) can't compete either: even if the one-third of a modern nuclear plant's capital cost that buys its nuclear steam supply system were *free*, the other two-thirds would still be far too costly. "Small modular" reactors don't scale down well and are decades behind their competitors' economies of mass production; they can never catch up.§ As I wrote in *Foreign Affairs* in summer 1980 (and is even more applicable now), nuclear power's "risks, including proliferation, are . . . not a minor counterweight to enormous advantages but rather a gratuitous supplement to enormous disadvantages."¶

The economic death throes of nuclear power offer a unique opportunity to reverse the policy muddle. Nuclear advocates claim in one breath that their option is competitive and in the next that it can't survive without escalating subsidies. But without being antinuclear, the U.S. Administration could simply accept the market's sad verdict on this sixty-year-old technology, reverse the "subsidy arms race,"

---

*March 8, 2010, speech to the OECD's International Conference on Access to Civil Nuclear Energy, http://ambafrance-in.org/france_inde/spip.php?article 6264.

†Released November 9, 2009, www.citigroupgeo.com/pdf/SEU27102.pdf.

‡Released October 6, 2009, www.iiasa.ac.at/Admin/PUB/Documents/IR-09 -036.pdf.

§www.rmi.org/rmi/Library/2009-07_NuclearSameOldStory.

¶www.rmi.org/rmi/Library/S80-02_NuclearPowerNuclearBombs.

and start moving toward a subsidy-free energy system, cutting budget deficits by many tens of billions of dollars per year.

Acting as if the U.S. needs nuclear power gives all countries with less fuel, wealth, or skill an ironclad excuse for claiming they need it too. Instead—applying abroad its domestic emphasis on efficiency and renewables—the U.S. should spread those nonviolent technologies freely and widely to fulfill the developing world's need for secure and affordable energy services. (Let countries wanting specifically *nuclear* technology explain why they want the costliest, slowest, hardest energy option.) Developing countries sought that same help in Copenhagen to protect the climate, and many to get off oil. Answering their plea with options far cheaper and faster would undercut claims to need nuclear power, just as reducing nuclear weapons undercuts claims that non-weapons states should get the same arms that the weapons states have broken their promises to retire.

Most important, a best-buys-first energy investment strategy, at home and abroad, would stop the spread of do-it-yourself bomb kits in innocent-looking civilian disguise. This would not make proliferation impossible, but would make it far more difficult: if bomb ingredients were no longer major items of commerce, they'd become harder to get, more conspicuous to try to get, and more politically costly to be caught trying to get, because now their purpose would be *unambiguously* military. This disambiguation, based on taking economics seriously, is our best and perhaps last chance to corral nuclear bombs, stabilize climate, and achieve just global development.

As a physicist studying nuclear issues since the 1960s (when, like Stephanie Cooke, I thought nuclear power sounded like a good idea), active in nonproliferation since the 1970s, knowing many of the people and events featured in this book, I am struck by how its startling, complex, intertwined events hold a profoundly simple lesson.

The world is held hostage by manmade substances so powerful that rapidly crushing a piece the size of an orange can instantly incinerate a city. Releasing that energy slowly enough to light the city instead has proven difficult, risky, and very costly. The myth that this energy option must nonetheless be promoted and adopted at the expense of all others—worsening climate change, weakening free markets, undermining free societies, and making proliferation unstoppable—is the greatest obstacle to achieving a safer, cooler, richer, fairer world. Stephanie Cooke's brilliant synthesis of the *whole* nuclear story provides the insight we need today to turn that obstacle and threat into opportunity and hope.

Amory B. Lovins
Chairman and Chief Scientist
Rocky Mountain Institute (www.rmi.org)
Old Snowmass, Colorado
May 23, 2010

Introduction

O N AUGUST 5, 1945, AS AN Army Air Forces pilot and his crew loaded a nuclear weapon called "Little Boy" into a B-29, a young British woman named Mary Buneman, nine months pregnant and living in Berkeley, California, felt the first unmistakable pains of labor. Across the Pacific on Tinian Island, where the loading operation was under way, a softball game also was in progress. The pilot, Lieutenant Colonel Paul W. Tibbets, asked a sign painter to leave the field so he could apply his mother's name beneath the cockpit window—"nice and big," Tibbets had said. That day and whenever he got anxious, Tibbets remembered how his mother had assured him he would not lose his life as punishment for arguing fiercely with his father about becoming a pilot. Her name was Enola Gay.[1]

Sleep was impossible for some of the *Enola Gay* crewmen that night, just as it was for Mary Buneman at the Berkeley General Hospital. Tibbets and his crew began the fifteen-hundred-mile journey to Japan at 2:45 the following morning. While the *Enola Gay*, with Little Boy on board, flew through the darkness on a mission that would immediately end some seventy thousand lives, Mary gave birth to her second son. It was still Sunday in Berkeley, in the late afternoon. "Nothing was further from my thoughts than the time and the date in Japan," Mary later recorded in her diary.[2]

Not yet twenty-five, Mary Buneman (pronounced Bune-a-man) had lived with the secret of the bomb project since 1943, when her husband, Oscar, told her about it "in hushed tones of deathly secrecy." The couple, still in England then, was about to move to the United States with their first son. At Berkeley, Oscar Buneman's expertise in mathematics and physics was applied to work on uranium enrichment, the process used to make the fissile material inside the core of "Little Boy."

The bomb was dropped from an altitude of about ninety-six hundred meters and exploded five hundred and eighty meters above Hiroshima, a little to the northwest of the city's center. Later, a nineteen-year-old woman who survived reported a remarkable sight near a public garden. Amid the bodily remains, burned black and immobilized at the moment of impact, there was, she said, "a charred body of a woman standing frozen in a running posture with one leg lifted and her baby tightly clutched in her arms."[3]

On August 9, a second nuclear weapon, called "Fat Man," was dropped on Nagasaki, immediately claiming another estimated forty thousand lives. The total death toll from both bombs would climb over the next five years to more than two hundred and fifty thousand.[4]

At the hospital in Berkeley, flowers and gifts arrived, along with the grim headlines from Japan. Mary shared a room with a Venezuelan lady named Mercedes, who had given birth to a girl a few hours after Mary's son was born. Mercedes was married to an American sailor stationed on a ship somewhere near Japan. The decision to drop the bombs was made in part to prevent soldiers and sailors like him from risking their lives by invading Japan to force surrender. But Mary's roommate was crying.

"Why did they have to go and drop another?" she protested through her sobs. "The first one would have finished the war off."[5]

WHY INDEED?

Physicists had known the answer, or so they thought, as far back as the early 1900s: the first nation to detonate a weapon based on the energy inside an atom would control the world. Everything changed in the vortex of life-and-death events that surrounded August 6, 1945. The newborns would never know life without nuclear weapons; a mother and child were already among its victims; and a pilot, comforted by the memory of his mother's words, thought that all he was doing was bringing an end to war. The United States had emerged as the leader of the non-Communist world.

To some prescient observers, however, the bombing of Hiroshima signaled the end of democracy as it was experienced then and the beginning of the modern superstate.[6] The natural order of things had been overturned; for the new order to take hold and flourish, security and secrecy were essential. America became a classified nation, at once fearsome and fearful.[7] While her husband worked on the bomb, Mary Buneman was instructed not to make friends with her neighbors, a request, by the way, that she ignored. Then, after the war, when the couple returned to England, Mary was isolated from the rest of society in one of the newly built, heavily guarded "atomic villages," where she lived under the watchful eye of security officials. Even back then, though, the fences were not as secure as they looked, and the secrets were leaking.

The scientists and their government overseers were at a crossroads. Thousands were now employed in the business of making nuclear weapons, but the war was over. What next for them?

Within less than two years, they knew the answer. The term "cold war" had been invented to describe deteriorating relations between the United States and its wartime ally the Soviet Union. That became the galvanizing force for building more bombs. Soon the scientists were inventing the thermonuclear weapon, with an explosive force a thousand times more powerful than that of the bombs dropped on Japan, and these weapons had in theory unlimited destructive potential. The Manhattan Project never really stopped.

Governments saw that there could be a positive side to nuclear and began to promote it as a way of producing electricity. In the United States this "peaceful uses" aspect not only provided a welcome antidote to the government's determination to rapidly escalate nuclear weapons production but was part of a program designed to win public acceptance of the expensive new arsenal. In other countries, like Britain and France, the primary purpose of so-called dual-use reactors was to produce plutonium for bombs. Yet the public was sold on the idea that the reactors were meant for electricity. In this heady atmosphere, when nuclear was seen as cutting-edge technology and the public's appetite for such advances ran high, officials could get away with promises that nuclear energy would eventually prove "too cheap to meter." That this next chapter in the nuclear story might lead to covert nuclear weapons programs was widely recognized within the elite circles of scientists and government officials advancing the cause, but they convinced themselves that a solution would be found. It was easy enough to downplay the problem to the public, which is precisely what President Dwight D. Eisenhower did in his famous 1953 Atoms for Peace speech, because the issues were so complex. Nuclear energy would not come cheap, nor would it ever be freed of its link to nuclear weapons, because the critical technologies associated with both were one and the same, and both these facts were understood at the time.

Money for nuclear development was plentiful in just about every industrially advanced country, even though budgets were stretched in other areas because people were still recovering from war. With governments lavishing generous salaries and other benefits on them, the nuclear scientists and engineers tended to develop a sense they were special and "above" the rest of society. Language became detached. Meeting with defense officials about the hydrogen bomb in 1949, one well-known physicist talked about how nuclear war could be waged through the use of "radioactive products"—as if he were a Madison Avenue advertising executive.[8]

Naturally, with so much money coming their way, the scientists went wild with ideas. They thought they could use this extraordinary energy to make deserts bloom by hooking up desalinization plants to reactors. Controlled nuclear explosions would divert mighty rivers, create canals, and carve tunnels through hard granite mountains. Most seriously advanced was a plan to excavate a new sea-level canal, to supplement or replace the Panama Canal, accommodating larger ships.[9]

The essence of the nuclear dream lay in the man-made production of plutonium, a chemical element created in great secrecy during World War II, and one that is lethal when inhaled in microscopic amounts. Because it is both radioactive and fissile, meaning it can sustain a chain reaction, access to it even after the war remained tightly restricted, so a mystique grew up around plutonium that uranium never had. Even its name, derived from the planet Pluto, had dark connotations because of its association with the Greek god of the underworld.[10]

Nevertheless, with electricity use bound to increase, the idea was to produce plutonium in large quantities by separating it out from conventional used nuclear fuel, then burning it in advanced "breeder" reactors. The plants would generate electricity while breeding more plutonium. The plutonium and residual uranium in the spent breeder fuel could then be recovered for use in more fast breeders. Nuclear people believed that through modern alchemy they could create a cycle of endless energy. It was a tantalizing prospect, so much so that breeders were expected to be dominant over conventional reactors by 2000. The prospect of breeders created a new danger by encouraging utilities to reprocess spent fuel instead of directly burying it in the ground. That put tons of plutonium into commercial circulation, raising the prospect for some that it might be diverted for use in illicit bomb programs. The breeders that were eventually built proved more costly and accident-prone than expected, and, moreover, unnecessary since huge uranium deposits were being found.[11] Breeders were symptomatic of the larger nuclear story—a big prize that kept everyone going but in the end proved too dangerous and expensive, and disappointed.

THE GLOSS HAD already begun to fade in 1980 when I began reporting on the industry for the McGraw-Hill newsletters *Nucleonics Week* and *NuclearFuel*, well-known within the nuclear world. India had exploded a bomb using plutonium from a U.S.-assisted reprocessing program. The Europeans were trying to figure out what to do about Abdul Q. Khan's theft of nuclear secrets from Holland and his flight to Pakistan. The accident at Three Mile Island had occurred one year earlier, and reactor orders in the United States had ended. In short, there was mounting evidence that the nuclear dream was not only fading but giving way to a fitful, troubling sleep. The costs—financially and politically—were climbing, and the threat of unwanted clandestine nuclear weapons programs was increasing. Pakistan was an ongoing worry. Then, in 1981, Israeli fighter jets bombed the Osirak reactor in Iraq. This set the scene for a lengthy nuclear-centered drama that culminated initially in the 1991 Gulf War and finally in the Iraq War.

The civilian nuclear enterprise is more politicized than any other industry, even oil, because of its close link to nuclear weapons. Power, secrecy, fear, and greed run like currents through the underbrush, and that has always drawn people in. It drew me in. There is a dark allure about the hidden channels of nuclear commerce and the people who do not want to talk about them. Nuclear people at first seemed cold, distant, and arrogant, and that was a problem for their public image. It was also a problem for me when I first started reporting on the industry. Covering conferences was a daunting prospect. But the individuals were not always like that once you got to know them. The late Bertrand Goldschmidt, one of the architects of the French nuclear program and a leading light among the safeguards crowd, was charming and irreverent. He would say things like "I can never remember what is classified and what is not."[12]

Naturally reporters were not entirely welcome among people who wanted to keep things secret, but Goldschmidt was different. Upon introducing himself to me at a conference in Mexico City, he immediately invited me to sit with him at lunch. While we ate, he told me how he had started his career by separating isotopes for Marie Curie in 1933, the year before she died. He was also the only Frenchman to have worked inside the United States on the Manhattan Project. This lasted for only a few exciting months, but he was there to witness Glenn Seaborg tell the scientists at the Met Lab in Chicago they had successfully separated plutonium. Seaborg became a friend and Goldschmidt a great believer in, and promoter of, breeders and plutonium recycling. Early in his career Goldschmidt played an important role in assisting the Israelis with their plutonium-based secret nuclear weapons project.

In the 1990s, after I had stopped regularly covering the industry for the newsletters, I wrote occasional articles about nuclear developments, in particular the discovery of a covert nuclear weapons program in Iraq. Naturally I talked with friends in London, where I was living, about what I was doing, dropping in stories about the people I had known in the past and the nuclear plants and uranium mines I had visited—and explaining with a great deal of anger how nuclear supplier nations like the United States were complicit in Iraq's nuclear effort. One of those friends, the author James Thackara, urged me to write a book. Through his nuclear parable, the novel *America's Children*, Jim brought literature to bear on an inscrutable subject whose moral and technical complexities might seem beyond poetic vision, and this work launched him on a lifetime of activism in the field.

We had talked for hours and hours about the situation in Iraq and North Korea, and the failings of governments and the International Atomic Energy Agency (IAEA), and had even penned a joint op-ed piece for the *International Herald Tribune*.[13] I protested that I wasn't really qualified to go ahead with a book. He pointed out that I had been on the inside, socially, journalistically, and technically, and still emerged not yet in a state of denial about the industry's seemingly intractable problems. In fact, my path had followed precisely the opposite course. I started out as a believer in nuclear energy, basically thinking reactors were safe and having little understanding of the relationship between the civilian side of nuclear energy and nuclear weapons. Gradually my views changed.

Jim pointed out that in adapting Terry Southern's script for *Dr. Strangelove*, Stanley Kubrick decided to make it a black comedy. He needed to get to the heart of the absurdities of the new situation—that mutually assured destruction was all that lay between survival and extinction—and comedy was, in a sense, beyond serious. Outrage and the ability to communicate from the inside could go a long way toward explaining the enormity of the situation to people unequipped with the technical knowledge to understand it.

As we sat on a playground in north London, watching my then two-year-old son tear from the slide to the swings, Jim said I should explain the quandary: it was not just that Iraq had abused the system to acquire nuclear weapons but that here was one more example of a breach of faith in the people and organizations most counted on to contain the spread of nuclear weapons. We talked like this for a while, sitting on a bench, our eyes on James, and I guess you could say a tiny seed was planted. The idea nibbled away at me until I began to agree with my friend Jim. I called an old friend that night, who urged me on. And after talking awhile with her, I could see that my mental scrapbook of memories offered a kind of close-up history of the nuclear era. Perhaps I did have something to offer, a story to share.

During the 1980s, when I started out, Hans Blix and Mohamed ElBaradei were not household names. As the International Atomic Energy Agency's two top officials, they were key players in the nuclear dramas that were beginning to unfold in Iraq and North Korea. Soon after the 1991 Gulf War I interviewed ElBaradei, and later I talked to Blix. ElBaradei, his deputy, has since replaced him as director-general, and Blix went on to be chief UN inspector in Iraq during the buildup to the Iraq War. In the early 1990s, I met Rolf Ekeus and David Kay just after they uncovered in Iraq what IAEA inspectors had been missing for years, the seeds of a full-blown nuclear weapons program. Ekeus is the Swedish diplomat who oversaw the special United Nations inspection effort in Iraq after the 1991 Gulf War. His willingness to stand up to the Iraqis, backed by a coalition of determined governments, resulted in remarkable discoveries of secret chemical, biological, and nuclear weapons and missile programs—without the need for military action. Kay was employed by the IAEA but worked closely with Ekeus, and he spent hours with me discussing the way the inspections were carried out.

While researching this book, I met people I had not known before, including, in London, Lord Flowers, a leading industry figure whose seminal 1976 report on the future of nuclear energy in Britain laid down the gauntlet and provoked a fury of accusations that he had betrayed his own.[14] Our first meeting resulted in an introduction to his wife, Lady Flowers, the former Mary Buneman, whose diary I have relied upon for its personal insight into life in the nuclear world both during and after the war, on both sides of the Atlantic. Flowers introduced me to another extraordinary man, Sir Joseph Rotblat, a nuclear physicist and tireless campaigner for peace. He and the philosopher Bertrand Russell created the Pugwash Conferences on Science and World Affairs. In 1995, Rotblat and the organization were jointly awarded the Nobel Peace Prize. Some newspapers identified him then as only a "little-known" physicist, but scientists and officials in many countries knew him well.[15] He left the Manhattan Project on moral grounds and dedicated his life to eliminating nuclear weapons. Sadly, he died August 31, 2005, just eight months after I last interviewed him. He was ninety-six.

Because of the relatively brief time span of the nuclear industry and the fact that I began reporting on it in 1980, I am fortunate in having gotten to know many people associated with the very early days of postwar nuclear development. Over that period and in the course of researching and writing this book, I have interviewed countless nuclear scientists, industry leaders, and government officials, past and present, and read through hundreds of documents and magazine, newspaper, and newsletter articles.

My own career has not been exclusively devoted to the nuclear issue, but I found myself continually drawn back to it, in part because the subject was so fascinating and there were always stories that a magazine or newspaper wanted. For example, in 1994, still in London, I flew to Texas to take advantage of an unprecedented opportunity: the U.S. government had invited journalists to tour the Pantex nuclear weapons assembly plant, something that had never happened during the long years of the cold war.[16] Nuclear energy had already gone out of fashion by then, and it was during that fallow period in the late 1990s, when even news about Iraq's nuclear program had temporarily receded to the back pages, that my friend Jim convinced me it was time to tell the story of why and how the nuclear genie had flown so far.

Since then, with the issue of global warming high on the international agenda, nuclear energy is again a top priority. Equally if not more pressing is the continuing flow of news about suspected or existing nuclear bomb programs in the Middle East and North Korea and the prospect of others that might follow—significantly, as a result of the resurgence of "peaceful" nuclear energy. All of this makes the book even more relevant and timely than it seemed when I began writing it.

At a conference on nonproliferation in 1980, when I was just beginning to understand the familial connection between the civilian and military uses of nuclear, I asked an industry official what he thought the gathering was really all about. "These are the war and peace issues of our time," he gravely replied.[17] And so I have spent the past several years putting all my notes back together and adding many more to produce this book—a look back at the people who kept the industry going in spite of the dangers, with a cautionary note for those who would keep it going forward. Today, with the advent of "combat proliferation"— threats of military action against Iran, and the aftermath of a war in Iraq over suspect nuclear programs—these issues are even more pronounced.

Understanding how we got to this point also requires a grasp of the basic science and the early key discoveries. These were so extraordinary that they changed our fundamental understanding of how the universe works—in the same way the advent of nuclear weapons, which the science made possible, led to a new geopolitical order and a common understanding that for the first time in human history we had brought about the means for destroying life as we know it. Every person concerned about national security and future energy policy will find it helpful knowing these basic facts.

NUCLEAR ENERGY IS the term used to describe the release of heat that results when the nuclei of atoms are split apart or combined. When the strong forces that hold the nucleus together are disturbed, energy is unleashed. Scientists believe that nuclear energy was at work during the first split seconds of the universe, when all that existed was darkness. They estimate that cosmic burst of force occurred approximately fifteen billion years ago. Many billion years later, when the gases of our proto-planet coalesced into the recognizable shape of the earth, the thermal heat from radioactivity may have provided some of the energy it took to form volcanoes, sculpt mountains, shape continents and oceans, and turn the atmosphere into breathable air.

The sun runs on the nuclear energy that is freed when lighter nuclei combine to make heavier ones. This is called fusion, which has been used in advanced thermonuclear weapons but which proved too problematic for reactors. So for practical purposes, the nuclear energy discussed in this book primarily refers to activities relating to the heavier nuclei, mainly uranium. Heavy nuclei also generate energy when split into lighter ones. This is a unique process called fission, which occurs in radioactive elements such as uranium and thorium. The process is accelerated and becomes a self-sustaining chain reaction in reactors and nuclear weapons. In a reactor the chain reaction is controlled—in a weapon it is uncontrolled.

To see how this happens, first picture a space filled with white balls and a few black ones mixed in. A few bullets (neutrons) fly through the space. When they hit a white ball they are absorbed, but when they hit a black ball it splits and shoots a few more bullets. That is basically what happens inside natural uranium. It contains less than 1 percent of the isotope that fissions—U-235, represented by the black balls. The rest is known as U-238, the numbers being an expression of atomic weight. Now imagine a mix with a higher percentage of black balls. The bullets released by their explosions would hit other black balls, causing further explosions more frequently. That is what happens when uranium is "enriched." The U-235 is concentrated so that a chain reaction can occur.

To be effective in a weapon, the uranium has to be so loaded with U235 that an explosion occurs. That requires boosting the isotopic content to more than 90 percent. A reactor, on the other hand, requires some means of controlling the colliding balls. This is accomplished in two ways. To begin with, the uranium is only enriched to about 3 percent. (Some reactors still run on natural uranium, although they tend not to be as efficient.) Then, inside the reactor, neutron-absorbing rods are used to control, and if need be stop, the chain reaction. The "moderator"—ordinary water in most reactors—slows the neutrons, which also increases the likelihood that they will be absorbed by U-235 rather than U-238.

Seaborg and his colleagues at the University of California in Berkeley first discovered plutonium in 1941 and made giant leaps in their work at Chicago. A chemical element, plutonium occurs in only minute traces in nature, but by burning uranium in a reactor it can be artificially produced. To harvest the plutonium, the fuel has to be removed from the reactor and then subjected to a chemical separation process known as "reprocessing." Plutonium was first used in the July 1945

Alamogordo test in the New Mexico desert and then again in the bomb dropped on Nagasaki.

When unstable nuclei disintegrate, they give off alpha particles, beta particles, neutrons, gamma rays, and often a lot of heat, depending on their properties. Alpha emitters travel extremely short distances, losing all their energy in just a couple of inches in air, but inside the body they can damage living tissue and be lethal. Beta rays are high-energy electrons from the nucleus that move farther than alpha particles but less than gamma rays. Like alpha particles, beta rays pose the greatest danger if the material emitting them is ingested. Such unstable nuclei are said to be "radioactive," and the energy they emit is called "radiation." Whereas beta rays can be stopped by a sheet of aluminum, gamma rays are only blocked by thick lead. These unstable nuclei are usually called "radionuclides" or just "nuclides." Each nuclide has a signature property—how long it remains radioactive—from a millionth of a second to billions of years.

Exposures to radiation can cause damage to cells and to DNA and, if the exposures are great, immediate radiation burns, radiation sickness, and death within days or a few weeks. The effects depend on the amount and type of exposure, the rate of dose absorption, and the sensitivity of the exposed tissues. The Soviet ex-spy Alexander Litvinenko's death in November 2006 was attributed to the presence of a major dose of radioactive polonium-210 in his body. Litvinenko fell ill in London on November 1 and died twenty-three days later. Large concentrations of alpha emitters were found in his urine, and those who treated him also required monitoring since alpha emitters can enter the body through inhalation and cuts in the skin. Although some scientists claim that a little radiation is not harmful—and even may be beneficial—it has long been regarded as detrimental to health, in any amount.

WITHOUT RADIOACTIVITY, THE planet as we know it would not exist. Thermal energy from radioactive decay acts like a great heat exchanger, driving plate tectonics and forming part of an interacting system of matter and energy that shapes mountains and continents, carves out ocean and river basins, and produces volcanoes and glaciers.[18] Robert Oppenheimer called fusion energy "the power that drives the universe," but fission, or radioactivity, occurs in products created by fusion and the neutron absorption that takes place in supernova explosions.[19] When scientists finally began unraveling these complexities in the late nineteenth century and the early twentieth, they were continually confounded. "The spontaneity of the radiation is an enigma, a subject of profound astonishment," wrote Marie and Pierre Curie in 1900, two years after announcing the discovery of radium.[20] The couple mistakenly argued that the strange force was externally caused, until Ernest Rutherford and his collaborator Frederick Soddy proved them wrong. In 1899, Rutherford first declared the possibility that the answer to the puzzle lay within the atom, and three years later he suggested "an atomic phenomenon . . . in which new kinds of matter are produced."[21]

He and Soddy discovered a pattern in the way atoms disintegrated, with half the atoms in a given sample decaying over a specified period. He called this a half-life. So half the atoms in a radium sample would decay into atoms of radon gas after 1,602 years. In the next 1,602 years, half of the rest of the sample would decay, and so on. Uranium-238, the most common form of uranium, has a half-life of 4.51 billion years. It produces a number of progeny in the process, until it reaches a stable state by becoming lead.

Soddy talked about how the "new alchemists" could "transform a desert continent, thaw the frozen poles, and make the whole world one smiling Garden of Eden." But he also told a military audience in London in 1904 that the first nation that developed nuclear weapons would control the world.[22]

Gradually scientists observed that packets of energy, known as quanta, were released by the splitting apart of the atomic nucleus. The behavior of these rays could not be precisely predicted, or explained by the existing laws of physics. The discovery of radioactivity revolutionized our understanding of the physical universe. Some felt as if they had come face-to-face with the cosmic puzzle of all time. The German physicist Werner Heisenberg remembers feeling near despair after hours of discussions with his Danish colleague Niels Bohr during a 1926 conference in Copenhagen. Afterward Heisenberg would walk alone in a nearby park, repeating the same question over and over: "Can nature possibly be as absurd as it seemed to us in these atomic experiments?"[23]

While the investigations proceeded, a radium boom launched the first atomic age, marked by the same kind of optimism that characterized the early postwar nuclear boom. Radium was sold as a cure for just about everything, even cancer. The luminous paint industry used it for glow-in-the-dark dials, light switches, electrical outlet covers, and a number of other household fixtures. In 1916, the journal *Radium* claimed that the metal had "absolutely no toxic effects," and while this was not universally believed, warnings about radiation hazards came too late for its victims, who included dial painters, scientists, and patients. Marie Curie suffered a miscarriage because of radiation poisoning, and both she and her daughter Irène eventually died of its effects.[24] In 1929, the *Literary Digest* warned that radium "deserves to be considered the most dangerous material in the world."[25] Today, most scientists would say that plutonium merits that dubious accolade.

THE REALITY OF nuclear energy, of harnessing the atom's awesome power, held great promise for mankind. But it also harbored unprecedented peril. Atomic bombs might bring wars to a close, as they did World War II, but as stockpiles grew they soon contained enough combined explosive force to incinerate all of mankind many times over. Nuclear reactors could in theory provide abundant electricity, but they opened pathways for proliferators and risked harmful, widespread exposure to radioactivity. The lure of this power was irresistible even as it came loaded with risk. And central to this risk was nuclear energy's two-sided nature—and the fact that preventing its "peaceful" side from being exploited to make weapons was not a simple matter.

As the nuclear community grew, driven by the desire for scientific advancement, status, and money, this ambiguity meant trouble. From the beginning, nuclear establishments charged with developing nuclear technology also were protected by secrecy and a lack of accountability. Without the checks and balances derived from informed public debate, basic human motivations made it not only possible but probable that the positive aspects of nuclear energy would be advanced, the negatives downplayed or ignored. This was beneficial to governments embarked on massive expansions of their nuclear weapons programs, and it also led to lucrative contracts in the private sector. Their experience with the military side of nuclear energy allowed multinational corporations to parlay their expertise into a new line of business— selling reactors and nuclear fuel plants for electricity production. The entire nuclear endeavor was fertile ground for human fallibility, wishful thinking, deception, and plain naïveté. The temptations proved too irresistible, and the dangers too large, for mere mortals to control.

On the most practical level, the first postwar report on preventing nuclear proliferation, whose drafting was guided by Oppenheimer, stated the basic problem unequivocally: "The development of atomic energy for peaceful purposes and the development of atomic energy for bombs are in much of their course interchangeable and interdependent."[26] It was talking about nuclear fuel cycle activities. For example, any country with access to uranium ore and the means to enrich it can, by adjusting enrichment levels, use the resulting fuel either in a reactor, for electricity, or in a nuclear weapon. That is why there has been so much controversy over Iran's enrichment program. If such a country also has a reprocessing plant, the fuel inside the reactor, once it has been burned, can be removed and chemically processed to recover plutonium. The country might claim the plutonium is for a benign purpose—namely, use in a breeder reactor for electricity production—and it might be. But the material also can be used inside a weapon. Once it can produce, or gain access to, enriched uranium or plutonium, a country (or terrorist organization) is over the biggest hump in terms of making a bomb. In other words, the activities that surround the manufacturing of nuclear fuel constitute the blurred seam along which the "good" side of nuclear runs with the "bad."

Imagine building an auto industry if gas could be used to make a weapon like the one dropped on Hiroshima, or if the oil running through an engine could be removed and chemically separated to produce plutonium. That is not a perfect analogy, but it is a simple way of looking at the problem governments faced when they decided to promote nuclear energy for electricity. How do you keep the fuel products from being used for weapons?

The United States tried to resolve the dilemma in several ways. Presented to the United Nations in 1946, the Oppenheimer-inspired plan proposed an international authority to control all nuclear fuel production and distribution, including even uranium mines. This agency would be like a central bank, leasing nuclear fuel to national governments as they needed it but never allowing them to own it. The plan was idealistic and had little chance of succeeding. This first attempt to control the power of the atom also immediately ran into an event that tapped into the countervailing motivations within the bigger package—the expression of power and geopolitical might. This was Operation Crossroads, the first postwar atmospheric bomb test, an extravaganza in the South Pacific to which representatives from other countries were invited as witnesses by the U.S. government. Hundreds more atmospheric tests would take place, but as a public display of atomic power, Crossroads was unprecedented and never to be repeated. The two highly publicized explosions during this operation only served to emphasize the inescapable connection between the military and civilian sides of nuclear energy. Not surprisingly, the U.S. plan eventually failed in the UN, the Soviets got the bomb, and scientists in both countries began developing thermonuclear weapons with far greater yields than conventional fission weapons.

Then, as the cold war arms race began in earnest, Eisenhower announced his Atoms for Peace project in 1953. The U.S. government started providing technical assistance to other countries to promote nuclear's "peaceful uses," and Congress passed legislation aimed at promoting reactor development at home. This accentuation of the atom's positive side was in the very broadest sense the culmination of the idea, around since at least the Renaissance, that there is good in reason and that we owe it to science to let it lead us where it may. But in the context of the times it was also a brilliant public relations gamble and a perfect example of how the atom has constantly been reframed to accentuate its supposed benefits. It was used to seduce an unsuspecting public with its promises of inexpensive electricity, while governments driven by power motives were in reality consummating their relationship with the atom's dark side—and courting nuclear disaster. The awful irony is that this deceit was intended in part to bring about public acceptance of the permanent presence of nuclear weapons, the atomic age.

The United States gambled away much of the technology on the thin premise that generosity would yield nuclear obeisance. In other words, the promotion of nuclear electricity became a way for countries that had bombs, or the technology to acquire them, to prevent those who did not from getting them. Yet it did not entirely work out that way. The largesse that flowed from Eisenhower's program led to an atmosphere of tolerance that allowed countries all over the world to acquire the technology and expertise necessary for bomb-making. The Israeli and Indian efforts took root in the Atoms for Peace firmament, while the Soviet Union and then Britain, France, and finally China became declared nuclear weapons states.

By the late 1950s, the United States began putting on the brakes. Safeguards agreements were stiffened, and in 1957 the IAEA was set up. But the nuclear world was still by and large a gentlemen's club where promises were politely made and discreetly broken. A decade later, the Non-Proliferation Treaty was signed, and then a Nuclear Suppliers Group was formed to limit exports. None of this stopped proliferators intent on securing the necessary technology, equipment, and material for bomb programs. Most notorious among them was A. Q. Khan, the Pakistani engineer whose efforts enabled Pakistan to develop nuclear weapons, and who then went on to sell the technology to other countries, including Iran, Iraq, Libya, and North Korea.

Meanwhile, large quantities of plutonium were shipped across oceans as the nuclear power industry prepared for the day that never came—the advent of economic and safe advanced breeders. As this took place, countries that were interested in developing a nuclear weapon option, such as Brazil, Argentina, South Korea, and Taiwan, pursued advanced fuel cycle technologies, using the peaceful-uses argument as cover. The United States gradually turned against breeders after India exploded its first nuclear bomb, with plutonium recovered by a U.S.-assisted reprocessing program, in 1974. That helped discourage enthusiasm for breeders in South America and the smaller Asian countries, but breeder programs continued in Europe and Japan.[27] However, because commercial breeders never materialized as expected, and commercial reprocessing continued, plutonium stockpiles grew to the point that there is now enough excess in the world to be converted into forty thousand first-generation (Nagasaki-type) nuclear weapons. That also includes unused military plutonium, but most of it is from the civilian program.[28]

In early 2006, the Bush administration made an ill-conceived attempt to revive reprocessing, claiming scientists would develop a more "proliferation-resistant" means to traditional reprocessing methods. The program faced stiff opposition in Congress and an uncertain future, but it demonstrated the tenacity of breeder promoters; after decades of failure and low levels of funding they could still attempt a comeback. Meanwhile the resurgence of plutonium recycling, or reprocessing, for "peaceful" purposes, and the insistence of the United States and the other four "legitimate" nuclear weapons states on maintaining their arsenals, is making it tempting for other countries, particularly in unstable regions of the world, to reconsider the nuclear option. Attention in recent years has focused on Iran and North Korea, but it is generally assumed among those who follow the issue that as many as forty countries now have the capability to develop nuclear weapons should they choose to do so.[29] This is the situation we live with today, and it is one of our own making.

Proliferation is not the only challenge faced by the nuclear industry. The civilian and military sides of nuclear grew in different ways but shared many other basic problems. For example, they both produced waste with long-lived radionuclides, and there was no obvious place to put it. Uranium mines, fuel production facilities, and fallout from weapons testing contaminated land, rivers, lakes, and underground aquifers. Safety problems led to serious accidents, which further hurt the environment and claimed lives. Many people remember Three Mile Island in 1979 and Chernobyl in 1986. But there were other earlier accidents with serious consequences and hundreds of narrow escapes. Within just the last five years these included earthquakes in Japan and China that damaged nuclear plants. Little is known about the fate of several key military nuclear installations after the May 2008 earthquake in China, but the quake in Japan a year earlier forced the shutdown of the world's largest civilian nuclear installation in terms of output capacity, with seven reactors, and left the operator struggling with an awkward challenge: the earthquake was more severe than the plant had been designed for. That single event was responsible for roughly half of a 1.9 percent decline in nuclear power output worldwide during 2007.

Fear was another "by-product" of the nuclear age. For the baby boomer generation, this came to a head during the Cuban Missile Crisis, but anxiety was never far away in other places, at different times. In the 1960s, for example, Spanish villagers watched four weapons fall to the ground after the plane that was carrying them turned into a fiery ball during an in-flight refueling operation. Only later was it revealed that the payload consisted of thermonuclear weapons. Thousands of people would learn over time that they had been exposed to life-threatening radiation, including adults who as children at a Massachusetts school had been subjected to secret radiation experiments. As the Three Mile Island accident unfolded, and people were not sure whether the reactor would explode, a Nuclear Regulatory Commission official taking a break at a coffee shop listened with dismay as a young waiter planning a trip to Paris asked whether he would make it.

"We will be judged upon the facts and upon our achievements," proclaimed Sir John Hill, former chairman of the UK Atomic Energy

Authority, in 1979 on the occasion of the organization's twenty-fifth anniversary, "and not upon the plaintive cries of the fainthearted who have lost the courage and ambitions of our forefathers which made mankind the master of the earth."[30]

Sir John was right in one respect. Nuclear certainly was not for the fainthearted.

AS WE ALL gradually came to understand the phenomenal powers of nuclear energy, we also came to realize that its by-products created continuing threats that would not go away. In September 2007, Israeli fighter planes bombed a suspected Syrian nuclear installation possibly delivered from North Korea, and we were once again reminded of what the physicists have known for the past century—that nuclear weapons in menacing hands threaten us all. But everyday hazards exist in the form of nuclear waste, further proliferation, the possibility of more serious accidents, and radiation contamination and exposure.

Today, after a twenty-year lull caused by a slowdown in energy demand and the Three Mile Island and Chernobyl accidents, countries all over the world are talking about a nuclear "renaissance." In the era of global warming, this is in part a legitimate attempt to provide an alternative to carbon-based fuels. Nuclear energy is unlikely to fulfill those expectations. Over the last fifty years, trillions of dollars have been poured into nuclear development; yet today nuclear reactors account for less than 15 percent of worldwide electricity output, and in advanced countries such as Japan and Britain the contribution has declined in recent years because of unexpected shutdowns triggered by earthquakes and technical failures.[31] The number of reactors needed to make an impact on carbon emissions is so high that even nuclear industry officials are skeptical they can be built.

This book will detail how and why nuclear energy failed to develop in the way its planners hoped, providing relevant reminders of what could happen in the future. A key element is the relationship between the military and civilian sides, and the fact that one sprang from the other, more for political reasons than because nuclear electricity was necessarily the best way forward. This in turn encouraged fanciful thinking about risks and costs and created a situation in which safeguards against proliferation were essential, yet never adequate to the task. The book explores why safeguards failed, why waste is a problem we are not yet close to solving, and how the billions spent by governments on nuclear over the past sixty years crowded out other energy options. Finally, this book will explain why for practical reasons nuclear reactors are unlikely to provide a much hoped-for solution to the climate change problem, making it all the more important to devote substantially greater effort and resources to energy alternatives—wind, solar, decentralized distribution, and conservation—than we have in the past.

The world has not been destroyed, but the nuclear enterprise developed in a way that offers us no guarantees for the future. What follows are stories about the mistakes, their whys and hows, their consequences, and a brief look at alternatives. These deserve especially close attention right now.

CHAPTER 1

A Voice in the Wilderness

"Sixteen hours ago an American airplane dropped one bomb on Hiroshima, an important Japanese Army base. That bomb had more power than 20,000 tons of T.N.T. . . . It is an atomic bomb. It is a harnessing of the basic power of the universe. The force from which the sun draws its power has been loosed against those who brought war to the Far East."[1]

AND THAT WAS IT. President Harry S. Truman had introduced two words—atomic bomb—to the human race. A day earlier, those words had been a secret, although not as well kept as was supposed by those who knew about it. Originally conceived as a deterrent against a German bomb, the weapons instead were dropped on Japan.

Truman heard—more accurately, read—the news while eating lunch on board the heavy cruiser *Augusta*, returning from the postwar settlement conference at Potsdam, a city near Berlin. The watch officer in the Advance Map Room, Captain Frank Graham, entered the mess and handed him a telegram. It was from War Secretary Henry L. Stimson, who had flown back from the conference to the United States:

Big bomb dropped on Hiroshima August 5 at 7:15 p.m. Washington time. First reports indicate complete success which was even more conspicuous than earlier test.

Truman looked up at the crew members sitting at his table and, without revealing the telegram's contents, said, "This is the greatest thing in history. It's time for us to get home." Later, he gathered all the sailors on the ship and told them of a "powerful new bomb."

They applauded.[2]

Thousands of miles away, as the news reached Los Alamos, there were conflicting emotions. Should the men be proud of their work or ashamed of what it had brought? One scientist remembered hearing yells of "Whoopee" among his younger colleagues, but he thought those were "inappropriate." After the Japanese surrender was announced on August 11, emotions ran almost out of control among the scientists and mathematicians who had built the bomb. They rushed to hidden supplies of whiskey, gin, and vodka, and in pouring the drink that was forbidden them during war they poured out all the anxiety, guilt, and pride stored up during years of living in isolation and secrecy. Someone wired up a few dozen munitions dumps and pushed the detonator to make fireworks. The litany of explosions accompanied the tumult of feeling: for many, waves of relief and accomplishment; for others, a profound sense of anguish.[3]

One man, Joseph Rotblat, living in London by then, felt only profound shock and dismay. Rotblat had quietly left the mesa in New Mexico in late 1944, after he discovered the German bomb program had stalled and was unlikely to succeed. His reasons for leaving were known only to his superiors. A story was invented to keep the others from finding out. The truth was that Rotblat and some of his colleagues had a keen sense of what lay ahead when the military conflict finally ended—an arms race between the two superpowers. Unlike the other scientists, Rotblat acted on his convictions. In his native Poland, Rotblat's wife already had been claimed by one holocaust; he did not wish to contribute to the possibility of another. Rotblat's moral choice—to have nothing to do henceforth with designing or building nuclear weapons—also was a repudiation of the hypersecure world the scientists had helped to create when they signed on to the project. Inside Los Alamos and the other nuclear laboratories they had become protected—and marooned—from the rest of society.

The effort and the war had changed them, and their role in society as well. They were no longer pure researchers. In fact, at least since they had begun voluntarily withholding the fruits of their efforts from German physicists in 1939 the scientists had become politicized. Their circle had been so intimate then that the German scientist Werner Heisenberg later contended the atomic bomb was not inevitable. "In the summer of 1939 twelve people might still have been able, by coming to mutual agreement, to prevent the construction of atom bombs," Heisenberg said.[4] Whether he was right or not can never be known. But the German-born writer Robert Jungk strongly criticized the scientists for not trying. "Their powers of political and moral imagination failed them at that moment as disastrously as did their loyalty to the international tradition of science. They never succeeded in achieving thought and action appropriate to the future consequences of their invention."[5]

During the war many of the scientists grumbled about the elaborate security arrangements; afterward some sounded the alarm publicly when they felt their colleagues were pursuing programs that were morally wrong, such as the development of thermonuclear weapons. Or they criticized the government for failing to adequately address the issue of nuclear fallout from atmospheric weapons testing. But for project managers pushing for big-ticket programs, secrecy and ambiguity had certain advantages. For one thing, it kept political leaders conveniently ignorant of the complexities and therefore more pliable when it came to approving budget requests.

Sixty years later, as I sought answers to the many nagging questions I had about nuclear energy, I met Rotblat at his home in north London.[6] The bombs in 1945 destroyed two cities. But in the intervening years, the existing U.S. and Soviet nuclear arsenals had become so large "that if the weapons had actually been detonated the result could have been the complete extinction of the human species, as well as of many animal species," he observed.[7] Rotblat had devoted his life to seeing that this did not happen. Much of his work was through Pugwash, the scientific organization he founded with philosopher Bertrand Russell in 1957 dedicated to alleviating cold war tensions.

I wanted to know the trajectory of Rotblat's moral choices, how and why he had made them, and his thoughts on why scientists were willing to work on nuclear weapons. The questions seemed more urgent in 2004 when I first interviewed him. The cold war had been over for more than a decade, yet the United States was actually increasing spending on nuclear weapons. Why would scientists want to do this work, and why were we spending more on it?

———————

ROTBLAT OPENED THE door to his 1930s-style West Hampstead home with a big smile. He had warm blue eyes and white hair and was tall, with a sturdy frame. Mostly, though, I noticed a quality of lightness, as if he had shed a burden a long time ago, not a characteristic I found very often in nuclear people. In fact, most seemed just the opposite, as if they were heavy with a weight they could not lose.

Rotblat showed me to his large study, a long, dark room with a bay window at one end. Stacks of books, papers, letters, and documents lined the walls, filled the tables, and spilled out of the room into other areas of the house. His dining room, too, was filled with papers. This was not clutter in any conventional sense. The large sturdy piles had become the furniture of Rotblat's daily life, more than the tables and chairs, and he still knew where to find something if he needed to. Outside the lead-mullioned window, a few pale pink roses fluttered in a cool June breeze.

Rotblat was ninety-five at the time. He had just suffered a stroke that slowed his movements but not his mind.

As a young man in Poland more than a half century earlier, Rotblat was at Warsaw's Radiological Institute. He harbored dreams of building on Polish-born Marie Curie's legacy, furthering her work on radioactivity and perhaps winning his own Nobel Prize one day. (He never won the award for science, but in 1995 he received the Nobel Peace Prize.) His life changed in 1939, the year German scientists unveiled the secrets of fission, the spontaneous splitting of atoms. Rotblat got a scholarship to study in Britain that year, but the discovery in Germany filled him with unease. He was, he wrote later, "like a person trying to ignore the first symptom of a fatal disease in the hope that it will go away."[8]

In Britain he studied at Liverpool University under James Chadwick, already famous for his 1932 discovery of the neutron—one of the three primary parts of the atom, along with protons and electrons. This elementary particle can penetrate the atomic nucleus in spite of the electric barriers surrounding it, because the neutron is electrically neutral and is therefore not repelled.[9] The discovery helped to unravel the mystery of fission because it is neutrons that induce the splitting apart of atoms.

Rotblat's wife, Tola, had had to stay behind in Warsaw because there was not enough money for two train tickets. Chadwick soon offered Rotblat a more prestigious scholarship with more money, and in

August 1939 the young scientist returned to Warsaw to collect ..... But fate intervened. On arriving in Warsaw, Rotblat discovered that Tola had just suffered appendicitis. She was not fit to travel. She urged him to return to England and carry on with his work.

So the young scientist with all his dreams left for Liverpool, once again leaving his young wife behind. A few days later, the Germans invaded Poland. "What happened after that is long and complicated, and as with so many Eastern European Jews of that era the story ends in tragedy."

Rotblat's voice had softened. He paused, and then his speech slowed and he choked before his voice broke, like a branch from a tree. "She died in one of the gas ovens."

His eyes welled with tears and his head dropped forward, involuntarily it seemed, as the memory caught up with him. He remained that way for a while, head forward, eyes closed, vanishing from the shared space of our conversation, until I felt he might disappear altogether.

ROTBLAT CAME TO life as suddenly as he had seemed to leave it, now back at Liverpool. There had been stories that Hitler's military strength was all bluff and that his tanks were painted cardboard. But with news of the Nazi advance into Poland, those tales had been exposed as just wishful thinking. Rotblat's country, his wife, and the entire European continent were in mortal danger.

Rotblat no longer tried to suppress the "fatal disease" he had so dreaded when he first heard about fission. Before too long he was working on a nascent weapons project, joining other scientists in Britain who shared a fear that their colleagues in Germany would build a nuclear weapon for Hitler. If they could build one first, they might check the German effort, or prevent Hitler from using a bomb if his scientists managed to build one. This was an early version of the deterrence doctrine that shaped defense policy throughout much of the cold war.

In January 1944, Rotblat joined a team of British scientists in the United States working on the Manhattan Project. He was sent to Los Alamos, where he stayed with Chadwick and his wife, Aileen, for a few months before moving into the single men's quarters. The Manhattan Project leader, General Leslie R. Groves, frequently came to the Chadwicks' for dinner on visits to Los Alamos. On one of these occasions, Rotblat was invited to attend. During the dinner, he listened as

Groves said, "You realize, of course, that the main purpose of the project was to subdue the Russians."

As Rotblat quietly digested this conversational snippet, something akin to a compass needle inside him lost its bearing. "I was completely shocked." Russian soldiers were dying by the thousands in order to defeat the Germans, and Groves was speaking of them as if they were the enemy, more than the Germans. "This was still at a time when Hitler could win the war," Rotblat said. "People I told later wouldn't believe it." After that, he said, "there was never any doubt in my mind that Russia was the main enemy."

The Polish émigré thought then that he should leave the project. Instead, still worried about a German bomb, he remained. Around this time he received a letter from a friend in England telling him that a mutual acquaintance from Liverpool, a well-off half-American woman named Elspeth, had moved to Santa Fe, hoping the clean air would be conducive to slowing the progress of a congenital deafness. Rotblat started seeing Elspeth regularly, usually on Sundays after the flying lessons he was taking with a few friends from Los Alamos. Inside his new friend's spacious adobe house, conversations about art, literature, and the course of the war took place in elevated tones to accommodate Elspeth's poor hearing. But Rotblat, like all the other scientists, was being closely watched, especially when he ventured outside the gated community of Los Alamos. Inside his friend's house a male Hispanic housekeeper apparently took notes, sending in badly mangled reports of what he thought he had heard.[10]

At Los Alamos, Rotblat's concerns about the project grew during conversations with the Danish laureate Niels Bohr, who came to his room every morning to listen to the BBC news bulletins on a specially equipped radio Rotblat had purchased in New York. Bohr too was worried about a postwar arms race. His concerns ran so deep that the Dane had sought and obtained meetings in 1944 with both the British prime minister, Winston Churchill, and President Franklin D. Roosevelt. He urged them to start a dialogue with the Soviets on atomic control before it was too late.

Rotblat remained at Los Alamos, clinging to the thread of reasoning that had brought so many scientists, Bohr included, there in the first place—the threat of a German bomb. What neither man realized then was that Groves knew as early as March 1944, the same month as the fateful dinner at the Chadwicks', that the supposed German threat was virtually nonexistent. This information was delivered by a special team sent into Italy in December 1943, the first of the so-called Alsos missions. The group gathered evidence from sources knowledgeable about the German bomb program that the effort had not progressed very far. In November 1944, a second team moved into Germany, arrested scientists at the University of Strasbourg, and raided their offices, laboratories, and homes. "The information gained there indicated quite definitely that Hitler had been apprised in 1942 of the possibilities of a nuclear weapon," Groves wrote in his book, *Now It Can Be Told*. "Nevertheless, all evidence from Strasbourg clearly pointed to the fact that, as of the latter part of 1944, the enemy's efforts to develop a bomb were still in the experimental stages, and greatly increased our belief that there was little probability of any sudden nuclear surprise from Germany."[11]

Chadwick relayed the news to Rotblat. The thin thread that was his rationale for staying at Los Alamos finally broke.

But leaving would not be so easy. The chief of security at Los Alamos, Major Peer de Silva, had already targeted Rotblat as a suspected Communist, and thus someone who might sell the secrets of the bomb to the Soviets. Rotblat heard this news from Chadwick. He was, of course, furious. Like many Europeans terrified of Hitler during the 1930s, Rotblat was a Communist sympathizer because the Soviets seemed to offer the only viable alternative to encroaching fascism in Western Europe. That made him a prime target for someone like de Silva, who was fast gaining a reputation as a Communist witch-hunter. De Silva was convinced that Robert Oppenheimer, the chief scientist at Los Alamos, also was a Communist spy.[12]

Chadwick confronted de Silva and demanded that he immediately destroy the dossier on Rotblat. De Silva agreed, and Rotblat was allowed to leave. But he had to promise not to tell his colleagues the reasons, presumably to protect either the secret of Alsos or the fantasy of the German bomb, or both. Rotblat was to say only that he was returning to Britain because he would be in a better position to look for his wife. Rotblat found out several years later, when he had trouble obtaining a U.S. entry visa, that de Silva had not kept his end of the bargain. Moreover, the charges against him, obtained under the Freedom of Information Act, were so bizarre that as Rotblat read the dossier, he could feel only incredulity and astonishment. The story according to de Silva was that Rotblat's flying lessons were far from innocent fun. Instead, he was learning to fly so he could return to Britain, join the Royal Air Force, hijack a plane, fly to Poland, parachute behind Soviet lines, and deliver the secrets of the bomb to the Communists. It had never occurred to Rotblat during his frequent visits to Elspeth that someone was always listening, but he surmised that with his poor English, the Hispanic housekeeper had taken snippets of conversation and "made up with his imagination what he did not understand."[13]

The shadowy security people apparently did not leave it there, either. Rotblat was followed across the country. Arriving by train in New York just prior to boarding a ship for England, he realized that a box containing all of his published papers, personal correspondence, and photographs had been taken from the luggage car. He never saw it again. This was just one man's brush with the new hypersecurity of the nuclear state. "I had to reconcile myself to the loss of my treasured belongings," Rotblat wrote. "By that time the war in Europe was over, and with this word reached me of a far greater loss, the death of my wife . . . Stalin is alleged to have said: 'A single death is a tragedy, a million deaths is statistics.' So Tola became a statistic. One of the six million who perished in Poland in World War II. During that period I was busy helping to design weapons which would increase a hundred-fold the death toll in World War II."[14]

ROTBLAT MADE, AND acted upon, his moral choice months before Truman even knew about the bomb. Truman was still a Democratic senator from Missouri when Rotblat left Los Alamos, and while he had an inkling something big was going on, he had no idea what it was. When he tried to investigate, as chairman of a special committee on defense spending, the flow of millions of unaccounted-for dollars into some mysterious military pothole, he was warned off by the same white-haired eastern establishment figure who had once called the former Missouri haberdasher a "pretty untrustworthy man." War Secretary Stimson told Truman very grandly (and misleadingly) that the spending was "a matter which I know all about personally and I am the only one of the group of two or three men in the whole world who know about it."[15] Actually, a good number of people in Moscow knew, but Stimson had no way of knowing that. Secrecy whirled around the new atomic era like a wind blowing in many directions, but the biggest secret—the one that gave birth to every other secret—was known about by the Soviets almost from the beginning.

When Roosevelt died of a massive cerebral hemorrhage on April 12, 1945, Truman was finally admitted to the select group of knowledge bearers. But the information was passed to him cryptically. First Stimson told him "about an immense project . . . of almost unbelievable destructive power," Truman wrote in his diary the day he took the oath of office, but "he gave me no details." A day later, James F. "Jimmy" Byrnes told him a little more. Byrnes had been a private citizen of South Carolina since April, but for the previous two years he was Roosevelt's director of war mobilization. He knew about the bomb even though he was not part of the Military Policy Committee that was making its mind up about whether to use it. Byrnes told Truman two important things. One was that the scientists were "perfecting an explosive great enough to destroy the whole world." The second was that "the bomb might well put us in a position to dictate our own terms at the end of the war."[16]

The veil only partially lifted, Truman had little time to weigh the consequences of using the bomb. He had not heard Bohr's personal plea to Roosevelt against it, and Bohr had been kept out of the meetings at which the critical decisions were made. Moreover, after the German surrender in May 1945, when Truman had been in office less than a month, there was still the problem of how to end the conflict in Japan.

By then, the Manhattan Project had taken on a life of its own. Over three years it had absorbed roughly two billion dollars, none of which was publicly accounted for. No one wanted more American lives lost at the hands of the Japanese enemy, still divided over surrender. Truman leaned heavily on his military advisers, who viewed the new weapon as a more effective means of achieving their overall objective. At the same time, there was a natural urge among scientists and their overseers to see if the thing they had created worked. This was the unspoken current that ran through the decision-making process as options were weighed.

At Potsdam on July 24, 1945, Truman told Soviet leader Joseph Stalin about a weapon of "unusually destructive force."[17] Two days later the remaining parts for Little Boy and Fat Man left the United States in air transport command cargo planes for Tinian Island, while others arrived on the USS *Indianapolis*, docking at Tinian that day. Also on July 26, Truman, Churchill, and the Chinese Nationalist leader Chiang Kai-shek issued a joint declaration to the Japanese government threatening prompt and utter destruction unless its armed forces agreed to unconditional surrender.[18] The Soviets tried to delay the declaration. They feared the Japanese might surrender before they could enter the war in the Pacific, thus preventing them from achieving the regional strategic aims that had been agreed upon at the Yalta conference that February.

In this crucible of geopolitical and military maneuvering, Truman found himself confronted with an enormity for which he was little more psychically prepared than the average citizen. He reached for a biblical perspective to help him come to terms with the meaning of what lay ahead. "It may be the fire destruction prophesied in the Euphrates Valley Era, after Noah and his fabulous Ark," he wrote in his diary. At least, he managed to convince himself, the bombs would hit only the war factories and "soldiers and sailors," and "not women and children." He had Stimson's assurance on that, and allowed himself to believe it. The two men agreed that the target would be "a purely military one and we will issue a warning statement asking the Japs to surrender and save lives. I'm sure they will not do that, but we will have given them the chance. It is certainly a good thing for the world that Hitler's crowd or Stalin's did not discover this atomic bomb. It seems to be the most terrible thing ever discovered, but it can be made the most useful."[19]

On July 30, Truman received a message from Washington asking for a "statement for release by you." In response, he scrawled cryptically: "Release when ready but no sooner than August 2 HST."[20] The first bomb was dropped a little less than four months after Truman took office. Truman must have drawn breath as one does when taking the next step in a dark, dense forest, having no idea what lies ahead. Three days after the bravura on board the *Augusta*, after arriving back in Washington from the conference in Germany, the president delivered an address over the radio. This time he spoke of the bomb's "tragic significance" and the "awful responsibility which has come to us."[21]

And he began thinking about the burdens and obligations of such power, and the immensely complex issue of control. "We must constitute ourselves trustees of this new force—to prevent its misuse,

and to turn it into the channels of service to mankind," he said in a radio speech on August 9.[22]

WHILE HE WAS still at Los Alamos, Rotblat and other scientists believed that the government had an implicit moral contract with them
never to use the bomb, other than for its deterrent effect. Naive as that
may now seem, the sense of betrayal is why, in London, the news of
Hiroshima had "a terrible effect" on him, Rotblat said. "I always felt
the whole purpose of my starting this project was to prevent its use. If
it would be used it shouldn't be used against civilian populations."

It was a cautionary lesson for the scientists, although many never
learned it. Shut off from the rest of society, without feedback or debate,
they went on working for the government, utterly absorbed in their
work. Either inured to the ethical implications or believing their work
was justified by national security demands, the scientists were also in
awe of the nature of their work. This made their rationales peripheral to
the invisible pull of just being part of the excitement. In her book *Secrets*, Sissela Bok writes: "Their isolation, and the power they shared
through this most devastating of all secrets, even the sense they describe of having it within their grasp to unleash the most extraordinary
physical burst of violence the world had ever seen: these were intoxi-
cating and, for some, utterly corrupting elements."[23]

Rotblat eventually concluded that even the deterrence justification
was flawed—he did not think the threat of atomic retaliation would
have prevented a "psychopath" like Hitler from hurtling a nuclear
weapon toward his enemies first. "It is very likely that his last order
from the bunker in Berlin would have been to destroy London, even if
this were to bring terrible retribution to Germany. Indeed, he would
have seen this a heroic way of going down, in a Götterdämmerung,"
Rotblat said.

Why did Rotblat's colleagues continue working on the bomb? "The
most frequent reason given was pure and simple scientific curiosity—
the strong urge to find out whether the theoretical calculations and
predictions would come true," Rotblat explained. "These scientists
felt that only after the test at Alamogordo [in July 1945] should they
enter into the debate about the use of the bomb. Others were persuaded by the argument that many American lives would be saved if

the bomb ended the war more rapidly—they would work to see that it was not used again once peace was restored. Still others, while agreeing that the project should have been stopped when the German factor ceased to operate, were not willing to take an individual stand because they feared it would adversely affect their future career."

In a speech to Los Alamos scientists in November 1945, Oppenheimer admitted that some of these early justifications "wore off a little as it became clear that the war would be won in any case." He talked about other reasons, similar to the ones Rotblat discussed. But the essence of the project, he said, was "an organic necessity."

> If you are a scientist you cannot stop such a thing. If you are a scientist you believe that it is good to find out how the world works; that it is good to find out what the realities are; that it is good to turn over to mankind at large the greatest possible power to control the world and to deal with it according to its lights and values.[24]

This is similar to what Thomas Henry Huxley told English audiences in the late nineteenth century when Darwinism had been foisted upon them and they had to contemplate for the first time that they might be descended from apes and not angels. Defending the necessity for truth, Huxley wrote a friend, "Sit down before fact as a little child . . . follow humbly and to whatever abysses Nature leads, or you shall learn nothing."[25]

Discovery and truth were one thing, but development—the power to control the world—was another. Rotblat was not so easily persuaded by Oppenheimer's apparent willingness to absolve the scientists of moral responsibility, or so convinced of the innocence and necessity attributed to their pursuit of knowledge. "The majority [of scientists] were not bothered by moral scruples; they were quite content to leave it to others to decide how their work would be used."

For many scientists, the Manhattan Project was the start of a long career. It also contributed to an exponential rise in the number of physicists in the United States. From a few thousand immediately after the war (and many of those émigrés from Europe) their number grew to between twenty-five thousand and thirty thousand by 1970, after which it leveled off, according to Spencer Weart, a noted nuclear historian and director of the Center for History of Physics at the

American Institute of Physics. Between 40 and 60 percent of all physicists in the United States at any given time were involved in work directly related to military concerns, Weart estimates. "The nuclear weapons program employed a lot of people especially in the early years because it lent a lot of prestige. We certainly would not have put as much money into it [physics] if the bomb had not existed."[26]

At Los Alamos, as the men headed for their bottles of spirits and the makeshift fireworks to celebrate the news about Hiroshima, there were some among them who, like Rotblat in London, felt more shock and shame than pride. A thirty-four-year-old electronics specialist named Willie Higginbotham, son of a Protestant minister, wrote to his mother: "I am not a bit proud of the job we have done . . . The only reason for doing it was to beat the rest of the world to a draw . . . Perhaps this is so devastating that man will be forced to be peaceful."[27]

Another man on the mesa that night confessed that after Hiroshima he had mixed feelings about using the more powerful plutonium bomb on Nagasaki. "I hoped that it would not be used and trembled at the thought of the devastation it would cause. And yet, to be quite frank, I was desperately anxious to find out whether this type of bomb would also do what was expected of it, in short, whether its intricate mechanism would work. These were dreadful thoughts, I know, and still I could not help having them."[28]

Most Americans were elated by the apparent success of the bomb in hastening the war's end, although within days they also heard reports of its horrific effects. These accounts "made the menace and promise of atomic energy an instant public reality," wrote McGeorge Bundy, Stimson's assistant just after the war. "The awe that had been shared in secret by a few became in some degree the common property of all within reach of these announcements. The bomb had gone public with a bang."[29]

But could such supremacy, with its requirements for excessive secrecy, coexist with democracy? Or would the new atomic establishment, starved of the oxygen of normal public discourse and debate, take root as a new order, handing down from one generation to the next the power over life and death? Bok and others argue that people are both isolated and transformed by excessive secrecy because they are not tested by the rigors of outside questioning. The process is strongest when it is linked with great power. These elements, secrecy and power, nourished the soil in which the atomic establishment took root and grew strong.

In his speech at Los Alamos, Oppenheimer went on to argue for more openness, saying it would be wrong to "attempt to treat science of the future as though it were rather a dangerous thing, a thing that must be watched and managed."[30] Yet Oppenheimer more than anyone understood the need for watching and managing nuclear development in order to prevent other countries from acquiring nuclear weapons, and he recognized the dangers of letting too much information out. When he told the bomb makers at Los Alamos they could not stop such a thing, he was speaking as much for himself as he was for them. He was a part of their world and, at least for a few years more, protected by the majesty and secrecy of the bubble in which it existed. He was also at least partially exonerating them from guilt. Their job was to "find out what the realities are" and let the rest of mankind deal with them—the path Rotblat had rejected. Bok suggests this rationalizing process demonstrated the delusional effects secrecy had on their ethical choices and the view they had of themselves. "The inability to stop [working on weapons] for which Oppenheimer adduced so many reasons came in part from the secrecy that he wished to conjure away through the production of his new knowledge, and demonstrates the debilitating effects that secrecy can have on reasoning and moral judgment," Bok writes. "The scientists at Los Alamos were in its power, and it had transformed them."[31]

Secrecy to some degree is necessary both individually and collectively. The question for the future would be this: in the yin-yang between the need for both secrecy and openness, with the threat of the atomic bomb hanging over the world, could the proper balances be achieved—or would excessive secrecy with its power to numb conscience and moral choices win out?

The nuclear bomb was part of a trend toward greater and greater destructive power. It had its antecedents in the massive aerial bombings during World War II and the use of poison gas before that. But as the writer Jonathan Schell points out, "Nuclear weapons and nuclear strategy, which actually trade on genocide for political purposes, called mutually assured destruction, threaten not just individual people, in however large numbers, but the order of creation, natural and human, and this is something new."[32]

Such power the United States would move heaven and earth to protect and exclusively maintain, at least for the next few years, as it moved into the cold war period. "There was never, from about two weeks from the time I took charge of this project, any illusion on my part but that Russia was our enemy and that the project was conducted on that basis," Groves testified in 1954.[33]

That is what lay at the heart of Rotblat's morbid reaction to the news about Hiroshima. "I was afraid. I knew at that time the atomic bomb was only the beginning," he said. It had been like that ever since the Polish physicist first heard Groves's menacing words over dinner. Americans of a more liberal persuasion would have tended to brush off the general's remarks then as the blusterings of a gruff, conservative military man. Rotblat did not. And time proved him right.

CHAPTER 2

Rites of Passage

FROM THE EARLIEST DAYS OF ATOMIC discovery, scientists knew that the new energy source had the potential to upset the normal order of things, not unlike what geneticists face today. They grappled with the issue of how to safely control development, even questioning whether they should continue with their experiments, and they had had no sure answers. "One may suppose how radium could become very dangerous in criminal hands," Pierre Curie cautioned in 1905, "and here we might ask ourselves if it is to mankind's advantage to know the secrets of nature, if we are mature enough to profit by them or if that knowledge will harm us."[1]

But Curie and his colleagues wanted to continue with the work, and as time went on and the stakes grew higher, a new generation of physicists convinced themselves that however perilous the results, their efforts would eventually be for the good. In 1939, the Hungarian émigrés Leo Szilard, Eugene Wigner, and Edward Teller had no desire to see themselves as creators of "a horrible military weapon" when they informed Roosevelt that year about the possibility of building an atomic bomb. So they justified their work by convincing themselves it would not only save the world from the threat of a German bomb but eventually lead to world peace. "We realized that, should atomic weapons be developed, no two nations would be able to live in peace with each other unless their military forces were controlled by a common higher authority," Wigner wrote. "We expected that these controls, if they were effective enough to abolish atomic warfare, would be effective enough to abolish also all other forms of war. This hope was almost as strong a spur to our endeavors as was our fear of becoming the victims of the enemy's atomic bombings."[2] Wigner's thinking proved wishful to say the least, but it was a compelling line of thought for scientists genuinely worried about the Germans and intent on bringing years of labor to fruition with their consciences clean.

When the first bomb was little more than a year away from completion, the idea of some form of world government took on a more complete shape. Its main thrust was still on eliminating nuclear weapons, and little was said about nonmilitary applications. The architect was Niels Bohr, whose deep concerns about the postwar world grew as the war progressed. Bohr pressed for common control over all atomic energy applications, seeing this as a possible means of reconciliation between East and West, whose political and economic systems were so fundamentally different. However unrealistic his hopes for cooperation with the Soviets may have been, Bohr was driven by one thought as he prepared to present his case to both Churchill and FDR that year: "We are in a completely new situation that cannot be resolved by war."

Churchill did not agree, and he convinced Roosevelt not to allow Bohr to travel to the Soviet Union, where the scientist hoped to use his influence to persuade his colleagues to cooperate in pushing Stalin for a postwar control plan. The British leader even went so far as to suggest putting the Dane under some form of house arrest to prevent him offering secrets to the Soviets.[3] The following year a group of seven scientists in Chicago, led by James Franck, another Nobel laureate, proposed the idea of controlling nuclear development by rationing uranium in a way that would prevent any country from getting enough of it to build a bomb. Franck's June 1945 report argued against dropping an atomic bomb on Japan. Instead, it suggested demonstrating the weapon's power in a remote location, with representatives of the newly formed United Nations observing. In this way he hoped to persuade Japan to surrender, as well as to achieve an international agreement in which all nations, including the United States, would renounce the future use of atomic weapons. A panel of experts that included Robert Oppenheimer rejected the Franck report on the grounds that scientists were not qualified to decide on strategic matters concerning the bomb's use, which was a convenient response to a proposal that was made after the decision to drop the bomb on two Japanese cities without any warning was more or less final.[4]

At the end of the war, the bomb had become a reality and the use of nuclear energy to produce electricity was still only on the horizon. Scientists had been thinking about such nonmilitary applications for years, and many were anxious to explore the possibilities now that the war was over. They knew, however, that even these presented dangers. Bohr and Franck had focused almost exclusively on the challenge of outlawing atomic weapons, more or less ignoring the issue of "peaceful uses." Oppenheimer, who became imbued with Bohr's ideas during the war, would take up the idea of international control only after the war ended and the damage was done. During Christmas week in 1945, he and the prominent American physicist Isador Rabi sketched out the basic ideas at Rabi's New York apartment overlooking the Hudson River.[5] This time, instead of skirting around the peaceful uses issue, the two scientists made it central to the new plan.

Oppenheimer questioned the economic viability of using nuclear energy to generate electricity, but he was in little doubt about the need to pursue the idea. Again he suggested scientific inevitability as a reason, closely linked to the issue of controlling development. "The point I have tried to make is that if you don't try to develop atomic energy, you can't control it," he wrote in the June 1946 edition of the *Bulletin of the Atomic Scientists*, which had only recently been created to warn the public about the dangers of nuclear catastrophe. "You can't say, first we will control it and then we will develop it, because the developmental functions are an essential part of the mechanism for control." These were pivotal statements. Not only was he advancing the idea that scientists must "find out what the realities are," he was shifting the argument for scientific inquiry onto a promotional platform. Scientists were now no longer wholly truth seekers; henceforth, they would be designers, builders, and promoters. Pushing nuclear development was self-serving, because it would assure scientists like Oppenheimer the funding and national laboratories necessary for prestigious programs and lifetime careers. His logic was no more compelling than Franck's and, viewed cynically, little different than suggesting that the country, and the world, had to be sold on nuclear energy before they could learn how to control it.

Under Oppenheimer's plan, peaceful nuclear energy would become the chalice from which all nations could sip so long as they agreed to the larger strictures of a universal, controlling church. That vision required an enormous leap of faith. Its underlying premises were that the benefits of nuclear power were so great they would discourage other nations from developing atomic weapons, and that by yielding authority to an international agency, nations actually could prevent unwanted proliferation. It was rooted in the long-held axiom that science, besides pursuing truth, should also be useful, and it had little chance of succeeding. Instead the idea eventually spawned an international nuclear bureaucracy that promoted nuclear growth in the civilian arena, and that in turn facilitated the spread of nuclear weapons.

Scientists were many things, but policemen they were not. When political leaders turned to them for answers to the problem of proliferation, they had no magic answers. Laypeople within the political establishment, grappling with the complex basics of nuclear energy and the dangers inherent in the production of nuclear fuel, failed to understand the limits of what science could achieve. The scientists, flattered by all the attention they were receiving, never really faced up to their own shortcomings, particularly in their naive assumptions about human motivations and the dynamics and pressures of international politics. As a result, the momentum proved unstoppable, and the failure to adequately address the challenges posed by the links between the civil and military uses of nuclear energy made the world a more dangerous place.

FROM HIS PERCH in the Oval Office, Truman looked out upon a world vastly changed by the war and the advent of Communism. There was civil war in Greece, the threat of Communist takeovers in Italy and France, a divided Berlin, and a new Red China. The United States held the trump card in being the only country in the world with an atomic weapon, but everyone knew that would not last forever. Truman needed to reshape the government, consolidate American power, and have constant access to information from all corners of the globe. Within two years of the war's end, the Central Intelligence Agency (CIA) was formed to coordinate intelligence gathering, and a fractious army and navy united under the Department of Defense. The advent of the bomb had changed everything. Within the military, the Army Air Corps was able to argue for independence from the army chiefly because of its role in delivering the atomic bombs in Japan and its perceived importance going forward (prior to the advent of missiles) as the nation's premier nuclear delivery force. It became the independent U.S. Air Force under the 1947 defense reorganization authorized by Congress.

As the steel beams of a modern superstate were hoisted into place and those in power jockeyed for position and influence, the issue of both developing and controlling nuclear energy was enormously important in determining how the United States positioned itself as a nuclear power in a postwar world. As policy-makers sought answers, there were two pivotal questions. One involved the matter of the Soviets—what to tell them, how far to trust them. The second was whether nuclear development in the United States would continue to be under the military or transferred to a new civilian organization. These were both highly contentious topics central to debate over the larger conundrum highlighted by Oppenheimer. Besides shaping the framework within which the cold war played itself out, the choices made in the first ten to fifteen years after the war would bear fruit in all sorts of other unwelcome ways well after the cold war ended.

Groves single-handedly ruled the nuclear establishment during and immediately after the war. Knowing there was a push on to wrest that control from him, he lobbied for legislation to establish a new Atomic Energy Commission (AEC), dominated by the military. But a freshman Democratic senator from Connecticut, Brien McMahon, introduced competing legislation, making the new AEC completely civilian. At that point, people in Washington were beginning to isolate a bigger issue: Who was in charge of the atom? Was it the elected representatives or men in uniform? In December 1945, Commerce Secretary Henry Wallace was shocked to hear that neither Truman nor the new secretary of war, Robert P. Patterson, apparently knew how many atomic bombs the country had. (The answer, evidently, at that point was none.) "I thought it utterly incredible that Patterson and the President should be willing to trust full information and responsibility on this to a man like Groves and his underlings without knowing what was going on themselves," Wallace later said.[6]

McMahon eventually prevailed, but putting the nuclear establishment under civilian control really offered no great panacea, if the idea was to reduce the dangers posed by nuclear energy. When it began operating in January 1947, the AEC's main job was to produce nuclear warheads for the military. That demanded ultrasecrecy; moreover, it absolved the Defense Department from having to include the tab for running the huge nuclear weapons plants in its yearly budget requests, thereby making defense spending look lower than it actually was.

There was a fallacy in believing that civilians could control nuclear energy in the same way they could regulate, say, the medical or financial services industries. The dangers were too great, the stakes too high. The officials who ran the AEC might not wear uniforms, but they would have to adopt a garrison mentality to protect information that under the 1946 Atomic Energy Act was deemed "born classified"—meaning it was considered classified from the moment of inception. This posed another conundrum: how could an enterprise whose dangers demanded so much secrecy exist in a democracy without constantly challenging its very principles of openness and accountability? If everything related to nuclear energy was secret, the citizens who supported the enterprise with their tax dollars would have no way of knowing the real risks, unless the government decided to be truthful about them—and to think that would happen was just plain naive. Added to this was the question of how America would handle nuclear issues with its allies and the rest of the world.

TRUMAN APPROACHED THESE issues cautiously, fearful of turning Groves and his supporters into enemies, yet conscious of the need to move forward. And in November 1945 he met with his British and Canadian counterparts, Clement Attlee and Mackenzie King, to establish a United Nations Atomic Energy Commission. That was the beginning of a multilateral effort to find a means of developing nuclear energy for beneficial uses in a controlled manner. Secretary of State James Byrnes made a last-ditch effort at a cooperative agreement with the Soviets, traveling to Moscow in December 1945, and although that led nowhere (amid much discord over what he should offer), Stalin agreed to join the new commission. At the same time, the Soviet leader—who doodled by drawing wolves on his paper, Byrnes observed—made a crafty strategic move, insisting that the new commission reside within the Security Council, rather than the General Assembly, so the Soviets could exercise the right of veto.[7] With the first international mechanism for controlling atomic development more or less in place, the UN became the official negotiating forum for future cold war confrontations.

The work on a nuclear control plan began after Byrnes returned to

Washington, when he appointed a new Committee on Atomic Energy to draft a proposal. He put Undersecretary of State Dean Acheson in charge. That in itself was a clear signal that changes were afoot among the power elite in Washington. Acheson, who was just at the beginning of a long career as the first and arguably most important craftsman of America's foreign policy as a nuclear weapons state, was the only committee member without a connection to the wartime bomb project.[8] He was acutely aware of the fact that once his country lost its exclusive hold over nuclear weapons technology the power balances would change. Groves believed a Soviet bomb could take as long as two decades to materialize. Acheson moved to dethrone the Manhattan Project leader by forming a second group, a board of consultants, led by Tennessee Valley Authority chairman David Lilienthal, to write the report. His argument to the committee was that this would save time for its busy members. Groves saw through the ruse and protested, but he was outvoted.

The idea for the board came from Acheson's assistant, a smart young lawyer named Herbert S. Marks, who had known Lilienthal when the two enforced government land sequestration efforts in the Tennessee Valley during the war. "They'd bought land from people who would come out of their houses with guns," said Anne Wilson Marks, a former wartime secretary to Groves, then Oppenheimer, who eventually married Marks.[9]

Lilienthal was surprised by what Acheson said when the two men first met to discuss the assignment January 16, 1946. "He talked frankly and in detail," Lilienthal wrote in his diary after the meeting. "Those charged with foreign policy—the secretary of state and the president—did not have either the facts nor an understanding of what was involved in the atomic energy issue, the most serious cloud hanging over the world. Commitments, on paper and in communiqués, have been made and are being made . . . without a knowledge of what the hell it is all about—literally!" Acheson further complained that the War Department, and "really one man in the War Department," had been "determining and almost running foreign policy" on the grounds of "military security."[10] That, of course, was General Groves.

THE MANHATTAN ENGINEER District, or MED, was like a separate state. It had been administratively cut off from the other wartime departments, and the handful of people who knew about it in its entirety had been sworn to secrecy. The MED's money came from taxpayers, but its budget was hidden from their representatives in Congress, which meant it was not accountable for how it allocated resources; sometimes it was a cash-only enterprise. "I came in one day and on his [Groves's] conference table there was about one million in cash for Sengier," Anne Marks recalled. Edgar Sengier was a Belgian mining company executive whose Congolese-origin uranium provided roughly three-quarters of the MED's total uranium needs.

Groves had gone to great lengths to protect information. All key aspects of the project, including geographical locations and strategic materials such as uranium and thorium, were assigned code names or letters, and every effort was made to keep the existence of the plants secret. Correspondence to scientists at Los Alamos, known as "Site Y," was sent to "P.O. Box 1663, Santa Fe." Letters sent from Los Alamos had to be put into a mailbox unsealed, so that the censors could read them to ensure they contained nothing affecting the project's security. Scientists joked or complained about the security arrangements and found clever ways to expose the gaps, but they knew that an unguarded phrase, a misplaced sentence, or a political comment could raise red flags among the censors and agents who kept them under constant surveillance. More serious transgressions were, in principle, punishable by imprisonment or death.[11]

A lot of secrets got out anyway. The Soviets knew about the MED during the war because of an extremely effective network of spies in Europe and North America. British and French scientists returned to their countries after the war with enough knowledge to start their own nuclear programs. Then, only weeks after the bombings in Japan, Groves himself decided to allow publication of a report describing the step-by-step development of the bomb. The report caused quite a stir, and there are varying views on why he allowed it to be published. Groves justified the decision by saying it drew a line under what could and could not be released to the public. Nevertheless, it helped fill in knowledge gaps for nuclear scientists in other countries.[12]

Groves held stark, black-and-white views about postwar atomic development. He paid lip service to developing nonmilitary nuclear applications, but for him the raison d'être for atomic activity was bombs. He could not take a nuanced approach such as Oppenheimer would. "Either we must have a hard-boiled, realistic enforceable world agreement ensuring the outlawing of atomic weapons or we and our dependable allies must have an exclusive supremacy in the field," he told Congress in a January 1946 memorandum. "We must have the best, the biggest and the most." Groves went further, suggesting a preemptive nuclear strike against prospective foreign atomic facilities to guarantee American atomic supremacy, envisioning what cold war historian Greg Herken describes as an American-administered Pax Atomica—"an atomic league of nations, founded upon the West's supposed technological superiority and the secret, preclusive monopoly of atomic raw materials."[13]

ACHESON GATHERED A group around Lilienthal that would come up with a very different view of how America should play its nuclear card, largely shaped by the ideas that Oppenheimer and Rabi had come up with the previous December. Besides Lilienthal, the board's members were Harry A. Winne of General Electric, Charles Allen Thomas of Monsanto Chemical Company—both of whom had worked on the bomb project during the war—and Chester I. Barnard, president of New Jersey Bell and a veteran of wartime cooperation between industry and government. "So these were all sorts of big types, a very remarkable group of people," said Anne Marks. Oppenheimer, who had already been tutoring Acheson before the meetings started, would be the board's primary consultant.

Groves could not hide his disdain for a panel that he knew threatened his hold over the MED and the nation's atomic affairs. Although Thomas and Winne had some knowledge of the processes involved in making the bomb, he wrote, "as far as I know Mr. Lilienthal and Mr. Barnard had little or no knowledge of the subject whatever."[14] Groves had a point. Lilienthal had virtually no experience in the nuclear field. Yet, like Groves, he had overseen big industrial projects, including dams and power projects; the TVA, among other things, supplied power to Oak Ridge, the vast industrial complex in Tennessee that had enriched uranium for the Hiroshima bomb. Groves exercised authority through compartmentalization and centralized command. Lilienthal preferred a collegial style of governing, sharing both power and information. Lilienthal's new assignment, however, would take him well away from the world of progressive liberalism. A man born in a grocery store knew he was doing something right when he improved lives ravaged by the Depression. Inside the MED, the moral calculations would be quite different.

THE GRADUAL TRANSITION of control over the MED arguably began on January 23, 1946, when Lilienthal's board met for the first time with Acheson's committee at the State Department. Lilienthal did not wait long to ask the crucial question. Would his panel be let in on the secrets? Groves pretty much knew then that the game was up and that he could not get away with the national security argument he had used a month earlier to keep McMahon and his congressional reformers at bay. However reluctantly, Groves agreed that the board "would have unrestricted access to any and all facts and facilities, including the very 'top secrets,' all of which, taken together, are now known to only a handful of men on this earth."[15]

Lilienthal, who recorded that passage in his diary, and the members of his panel were on the inside now, and another link in the general's security chain was broken.

Guided by Oppenheimer, Lilienthal and the other consultants started that day to learn facts about the Manhattan Project. They became not only bearers of secrets but their keepers as well. Lilienthal began to censor himself, explaining in his diary that he would not record the details of the discussion because "the records will show the results." At the same time, he sensed for the first time a great weight, for he knew that possession of atomic secrets could "change my prospects for peace of mind for a long time to come."[16]

Then, beginning with a long, one-day meeting in New York, and moving on to Oak Ridge and Los Alamos, Lilienthal and his fellow committee members saw and heard things about which the vast majority of Americans knew nothing. "No fairy tale that I read in utter rapture and enchantment as a child, no spy mystery, no 'horror' story, can remotely compare with the scientific recital I listened to for six or seven hours today," Lilienthal wrote after the New York encounter. "Mixed with that the constant element of international rivalry and intrigue, and I feel that I have been admitted, through the strangest accident of fate, behind the scenes in the most awful and inspiring drama since some primitive man looked for the very first time upon fire."[17] His writing was overblown, but it reflects the extraordinary sense of awe and self-importance Lilienthal felt upon being ushered

...o the secret world. He was not unique in that respect: the allure of what was hidden from everyone else and the power that swirled around the world of nuclear energy captivated many newcomers over the next several decades, even if they turned critical of it, as Lilienthal eventually did.

The industrial nuclear sites were in remote deserts and scrubland, sometimes in places where farmers and homeowners had been rushed off land so the building could commence. High wire fences had been thrown up around thousands of acres, while well inside the peripheries, factories at places like Oak Ridge and Hanford, in a remote part of Washington, performed a modern form of alchemy, spinning uranium into military gold—highly enriched uranium and plutonium, the fissile material needed for atomic bombs. These sites were linked by road, rail, and specially designated military aircraft, and by the rules, norms, and codes of a system designed to ensure that no outsider would know what the people inside were doing. Marks himself memorably recorded: "The Manhattan District bore no relation to the industrial or social life of our country; it was a separate state, with its own airplanes and its own factories and its thousands of secrets. It had a peculiar sovereignty, one that could bring about the end, peacefully or violently, of all other sovereignties."[18]

Nuke initially intentional or not - could now be Mechanism to achieve World Gov?

BACK IN WASHINGTON, the Dumbarton Oaks mansion in Georgetown, with ten acres of formal gardens and European antiques and paintings inside, provided a rarified setting for the exercise ahead. The report writing took place in the music room, where the UN charter had been drafted only two years earlier, and light and dark played off the heavy tapestries and gilded furniture. A religious painting, El Greco's *The Visitation*, caught sunlight directly from the great French doors leading to the garden. It was still only March 1946. After two months of fact-finding, the group was sitting down to propose a means of doing what Oppenheimer had always believed necessary, namely finding a means to develop nuclear energy for peaceful purposes while also preventing it from leading to disaster.

The crux of the challenge lay in finding some way of managing the two key nuclear fuel manufacturing processes—enrichment and reprocessing—that are critical to manufacturing nuclear weapons but also are used to produce the fuel to run reactors. Oppenheimer convinced the panel to propose international jurisdiction over all fission-able materials and the elements that can be used to produce them, in-cluding uranium, plutonium, and thorium. The new organization would be called the United Nations Atomic Development Authority.

Oppenheimer used the terms "dangerous" and "safe" to distinguish between activities that would be placed under the authority's control and those that in his opinion could safely remain within national juris-dictions. Even uranium mining, in his view, was not safe under national government controls. After all, uranium ore could be inconspicuously transported to hidden facilities and made into bomb-grade nuclear fuel. So the report proposed that any national or private effort to mine uranium would be henceforth illegal. The same was true with tho-rium, which could be used to make U-233, which is fissile.

Oppenheimer also emphasized that inspections alone could never be relied upon to prevent a nuclear facility from illicit use. Instead, if one country seized the nuclear fuel plants within its borders, intent on making nuclear weapons, other countries would be in a position to take counteractions, presumably by gearing up their own nuclear fa-cilities to make weapons. "The security which we see in the realiza-tion of this plan lies in the fact that it averts the danger of the surprise use of atomic weapons," the report said.[19] Of course, that still left the theoretical possibility of nuclear war.

On Thursday, March 7, the report was ready. Lilienthal and Ache-son took turns reading it to the members of their respective com-mittees. After finishing the final paragraphs, Lilienthal declared, "This, gentlemen, is our recommendation of a plan for security in a world of atomic energy." At the other end of the long table, Acheson removed his glasses. In a warm, low tone he said, "This is a brilliant and a profound document."[20]

AS THE FINAL touches were applied to the fifty-five-page report and it was readied for submission to Byrnes and Truman for approval, a strange thing happened. The secretary of state appointed Bernard Baruch to take the process to the next stage. He would be the U.S. am-bassador to the new UN Atomic Energy Commission.

Baruch was by instinct and temperament a gambler, a fighter, and a believer in unbridled capitalism. He was everything that Lilienthal and Acheson were not. An inside trader on Wall Street when it was not yet illegal, Baruch became a statesman after parlaying his great wealth and circle of contacts into a job as head of the War Industries Board during World War I. Then he worked his way into international diplomatic circles and gained the admiration of world leaders as politically distant as Winston Churchill and Woodrow Wilson.

Lilienthal could not sleep after he heard on March 18 about Baruch's appointment. "When I read this news last night, I was quite sick," he confided to his diary. "We need a man who is young, vigorous, not vain, and whom the Russians would feel isn't out simply to put them in a hole, not really caring about international cooperation. Baruch has none of these qualities."[21] Oppenheimer recalled later that he realized then the plan would never be put into action, according to Anne Marks. "Hope just sank," she recalled. Baruch was not only of a different generation but cut from an entirely different political cloth.

True to form, Baruch approached the job with a combination of brinksmanship and swashbuckling. He tapped into a network of like-minded conservative investment bankers and industrialists. They revisited Groves's idea of a U.S.-dominated atomic league. Since acquiring uranium was critical to a bomb program, they also suggested an immediate survey of world uranium reserves as a backdoor way of finding out what the Soviets had.

By mid-May, Baruch and his team had redrafted the Acheson-Lilienthal report, making four major changes. The new version incorporated the possibility of punishment, including nuclear attack, for violating the scheme. It also proposed total disarmament rather than just international control over nuclear weapons or the means of producing them. It shifted responsibility for mining and refining of fissionable materials back to private industry. Most significant, Baruch advocated abolishment of the veto power in the Security Council, the advantage the Soviets had gained in their original negotiation with Byrnes over the new UN Atomic Energy Commission. Baruch argued that as long as there was veto power, the proposed new authority would be hamstrung when it came to punishing violators.

Although even the original report was bound to fail, the revised edition made the chances of success even slimmer. It contained no timetable for the United States to relinquish its hold over nuclear weapons and called for total disarmament. This last condition, Lilienthal and his allies argued, "would hopelessly confuse and mix issues, and obscure the hope of working out something on the atom bomb."[22]

Moreover, it placed an emphasis on punishment that he thought was premature and possibly fatal to the proposal's acceptance. Oppenheimer and Lilienthal worked on the plan for another month, but with a growing sense of despair. On the eve of Baruch's June 18 speech to the UN, even Byrnes was worried. He confided to Acheson that choosing Baruch was "the worst mistake I have ever made."[23] In truth, though, with Stalin in charge, there probably wasn't any "right" way of achieving his objectives.

IN NEW YORK, Baruch was dressed for the occasion in pinstripe trousers and a dark, double-breasted jacket, befitting his distinguished elderly statesman role. His hair was white, and a voice once shy of public speaking occasionally faltered, although now more from age than from nerves. He was seventy-five.

"My fellow citizens of the world," he began, "we are here to make a choice between the quick and the dead. That is our business. Behind the black portent of the new atomic age lies a hope which, seized upon with faith, can work our salvation." The overblown oratory continued. "The peoples do not belong to the governments but . . . the governments belong to the peoples . . . War is their enemy . . . We find ourselves here to test if man can produce through his will and faith the miracle of peace, just as he has, through science and skill, the miracle of the atom."[24]

Listening to the speech from his radio back home in Tennessee—he had been in Washington days earlier arguing over its final touches—Lilienthal began to relax. Baruch had made some concessions. The outlawing of war was purposely understated, accompanied by an acknowledgment that progress toward that goal would depend first upon abolition of the atomic bomb. The timing of stages was left unresolved, and there was no mention of an atomic league or using atomic bombs against violators. Baruch had also toned down and made vague the proposal on ownership of uranium assets. But the proposal to eliminate the veto remained.[25]

After the speech, Baruch treated UN Atomic Energy Commission delegates to a dinner at the Stork Club. As the cocktails went around, Baruch declared, "We're going to forget the bomb and all other troubles." After grilled steaks, his guests ate ice cream laced with brandy and topped with fresh strawberries. Then the American diplomat took

them to Madison Square Garden to watch Joe Louis knock out Billy
Conn to retain the world heavyweight crown. Afterward, enjoying a
final libation at his apartment, Baruch and Soviet UN delegate Andrei
Gromyko posed, arm in arm, smiling. "Baruch and Gromyko in Ac-
cord on Louis," read the picture caption in the *New York Journal-
American* the next morning.[26]

STATESMEN AND PUNDITS from many parts of the world lavished
praise on Baruch. Gromyko remained silent, then delivered his coun-
terpunch in the form of an alternative proposal June 19. The Soviet
proposal was weak and unrealistic and seemed mainly aimed at scor-
ing diplomatic points. It asked for an international convention within
ninety days of an agreement, outlawing atomic bombs and the means
to their production—a proposal the Soviets knew the United States
would never accept. With their own bomb program now moving ahead
at top speed, the Soviets naturally also were hesitant on inspections,
insisting on only "periodic" visits by inspectors. Most important, however, they adamantly opposed the elimination of the right of veto.

In December, Baruch forced through a preliminary vote on his plan
in the Security Council over the objections not only of the Soviets
but also of the British, French, and Canadian UNAEC delegates, who
wanted more time in hopes of reaching a workable agreement. With
only Russia and Poland abstaining, the eleven-member council voted
in favor of continuing negotiations on the U.S. plan. "America can get
what she wants if she insists upon it," Baruch told Lilienthal tri-
umphantly. "After all, we've got it [the bomb] and they haven't and
won't have for a long time to come."[27]

With his vote secured, Baruch submitted his resignation and walked
off the international stage. He offered a last piece of advice to Truman—
the United States, he said, should dramatically increase production of
nuclear weapons.[28] Two years later, negotiations over the Baruch plan
collapsed and the UN Atomic Energy Commission was abandoned. It
would take almost a decade for a new international organization, the
International Atomic Energy Agency, to take its place, bearing little re-
semblance to the global authority Oppenheimer, Acheson, and Lilienthal had envisioned.

As a step toward international cooperation in the nuclear field, the Acheson-Lilienthal report was a masterpiece of fine and delicately poised legal thinking, reflecting the spirit of the times when international institution-building was seen as a way of preventing further war. Looked at from the vantage point of five decades, the report seems naive in its assumptions about the way nations would behave once they had access to nuclear technology. The idea that illicit bomb programs could be prevented by putting nuclear fuel processing plants all over the world also tempted fate, since that would increase the spread of the technology and the opportunity for making weapons by anyone with access to the facilities. The report advocated nuclear development on an international scale, without any assurance that the proposed safeguards would work. This was the necessary order, Oppenheimer had said, because you could not have one without the other.

Oppenheimer saw the civilian side of nuclear energy as a cornerstone to the whole question of control over military uses: the promise of benefits, however far off in the future, could be used to persuade other countries to forego nuclear weapons. Nevertheless, he was uncertain about the prospects for peaceful uses and understood that bomb programs would be a higher priority; and in this he was correct. It was only among the scientists, he said, where the interest in peaceful nuclear development was more immediate, that they had developed "an enlightened enthusiasm for cooperation."[29]

The question of whether nuclear energy should be further developed was not considered, and a lot of questions were left unanswered. For example, how accountable would the proposed new authority be to national governments, and to individual citizens? Also left for others to decide was the issue of how and when the United States would transfer control over existing nuclear facilities to an international body. Lilienthal's group understood the problems but did not try to resolve them. Their report, they emphasized, was only a place to start. And they had a point.

Six months after Baruch delivered his speech, on December 31, 1946, Lilienthal stood with Truman in the Oval Office. As the motion picture cameras clicked and whirred, Truman signed the order transferring the MED to the newly created Atomic Energy Commission as mandated by McMahon's legislation. Lilienthal, the commission's new chairman, was now in charge of the empire that Groves had built and tried to own.

Lilienthal hoped he could turn the atom into a force for good, penning a prayer in his diary that night: "God grant that in the coming year I may by a bit lessen the cloud of dread and fear that hangs over the world since Hiroshima. For I am sure that if we have some wisdom and patience, and divine guidance, we will find, we mortals, that the cloud has indeed a lining of silver."[30]

He was, like Voltaire's Candide, putting optimism and faith on trial, hoping man's technology would prove every bit as miraculous as God's. But the scientists were already thinking ahead to the next stage of weapons development—the thermonuclear, which would make Little Boy and Fat Man look like atomic relics.

CHAPTER 3

Crossroads

As he stood on board the *Panamint*, Bertrand Goldschmidt thought it had to be the strangest ship he had ever been on. Radio and radar antennas, like the ears of an elephant, topped the twelve-thousand-ton U.S. Navy vessel, scanning the airwaves for signals. Representatives from a host of the world's nations walked two by two up the gangplank, reminding the French scientist of the animal pairs in Noah's Ark.[1] A World War II flagship communications vessel with one battle star to her name, the *Panamint* was a survivor, like the ark. Her name derived from a mountain range that looks down on Death Valley.[2]

The *Panamint* headed out into the Pacific again on June 12, 1946, for a two-month voyage to the Bikini atoll so the passengers could watch two atomic bomb tests. The first would be dropped from the undercarriage of a plane; the second, twenty-four days later, would fulminate from below the water's surface. The observers on board the *Panamint* would not see goats tethered in iron holds on the target ships, contentedly chewing hay or having their last sips of water before the detonations. But a photographer, probably from the navy, caught the scene, and the picture is still in the National Archives.[3]

The Bible says that in Noah's six-hundredth year "all the fountains of the great deep burst forth, and the windows of the heavens were opened." After the biblical flood receded, life would be more precarious, no longer as secure or stable, and the average life span would be shorter.[4] There were only eight human survivors of the Flood, according to the legend. An old world was destroyed, a new one created.

In Operation Crossroads, this first and only postwar nuclear test exercise openly displayed for the world's media, people from the preatomic world voyaged to the South Pacific to witness the beginning of a new era. They were a mix of military men, intelligence experts, parliamentarians, academics, and scientists, from a total of twenty-two countries, including China, Russia, Poland, Mexico, and Brazil. Britain and Canada were allowed to send more than two representatives because of the close alliance they shared with the United States.

CROSSROADS WAS CONCEIVED and organized at a delicate moment in the nuclear age—the point at which it was just beginning, and therefore when no one knew how it would evolve. Americans were still trying to decide whether having an atomic bomb was a good or bad thing. If they were uneasy about it, the rest of the world was even more so. The tests were originally scheduled to take place in May, when by coincidence foreign ministers of the Big Four had organized a meeting in Paris to discuss peace treaties for Nazi Germany's European allies.[5] Instead, because the tests were postponed to July, the *Panamint* would leave San Francisco at an even less propitious moment, during the month Baruch presented his proposals ostensibly aimed at eliminating nuclear weapons, to the United Nations. Like Goldschmidt, many of the ship's other passengers were members of the UN Atomic Energy Commission and would later be involved in negotiations over the American plan.

Coming when it did, and surrounded by massive publicity, Crossroads was a bizarre spectator extravaganza that conveyed a mixed message. What was the United States trying to tell the world—pressing for an international control plan while demonstrating little intent of its own to curb further development of atomic weapons? To outsiders the timing seemed less than coincidental.[6] Although Crossroads was not originally conceived to show off America's new technological and military strength, it gave that impression, with conflicting results. It heightened admiration toward the United States on the one hand and jealousy and resentment on the other. These sentiments had already taken root among America's allies during the war, especially in atomic circles. Imagine the reaction within countries who would be enemies.

Planning for Crossroads began in an outburst of rivalry between the U.S. Army Air Forces and the U.S. Navy and Navy Air Force less than one month after the war ended in August 1945, and a push by the air forces for independence from the army. Within the navy there was a deep-seated fear that the new weapon would make the military branch obsolete. After all, what use were battleships and navy planes when atomic-armed army planes had won the war? While the army air forces jealously guarded its special relationship with the atomic bomb, the navy had begun making plans for atomic aircraft that could be launched from carriers.[7] The navy got its way on Crossroads, though, by proposing a joint task force, and the Joint Chiefs agreed.

Truman approved the exercise in the pivotal month of January 1946 when U.S. policy toward the atomic bomb began taking shape, often around contradictory objectives. In order to reduce concerns about military dominance over atomic power, Truman set up a civilian commission to report on the tests, promising to make the panel's report public. That promise was not kept, for two basic reasons: the panel put forth proposals that made the U.S. position at the UN look hypocritical, and its assessment of the horrors of nuclear war were so frightening that the government decided it was best to keep them from the public.[8] The bomb was not yet central to military strategy—that would not happen for another eighteen months—but policy planners were beginning to understand its importance in strategic terms.

Commanding the vast operation, officially known as Joint Task Force One, was Vice Admiral William Henry Purnell Blandy, the navy's ranking expert on missile and nuclear weapons development.[9] He defined the mission's official purpose, which was to determine the effects of atmospheric and underwater nuclear blasts on U.S. Navy vessels. Thousands of documents were created in the planning phases as Blandy considered how many target ships to put in place, where they would come from, how they would get there in time, and where they would be positioned in the lagoon. Blandy approved the code name Crossroads not for its symbolism but because of its "brevity in despatches."[10] He grappled with major issues, such as whether there would be two or three tests, and minor ones that seem ludicrous given the destructive nature of the exercise, such as what to do about mosquitoes. Several months before the exercise he ordered the entire test area sprayed with DDT.[11] Animals would be used to study physiological effects, Blandy wrote, with two exceptions. "No dogs or cats will be used."[12] The war being over, there was a shortage of naval personnel. Could "Jap" stewards be used, one previously classified telex asked? "Absolutely not," came the reply.[13]

There was even a relatively minor flap in which the Soviets expressed concern their representatives would be assigned the smallest cabins on board. They were assured this would not be the case.[14]

The bombs were produced and assembled at Los Alamos, still under the direction of General Groves, and a Los Alamos team would oversee key aspects of both tests, particularly the detonations. A third, deep underwater test was planned but never carried out. When the postponement was announced (mainly to let Congress finish its business ahead of the summer break), several leading Democrats argued for outright cancellation. So too did Byrnes, the secretary of state, who feared Crossroads would make his country look like an "atomic dictator." Also leading opposition to the exercise was the Federation of American Scientists, an organization of Manhattan Project scientists set up in 1945 to warn the public about potential dangers from scientific and technical advances.

Secretary of the Navy James Forrestal, one of the earliest advocates of the tests, argued they were necessary to obtain information about the effect of atomic bombings on ships, although Oppenheimer and other leading nuclear scientists maintained that laboratory experiments and existing data could provide all the information the navy needed. Coalescing around military proponents of the operation was a body of public opinion, including a large number of World War II veterans, that already saw nuclear weapons as necessary for America's defense. "The advocates of canceling the tests," argued conservative syndicated columnist Ernest Lindley, "seem to be walking along the trail which nearly led us to disaster after the First World War."[15]

But the atomic bomb had put us well past that era because its use in future wars, as policy-makers and the general public would gradually come to understand, was inconceivable, particularly once other countries had it. Beyond that, test enthusiasts utterly ignored, or failed to comprehend, the extent to which atomic testing, beginning with Crossroads, would destroy another world far away from theirs. That wasn't their concern—but it should have been, if for no other reason than it provided a glimpse of what might happen in a nuclear war closer to home. The Bikini islanders were moved some four hundred miles from their home to a less hospitable island called Kili. They were returned to Bikini in 1972, but after five years they had to be reevacuated because the atoll was still too contaminated. Today they remain on other islands.[16]

This was how power was displayed in the new atomic age. It ruined lives. It made land uninhabitable. It made fishing unthinkable. The atomic bomb delivered total annihilation. Still, a lot of people like Lindley wanted it, and so did the leaders they elected and supported. Testing was a way of demonstrating there was no intention of giving it up—the bomb was here to stay. No one understood these motivations more than Goldschmidt, whose personal and professional journey followed the vector of these emotional and political turnings. During the war, while he was in the United States and Canada, he learned the secrets of plutonium production. Afterward, he used that knowledge to start a French program.[17] Over time, France's behavior in the nuclear world—in particular the way it shared technology in unwelcome ways with other countries—would be sharply criticized by successive U.S. administrations. But it was precisely because of American nuclear exclusivity and exercises like Crossroads—plus France's own prewar nuclear legacy—that France would feel justified in its actions.

PRIOR TO THE war, the French government had poured more money into nuclear research than any other country in the world, and in the race to build and operate the world's first reactor France's scientists, led by Frédéric Joliot-Curie, had got closest. Instead, the distinction became Enrico Fermi's after he and his team successfully completed the world's first chain reaction in December 1942. "But it is probable, had it not been for the invasions of France and Norway, that Joliot-Curie and his co-workers would have won," Goldschmidt later contended.[18] The feeling that war had cheated the French scientists of this distinction was only enhanced by their effective demotion to third-class status as participants on the periphery of the Manhattan Project.

Goldschmidt experienced this personally after suffering the humiliation of exile from his native country for being Jewish. But once he was in North America, his professional life proved doubly frustrating because he found himself trapped in a cycle of exclusion and inclusion from the only project that mattered to a scientist of his caliber. This he blamed on a combination of bureaucratic ineptitude and autocratic political decisions. For example, after new security regulations prevented him from working with Enrico Fermi when both were still in New York, a loophole in the rules allowed Goldschmidt to take up a short-lived post at the Metallurgical Laboratory (Met Lab) at the University of Chicago. Because of that he not only witnessed the meeting on August 20, 1942, where Glenn Seaborg momentously announced that his team had isolated a tiny sample of plutonium, but gained the contacts and expertise that would help him replicate the reprocessing effort once back in France.[19]

That was a high point in the Frenchman's early career, but it ended after only three months when he was called to Canada to join a team of scientists that had just moved over from Britain, including a handful of French physicists. Shortly after their arrival, however, on January 2, 1943, they were informed that the U.S. government would no longer be sending them critical information about the project. This infuriated the scientists in Canada, who wondered why they had bothered to cross the ocean and suspected that more than wartime security arrangements were at stake. "As far as the Canadian-based scientists were concerned, the U.S. government was doing more than protecting its greatest military asset; it was also attempting to monopolize technology that might prove valuable once the war was over. In the Anglo-Canadian group, still waiting to move into their laboratories, feelings ran high," Goldschmidt wrote. "We had but one thought in our minds: cooperation. We had but one obsession: to resume our collaboration with the Americans."[20]

Although some cooperation resumed in August 1943, the United States continued to constrain the flow of information. And it was in this hothouse atmosphere of mutual collaboration and mutual distrust that both the British and French bomb projects effectively began. British scientists at Los Alamos and the other labs had taken to discreetly jotting down valuable information. As Brian Flowers, who was with the team in Canada, recalled, "Sir John Cockcroft used to keep a little black notebook in which he recorded every fact that came his way. A number of us followed his example, including me."[21]

The French scientists more dramatically—and in violation of secrecy oaths—told General Charles de Gaulle about the existence of the bomb project during a visit to Ottawa by the leader of the Free French Forces in July 1944. As temporary British citizens, the scientists debated the morality of violating their oaths, but they quickly overcame their reservations when they considered the way in which they had been treated and the unwelcome prospect of a postwar world in which the United States alone possessed an atomic weapon. "We did not want to see the Americans appropriate a monopoly over this new force, to whose discovery France had made such an important contribution. This is what finally emboldened us to commit the very violation of secrecy that Groves had feared. The fact that we had been treated like potential traitors contributed to pushing us toward the 'crime' itself," Goldschmidt revealed years later.[22]

Jules Guéron was chosen to do the telling because he knew de Gaulle and, being in the pay of the Free French, was theoretically less honor bound than the others. On July 11, 1944, at the French delegation's Ottawa villa, Guéron walked into a small room at the end of a corridor and told de Gaulle that a "weapon of extraordinary power, based on uranium, should be ready in one year and [was] to be used first against Japan. The possession of the weapon, perfected in the United States, was going to give that country a considerable advantage in the world after the war. It was absolutely necessary to resume atomic research in France as rapidly as possible."

The meeting lasted three minutes. Afterward Goldschmidt and the other French scientists were introduced to de Gaulle for the first time. "It was a moving moment," Goldschmidt recollected, "and I have often boasted about it because, when it was my turn, he addressed me as 'Monsieur le Professeur,' the first time in my life anyone had used that title for me, and said to me simply, 'I thank you. I understood you very well.'"[23]

Just before returning to France in February 1946, Goldschmidt requested a meeting with Groves. The general knew he could not prevent the French scientists from using their knowledge or from passing it on to their teams, "but he asked me that it be done without publication and only gradually as our work evolved." Evidently, Groves knew nothing of the exchange with de Gaulle.[24]

Goldschmidt was relieved to be leaving, and he had enough information to start a plutonium program in France when he returned. Through the crucible of his wartime experience in North America, he, like other returning European scientists, adjusted his moral and political compass to the emerging realities of the postwar world in a nuclear age. Every country would have to fend for itself in the rush to claim a stake. As far as Goldschmidt was concerned, the "true genesis of U.S. nuclear policy" lay in the decision to sever collaboration with the team in Canada after Fermi's chain reaction. It amounted to "split the atom, but do not share it . . . not even with your closest ally." That moment also marked "the beginning of the United Kingdom's vassalage to the United States in nuclear affairs." [25]

AS THE *PANAMINT* made its way toward the Marshall Islands in June 1946, Goldschmidt had a lot of time to reflect on the tumultuous past few years. Life on board was anything but pleasant. The men lived in close quarters, with little to do but watch second-rate movies in an open-air cinema on the afterdeck and search for alcohol in the privacy of staterooms, since open consumption was forbidden. Only seven years earlier, the French chemist had sailed to Taihiti to study cosmic rays. He marveled at its stunning mountains, "the perfume of the frangipani . . . the color of the flowers, of the butterflies, and especially of the fishes in the lagoon."[26] This time he would travel to the Bikini atoll, where the gray hulks of naval vessels would impose themselves on verdant shorelines like ungainly leviathans from the deep. An inno- cent world of palm trees, grass huts, and calm seas would soon be transformed; natives numbering fewer than two hundred, Blandy as- sured those back in Washington, could "be readily moved to another atoll"—banished, we now would think, as if from the last remaining Eden.[27] "For me, the name Bikini summons up the memory of a hallu- cinatory vision, as well as the only exotic cruise on which I was bored," Goldschmidt later wrote.[28]

Often we imagine that the Marshall Islands were selected for the bomb tests because of their remoteness from the continental United States, five thousand miles from California and half that distance again from Hawaii, to its southwest. While that was certainly a factor, there were others. The Marshall Islands are divided into eastern and west- ern chains of atolls, or island groups, comprising an area slightly larger than Washington, D.C., although spread out over a much larger expanse of sea. They are made up of coral reefs rising a few feet above sea level. The Bikini and Eniwetok atolls, part of the western chain, were selected as test sites in part because of their proximity to a major U.S. military airbase, on the Kwajalein atoll, also on the western chain. But they had the added advantage of being far from commercial shipping lanes, air routes, and, theoretically at least, fishing grounds.

They were also out of the way of most western Pacific typhoons, and military planners believed that the prevailing northeastern winds would prevent or at least limit the threat of radioactive fallout to nearby inhabited islands.[29]

On the eve of the first test Goldschmidt got lucky, or so it seemed. He had run into an old acquaintance from Chicago, Karl Compton, president of the Massachusetts Institute of Technology and a presidential adviser on the atomic bomb during the war. Compton now headed Truman's civilian review panel, formally known as the Joint Chiefs of Staff Evaluation Board, which would write reports on the tests—code-named Able and Baker and alphabetized for the order in which they would take place. Compton asked Goldschmidt if, after the Able shot, he would join his team on a research excursion to Australia and New Zealand in the weeks before the second test. Goldschmidt was delighted to accept.[30]

The morning of July 1 dawned clear and bright, a good omen. Most of the forty-two thousand participants and observers, mainly navy personnel but also including five hundred civilians, were spread around more than one hundred and fifty vessels that provided quarters, experimental stations, and workshops. Others were in the air. For most, this would be the first sight of an atomic bomb explosion. A further ninety target vessels, including battleships, destroyers, light cruisers, transport ships, and submarines, were in their assigned moorings, designed to provide the technical information the navy wanted on the effects of an atomic blast.

The main target ship had been painted bright red. Goats numbering 176 were unloaded onto ships and placed in iron bar tethers, securely fastened to either end by rope. There were also about as many pigs and an equal number of mice, as well as guinea pigs and more than three thousand white rats. The animals were spread around some of the target ships, placed in positions that crew members would normally occupy, to check afterward for the effects of gamma radiation. During Baker, two hundred white rats and twenty pigs were used.[31] The *Panamint* was about twenty-five miles from the target sector. The passengers were told to put on dark glasses to protect their eyes from the intensity of the fireball.

At thirty-three seconds after the appointed hour of 9:00 A.M., a modified B-29 dropped the first bomb, a replica of the plutonium weapon used on Nagasaki, over the sea. Almost instantly the classic mushroom shape appeared, "white with peach-colored bands," Gold-schmidt noted. Pilotless planes soon flew through the cloud collecting samples. "Nearly two minutes later, the sound from the explosions reached us in a distant muffled roll," Goldschmidt wrote. "Among the twenty or so vessels located less than one kilometer from the vertical under the explosion, five sank immediately or within twenty-four hours." Fires broke out on ships farther away, and subsequent studies showed virtually all of them had been made intensely radioactive.[32]

But the bomb missed the bright red ship that was its intended tar-get, bursting instead about two thousand feet to the west, in a sector with relatively few ships. The Russian observers were heard to mutter "pooh," while news reports labeled the exercise a semifailure. Blandy tried to make the best of it, pointing out to reporters that although the force was less than realized at Nagasaki, it was greater than the first test at Alamogordo, where a plutonium bomb also was used. But the reporters were not persuaded. And, as Goldschmidt noted, "What was feared actually happened: the public tended to minimize the impor-tance of the atomic bomb."[33]

Blandy could only hope that Baker would turn out better. He had twenty-four days to prepare.

THE TEST OVER, Goldschmidt looked forward to his break from ship-board tedium. Just as he prepared to leave for the trip to Australia, however, an army colonel appeared and started shouting at him. He accused him of circumventing the chain of command in order to join Compton's group on their trip. Blandy had vetoed it, and, of course, Goldschmidt instantly understood why. "Actually," he wrote, "no-body wanted to see me spend three weeks with the scientists who were charged with evaluating the quantitative results of the tests, and learning all their most secret data."[34]

So he was forced to remain on the ship with the other non-Americans for another month. By the time the trip was over, he had seen movies fifty-seven evenings in a row, seated between the same two neighbors, both physicists—Stefan Pienkowski, president of the Univer-sity of Warsaw and one of the organizers of student resistance during the war, and Chung-yao Chao, a future leader of China's nuclear weapons project. The only news the passengers received arrived on mimeographed sheets at breakfast. There was no attempt to censor the news, and little concern for its effect on the already touchy Russians. One morning, the passengers arrived at their tables to read the headline: "Ambassador Bullitt Declares Soviet Union Wants War," referring to William C. Bullitt, who was the last U.S. representative to France before the Vichy government came to power. "When the two Soviet delegates came to breakfast, their faces turned purple; they got up from the table and demanded to be let off the boat immediately," Goldschmidt recalled. That wasn't possible, so the Soviets were forced to make do.[35]

As SCHEDULED, AT 8:35 A.M. Bikini time on July 25, a second plutonium bomb, lodged under a barge in the lagoon, was detonated remotely by radio signal. The closest battleship, *Arkansas*, lay about one thousand feet away; the aircraft carrier *Saratoga* was farther still. A dome rose upon the lagoon's surface, showing the light of the incandescent material within, and an opaque cloud that followed the blast wave enveloped about half of the target ships.[36]

The cloud vanished in about two seconds. Then the roiling water beneath sent a column of water—ten million tons, Compton's people estimated—high above the lagoon's surface. It climbed at a rate of thirty-two hundred feet per second (the rate of ascent was not made public at the time). Within a few seconds the water column was fifty-five hundred feet, more than four times the height of the Empire State Building; its diameter was less than half the height, about twenty-two hundred feet. For several minutes after the column reached maximum height, water fell back, forming an expanding cloud of spray, which now engulfed the ships that had been enveloped by the cloud. A wall of foaming water, several hundred feet high, surrounded the base of the column, forming huge waves, eighty to one hundred feet high, which gradually became smaller as they moved toward land.[37] When the waves receded and the column finally collapsed, the *Arkansas* had disappeared. The column of water had lifted the twenty-six-thousand-ton battleship "like a piece of straw," Goldschmidt recorded. The *Saratoga* sank within seven hours, as did many other vessels.[38]

The terror and beauty of this event made an instant impression. "This was the most beautiful and awe-inspiring open-air spectacle I had ever seen," Goldschmidt wrote. In a report to his superiors in France he said that the only defense against such a weapon was "distance and dispersion." The war that had ended in Europe only one year earlier, and the way it had ended, he realized, was now a relic of history—"a landing like the one in Normandy is inconceivable against a country possessing the atomic weapon."[39]

If the American military wanted to impress foreigners with the message that there was a new way now of waging war, or defending one's country from attack, they had achieved their goal. But the *Panamint*'s passengers reacted to the spectacle in completely contrasting ways, demonstrating that even within one country—in this case, Brazil—the gamut of emotional and, eventually, political reactions to the bomb could be irrevocably divided. "We've got to have one of these," exclaimed Brazil's Admiral Alvaro Alberto, or words to that effect. His compatriot, Senator Arnon de Mello, on the other hand, was deeply troubled by what he had witnessed. Brazil's military did indeed embark on a secret weapons program, though many years later. But in 1990 the effort was stopped on the order of Brazil's newly elected president, Fernando Collor de Mello, the senator's son. Brazilians who know de Mello say that his father's influence, stemming from the sight of the Baker explosion all those years earlier, had prompted the reversal.[40]

WHILE THE OBSERVERS focused on the sheer force of the explosion, still thinking in preatomic ways, Compton, reporting to the Joint Chiefs, understood very quickly where the real, long-term damage lay. In a top secret dispatch four days after the test, he wrote that compared to the previous air burst, in which much of the fallout was sucked into the atmosphere by clouds and then widely dispersed, the underwater explosion was more deadly. It "threw large masses of highly radioactive water onto the decks and into the hulls of vessels. These contaminated ships became radioactive stoves, and would have burned all living things aboard them with invisible and painless but deadly radiation. It is too soon to attempt an analysis of all of the implications of the Bikini tests. But it is not too soon to point to the necessity for immediate and intensive research into several unique problems posed by the atomic bomb. The poisoning of large volumes of water presents such a problem."[41]

Despite warnings from the chief radiation safety expert that the target ships "may remain dangerous for an indeterminate time," the first patrol boats reentered the lagoon just forty-one minutes after the blast to measure radioactivity and to retrieve instruments. Salvage crews on other ships were boarding target ships within a couple of hours of the blast, and by the end of the day forty-nine ships with fifteen thousand men on board were in the radioactive zone. All were forced to return to the ocean because of high readings.

Decontamination efforts started on July 27 in hopes that some of the vessels could be reboarded and returned to their home ports. The first ship was hosed down with saltwater, and when that didn't work a variety of detergents, chemicals, and finally foodstuffs, such as cornstarch, flour, and coconut shells, were tried. Finally it was discovered that prolonged washing with an acetic acid solution worked reasonably well, but it was not feasible for mass application. Other reagents worked only to the extent they could remove paint or corrosion.[42] "When you realize that even a small destroyer . . . had a superstructure that was about three acres," recalled the radiation safety (radsafe) director, Stafford Warren, "the job of cleaning the radioactivity off was just impossible."[43]

The desperate measures reflected a total absence of decontamination planning by the navy. Cleanup crews were two thousand miles from any well-stocked port facility and had never attempted even experimentally to irradiate and then decontaminate a ship, or parts of one. Navy cleanup crews worked without shirts. The "safety culture" we now have did not exist. Radiation safety personnel tried to warn the sailors but never insisted on making them wear protective clothing, and there were shortages of monitors and other protective gear. The radsafe monitors, on the other hand, were well protected, and astounded at the attitude of the navy men. A captain unsuccessfully seeking permission to reboard one of the target ships was "completely bewildered" by all the seeming fuss, according to David Bradley, one of the radiation monitors. "The deck was clean, anybody could see that, clean enough for the Admiral himself to eat his breakfast off of. So what was all this goddamn radioactivity?"[44]

On August 10, most of the fleet was towed to the military base at Kwajalein so the work could be done in uncontaminated water; that effort continued into 1947. But some of the ships were never moved. They were simply sunk off Bikini, while others were towed back to the United States and Hawaii for radiological inspection. Twelve less-contaminated target ships were remanned and sailed back with their crews to the United States.[45] Warren knew the exercise—Baker in particular—had been a disaster from a radiation safety perspective and told one of his monitors, "I never want to go through the experience of the last three weeks of August again."[46]

POLITICAL SANITIZATION BEGAN in Washington, when the government decided to withhold a critical final paragraph from Compton's initial report. It suggested that in an actual nuclear attack the destruction would be so devastating that Americans should be ready to consider preemptive nuclear strikes in order to prevent that from happening. This proposal was the stark and understandable reaction to what Compton and his panel had just witnessed—in a nuclear war, defense might not be an option, so the best thing would be to strike first before the enemy does. But the suggestion was diplomatically loaded, particularly since a parallel effort for an international nuclear control treaty was under way in the UN. So when the preliminary report was made public, the paragraph was deleted. Compton and his fellow board member Bradley Dewey were furious, both still being old-fashioned enough to believe in being up-front with the public about matters of such grave importance. They also believed that public knowledge of what was at stake would increase support for nuclear weapons and a policy of preemption. Compton threatened to resign over the omission, while Dewey told the Joint Chiefs that he reserved the right to state publicly "at any early and appropriate moment" the contents of the excised paragraph.[47]

The Joint Chiefs apologized but said that they feared that its publication would imply their official approval. This was unacceptable, they said, "in view of the fact that a national policy on the control of atomic energy has been announced and is now the subject of international negotiation."[48] That did not mean the recommendation would be ignored. It only meant that the United States could not afford to be seen talking about the need for preemptive nuclear strikes while arguing in the United Nations for a plan to prevent other countries from acquiring nuclear weapons.

A year later, in June 1947, the board sent its final report on Crossroads. It made grim reading and was not made public:

> We can form no adequate mental picture of the multiple disaster which would befall a modern city, blasted by one or more

atomic bombs and enveloped by radioactive mists. Of the survivors in contaminated areas, some would be doomed to die of
radiation sickness in hours, some in days, and others in years.
But, these areas, irregular in size and shape, as wind and topog-
raphy might form them, would have no visible boundaries. No
survivor could be certain he was not among the doomed and
so, added to every terror of the moment, thousands would be
stricken with a fear of death and the uncertainty of the time of
its arrival.[49]

This time, the board was explicit about the need for preemptive
measures: "Offensive measures will be the only generally effective
means of defense, and the United States must be prepared to employ
them before a potential enemy can inflict significant damage upon
us." Thus Congress should enact legislation allowing the commander
in chief to engage in "prompt and effective atomic bomb retaliation
should another nation ready an atomic weapon attack against us."[50]

The following month, the report was formally presented to the Joint
Chiefs of Staff, along with two dozen or more military officials and
the five members of the U.S. Atomic Energy Commission. By October,
news of the report's existence, and its suppression, had leaked. The
New York Times Herald quoted a "high placed military source" describing the report: "Some of the findings about the effects of the atom
bomb are so disturbing and frightening and the recommendations are
so sensational that the White House won't permit it to be made public
at this time."[51]

After the article appeared, an attempt was made to publish a less
sensational version, but even that remained top secret. Eventually it
became obvious to both Compton and Dewey that with the ongoing
attempt to promote Baruch's nuclear control plan in the United Nations "the effectiveness of the report was being neutralized by someone, either in the State Department or in the office of the President
(U.S); the report 'kept bouncing back and forth' between these two offices."[52] In fact, their report had fallen victim to one of the central co-
nundrums of the nuclear age—how to retain a military nuclear option
while promoting "peaceful" nuclear power in a manner intended to
prevent other countries from obtaining the same perceived advantage.

Compton and Dewey refused to relinquish their own copies when requested to do so by the Joint Chiefs, and the battle over the documents

continued for almost a decade, during which Compton died. Compton's widow was persuaded to return her husband's copy, but Dewey's remained outside the Joint Chiefs' ambit. In 1955, Dewey was once again requested to return his copy of the report, this time by the Defense Department's Armed Forces Special Weapons Project, an interservice advisory group on nuclear weapons set up after the war. He replied in "shock" that "the report as written was to be a public document, to record for the benefit of the public the facts brought out by the spending of the millions of dollars that were involved in this elaborate and wonderfully conducted operation."[53] Interviewed by an agent of the U.S. Army's Counter Intelligence Corps (CIC), Dewey stated, according to the agent's report, that "he had seriously contemplated 'exposing' the matter to the press and that he 'will fight the highest court in the land, if necessary, to retain his copy of the report.' "[54]

By early 1947 the bomb was already playing a significant role in U.S. military thinking, even more so as strategists grappled with the uncomfortable prospect of a Soviet bomb, whose advent, they knew, was only a matter of time.[55] The question of how much the public should be told about nuclear weapons policy would be under continual debate, while discourse about the role of nuclear weapons in the nation's defense coalesced around a powerful, narrow, and secretive community of military and political advisers. Among members of this power elite, the notion took hold that nuclear weapons were essential to national security; over time that conviction would devolve downward into the public consciousness through a combination of censorship and media manipulation. The way in which the message traveled either numbed people to the pain of life in the nuclear age or convinced them of its necessity. Informed decision-making became more difficult, if not impossible, which meant ordinary citizens were effectively absolved of the responsibility of weighing such dark matters. Nuclear weapons became something for "experts" to worry about.

Compton and Dewey had welcomed the atomic bomb, not as an instrument of human extinction, but as a symbol of power that accrued to the United States as its sole possessor. But they bridled at the censorship that was its natural partner in this new age. This they had not anticipated. Ironically, the military investigation that made Dewey a target in 1955 was itself trapped by the same codes of secrecy. If the

Crossroads report was to be kept secret, there was no question of arresting Dewey and dragging the matter through the courts. Dewey was allowed to keep his copy, and the matter rested there. The report remained buried. This time, the reasons for suppression were not related to the conflict over the effort to promote "peaceful" nuclear energy. Instead, the military had cryptically concluded that the document "contains conclusions and recommendations pertaining to national policy, some of which have been subsequently adopted."[56] Four decades after it was written, on June 13, 1986, the report was released.[57]

APART FROM THE feud over the report's publication, Compton's board viewed the tests themselves as a complete success. They congratulated Blandy on a job well done and said the exercise had achieved its military objectives. Goldschmidt was less impressed. "An effort had been made to give these experiments a scientific character that they did not really have. They could produce no new data on the civilian production of atomic energy, and the hoped-for biological results could have been obtained at considerably less expense."[58]

In 1985, and again in 1996, follow-up tests conducted on forty-two thousand participants in Crossroads showed a higher than normal incidence of leukemia and prostate cancer. Although no direct link to the fallout could be established, an analysis of the exercise concluded that some of the personnel were likely to have experienced high internal exposures because of widespread contamination, poor safety practices, and the "hairy-chested" attitudes of naval officers. In the islanders' new home on Kili, the living conditions were more crowded and there was no lagoon or sheltered fishing grounds, so food supplies ran critically low. The Able and Baker explosions were only the beginning of extensive atmospheric and underwater nuclear testing that left the coral atolls of Bikini and Eniwetok poisoned with radiation.[59]

When the *Panamint* reached Hawaii, Goldschmidt received a telegram requesting his presence in New York to monitor the UN talks on atomic control. In the middle of August, he watched the protracted negotiations over the Baruch plan with a growing sense of hopelessness. "I felt even more vividly the contrast between the two projects," he recorded, "the one inhuman and useless, the other unrealistic but indispensable."[60]

Later France would test its own atomic weapons near Tahiti, resulting in an influx of money and a tripling of the island's population—"an unexpected consequence of uranium fission," Goldschmidt ruefully admitted, and one he could not have imagined during his prewar visit to the island that had so enchanted him.[61]

CHAPTER 4

The *Hausfreund*

WHEN MARY BUNEMAN FIRST SAW her new home at Harwell, her misery was complete. The Atomic Energy Research Establishment (AERE) was built on a former airfield beside a typical English country village just south of Oxford. But unlike the thatched cottages, pubs, and shops nestled around the village's Norman church, the houses where the atomic people lived were, as she put it, "aluminum toolboxes," near a compound surrounded by a high barbed-wire fence and concrete uprights.

"It looked forbidding, and served to emphasize the feeling that our environment was abnormal," she wrote in her diary in 1946. And indeed, Mary Buneman's new "town" was abnormal. It was an artificial community made up of scientists and mathematicians who had worked on the Manhattan Project and returned home to work the new alchemy for their own country.[1] The villagers nearby came from families that had lived in Harwell for generations. The area was famous for its orchards of Morello cherry trees. But it would not be any longer. Henceforth, Harwell would be associated with the grim atomic enclosure.

Across the English Channel in France, scientists set up a research center on a four-hundred-acre plain at Christ-de-Saclay, near Versailles. The land was expropriated from local wheat farmers and landowners, who naturally protested, not just because of the loss of their land but because of what such a facility might do to their lives. They feared the influx of then mostly left-leaning scientists into their politically conservative community. One parliamentarian went so far as to suggest that the palace at Versailles might be destroyed in a future war because the research center would be a certain target.[2] Irène Joliot-Curie, quiet, shy, and very inward, responded to the furor by ordering five thousand trees planted. They would shield the scientists from the locals, and hopefully keep everyone happy.[3]

Such communities existed in every country that developed nuclear weapons after the war. They were an indication of what nuclear, whether for military or peaceful purposes, would demand. Tight security and the nature of the work would isolate one segment of the population from another. At Harwell, the scrutiny became especially intense because of the presence of several scientists with Communist affiliations, including one who would become history's most famous atomic spy, Klaus Fuchs. Anyone connected with the British nuclear program was required to sign the Official Secrets Act, commonly considered one of the world's most draconian pieces of censorship legislation.

This exclusiveness was not good for anyone. Scientists locked away with each other by day, socializing with each others' families by night, could easily lose touch with "real" life. For a number of years, while the bomb development was under way, people in the village who lived "real" lives—farming, banking, teaching—would know nothing of what the scientists did. Isolation and secrecy discouraged informed public discussion about the value of nuclear weapons. That allowed "peculiar sovereignties," beyond the one described by Herbert Marks on seeing the Manhattan Project enclosures, to grow and flourish until they became so entrenched that no political leader would be brave or foolish enough to seriously challenge their yearly budget requests, let alone their existence. The irony is that secrets continued to leak, particularly from Harwell, and as the secrets leaked, the rise of new nuclear states became inevitable. If nuclear weapons offered security, they also tempted fate. Once other countries had them, the possibility of nuclear war increased.

To affect a sense of normalcy, atomic villages often had their own schools and hospitals, as well as small orchestras, theaters, and sports teams. However, behind the scenes addiction and promiscuity were not uncommon. "Some of us looked forward to these rather pathetic social events as if they were gala evenings, such was the distance between us and a normal social life," Mary recalled. Such isolation, combined with the postwar letdown and youthful adventurousness, fed an atmosphere that Mary described as sometimes verging on mild hysteria. "If we could lay our hands on alcohol we tended to drink it with undue haste and relish; sexual adventures were common and scandal was our daily diet," she recorded. This was hardly what the security apparatus would deem an ideal climate for protecting secrets.

To the scientists, though, AERE's separateness from the rest of society only underscored its importance, and by extension their own. However odd they might have seemed to "normal" people, the scientists were masters of their own universe, at the leading edge of their discipline. "There was an air of excitement and expectation about what lay ahead," wrote Terry Price, a Cambridge-educated physicist who arrived at Harwell a few months after the Bunemans in 1946. Price continued: "We knew we were the standard-bearers for the country—and needed no further proof than the 'mystery tours' run by London Transport. At weekends, these brought red double-decker buses to the Harwell runways, with passengers gaping at scientists digging their gardens, as though we were denizens of a zoo. Newspapers ran headlines like, 'Atom Man Was There' when one of us attended any meeting that was remotely in the public eye. It was all very heady and enjoyable."[4]

But the security demands could rattle nerves and topple careers, as Price himself would later discover. In France, Bertrand Goldschmidt recalled being "seized by panic" when in 1963, at a dinner in honor of the duke and duchess of Windsor, he was summoned to speak in private to the two guests of honor. Exiled from Great Britain, the former King Edward VIII and his American divorcée wife, Wallis Simpson, had taken up residence at Gif-sur-Yvette, adjoining the Saclay research site. Goldschmidt was afraid they would ask him about "some delicate point covered by atomic secrecy, probably some aspect of our military program." Luckily for him, the displaced couple were not remotely interested in such matters. Instead, the duchess asked Goldschmidt how much the gardeners at Saclay were paid and whether they were given pensions. "She explained that her gardeners had left her, one after the other, for a less noble but probably more lucrative position," Goldschmidt wrote. Barely able to contain his laughter and relief, Goldschmidt told the duchess that the French atomic energy commission "gave a pension to all its employees, and probably a better salary than she paid."[5]

In the new nuclear kingdom, even Windsor wealth was evidently hard-pressed to compete with that of modern technocracy. There was no shortage of funds flowing into the nuclear coffers, but the scientists

who benefited from them paid a price in other ways. They were no
longer free men. Before the war, they openly explored the nuclear questions. Now they were harnessed to the state and its security requirements. Within that secret environment, as everyone at Harwell would
discover, lurked tremendous personal and professional dangers.

MARY WAS ALREADY part of this world when she first met Fuchs in
New York in December 1943. She and her first husband, Oscar Buneman, were traveling with other British scientists to continue working
on the bomb project started in Britain. Filling out forms at the British
Supply Mission, she had been flustered, keeping one eye on what she
was writing and the other on her toddler son, who was crawling into
everything. She was in a new country. Christmas was approaching. A
war was on, and she had spent the last week crossing the Atlantic. She
hoped, or at least thought, that the tall, slim man standing closest to
her might make a gesture of help, humor her or amuse the child. There
was nothing but a nod, a smile, and silence. Fuchs stood there, pale and
slender, with round spectacles and full, sensitive lips. He was young
but his hairline was receding, a feature that echoed his reticent behavior. "My first impression was of failure to make contact," Mary observed. "Everything I said, every attempted conversational opening
was greeted with benign silence. He didn't seem to find it necessary to
make any reciprocal comment. It was like talking to a faintly smiling
mask."

Three years later, in 1946, having just arrived back at Harwell, she
was unpacking her china and glass when Fuchs stopped by to say
hello. They had not seen each other since that brief encounter in New
York. Fuchs had remained in New York for several months and then
went to Los Alamos, while Mary and her husband left almost immediately for Berkeley. After the war, Fuchs returned to Britain shortly
after the Bunemans did to become Oscar's immediate supervisor as
head of theoretical physics at Harwell. This was an enormously prestigious position, which meant that Fuchs would easily command the
respect and admiration of his colleagues. "His personality seemed to
have developed since our first brief meeting in New York and he had
acquired something of an aura of authority," Mary recorded in her unpublished diary. "The sun of New Mexico, which he had recently left,

had burnished his pallid complexion, and he was wearing rather more stylish, lighter-colored clothes, and they suited him."

By then Fuchs had passed on information of such critical importance to atomic-bomb-making that the Soviets would have their first nuclear weapon one year earlier, possibly two, than might otherwise have been the case.[6] Included in the packets of material he handed off to couriers, first in England, then later in New York and Los Alamos, were vital reports on the gaseous diffusion uranium enrichment process and, later, a detailed design of the plutonium bomb tested at Alamogordo on July 15, 1945.[7] Before he left the United States, Fuchs attended an important conference at Los Alamos in April 1946 on developing thermonuclear weapons. He passed on Edward Teller's preliminary design for the weapon, which seems to have prompted the Soviet government to authorize thermonuclear weapons research the following year, in 1947, two years before a decision on developing these weapons was taken in the United States.[8]

Now back in England, Fuchs was assigned a new handler, one of the Soviet Union's most celebrated espionage agents, Alexander S. Feklisov, and his subterfuge would continue for another two years.[9]

FUCHS'S DECISION TO "turn" facilitated the cold war and the arms race in the way that Abdul Qadeer Khan's activities several decades later would lead to the commoditization of nuclear weapons. Both were master proliferators. More than that, though, by helping countries toward which they felt a prime allegiance, they each contributed to enormous power-balance shifts. Through the theft of nuclear technology, they proved that men could move geopolitical mountains.

Fuchs's tipping point came shortly after his arrival at Birmingham University, when Germany launched its surprise attack on the Soviet Union on June 22, 1941. A year later he signed a standard form placing him under Britain's Official Secrets Act and became a naturalized British citizen. But by then he had established contact with a military intelligence officer at the Soviet embassy in London and was periodically delivering reports through a courier on Tube Alloys, the code name for the British bomb project.[10]

Although Fuchs seems to have acted independently, he was not alone. Dozens of Soviet sympathizers in the United States, Canada, and Europe passed atomic secrets to the Soviets during the war. Their activities were motivated in part by misguided notions about life under Communist rule in the Soviet Union but also by a desire to check the concentration of atomic power in one state.

Fuchs's real importance as a spy came after he arrived in the United States in December 1943, when he started passing on information about the gaseous diffusion uranium enrichment process at Oak Ridge. Although the Soviets later adopted a better technology, they quickly made the American process a top priority in the early bomb effort. But it wasn't until Fuchs went to Los Alamos in August 1944 that the Soviets began receiving the most valuable information of all, the critical calculations needed to build and successfully detonate a plutonium bomb.[11]

After the war, Fuchs moved into Ridgeway House, the quarters for single men and women at Harwell. At Moscow Center, Soviet officials were laying the groundwork for a postwar espionage operation in England, and naturally they kept tabs on Fuchs. In 1947, they arranged for Feklisov, who had earlier directed the atomic spy ring in the United States, to meet him at a north London pub. "At his own initiative," Feklisov wrote after he retired, "Fuchs brought important materials on the technology of plutonium production which he had failed to acquire in the United States." Every three or four months, Fuchs slipped through the security gates without being detected to meet with Feklisov. "All the meetings were carefully prepared," Feklisov disclosed. "Moscow approved each plan."[12]

At Harwell, Fuchs continued to enjoy Mary Buneman's company at parties and visits to her house, but he remained cool and reserved. "Although he was a deft and competent dancer, he never let himself go at any of the parties, remaining always the smiling onlooker. He kept up with the rest of us, drink-by-drink and smoking Councillor cigarettes, but I never saw him lose an ounce of his formidable self-control," Mary remembered. "In all the years during which I knew him, I could never describe his manners as being anything but perfect."

Harwell's director at the time was a taciturn British northerner named John Cockcroft. He was one of three people critical to the British bomb effort, which had been approved on January 8, 1947, by a small ministerial committee operating in total secrecy. The other two were Christopher Hinton, who was in charge of designing and building plants to produce fissile material, and William Penney, who would oversee the making and testing of a weapon. Penney had been at Los Alamos, and his establishment would eventually be placed at an airfield at Aldermaston in Berkshire, west of London. Hinton's main base was at Windscale in Cumbria, along England's northwest coast.[13]

Cockcroft and his wife entertained only modestly, offering guests a discreet sherry or two. The task of throwing wild parties was left to his deputy, Herbert Skinner, and his exuberant Austrian-born wife, Erna. Their home became the site of memorable gatherings. At the Skinners' parties, Mary and Klaus Fuchs flirted with each other while enjoying conversation, jazz, and a steady flow of drinks. "In spite of his immensely detached personality, he smiled at me in the way that men do when attracted by a young woman, and I in turn was fascinated by him. His very aloofness represented something of a challenge. I was determined to try to crack the veneer he presented to the world," she confided to her diary. "Whatever was thought about him later on, I found him overwhelmingly charming and gentle at the time, betraying nothing of the opinionated conceit that his colleagues noticed," she wrote.

A handsome young physicist, Brian Flowers, who directed the Harwell orchestra and played cello, also caught Mary's eye. She had become increasingly despairing about the state of her marriage and soon fell in love with the attractive, musical physicist. Her husband was threatening to keep their sons if she divorced him (which she eventually did). Her parents were disapproving.

Living at Harwell posed significant risks for a person like Mary Buneman, who would hear rumors about atomic spies but never conceived that, if true, any of them were friends of hers. While she entertained Fuchs at her home from time to time, she also turned to the security chief, Henry Arnold, who struck her as kindly and avuncular. If Mary's phone was being tapped, as she later suspected, Arnold probably had authorized it. Arnold undoubtedly liked Mary, but there was value for him in his friendship with her and, in turn, her friendship with Fuchs. Sometimes when he stopped by her house, Fuchs would be there too. By 1949, unbeknownst to Mary, Fuchs was under round-the-clock surveillance. The British had received a tip from American intelligence sources about Fuchs's treachery.

As THE END of the decade approached, Herbert and Erna Skinner were preparing for one of their legendary pre-Christmas parties. The whispers

were growing more frequent: someone inside the compound was passing information to the Soviets. Mary Buneman was certain by then
that her phone was bugged. From time to time she'd hear a sound like
an echo, followed by a soft click that temporarily interrupted her conversations.

Fuchs had moved in with the Skinners and started an affair with his
friend's wife. Fuchs helped with the Skinners' household chores and
served drinks at the couple's innumerable parties. He became known,
in the central European tradition, as a *Hausfreund*, which means
"friend of the house," or more explicitly, friend of the wife with the
concurrence of the husband. British surveillance reports recorded that
Fuchs and Erna Skinner would spend nights together in London while
her husband was away.[14] "One man had never been enough for Erna,"
Mary wrote in her diary, "and she was frequently involved with a sup-
plementary companion . . . the marriage had already survived a few
such adventures."

At the Skinners' Christmas party, Fuchs played his usual role of
deputy host, pouring drinks. After a few glasses of wine, Mary was feeling in high spirits, and she threatened his cover with an unwittingly
pointed question.

"I thought it might be rather fun to tease Klaus, so I sidled up to
him and asked in a voice which I did nothing to subdue: 'Why do you
give all those secrets to the Russians?'

"He never as much as batted an eyelid. 'Why should I?' was his reply; but what a cacophonous chord I must have struck. Already up to
his neck in espionage, he might well have supposed that I was planted
there purposely by the security services, but that the drink had loos-
ened my tongue and impaired my caution."

A short time later, in early 1950, Mary collapsed in a state of mental exhaustion and depression, weighed down by what seemed an impossible situation in her personal life. She was admitted to a mental
institution in Oxford. Brian Flowers came to see her, and to her great
surprise, Fuchs was with him. Ever since her remark at the party, he
had been frosty to her. Now he showed another, more compassionate
side, reflecting some of the moral fiber that guided his own actions,
however misconstrued. "He advised me to make up my mind and
stand by my convictions. He told me that he had been brought up to
believe that if one was sure beyond any doubt that a certain course of

action was right, it should be followed, and the opinion of those opposed to it disregarded," she wrote.

Fuchs knew the net of criminal suspicion was tightening around him.

Two nights later, on February 3, 1950, the hospital radio was switched on as usual for the nine o'clock news. "I felt as if I had been punched in the stomach as I heard that Klaus Emil Julius Fuchs had been arrested in London, and remanded in custody on a charge of spying and passing secret information to Soviet Russia. So it was TRUE."

FUCHS WAS THE first major spy to be identified by Venona, the American operation that cracked Soviet coded messages during World War II. The Soviets, as it happened, already knew about Venona, but since the British and the Americans did not know this, they viewed a confession from Fuchs as absolutely paramount because they did not want to reveal Venona's existence at a public trial. That finally came during his fourth interrogation on January 27, 1950, after a pub lunch near Harwell. The formal arrest took place on February 2. Fuchs was charged with betraying the Official Secrets Act. He was given the maximum sentence, fourteen years in prison. He could not be tried for high treason, which called for the death sentence, because the Soviet Union was an ally during the period in which his offenses took place.

At Harwell, Price heard of the arrest during the BBC lunchtime news in the mess at Ridgeway House. He went back to tell his immediate boss, Bruno Pontecorvo, one of many left-leaning scientists at the facility. "His immediate reaction was to speak to Fuchs's secretary," Price recalled. "Reassured, he told me that Fuchs was at a meeting in London. Indeed he was, but no longer as a free man."

Everyone who knew Fuchs was shattered by the arrest. Rudolph Peierls, a fellow German native who had first invited Fuchs to Birmingham back in 1941, went with his wife, Genia, to visit Fuchs in prison. Back in 1941, he had helped organize Fuchs's release from internment during the so-called fifth column scare when thousands of German refugees were put in camps; they had worked on the problems of enriching uranium. When the Peierlses asked Fuchs why he had not denounced the Soviets and the horrors of Stalinism, Mary recalled, "Klaus replied that he was going to wait until the power of the Soviet Union had achieved world supremacy and then point out their errors to those in authority. He had been reported widely as having said that he thought that Russia was going to build a new world, and that he would play a leading part in it."

But those beliefs had slowly disappeared. "To me, the most tragic thing about his whole career was that by the time of his arrest his beliefs had evaporated, and were no longer able to sustain him at his trial," Mary wrote.[15]

In his confession, Fuchs said he had compartmentalized his personality, concealing his secret side from his friends. "I could be free and easy and happy with other people without fear of disclosing myself because I knew that the other compartment would step in if I approached the danger point . . . Looking back at it now the best way of expressing it seems to be to call it a controlled schizophrenia."[16]

Mary Buneman had seen the two compartments close in on each other after her joking remark at the Skinners' party.

AFTER FUCHS'S ARREST, the American government bore down harder on the British for being too lenient with Communist sympathizers, and Senator Joseph McCarthy of Wisconsin kicked off his infamous Communist witch hunt with a speech in Wheeling, West Virginia, February 9, 1950. In it he claimed to have a list of more than two hundred Communists working in the State Department. The witch hunt at Harwell had only just begun. Pontecorvo was apparently not yet suspected but soon would be.[17]

The summer immediately prior to Fuchs's arrest, Pontecorvo traveled to Italy, accompanied by his wife, Marianne. Traveling with them were Mary and Oscar Buneman and Brian Flowers. Mary and the others believed that during the trip Ponte, as his friends called him, "turned." The trip had started on a high note, but after they arrived in Rome, Pontecorvo's mood inexplicably changed. Tall, broad-shouldered, and charismatic, Pontecorvo was just the opposite of his small and frail wife, Marianne. In Rome he became nervous and irritable, but his fragile wife seemed distraught. "Marianne seemed to be near to breaking point. She frequently wandered off, or shut herself in the car and burst into tears. Her small face looked pinched, and her eyes were nearly always red and swollen. It was obvious that something had affected them profoundly," Mary wrote. Someone, possibly Pontecorvo's brother-in-law, an associate of the Italian Communist Party, had "turned the screws."

Over the next several months, it became clear that "Ponte" was not planning to stay long at Harwell. He was offered a prestigious position at Liverpool University, the chair in the physics department, but he demurred, not relishing the idea of living in the dreary northern city. After a grilling by Arnold he finally agreed to accept the post, but not until January 1951. In the meantime, as a group leader at Harwell, he oversaw an experimental physics group that was preparing an expedition to France to study cosmic rays. He asked Terry Price to head the effort, so Price happily packed his bags in the summer of 1950 for a laboratory high on Mont Blanc above Chamonix. Dazzling white in the August sun, the facility was set on a rocky ridge about a half mile long. For three months, Price and his colleagues slipped into a world that seemed far removed from the anxiety-ridden one below. In reality, though, there was no escaping it.[18]

Pontecorvo was scheduled to join the team on his way back from a holiday in Italy with his wife and three sons in late August or early September. "His parents had not been to Chamonix for years, and it was arranged that we should all meet in the valley for dinner," Price recalled. Price dined with Pontecorvo's parents at the restaurant, but Ponte and his family never showed up. "A couple of weeks later I received a letter from Ponte's father, asking if I had any news: he had heard nothing further. I rang Henry Arnold, the security officer at Harwell. He sounded worried but tight-lipped. He knew something of Ponte's movements from the traveler's checks that had been cashed; but there had been no clues during the last few days," Price wrote in his memoir, whose title, *Political Physicist*, reveals something about the world he lived in. "We now know that it was on the day that we should all have had dinner together that Ponte flew from Rome to Stockholm, on his way to Moscow. At the time nothing was further from my thoughts."[19]

Two weeks after that, a French policeman acting for what is now known as Interpol (International Criminal Police Organization) questioned Price about Pontecorvo's disappearance and the Italian's relationship with Fuchs. Price responded that Pontecorvo knew Fuchs, a disclosure that he did not regard as particularly significant since most people at Harwell did. A short while later, Price found himself face-to-face with Pontecorvo's boss, Egon Bretscher, who had flown down from

England. The two men sat on the porch of a hut, and Bretscher took off his shirt to enjoy the sun. Price was wondering why he'd come.

"He [Bretscher] then asked: 'What's this about Fuchs?'" Price had no idea what he was referring to, so Bretscher explained: "When you spoke to the French police you said you thought that Pontecorvo was an accomplice of Fuchs. The French police are too close to their newspapers for our liking. We are trying to negotiate a new agreement with the Americans. If that kind of thing gets into the papers we could kiss all that goodbye."

Price felt a chasm opening beneath him. Was Bretscher implying that he, Price, was a security risk?

Price explained that he had not said anything that definite, and that his French interrogator had embroidered his reply. Bretscher asked him to put his explanation in writing so it could be reviewed by the Harwell security chief. After he left, Price spent the next three weeks wondering if his Harwell career had been irretrievably sunk.

Back at Harwell, Henry Arnold reviewed Bretscher's notes. He was satisfied that Price had not intentionally breached security regulations and sent him a note of reprieve.[20]

This was the precipice on which nuclear careers could falter. Prying was sanctioned by governments in the name of national security, and anyone who had signed on to a nuclear career could suddenly be on the receiving end of a police visit. The extraordinary attention to personnel vetting and monitoring did not apply only to military nuclear research: Three decades later, in the mid-1970s, the civilian-run U.S. Nuclear Regulatory Commission (NRC) set up the so-called two-man rule so that workers in sensitive areas of a nuclear plant would work in pairs, in order to keep a close watch on each other. The NRC staff faced a dilemma. As they looked for ways to protect nuclear facilities from aberrant, unstable, or even violent people, observed *Nucleonic News*, they were dealing with "one of the touchiest things the agency has ever handled, something with considerable potential civil rights impact and which nuclear opponents see as the sure road to 1984, with its 'Big Brother' and other societal horrors that George Orwell wrote about thirty-odd year ago."[21]

PONTECORVO WAS SUSPECTED of having spied for the Russians while working for the Anglo-Canadian atomic team in Canada, but he was never charged because nothing against him could be proved. He was not heard from again until 1955, when he held a press conference in Moscow and announced he had become a Soviet citizen three years earlier and worked at the Institute of Nuclear Physics, part of the Soviet Academy of Sciences. In 1963, he was awarded the Lenin Prize for "great services in physics" and was elected a full member of the academy, thus attaining the status that Fuchs had sought but never gained. Fuchs spent nine years in prison and went to East Germany, where he led a distinguished career as a scientist.[22]

Pontecorvo's wife suffered a far sadder fate. Marianne was diagnosed with severe schizophrenia and committed to a Soviet mental institution.[23] The stressful nature of Pontecorvo's duplicitous life surely did not help his wife's mental state, any more than the pressures of living beside a barbed-wire compound helped a young woman in an unhappy marriage. But this was one side of atomic energy's future. Wherever a nuclear facility arose, it would need gates and guards, sometimes wiretapping, and other policing apparatus because of the risk of spies, surprise attacks, or sabotage. To the writer Robert Jungk, that suggested a "nuclear state" coexisting with the society that supported it, possibly robbing that society of the freedoms it was meant to secure. "If our nuclear power plants are to be well-enough protected to be totally immune to these risks, the inevitable consequence is a society dominated by prohibitions, surveillance and constraints, all justified by the magnitude of the danger," the Berlin-born Austrian writer warned in 1979.[24]

Mary and Brian Flowers married in October 1951. They moved to Birmingham, where Flowers had taken up a university teaching post. Harwell was expanding. It now had fifteen divisions, but Cockcroft had not found a satisfactory replacement for Fuchs as head of theoretical physics. He had his eyes on Flowers, who had worked under Fuchs. So, in the autumn of 1952, the couple was invited back so Cockcroft could see if Flowers was the right man for his former boss's job. In December, Cockcroft announced the appointment. Flowers was only twenty-eight. Britain's major newspapers and tabloids paid considerable attention to the appointment. One tabloid headline read: "Scientist of 28 Is Given Fuchs's A-job." Mary cut out all the articles and photographs and placed them in an album, which now lies in a small room on the second floor of their north London home.[25]

After Harwell, Flowers had a distinguished career in the academic and political world. He was knighted and eventually made a peer of the realm, which gave him a seat in the House of Lords. Mary's first husband, Oscar, moved back to California and became a professor at Stanford University and an expert in space physics and mathematics, building one of California's first solar-heated houses, according to his second wife, Ruth.[26]

The memories of those early years are still vivid for the Flowerses, now in their eighties. They had veered perilously close to danger without always knowing it, and had come out ahead. Their lives are no longer bound by secrecy in the way they were, but the habits it fostered never completely disappeared. "Wherever we go and whatever we do, we have been taught through the lessons we learnt so early in our lives, to be careful in our actions and our utterances," Mary wrote. "The old saying 'You can't ride a tiger and expect to dismount' is very telling."

CHAPTER 5

Two Scorpions

I T MIGHT HAVE BEEN THE WAY the Russian looked at him and smirked, or perhaps it was the Soviet's emphasis on the word *can*, as in "You Americans *can* keep a secret when you want to," but it was then that W. Averell Harriman, America's ambassador to Moscow, understood the awful truth. The Soviet foreign minister, Vyacheslav Molotov, was basically telling him what U.S. intelligence almost certainly already knew, that the Soviets had been onto America's "secret" far longer than he cared to imagine.[1]

On the evening of August 8, 1945, when the exchange may have taken place, Harriman and his counselor, George Kennan, met with Stalin and Molotov at the Kremlin.[2] The Soviet leader was acutely aware of the position he was in, now that the Americans had the bomb and his country did not, but he was careful not to show it. His troops had just crossed into Manchuria, where it was just after midnight, August 9. A second American atomic weapon was about to be unleashed on Nagasaki. Harriman and Stalin talked about the new weapon, evidently keeping the tone of the conversation as casual as they could.[3]

Harriman was dancing on the head of a pin. If he hoped to subtly persuade the Soviets against developing their own bomb, which he apparently tried by mentioning the tremendous cost, his cause already was lost. A nascent Soviet bomb project, long an object of suspicion, skepticism, and even derision within the Politburo, was now a top priority. Having seen that the bomb worked, Stalin was intent on rapidly trying to catch up. He wanted to redress the power balances, demonstrating the predictable political consequences of "scientific inevitability," that if one country has it, another one, particularly its chief rival, would want it too. The scientists had done their job and, as Oppenheimer suggested should happen, transferred their discovery—"the greatest possible power to control the world"—to mankind. In the political sphere there were certain "inevitabilities," too, but they bore little relationship to the meaning of the word as it applied to scientific discovery and the search for truth. Truman and Stalin would now have to deal with the new power according to their own "lights and values." And it is doubtful that any amount of lobbying by well-meaning scientists beforehand could have prevented the course of action on which Stalin had embarked. "These reasons for building the bomb—to restore the emerging balance of power, and to acquire a new and potent symbol of power—would have existed even if Niels Bohr's advice to inform Stalin had been followed . . . ," writes David Holloway in his account of the Soviet bomb project. "Stalin would still have wanted a bomb of his own."[4]

This was the world as it was, not the world as the scientists wanted to see it. And from there the stakes would only get higher. The drive for power balancing set the stage for the cold war, and that in turn spawned a nuclear enterprise in both countries that churned out thousands of warheads of unprecedented destructive power, together with any number of ways to deliver them. Henceforth, the two sides would vie for regional influence all over the world, using their nuclear muscle to achieve their aims, with mixed results. The titanic struggle, fueled by fear and vast sums of money, led to the placement of American nuclear weapons in Europe. And that prompted the Soviet decision in the late 1950s to virtually build China's first atomic weapon, thinking, mistakenly as it turned out, that it could retain influence over the Asian behemoth in the way the Americans did Europe through the North Atlantic Treaty Organization (NATO). Atoms for Peace, the program ostensibly started to promote the benefits of nuclear energy, also was a cold war product. It resulted in widespread nuclear proliferation. And as other countries were let in on the secrets, they acquired the capability, if they chose to exercise it, of building their own nuclear weapons.

The superpowers, Oppenheimer famously said in 1953, were "two scorpions in a bottle, each one capable of destroying the other, but only at the cost of its own life."[5] In the next phase of this struggle—a direct response to the first Soviet bomb—the United States would invent a weapon that could potentially annihilate the planet.

A CLOSED SOCIETY, such as then existed in the Soviet Union, made a perfect host for bomb developers. Stalin's first step was to put his "evil genius"—Lavrenty Beria—in charge, replacing Molotov. Beria ran the three most vital components of the Soviet security apparatus: the internal police, the prison camp system, and the global espionage network.[6] The Soviet bomb project would depend on all these elements to succeed, effectively coupling scientists to a system of legitimized criminality. But the marriage of technology to ruthless, corrupt, and publicly unaccountable overseers also would have devastating consequences. Most notably these included an explosion at the Mayak nuclear fuel plant in 1957 and three decades later, in 1986, the Chernobyl catastrophe. Both these events caused incalculable damage to the environment and "fallout footprints" that will be traceable for centuries.[7]

The project's scientific leader, Igor Kurchatov, stopped shaving around the time he was chosen by Molotov for the job in 1943. Friends attributed this to a spiritual transformation they believe he went through in this period. His fellow scientists began calling him "the Beard."[8] Whatever his private thoughts were, Kurchatov did not let them get in the way of his work, and he proved a skillful operator in a treacherous system. His talents enabled him to ensure that the right player was in place when the time came—it was Kurchatov who had orchestrated Beria's elevation, and Molotov's demotion, in the weapons development hierarchy. He was "a charmer," Anna Kapitsa, whose husband, Peter, was one of Kurchatov's mentors, said. "That's why he could manage not only his dealings with scientists, but he was very clever in dealing with people at the top, which was much more difficult."[9]

While Molotov was still in charge, Kurchatov had access to Beria's vast network of intelligence gathering, and as a result soon realized the extent of the bomb effort in the United States. At its height, the Manhattan Project employed more than a hundred thousand people. Kurchatov had roughly a hundred. He was having difficulty obtaining uranium and other raw materials, and he blamed Molotov for these shortages. In short, he wanted more than Molotov could deliver. As a consequence, eighteen months after his appointment, Kurchatov made an extraordinary move. He did an end run around Molotov by making a direct appeal to the only man he thought could give him what he needed—Beria. In a letter dated September 29, 1944, Kurchatov told Beria that the Manhattan Project was being conducted "on a scale unseen in the history of world science." Pointing out the deficiencies in the Soviet program, Kurchatov said, "Knowing that you are exceptionally busy I nevertheless decided, in view of the historic significance of the uranium problem, to bother you and to ask you to give instructions for the work to be organized in a way that corresponds to the possibilities and significance of our great state in world culture."[10]

But Beria and Stalin, who had a mutual suspicion of each other, also shared in common a distrust of the physicists' claims. They found it difficult to comprehend atomic energy because it was something they could not touch or see. This even extended to skepticism about information delivered by Beria's agents during the war. Beria half believed that "the enemy was trying to draw us in this way into huge expenditures of resources and effort on work which had no future."[11] Kurchatov was given enough money to keep the program afloat, but Beria remained on the sidelines, probably intentionally, until after Hiroshima.

Doubts persisted after the war, but Stalin nevertheless ordered that work commence on a broad scale "with Russian scope," promising the "broadest all-round help" he could give.[12] He tripled the science budget in 1946, breathing life into a large community of Soviet physicists scattered around various Soviet institutions and universities, with promises of status, jobs, and good pay. If there was any question about the esteem in which they now were held, Stalin had erased it with an admonition to Kurchatov to ask for all that he needed. "If a child doesn't cry, his mother doesn't know what he wants," Stalin said that September. "Ask for whatever you like. You won't be refused."[13] Kurchatov had the equivalent of a blank check. But the deadline for completion was 1948. That gave him a little more than three years to meet Stalin's demand.

Kurchatov and his band of followers knew their lives were at stake if they failed to deliver. In 1949, Stalin is reported to have said to Beria about the physicists: "Leave them in peace. We can always shoot them later."[14] And despite the flow of money, the paranoid tendencies of the man Kurchatov reported to persisted. Thus, sometime toward the end of 1946 or very early the next year, Beria approached Kurchatov's Laboratory No. 2 in Moscow, the principal center for Russian atomic research since 1943, for what promised to be an exciting event—a repeat performance of the first self-sustaining chain reaction outside the United States. That had occurred on December 25, 1946, in a small graphite-uranium "pile," modeled after the Fermi reactor, after more than a year of hard work. The occasion had merited warm smiles and hearty congratulations.

Beria spoiled the party organized for his benefit. As he stood by the control panel and watched one of the men push the button to lift the control rods, he heard only clicks of the first reactions, then a wail as the neutron bombardment intensified, but nothing else.

"Is that all? Nothing more? Can I go to the reactor?" he asked.[15]

Kurchatov told him it would be dangerous for his health because of the radiation hazard. Beria did not entirely believe him; perhaps he was being duped. "Beria began suspecting that Kurchatov was swindling him," according to two Soviet scientists who later wrote about the episode.[16]

THE SOVIET NUCLEAR complex would eventually consist of ten closed, secret cities, but to begin with there were only two that mattered: a plutonium production complex near Chelyabinsk and the warhead development and final assembly facilities at Sarov.[17] For fifty years, outside the Soviet Union, little to nothing was known or written about these places. And for the entire duration of the cold war, even within the Soviet Union, the second most important scientist in the weapons program after Kurchatov, Yuli Khariton, was invisible. A filmmaker in Moscow interviewed Khariton just after the Soviet collapse and produced a documentary detailing his efforts at Sarov, where the first Soviet bomb was designed and partially assembled.[18]

Khariton, a tall, contemplative, and seemingly shy man with aquiline features, chose the site of a former monastery for his work in April 1946, coincidentally the same month Mary Buneman was unpacking boxes at her prefab house at Harwell. Located in a vast area of forest, lakes, and rivers, Sarov had been home during the early nineteenth century to Seraphim, a monk celebrated, and later sainted, for his legendary healing powers and predictions of Russia's future, including revolution, wars, and finally the destruction of monasteries and churches.[19] He was so important in Russian folklore that after the Soviet collapse, when priests were once again tolerated, President Vladimir Putin traveled to

Sarov to dedicate a new Cathedral of St. Seraphim. Putin described Seraphim as "one of the brightest" of Russian Orthodox saints.[20] The cathedral stood within the barbed-wire compound where eighty thousand security-cleared employees now lived.

Gentle and civilized, Khariton evidently found it difficult to speak after so many years of silence, but gradually the story was pried from him. He told the filmmakers that he realized Sarov was his spot, in part because it stood on the edge of a large forest, offering privacy and concealment, but also because the monastery buildings could be converted into laboratories, offices, a canteen, and a library. A labor camp lay nearby, with a supply of able, if unwilling, workers. "Of course there was little joy in watching the columns of prisoners who built the installation initially," Khariton said in an occasionally faltering voice. "But all that receded into the background, and people had little regard for the difficulties of everyday life—they were trying to achieve success in the best and quickest way. They knew that the country was in danger, and they understood that the state was relying on them and giving them everything necessary for their work and their daily life. And they carried out their task splendidly."[21]

Sarov was a healthy distance from Moscow, about two hundred and fifty miles, but reachable by train, and the city of Arzamas was about thirty miles to the north. By 1948, Sarov had been surrounded by perimeter and access control facilities, its name erased from all maps and documents. Henceforth, Sarov would be called Arzamas-16, in accordance with the Soviet practice of naming the secret communities after a nearby city with a post office box number. Inevitably, it would also be referred to as "Los Arzamos."[22]

Not wanting to deal with the detailed management issues of such an installation, Khariton requested that someone else be assigned the job. Beria tapped General Pavel M. Zernov, who had helped in the mass production of tanks during the war. The scientist and the general were an odd couple, not having known each other, but soon formed a good working relationship. Once the operation got under way, Khariton concentrated on the science with zeal. He was supplied with plenty of technical information from Beria's intelligence-gathering effort, but Khariton insisted on checking and rechecking every detail to ensure its accuracy. "We have to know ten times more than we are doing," he told his scientists.[23]

While Khariton ran the complex at Sarov, Kurchatov and Boris Vannikov, the man in overall charge of the project's industrial aspects, moved to the southern Urals to oversee construction and operation of a plutonium complex near Kyshtym. There, also in a region of lakes, mountains, and forest, he and Vannikov relied upon seventy thousand prisoners to build the plants and the security apparatus around them. This place would be known as Chelyabinsk-65. Vannikov, well grounded in the principles of engineering, struggled to grasp the concepts of the atom. "We engineers are used to touching everything with our hands and seeing everything with our eyes, and, in extreme cases, a microscope will help," he had said during a meeting in 1945. "But here it is powerless. It makes no difference, you won't see the atom, and even less will you see what is hidden inside it. And on the basis of this invisible and intangible thing we have to build factories, and organize industrial production."[24]

There were immense challenges. The biggest of all was finding enough uranium for an industrial-scale project. Acting on a "broad front," geologists fanned out across the Soviet Union, from Siberia to the Urals and Central Asia, to explore prospects. And by 1948 there were mines in these areas as well as in Ukraine, Estonia, and other parts of Eastern Europe. What proved the most prized area of all was the Soviet zone of Germany and Czechoslovakia in the Erzgebirge and Harz mountains, the area where Martin Klaproth first discovered uranium, Curie secured ore for her radium experiments, and Oppenheimer fell in love with science.[25]

Kurchatov, tall and saintly looking with his beard much longer then, had taken on the role of chief nuclear prophet and propagandist, in a distinctly Russian manner. In March 1948, while a plutonium production reactor was being assembled, he gathered the workers together for a speech. "Here, my dear friends, is our strength, our peaceful life, for long, long years," he said. "You and I are founding an industry not for one year, not for two . . . for centuries." Then he quoted lines from a Pushkin poem, "The Bronze Horseman," in which Peter the Great promises revenge for a recent defeat by the Swedes:

> *Here a town will be established*
> *To spite our arrogant neighbor.*[26]

Three months later, when the reactor went online, there were problems. The intense heat had started to corrode the aluminum cladding on the fuel rods. Even more ominously, the uranium pellets themselves began to swell, forming wrinkles and lumps on the surface, which in turn caused them to stick to the discharge pipes. The reactor, called Annushka, had to be shut down.

Beria suspected sabotage. Kurchatov had to explain the basic problem of finding metals that would withstand the corrosive effects of heat and still allow neutron bombardment to continue at the desired rate. The same difficulty had bedeviled scientists and engineers at the Hanford and Windscale plutonium plants during and after the war. Kurchatov noted that it was mentioned in the Smyth account of the Manhattan Project that had been sanctioned by Groves. "It was definitely not a simple matter to find a sheath that would protect uranium from water corrosion, would keep fission products out of the water, would transmit heat from the uranium to the water, and would not absorb too many neutrons," the American report explained. "Yet the failure of a single [nuclear fuel] can might conceivably require shutdown of an entire operating pile."[27]

The report offered no solution, so the Soviet scientist reached out through the espionage network to see if Fuchs, in England, could find an answer. That too proved futile. The fuel had to be removed, along with the plutonium that had built up, so the problem could be studied. This resulted in design modifications to the reactor, and the problem was solved.[28] Meanwhile, a separation plant was completed in December 1948. It began producing plutonium early the following year. In April 1949, a chemical-metallurgical plant was converting the plutonium into metal for use in bombs, and by June there was enough for a first atomic bomb.[29]

KURCHATOV AND KHARITON chose an isolated spot on the stony, sandy steppes of Kazakhstan for the finale of this first chapter in the story of Soviet nuclear weapons development. In an area devoid of houses and trees, with only black starlings and the occasional hawk providing signs of life, a small settlement was built on the banks of the River Irtysh, about ninety miles northwest of the city of Semipalatinsk. Intense heat during the day created a haze over the roads, and mirages of mountains and lakes made the area seem all the more eerie.[30]

By August 1949, a tower rose almost one hundred feet from the ground at the detonation site in a valley between two small hills, about forty-five miles to the south of where the scientists, Red Army units, and other test personnel lived. An assembly hall was built at its base, with rails and a traveling crane. Around the tower, final work took place on buildings and houses made of wood, stone, and brick and on bridges, tunnels, and water towers. Soviet generals oversaw the placement of railway locomotives, tanks, and artillery. Like children building sand castles on the beach, they did all of this to see how much would disappear when the shock wave swept through.

In the second half of the month, Kurchatov announced the test would take place at six in the morning on August 29. Just prior to the test, Stalin called Beria, Kurchatov, Khariton, and other scientists back to Moscow. He asked to see each individually for a progress report. When it was Khariton's turn, the Soviet leader threw out the interrogator's equivalent of a hand grenade: "Couldn't two less powerful bombs be made from the plutonium that is available, so that one bomb could remain in reserve?"

Khariton answered calmly that he had only enough plutonium for one bomb and that trying to turn it into two would take too much time and pose unacceptable risks. "We understood that the sooner the world knew we had a bomb, the better for everybody. So I said it is better to do one bomb than two," Khariton told his film interviewer in the early 1990s.[31]

Stalin accepted his response.

Beria arrived at the test site about two weeks before the event itself, and through his wire-rimmed glasses surveyed workers in the assembly hall checking and rechecking the bomb components. Outside, he could see men installing instruments and high-speed cameras at various distances from the tower. They would measure the pressure of the shock wave and the intensity of radiation. Then, as the time drew nearer, animals were placed in open pens and covered houses. Khariton himself accompanied the two bomb hemispheres on the final leg of their journey from Arzamas to Semipalatinsk, riding in a special train along a dedicated rail line, with armed guards front to back.[32]

At daybreak, a sharp north wind was blowing. The clouds hung low, occasionally separating to let the sun peek through. The top officials gathered in a command post about six miles from the tower, while military officers were farther away in two command posts. Khariton gave the order for the detonation and someone else pushed the button. Then they got what they had waited for, a white fireball of "unbearably bright light" that briefly dimmed, gathered new force, and quickly grew. It consumed the tower and assembly hall as if they were toys in a field. Magnificently, the blazing mass changed color and rushed upward, while the blast wave at its base swept the houses and army equipment in its path, churning up stones, wooden logs, metal fragments, and dust into a universe of chaos.[33]

PEOPLE WHO HAVE experienced bomb tests, facing away from the point of explosion, say that the first thing they notice after the explosion is heat hitting them in the back of the neck. Very soon after that they feel the sensation of the blast wave and then, in quick succession, they hear the sound. A high wind travels initially away from the explosion and then reverses itself and travels into it—air rushing into the vacuum created by the initial rapid expansion of gases.[34]

At Semipalatinsk that cool August morning, the strong wind seems to have suppressed the sound. What observers heard instead was like the muffled roar of an avalanche. The atomic mushroom formed a gray column of sand, dust, and fog with a cupola-shaped, curling top, intersected by two tiers of cloud and layers of inversion. It reached a height of up to five miles, and then it blew away to the south, lost its outline, and became a formless mass.[35]

For Khariton and Kurchatov, there were kisses on the forehead from the man with the wire-rimmed glasses. Now, at last, Beria knew their science was not fiction. Khariton said that "when we succeeded in solving this problem, we felt relief, even happiness—for in possessing such a weapon we had removed the possibility of its being used against the U.S.S.R. with impunity."[36]

Beria almost immediately called Stalin, who was sleeping. He ordered the assistant to wake him and waited. Then came the voice he was waiting for on the other end.

"I know already."[37]

THREE WEEKS AFTER the Soviet test, on a Monday night, David Lilienthal and his wife, Helen, were in Martha's Vineyard, driving back from dinner in a heavy fog. Suddenly, their headlights picked out the figure of a man, hatless, squinting into the lights, standing at a traffic circle. At that hour, the landscape looked like a windswept moor, which added to the surreal atmosphere. The man hooked his thumb in the manner of a hitchhiker. He appeared bemused.

The AEC chairman peered closer. "It's Jim McCormack," he said to Helen. Brigadier General James McCormack was director of the AEC's division of military applications. Lilienthal was accustomed to seeing him in his Washington office, but not here, late at night, on this island south of Cape Cod while the couple vacationed. How had he got there? Had he parachuted in?[38]

McCormack was there to give him the bad news, based on an analysis of aircraft samples collected after the test halfway around the world. In Washington's still-rarefied atomic circles, people had been speculating about a Soviet test for the past several years but misjudged how quickly it would come about. Groves testified in November 1945 that, without aid from the West, it would take "fifteen to twenty years." The Soviets had of course benefited from such "aid," as Groves had feared they might, so his forecast could only be based on hope. In that he had much company, among military officers, political leaders, and industrials. Nuclear scientists tended to think it would take a lot less time, but even they kept pushing the date out into the future. Wishful thinking meant the United States government had no plan in place to deal with the inevitable. "The fact the present development has been freely predicted by no means proves that we are prepared to meet it," wrote Eugene Rabinowitch, cofounder and editor of the *Bulletin of the Atomic Scientists*, at the time. "Like metastasis in an incurable cancer, it may merely mean that the deadly disease is taking its foreseeable course unchecked."[39] And that was only the beginning. Over the next six decades, government leaders and their advisers would continually underestimate the speed with which less advanced countries could develop and assemble nuclear weapons.

The afternoon after McCormack's strange visit, Lilienthal was called to the White House. Truman wanted to play down the event, just as Stalin had the bombings in Japan. Lilienthal and others persuaded him not to. Oppenheimer was particularly voluble. He saw it as an opportunity to "end the miasma of secrecy—holding a secret when there was none."[40] Truman's statement September 23 pleased Lilienthal, especially the opening, "that the public is entitled to know."[41] But the scientists had not yet told anyone about the biggest secret of all, the weapon many of them had wanted to produce since the outset of the war but for technical reasons could not: the thermonuclear.

Now at last, with the news from the Soviet Union, they might get their chance.

"KEEP YOUR SHIRT on," Oppenheimer advised Edward Teller in a phone call immediately following the Soviet test. Teller had been languishing in a kind of purgatory since the end of the war, convinced, he later testified, that working on a thermonuclear bomb had become impossible with the reduced staffing levels at Los Alamos.[42]

The idea of such a weapon had been around for at least two decades. In 1934, scientists in Britain produced a paper describing the "enormous effect" that would result from the fusion of two nuclei of deuterium, the heavier form of hydrogen. But fusing nuclei together to produce energy would require a seemingly impossible feat—overwhelming the positive electrical field that keeps the two particles apart. In other words, neutralize the electrical charge and fusion can occur. The solution is heat, although the heat of a furnace or even of fire would not be enough. To drive fusion at a significant rate, the temperature would have to exceed that in the center of the sun. The weapon they envisioned derived its explosive force from a thermonuclear, as opposed to fission, reaction— hence its name. But the weapon also came to be known as the "Super" or "hydrogen bomb."

At the outset of the Manhattan Project, Teller, whose mind soared with the possibilities of nuclear fusion, thought fission would be a cakewalk. Once fission was conquered, he would have the heat he needed to produce, and sustain, fusion, or thermonuclear burning. A scientist named Robert Serber remembered seeing a list of possible Supers on Teller's blackboard at Los Alamos, with differing design characteristics, yields, and delivery methods. Someone had written "backyard" for the one with the biggest yield. "Backyard" simply meant the weapon did not require a missile or airplane to deliver it because, as Serber put it, "Since that particular design would probably kill everyone on earth, there was no use carting it elsewhere."[43]

In Teller's mind, at least initially, there was no limit to the theoretical force of the explosions. The effects of a fission bomb were constrained by the size of its critical mass. But a Super might burn for as long as a star, because it would work like one, so long as a way could be found to ignite and sustain thermonuclear burning. Teller eventually realized that even thermonuclear explosions had limits, but he liked to speculate about the effects of different yields. At around a hundred megatons, he estimated, the Super "would simply lift a chunk of atmosphere—ten miles in diameter, something of that kind—lift it into space. Then you make it a thousand times bigger still. You know what would happen? You lift the same chunk into space with thirty times the velocity."[44]

But the fission bomb proved more of a challenge than he had anticipated. Teller had to put his dream aside. After the war, he and six other colleagues from Los Alamos picked up where they left off, writing a fifty-nine-page document explaining how such a weapon could be built and why it was worth spending a lot of money to do it: if approved, it would require a substantial portion of the national nuclear weapons budget for many years. The report was called *prima facie proof of the feasibility of the Super*. The morality of such a weapon figured only as a political calculation, with the authors noting "that further decision in a matter so filled with the most serious implications as is this one can properly be taken only as part of the highest national policy." But it recommended that the AEC organize a way to produce tritium, which, in combination with deuterium, would produce an optimal fuel for fusing.[45]

On April 18, 1946, thirty-two scientists met at a secret three-day conference at Los Alamos to discuss the Teller document.[46] Fuchs attended and contributed to the design work. Only one month earlier, Lilienthal's committee had made its recommendations for controlling nuclear energy development in a way they hoped would protect people from the threat of nuclear war. In other words, while the men at Dumbarton Oaks looked for ways to prevent nuclear holocaust, the scientists in New Mexico considered how they might advance the bomb project to its next technological stage of development.

The man who straddled these seemingly contradictory efforts was Oppenheimer, whose famously conflicted mind and moral sensibilities now extended to debate over the Super. Two weeks prior to casting his vote against the bomb, in October 1949, he was still undecided, and he again expressed his belief in scientific "inevitability" in a letter to Harvard president James B. Conant, a staunch opponent of the Super: "It would be folly to oppose the exploration of this weapon," Oppenheimer wrote. "We have always known it had to be done; and it does have to be done, though it appears to be singularly proof against any form of experimental approach. But that we become committed to it as the way to save the country and the peace appears to me full of dangers."[47]

By the time he made up his mind to vote against it, influenced by Conant and others, it was too late, although it is doubtful that Oppenheimer could have made a difference to the outcome. In the fetid atmosphere that existed after Joe-1, as the Americans called the first Soviet test, the forces already were lining up against him. Washington was becoming increasingly conservative, and he was politically liberal, had Communist friends, and could be woefully arrogant. Those factors, together with his vote against the Super, would prove his undoing five years later. In the meantime, the Joe-1 test in August had provided the political fodder needed by the Super's proponents, and Truman's mind was made up by the time the nation's most eminent scientists voted on the matter.

THE SMALL CIRCLE of people involved in what was arguably the most momentous decision ever taken by a single nation—whether to build weapons with the potential for planetary annihilation—included the Joint Chiefs, members of the congressional Joint Committee on Atomic Energy (JCAE), the five commissioners of the AEC, and a panel of nuclear scientists, known as the General Advisory Committee, or GAC, which dispensed advice on nuclear-related matters. Most often the GAC's recommendations were accepted; this time would be different, in part because there were other influential scientists who supported the idea. But it was as chairman of this august panel, on which sat men like Conant, that in 1954 Oppenheimer became a target and victim of accusations that he was a security risk, and wrongly accused of leading the committee's opposition to the Super.

The Super needed promoters in Washington other than Teller, and that job fell to Ernest O. Lawrence and his protégé, Luis Alvarez, both of whom felt, along with many of their colleagues, that Joe-1 almost certainly meant the Soviets would be working on a Super, and they were correct in that view.[48] One of America's earliest Nobel winners, Lawrence founded what is now known as the Lawrence Berkeley National Laboratory in the hills above the University of California's Berkeley campus and had long been admired in nuclear circles on both sides of the Atlantic. When the Australian physicist Marcus Oliphant traveled from England early in the war to rally American support for the first bomb project, it was Lawrence he had turned to. Once again, Lawrence was the point man on a matter of supreme importance.

The fact that Washington was thick with talk of Soviet spies only made Lawrence's job easier. Fuchs had not yet been arrested, but he was under FBI investigation. Some of those who knew about the probe, like politically conservative AEC commissioner Lewis Strauss, had already started wondering whether Oppenheimer himself was a spy. Acheson too would soon be under pressure because of his association with convicted spy Alger Hiss and his friendship with Hiss's brother, Donald.

As debate over the H-bomb escalated in the autumn of 1949, secrecy remained its silent co-conspirator, leaving policy-makers lacking facts with which to plead their case. For example, George Kennan, then head of the State Department's Policy Planning Staff and senior adviser to Acheson on nuclear policy issues, was not privy to the stockpile numbers; neither was the JCAE. (There were believed to be some two hundred nuclear warheads by then.) "In this and many other ways most of those who were asked to help in thinking about this awful decision were flying blind," writes McGeorge Bundy.[49]

Meanwhile, the AEC had become little more than a commissary for a bomb program run by the military, and was also fast sinking into the mire of snake-pit politics afflicting much of the rest of Washington. Sensitive, irritable, and not very well liked, Strauss undermined Lilienthal's collegiality, especially as he, Strauss, took on the cause of the H-bomb. Like Baruch, Strauss was a southern Jew who had made a fortune on Wall Street, but he lacked Baruch's charm and persuasive powers. Instead he used back channels to get his way, and it was by this method that he was able to indirectly appeal to Truman and influence his decision.

As Lawrence geared up for a trip to Washington in early October, Strauss (pronounced *Straws* in the southern fashion) moved in two directions to garner support for the Super. To begin with, he penned a memo for an October 5 meeting with his fellow commissioners propounding the need for a "quantum leap" in the nation's nuclear weapons technology. There are differing views as to whether he read it at the meeting or distributed it afterward.[50] But Strauss wasn't taking chances. Knowing he would run into opposition from Lilienthal, he headed straight from the meeting for a prearranged lunch with Rear Admiral Sidney Souers, executive secretary of the National Security

Council (NSC), and the man on whom the president relied for national security and intelligence briefings. Strauss had helped Souers get his job; now he would use Souers to lobby Truman for the H-bomb. When Strauss told Souers about the Super, the admiral wondered why the AEC was not building one. Strauss blamed his chairman. "Well, I don't think [the President] has been informed because Lilienthal is opposed to it," Souers later recalled the AEC commissioner saying.[51]

The next morning, Truman learned about the hydrogen bomb for the first time. When the rear admiral asked Truman if he knew anything about the Super, the president replied, "No, but you tell Strauss to go to it and fast." Souers called Strauss the next day and passed on the message.[52] It would take another four months before a formal presidential approval was given, but the decision to move quickly to develop the Super had effectively been made—almost literally overnight.[53]

LAWRENCE AND ALVAREZ had little trouble lining up the military brass and the right people in Congress. Uniformed men, Lilienthal noticed at one meeting with them, had adopted a new way of talking about warfare since the advent of the bomb. "Soldiers and sailors weren't boys and men, but 'personnel' . . . Hitting a potential enemy . . . becomes 'anticipatory retaliation,'" he noted in his diary. "The whole thing seemed quite unreal and stuffy."[54] But Lawrence had caught on. When he visited defense officials on October 9, according to Alvarez, he "made serious proposals . . . that warfare could be waged effectively by the use of radioactive products." That same day, in California, his wife gave birth to the couple's sixth child.[55]

The new weapon raised other interesting questions. Would the Super be worth two, five, or fifty existing nuclear weapons? What would it cost in relation to improving existing fission weapons? These were important questions because, apart from anything else, for technical reasons the problem of finding enough tritium potentially threatened the supply of plutonium for conventional bombs. The questions were raised and put aside.[56]

Lilienthal, sensing he was in a losing battle, had become immensely dispirited. After meeting with the Berkeley promoters October 10, he wrote: "Ernest Lawrence and Luis Alvarez in here drooling over the same [super-bomb]. Is this all we have to offer? . . . We keep saying,

'We have no other course'; what we should say is 'We are not bright enough to see any other course.'" The AEC chairman had been through another grueling congressional investigation for alleged incompetence, but Lilienthal's real problem was that he could not leave his moral values aside for the job. The following month he offered his resignation to Truman, to take effect February 15, 1950, and the president accepted it.

The strongest opposition to the Super surfaced during the GAC meeting that Oppenheimer opened on the weekend of October 29–30. Typical of what was said during this gathering was the statement "We already built one Frankenstein," by GAC member Hartley Rowe, one of the leading engineers on the Panama Canal project: "I may be an idealist, but I can't see [how] . . . any people can go from one engine of destruction to another, each of them a thousand times greater in potential destruction, and still retain any normal perspective in regard to their relationships with other countries and also in relationship with peace," Rowe explained later. "If a commensurate effort had been made to come to some understanding with the nations of the world, we might have avoided the development."[57]

All eight GAC members present, including Oppenheimer, voted against the crash program. But two members, Fermi and Isidor Rabi, dissented from the majority view by not completely ruling out development.[58] The Joint Chiefs were unanimously in favor of the program, and the five AEC commissioners were divided, with two in favor and three against. For nearly three weeks after the GAC meeting, the public knew nothing about the deliberations. However, a leak by a JCAE member resulted in a front-page story in the *Washington Post* November 18, causing an uproar in the Oval Office because it intensified pressure on Truman to make a decision before Congress preempted him. Truman set up a panel, consisting of Acheson, Lilienthal, and Defense Secretary Louis Johnson, to advise him, but because Lilienthal and Johnson stood on completely opposite sides of the debate, it would be Acheson who would cast the deciding vote.[59]

Within the State Department, Kennan was at work on the last great statement of his career, an eighty-page document outlining his reasons not only for opposing the Super but for challenging the idea that nuclear weapons would be diplomatically, if not militarily, useful.

Kennan found himself increasingly at odds with both Acheson and Paul Nitze, who was about to unseat him as the State Department's chief policy-maker.

Kennan pleaded for mental balance, famously writing that to rely on the Super or indeed any atomic bombs in war was to "reach backward beyond the frontiers of western civilization, to the concepts of warfare which were once familiar to the Asiatic hordes." Kennan begged for "a clean and straight beginning" in American policy toward nuclear weapons. That would include announcing that the United States would never again be the first to use a nuclear weapon, and that it would once again devote serious efforts to achieving international control. Kennan hoped he would be able to show his statement to Truman before leaving his last official job, but he never got that chance, because Acheson prevented it. Acheson viewed Kennan's hopefulness with caustic skepticism. "If that is your view of the matter,'" he said to diplomacy's sage, "I suggest you put on a monk's robe, put a tin cup in your hand, and go on the street corner and announce the end of the world is nigh."[60]

That Acheson's mockery conjured up a monk is altogether fitting. During the Middle Ages, when lawlessness abounded, secret tribunals like the Holy Vehm were formed to dispense rough justice in the name of Christianity and the Ten Commandments. Over time, more people, criminals included, found it safer to join up rather than risk persecution and execution.[61] When Alger Hiss, accused of spying for the Soviets, was sentenced January 25, 1950, to two concurrent five-year sentences in a federal penitentiary for perjury, a reporter asked Acheson to comment. He famously answered, "I do not intend to turn my back on Alger Hiss."[62] That remark was made just six days before Acheson, Lilienthal, and Johnson were scheduled to make their recommendation on the Super to Truman. Hounded by the "yelping pack" for his defense of Hiss, Acheson may have found it more expedient to join the new holy order. He had scratched around for alternatives but could find none. Instead, he concluded there should at least be a program to determine whether an H-bomb was feasible.[63]

Truman had pretty much made up his mind by then, anyway. On January 19, 1950, he told Souers that crash development "made a lot of sense and that he was inclined to think that was what we should do."[64] Lilienthal, Johnson, and Acheson met with the president on January

31. The meeting lasted seven minutes. After listening to Lilienthal's objections, Truman rather weakly said he did not have any choice but to proceed. And he affixed his signature to a press statement announcing that he was directing "the Atomic Energy Commission to continue its work on all forms of atomic weapons, including the so-called hydrogen or super-bomb."

Lilienthal wrote in his diary entry afterward of his "night of heartache." Fifteen days later he left the AEC for the last time.

FOR MICROSECONDS AFTER the world's first hydrogen bomb was detonated on November 1, 1952, it became the closest thing to a star that man has ever invented. The device itself was shaped like a sausage, twenty feet long and six feet in diameter. It contained a so-called primary at one end, consisting of a fission device to provide the heat needed to ignite the "secondary," a large thermos-shaped container filled with liquid deuterium, surrounded by natural uranium. Although Teller is often described as the "father" of the H-bomb, his colleague, the brilliant mathematician Stanislaw Ulam, played a pivotal role. According to some accounts, Ulam came up with the breakthrough idea of a two-stage device that used the shock waves from a fission bomb to compress the hydrogen and ignite the H-bomb.[65]

The weapon, nicknamed Mike, was assembled and detonated on Elugelab Island, on the northwest quadrant of the Eniwetok atoll, a necklace-shaped string of small coral islands around a fifty-mile wide lagoon, about halfway between Hawaii and the Philippines. The joint task force that conducted the exercise consisted of more than eleven thousand mostly military personnel. The radio signal was sent at less than a second before 7:15 A.M. from a control ship about thirty miles from ground zero. When it reached Mike, the capacitors, already charged by a battery, sent high-voltage electricity through a mass of cables into the primary's ninety-two detonators. Within a few millionths of a second, it had become a fission fireball hotter than the sun. Mike yielded 10.4 megatons of explosive power, approximately 750 times greater than the bomb at Hiroshima. Only three of the sixty-seven U.S. tests that would be conducted in the Marshall Islands would be larger than Mike. By comparison, the largest yield during the Plumbbob series of nuclear tests in 1957 was seventy-four kilotons.

Mike was somewhat less than a true thermonuclear because more than 75 percent of its yield was attributed to fissioning uranium, instead of fusion, which should in theory produce the bulk of a thermonuclear blast. But that was only a technicality. A Los Alamos radiochemist, George Cowan, noted that Mike's neutron density was ten million times greater than a supernova, making it "more impressive in that respect than a star."[66]

The expanding fireball began to rise on a stem, casting what from afar appeared to be a purplish light. It kept rising until the stem was thirty miles high and the billowing cloud spread out for a hundred miles, brushing up against the earth's stratosphere. The base of the stem, now eight miles across, had become a fountainhead, showering a ring of radioactive water back into the ocean. The water fell not onto the island, for it had vanished, but into the crater left in its place. The hole, about a mile wide and two hundred feet deep, quickly filled with water. The coral and sand of what had been Elugelab, as well as bird, animal, and vegetable life of nearby islands, and the concrete, steel, and other equipment at the test site, were vaporized or burned in the explosion and converted into a mass of radioactive particles weighing an estimated eighty million tons. All of that was lifted into the air, and some was carried on stratospheric air currents around the world. What remained on islands farther away were birds too sick to fly, their feathers singed, and radioactive stumps of vegetation.[67]

Less than two hours after the explosion, four sampler pilots flew into the stem of the cloud because their planes could not fly any higher. They flew in pairs, staggering their entries, and remained in the stem for only a few minutes. Their cockpits were bathed in a red glow, the needles on their monitoring equipment "went around like the sweep second hand on a watch," and they quickly lost sight of each other. One of the pilots, Captain J. P. "Jimmy" Robinson, spun out upon entering and started rapidly descending. He recovered, but with fuel running low, he did not make it back to the runway on Eniwetok, crashing less than three and a half miles away. Helicopters searched the area for several hours, but his body was never recovered.[68]

The official accident report notes that all of the pilots on the mission wore lead gowns weighing approximately fifty-five pounds and helmets containing six pounds of lead coating. Air force experts say it would have been virtually impossible for Robinson to get the lead covering off in the confines of an F-84 cockpit, and that while the suit might not have prevented ejection, it would almost certainly have caused him to drown had he ejected successfully.[69]

IN THE SOVIET Union, scientists were already at work on a hydrogen bomb. They had been since 1947, spurred on by the notes Fuchs had passed on after the secret meeting on the Super at Los Alamos the previous year. Again, what had been viewed as inevitable scientifically had transferred to the political realm and proved impossible to stop. The senior Soviet theoretical physicist Igor Tamm was put in charge of the effort in 1948, and he turned to a rising star, Andrei Sakharov, for assistance.[70] On August 12, 1953, less than a year after Mike, the Soviets tested Sakharov's "layer cake" device, in which "alternating layers of light elements" produced a three-stage process of fission, fusion, and fission—and a yield ten times greater than their last fission test, but not even approaching Mike's power.[71]

The Teller-Ulam configuration still eluded the Soviet scientists, but the rivalry was escalating.[72] Sakharov was only twenty-seven when he began his work on the hydrogen bomb. A colleague who worked for him described a "simple, modest, childlike man . . . who distinguished himself through the clarity and correctness of his thought, and the conciseness of expression of his ideas." But the youthful Sakharov often could not sleep. "You know," he told a colleague then, "I have internal hysterics."[73]

Sakharov later became one of the Soviet Union's most prominent dissidents and in 1975 won the Nobel Peace Prize. He understood more about that early period: "Our world was bizarre and fantastic, a striking contrast to everyday city and family life, and to normal scientific pursuits." The scientists were convinced their work was essential, he wrote. "We were possessed by a true war psychology."[74]

CHAPTER 6

A Certain Wildness

I N SEPTEMBER 1956, a young entrepreneur named Sam Edlow stood at a trade booth on Chicago's Navy Pier. His wife, Frances, was at his side. Attractive, friendly, and quieter than her occasionally brash and temperamental husband, she had accompanied him on business jaunts since his days as a scrap dealer in Fort Wayne, Indiana. Now he was in the lead business, and lead containers were displayed on the velvet-covered table. A draping banner read EDLOW SHIELDS THE WORLD.

The claim was a bit of an exaggeration since, geographically speaking, Edlow's business extended only to clients near his foundry in Columbus, Ohio. But it was in keeping with the spirit of the times, and Edlow had not done too badly. He had started his commercial life driving a truck to filling stations and junkyards, collecting batteries to re-sell to recycling companies that removed and resold the lead. Then the National Lead Company, looking for "competitors" to get around antitrust problems, set him up in business with his own lead foundry. National Lead also introduced Edlow to Atomic Energy Commission officials in Portsmouth, Ohio, where a new uranium enrichment plant was under construction. A lot of lead protective equipment was needed. Edlow had found his next big client, the United States government.

"On the last day of the show, a guy walked in," Edlow recounted. "He was tall and well dressed. He said, 'Why don't you come in and talk to us?' It was Myron Kratzer from the AEC."[1]

Kratzer told Edlow about Eisenhower's Atoms for Peace program. He said the AEC had plans to ship a lot of nuclear material—enriched uranium and plutonium—to destinations in the United States and around the world. But the AEC needed someone to help develop systems for packaging and transporting the fuel and for dealing with customs inspections. Would Edlow come to Washington to do this? That was the beginning of a new line of business for the Ohio lead merchant. "I took him up on it and spent the next four to six months working with one of the [AEC] men to draw up shipping regulations," Edlow said. Within a few years, Edlow was at the front line of nuclear commerce, shipping fissile material by the ton, on trucks, trains, airlines, and oceangoing freight ships, across thousands of miles to other countries.

The nuclear scene and its cast of characters were changing. Edlow exemplified a new entrant: a man who had secured entrée by chance, circumstance, and what he had to offer, irrespective of his educational background. Bright young people with a penchant for science were choosing nuclear physics and engineering courses at universities because they knew that prestigious careers awaited them after that. Nuclear in the 1950s was like the dot-com boom in the 1990s. A lot of people wanted to be part of it.

WHAT HAD BROUGHT about these changes?

The answer in two words is nuclear weapons. On Eisenhower's first day in office, a document known as the Candor Report awaited him. It contained the seeds for the program that became known as Atoms for Peace, although its authors probably did not intend it that way. The report was requested by Acheson in the waning days of the Truman administration to help him shape the U.S. role in the UN Disarmament Commission. It was written by a panel headed by Oppenheimer, and its main message was that the American public was not adequately prepared for life in the nuclear age. "The present danger is not of hysteria but of complacency," said the report. The public had to overcome the "apparent reluctance to face the simple but unpleasant fact" that nuclear weapons in their "power to end a civilization and a very large number of people in it worked both ways."[2]

Candor was the first declaration by a government panel of both the danger and the necessity of nuclear weapons—and the likelihood that the Soviets would soon have enough of their own to destroy the United States "no matter how many more we ourselves have." Not all the report's warnings were followed, particularly the admonition against becoming overly reliant "on the unlimited use of the largest possible weapons." But Eisenhower picked up on the report's recommendation to place the meaning of nuclear armaments "fully on a level with the menace of the Soviet Union and the urgency of the defense of the free world." That became the genesis of Operation Candor, a yearlong media campaign designed to get Americans used to the permanent presence of nuclear weapons, culminating in the president's Atoms for Peace speech at the United Nations.[3]

In April, with the Soviet Union only a month into the post-Stalin era, Eisenhower delivered a speech entitled "Chance for Peace." In reality, it was little more than an effort to secure a cold war triumph by proposing a way out of the nuclear dilemma through disarmament talks. Since it required almost complete Soviet acquiescence to American demands, the proposals had little chance of succeeding. That spring Eisenhower also put together a team to reverse public apathy toward nuclear weapons and to drive home the point that the United States was permanently in danger of a "knock-out blow" from the Soviet Union. At the same time, he wanted to balance fear with hysteria avoidance, what historians have variously called "apocalypse" or "emotion" management.[4]

The idea of "peaceful" nuclear energy was not new—Eisenhower had talked about the possibilities with scientists well before taking office—and it was part of the long tradition that equates scientific discovery with improvements in our material lives. Under the new regime, however, it would become the necessary correlative. Nuclear weapons were at once fundamental to the nation's defense and the progenitor for nuclear energy's peaceful uses. But in their determination to get the public used to living with nuclear weapons, Operation Candor and its offspring, Atoms for Peace, led to the conflation of two apparently contradictory messages (peace now, war later?) and, in the process, an overselling of the supposed benefits. Atoms for Peace permanently fixed in the public's mind not only the concept of the trade-off between the two sides of nuclear energy, but also the idea that the world would be a far better place in which to live because of the many gifts that would flow from it, irrespective of the fact that activities associated with these benefits could (and did) lead to the presence of nuclear weapons in a greater number of countries.

Beginning in the spring of 1953, the process of "persuasion" was controlled by savvy media men, led by Charles Douglas Jackson, an expert in wartime psychological operations, or "psy-ops," on leave from Henry Luce's Time-Life Corporation, where he was an editorial executive. Jackson's job at the White House was to figure out ways of putting the United States and its allies in the best light, "exploiting incidents which reflected negatively on the Soviet Union, Communist China and other enemies in the Cold War."[5] Now Jackson's office would reach out to top opinion makers—journalists, educators, and national organizations—to convey to the public the seriousness of the nuclear threat. These efforts would be supported by an ad campaign that used media of every kind, even comic books, and a series of six radio-television talks by the president and top administration officials. The centerpiece of the campaign was a major presidential address to be given later in the year. The plan was in play by early July.

As the speechwriting began, Eisenhower did not think the right message was coming across. He would be okay with the sentence "We live not in an instant of peril but in an age of peril," but there was too much emphasis on weapons. He needed an antidote, something reassuring and uplifting—a better ending. After reading an early draft, the popular World War II general shook his head and said, "This leaves everybody dead on both sides, with no hope anywhere? Can't we find some hope?"[6]

As the psy-ops men looked for optimal ways of balancing fear and hope, the defense establishment's policy-making machinery weighed in with a new National Security Council document, a "new look," on October 30, 1953. The document contained ten thousand words, but a single sentence summed up its central chilling message: *In the event of hostilities, the United States will consider nuclear weapons to be as available for use as other munitions* (author's italics).[7] To those who knew about it, the need for public acceptance of nuclear weapons was critical since it would be taxpayer money that paid for them.

By early December the speech was almost ready. Eisenhower flew to Bermuda for a summit meeting and showed a draft to British prime minister Winston Churchill, who pronounced it a "very fine speech" and predicted that it would "resound through the anxious and bewildered world." When his plane left Bermuda for New York December 8, the president reportedly asked the pilot to circle before landing so finishing touches could be applied.

The address delivered that afternoon dealt a good deal with the threat of a nuclear exchange between the United States and the Soviet Union. It moved brilliantly between the twin themes of fear and hope—a public relations ploy, to be sure, but one that resounded with American optimism, and the belief and yearning for something better. To accept a situation in which "two atomic colossi are doomed malevolently to eye each other indefinitely across a trembling world" would be to accept "the condemnation of mankind to begin all over again the age-old struggle upward from savagery towards decency, and right, and justice," the president told a receptive UN General Assembly. Therefore the United States wanted to offer a way out, "to help us move out of the dark chamber of horrors into the light, to find a way by which the minds of men, the hopes of men, the souls of men everywhere, can move forward toward peace and happiness and well-being."

Eisenhower promised to submit to Congress a plan, "with every expectation of approval," that would "encourage world-wide investigation into the most effective peacetime uses of fissionable material, and with the certainty that they had all the material needed for the conduct of all experiments that were appropriate." Eisenhower proposed setting up a joint U.S.-Soviet stockpile of fissile material that would be controlled by a new international atomic energy agency. But the agency's main role was "to devise methods whereby this fissionable material would be allocated to serve the peaceful pursuits of mankind" and provide "abundant electrical energy in the power-starved areas of the world."[8]

THE APPLAUSE CAME in waves, rippling across the floor of the General Assembly in an ocean of gratitude and admiration. Ike beamed his famously modest smile. He had managed to deliver sunshine in the news about mass-destruction weapons, making the United States appear peace loving and progressive all at the same time. For an unborn nuclear energy industry, the speech was a critical step toward advancement. Less than one year later, the AEC would announce a program of incentives to encourage American utilities to build nuclear reactors; at the same time, it began developing plans for assisting other countries with new nuclear programs. Moreover, issues concerning a nuclear future—military and civilian—had been placed before an uncertain worldwide public for the first time.

In other ways, however, the speech was disingenuous. The stockpile suggestion, which in any case never worked, would have done nothing to stop the arms race. Eisenhower had not proposed donating all the fissile material produced by either country, which meant that both sides could continue producing whatever they needed for nuclear weapons. Meanwhile, the arms race was vastly accelerating. The Soviets had detonated their first version of a hydrogen bomb only four months earlier, in August 1953. And for the rest of Eisenhower's two terms, the number and destructiveness of the nuclear weapons in both countries would grow stratospherically, to levels capable of decimating each side several times over. The notion that "peaceful uses" might help turn the corner from danger to hope was, in McGeorge Bundy's words, no more than "a mirage whose temporary persuasiveness was evidence not only of the general respect for the president's sincerity, but also of the degree to which his hearers found it comforting to share his optimism."[9]

In one seemingly positive development, Eisenhower set the stage for the eventual formation of the International Atomic Energy Agency, a key step in the government-backed worldwide promotion of civilian nuclear energy. Plans were also laid for an international conference on nuclear energy to be held in Geneva in 1955. But, as many nuclear scientists quickly realized, if the theme was salvation through peaceful atoms, the outcome might not be what the psy-ops people had promised.

"What about security?" asked British nuclear physicist Terry Price, one of the Harwell scientists called into Whitehall to discuss the implications of Eisenhower's proposal the day after the speech.

"What do you mean?" asked a minister.

"U-235 can be bomb material," Price explained.

If power reactors were going to be built all over the world, as Eisenhower proposed, they would need nuclear fuel, and the processes involved in producing it could also be applied to making nuclear weapons. That was only one danger. Once the fuel was burned in reactors, it would contain plutonium, which could be separated and used in bombs.

Others too were beginning to worry that the widespread use of nuclear energy to produce electricity would make it easier for other countries to develop nuclear weapons. But Eisenhower, like most of his advisers, was preoccupied with the threat of "vertical" proliferation, meaning the growth of nuclear stockpiles in the Soviet Union. He had hoped his proposal to use the IAEA as a fuel bank would lead to a treaty in which both sides would agree to limiting and eventually stopping the production of fissile material for bombs.[10] But he was working at cross-purposes with the Soviets, who were more worried about catching up with the United States in the arms race while also concerned about the "horizontal" spread of nuclear weapons.

The Soviet foreign minister, Vyacheslav Molotov, raised the safeguards issue with his American counterpart, Secretary of State John Foster Dulles, when the two met in Geneva in the spring of 1954. Just as the Soviets had opposed the Baruch plan, now Molotov was objecting to Atoms for Peace and the proposed international agency. In part, his objections were inspired by cold war politicking, but Molotov raised a legitimate concern. He based it on a report drafted by Kurchatov and four colleagues, presented to him just prior to his meeting. "The development of the industrial use of atomic energy by itself does not only not exclude, but leads directly to, an increase of military atomic potential," said the Soviet report, echoing points made in the Acheson-Lilienthal plan. Furthermore, nuclear fission, the basis of electricity generation, produces isotopes such as plutonium and uranium-233, which "are themselves powerful atomic explosives."[11]

None of this should have been news to him, but Dulles was taken aback when Molotov, in a long note to him, stated that producing electricity by means of nuclear energy "not only fails to lead to a reduction of the stocks of atomic material utilized for the manufacture of atomic weapons, but also leads to an increase of these stocks." Molotov told him that the Atoms for Peace proposal would not only *not* save the world from nuclear war but might actually increase its possibility.

Flummoxed by what the Soviet was saying, Dulles asked Molotov what he meant. The Soviet foreign minister explained that "parallel with the peaceful use of atomic materials, as in power plants, it was possible concurrently to increase the production of material needed to produce bombs." Dulles rather weakly answered that "he would seek out a scientist to educate him more fully."[12] Gerard Smith, leader of many U.S. delegations to disarmament talks, was present at the exchange. "I had to explain to Dulles that Molotov had been better informed technically than he," Smith later wrote. "Subsequently, the Soviets asked how we proposed to stop this spread. The best we could reply was that 'ways would be found.'"[13]

THE ISSUE WOULD be put to the test directly following the international nuclear conference in Geneva in August 1955. This was an extraordinary event whose preparations were overseen by the nuclear luminaries of the day, including France's Bertrand Goldschmidt, whose career was now almost exclusively devoted to international nuclear politics; Isador Rabi, the Austrian-born American physicist who had come up with the idea of the conference in the first place; and Sir John Cockcroft, the staid head of Harwell and Goldschmidt's last overseer in Canada. Homi Bhabha, founder and head of India's Atomic Energy Commission, also was on the United Nations preparatory committee. There was camaraderie among these scientists and finally even the Soviets decided they wanted to be part of the scene. They abandoned their opposition to the IAEA in June 1955, just two months before the meeting.

When the conference opened on August 8, fifteen hundred delegates from all over the world showed up, with a thousand scientific papers between them. "It was the largest gathering of scientists and engineers the world had ever seen . . . a landmark in the history of science, the first intergovernmental conference ever held to illuminate progress on a new technology," raved David Fischer in his official history of the IAEA. The meeting "lifted the blanket of secrecy that had descended on nuclear research in the dark days of 1939, and did much to restore the international character of science." Most notably, Soviet scientists were allowed to mingle with their Western colleagues for the first time in twenty years.

The atmosphere would be described, aptly, as "euphoric," an adjective defined by Webster's Dictionary as meaning "exaggerated . . . without an obvious cause." AEC chairman Lewis Strauss told the assembled scientists and government officials, "It is not too much to expect that our children will enjoy electrical energy too cheap to meter . . . will travel effortlessly over the seas and under them and through the air with a minimum of danger and at great speeds."[14] Others predicted that the nuclear chain reaction would propel cars and trains, and that deserts would turn green with the desalting of ocean water filtered through fission-powered plants. Bhabha confidently predicted that over the next two decades scientists would find a way of "liberating [thermonuclear] fusion energy in a controlled manner . . . When that happens, the energy problems of the world will truly have been solved for ever."[15]

The British team arrived in particularly high spirits, checking into the Beau Rivage Hotel, where they enjoyed breakfast at the outdoor café.[16] By 1975, one British speaker predicted, almost half of the United Kingdom's electricity needs would be supplied by "the peaceful atom."

Shortly after the meeting, the Canadians struck what would prove a history-making deal: they agreed to build one of their natural uranium reactors at Trombay in India. As part of the agreement, the U.S. AEC promised to provide heavy water for the reactor, which was needed to moderate the chain reaction. This was absolutely critical since heavy water is both expensive to produce and rare. It is chemically the same as normal, or "light," water except that hydrogen is replaced with deuterium atoms. The reactor was named CIRUS, which stood for "Canada-India-Reactor United States."[17] By agreeing to this contract, the Americans and the Canadians had paved the way for India's early bomb effort. CIRUS would produce plutonium for the country's first nuclear weapon.

After the main meeting, representatives of six nations—Bhabha was not among them—met to discuss the increasingly vexing issue of how in a world of flourishing nuclear commerce governments could prevent would-be proliferators. Newspapers learned about the exclusive gathering, dubbed "Little Geneva," through a communiqué. They reported growing uneasiness among the diplomatic representatives of countries that had not received invitations, which, of course, was most of them. At least one account even suggested that Little Geneva might be the equivalent of "an atomic Yalta," referring to the exclusivity that prevailed at the World War II meeting where the Great Powers divided up their postwar spheres of influence.[18]

The comparison with Yalta was not altogether misleading. Of the countries represented, three were nuclear weapons states—the United States, Great Britain, and the Soviet Union. France would soon make four, while Canada (which had decided to forgo nuclear weapons development) and Czechoslovakia were important because of their indigenous uranium reserves. Complaints about the meeting's exclusivity foreshadowed future difficulties. When a safeguards system was finally established, the nuclear "haves" (those with nuclear weapons) basically dictated the rules that everybody else—the "have-nots"—had to follow.

But for all the bad feeling generated by the meeting, not to mention the assembled expertise, not much progress had been made on the issue of safeguards since the Eisenhower speech. The lack of preparation quickly became evident once the preliminaries had been dealt with and the core discussions began. Price, who attended the meeting, recalled it in a memoir he shared with me just prior to its publication.[19]

"No one wished to speak. Several times we sat for ten minutes on end, eyes cast down, doodling. The stenographers' fingers remained poised over the keys. The interpreters sat alert but silent in their booths. The tension grew. Occasionally a delegate would make a short comment; but nothing ran, and Trappist silence descended once more on the conference chamber."

It took Rabi to break the ice. Since the problem was to know where stockpiles of uranium—potential bomb material—were being kept, the American laureate suggested that "tagging" them with small quantities of an easily identifiable isotope such as uranium-232 might be an answer. But the scientists in the room knew this would not really work. Who would do the tagging and the monitoring? How would they "tag" uranium that already had been produced and processed? How could such a system work within the complicated machinery of a chemical reprocessing plant, producing plutonium?

"The scientists present—Rabi most of all—knew the hollowness of the proposal, but gave no sign: their professional reputation within the world of diplomacy was at stake," Price wrote. No one else present at the meeting—diplomats, interpreters, or UN officials—appeared to see through the facade. They assumed Rabi's suggestion was a breakthrough "of the kind that could advance careers." So they leapt into action, supported by the scientists who "did what they could to help spin the web, heaping hypothesis on hypothesis, taking care whenever possible to use incomprehensible jargon while conceding only a minimum of clarity," Price recounted.

Much of what followed came from the U.S. team. Its members said that Rabi's "safeguards" could be incorporated into the new international agency, although its role and method of operating were still not clearly defined. They assumed, incorrectly as it turned out, that the agency would have a high degree of authority over the design and operation of nuclear fuel plants, making clandestine diversion difficult.

"This splendid game could not last," Price records.

The failure at Little Geneva was unsurprising. Scientists were not accustomed to thinking like security guards, but much was at stake, and they knew that too. Price and a colleague returned to Britain determined to explore ways that an inspection system might work, even conducting an elaborate experiment at Windscale involving a team of mock inspectors and a management team that devised ways to falsify records. From this lengthy exercise, they concluded that round-the-clock inspectors could go some way toward thwarting illicit diversions but that no system would be completely foolproof.

As SCIENTISTS COOKED up schemes to thwart secret bomb programs, the civilian industry they were intending to protect existed mainly in the minds of scientists, engineers, and a few bold utility executives willing to pioneer the new technology. Inspired by Eisenhower's Atoms for Peace speech, Congress tried to goad the nation's utilities by passing the 1954 Atomic Energy Act to "encourage widespread participation in the development and utilization of atomic energy for peaceful purposes."[20] But the truth was that most power companies were not ready for a risky, undoubtedly expensive new technology. And even the daring handful willing to move forward attached conditions: they wanted the government to shoulder some of the risk in the form of taxpayer-funded insurance against major accidents. That would take another three years to legislate. "In the 1950s, after '54, there were a lot of unknowns about [nuclear] safety but especially about economics and there was no pressing need for power at that point," said Samuel Walker, the U.S. Nuclear Regulatory Commission's official historian.[21]

The 1954 law had another, more immediate effect. The AEC began a massive declassification program, flinging the doors wide open to what once had been the most heavily guarded enterprise on earth. "The thing that permeated everything in those days, of course, was classification," said Kratzer. "The real crucial step to make the separation between military and civilian applications was declassification and the thing that moved that forward was the Geneva conferences, which had a very competitive flavor. Things got declassified to enable people to demonstrate their expertise."[22]

In line with Eisenhower's admonition to ensure that scientists in other countries "had all the material needed for . . . experiments," the AEC, with assistance from the Export-Import Bank, began directly distributing funding to dozens of countries so they could build small nonpower-producing reactors for research and training purposes. The largesse displayed by the AEC during this period contributed to further spreading technology that could be, and in some instances was, used for secret nuclear weapons programs. The research reactors were designed to run on highly enriched uranium (HEU)—that is, material in which the proportion of U235 was boosted above 90 percent. Aware of the sensitivity of shipping weapons-grade uranium all over the world, the AEC tried to satisfy the recipient countries with uranium enriched to a lower level, but the scientists operating the reactors complained. "People began to say, 'These don't work well with twenty percent enriched material, and they worked better with HEU,'" Kratzer explained. "So we began to put into these agreements provisions for named quantities of HEU—you had to see how much was available for this after military requirements."[23] Harold Bengelsdorf, who worked closely with Kratzer, put it this way: "Going back to first principles— the Eisenhower philosophy—people reached the judgment we couldn't monopolize the stuff, that other bright people could figure out how to get involved. The philosophy, right or wrong, was that if you wanted to influence and shape the regime, you had to collaborate, be proactive and engage with them."[24]

Research reactor recipients included countries with unstable political profiles in volatile regions, such as Vietnam, Taiwan, the Belgian Congo, the Philippines, and South Africa. By the end of 1959, the United States had provided forty-two countries with these experimental units, together with the fuel necessary to run them. The Soviet Union, anxious to compete for influence, followed suit, and the French, British, and Chinese eventually got into the game. In all, enough highly enriched uranium for at least one thousand Hiroshima-like bombs ended up at small reactors all over the world, often in urban locations with moderate or poor security, presenting—in theory, at least—inviting targets for terrorists.[25] "There was a certain wildness to it," admitted Kratzer's colleague Bengelsdorf. "Everybody wanted an agreement for technology."[26]

In only two key areas—bomb design and technology related to producing weapons-grade fuel—did the U.S. government hold back. But even this was not total. For example, when the Organization of Economic Cooperation and Development (OECD) proposed a reprocessing plant (for plutonium separation) in Belgium, the United States raised no objections and even provided financial assistance for the project. Kratzer and an AEC official named Floyd Culler negotiated the deal, said Kratzer, on "the principle that if there was going to be European reprocessing, it was much better that it be under international auspices." Kratzer also noted "a rather curious episode that came even earlier" involving "a classified exchange of reprocessing information for the benefit of the Belgians." This, he said, was a direct result of the close relationship the United States had with Belgium at that time, stemming from the fact that most of the Manhattan Project uranium came from a Belgian Congolese uranium mine. Added Kratzer, "One of the reasons for the sympathetic attitude to Belgium, I'm quite sure, was that the AEC chairman, Lewis Strauss, got his start in government positions as an assistant to Herbert Hoover running Belgian war relief after World War I, and he clearly had a soft spot for Belgium."[27]

There was a commercial logic to this decision, even if it was not wise from a proliferation standpoint. The AEC wanted to promote new American "light-water reactor" (LWR) technology and this was seen as a way to do it. The LWR designs, which used ordinary, as opposed to "heavy," water as a neutron moderator, were deemed more proliferation resistant than the European models because they required enriched uranium fuel. Since the AEC was then the only Western supplier of enrichment services, AEC officials believed they could use the promise of fuel supply as a lever to insist on recipient countries accepting safeguards. "We wanted to make LWR technology and dependence on enrichment the world choice," Kratzer said. "I would not deny that there was a commercial attraction to it, but the big reason was this was good nonproliferation policy."[28]

As Kratzer suggested, the supply of U.S. nuclear fuel enrichment services became one of the main levers in applying safeguards. Through its agreements for cooperation in the nuclear field, the U.S. government gradually came to insist upon the right of prior consent over all subsequent transfers of U.S. nuclear fuel once it was shipped overseas, and in that way kept track of the material. But commerce and politics almost always took preference over nonproliferation concerns—the reactor deal with India being one of the first and, as it turned out, most egregious examples. And over time the prior consent levers were gradually weakened, in part because of policy changes under the Reagan administration and the gradual loss of the U.S. enrichment monopoly. But as many critics have noted, the policy's architects also played a role. For example, when nonproliferation activists tried to stop further

U.S. fuel shipments to India after the 1974 explosion, Kratzer argued in favor of continuing them. In the early 1980s, Bengelsdorf was instrumental in ensuring that South Africa received nuclear fuel from foreign sources when further shipments from the U.S. were barred because of the apartheid government's refusal to allow inspectors into a suspect enrichment plant. After leaving government, both Kratzer and Bengelsdorf worked at an international nuclear consulting firm in Washington, D.C., which specialized in smoothing the way for other countries seeking U.S. government nuclear export approvals.

WITH "APOCALYPSE MANAGEMENT" in full swing, public enthusiasm for nuclear power during the 1950s is difficult to exaggerate. In 1955, *Newsweek* hailed the first privately owned, publicly accessible, and completely unclassified nuclear research reactor at a college in North Carolina.[29] The following year, Walt Disney Productions published a book for children, *Our Friend the Atom*, in which a genie promises to make the atom "our friend and servant" and ultimately bring peace to the world.[30] Nuclear energy was an empty vessel into which almost any dream could be poured. Imaginations soared with possibilities, propelled by what seem now like wild and outlandish predictions. If nuclear weapons had reached mythical dimensions because of their power to end life, the peaceful atom offered a fantasia of possibilities for making it better.

In the headlong rush to "go nuclear," caution was an unwelcome interloper, and promotion generally took precedence over regulation, just as it did over efforts to prevent nuclear proliferation. Young AEC officials, looking forward to long careers and a rapid climb up the bureaucratic ranks, were empowered by the prevailing optimism of Eisenhower's message. "Our great hazard is that this great benefit to mankind will be killed aborning by unnecessary regulation," AEC commissioner Willard Libby declared during an early 1955 meeting with colleagues as they set about establishing a regulatory framework.[31]

But for all the hoopla, the AEC still had to find a way to entice private utilities to "go nuclear." Four months after the 1954 Atomic Energy Act passed, the commission set up its Power Demonstration Reactor Program, offering incentives such as free nuclear fuel and research and development assistance. There were only four responses.[32]

By then at least a half dozen or more reactor designs, mostly based on

the light-water concept, lay on the drawing boards of the national laboratories. Among the most promising was a so-called pressurized-water
reactor (PWR), the brainchild of scientists at Oak Ridge led by the
physicist Alvin Weinberg, and General Electric's boiling-water reactor
(BWR), which drew heavily on research from the Argonne National
Laboratory. The PWR, first championed by the AEC at Shippingport,
Pennsylvania, with Westinghouse as the contractor, used a steam generator to boil water before it was fed through to the turbine. GE, on the
other hand, offered an ostensibly lower-cost model that did away with
the need for a steam generator. In its BWR, the coolant was allowed to
boil directly in the core, with the steam fed to the turbine generator
through a steam drum. The first BWR would be showcased by Commonwealth Edison at Dresden, Illinois, one of the four utilities that
responded to the AEC's incentive program (although it eventually
dropped out and built the reactor with entirely private capital).[33] Over
time, however, the PWR became the industry standard-bearer, and
was adopted by reactor manufacturers in France and many other
countries.

Even among the small crowd of utilities and reactor vendors eager
to push ahead with nuclear projects, however, none were willing to go
the whole way without publicly funded risk insurance. For the vendors, this was nothing new. Since the early days of the Manhattan
Project, wartime government nuclear contractors such as Westinghouse and GE had insisted upon full government liability coverage,
noting that nuclear hazards were, as an early GE contract stated, of
"an unusual and unpredictable nature."[34] The deals these companies
secured kept them completely free of the threat of lawsuits—even in
the case of their own negligence—in return for building and operating
the government's large laboratories and nuclear fuel plants. GE's contract went even further, insuring it against any future legislation that
GE, in its "sole judgment," considered unacceptable.[35] That might,
for example, include a new law requiring the operator to clean up
waste.[36] Now that the government wanted private utilities to get into
the nuclear game, these companies expected the same treatment.

Not surprisingly, a GE official, Francis K. McCune, was in Congress
to testify on the issue when it first came up during the Joint Committee on Atomic Energy's hearings on the pending atomic energy legislation in 1954. McCune ran GE's atomic products division. He said
that while private industry should, and presumably would, contribute

what it could to nuclear insurance, the amounts would never be enough to cover a major accident, because it was "entirely possible for damage to exceed the corporate assets of any given contractor or insurance company." In other words, a serious nuclear accident could bankrupt a company even as big as GE.[37]

Some insurance company executives wondered why Congress was even considering nuclear if the risks were so great. "We have heard estimates of catastrophe running not merely into millions or tens of millions, but into hundreds of millions and billions of dollars," complained Liberty Mutual Insurance Company vice president Henry Young in his congressional testimony. "It is a reasonable question as to whether a hazard of this magnitude should be permitted, if it actually exists. Obviously there is no principle of insurance that can be applied to a single location where the potential loss approaches such astronomical proportions." Young added, "Even if insurance could be found, there is a serious question whether the amount of damage to persons and property would be worth the possible benefit accruing from atomic development."[38]

The AEC took note of such worries. Unable to offer up any meaningful data to executives like Young, it did the next best thing. In March 1955, it invited ten insurance executives into its sanctuary of still-classified records. It cleared them to visit sensitive facilities and talk to officials not otherwise authorized to speak to people outside the agency.[39] This glimpse into the AEC's inner sanctum mollified the insurers somewhat but also seems to have solidified their view that the private sector could never be wholly responsible for assuming nuclear risk. That June the insurance chiefs wrote a preliminary report concluding that the "catastrophe potential, although remote, [was] more serious than anything [then] known in industry." The biggest area of concern, requiring further investigation, was the radioactive contamination that might result from reactor failure, the group said. This would affect not only the reactor and surrounding buildings but other nearby facilities. The most serious problem would be third-party liability in the event of widespread damage to people and property outside the reactor site.[40]

NONE OF THESE concerns were news to the AEC, which had been pondering the question of reactor safety since 1947, when Lilienthal, ng to turn the dark task of building more weapons into something positive, set up a group to investigate commercial reactor development. He put Edward Teller in charge of probing the issue of accident risk. Disasters involving reactors, the hydrogen bomb's chief advocate concluded, were nothing to smile about, particularly because most reactors, to reduce transmission costs, would be located near large urban areas:

> An error in the manufacture of an automobile, for instance, might kill one to ten people. An error in planning safety devices for an airplane might cost the lives of 150 people. But an error allowing the release of a reactor's load of radioactive particles in a strategic location could endanger the population of an entire city. In developing reactor safety, the trials had to be on paper because actual errors could be catastrophic.[41]

The temperamental but powerful admiral Hyman Rickover had long been a nuclear enthusiast, but he too was wary of the dangers. Assigned to Oak Ridge during the late 1940s, Rickover helped oversee work on the PWR. Later, as head of the AEC's naval reactors branch and nuclear submarine development, Rickover was also put in charge of the commission's civilian model project at Shippingport, which had originally been intended for an aircraft carrier but fell victim to an Eisenhower budget cut. Rickover left nothing to chance. When the PWR was powered up on December 2, 1957, Rickover insisted on retaining operational control.[42] "The whole reactor game hangs on a much more slender thread than most people are aware," he warned during the unit's construction. "There are a lot of things that can go wrong and it [a nuclear reactor] requires eternal vigilance. All we have to have is one good accident in the United States and it might set the whole game back for a generation. We do not want that to happen."[43]

Already, though, the prognosis was not particularly encouraging. For example, on December 12, 1952, an assistant operator at a Canadian reactor (known as NRX) at Chalk River, Ontario, pushed a wrong button, causing a four-ton lid to lift off the top of the reactor vessel four minutes later, flooding the building with radioactive heavy water. Within the space of those four minutes, a series of errors, miscommunication, and defective parts led to an apparent explosion inside the reactor core, the jamming of control rods, and a fuel meltdown. What

remained were the shards of a reactor core—melted fuel, twisted s†
and radioactive water everywhere.[44] *Accid #2*

Three years later, on November 29, 1955, a series of operator errors
at Experimental Breeder Reactor No. 1 (EBR-1) in Idaho caused a partial meltdown. Once the "scram" order was given, the control rods
were not lowered fast enough. In less than two seconds, temperatures
inside the core reached two thousand degrees Fahrenheit. Nearly half
the uranium fuel in the core melted.[45]

News of that accident unsettled the nuclear community. Only a few
years earlier, on December 20, 1951, EBR-1 had become the world's
first reactor to generate electricity, turning it into a beacon of hope
for the industry's backers. Moreover, EBR-1 epitomized the nuclear
dream of providing unlimited electricity, other than by fusion, by producing more plutonium than it consumed. The breeder reactor was
considered advanced technology that the utility industry would eventually move to, once it had been successfully demonstrated commercially. At the time of the accident, Detroit Edison, hoping to lead the
way, was already three years along in the planning phases of an industrial-scale version of EBR-1. The utility's chief executive, Walker L.
Cisler, was a fan of Argonne's director Walter Zinn, and both were
convinced that the industry's best hopes lay with breeder. Now the
celebrated Idaho unit was an object lesson in what could go wrong
with such complex machinery.

Yet Cisler did not let it slow his own effort. So in January 1956, just
two months after the accident, while engineers in Idaho were still trying to figure out what had happened to EBR-1, Cisler's engineering
team, keeping to their schedule as best they could, hurriedly folded the
available accident data into their reactor design and filed for a construction permit.[46] Named after Enrico Fermi, the plant would be sited
at Lagoona Beach in Monroe, Michigan, on the shores of Lake Erie,
about thirty miles from Detroit. Cisler had persuaded fifteen other
utilities plus Dow Chemical to share in the capital expenses; a lot was
at stake.

At the same time, Cisler moved forward on another front, pushing
Congress for nuclear insurance legislation. A month after filing the
permit application, he joined other utility executives for hearings on
the issue in Congress. Commonwealth Edison's chairman, Willis Gale,
told the JCAE that utilities had to be indemnified against catastrophe
in order to build reactors—the utility's Dresden reactor was under

construction at Morris, Illinois. Cisler wholeheartedly backed Gale: "the absolute necessity of insurance against a catastrophe involving extensive public liability, in adequate amount, cannot be overstressed," he said.[47] Consolidated Edison's president, Hudson R. Searing, told the committee that fuel rods would not be inserted at the utility's planned Indian Point unit on the Hudson River, about thirty miles north of New York City in Westchester County, until the insurance problem was resolved.

But how could Congress come up with legislation when no one was able to quantify the amount of risk it was being asked to cover? The JCAE, under the leadership of Senator Clinton P. Anderson of New Mexico, a former insurance executive, and Representative Melvin Price of Illinois, both Democrats, sought a compromise. They would place an upper limit on federal liability of $500 million, with provisions for the government paying out more after further congressional consideration. Utilities would create a pool of $60 million in addition to the federal funds—but the vendors were off the hook in the event of an accident. They could be sued but only the operator would pay. This system, known as "economic channeling" (still in place today, although utilities now pay into a larger fund no longer supported by the government), was completely unique to the nuclear industry. And the amounts were completely arbitrary: the committee's staff director, James T. Ramey, realizing there was no "realistic" number that could be supported by hard evidence, chose the halfway point between zero and one billion. And that is how the figure got into the legislation.[48]

The AEC's chief regulator, Harold L. Price, argued for unlimited liability. Price was a lawyer from Virginia, and his logic was difficult to dispute. "Since the size of risk involved cannot be accurately estimated, we recommend that the legislation not place any ceiling on the amount of the indemnity," he said. The limit of five hundred million or "any other particular figure," he said, had "no sound basis."[49] But the congressmen knew they could never get away with asking the public to protect an industry from the consequences of what might be its own mistakes, with no upper limit on how much the American taxpayer might be forced to pay out. There had to be a limit, even if it was just one man's best guess.

Anderson probably knew he was on a fool's errand, but with his background in insurance he figured the best way to get support for the legislation was to get risk estimates—probability statistics, the kind that insurance companies use to set rates for automobile and health coverage. So the AEC asked the Brookhaven National Laboratory to quantify the chances of a catastrophic accident, as well as the number of deaths and total damages. The report came back with various hypothetical scenarios but the authors refused to set an upper limit on the potential damages because they did not have the data necessary to estimate them. They said the "entire study hardly constitutes more than an identification of the factors that are important . . . and a rough approximation of the magnitudes of the composite results."[50]

The Brookhaven effort did little to help Anderson's cause because it implied the AEC's argument for unlimited liability was correct.[51] But the report's existence gave Anderson the grist he needed for a new round of hearings on the insurance bill. They started on March 25, 1957. Once again, the industry's titans strode onto the committee hearing room floor, determined to see action. GE's McCune told the lawmakers that if legislation did not pass during that session, GE's work on the Dresden reactor would cease. He noted that all of GE's contracts in the civilian field contained provisions for stopping work if liability protection could not be obtained. When asked if GE would remain in the civilian nuclear business without cover, McCune answered that in such a case there would be no market, and that, as a consequence, no one would remain in the field.[52]

The five-hundred-million-dollar figure stuck, and the Price-Anderson bill was voted out of committee in May. It passed both the House and the Senate, and Eisenhower signed it into law on September 2, 1957.[53]

Accid #5

LUCKILY FOR THE U.S. industry, the next serious accident, this one involving fatalities, occurred on government property. It demonstrated another unquantifiable risk, namely the potential for unsafe technology, coupled with unpredictable human behavior, to lead to disaster. On a cold January night in 1961, three of the oldest, most violent emotions known to man—heartbreak, anger, and jealousy—may have been at work as three military men took up their posts at a small experimental reactor in Idaho Falls known as SL-1. Investigators would

later report rumors, never conclusively proved, that one of the men
had been involved with the wife of one of the other men, and speculated that the accident could have been a murder-suicide.

The small crew was tasked with "exercising" control rods that had
been sticking and jamming over the past few months. Evidently one
of the rods was pulled out too far, too fast—almost certainly intentionally, according to an AEC investigation.[54] The alarms sounded
just after 9:00 P.M. on January 3, with all radiation meter needles at
full scale. Firemen and other emergency workers rushed to the scene.
After kicking and pounding on locked doors and finally forcing their
way in, they encountered only silence. Shortly before 11:00 P.M., two
bodies were discovered lying near the side of what had once been the
top of the reactor. One of the men was still breathing, although he
died on the way to the hospital. The second body still lay on the floor
when another emergency worker raced in. Then someone looked up
and saw the third member of the team impaled on the ceiling, one
story above the reactor floor. Part of the fuel rod had shot through his
groin and out one shoulder.

More than a week later, it took a crane and other special equipment
to remove the body, and one man climbing to the ceiling to pry it
loose so it could fall into a stretcher below. Then, along with a massive
clean-up and decontamination operation, came the gruesome job of
preparing the bodies for burial. Nine days after the accident, on January
12, the body parts most exposed, including their heads and limbs, had
to be severed from the bodies and buried with other radioactive waste
on the test station grounds. Radiation had robbed the men of a digni-
fied final rite of passage. What remained of the corpses was wrapped in
plastic, cotton, and lead and put in special hermetically sealed steel
coffins. Black-and-yellow radiation caution signs were slipped inside
the coffins. At Arlington National Cemetery, where one of the men
was buried, a permanent record states: "Victim of nuclear accident.
Body is contaminated with long-life radio-active isotopes. Under no
circumstances will the body be moved from this location without prior
approval of the Atomic Energy Commission."[55] Several of the emergency crew and a nurse who had accompanied one of the victims to the
hospital later developed cancers, in some cases fatal. They and their
families blamed their illnesses on the excess radiation they too had
been exposed to that night.[56]

The first official AEC report on the accident mentioned nothing specific about the love triangle rumors, but it hauntingly concluded that the control rod may have been removed for one of two reasons: "involuntary performance of the individual manipulating the rod as a result of unusual or unexpected stimulus, or malperformance motivated by emotional stress or instability."[57] A later investigation speculated more definitively about the possibility of a murder-suicide, but the author of the report, an AEC official named Stephen Hanauer, was equally critical of the reactor design, which lacked safety features that might have prevented the removal of a single control rod from causing catastrophe.[58] The real story, he told the author of a book on the incident, William McKeown, is that "you can wreck one of these plants. Something went very badly wrong, either in somebody's head or in some piece of machinery or in the execution of commands that never should have been given . . . This technology really depends on people and machinery. I don't know if people really understand that or not. Both can make trouble."[59]

THE IDAHO CATASTROPHE received worldwide coverage at the time, but the AEC did its best to see that it was quickly forgotten, keeping the results of its investigations secret, and the media soon lost interest. By 1966, the commercial nuclear industry appeared poised to take off as concerns grew about pollution from coal-fired plants and dependence on foreign oil. That year, construction permits were issued for five proposed reactors in the United States, all of which were eventually built and operated. Two years later, a total of twenty-three projects were approved for construction, the highest in any year, and they too all eventually received operating licenses. The boom lasted until 1974, but the number of reactors that eventually operated, compared to the number that were ordered, began falling. Construction delays, regulatory hurdles, higher interest rates, and a reduction in energy demand forecasts were blamed for the decline. The accident at Three Mile Island in 1979, followed by Chernobyl in 1986, sealed the industry's fate. The last operating license was granted in 1996, by which time more than one hundred reactors were generating roughly a fifth of total U.S. electricity output. That was impressive, to be sure, but hardly what the early promoters had promised. None of the total 259 units ordered were ordered after 1978. By 2000, 124 units had been cancelled, representing 48 percent of all ordered units.[60]

1966 near Acc'd could Be considered mke Accid # 6

Acc'd #7

Ironically, the dream of endless electricity from advanced "breeder" reactors ended, at least in the United States, the very year the boom in first-generation reactors took off, although more than a decade would pass before the breeder's official demise. On October 5, 1966, just as the Fermi reactor was being brought up to full power, a number of things went wrong and the core started to melt. A "Class I" emergency took effect and the reactor was shut down before it had produced a kilowatt of electricity. It took experts from all over the world, working with Fermi's own engineers, more than three years to sort through the technical difficulties before they felt confident enough to attempt a restart. In May 1970, preparations again were under way to bring the unit to full power when two hundred pounds of radioactive liquid sodium coolant burst through the pipes. Other pipes containing water broke loose, spilling onto the sodium and igniting it. The fire and explosion were contained, but it was another ill omen for the troubled plant. Most of the original partners in the consortium began backing out. They had spent a total of $132 million on a power plant that had still not produced any electricity.[61]

The reactor was restarted in July and ran for a little more than two years after that. In 1972, the AEC refused to further extend the reactor's operating license. The Fermi accidents left no one dead, but they demonstrated the high cost of mistakes. Detroit Edison built a second reactor at Lagoona Beach that began operating in 1983. Beside it sat the crippled breeder, whose decommissioning costs grew until, three decades after the accident, they stood at some thirty million dollars.[62] Quite possibly, by the time the reactor is finally declared free of radioactivity, one hundred years will have passed since the event that prompted the reactor engineer's famous remark (and the title for John Fuller's book): "Let's face it, we almost lost Detroit."[63]

THERE WERE OTHER stories, other consequences, of this early period of nuclear history. An AEC-inspired uranium boom that began in 1948 left a few people rich and thousands of others—unemployed men, housewives, and weekenders—stalking the countryside looking for ore containing the silvery-gray metal, without success. Speculators invested in "penny stock" uranium companies, often start-up ventures with little or no mining expertise that were doomed to fail. One of the lucky prospectors, an unemployed electrician from the Midwest named Vernon Pick, was smart enough to watch government survey planes as they flew in over the mountain rims in Utah. If they made several passes, he would make a note of the position and head over to the area in his small truck, equipped with shovel, pick, and Geiger counter, to see what he could find before the official survey results were tacked up in the nearest post office. Pick got lucky in 1950 at a site near the Dirty Devil River, in the central part of the state. It proved rich in uranium, and became the Hidden Splendor Mine. A start-up company, the Atlas Corporation, offered Pick nine million dollars for the property—four million more than the AEC was willing to pay— and Pick flew off to South America with his own geophysical survey plane and the promise of even greater riches.[64]

Pick became one of the legends of a boom that lasted about ten years. But in the midst of it, few people concerned themselves with the risk of exposure to the cancer-causing radon gas emitted by uranium ore. Debra Munkers was a child in Uravan, Colorado, a uranium-mining town owned and operated by Union Carbide and Carbon Corporation. Her father worked at one of the mines. "I remember him bringing uranium into the house in a jar and us kids playing with the Geiger counter," Munkers recalled three decades later on a Web site for former Uravan residents. The drinking water was bad, but Munkers thought Uravan was a great place to grow up. "What better place to be a child? We could run, and jump, and scream and holler—explore the rocks, the river, the creek."[65]

Life in Uravan seemed just like what Union Carbide promised in the magazine ads it ran at that time. In one, the painted image of a man's hand clenches a chunk of rock against a background vista of mesas and canyons with a river winding through the middle. Below, in big, bold text, the ad reads: "Promise of a golden future. Yellow uranium ore from the Colorado Plateau is helping to bring atomic wonders to you."[66]

This was one way the spin-doctoring in Washington, D.C., reached down through the corporate sphere to local people. Although uranium would eventually be needed for commercial reactors, the uranium boom was really started to ensure the country had enough fuel for the rapid buildup of its nuclear weapons stockpile. Miners and their families could hardly be expected to know that, or the fact that there were fierce debates then taking place in national and international scientific and political circles about the risks of excess radiation exposure. By 1956, the National Academy of Sciences advised: "We ought to keep all our expenditures of radiation exposure as low as possible. From the point of view of genetics, they are all bad."[67]

THE URANIUM BOOM was part of an AEC program to significantly increase fissile material production. That required expanding the plutonium facilities at Hanford in Washington and Savannah River, South Carolina, and building new enrichment facilities at Portsmouth, Ohio and Paducah, Kentucky.[68] These plants posed great risks to workers and generated enormous amounts of radioactive waste and contamination. Alan Labowitz caught a glimpse of the challenges at the Oak Ridge enrichment plant just after the war when he secured a job in the main K-25 facility, which was the size of several football fields and processed hot, corrosive uranium hexafluoride gas (UF6) to turn it into bomb-grade uranium. On his work sheets, Labowitz recorded mechanical failures: the rotating shafts would get stuck, pumps would break down, and seals would wear out. Repairs and replacements had to be made quickly because of the possibility of the corrosive UF6 gas leaking, or coming into contact with water and generating hydrofluoric acid. Lubrication could not be used on the pump seals "because UF6 is corrosive as hell," he recounted. "As you can imagine with this half-mile-long plant filled with all this equipment, something is going wrong all the time."[69]

Later, in the early 1950s, Labowitz moved to the AEC's headquarters in Washington, D.C., and as head of the commission's feed materials branch became an overseer and troubleshooter at all of the nation's nuclear fuel facilities. Builders were dumping excess material—parts of steel beams and metal piping—wherever there was space. A lot of it was contaminated because it had been exposed to the radioactive feed material during test runs. "We had to get rid of this stuff. It was occupying huge amounts of space. The reason it hadn't been disposed of earlier was that it had come into contact with UF6," Labowitz said.[70]

By the time Labowitz realized there was a problem, the contractors had taken matters into their own hands by selling the excess metal to scrap dealers, who in turn sold it to smelters. The smelters mixed the radioactive metal with virgin iron and sold it through normal channels. Kodak officials had already complained to the AEC that radioactive fallout from atmospheric bomb tests threatened to damage film stocks and cause heavy financial losses.[71] They did not want the same problem from contaminated steel. "Eastman Kodak and other manufacturers said that if they buy any kind of steel, if there was any trace of radioactivity, it would screw up their film processing," said Labowitz. "So we had to develop a system of putting used steel on the market in a way that didn't jeopardize their industrial processes . . . We set up certain guidelines for each of our AEC sites that they could only sell a maximum quantity per day or week, or whatever time period there was."[72]

But, where Does this Radioactive metal GO?

IN THE EARLY 1960s, after the uranium boom ended, many mill operators in the West walked away from their plants, leaving tailing ponds the size of small lakes, filled with radioactive effluent from the ore-processing operations. Over years, the sludgy waste was left to bake in the sun until it turned into a spread of fine white sandlike material. Much of it was tucked up in mountain fastnesses or on Indian reservations. Wind blew some of it across the land, but contractors became even better agents for spreading it about. They used the dried-up tailings to make concrete. People began picking up high radiation readings in the most unlikely places—the foundations of their houses, schools, offices, and hotels. Not surprisingly, the tailings also ended up under roads. Since the tailings emitted radon gas, which can cause lung cancer, the discoveries were of great concern.

After almost two decades of lobbying by state officials, Congress finally was persuaded to act. In 1978, it passed the Uranium Mill Tailings Remedial Action (UMTRA) law. The legislation required the government to remove and secure nearly forty million cubic yards of mill tailings—enough material to cover twenty-three hundred football fields—from abandoned mill sites in eleven states and four Indian reservations.[73] The cleanup project lasted more than two decades and even then it was not complete. Decontaminating groundwater proved impossible in some places; in others the government said the effort would have to continue well into the twenty-first century. The cost so far, naturally much higher than original estimates, was calculated in the mid-1990s at approximately $2.5 billion. That is roughly comparable to the $3 billion value of all the uranium that was processed in the United States between 1948 and 1971, when the worst offenses occurred.[74]

In the 1980s, the Uravan operation was shut down and the town torn down so the land could be reclaimed. The children had grown up, but some, like Munkers, reminisced with old friends through the Web site about happier times. Their stories were interspersed with less cheerful news of thyroid cancers that some had developed and others had heard about. They knew by then they had paid a price for drinking the foul-tasting water, swimming in the streams, and playing with the ore samples their fathers brought home from the mines.[75]

The dispensation of research reactors also came back to haunt. In 1975, when the North Vietnamese were about to overrun Da Nang, where an American research reactor was located, Kratzer became concerned. By then deputy secretary of state for nuclear energy, he helped organize an operation to get the fuel out. He said his primary concern was the political backlash he would face if nothing was done, since naturally there would be people in Congress concerned that the Communists might hijack the fuel, or that U.S. military planes would mistakenly bomb it. A top secret retrieval mission was arranged with the air force and a senior government nuclear expert. "They got there before the North Vietnamese and got the fuel out," said Kratzer.[76]

With so much bomb-grade fuel lying around the world at various other reactor sites, Congress passed legislation in 1978 to encourage countries to return highly enriched uranium and convert their reactors to using low enriched uranium. Until very recently progress has been slow. Even so, experts estimate that roughly only half of the twenty tons of HEU the United States sent overseas has been returned.

The nuclear industry, whether it served the military or civilian sector, or both, had been built on uncertain assumptions and jury-rigged solutions to dangers that no one fully understood. The problem of recycling radioactive metal that Labowitz tried to resolve is a case in point. Had there been any attempt to set standards for the maximum amount of allowable radioactivity in the material sold for scrap, based on sound scientific principles? I asked Labowitz. "There must have been [radioactive measurements], but I don't recall," he replied. "I was only using this to illustrate the curious sidelines we had to get into because we were moving into whole new frontiers . . . We had to satisfy particular concerns that no one had identified yet."[77]

CHAPTER 7

Caviar Electricity

[handwritten: Accid #3 → Oct '57]

ONE MONTH AFTER THE PRICE-ANDERSON bill became law, disaster struck the nuclear industry—but this time on the other side of the Atlantic. Fire swept through the first of the two early Windscale reactors, sending a radioactive plume into the air that showered radionuclides over parts of England and northern Europe. It seemed impossible to imagine that only one year earlier, almost to the day, on October 17, 1956, a smiling Queen Elizabeth had opened a larger reactor nearby at Calder Hall, yielding one of the most iconic photographs of the Atoms for Peace era. Although the Soviets had been producing nuclear electricity since 1954, this was generally unknown in the West, and the Calder Hall reactor was billed as the first commercial unit in the world. The Soviets were having their share of problems too. A month before the Windscale fire, an explosion occurred at a nuclear fuel plant in Kyshtym in the southern Urals—with far greater consequences than the accident in Britain. *[handwritten: Accid #4 sept '57]*

For a brief period, Britain seemed to be advancing faster than any other nation in the race toward commercial nuclear energy. Across the English Channel, though, a confident group of *polytechniciens*, graduates of the elite French engineering university, the Ecole Polytechnique, were rapidly catching up. "The use of atomic energy can command the future of France," declared a parliamentary deputy named Félix Gaillard, after his appointment as state secretary for atomic energy in January 1951. That year the young *polytechnicien* pushed through a big five-year development program, costing a total twenty billion francs—and the young Commissariat à l'Energie Atomique (CEA) never looked back.

Inspired by Eisenhower's example, the atomic establishments in both countries—Britain and France—presented their sunnier side to the public while deceiving it about the true purpose of the early reactors, which was to produce plutonium for weapons. In every country where nuclear energy was under development, the public was misled into thinking that the division between military and so-called peaceful uses was real. The illusory nature of this concept was particularly evident in countries with reprocessing plants, but any country with a reactor—even one designed purely for electricity production—had the means to produce plutonium. The push for breeder reactors, specifically designed to increase plutonium output, presented even greater opportunities for countries—for instance, Japan and Germany—to appear peaceful while developing the means, if they chose, to eventually produce nuclear weapons.

Encouraged by inept or unquestioning government ministers, atomic establishments in most countries engaged in highly questionable methods of bookkeeping and phony economics to justify large expenditures. The Windscale and Kyshtym catastrophes meanwhile pointed to another inconvenient truth: the concentration of dangerous nuclear activities in even outlying areas threatened the surrounding populations, sometimes extending to those across national borders. But powerful national governments, increasingly dominated by technocrats, were able to disguise the harm, at least insofar as the wider public was concerned, thus preventing, at least for a number of years, serious challenges to continued nuclear expansion. The Kyshtym explosion was almost completely covered up, providing an excellent example of how a totalitarian state wedded to a nuclear industry could mute warnings or protests. Even in Britain, where an inquiry into the fire was held, the site was renamed Sellafield and the event itself in no way threatened to impede the industry's advance. There were too many dreams, too many vested interests, and too much secrecy to stop the momentum.

THE BRITISH FIRE also demonstrated the repercussions of not working out potential safety problems on paper, as Teller had suggested was necessary before building reactors. The blaze was blamed on a series of operator errors, but the problems really started when the unit was still on the drawing boards and its designers failed to fully understand all its operating characteristics. The result was a plant that left its operators without the instruments needed to measure power levels and temperatures inside the core during an operation necessary to release a buildup of excess energy—called "Wigner energy" after the Hungarian-born physicist Eugene Wigner, who discovered it. The fire started during an attempt to perform one of these Wigner releases, but it was not discovered for another three days, on October 10, 1957, because operators were unable to accurately read or interpret trouble signs.[1] In that time, what had started as smoldering fuel rods burst into flames that spread to about one hundred and fifty fuel channels and sent a plume of hot radioactive particles up a four-hundred-foot brick chimney stack and out into the open air.

As men battled the fire, health physicists drove on narrow, twisting roads to take radiation readings on the windswept hills and lush meadows where cows and sheep grazed. William Wordsworth, who penned some of his most famous poems in the Lake District, wrote in 1800 that the advances of the Industrial Revolution blunted the mind "to a state of almost savage torpor."[2] The scene inside Windscale seemed to be the culmination of that progression. Crews worked in relays because the area around the burning core had become extremely radioactive. They agonized over how best to put out the blaze. Liquid carbon dioxide proved ineffective because the reactor core was too hot. Sand could smother fire, but there was not enough of it. Another option was to let it burn itself out, but that would have meant allowing more radioactivity to escape.

All day Thursday, as the reactor burned, the wind took the airborne particles over the narrow sea. Then it shifted, sending the plume in a southerly direction down the English coast, past the nearby village of Seascale, to Barrow-in-Furness, a city of steel mills and docks—and sixty thousand inhabitants. As the situation became more desperate, the deputy station manager, Tom Tuohy, talked with his colleagues about an idea almost too terrifying to contemplate: drowning the reactor in water. Mixed with the graphite moderator, water could produce a potentially explosive mixture of hydrogen–carbon monoxide gas, creating enough pressure to pop the filters off the chimney and allowing all the fission products to escape into the atmosphere. There appeared to be no other choice, so firefighters were called to the scene. The hoses were turned on just before nine o'clock Friday morning.

Luckily there was no explosion. The water stayed on until just after three in the afternoon of Saturday, October 12, by which time the pile was cold.

The worst affected areas were within a two-hundred-square-mile area of the reactor, and some of the radionuclides were carried in the currents of the Irish Sea. Researchers later discovered evidence of Windscale fallout in parts of Belgium, Germany, and Norway.[3] Until the early 1980s, when the Soviets revealed an even worse event had taken place that same year at the Kyshtym plutonium complex, the Windscale fire was considered the worst nuclear accident on record.

The first official statements gave little hint of what had gone on inside—and the fire was not visible from the outside. "There was not a large amount of radioactivity released. The amount was not hazardous and, in fact, it was carried out to sea by the wind," the UK Atomic Energy Authority blandly stated. The consequences would have been far worse if Terry Price had not successfully fought the chairman of the design committee, Leonard Owen, years earlier to install chimney filters. "Don't be so silly, lad," Owen had admonished Price. "Two tonnes of air go up chimney [sic] every second. Can't filter that."[4]

The filters trapped some of the heavier particles, but the iodine-131 proved too fine for them to prevent its escape. Over the next few days, high levels were detected in the grass where dairy cows grazed. Milk samples turned up readings six to ten times the internationally recommended guidelines, posing the threat of thyroid cancers to anyone who drank it, particularly children.[5]

Eventually, thousands of gallons of milk were dumped into sewers that emptied into the Irish Sea, and farmers were offered compensation in exchange. Even so, contaminated milk almost certainly was sold to the public. The effort to secure milk supplies started well after the first burst of contaminants was released through the stack, and then it took health officials even more time to gauge how far they had spread.

The Kyshtym explosion resulted in an even bigger release of radioactivity to the atmosphere. Located on the eastern edge of the southern Urals, the facility produced plutonium for Soviet nuclear weapons. It also generated enormous quantities of highly radioactive waste, which was routinely dumped into a nearby lake and the Techa River, the only drinking-water source for some twenty-four villages located along the river. On September 29, 1957, a cooling system in a liquid waste storage tank failed, causing the wastes to dry out, precip-

...d eventually explode with enormous force. Seventy
...tons of radioactive debris spewed into the air, equiv-
...e-fourth the amount later released by the Chernobyl
...posing more than a quarter million people to radia-
...government waited seven days before it began evacu-
...near the plant.[6] Much later a Soviet-born scientist
...merman, former head of the biophysical laboratory of
...stitute of Molecular Biology, who emigrated to Israel in
...a shocking sight after an official visit to the area: vil-
...ships had been leveled by the authorities to prevent the
...m returning to their homes.[7] But less than half of 1 per-
...at risk from the accident were ever moved, and some
...rs had passed. Much of the land was returned to agricul-
...1961, but eighty square miles remained off-limits for al-
...cades.[8]

...ments of fallout from atmospheric weapons testing that
...ed even higher as a result of the two industrial accidents,
...uting to increased cancer risks, according to health experts. Al-
...gh the Windscale accident pales in comparison to Chernobyl, some
...timates suggest two hundred extra cancers (over and above what
would normally be expected) still could be blamed on it, of which half
would have been fatal.[9] The situation was far worse in the Soviet
Union. Using records of radiation levels in the various towns and villages, the authors of a study on the Soviet bomb program estimated the
Kyshtym fiasco could have led to as many as one thousand additional
cancers—or roughly one in ten living in the path of the cloud.[10]

PEOPLE DID NOT hear about Kyshtym, and the Windscale fire was
quickly forgotten. Atoms for Peace was in full swing, and in some
countries, particularly Britain and France, public ignorance about the
darker aspects of this seemingly benign drive for nuclear energy was
useful. The military nuclear establishment needed positive publicity
as well as cover for its primary task of making atomic weapons. A
monarch's smile might have reassured British citizens that the Calder
Hall enterprise was there to keep the lights on, but the reality was just
the opposite. Those four units and a subsequent generation of gas-
graphite "Magnox" reactors (so called because of the magnesium used
in their fuel rods) were designed and built to produce plutonium for

weapons; electricity was only an added extra. "We need
deterrent and in order to get it you needed the by-produc
nuclear energy," said Eric Price, who had by then return
front lines in Germany and worked as a government energy

As Price (who is no relation to Terry Price) soon realize
ernment's nuclear game plan required economic inventive
the perpetuation of another myth, that nuclear electricity wou
both less expensive and more reliable than alternative energy s
Nuclear energy was seen as a means of weakening powerful c
terests in the grip of left-leaning miners' unions, feared and hat
the establishment. When the numbers failed to convey the story
way the leadership wanted it told, economists like Price were tol
rework them so that nuclear energy would come out on top. In c
study Price worked on, for example, the instructions were to build
patently misleading assumptions: new coal-fired generation plant
would be assigned the same British coastal locations marked out for
planned reactors, which needed the water for cooling. This had the effect of inflating fossil fuel costs because of the fictional expense associated with transporting coal from the mines to the plant. In truth,
coal-burning stations historically were situated near the mines, precisely in order to eliminate the need for transport.

Another trick was to allocate a notional "plutonium credit" as equivalent to the difference per unit of electricity between the cheaper fossil
fuel plants and the more expensive atomic plants, so that nuclear energy would at least economically match the costs of coal. Notional
was the operative word, of course, because there was no basis on which
to value plutonium other than for military use. The commercial-scale
advanced reactors that could use it for fuel still were decades off.[11]

"The decisions were not economic. In fact they were far from economic. In fact I would say they were gravely distorted," Price said.

IN FRANCE IT was much the same. While Gaillard publicly proclaimed
the benefits of nuclear's peaceful uses, the funding he secured for the
program was almost entirely devoted to nuclear weapons. The man he
put in charge of the CEA in 1951, a *polytechnicien* named Pierre Guillaumat, centered the new empire at Marcoule, near the city of Avignon. There Guillaumat built the reactors and fuel plants needed to

produce plutonium for a weapons program still several years away from being officially sanctioned.

During the chaotic years of the Fourth Republic, when France's leadership changed fourteen times in twelve years, Guillaumat had to be careful not to reveal Marcoule's true purpose. He not only succeeded in remaining above the fray but also, through a stunning mix of duplicity and arrogance, secured all the funding he needed to keep the program on track. He told the French Parliament that the reactors in his budget requests were prototypes for much larger power stations—in other words, that their principal function was to produce electricity.[12]

Inside the CEA, people were not fooled. "Even before the return of de Gaulle [as head of the Fifth Republic in 1958] they were laying the groundwork," said George Vendryes, a former senior CEA official who during the mid-1950s was offered and turned down a promotion to the weapons side.[13] André Finkelstein, a former high-level CEA official who later wrote an unpublished history of the commission, marveled at Guillaumat's gall. He could understand getting away with the story about the first two experimental reactors, named G1 and G2. But when it came time to requesting funds for a larger reactor, G3, he thought even Guillaumat would have to admit the truth. "Okay, G1 and G2 because they were prototypes, but everyone [inside the CEA] knew what G3 was for," he said. Finkelstein once asked Guillaumat how he succeeded. Guillaumat replied, "Do you believe political people understand anything about nuclear energy?"[14]

The tendency of politicians to accept the word of nuclear technocrats like Guillaumat was not limited to France. It was typical of nuclear development everywhere, reflecting the great difficulty facing political leaders whose decisions involved not only complicated issues but a cross-section of professional disciplines and experiences within the nuclear field, ranging from physics to chemistry and geology, nuclear engineering to weapons design, risk measurement to economics, and so forth. This made leaders and lawmakers susceptible to judgments based on a limited body of information, and on who had their ear. Secrecy, particularly when it involved nuclear weapons design, only compounded the problem.

The blurred distinction between the civilian and military sides led to confused methods of bookkeeping, which in a country like France meant that it became a practical impossibility to distinguish precisely how much the government spent on each of the civilian and military sides of their nuclear program. "We used to say their [the military's] budget was two-thirds civilian and two-thirds military. It is very difficult to adjust for what is civilian and what is military," said Finkelstein, who signed off on the expenditures as personal assistant to Francis Perrin, the CEA's scientific director. "Marcoule was mainly paid from the civilian side."

No one complained very loudly. The flow of funds into the CEA was arguably unprecedented in the annals of French government research and development expenditures. Exact sums remain obscured by the passage of time, secrecy, and the lack of accountability, but Finkelstein estimated that by the 1970s, the organization's annual budget had roughly quadrupled to twenty or twenty-five billion francs, from the still-large sums spent in the 1950s. Most of the early money went to plutonium production. "Until the mid-'70s we had a practically unlimited budget," Finkelstein told me over lunch near the Eiffel Tower, in a restaurant where semiprecious stones were artfully laid out on white linen tablecloths.

Guillaumat's operation was not immune to human error. In October 1956, ten months after G1 started, the reactor caught fire with one thousand fuel channels operating at full power. "I was sleeping in Avignon near Marcoule. They woke me," said Pierre Zaleski, who had overseen the reactor's start-up. Zaleski drove the thirty miles to Marcoule and discovered the source of the fire by peering down a fuel channel. "We found a big tissue like a cleaning rag."[15] The rag that caused a blockage had probably been left by one of the workers during construction and then caught fire. Once the fire was out, all the graphite and fuel bundles had to be taken out by a remotely operated boring machine.

Zaleski confirmed that the fire sent radioactive particles into the air, but the extent of contamination was never revealed. Perrin and other high-level officials were dispatched to investigate; their reports were buried. Just as they could spend money without restraint, the CEA's leaders could walk away from the scene of an accident that may have caused harm to the public without it ever being independently investigated or mentioned to anyone outside their own tight-knit circle of people.

FAR MORE WAS at stake, however. Duplicity over the aims of the early reactor programs not only stifled public debate about nuclear weapons but in Europe, at least, had the unintended effect of hindering development of commercially attractive nuclear reactors. It turned out that dual-use reactors created problems for their operators because of differing demands, depending on whether the aim was to optimize the output of plutonium or of electricity. For maximum plutonium production, the fuel rods are normally kept in the core for no longer than ninety days. Then they are removed and sent to a reprocessing plant. For electricity production, however, the fuel "burn-up" time is much longer, about eighteen months.

In France, these and other differing technological requirements led to intense conflicts between the CEA and the state-owned electrical utility, Electricité de France (EDF), which wanted more efficient reactor models along the lines of those being developed in the United States. In the process, compromises were made that resulted in reactors with less than optimal features for either purpose. "Relations between the CEA and EDF were difficult," said Finkelstein. "Their aims were not the same." Ultimately, in 1969 EDF rejected the CEA's gasgraphite reactor in favor of the American pressurized-water reactor.

The same problem existed in Britain, but national pride prevented a switch to American technology, and a market-based approach to development led to the spectacle of several domestically based consortia tripping over each other for a limited amount of business and no hope of achieving the economies of scale and experience that might have been possible with a centralized approach. So when it came time to improve upon the first-generation Magnox reactors, Britain ended up with five versions of an advanced gas-cooled reactor (AGR) design, instead of one, and only seven were ever built. Contracts were ordered on the irrational but equitable principle of what the British call "Buggins's turn," thus giving all the consortia a stake.

The pitfalls were evident to savvy reporters early on, even if the reasons for them were not. For example, in 1958 a writer in *Science et Vie*, a mainstream French science journal, criticized the CEA for making seemingly inflated promises about the potential for atomic energy, pointing out that the Marcoule reactors had so far only produced extremely expensive "caviar electricity."[16] The author of the article, Jean Boiset, ridiculed the hyperbole that surrounded the nuclear program. He described G1's cooling tower as "a 95-meter minaret topped by a lampshade." Three Arcs de Triomphe might be sandwiched into G2, but it was only "a marvellous stove which you only turn on to gather some precious slag (which isn't good for anything anyway) and which only incidentally heats things up a tiny little bit." Assuming the "slag" Boiset referred to was spent fuel, he was wrong. It was precisely what the military planners needed to produce plutonium. Possibly he did not know that.

YET MORE DISTRACTIONS came from a cadre of engineers and scientists devoted to the dream of advanced breeder reactors—the hoped-for route to endless electricity. As some nuclear historians tell it, people began believing that nuclear would develop so quickly that there would not be enough uranium around to satisfy demand, so this became the underlying rationale for breeders. But the vision persisted long after everyone knew there was plenty of uranium around, and the industry had not grown as quickly as anticipated. Something less rational was at work in this expensive, taxpayer-funded, politically contentious sideshow. The breeder had come to symbolize a belief in the promises of technology. More than that, wrote the physicist Walter Patterson: "The concept had an exquisite symmetry."[17]

Vendryes (pronounced *Van-dree-ayes*) became a convert after a visit to EBR-1 in Idaho before its terrible accident. Having turned down a promotion to the weapons side, he instead approached his superiors about starting a breeder program in France, with little to no concern that the much-vaunted advanced reactor itself could ease the path to nuclear weapons for countries that built them. There was no shortage of funds, which meant there was plenty of scope to experiment with new ideas; his superiors gave him the go-ahead. Zaleski, who had seen the Idaho reactor too, became Vendryes's deputy on the project, and they began looking for a suitable location on which to build. They were offered an old military site in eastern France—not what they had in mind, so they headed south to Cadarache, near the sunnier, more hospitable climes of Aix-en-Provence. "Of course I could not write to Mr. Francis Perrin and say this [original site] was too awful to house a nuclear center." In order to win approval for the site he wanted, Vendryes resorted to an old bureaucratic trick; he proposed criteria that only Cadarache would meet. The ploy worked. "The decision to open a new site was a tremendous boost for the breeder," he said. He omitted to mention, or perhaps simply did not know about, the earth-quake fault line running only a few miles from the site.[18]

Vendryes chose names for his projects that had musical or mythical associations, although this was a calculated move designed to secure approval for ever larger funding requests. "As long as I sent reports for an 'experimental fast breeder' I got no response. I had to give it [the first larger-scale breeder] a name, so I gave it the name Rapsodie, and that attracted the attention of the authorities, and I think that helped to get the decision made to build it and give the money," Vendryes explained, adding that the name stood for certain technical characteristics—*rapides sodium*. Rapsodie followed two experimental breeders named Harmonie and Masurca (like *mazurka*, the lively Polish dance). Finally, years later, came the two commercial-scale breeders, Phoenix and Superphoenix, after the legendary bird that rose from the ashes. "If something has a name and a good name, it begins to have life," Vendryes said.

Breeders were built elsewhere, in Germany, Britain, the United States, the Soviet Union, and Japan, and over the next few decades they would prove the industry's biggest and most extravagant folly. Because they mostly used sodium as a coolant, the plants were particularly vulnerable to leaks and explosions. In 1976, the year the French government approved Superphoenix, the CEA predicted that 540 reactors of its type would be operating in the world by the turn of the century, but when that year arrived not one commercial-size plutonium-fueled breeder existed anywhere. The industry's increasingly unfavorable public image was not helped by numerous breeder and reprocessing plant accidents and leakages in Europe and Japan. In 1977, when Superphoenix was still under construction at Creys-Malville, protests at the site left one person dead. And in the United States, the Clinch River project was the focus of heated debate before it was finally canceled in the early 1980s. Rickover summed up the basic problem with breeders. They were, he said "expensive to build, complex to operate, susceptible to prolonged shutdown as a result of even minor malfunctions, and difficult and time-consuming to repair."[19]

By the time Superphoenix was connected to the grid in 1986, the breeder era was really over and orders for conventional reactors had slowed to a trickle. There was more than enough uranium to satisfy existing and future demand for as far out as anyone could see. The breeder at Creys-Malville was designed to produce 1,250 megawatts of electrical output, but it was plagued with trouble and constantly forced into shutdown mode. To the quiet relief of people inside the French utility, EDF, the government decided to permanently shut down Superphoenix on Christmas Eve 1996.[20] It had operated for the equivalent of less than six months, which meant that the average cost of the electricity it generated was at least ten times higher than that from light-water reactors.[21] By one estimate, Superphoenix had already cost the equivalent of five billion dollars, but its true costs will not be known until it is decommissioned.[22]

The anticipation of dozens or even hundreds of breeders in commercial use led the British and French governments to build large reprocessing operations, at Sellafield in Britain and Cap de la Hague in northern France. Utilities in Europe and Japan signed long-term reprocessing contracts, which meant that shipments of spent fuel and plutonium increased. This opened up potential pathways for proliferators—and hazardous radioactive contamination. Reprocessing plants involve a lot of robotic equipment to maneuver the hot fuel rods through the lengthy process of chemical separation. Workers in heavy protective clothing—called "shaddoks" at La Hague—struggled to perform mundane tasks like operating equipment through glove boxes, screening off leaks, or putting radioactive waste and contaminated clothing into plastic bags. One misstep would set off alarm bells and send the offending employee to a "clean zone," where he or she would undress in panic and then be subjected to hours, or days and weeks, of exhausting medical examinations involving the analysis of blood, spittle, nasal mucus, and urine. Tiredness, irritability, and diminished love lives were side effects of dreary, dangerous working lives inside these fuel plants.[23]

Utilities in Europe and Japan were persuaded to sign long-term reprocessing contracts on the basis that breeders would miraculously appear as envisioned by their ardent promoters. When the breeders did not materialize, the utilities, locked into their commercial agreements, kept sending the fuel to be reprocessed anyway and began viewing Sellafield and La Hague as de facto waste dumps for their spent fuel, thereby alleviating themselves of the pressure to find a more viable means of intermediate or permanent disposal. But this was costly—by one recent French calculation, about 85 percent more expensive than direct disposal of the spent fuel. In 1989, EDF's fuel division concluded that reprocessing "does not have an economic basis and would have other significant international repercussions harmful for the entire nuclear sector."[24]

Meanwhile, the chemical separation plants churned out hundreds of tons of plutonium and, as a by-product of their operations, highly toxic radioactive waste. Used plutonium sat in a pure state, far more accessible to malevolent misuse than if it had never been separated in the first place. And it had no value. (The military establishments by then were sated with the stuff.) Today, some utilities, still sitting on their plutonium inventories, are opting for an intermediary route, known as mixed-oxide fuel, to use up some of it, but even that involves costly alterations to their reactors, dedicated fuel fabrication facilities, and the prospect of further commerce in plutonium-based nuclear fuel.

Reprocessing plants also leaked tremendous quantities of radioactive contaminants. In a scene reminiscent of the aftermath of the Windscale fire, French authorities on October 2, 1968, scurried around buying up milk from the local farms because of above-average amounts of iodine-131, dangerous to the thyroid gland, which had escaped into the atmosphere. The crabs at La Hague became unsalable, and the once sought-after "beurre de la Hague" had to be renamed "beurre du Val de Saire" because people refused to cook with it.[25]

ALTHOUGH THE BREEDER experiment proved costly and highly controversial, to begin with it was little more than an expensive dalliance, while the real money was on weapons research. In Europe only France and Britain would drive their programs through to actual warhead development with Britain conducting its first nuclear weapons test, with Australian government permission, off Australia's northwest coast near the Monte Bello Islands on October 3, 1952. The device was suspended beneath a frigate named the HMS *Plym* and detonated ninety feet underwater. The *Plym* was instantly obliterated, although its brass nameplate had been removed and is now kept at Aldermaston. Thirteen months after the exercise, the Royal Air Force received its first nuclear weapon for training and, ostensibly, actual use.[26]

In France, the defeat in Vietnam spurred the CEA into setting up a military bureau in 1954. A year later, a secret protocol was signed with the Armed Forces Ministry (Ministère des Forces Armées) authorizing the transfer of funds to the CEA. Relations between the two organizations grew stronger until, in November 1956, a protocol was signed ordering the CEA to conduct preliminary studies for a weapons test. Fittingly, it was Gaillard, who had been the first atomic energy minister, who on April 11, 1958, signed the order for bomb development. He had become prime minister in November 1957. A test date was set for the first quarter of 1960.

As the French prepared to take a fourth seat at the high table of nuclear weapons states, the Soviets tried to frighten them away. The incident took place late in 1959, during a lunch in London, ironically organized to discuss the issue of safeguards. The guests that day included the head of the French delegation, Jules Moch, the Soviet deputy foreign affairs minister, Valerian Zorin, and the CEA's Finkelstein. During the meal, Finkelstein recalled, Moch said, "You know, France still wants to play a major political role, and we probably will have to go nuclear."

Not skipping a beat, Zorin calmly replied, "We have no objections." Then the Russian paused and pointedly added, "Do you think it is safe in such a small country?"

Finkelstein said, "We were perspiring."

But the diplomatic intimidation did not have its desired effect. During his twelve-year absence from government, de Gaulle had kept abreast of nuclear developments. He remained convinced of the need for a nuclear *force de frappe* (strike force) and the importance of advancing nuclear energy. Without nuclear weapons, de Gaulle later explained, France "would hand over to the Anglo-Saxons our chances of life and . . . death on the one hand, and . . . our industrial potential on the other."[27] He could not have forgotten meeting the handful of French scientists in Canada in 1944 when they were still sworn by the British to protect the nuclear secrets—but didn't. De Gaulle looked upon technology the way kings and queens once viewed territorial conquests: it brought power and a sense of progress. And he was right in a sense. Henceforth, political dominance on the world stage would be purchased through the nuclear scientists and engineers. One by one France would lose its former colonies; nuclear would be the source of new prestige. "We are in the epoch of technology," de Gaulle declared. "A state does not count if it does not bring something to the world that contributes to the technological progress of the world."

Thirteen months after de Gaulle became the first president of the

Fifth Republic, and several weeks after the lunch in London, another desert became the setting for a nuclear explosion. It occurred just after seven in the morning, February 13, 1960, over the Sahara at Reggane, a town in south-central Algeria. As French planes took off to take radiation readings, they flew as far as the border with Libya, and then turned back. "The Americans took over, and they radioed the French pilots and said, 'Congratulations,'" said Finkelstein. "Libya was under U.S. control at the time."[28]

After the bomb exploded, Yves Rocard, father of the later prime minister Michel, took a piece of paper to measure the yield. "He simply looked at the way it blew and calculated it to within 5 percent of the [actual] yield," Finkelstein said. "The people with all the instruments were furious." The yield was more than sixty kilotons, three times larger than the first American test at Alamogordo.

Caviar electricity had finally paid off.

CHAPTER 8

Parlor Games

O N A WINTER'S DAY ALMOST fifty years ago in Oslo, British
and Israeli nuclear officials held a meeting at which neither
side spoke to, or saw, the other. The two delegations sat in
separate, though adjacent, rooms. In between, Norwegian business-
men scurried back and forth arranging a sale of critical importance to
a secret Israeli weapons program—twenty tons of heavy water. The
world would not know about that February 1959 exchange because
the Norwegians were paid providers of cover. Plus, the British knew
how to keep secrets, and the Israelis might have gone so far as to pun-
ish anyone silly enough to commit an indiscretion.

The two-room bargain says a lot metaphorically about the way the
nuclear industry developed. A degree of protection was needed in transactions between the civilian and military sides of nuclear, not necessarily because they were strictly illegal but because they looked bad. The
International Atomic Energy Agency was having a difficult beginning.
Countries resisted the idea of committing themselves to "peaceful
uses" and agreeing to international inspections, and exporters were
more anxious to win business than they were to play nuclear policemen. Although the United States itself was hardly a model of propriety
back then, AEC officials were applying more and more pressure on
countries to support the new agency. Hence the smoke and mirrors in
Oslo.

Heavy water was essential to the Israelis' program because they
needed it for the natural uranium reactor they were building with

French assistance. These reactors were ideal for fast-tracking plutonium production in part because they did not require expensive, time-consuming uranium enrichment.

Of course, everyone involved in the transaction that day understood these arcane, but important, details. Which is precisely why countries like Israel wanted the French reactor. So the deal worked like this: A newly established Norwegian company named Noratom took temporary ownership of heavy water owned by the UK Atomic Energy Authority (UKAEA). Then they resold it to the Israel Atomic Energy Commission (IAEC). The UKAEA would earn a tidy sum of one million pounds (about two million dollars) for the heavy water, out of which Noratom would pocket a 2 percent commission.

It was a case of nod, nod—and try not to wink. "An elaborate charade was played out," a former British defense intelligence analyst named Peter Kelly told an interviewer in 2005, the year the duplicitous transaction was finally revealed to the British public in a BBC documentary. "Noratom's people went back and forth ferrying the relevant documents so that UKAEA would be able to say it had not signed a deal with Israel."[1]

In that way, the British avoided the complications of having to confront the messy issue of safeguards—asking the Israelis to agree to periodic inspections—while at the same time divesting themselves of unneeded and extremely valuable strategic material. The British actually considered requiring the right to future inspections but in the end decided against it. "Our own view here is that it would be somewhat overzealous for us to insist on safeguards in the sale of this material to Israel, and unless I hear from you to the contrary . . . we shall proceed to complete the sale of the material, within the next week or two, without restrictions." The letter was from an official of the UKAEA named D. E. H. Peirson, and it was sent to the prime minister's Atomic Energy Office. It was dated September 22, 1958, and stamped CONFIDENTIAL. Peirson's views prevailed.

So Norway asked Israel for safeguards, and in the final exchange of documents on February 25, 1959, Israel promised to use the heavy water for "the peaceful uses of atomic energy and not for any military purposes." The Israelis gave Norway "the opportunity to ascertain to its satisfaction that the use of heavy water [is] in accordance with these guarantees." That meant, loosely speaking, inspections.[2]

The "peaceful uses" promise conformed to the safeguards etiquette of the day, but it was virtually meaningless. Two years later, in March 1961, Kelly reported to the prime minister's Joint Intelligence Committee that the Norwegian "safeguards were not stringent, nor was the agreement ever registered with the IAEA." As part of Britain's Defense Intelligence Staff (DIS), Kelly had specific responsibility for tracking covert nuclear facilities in the Soviet Union and other countries.

At this stage, you might ask, why Norway? The answer: Norway's Norsk Hydro was the only Western manufacturer of heavy water in the world, apart from the AEC in the United States. Noratom, partly owned by Norsk Hydro, was brought in after it became clear that the Israelis could not get what they wanted from either of the two primary suppliers; talks with the United States got bogged down over demands for safeguards, and Norsk Hydro could not deliver to the Israelis' tight timetable. By agreeing to front for the British and help the Israelis, Noratom hoped to secure a foothold in the international nuclear market, where it wanted to sell natural uranium reactors. The British had more heavy water than they needed, and the Norwegians knew that, so Noratom effectively brokered a deal. When the shipment took place, the duplicity was complete. "Two lots, of 10 tonnes each, of heavy water were consigned to Noratom in June 1959 and June 1960, not to Israel. The lots were, however, put on board Israeli ships at a UK port," according to British Foreign Office records.[3]

PRETENSE WAS VITAL to the industry's survival and growth, particularly when it came to the Israeli program. Ten years earlier, French nuclear scientists had reached out to help their Israeli colleagues, but they did it in a way designed to convince both themselves and anyone who found out about it that their joint undertakings were of an entirely innocent nature. "We weren't really helping them [the Israelis]," Goldschmidt told an interviewer years later. "We were just letting them know what we knew—without knowing where it would lead. We didn't know ourselves how difficult it would be."[4]

The "it," of course, was making weapons. At that time, neither Israel nor France had the technical capability to build a bomb, and influential people in each country opposed the idea on ethical and financial grounds. But Israel's fierce, white-haired leader, David Ben-Gurion, wanted nuclear weapons, and his ambitions coincided with those of the powerful *polytechniciens* in France making choices that virtually guaranteed France would have them. And then the physicists and chemists stepped in to play their part.

In 1949, the CEA's Francis Perrin traveled to Tel Aviv to visit with another war refugee, Ernst David Bergmann. The two scientists began talking about how they could help each other in the nuclear field. Perrin was a member of Frédéric Joliot-Curie's inner circle who had fled to England during the war. Bergmann, a rabbi's son, was an organic chemist who had studied in Berlin and was on the fringes of Europe's nuclear scene in the early 1920s. He escaped Nazi Germany and was now in charge of Israel's fledgling atomic program, supported by Ben-Gurion and his protégé, Shimon Peres. Bergman was well known among the French scientists, which was in part why Israel sought help from France, rather than the United States or Canada.[5]

The conversations between Perrin and Bergmann led to informal exchanges, and then in 1953 to a formal agreement of cooperation between the two countries in nuclear research. The partnership was like a childhood friendship—the nuclear programs in both countries were still in the formative stages. The French and the Israelis would hold each other's hands, metaphorically speaking, for more than a decade until each country had well-developed fissile production capabilities, and in France's case atomic weapons.

Meanwhile, proliferation continued in other more prosaic ways. Only two years after he succeeded in separating his first morsels of plutonium in France, Goldschmidt in 1951 discovered the Americans were using a new solvent. Again, there were dozens of likely candidates and he did not know which one. So he assigned two assistants to pour through American chemical publications. A few weeks later they spotted information on one solvent, tributyl phosphate, that seemed promising.

Before Goldschmidt could follow up, a colleague from across the Channel came to visit. The British visitor was designing reprocessing plants at Harwell for the Windscale facility. Naturally, Goldschmidt was eager to show off his new plant at Le Bouchet, and a trip like that would provide a more relaxed setting for informative conversation. On the way, Goldschmidt—without looking at his passenger—asked if the British were using tributyl phosphate. The man from Harwell could hardly contain himself. Goldschmidt recalled, "He could not keep from replying: 'Oh, you know!' We thus 'discovered' the exceptional properties of this solvent."[6]

Only six years later, in 1957, a London-based chemical company, Albright and Wilson, sold tributyl phosphate to Israel, with the understanding that it would be used to separate plutonium from spent fuel. The deal was not reported to the British government. Peter Kelly, the British defense intelligence officer, discovered it in 1961 when he was investigating his country's involvement with the Israeli nuclear program. Without knowing it, the Harwell official had helped not only the French improve their reprocessing operations, but the Israelis as well.

AFTER THE WAR, Goldschmidt gradually forgot about his assurances to Groves. He was naturally gregarious, and he had friends in nuclear circles all over the world. He would joke that he had a hard time remembering what was classified and what was not. Nuclear scientists and high-level government officials traveled everywhere, staying at fine hotels and dining at expensive restaurants. "It was a club. We knew the physicists from all over," said André Finkelstein, who was a personal assistant to both Goldschmidt and Perrin at the time. During the late 1950s, for example, Goldschmidt and Finkelstein flew together to the United States. Their plane stopped in Newfoundland. They got out to walk around the small airport, and in the men's room they ran into an American physicist they knew, Mason Benedict. The joke was, said Finkelstein, that "if you cannot wash your hands [without being] next to a nuclear physicist when you are traveling, then you are probably traveling too much."

Goldschmidt also had deep connections with Israel, both as a Jew and as a physicist. His wife was a member of the wealthy and well-connected Rothschild family, which made generous contributions to the young Jewish state. Sometime during the early 1950s—his memoirs do not reveal precisely when—Goldschmidt went to Ben-Gurion's home in the Negev Desert. He listened as Ben-Gurion spoke of his dream of making the desert bloom, but as both men gazed at the Negev from inside the Israeli leader's frame house, they knew what he really had in mind.[7] Groundbreaking in the desert, at a place called Dimona, was only a few years away.

The desire to become a weapons state was not uniformly shared by people inside the Israeli government at that time. Those who opposed the idea did so for much the same reason that Rotblat finally left Los Alamos. They could not sanction that a country built on the ruins of death camps should produce weapons of indiscriminate mass destruction.[8] Ben-Gurion, on the other hand, saw in nuclear weapons the key to Israel's survival—either that, or they would take the whole of the Middle East down with his people.

Besides the moral calculus, there was the financial question. Finance Minister Levi Eshkol feared that an all-out weapons effort could bankrupt the government, diverting the resources and money needed to build a new country. Ben-Gurion and Peres eventually set up a separate channel for financing the project and started a secret fund-raising effort in Europe and the United States, but they needed hundreds of millions of dollars to succeed and still relied upon a heavy amount of government underwriting. Ben-Gurion's insistence on investing Israeli money in the bomb project remained a major source of conflict inside his cabinet and the Mapai Party.[9]

In France, meanwhile, Israeli scientists were on hand to witness the drive toward a bomb, which, like a dance with many intricate steps, was helpfully disguised by the whirlwind of changing leaders and Guillaumat's artful dodging. Ben-Gurion wanted his own reactors and reprocessing plant, and he needed to strengthen his ties with France to get them. The Canadian-American deal to supply India with a natural uranium reactor provided a model for how the French could do the same for Israel. The 1955 deal with India lacked any demands for inspection. India had only to promise to use the CIRUS reactor for "peaceful purposes." If France agreed to provide a similar reactor to Israel, the argument ran, there was an example to follow, a precedent—a cover.

The following year, in July 1956, Egypt's Gamal Abdel Nasser nationalized and closed the Suez Canal, and France and Britain joined Israel in attacking Egypt that October. These larger events served to further strengthen the French-Israeli ties on the nuclear front. One month before the attack, Goldschmidt welcomed Peres and Bergmann to Paris. "They came to me and said they'd like to buy a heavy-water research reactor similar to the one the Canadians were building in India. They said that when the Americans will realize we have a nuclear capacity, they will give us the guarantee of survival," Goldschmidt told an interviewer.[10]

That was on September 13. Four days later, Guillaumat and Perrin met the two Israelis at the home of the Israeli ambassador in Paris. Between the meeting with Goldschmidt and the small dinner party, ties between the two countries, already strong, appear to have been cemented.[11] Ben-Gurion would get his reactor.

Now, too, within the Direction des applications militaires (DAM), the CEA's military division, there would be a separate organization to manage French relations with the Israelis. Cooperation with Israel "was dealt with in a very secret manner by a separate group within CEA," Vendryes told me. "The team that worked on the construction of Dimona never appeared on any [organizational] chart."

IN 1957, A young, very bright engineering student was asked to oversee the French nuclear effort in the Middle East. His name was Rémy Carle. Carle was not just any student. He was one of just five selected in his graduating year from the Ecole Polytechnique for a place at the Ecole des Mines, the highest honor a French engineering student can receive.[12]

Carle had dreamed of engaging in pure research after graduating, but those dreams were soon dispelled. Without knowing it, one of France's best and brightest had stepped into the organizational equivalent of a fast-moving elevator. In September 1955, at the start of his second year, he recounted: "I was told 'no, you have to be next Monday morning in Marcoule. There we are starting our first reactor.' They were in such a hurry. At this time I lost my idea to do research. My business was to be an engineer and build reactors."[13] Carle would learn on the job.

Retired now, Carle and his wife live in a château-style house in Sceaux, the smart Parisian suburb linked with the Curie family— Pierre grew up in the town, and Marie moved there with their two daughters after Pierre's untimely death. It was to Sceaux, to the home where Frédéric and Irène Joliot-Curie then lived, that Goldschmidt had traveled to show his first sample of plutonium, like an offering. Carle had wanted to follow in the Curie tradition, questioning and talking openly with fellow scientists to further knowledge. It was science at its noblest. But that wasn't the way things worked out. He became an industrialist helping Israel with Ben-Gurion's sacred project. In the process, Carle grew as secretive as the organization that hired him and the clients he worked for in the Negev.

When Carle opened the door to his house, the first thing I noticed besides the man himself—tall, gaunt, and very cool—was a glass cabinet in the large entryway filled with expensive-looking porcelain turtles. "My wife collects them," Carle explained in quiet tones. (She was out attending to her volunteer work at the Curie homes, now tourist attractions.) As I looked around, I realized there weren't just ten or twenty but several hundred porcelain turtles taking up the whole of the cabinet and every available surface in the hallway. A few were poised with their heads close to the shell, ready to disappear inside. Some were craning their necks up, or curling them sideways, or looking straight ahead. Cold and silent, the turtles had turned the wide entryway into a mausoleum. So too, in a way, had this man.

Inside, the house was as quiet as the gathering of years and settling of dust. Somewhere a clock ticked. Alone in the living room, while Carle disappeared to the kitchen to make the coffee, I surveyed the artifacts, paintings, and heavy brocaded furniture. Carle returned with two demitasse cups. After placing one on the small table next to me, he sat on an ornate wooden-backed chair. He had a thin mustache over the middle of his top lip, but it was almost invisible among the creases of his bony, grave face.

"My main problem was the secrecy," he explained about an early trip he had taken to the United States to visit nuclear facilities. "People were friendly, but behind this, we felt a barrier."

The irony of this statement, even if unintended, was impossible to miss. That trip was taken in 1956. In March 1957, Carle was put in charge of the CEA's activities in the Middle East. After that, he became very good at keeping secrets—especially on the topic of Israel. And decades later, as he sat erect in his chair, it became clear that what he knew would never be revealed, not by him anyway. Apart from acknowledging his role as chief French liaison on the Dimona reactor project, Carle offered that he had close links with Shimon Peres and made several trips to Israel while the reactor was being built. He also wanted to make clear that he had no moral qualms about his work. At the time of his hiring, he was asked if he had any objections to helping Israel with its bomb project. His reply was that, with memories of the Holocaust still fresh in his mind, "the only country I would support would be Israel."

And now? "Now I remain convinced that if Israel had no bomb, it would not exist."

Then he resumed his autocratic posture and withdrew into his

shell, until we found something else to talk about. The invisible wall
between us was as evident as any that would divide two rooms.

CARLE MUST HAVE been a busy man in 1957. That year hundreds of
French engineers and technicians moved to the ancient city of Beersheba to work on the nuclear plant nearby. Ben-Gurion transferred
money straight from his own secret account to Paris and the French
engineering firm Saint-Gobain, then two years away from completing
the reprocessing plant at Marcoule. In order to build such a facility in
Israel, the Saint-Gobain engineers were given access to the reactor designs, and they were reportedly "stunned" by what they learned. Although the reactor, known then as EL-102, was designed to produce
twenty-four megawatts of thermal (as opposed to electrical) power,
other specifications, such as those associated with the plant's cooling
ducts and waste facilities, suggested the plant might operate at two to
three times that level.[14] This was important because it meant that the
Israelis could ramp up plutonium production.

Finkelstein confirmed that the reactor's "upper limits" were indeed
more than the nominal design capacity. They equated to production of
some twenty to twenty-five kilograms of plutonium per year, depending on the amount of time the unit operated, enough for five or six
weapons. By comparison, at the lower level, the plutonium output
would amount to roughly seven kilograms a year—still enough for two
low-yield weapons. "But it didn't matter," said Finkelstein. "They only
needed a few bombs . . . You know, when you have military people
they always want more tanks and equipment. It's the same thing [with
nuclear weapons]. But it's meaningless."

Of course, the Israelis did not share Finkelstein's attitude. They
wanted more than a few bombs—a stockpile, in fact—and ultimately
hydrogen weapons. Dimona's security arrangements were as tight as
any devised by the Americans or Soviets. French workers were not allowed to write directly home to France; their mail was sent via a post
office box in Latin America. The equipment necessary for the reactor
and the reprocessing plant was assembled by the CEA in a secret
workshop in a Paris suburb and transported to Israel by truck, rail, and
ship.[15] The pace quickened. Groundbreaking at EL-102 took place
early in 1958.

Meanwhile, in France itself, dozens of Israeli scientists were benefiting from the early cooperation agreement. Some were at Saclay, and others roamed "at will" inside the perimeter fence at Marcoule, while French curiosity seekers had to be satisfied with viewing the facility from an open-roofed galley across from the main entrance. Israelis were present at the first French test at Reggane in 1960.

WHILE THE BOMB programs in France and Israel proceeded apace, the Chinese and Indians were developing their own nuclear capabilities, directly or indirectly helped by the United States or the Soviet Union. The sharing that took place was sometimes overt, as in the case of Soviet assistance to China, and other times conveniently trusting, or naive, as in the instance of further American nuclear exporting to India.

Mao Zedong is believed to have started thinking about nuclear weapons at the founding of the People's Republic in 1949, but it was not until 1955 that he and other Chinese leaders made the decision official. They were looking for an antidote to American "nuclear bullying" in Korea, Indochina, and the Taiwan Straits. "Now it is the time to pay attention to it [nuclear weapons]," Mao told a decisive gathering that year. "We can achieve success provided we put it on the order of the day." He was able to say that because his government had recently signed an agreement with the Soviet Union for nuclear assistance. Many Chinese nuclear scientists trained in the United States, but over a five-year period the Soviets basically designed and built the early Chinese nuclear weapons infrastructure. Jonathan Pollack, a prominent China expert, has said that "in scale and scope Soviet assistance to the Chinese weapons program is without parallel in the history of nuclear proliferation."[16]

Chinese nuclear weapons became even more important after the Sino-Soviet split in 1960, when all Soviet assistance was abruptly withdrawn. Two years earlier, Deng Ziaoping, the Communist Party general secretary, tellingly commented, "The Soviet Union has the atom bomb. Where does the significance lie? It lies in the fact that the imperialists are afraid of it. Are the imperialists afraid of us? I think they are not . . . The United States stations its troops on Taiwan because we have no atom bombs or guided missiles."[17]

Although Soviet assistance allowed the Chinese to leapfrog other nations on the way to achieving nuclear weapons capability, the cutoff in 1960 set the effort back by several years, according to a partially classified American CIA study in 1966. Nevertheless, the Chinese were able to detonate a twenty-two-kiloton fission weapon in 1964. "Without Soviet industrial help . . . it would have been impossible for us to have achieved such a rapid success in making the atomic and hydrogen bombs," said Liu Xiyao, vice minister of the Second Ministry (nuclear weapons).[18]

That same year, China began a massive effort known as the "Third Line" to duplicate infrastructure, including the nuclear plants. They built new nuclear fuel production lines, research reactors, and a weapons assembly factory in Sichuan Province, taking advantage of the mountains of central China to further protect the facilities from attack by either American or Soviet forces. Among these newer installations is a large weapons research and development center, known as the "Los Alamos of China," in Mianyang. At least four of these complexes, including the country's largest plutonium plant and the Mianyang center, were within one hundred kilometers of the epicenter of the May 2008 earthquake (7.9 on the Richter scale), and some are believed to have sustained severe damage.[19]

By superpower standards, the Chinese nuclear arsenal was relatively small, but it was enough to ensure China's international stature and not something that would easily be negotiated away. Marshall Nie Rongzhen, the overall director of China's nuclear weapons program, put it this way in 1959: "To get rid of imperialist bullying, which China had suffered for more than a century, we had to develop these sophisticated [nuclear] weapons. At least then, we could effectively counterattack if China were subject to imperialist nuclear attack."[20]

INDIA, ON THE other hand, was propelled forward by the United States and Canada, initially with the 1955 contract for the CIRUS reactor and the heavy water. But India also wanted nuclear electricity, in part to provide power to spur industrial growth, but also to lend respectability to a program whose aims were beginning to look suspect. Once again the United States stepped into the breach. In 1958, Bhabha met John McCone, then the AEC chairman, at a second Atoms for Peace conference in Geneva.

"Bhabha impressed McCone," Kratzer said.[21]

When Bhabha said he wanted a nuclear power plant, McCone was ready to listen. "We were anxious to get the business. We'd been beaten by the Brits on exports to Italy and Japan," Kratzer said. India would soon have two General Electric boiling-water reactors, with generous U.S. taxpayer-supported financing.

While the desire for two power reactors was perfectly legitimate, Bhabha made no secret of the fact that he was also interested in weapons, even if he never mentioned it explicitly. In 1956, Britain's Terry Price and a colleague traveled to Paris to discuss the results of the inspection exercise they had conducted at Windscale after the embarrassing failure at Little Geneva. In Paris, they were treated to dinner in a velvet-lined *cabinet particulier* at Lapérouse, an old restaurant famous for its privileged clientele and intimate settings; Maupassant, Zola, Hugo, and other French literary figures had held forth at its tables in earlier times. That evening, the collection of nuclear luminaries included the host of the occasion, Francis Perrin, as well as Bhabha, a Norwegian scientist, and the two British scientists.

The private alcove was a suitable setting for the delicate subject of nuclear safeguards. Bhabha, Price recalled, "made it quite clear that India would resist any attempt on the part of the international community to control her own future plutonium production." Bhabha wanted a strong International Atomic Energy Agency, but he could not agree to discriminatory controls. "He was not asking the Big Three to abolish all their stocks of nuclear weapons, because that would be unrealistic. He would, however, be impressed if they agreed to supervision of their own future production, because it would remove the element of discrimination that India found so objectionable."[22]

During meetings that same year to draft the IAEA statutes, Bhabha warned, "We will stand on the brink of a dangerous era sharply dividing the world into atomic 'haves' and 'have-nots' dominated by the Agency." If the purpose of a safeguards system was to build "a secure and peaceful world," he said, such a division would work against it by creating lasting tensions that would only get worse with time."[23] All of this was true, but Bhabha was also staking out the position he needed in order to secure nuclear exports.

By then, the Canadians had already begun work on the CIRUS heavy-water reactor at Trombay; Bhabha did not want anything to get in the way of his ability to reprocess the irradiated fuel. That plutonium from the Trombay facility would be used in India's first "peaceful" explosion demonstrated at least one reason Bhabha had been so adamant on the subject of controls while he dined in Parisian splendor.

IN 1960, MCCONE appointed a group of AEC officials to travel to India to make a recommendation. The trip was designed in part to find out more about India's nuclear intentions, but the Americans, led by Kratzer, were more concerned about whether India was technically capable of such advanced technology. Naturally, the group was predisposed to favorable findings, in part because they wanted to secure business for American reactor vendors, but also because they wanted to get the Indians hooked on light-water technology so they could persuade them to join the safeguards regime. The French and British were competing to sell natural uranium reactors, and the French were not requiring any safeguards at all.

Bhaba's deputy, Homi Sethna, escorted the American visitors to the proposed reactor site at Tarapur, on the west coast north of Bombay. The AEC representatives also traveled southwest from there and surveyed beaches with high concentrations of thorium, emitting radiation well above normal background levels. Although thorium itself cannot support a nuclear chain reaction, subjecting it to a barrage of neutrons inside a nuclear reactor converts the element to uranium-233, which can support fission. Thorium was seen as a possible alternative source of reactor fuel as well as a pathway to achieving bomb material. "Their plan was to operate several uranium-based reactors, either natural or enriched, and then extract plutonium as fissionable material to target thorium. The whole process depended on reprocessing," Kratzer said.

After returning to Washington, Kratzer and his team wrote a report recommending export approval for a proposed General Electric plant. But it cautioned that India could easily turn its program to making weapons. "We said their program [was] a very ambivalent one in the sense it could easily be redirected to weapons use . . . We said the Indian program could very easily go toward weapons." The deal went ahead, with a generous loan at almost no interest from the U.S. Agency for International Development.

BY THIS TIME, intelligence officials in Washington were becoming increasingly suspicious of what was going on in Israel. In late 1958, U-2 overflight photographs revealing activity in the Negev were rushed to the White House.[24] Eisenhower was worried enough to write Ben-Gurion about the evidence. Ben-Gurion replied it was all innocent, part of the young country's effort to make the desert bloom, or realize any number of other beneficial uses, and the American president who had promoted the peaceful-uses concept in the first place ultimately accepted his claims.

In London, government officials involved in the Oslo heavy-water transaction briefly considered telling their counterparts in Washington about it, but decided against it on the grounds it might lead to scuttling the deal. "On the whole I would prefer *not* to mention this to the Americans lest it lead them to ask us to take [what would] ultimately in fact be an untenable position vis a vis the Norwegians," a British Foreign Office official named Donald Cape scribbled in a memo.[25]

Cape and Kratzer knew each other well, and Kratzer almost certainly would have been one of the officials that Cape would have told. Yet on the face of it, Cape need not have worried. Kratzer, who was surprised to learn of the transaction almost a half century after it took place, sent me a long e-mail explaining why he probably would not have objected to the deal. The gist of it was that the Norwegian safeguards would have been considered adequate at that time. Kratzer himself approved an AEC export of 3.9 metric tons of heavy water to Israel in 1963. He said it was destined for a research facility at Technion, although other evidence suggests it went direct to Dimona. Whatever the truth, the U.S. shipment provided an added buffer to the material sent by the British.[26]

You could say that Cape and Kratzer had similar concerns. They worried about proliferation to some extent, but that went hand in hand with promoting exports.

At a January 1961 preinaugural meeting with top officials of the outgoing Eisenhower team, John Kennedy asked about the likelihood of nuclear weapons in other countries. Where should he direct his attention? Eisenhower's secretary of state, Christian Herter, may have thought about China, but there were two countries of more immediate concern.

"Israel and India," Herter replied to Kennedy's question.[27]

Oppenheimer had advanced the notion that without nuclear development you could not find a means of control. Under Eisenhower's Atoms for Peace program, development was outpacing efforts at control. But the problem was now in the hands of a new administration.

CHAPTER 9

Snow

IN AUGUST 1962, A GROUP OF NUCLEAR scientists gathered in Cambridge, England, to talk about ways of ending the arms race. They were part of the Pugwash movement started several years earlier to try to mediate the conflict from behind the scenes. At a final banquet, the American Isador Rabi climbed on a table and implored the gathering "not to waste Pugwash." Then the big, burly Lev Artsimovich, one of the inventors of the Soviet hydrogen bomb and a leading fusion expert, said he wanted to tell a story. Igor Tamm, the mathematical physicist and Nobel Prize winner, offered to act as interpreter.

Artsimovich told of an old man married to a young, beautiful woman. The man worried whether his wife was being faithful. He went to a soothsayer, who said, "It's really quite simple. You must spin a coin. If she's being unfaithful to you while you're away and she's at home, the coin will come down heads. If it's when you're at home and she's away, it will come down tails." Crestfallen, the old man asked, "What if she's being faithful?"

The answer was "Then the coin will hang in the air."

The audience was delighted with the story. When the laughter died down, Artsimovich said, more seriously, "Disarmament is like that. If the coin comes down heads, the Americans will make a proposal that the Russians will reject. If it comes down tails, the reverse will be true. As for 'general and complete disarmament,' that corresponds to the coin hanging in the air. But there is one further possibility—that the coin lands on its edge, which I interpret as some kind of accommodation between the two sides. We need to become so practised that we can make the coin land on its edge every time."[1]

AT THE TIME of the telling, a worldwide movement against nuclear arms had taken hold. The United States and the Soviet Union, having showered the planet with radioactive fallout for more than a decade, were under increasing pressure to agree to permanently halt the testing that caused that to happen. Two attempts had failed, one in 1960 and the other a few months before the Cambridge Pugwash meeting in 1962. Lack of progress could easily be blamed on either side, but here in Cambridge were some of the scientists that made the bomb programs and the testing possible. Tamm, after all, had headed the Soviet's early hydrogen bomb effort. Many scientists, including Rotblat, were speaking out against nuclear weapons, but thousands of others were still gainfully employed designing and building warheads. "Project swinging"—the ability to secure long-term government support for research and development programs—was becoming a highly honed skill.[2] Hundreds of thousands of others were employed in the weapons manufacturing process, and they, like the scientists, had a vested interest in maintaining the status quo. Military personnel in underground missile silos, nuclear submarines, or Strategic Air Command planes also were wedded to the arms race. No sane person wanted nuclear war, and as Artsimovich had implied, a nuclear exchange was not a foregone conclusion. The two sides would seek "some kind of accommodation" but the underlying dynamic would remain more or less as it was—assuming both sides could always land the coin on its edge.

The civilized gathering in Cambridge, with its soft laughter and warm atmosphere, offered some hope of a way out, because in the wash of conversation, views could change, and that in turn could influence the direction of nuclear decision-making back home. But the prospect of the scientists radically altering the course of the arms race was not something to bet on because they were not the ones with their fingers on the button. These were men in "a tragic situation," as Jungk observed in 1979. "They are compelled to hope for a happy outcome of the 'nuclear gamble' for they have invested in it their whole professional life, their self respect and their expectations."[3]

The war gamers and military commanders had other priorities, and they were busy figuring out ways to use what the scientists had invented. It might come as a shock to learn that in 1963, a multiple choice question on a U.S. Air Force nuclear weapons employment course exam asked students to calculate how many tons of nuclear force it would take to knock out a bridge in North Vietnam. The idea was to achieve, with 95 percent probability, severe structural damage, but without destroying a schoolhouse a few miles away. Most of the students, including an air force colonel, picked the highest number— five megatons—but it turned out the answer was lower, one hundred and twenty-five kilotons. The examiner, an air force captain, found himself apologetically explaining to his superior why the lower figure was correct, according to Victor Gilinsky, a scientist who took the test and observed the scene. Exasperated, the colonel asked, "Is that all we're gonna use, a li'l ole one hundred and twenty-five kiloton bomb?"[4]

For more than a decade, the real nuclear "wars" had been played out at test sites. Soldiers were ordered to lie in trenches at these sites and pilots flew sampling missions into the mushroom clouds. Much about what they experienced was revealed only after the cold war ended, and it was far from the cozy confines of a science gathering in Cambridge, or the sterile atmosphere of an air force exam room. After the collapse of the Soviet Union in 1989, filmmakers in Moscow recorded the memories of soldiers who had never before been allowed to talk about what they went through. The result, a documentary called Nuclear Tango, makes disturbing viewing. "It was like being in a swing, swinging with a girl. Everything was shaking," said one former Soviet soldier interviewed for the film, as he recalled through a translator the impact of a nuclear explosion in November 1954. "We were on a swing. Suddenly a light appeared in our underground bomb shelter—from behind closed doors a bright light."

Looking gentle and calm, and much older than he was at the time of the test, the ex-soldier smiled and cradled his arms, moving them from side to side, to demonstrate the effect. The film shifts from the soldier to official black-and-white footage of the aftermath, revealing what had been a lush green landscape, shown earlier in the film, turned cinereous white. Close to the epicenter, a horse is burned almost to a skeleton. The horse's coat has turned to ash. His fleshy lips have disappeared. He cannot see. And he is still alive, quivering and barely standing.

Another soldier, one of thousands ordered to lie in trenches, recalls his own grueling experience: "I began to see bloody red smoke. Then

I could not hear, see, or feel. Later I analyzed it. I was paralyzed with shock. I didn't hear the explosions. Slowly I began to hear friends. We realized we were alive. Still I couldn't see." (It appeared he eventually regained his eyesight.)

Soldiers ordered to drive into ground zero recorded the original scene on camera—first the horse and, farther on, what looked like a field of live mice. As they got closer, they realized they were not seeing mice. They were seeing birds without feathers. "Earlier this had been a green field full of birds, but when the explosion went off, they flew up towards what they thought was the sun," the narrator explains.[5]

The Soviet test took place in late 1954 near the village of Totskoye, in the southern Urals. Soviet military planners studied the official film footage because they wanted to find a way to use nuclear weapons in their battlefield plans after the United States positioned tactical nuclear weapons in Europe. The military film, with its stark reminders of what nuclear war might look like, remained classified until the Soviet Union disintegrated in 1989. That year journalists, researchers, writers, and filmmakers began searching government archives for the first time to learn secrets of their country's past. A documentary producer discovered the Totskoye footage, and *Nuclear Tango* was the result. Besides showing viewers the raw footage of the tests for the first time, the documentary film also recorded the fate of the thousands of soldiers who took part in the exercise and others that followed. They had been required to sign statements to remain silent about the tests for twenty-five years. In May 1992, the soldiers gathered for a victory parade and spoke publicly of their experiences for the first time. "We lived in an upside-down world of freezing deserts and blazing ice floes," one said. "Most of us were only twenty years old when we signed a paper promising not to talk," recalled another. After that, he added, "we simply didn't exist."

BUT THE SOLDIERS' stories were only part of a larger narrative. Among the nuclear elite, bomb tests were cause for celebrating. Scientists and top military brass watched from afar, protected inside bunkers, enjoying each event as if it were a spectacular fireworks finale. They downplayed the possible health effects because that might get in the way of the test itself. Marshal Georgi Zhukov, the Russian in charge of Totskoye and first deputy minister of defense, worried that taking too many precautions against radiation exposure would cause the troops to be afraid. There were forty-four thousand men in all, making the test the biggest ever in terms of personnel. Zhukov could not afford an outbreak of panic. So, as preparations for the blast got under way, he told the exercise commanders, "You have frightened people too much with your safety measures. Now you'll have to 'unfrighten' them."[6]

Zhukov's chutzpah was symptomatic of the cavalier way in which nuclear developers, whether on the military or civilian front, approached the whole issue of radiation exposure. Soldiers and the broader public were misled by official pronouncements that fallout posed little health risk, supported by "evidence" that was no more than a compilation of simplified risk assessments dressed up as fact. Zhukov's measures only partially worked. He avoided wholesale panic, but not fear. On the night before the test, one soldier recalled, "we were fed as if it was the last supper and given our clothes." The clothing, he said, consisted of a T-shirt, pants, two sets of thermal underwear, and a gas mask. "Our commander told us directly that if we were going to get our jobs done we had to work without radiation protection because it would impede our work . . . and that couldn't be allowed."

Some written accounts of the Soviet nuclear program claim that soldiers had instructions on how to defend themselves against the effects of fallout.[7] A soldier in *Nuclear Tango* recalled just the opposite: "There were no instructions as to how we were to protect ourselves. Me and my friend were proud we were asked to participate. We had no idea how it would end." Remembering how he watched his superiors retreat to their safer posts, another soldier remembered: "We hoped we too would be invited into the bunkers. The best we could hope for was a small trench." The trenches were between three and five miles from ground zero.[8]

The High Command was clearly pleased with the results. A celebratory banquet was held in an army tent. Kurchatov, his beard very long by then, introduced some of his leading scientists to the marshals and generals. An official report later stated that all the missions that had been assigned in the Totskoye exercise had been satisfactorily carried out, with the damage as predicted. The panic felt by soldiers was completely denied; they were portrayed as invincible warriors with skins as thick as lead. "And the troop units, which took part in these exercises," the document stated, "went without fear into the region of the atomic explosion, even to ground zero, overcame the zones of radiation and carried out the missions that had been set for the units and formations."[9]

EIGHT MONTHS EARLIER, on March 1, 1954, the United States conducted its biggest bomb test ever: a fifteen-megaton shot in the Bikini Islands code-named Bravo, in keeping with the gung-ho spirit of the times. Among the American nuclear weapons crowd, Bravo was Everest. Hence the lead scientist—protected in a concrete bunker on an island twenty miles away—felt like he had reached the mountain summit when the shot went off successfully. "I began to dance in my excitement," he said.[10]

But the winds suddenly shifted in an unfavorable direction—easterly toward other island chains where people still lived. They were showered with fallout, as were a Japanese fishing vessel crew and U.S. military personnel on ships. Whoever and wherever they were, the victims would remember the event as anything but cause for celebrating. "I wanted to die and I have never experienced anything like that," recalled Almira Matayoshi, a native of the Rongelap atoll, who was pregnant at the time and already had two small children.[11] Rongelap was the nearest large atoll to Bikini, about one hundred miles away.

The explosion destroyed the test island on Bikini, from which residents had been removed in 1946, and all living things on it. People living on Rongelap and other island groups soon saw radioactive ash falling from the sky and thought it was snowing. Children played in it. They drank contaminated water. Within days, they developed radiation sickness, hair loss, skin and mucous membrane lesions, and low blood count averages, according to U.S. Department of Energy records. "At that time we were really suffering; our bodies ached and our feet were covered with burns, and our hair fell out. Now I see babies growing up abnormally and some are mentally disturbed, but none of these things happened before the bomb. It is sad to see the babies now," Matayoshi told an interviewer more than twenty years later.

The crew of the *Daigo Fukuryu Maru* (Lucky Dragon) were so startled from the blast—they too were at least one hundred miles away—that they immediately headed back to their homeport of Yaizu, south of Tokyo, a journey that took about two weeks. All twenty-three men on board suffered the effects of radiation illness. One died several months later.

Bravo helped ensure that the entire chain of thirty-six islands in the central Pacific, as well as some neighboring atolls to the east, including Rongelap, would remain uninhabitable for decades, if not longer. Besides the Japanese fisherman, it claimed the life of an island boy, who was only three at the time, fifteen years later. He died of leukemia at a National Institutes of Health facility in Bethesda, Maryland, where he was being treated. The boy had lived on Rongelap, where Almira Matayoshi lived. Matayoshi gave birth the year after the test to a baby with no spinal system. She had a series of disastrous pregnancies after that. Children, like one of Matayoshi's little boys, alive at the time of the test, later developed thyroid problems and cancers. Testing in the Pacific overall would claim many other lives through thyroid and other types of cancer. In Japan, more than six hundred boats were found to have contaminated catches. They had to be discarded. Fish prices in Japan collapsed. And a wave of panic broke out over the advisability of eating tuna, in both Japan and the United States, which imported Japanese tuna.

BY 1956, THE AEC regarded the northern Marshall Islands, in the words of one official, as "by far the most contaminated place in the world." But the commission's attitude toward the residents was not unlike that of a plantation owner toward slaves. The official who described the devastation did so in support of the AEC's Advisory Committee on Biology and Medicine, which viewed the Rongelap experience as an excellent opportunity to study the uptake of radiation after a nuclear explosion. At an AEC meeting to consider putting islanders back on Utrik atoll for this purpose, an environmental expert named Merril Eisenbud made this remark: "While it is true that these people do not live, I would say, the way Westerners do, civilized people, it is nevertheless also true that these people are more like us than the mice."[12]

The AEC initially tried to keep the entire episode—explosion included—secret. However, because of growing controversy over its test program, it was forced to admit that the fallout was global and then explain the risks, a task it performed with considerable understatement. Presenting conjecture as solidly based scientific findings, the AEC declared that fallout "would not seriously affect the genetic constitutions of human beings."[13] Other test advocates like Edward Teller began to contend publicly that radiation from fallout "might be slightly beneficial or have no effect at all." This was another aspect of nuclear salesmanship—using the exalted status of scientists to camouflage the dangers with deceptive assurances that appeared to be based on fact but which were no more than educated guesswork. Experts had known for many years that radiation alters basic cellular structure, and they were pretty certain it caused genetic damage. Moreover, there was a real risk of excess cancers in areas of high fallout, where radionuclides would enter drinking water and the food chain. The whole of the continental United States had been showered with fallout, although in differing amounts, depending on the location. A National Cancer Institute map shows that people in parts of Nevada, Utah, Idaho, the Dakotas, Colorado, Kansas, and several other midwestern states received the highest average dose rates.[14] During the most intense periods of testing, strontium-90 levels in milk rose dramatically, according to the AEC's own data. Strontium-90 is considered one of the most hazardous products of fallout because of its relatively long half-life of twenty-nine years. It concentrates in bone surfaces and bone marrow and can cause tumors in the bone or in the organs that form blood cells. One area of the northern Great Plains—particularly the Red River Valley dividing North Dakota and Minnesota—became so heavily contaminated with strontium-90 that for a while the level in the region's milk supply was far in excess of the AEC's own limits for human consumption.[15]

Nothing was allowed to get in the way of the weaponeers' assault. The AEC's test program was the nation's answer to Communism. It complemented the conquering spirit of the 1950s. And it provided the nuclear establishment and its supporting cast with the primary justification for large annual budget requests. The momentum appeared unstoppable. "We must not let anything interfere with this series of tests—nothing," said AEC commissioner Thomas Murray at a 1956 hearing on further planned tests in Nevada and Utah.[16]

BUT BRAVO HAD stretched the limits of public credulity and inspired a movement to ban atmospheric testing. In Britain, as the year the test took place rolled to a close, the producers of BBC's *Panorama* news and topical issues program chose the topic of thermonuclears for their Christmas broadcast. It was not a cheery subject for the holiday, but the program had positive consequences: the two guests, Joseph Rotblat, the scientist who had rejected the world of nuclear weapons a decade earlier, and the philosopher and mathematician Bertrand Russell, met beforehand and out of that meeting formed Pugwash. Rotblat was by then chairman of the physics department at one of London's oldest teaching hospitals, St. Bartholomew's, still a widower and not remarried, dedicating his life to finding medical uses for nuclear energy. "I made the decision I didn't want anything more to do with nuclear weapons," he said. "I found myself being brought back to it after Bikini in 1954."[17]

As they waited for the program to begin in the BBC studios that December, Russell told Rotblat he wanted to start a group of the world's best scientists in order to effect an end to the arms race. They would start by holding conferences to explore ways the scientists could influence governments on immediate and longer-term issues associated with nuclear weapons. In order to give the group the visibility he felt it needed, Russell sought support from the greatest living scientist, Albert Einstein, and wrote to him with the request.

As Rotblat recounted the story, he stopped for a minute to make sure I was still taking notes. "This is the very important part," he said urgently. "On 18 April 1955, Bertrand Russell flew from Rome to Paris, and during the flight, the flight captain announced that he had received news that Einstein had died. Russell was shattered. He felt that without Einstein's support the whole project would die. When he arrived at his Paris hotel he found a letter that had been forwarded to him from London. It was from Einstein. It was one of the last acts of his life."

This brought tears to Rotblat's eyes, just as the recollection of his wife had. Then the aging scientist grew still again—and I worried he himself might be dying—but he awoke and started where he had left off. With Einstein's agreement, Russell drafted a statement calling on all scientists and the public to support the settlement of all political disputes by peaceful means, because "in any future world war, nuclear weapons will certainly be employed, and . . . such weapons threaten the continued existence of mankind."

Besides Einstein, Russell, and Rotblat, eight others put their names to what became known as the Russell-Einstein Manifesto. Nine of the signatories were Nobel laureates. Rotblat would receive the Peace Prize in 1995. Russell received a letter from Nova Scotia, postmarked "Pugwash," a fishing and salt-mining village on the island's north shore. Inside was an offer of financial backing from steel magnate and Pugwash native Cyrus Eaton. In Britain, "Pugwash" is also the name of a children's cartoon character—a clownish pirate. Russell almost threw the letter out thinking it was a hoax, Rotblat said, laughing.

Scientists from all over the world came to the first Pugwash conference, held in Eaton's hometown in July 1957. From then on, Pugwash held conferences every year, through critical stages of the cold war. It operated in a prestigious sphere of its own. Its meetings were kept out of the public eye, and some of its members were subject to vettings by their governments in order to attend. The Soviet participants generally came with minders. Critics complained with some justification that Pugwash was secretive and too much a part of the establishment it had been designed to confront. But some of the scientists who attended the gatherings themselves left with a greater understanding of a range of issues involving arms control and proliferation. They would in turn talk to government officials and journalists and in that way help to increase public understanding about the complexities of nuclear energy.

ALONGSIDE PUGWASH, THE antibomb movement also grew, increasing pressure on governments to disarm. Two months after the first Pugwash conference, a veteran British activist named Walter Wolfgang organized the first large-scale protest at Trafalgar Square. Four thousand people demonstrated against the British Labour Party's opposition to unilateral disarmament, but they had no immediate effect on a party that was out of power and felt that it could not afford to be branded soft on Communism. Neville Chamberlain's infamous prewar handshake with Hitler cast a long shadow: a month after the demonstration, at the party's annual conference, the shadow foreign secretary, Aneurin Bevan, famously said he did not want to have to go "naked into the conference chamber."

Bevan's remark fueled anger among a group of leading British left-wing intellectuals who had hoped their party would change its position. They met with Wolfgang and formed the Campaign for Nuclear Disarmament (CND) on January 16, 1958. Russell moved on to become its president, leaving Rotblat largely in charge of Pugwash. The philosopher joined forces with other left-wing intellectuals, such as Kingsley Martin, the long-serving editor of *New Statesman* magazine, the writer J. B. Priestley, and John Collins, the radical canon of St. Paul's Cathedral, who became the group's chairman.

Three months after the CND's formation, thousands of protestors took part in a four-day Easter walk from London to Aldermaston in Berkshire, where Britain's nuclear weapons were manufactured. It was there that the famous CND "peace logo," an upside-down Y contained in a circle, made its debut. Its designer, Gerald Holtom, once explained how he conceived it: "I drew myself: the representative of an individual in despair with hands palms outstretched, outwards and downwards, in the manner of Goya's peasant before the firing squad." He referenced the Navy's semaphores for N for nuclear and D for disarmament. "I formalized the drawing into a line and put a circle around it."[18]

Other scientists joined the crusade, warning the public about the threats posed by nuclear weapons and the factories that produced them. On April 24, 1957, Albert Schweitzer made a lengthy, damning radio broadcast from Oslo, Norway, explaining in graphic detail the very facts that the establishment had worked so hard to suppress. He spoke not only of the long-term consequences from fallout but also of the contamination from nuclear fuel plants like Hanford:

> From official and unofficial sources we have been assured, time and time again, that the increase in radioactivity of the air does not exceed the amount which the human body can tolerate without any harmful effects. This is just evading the issue. Even if we are not directly affected by the radioactive material in the air, we are indirectly affected through that which has fallen down, is falling down, and will fall down. We are absorbing this through radioactive drinking water and through animal and vegetable foodstuffs, to the same extent as radioactive elements are stored in the vegetation of the region in which we live. Unfortunately for us, nature hoards what is falling down from the air.[19]

Aware of the possibility of such an alarming broadcast, the Central Intelligence Agency had been keeping files on Schweitzer to try to discredit him, and Eisenhower himself apparently attempted to stop him from speaking out. Governments were under pressure, though, because too many scientists were saying the same thing. The chemist Linus Pauling released a petition calling for rapid action on a nuclear test ban treaty, with the signatures of eleven thousand other scientists from all over the world. Also in the United States, Norman

Cousins, editor of the *Saturday Review*, worked with Clarence Pickett, long-time leader of the American Friends Service Committee, to form the National Committee for a Sane Nuclear Policy, or Sane.[20]

These activities began to influence thinking in the Soviet Union. There, the angst and guilt felt by many American nuclear physicists over their involvement in nuclear weapons was virtually unknown, and the scope for genuine dissent was severely limited. Nevertheless, Sakharov, Kurchatov, and a few other scientists began pressing for an end to testing. Sakharov attributed his antinuclear views to statements by Russell, Einstein, Schweitzer, and Pauling, while others were undoubtedly influenced by the cross-pollination of ideas at Pugwash meetings and in nuclear journals.

The protestors could not be easily dismissed. They were a minority, to be sure, but a highly visible one. Ignoring government bans on travel and demonstrations, the activists marched into each other's countries, brandishing CND's peace symbol. By 1964, Easter marches were taking place in twenty countries with half a million people participating.[21]

WHILE THEY CONSPIRED against the "pavement sitters," as they were disdainfully dubbed by members of Britain's defense intelligence establishment, the leaders of the weapons states instinctively understood that the better public course was to support the drive for disarmament, with an initial goal of bringing an end to the atmospheric tests. The Soviets viewed the peace platform as a useful propaganda tool in disarmament negotiations and in March 1958 attempted to steal a public relations victory by declaring the first unilateral moratorium on such explosions. Later that year, President Eisenhower and British prime minister Harold Macmillan realized they had no other choice but to follow suit, so they too declared a moratorium.

The three countries also started looking for a way to end the testing altogether, and by May 1960 they were within reach of a compromise test ban treaty. But these efforts were continually rocked by political fallout in the contest between the two superpowers, and the French nuclear test that same year caused another shake-up. Shortly before a summit meeting to conclude the pact, U-2 spy pilot Francis Gary Powers was shot down over the Soviet Union, ending any chances of a treaty for the brief remainder of the Eisenhower administration.[22]

Tensions increased in 1961, John F. Kennedy's first year in office, after the disastrous American attempt to invade Cuba at the Bay of Pigs and Soviet threats on West Berlin, to the point that the Soviets decided to end their testing moratorium.

In the far reaches of the nuclear empires, highly trained and programmed military men were ready to pounce the moment trust broke down at the negotiating table. This time it was the turn of General Lieutenant G. Kudryavtsev of the USSR. For three long years, Kudryavtsev had been doing what he could to improve conditions at a dormant test site on an island archipelago in the Arctic Ocean. Life was anything but pleasurable in Novaya Zemlya, whose southern tip was roughly on the same latitude as the northernmost point of Alaska. Winds of near hurricane strength howled across the icy, mountainous landscape, and, during the winter months, darkness lasted for all the hours of day and night.

For centuries Novaya Zemlya had been home to the Nenets, nomadic tribes whose migratory cycles were adapted to hunting, fishing, and reindeer breeding. They had borne the incursion of traders in the previous century and Soviet efforts at collectivization in the twentieth. But in 1954 they faced an invasion of unprecedented strength when officials in Moscow decided they needed somewhere more remote than Semipalatinsk to test high-yield weapons. Novaya Zemlya became the focal point of the Soviet test program. The three hundred or so settlers were forced to leave and settle down to a static life on the mainland, leading many to succumb to disease, drunkenness, and suicide, while hundreds of military and civilian specialists moved in. Then came the cessation of testing and the long wait.

Relations between the superpowers so soured during that period that on the night of July 25, 1961, Americans turned on their televisions to hear Kennedy warn them for the first time, more than a year before the Cuban Missile Crisis, to begin preparing for a nuclear attack by the Soviet Union. That same month, Kudryavtsev got the telegram he had been waiting for, directing him to prepare for a series of new nuclear tests after September 1. This would be the Soviet reply to Gary Powers, de Gaulle's bomb, the Bay of Pigs, and the conflict in Berlin. General Secretary Nikita Khrushchev told the world of the decision on August 30, and the testing began two days later. Four tests took place at Semipalatinsk and Sary Shagan, another site in what is now Kazakhstan, but the action after that moved to the icy north. From mid-September and for the next several weeks, a once remote fishing outpost was the corpus callosum center of the Soviet nuclear empire: In a convulsion of noise and light, a bomb went off every other day, including a Super on October 30. It yielded fifty megatons, the biggest ever exploded anywhere and more than three times more powerful than the American Supers in the Pacific.

Two weeks after the first Soviet test, Kennedy responded by ordering an underground explosion at the Nevada Test Site. Eight more tests followed that year. Although the American president withstood pressure to test in the atmosphere, his forbearance wore thin and finally failed him as he gradually learned the full extent of the Soviet test program. A new round of atmospheric tests was ordered in the Pacific, far from the increasingly wary citizens of Nevada. The explosions began in April 1962, a month before Khrushchev would make a fateful decision to ship nuclear-tipped missiles to Cuba. The American tests lasted right through the Cuban crisis itself, with the last one taking place a month after it was over, in November 1962.[23]

Soviet testing ended a month later with a mushroom cloud on Christmas Day.[24]

KENNEDY NEVER LOST hope for a comprehensive test ban treaty and tried once again in early 1962, even as the tests continued. At home, the youthful leader challenged the existing atomic bureaucracy by setting up a new one, the Arms Control and Disarmament Agency (ACDA), whose sole concern would be furthering the interests of arms control and stopping the spread of nuclear weapons. This last challenge had taken on new urgency. France was now a nuclear power, there were grave concerns about the direction of the Chinese nuclear program, and there was outright hostility between Kennedy and Ben-Gurion over the Israeli leader's claims of a peaceful nuclear program. Apart from the threat posed by enemies going nuclear, there also were worries about America's nuclear allies embroiling the United States in a nuclear conflict that was not of its own making.

Official disarmament efforts, if only halfhearted, also continued. In March 1962, a few days before the new Eighteen-Nation Disarmament Committee was scheduled to meet in Geneva, the CND leader Canon Collins traveled from London to Jordans, a Quaker village less than an hour outside London. Terry Price, the former Harwell scientist now working for Sir Solly Zuckerman at the Defense Ministry, happened to live in the village, although he was not a Quaker. Price would soon be leaving for Geneva and decided to go to the meetinghouse to hear the famous cleric. "He [Collins] spoke fluently and to the point for about fifteen minutes, and I began to take a more favorable view of the people coming from his ministry who sat on pavements outside my own," Price recounted. "But he ran out of steam just as he was coming to the interesting bit: what should actually be done? He seemed to have nothing negotiable to say."

Yet when the professional negotiators met three days later on March 15, the Ides of March, they had little to offer either. The conference turned into a miasma of conflicting signals, strained humor, and language difficulties. The Soviets wanted it all—general and complete disarmament—at once, but there were too many differences on the pace of reductions and the application of control procedures to make that work. The Americans argued for a more gradual approach. The meeting ended without agreement. "We were back to a competition for the hearts and minds of the listening world, rather than the serious search for world stability that was our daily preoccupation back in Whitehall," wrote Price.[25]

By August, when Artsimovich told his amusing story to the scientists at Cambridge, the Soviet missiles were on ships bound for Cuba. And no one knew which way the coin would land this time.

CHAPTER 10

Any Fool Can Start a War

O N AN AUTUMN AFTERNOON IN 1962, Soviet foreign minister Andrei Gromyko and his ambassador Anatoly Dobrynin paid a long-planned visit to President John F. Kennedy at the White House. Kennedy greeted the two men as if nothing were wrong, the way a lover might an unfaithful partner who has not yet confessed. He smiled, they smiled, and photographers took pictures. That day, October 18, Kennedy had for the first time seen CIA photographic evidence of nuclear missiles in Cuba that could, as far as he knew, hit every city in the United States except Seattle, assuming they were operational. As bad as that seemed, it later transpired they had grossly miscalculated the range of these missiles, some of which, in fact, could strike as far away as Hudson Bay, Canada, and portions of Latin America. In less than a week, U.S. nuclear forces would be at their highest level of response readiness short of all-out war, the only time that happened in the forty-five years of the cold war.

Dobrynin did not know fully what was happening in Cuba. Gromyko, who did, turned the conversation to Kennedy's complaints the previous month about the movement of Soviet troops and military equipment in Cuba. His knees almost within touching distance of the young president, Gromyko accused the United States of pestering Fidel Castro's small island nation. "If it were otherwise," Gromyko assured Kennedy, who sat in his rocking chair, "the Soviet Government would have never become involved in rendering such assistance."

The deception was not entirely one-sided. After the miserable and embarrassing Bay of Pigs fiasco eighteen months earlier, Kennedy promised Gromyko that the United States would not again attempt another invasion of Cuba; he did not tell him about an existing covert government plan to overthrow Castro. Other topics were raised during the meeting—the ongoing tensions in Berlin and a planned visit to the United States by Soviet leader Nikita Khrushchev—but everyone knew that Cuba was the most potent issue that day.

Kennedy remained calm and self-contained throughout the two-hour exchange. "He gave no sign of tension or anger," wrote Kennedy aide Arthur Schlesinger Jr. of the meeting. Kennedy's impassivity was strategic: he had to know more; if the matter ended up in the United Nations, the Soviet deception would play into his hands. And he needed to win one over his adversary in Moscow; in June the previous year, Kennedy had ignored his advisers and rushed headlong into a meeting with Khrushchev in Vienna. The Soviet leader went on the attack for two days, lecturing Kennedy on American hypocrisy and cautioning him against supporting "old, moribund, reactionary regimes."[1] Kennedy had been humiliated not only in front of Khrushchev but before his own advisers. So this time he took a tougher stance, reading aloud part of a warning he had made in September against deploying offensive weapons in Cuba, musing later that Gromyko "must have wondered why I was reading it but he did not respond."[2]

On the diplomatic circuit that evening, it was business as usual, with the State Department hosting a black tie dinner for Gromyko. At the White House Kennedy started circling the wagons, warning his most trusted advisers, "Whatever you fellows are recommending today you will be sorry about a week from now." The president might have been speaking for himself. He was in the hollow of the nuclear furnace, confronted at once by the power of atomic weapons and the sense of abject powerlessness at the prospect of their use.

THE IDEA OF planting nuclear missiles on Cuban soil sprang into Nikita Khrushchev's mind during a beach stroll in the Black Sea resort of Varna in mid-May 1962. The trip to Bulgaria had been put off for three years, and when Khrushchev finally decided to go he took with him a large delegation of high-ranking officials from Moscow, Gromyko included. Khrushchev had much to mull—his country's lagging economy, tensions in Berlin, and requests from Cuba for stronger defense. In such a pretty place, the balding leader with the aging Pills-bury Doughboy face decided to take a walk on the beach with his de-fense minister, Rodion Malinovsky. Southeast from Varna, across the Black Sea in Turkey, fifteen American Jupiter nuclear missiles had just been put in place. These intermediate-range weapons, Malinovsky told Khrushchev, could destroy Kiev, Minsk, and Moscow within minutes.

"And why then can we not have bases close to America? What's the reason for such imparity?" These were questions asked of Malinovsky, Krushchev would later tell Castro. If he could send conventional mis-siles, as promised only a month earlier, why not nuclear? Could Mali-novsky do that without being detected? The defense minister said that he could, an assumption that proved woefully incorrect.[3]

The irony was that the Jupiters were obsolete the day they were in-stalled. They were vulnerable and cumbersome and used liquid fuel. The better alternative was the submarine-based Polaris nuclear missile, which was mobile and used solid fuel. Replacement of the Jupiters had been discussed for some time, but the Turkish government and NATO were resistant.

Khrushchev had other concerns. He led a nation that was geograph-ically the largest on earth, encompassing fifteen resource-rich but in-dustrially backward republics. The Soviets, per capita, were among the world's poorest populations. For the past several years, a myth had de-veloped of a supposed gap, unfavorable to the United States, in the rel-ative numbers of intercontinental ballistic missiles (ICBMs) between the two rivals. Kennedy had used the "missile gap" as a campaign is-sue, but within a few months of becoming president he discovered it was nonexistent. If anything, the disparity was the other way around. Although they had a much bigger nuclear submarine fleet, the Soviets had many fewer nuclear-tipped missiles and strategic bombers than did the United States.[4]

Khrushchev also knew the truth about the missile gap, and the So-viets' inferior position was a source of concern. Moreover, he was faced with the threat posed by thousands of American and NATO tactical weapons stockpiled across Europe, in addition to nuclear-tipped mis-siles that could be launched from Turkey, Italy, the United Kingdom, or West Germany. By then, nuclear weapons could be produced in all sizes, from battlefield artillery shells with relatively small yields to thermonuclear bombs more than two thousand times as powerful as the weapons dropped on Hiroshima and Nagasaki. And a range of delivery options offered military planners speed and flexibility. Mobile launchers would keep the enemy constantly off balance, while bombers with vertical takeoff capability meant they could be airborne from nearly anywhere. Under the oceans, nuclear-armed submarines stealthily glided with ease from one land mass to another.

Military personnel who handled nuclear weapons were subjected to psychological tests and other types of screenings, but the weapons then lacked the systems they now have to avert accidental or unauthorized arming or firing. Although it was up to the president to authorize the use of nuclear weapons, the actual timing of delivery and selection of targets were left to commanders in the field. "Statesmanship," Henry Kissinger had declared in 1957, "has never faced a more fearful challenge."[5]

In the first instance of nuclear brinksmanship potentially affecting the entire planet, a man born in 1894 to peasant farmers near the Russia-Ukraine border and famed for his public outbursts evidently believed he could win against the young wealthy Massachusetts man of Irish Catholic origins. He had, after all, verbally trounced him in Vienna. An aide had told him after that first day that the American president seemed "very inexperienced, even immature," and Khrushchev concurred. Kennedy, he said, was "too intelligent and too weak."[6] That summer, in August 1961, Khrushchev gave the nod to East German troops to begin building a wall through the heart of the old German capital. The Berlin Wall quickly became the most visible symbol of the East-West divide.

Nikita Sergeyevich Khrushchev began his political career in the rough-and-tumble of the Bolshevik Revolution; just prior to 1917, as a young man, he promoted labor strikes among his fellow factory workers, and he joined the Bolsheviks for the civil war. As Stalin rose to power, so did Khrushchev, taking on political jobs that included the extermination of much of the Ukrainian intelligentsia. Khrushchev was an uneven henchman, though, with a limited education and great political instinct. During the famine of 1946, Stalin demoted him for feeding Ukrainians, with whom he had close connections and sometimes identified, rather than sending food to the rest of the Soviet Union. After Stalin's death in 1953, Khrushchev was put in charge of the Communist Party as first secretary. The following year, he shook the Communist Party to its core by condemning Stalin's intolerance, brutality, and abuse of power. He released eight million political prisoners. Until Hungary hinted at withdrawing from the Warsaw Pact in 1956, Khrushchev even flirted with the idea of allowing more independence for the satellite states. Instead, he sent in the Red Army to quash the rebellion, and some twenty-five hundred protestors were killed. Having purged opponents within his own party, he became prime minister and the undisputed leader of both state and party in 1958. In August 1961, as tensions over Berlin rose, Khrushchev's decision to cut the Communist sector off from the rest of the city precipitated a crisis that led Kennedy to briefly consider using nuclear weapons in Berlin.

There is no other leader who embodies the Soviet side of the cold war as much as Nikita Khrushchev. For Americans, the lingering images of him were as a bully and a buffoon. In the so-called Moscow Kitchen Debate of 1959, Khrushchev argued with Vice President Richard M. Nixon over whether capitalism or Communism was better. At the United Nations General Assembly in October 1960, Khrushchev pounded his fists on the desk, shouted in Russian, and pulled off his right shoe, brandishing it at the Philippine delegate across the aisle.

Americans held these memories as defining characteristics of the Soviet leader as strongly as they clung to the belief that Kennedy, with his charm, wit, telegenic smile, and elegant wife, Jacqueline, was the embodiment of a strong and youthful nation. However, much of Kennedy's image was more myth than reality. He had back pain as well as several chronic illnesses—including colitis and Addison's disease—that often required him to wear a back brace and to take a daily infusion of medicines including a "feel-good" cocktail of vitamins, amphetamines, and other drugs to increase his energy levels. "At no time during the crisis was President Kennedy not in pain or not being medicated to deal with the discomfort," wrote the authors of *DEFCON-2*, a detailed account of the crisis. Khrushchev, while older than Kennedy, was in relatively good health. He drank a lot, as did most Russians, but he was not heavily medicated, according to his son, Sergei, who is now an American citizen and a senior fellow at the Watson Institute for International Studies at Brown University in Rhode Island.[7]

Although the fate of the world ostensibly rested with these two men, the crisis as it unfolded demonstrated an uncomfortable truth: that the leaders of the two most powerful nations on earth had relatively little power over how men responded to tensions in the field. And it was this that could have spelled the difference in the ultimate outcome.

WITHIN WEEKS OF Khrushchev's return from Varna, a plan was in place, code-named Anadyr, after a river in northeastern Siberia, five hundred miles from Nome, Alaska. Anadyr called for sending a total of twenty-four medium-range ballistic missiles that could strike New York City, Omaha, or Dallas, and sixteen intercontinental-range ballistic missiles to reach as far away as Seattle and San Francisco, and even the northern reaches of Canada. One hundred and sixty-two nuclear warheads would accompany these delivery vehicles. Forty thousand Soviet personnel, troops, advisers, and military technicians would build, operate, and defend the missile bases, reinforced by military aircraft. Except for the nuclear missiles placed in East Germany in 1959, the Soviet Union would have its first nuclear foothold beyond its borders and first ground combat troops outside the Warsaw Pact states. This massive movement of men and matériel some eight thousand miles from Soviet ports to Cuba would require a fleet of military and commercial ships.

Soviet military leaders took no chances. They turned to an age-old Russian tactic called *maskirovka* that relied upon duplicity and concealment to catch an enemy unaware. To begin with, the mission's code name pointed thousands of miles away from Cuba, in the opposite direction. The planners used no secretaries and took their own notes. Troops would not know their destination. Cuba-bound weapons would be stored under metal sheets that infrared cameras could not penetrate, or covered by wooden planks that, from a reconnaissance plane, would look like a ship's superstructure. While in Cuba, Soviet personnel would be described as agricultural advisers or disguised as tourists.[8]

Castro's brother Raúl traveled to Moscow to seal the deal and left with the final agreement on July 17, 1962. In a matter of days, at Soviet ports along the Baltic Sea, Black Sea, and Arctic Ocean, men, munitions, equipment, and provisions were loaded onto ships, so quickly that Western intelligence failed to grasp anything was going on. Issued with snowshoes, skis, and parkas, some of the military personnel were misled into thinking their destination was the cold Anadyr region itself. Crew members were banned from writing or telephoning home. At specified navigational coordinates in the Atlantic, often beside a member of the KGB, the Soviet secret police and intelligence agency, each captain opened a sealed envelope revealing the destination. *Maskirovka* worked well at the outset.

The trip took twenty grueling days. Even though seas were calm, crews sweltering below deck in temperatures above one hundred degrees Fahrenheit were frequently seasick, overpowered by the heat and the stench from rotting food and overflowing toilets. Crew members who could eat got two meals a day. They were allowed above deck only at night and when they could not be seen by NATO ships and aircraft. The first ships arrived at the end of July; they kept on arriving through the first half of October. One man died on the voyage.[9]

ANADYR WAS AUDACIOUS by any standards and totally out of keeping with the Soviet Union's historical tendencies—it had almost never been an aggressor beyond territory adjacent to its immediate borders—which is partly why the Kennedy administration took so long to recognize the buildup for what it was. United States and NATO forces began monitoring the Soviet fleet as soon as it rounded the northern tip of Norway, and intelligence analysts in the arcane field known as cratology examined photographs of shipping crates on the decks, using their size and shape to guess at the contents.[10] U-2 flights over Cuba picked up other evidence—troops blocking roads and clearing streets for convoys of Soviet trucks, and then missile sites.[11]

John McCone, the former AEC chairman who was by then head of the Central Intelligence Agency, was the first to guess what was going on. But when, on August 17, McCone said that he believed the Soviet Union was constructing offensive missile installations in Cuba, important people in the Kennedy White House, including Secretary of State Dean Rusk and Defense Secretary Robert McNamara, roundly dismissed him. They argued, just as the Soviets would, that the buildup was purely defensive. And Kennedy publicly supported that position. There were a number of major intelligence failures during that period, including a gross underestimation of the number of Soviet troops in Cuba—but the biggest lapse was the failure to recognize the arrival of nuclear warheads there.

The big break for the United States came on October 14 after a U-2 flew an early morning pass over western Cuba and delivered canisters of film with irrefutable evidence of offensive missile capability. It took photo interpreters about twenty hours to satisfy themselves of this fact; thus it was not until the evening of October 15 that the information was conveyed to Kennedy's national security adviser, McGeorge Bundy. Bundy decided to wait until the following morning to tell the president, holding the secret under wraps to prevent too many people knowing, even if it meant that the country's leader was himself ignorant during those hours. "If I had called him," Bundy explained later, "one of two results would have followed: Either he would have had a terrible night alone with the news, or he would have stirred up his administration by telephone calls and meetings that could easily have led to leaks. It seemed better to wait twelve hours and protect both his sleep and the secret."[12]

Kennedy was in his dressing gown, scanning the morning newspapers, when Bundy finally told him what the photo interpreters had determined. Having spent the past several weeks trying to quell a rising panic brought on by critics who suspected the worst, Kennedy now realized he had been misled, and McCone had been right all along. A meeting was held in the Cabinet Room just before noon that day, where Caroline, not quite five, had been playing with her father. She was sent back to the residence. Gathered around the table were the men who would serve in what became known as ExCom, or the Executive Committee of the National Security Council.

The group's composition would fluctuate throughout the crisis, and it would split up into subgroups to consider different options. Its members included the president's brother and most trusted adviser, Attorney General Robert F. Kennedy, eight years the President's junior, McNamara, Rusk, and Bundy. There were others, too: Acheson, Vice President Lyndon B. Johnson, and General Maxwell Taylor, the only military man Kennedy really liked and trusted, recently sworn in as chairman of the Joint Chiefs. Assistant Defense Secretary Paul H. Nitze also sat at this most important table, keenly aware of the dangers; he had drafted a secret plan to use nuclear weapons during the Berlin crisis the previous year. There were a number of others at the meeting as well, including Theodore "Ted" Sorensen, the president's policy adviser, legal counsel, and speechwriter.

The men viewing the briefing boards of chief photo interpreter Art Lundahl could not deny the meaning of the stark images; many believed they were looking at the beginnings of a preemptive strike—a nuclear Pearl Harbor. But the photos left many questions unanswered and part of the story untold. Lundahl's people had underestimated the missile ranges by 20 percent and did not realize that nuclear warheads were actually in Cuba, some at the missile sites. They would later learn that the intermediate-range SS-4s could have hit much of the United States, including most cities in the eastern and central regions, and were operational. The SS-5s, though nonoperational during the crisis, could strike all forty-eight states in the contiguous United States, much of Canada, all of Central America, and part of South America.[13]

THIS WAS NOT the first time the two superpowers had threatened or considered using nuclear weapons. In 1950, during the Korean War, General Douglas MacArthur pushed for an invasion of China and the use of nuclear weapons, and there had been at least ten instances of nuclear saber rattling since that time.[14] The difference was that on previous occasions the threats were made mainly through proxy battles rather than directly against each other.[15] Recently evidence has come to light that when Kennedy publicly warned of nuclear war in July 1961, during the Berlin crisis, his advisers had drawn up plans to use nuclear weapons if all else failed. The one crafted by Paul Nitze laid out a series of escalating conventional military response measures, followed by a graduated nuclear response if none of those worked. The final result, Nitze wrote, might be "general nuclear war." A separate proposal outlined the pros and cons of a first strike against the Soviets. It was drafted by Bundy's assistant, Carl Kaysen, and Henry Rowen, a nuclear strategist with the RAND Corporation, then serving as deputy assistant defense secretary under McNamara.[16]

To most people the idea that nuclear weapons might actually be used—in this case to protect half a city from Communist rule—is unthinkable. But among the higher political and military echelons the unthinkable became not only thinkable but doable, and for some even acceptable. Nitze's plan did not develop in a vacuum. By then wargaming with nuclear weapons had become a secondary industry, fostered by an international salon of think tanks stretching from Santa Monica, California, home of RAND, to the major cities of Europe. People made careers out of thinking, talking, and writing about nuclear weapons and ways to use them, and within military circles there were generals and admirals who would not have hesitated to push the

button if the order came. Think-tankers like Henry Kissinger had no
direct experience in war planning; yet in 1957 he made his mark with a
book propounding the possibilities of "limited" nuclear war.[17] (He
now advocates the total elimination of nuclear weapons.) Then Her-
man Kahn, reputedly the model for the main character of the film
Dr. Strangelove, Stanley Kubrick's nuclear satire, advanced the notion
that "all-out" nuclear war would be winnable; dark-haired, balding, and
overweight, Kahn also was credited with the theories that led to the doctrine of mutually assured destruction, or MAD, which depended on each
side having enough nuclear firepower to inflict maximum harm on the
other, thus effectively preventing either side from using the weapons.

In Britain, Solly Zuckerman, the Defense Ministry's scientific adviser, was dubious of these ideas and concerned about the rise of the
"nonmilitary weaponeer." In his view, the military was being over-
taken by people without battlefield planning experience who had enormous influence on decisions about whether and how much money
would be spent researching and developing new and complex weapons
systems. Zuckerman had been a battle strategist in World War II, with
a leading role in planning the air support operations of the Normandy
invasion and before that the Allied landings in Italy. He was skeptical
that nuclear weapons could be used in any fashion without causing total devastation. Meeting in London with Eisenhower's science advisers
in 1960, Zuckerman posed the question "Could the use of nuclear and
conventional weapons be so integrated and controlled, that given a
war, all-out escalation did not occur?"[18] His answer was basically no,
which meant that "the deployment of nuclear weapons in the field
was of little, if any, value to either NATO or the Soviet forces, except
in an abstract military sense." The debate, he cautioned, would lead
everyone in "ever decreasing circles. We have got to break the circle either by reexamining the postulates of the argument, or by introducing
into the circle some new considerations."

One military study in Britain to which Zuckerman took particular
exception suggested that as many as twenty one-megaton nuclear warheads would be needed to prevent a Russian army corps from crossing
the Weser, a 282-mile-long river in northwest Germany. In what sense,
Zuckerman asked, could "twenty Hiroshimas between lunch and tea"
be regarded as a meaningful defense of Germany, since the damage to
the country and people would destroy the operation's political purpose?
As the piles of NATO war-gaming studies mounted, Zuckerman grew

increasingly alarmed by what he saw as the organization's unthinking reliance on nuclear weapons. Furthermore, Zuckerman knew that as far as NATO's supreme commander, Lauris "Larry" Norstad, was concerned, policy would be translated into action if necessary. Zuckerman had worked and lived with Norstad in North Africa in 1943. "I knew him well enough to realize that he meant what he said when he declared that he would not hesitate to initiate a nuclear attack."[19]

Quirky and unconventional, Zuckerman was widely read, quick to grasp complex points, highly secretive, sometimes devious, and extremely distrustful of civil servants. He had a healthy-size ego and was naturally controversial. Some quarters of the British political and military establishment viewed him as defeatist and, therefore, suspect. But he got a chance to put his views before the audience that counted in the summer of 1961 when he was invited to speak at a NATO symposium. "Prepare a real shock piece," his supporter Lord Mountbatten advised him; and Zuckerman did not disappoint. His speech described scenes of devastation following an imaginary nuclear attack on the British cities of Birmingham and Carlisle. "I knew of no nuclear wargame that had ended in victory for the defenders, only in devastation and disaster. Nuclear weapons, I insisted, could not be categorized as tactical or strategic . . . A few Soviet 'tactical' nuclear strikes could remove from the map some of the smaller member states of NATO."

When he finished speaking and sat down, silence enveloped the room. Germany's General Adolf Heusinger was shaken, Zuckerman later recalled, and "rose to express his disquiet about NATO nuclear policy." Heusinger knew when he was facing an impossible situation: he had been directly to Hitler's right when a bomb went off in a famous 1944 assassination attempt at the German leader's headquarters in Rastenburg. As people began to leave, Lieutenant General Earle G. Wheeler invited Zuckerman to his room for a drink. Then director of the joint staff of the Joint Chiefs, Wheeler's daily responsibility was the rank and file; the following year he became army chief of staff. "We have painted ourselves into a corner," Wheeler said to Zuckerman. "How do we get out of it?" Zuckerman had no answer.[20]

Zuckerman influenced thinking in both the Eisenhower and Kennedy administrations through his contacts with the chief scientific advisers and military men such as Wheeler. McNamara told a British interviewer, "He was huge . . . he has no counterpart in your country or in mine today."[21] When Kennedy was presented with the Kaysen-Rowen memo, he responded with a request for alternatives: "I am concerned over my ability to control our military effort once a war begins," the president wrote.[22] Zuckerman could not have said it better.

Kennedy could not think about such questions without losing sleep, he once confided to the political columnist Joseph Alsop.[23] Bundy does not mention the Kaysen-Rowen plan in his book *Danger and Survival: Choices About the Bomb in the First Fifty Years*. But he alludes to it in a brief passage about an exchange that occurred between Acheson and Kennedy at the end of a cabinet meeting on Berlin during that period, which only he, Bundy, witnessed:

> The president asked Acheson just when he thought we would have to use nuclear weapons. Acheson's answer was more measured and quiet than usual. He said that he believed the president should himself give that question the most careful and private consideration, well before the time when the choice might present itself, that he should reach his own clear conclusion in advance as to what he would do, and that he should tell no one at all what that conclusion was. The president thanked him for the advice, and the exchange ended.[24]

Kennedy rejected the nuclear option in 1961 and the immediate crisis over Berlin ended that October after a standoff between troops from both sides, without a shot being fired.

NOW, TWELVE MONTHS after the crisis over Berlin, as the nuclear sabers rattled again, this time in Cuba, Kennedy and his advisers grappled with the question: how to get the Soviets to withdraw? It was like Berlin all over again, except the stakes now seemed so much higher. American cities were directly threatened. "I hope you all will choose the least violent course you can," an anxious Mary Bundy told her husband after he returned home one evening.[25] She could only hope. More than five hundred and fifty American conventional combat aircraft were positioned at southeastern U.S. military bases and aboard aircraft carriers, part of a long-planned mission originally designed to simulate the overthrow of an imaginary tyrant named "Ortsac"—Castro spelled backward. Now they were on the front line of an effort to frighten the Soviets into taking their missiles back home.

Kennedy opted for the least confrontational option, a blockade of Soviet ships, while allowing plans for an air strike to move ahead as backup. After a previously scheduled campaign trip to Chicago—he conducted business as usual to make things appear normal—he prepared once again to address the nation. While Sorensen put the finishing touches on the speech, set for Monday night, October 22, the U.S. Information Agency set up radio connections and arranged for broadcasts in Spanish to Cuba and the rest of Latin America. Kennedy asked his wife and their two young children to return to Washington from their Virginia horse farm so the family could be together in the deepening crisis. In Moscow, Khrushchev, also wanting to keep a calm facade, told his fellow Soviet leaders to take a night off and join him at the Bolshoi theater. "They'll say if Khrushchev and our leaders are able to go to the opera at a time like this then, at least tonight, we can sleep peacefully."[26]

MOST PEOPLE WHO lived through the tensions of that time tried to ignore as best they could the ever looming threat of nuclear war. In a 1959 *Foreign Affairs* article propounding the existence of a missile gap, Albert Wohlstetter, an emerging name on the think tank circuit associated with RAND, complained of America's "deep pre-Sputnik sleep." But for the majority of people, salvation lay, symbolically speaking, in just that, sleep. Television provided another anesthetic. By 1962, more than 90 percent of the nation's nearly fifty million homes had a set, an all-time high and a tripling of television ownership in a decade. TV was black and white. Programming that autumn included a mix of westerns where the good guys of *Bonanza* and *Gunsmoke* talked down, or gunned down, the bad guys; dramas where the stars of *Dr. Kildare* and *The Nurses* always made things better; and comedies where *Ozzie and Harriet* and *Father Knows Best* depicted what was great about family life and small-town America. On *The Jetsons*, rockets were our friends and would someday take us to the supermarket. The viewing public of 1962 was comprised of generations who had lived through World War I, World War II, and the Korean conflict, as well as the postwar baby boom generation, the oldest of whom were about to graduate from high school and had spent years practicing the cold war civil defense technique of duck and cover. Despite the havoc Americans knew war could wreak, they still wanted to see war on TV. Though *Combat* showed the gritty life of a soldier, TV viewers preferred *McHale's Navy*, which made war seem nothing but zany fun.[27]

But this medium of enjoyment and relaxation would now become the conveyor of a real-life drama that threatened to turn the average citizen's suppressed nightmare into a horror of unimaginable consequence. They might have learned about the crisis first from the *New York Times* and *Washington Post*, each ready to publish detailed accounts, but Kennedy, who feared panic and confusion—even mass exoduses from American cities—asked that the stories be held until he could address the American people, and the newspapers reluctantly agreed. The morning of October 22, the White House requested the then three national television networks, ABC, CBS, and NBC, to set aside time for a presidential address that was a matter of the "highest national security." White House press secretary Pierre Salinger took care of the staging, calling a television director to secretly come from New York to advise on lighting and camera lenses. Kennedy's multiple medicines sometimes caused puffiness in his face, and Salinger wanted him to look as commanding as possible.

Before the speech, the president briefed Democratic and Republican congressional leaders, the secretary of state, and an intelligence officer; most of the congressional leaders supported the quarantine but argued that an air strike would eventually be necessary. That evening Rusk told his Soviet counterpart, Dobrynin, that the missile deployment was "a gross error" and gave him an advance copy of Kennedy's speech. Rusk said he saw Dobrynin age "ten years right in front of my eyes." Only later did Rusk conclude that the Soviet ambassador, like the members of the Kennedy administration, had been duped by the government in Moscow into believing the Cuban missiles were not offensive.

That evening, viewers who tuned in minutes before seven o'clock eastern time heard an announcer say that *To Tell the Truth, I've Got a Secret*, or other regularly scheduled programming would be interrupted. Kennedy, in a dark suit, seated and holding several sheets of white paper on a small, sloping lectern with two microphones, began to speak. Explaining that "unmistakable evidence" had established the presence of Soviet missile sites and nuclear-capable bombers on what he called "that imprisoned island," he announced the naval quarantine and warned that any nuclear missile launched from Cuba would result in full retaliation against the Soviet Union. When the klieg lights went out, Kennedy, apparently referring to Khrushchev, was heard to say, "Well, that's it unless the son of a bitch fouls it up."[28]

Kennedy's speech, lasting less than seventeen minutes, was the first public official acknowledgment of what had become the Cuban Missile Crisis. The nation and the world were transfixed. Americans realized that war was not a TV drama or a situation comedy. A good portion of the planet was on the brink of thermonuclear holocaust. Besides warning of the imminent danger, the forty-five-year-old president also was sending a message to Khrushchev, halfway around the globe in Moscow, where Kennedy's voice came over international radio.[29] Americans were not sure what would happen next. In a Gallup poll taken the next day, one in five said they believed that World War III was imminent.[30]

Just before delivering his speech, Kennedy authorized the United States armed forces around the world to go to Defense Condition Three (DEFCON-3), the nation's third highest military alert—DEFCON-1 means war. At Guantánamo, navy dependents and nonmilitary personnel already were packing to leave. Before boarding buses for ships or flights to the United States, they were told to tie their pets in their yards and to leave their house keys on dining room tables. Sixteen hundred officers and other military personnel remained to defend the base, while Castro readied some 270,000 troops to repel an invasion.

"I would not be candid and I would not be fair with you if I did not say that we are in as grave a crisis as mankind has been in," Dean Rusk told Latin American ambassadors in Washington that night.[31] On Tuesday, the United States would learn of a 19–0 vote by the Organization of American States approving the quarantine.

As U.S. AIRCRAFT carriers, cruisers, and destroyers moved into position, setting up a quarantine line first eight hundred, then five hundred, nautical miles from Cuba, the Soviets put their own forces on higher alert and ordered weapons and facilities in Cuba camouflaged to avoid further detection. Kennedy knew his quarantine line greatly exceeded the distances established by international norms in preatomic times; he simply ignored those. In Washington and Moscow, the leaders and their advisers worked around the clock, often grabbing only minutes of sleep in their offices. Khrushchev too said he was sleeping in his office, still in his clothes, so that if an emergency happened, he would not be caught with his pants literally down.

Then came a series of events on both sides that demonstrated how in a ripening conflict certain immutable laws take hold, beginning with the one that says a national leader can quickly lose control over his military chiefs; this can lead to a widening of the conflict with unintended consequences, but add the nuclear ingredient and burgeoning chaos becomes a recipe for planetary disaster. This happened to Kennedy two days after he spoke to the American nation, when General Thomas Power, commander in chief of the Strategic Air Command, moved SAC to DEFCON-2—the nation's highest level of readiness short of actual war. Power not only acted without the approval of the president, he transmitted the unprecedented order—unencrypted—to SAC's thirteen hundred bomber crews (on the ground and in the air) around the world, purposefully enabling the Soviets to intercept the message. This had the effect of immediately readying hundreds of bomber crews, otherwise engaged in training or other activities, for combat. Within hours of the DEFCON-2 alert on October 24, Power used the SAC worldwide broadcast network to deliver a long message in which he declared the bomber planes ready to strike and said that he expected every man to do his duty. When the message reached Kennedy and the members of Ex-Com, all were outraged. The United States was now on the brink of nuclear war. "It looks really mean, doesn't it?" the president said, who nevertheless allowed Power's controversial move to remain unchallenged. "But then, really, there was no other choice. If they get this mean in our part of the world, what will they do next?"[32]

With the nation so close to nuclear war, the president and his brother worried there could be calls for Kennedy's impeachment. Moreover, there was evidence the quarantine would have worked without Power's drastic step. At 10:25 A.M., five minutes before the DEFCON-2 alert, U.S. intelligence sources had preliminary evidence that some of the Russian ships had stopped dead in the water, within a few miles of the line. By that afternoon, a number of Soviet cargo ships had changed course or stopped. Secretary of State Dean Rusk told Bundy, "We're eyeball to eyeball, and I think the other fellow just blinked."[33]

But the crisis was far from over. On Thursday afternoon, October 25, many Americans were back in front of their TVs watching U.S. ambassador Adlai Stevenson in the United Nations confront his Soviet

counterpart, ambassador Valerian Zorin. In a sharply critical statement, Stevenson, who had twice been a presidential candidate, said he
had one simple question: "Do you, Ambassador Zorin, deny that the
U.S.S.R. has placed and is placing medium- and intermediate-range
missiles and sites in Cuba? Yes or no—don't wait for the translation—
yes or no?" The usually solemn Zorin squirmed and attempted to use
procedural delays. Zorin, like Dobrynin, had not been told about the
missiles.

"I am not in an American courtroom, sir . . . You will have your answer in due course," Zorin responded.

Stevenson hammered back that Zorin was in the court of world
opinion. "I am prepared to wait for an answer until Hell freezes over, if
that is your decision. I am also prepared to present the evidence in this
room."[34]

Zorin insisted that United States had falsified claims of Soviet mis-
sile programs. Stevenson had the opening he needed. As laughter over
Zorin's grilling subsided, he lifted the coverings on poster-size aerial
photos propped up on easels, revealing the stunning photos of the
Cuban countryside before and after the installation of Soviet missiles.
Should the United States decide to invade Cuba, the justification
America wanted was there, in front of a worldwide audience, in black
and white.

KENNEDY HAD HOPED his speech would help quell the rising panic.
But as the week wore on, the public's impression was that the threat
of nuclear holocaust was only intensifying. People began thinking seriously about leaving towns and cities, and New York City officials
drew up evacuation procedures. As a sense of doom settled over the
country, however, Robert Kennedy secretly met with Dobrynin that
Friday night (one day after the UN showdown) and suggested a deal:
the United States would remove the Jupiters from Turkey in exchange
for Soviet withdrawal from Cuba. The same night, the Soviets sent a
peace offering via a lengthy telex that took some twelve hours to get
through. Meanwhile, several back-channel sources were being used to
get messages between the two sides, and U Thant, the UN's Burmese
acting secretary-general, stepped into the crisis, sending identical private appeals to Khrushchev and Kennedy.[35]

But the glimmers of hope that the situation was improving quickly ᵤ the next day because of a series of provocations, intended and unintended, on both sides—and again, a failure by leaders in Washington and Moscow to keep a firm grip on their forces. Early Saturday morning, far away in Alaska, an American U-2 strayed into Soviet airspace, prompting both American and Soviet fighter planes to scramble toward the area. The American plane eventually managed to return to U.S. territory without being fired upon, but had signals somehow crossed differently the outcome could have been the start of nuclear war. Kennedy later apologized. That same day in Cuba, Castro, against the wishes of leaders in Moscow, ordered his antiaircraft gunners to fire on U.S. reconnaissance planes—even as the Soviets began removing nuclear warheads positioned near the missiles.[36]

Far worse was in the offing. Around noon, Kennedy learned that a U-2 had been shot down and that its pilot, Major Rudolf Anderson, who had flown one of the first U-2 missions responsible for detecting the Soviet missiles, was dead. ExCom's members assumed the Kremlin had ordered the attack. Not until decades later did Soviet and Cuban officials admit that Soviet commanders in Cuba ordered the attack, without Kremlin authorization. Even more telling was this recollection by Khrushchev's son Sergei of his father's reaction on hearing the news from Cuba: "It was at that very moment—not before or after—that Father felt the situation was slipping out of his control."[37] After Anderson was downed, additional U.S. reconnaissance planes flew over Cuba, discovering that five medium-range missile sites were fully operational and that Castro was rapidly mobilizing forces. Cuban troops opened fire with antiaircraft guns and small arms. Another U.S. plane was hit but was able to return to its base. Kennedy waited and did nothing; his military advisers stood by in amazement. "We had not abandoned hope, but what hope there was now rested with Khrushchev's revising his course within the next few hours," Robert Kennedy would later recall. "It was a hope, not an expectation. The expectation was a military confrontation by Tuesday [October 30] and possibly tomorrow."[38]

Meanwhile, in the Caribbean itself U.S. warships played potentially perilous cat-and-mouse games with Soviet submarines, whose crews were under tremendous duress. Having made the eight-thousand-mile voyage in cramped quarters, the Soviet sailors hit the tropical climes and suddenly discovered their submarine batteries running dry because of the buildup of heat and humidity. They were running short of fresh air and clean water, and crews began to dehydrate and suffer other severe health problems, including skin lesions and rashes. Unknown to the U.S. Navy at the time, each Soviet sub, in addition to as many as twelve conventional torpedoes, carried one nuclear torpedo with a yield approximately half the force of the bomb that leveled Hiroshima.[39]

The same day that Anderson was shot down, Soviet submarine captain Valentin Savitsky ordered the officer assigned to the nuclear torpedo to prepare it for firing. "Maybe the war has already started up there, while we are doing somersaults here," the hot and emotional captain reportedly screamed as the U.S. depth charges rattled his vessel, and his nerves. "We're going to blast them now! We will die, but we will sink them all—we will not disgrace our navy!" His submarine reduced to emergency lighting, with dangerously high carbon dioxide levels and scorching interior temperatures, Savitsky was beside himself. His second in command apparently calmed him, and another officer ordered the sub to surface, without the torpedo being fired. But for those few minutes, "all that stood between tense peace and a small nuclear war in the Caribbean Sea was a rattled, exhausted, dehydrated, and desperate submarine captain," state the authors of *DEFCON-2*.[40]

There were yet more sharp turns on the diplomatic circuit, but the same day that Anderson was shot down Kennedy made an offer: the Soviets would remove the Cuban missiles, the United States would not invade Cuba, and the Jupiter missiles would be out of Turkey within six months, provided nothing was said publicly about the last concession. The Soviets had one day to accept the offer. That came the next day via a Radio Moscow broadcast—and nothing was said publicly about the Jupiters until Robert Kennedy's memoir, *Thirteen Days*, was published six months after his June 1968 assassination.[41]

The quarantine was not ended until November 20, while the two sides argued over what equipment could stay in Cuba and what had to go. On that day, the DEFCON-2 alert was canceled, and the world moved a step back from the nuclear brink. A month after he ended the blockade, Kennedy announced to the world that all strategic missiles and IL-28 bombers were out of Cuba. Because of Castro's objections, the United Nations did not verify the removal, but American reconnaissance showed the missile sites plowed under.

The Soviets viewed the end of the crisis as a terrible defeat. Ultimately, it cost Khrushchev his job and reportedly almost his life. He was ousted in a bloodless coup in October 1964, two years after the momentous events and one year after Kennedy's assassination. Despite repeated U.S. moves against him, Fidel Castro remained El Commandante as eight other American presidents took the oath of office. In 2006, severe illness forced Castro to relinquish control to his brother Raúl.

For decades most Americans assumed the crisis ended because intelligent, wise leaders sought a way out. While this was partly true, it obscures another more unsettling fact, and one that runs through every other aspect of the nuclear story, namely that on many occasions bright men stumbled, made serious mistakes, and lost control over a dangerous technology. Shortly before he died in 1971, Khrushchev famously said, "I want to make one thing clear: when we put our ballistic missiles in Cuba we had no desire to start a war. Any fool can start a war, and once he's done so, even the wisest of men are helpless to stop it— especially if it's a nuclear war."[42]

CHAPTER 11

Fire in the Air

S OMETIME IN THE EARLY 1960S, Gaston Palewski decided he wanted to see a bomb test. De Gaulle's chief of staff during World War II, Palewski had become France's minister of research and technology, thus nominally in charge of nuclear affairs. But he was better known as a great womanizer and for his long and celebrated affair with the British novelist and biographer Nancy Mitford. When he finally settled down it was with a rich and beautiful socialite, Violette de Talleyrand-Périgord, the granddaughter of the roguish American financier Jay Gould.

If Palewski broke Mitford's heart, as has been reputed, he evidently got a taste of what it is like to be jilted—while he watched an underground test in the Atlas Mountains. When the explosion accidentally "vented," showering the area near the Algerian-Moroccan border with radioactivity, everyone ran for cover, leaving him behind. "The mountain shook," said André Finkelstein, the former CEA official who watched it happen. "A crack and a radioactive plume went up, so everyone left very quickly." All the other officials had scurried away in cars, but Palewski never made it. "Then someone said, 'We forgot the minister!'—and when they returned Palewski was green." Finkelstein rolled the r and stretched out the double vowels—*gar-eeen*—as he recalled the episode. "The health physics people had a field day scrubbing down the minister."[1]

Life on the precipice made nuclear people careless. But that was not the way they saw themselves, or how they wanted to project their public image. In 1965, around the time of the French test, the American AEC commissioner Willard Libby spoke of the nuclear enterprise in grandiloquent terms, as if its leaders were godlike, capable of dominating the earth. "Man's place is to be its master or at least to be the master of the part he inhabits," declared the Nobel Prize winner. "It is his place by controlling the natural forces with his intelligence to put them to work to his purposes, to build a future world in his own image. The possibility of doing this is exciting. This to me is man's place in the physical universe, to be its king through the power he alone possesses: the principle of intelligence."[2]

For a time after the Cuban crisis, it seemed as if the nuclear dangers were subsiding. Finally a test ban treaty was agreed upon, and steps were taken to improve communications between the two superpowers to prevent an accidental nuclear war. McNamara ordered that locks known as permissive action links (PALs) be placed on all Minuteman nuclear weapons to prevent their unauthorized use. But the test ban treaty was only partial and simply pushed the test programs underground. This presented other challenges and no foolproof way to prevent further venting episodes like the one Palewski experienced.

Being "king" was only relative to a person's vantage point in the nuclear age. People in Spain who witnessed a B-52 crash and explode, then drop its payload of thermonuclear weapons on their land, could hardly think of SAC pilots as "king" of the skies in the way the pilots thought of themselves. From their perspective, and in a very tangible way, it looked as if the people in charge were *losing* control. People inside the military knew another secret: the PALs and other emergency systems designed to maximize presidential authority during a nuclear crisis had just the opposite effect. They left effective control over the nuclear missiles with the people who had access to the buttons.[3] This meant that the decision to launch nuclear war was as far removed from the president as it ever had been, and the missiles as vulnerable to an unauthorized release.

THE CUBAN CRISIS, for all its tense moments, did little to advance the chances of a comprehensive test ban treaty such as Kennedy, Rabi, and Zuckerman had hoped for, because the cold war rivalry still revolved around the power of the atom. The special interests supporting that dynamic had little desire to see it radically changed. To be sure, there was an uplift to the test ban talks, but the nuclear bomb lobby moved in to thwart the chances of a comprehensive sweep. After it was signed on August 5, 1963, the limited test ban treaty still faced a rough passage through the U.S. Congress and only made it through after the defense lobby extracted concessions to ensure a robust future for the vast nuclear weapons research and development complex.

Critically, the AEC chairman, Glenn Seaborg, a Kennedy appointee, supported the test ban effort. Kennedy also had important senators on his side, including the aging Senate Minority Leader, Illinois Republican Everett M. Dirksen, who spoke in the treaty's favor, thinking about posterity and his own reputation. Dirksen recalled that "bright, sunny day" in August 1945 when the *Enola Gay* opened its bomb bay doors over Hiroshima and "for the first time, the whole bosom of God's earth was ruptured by a manmade contrivance that we call a nuclear weapon. I want to take a first step, Mr. President," Dirksen said. "I am not a young man. One of my age thinks about his destiny a little. I should not like to have written on my tombstone, 'He knew what happened at Hiroshima, but he didn't take a first step.'"[4]

Anxious to ensure smooth sailing for future budget requests, the bomb lobby pushed back with arguments about the need for national security "safeguards" to guarantee the nation's nuclear arsenal remained safe. There were four broad requests: support for a vigorous underground test program; high-level maintenance of the nation's weapons labs; continued readiness to resume atmospheric testing; and improving national technical means for detecting Soviet treaty violations. To a moderate politician these requests sounded reasonable, and some were valid in the context of the times, but the overarching concern was to maintain business more or less as usual.

Kennedy secured Senate approval by a wide margin of 80–19 on September 24, 1963, and the treaty went into force the following month, on October 10, a year after the Cuban Missile Crisis. It banned explosions in the atmosphere, under the sea, and in outer space but not underground. Still there was no abating the nuclear defense lobby's voracious appetite for funds. One day after the Senate vote, California congressman Craig Hosmer wrote Kennedy to complain that the AEC budget for weapons testing was not enough. An unsuccessful Republican candidate for Congress in 1950, Hosmer was elected two years

later and became a front man for the bomb lobby. He was seeking a billion dollars in additional funds. Hosmer had a shopping list that would
make modest men blush, but his state, home to the Lawrence Livermore National Laboratory and a host of defense contractors, had a lot
at stake. Hosmer's list included a new town at the Nevada Test Site
and—for readiness—a completely new missile range for atmospheric
testing, should that be resumed. He also urged that other Pacific islands, in addition to those that had already been used, be readied for
testing. Hosmer wanted diagnostic ships for test sampling and a fleet
of twelve planes for gathering radioactive air samples—all of which
would have to be developed and built.[5]

Hosmer had overreached. His demand was well above the AEC's
own budget request and Kennedy, with Seaborg's support, fended off
the request. Nevertheless, pressure for vigorous implementation of
the "safeguards" to support the sprawling nuclear weapons research
and manufacturing base was maintained. As a thematic pitch, the notion of stewardship would become especially important after the cold
war ended and the weapons lobby had to invent new ways of securing
funds. The bomb builders had become like the automakers, continually upgrading existing models and designing new ones, except their
products were essentially obsolete before they ever got off the factory
floor because in theory they were never supposed to be used. And their
Sisyphean task continued to be rewarded. The weapons establishment
and its lobbyists in Washington became so entrenched that even after
the cold war ended, spending on nuclear weapons, after allowing for
inflation, actually increased.[6]

DIRKSEN DIED SIX years after his ratification speech, in all likelihood
assuming he and his Senate colleagues had taken a small step toward
ridding the world of nuclear weapons. In the long run, history may
prove him right. But the treaty was in trouble barely a year after it had
been signed. China conducted its first nuclear test, and suspect nuclear
programs were well under way in India and Israel, while at earlier stages
in countries such as South Africa, Taiwan, Brazil, and Argentina. The
treaty had done nothing to halt the spread of nuclear weapons among
those countries determined to have them, nor had it prevented further
nuclear testing in the atmosphere among the two newcomers to the

nuclear club (but not to the treaty), France and China. Seaborg viewed the partial test ban as a failure—a "pyrrhic victory," he wrote.

Among the three other nuclear powers, the treaty should have ushered in a period of restraint. In fact, the opposite was true, particularly in the United States. With the stigma of atmospheric tests no longer causing a public relations problem, testing underground resumed with gusto. But underground testing came with its own set of problems. Preparing explosions underground was expensive. Rather than hoisting a bomb onto a tower or dropping it from the hold of a plane, vertical shafts and, sometimes, horizontal tunnels had to be dug, six hundred to twenty-five hundred feet underground, depending on the expected yield. Each test required a complicated series of steps designed to ensure success and to minimize disturbance to the earth's surface.

After the tests, a second hole had to be dug in order to obtain samples, which, of course, were highly radioactive, from the area around the explosion. Not surprisingly, the costs of the U.S. testing program substantially rose. In the five years 1964 through 1968, the United States conducted 140 underground tests in Nevada, according to official records, with a price tag of roughly $1 billion per year, compared to $473 million U.S. taxpayers spent in 1958, or less than half, just before the moratorium on atmospheric testing took effect. The Soviets conducted twenty-five underground tests in the same period but ramped up their program later.[7]

Underground testing was not a cure-all in terms of the environment, either. Venting occurred when cracks unexpectedly developed in the geological structures where the tests took place. This caused radionuclides to escape into the air, posing a potential problem not only environmentally but politically. If the radioactive debris blew outside the territorial limits of the treaty's signers, the government would be in violation of the treaty's terms. In one venting episode in 1964, after the so-called Pike test, the air force flew forty-four tracking sorties and picked up increases in radioactivity in Las Vegas and Boulder City, Nevada, as well as in Colorado and Arizona. Seaborg believed a small amount of radioactivity had crossed into Mexico, but the planes were not allowed to continue over the border to find out. Later, radioactive contamination was found in milk samples ten miles inside the U.S. side of the border with Mexico, but there is no public evidence that anything was done to prevent children from drinking the milk. "We promised to be more careful about our geological evaluation in the future and, if possible, to conduct tests only when the wind was blowing away from Mexico," Seaborg later wrote. "Yet, there could be no guarantees."[8]

Venting underscored a fact of the nuclear age: the pathways of airborne radionuclides were beyond human control and, depending how far they went, made a mockery of national boundaries. The same was true even without venting because the radionuclides from an underground blast could migrate to aquifers and from there enter the food chain, either through drinking water supplies or through grazing or farmland. Some environmental groups began to take an interest, but tracking underground migration was an expensive, time-consuming job, not guaranteed to yield conclusive results. And the funding levels of such organizations were no match for what those in the test programs had to spend.

TESTING WAS ONLY one way in which the nuclear weapons establishment caused problems for people it should nominally have been protecting. In the skies, the Strategic Air Command's B-52s, like dark-winged whales, flew around the clock, seemingly invincible. They could traverse a third of the earth's circumference in little more than eighteen hours without refueling, carrying in their underbellies the means of planetary devastation. Flying at forty thousand feet, their pilots felt as if they owned the air. They carried target folders on board, knowing that with the authenticated "go" code they would light out toward, and through, a fail-safe line, and proceed toward preassigned targets. Such technological supremacy was intolerant of error. But mistakes were made, with grave consequences, and these mighty airborne fortresses came hurtling to the ground like any ordinary plane.

Two of the most famous crashes—and there were at least a dozen—occurred outside the United States, one on January 17, 1966, over the village of Palomares in Spain, and the other on January 21, 1968, at an airbase in Greenland. In both instances, the planes carried four thermonuclear bombs. In Spain, the U.S. Air Force bomber exploded on contact with a KC-135 refueling tanker at thirty thousand feet. The accident left indelible impressions on the people who witnessed it. "I remember all this fire in the air and pieces of airplane falling to the ground," recalled Antonia Flores, a young girl at the time. "I remember all the neighbors running to the place where the smoke came from. We thought that what had fallen there was still burning."

Both aircraft were destroyed, and seven of the eleven crew members perished. One of the unexploded bombs dropped into the Mediterranean. "I saw it very clearly: The bomb fell into the sea very close to me," a fisherman named Francisco Simó Orts told a CNN television crew years later. It took thirty-eight U.S. Navy ships three months to find the missing bomb. Despite the fact that people like Orts witnessed it falling into the sea and residents all over the area knew about the search effort, the U.S. Defense Department refused for forty-four days to admit that one of its thermonuclear weapons was missing.[9]

In the other accident, a B-52 over Thule, Greenland, caught fire, turning itself into an inferno before crashing thirty-five thousand feet into a sea of ice in the Wolstenholme Fjord, about eight miles west of the Thule airbase. Six of the seven crew members ejected safely.[10]

Safety devices prevented thermonuclear explosions in each of these instances. But the high explosives that formed part of the triggering mechanism detonated on impact in all four of the bombs near Thule, and in two of the four around Palomares. The detonations caused plutonium, tritium, and other radionuclides to disperse for miles around. The cleanup efforts took months and involved thousands of military and civilian personnel, often wearing little or no protective clothing.

"Cleanup" is a bit of a misnomer in nuclear terms. What it actually means is that radioactive debris is shipped from one place to another, where it will sit, in theory, for the hundreds, thousands, or millions of years it needs to decay and lose all its radioactivity. In both Spain and Greenland, the waste transference operation was breathtaking in scope and impossible to hide. In Spain, fourteen hundred tons of earth were lifted and emptied into forty-five hundred barrels. The fisherman Simó Orts recalled, "There were five thousand soldiers living on land in tents—generals, colonels, so many important people from North America."

Two years later, Danish and American crews labored in almost total darkness, against near hurricane-force winds howling across a frozen landscape, to put contaminated snow, ice, and debris—weighing 10,500 tons—into barrels. The containers from Greenland and Palomares were sent to one of America's primary de facto nuclear waste sites, the Savannah River plant in South Carolina.[11]

In Greenland, health monitoring by the Americans was evidently

scant to nonexistent. In Palomares, records of nasal swabs, urine samples, and air sampling information were kept locked up. Secrecy was
blamed initially on pressure from the United States and, later, on the
Franco regime wanting to avoid trouble.[12]

"They started doing medical checkups here in the town with a
Geiger counter," said Flores, who became the village's mayor in the
1980s. "Some people had to throw away their clothes because they
were contaminated. The houses were washed down with detergent or
water. At no stage did the Americans tell us anything. People were
scared, because no one knew what was happening; all you knew was
that you were forbidden to eat things, that you couldn't go out on the
street, you couldn't touch anything—everything, but everything, was
permanently prohibited."[13]

When the records were finally released in 1985, more than five hundred residents of Palomares brought claims against the United States,
pushing the accident's final official cost, not including the price of the
aircraft, to more than $120 million. At Thule, the wife of a Danish per-
sonnel manager began collecting the names and medical histories of the
eight hundred Danish workers involved in the eight-month cleanup.
Ailments ranged from cancer—she recorded ninety-eight cases—to
sterility. In December 1986, Denmark's prime minister, Poul Schlüter,
launched a formal investigation of surviving Thule workers. Radiological experts from Denmark's Institute for Clinical Epidemiology
examined them and reported eleven months later that Thule workers
who had participated in Project Crested Ice (the name of the cleanup)
experienced a 40 percent greater incidence of cancer diagnosis than a
cohort of three thousand workers who were at the base before and after
the accident but not during the cleanup.

Nearly two hundred Danish workers also took legal action in the
early 1980s, seeking damages under the Foreign Claims Act; their suit
was "disallowed." However, secret documents released during the
discovery process revealed another startling fact: U.S. military personnel who worked alongside the Danes had not undergone any long-
term monitoring.[14] Finally, the air force began paying attention to the
litany of complaints and undertook a review of its own methodologies
and data, using modern modeling methods. But the conclusions, announced May 22, 2002, only confirmed the original conclusions that
the exposures were not significant.

These were the two extremes of the "peculiar sovereignty" twenty years after Herbert Marks coined the term: Stratofortresses peeling across the skies, impervious, vigilant, ready to strike, and barrels of radioactive crushed ice.

TWO YEARS BEFORE the crash in Spain, America's nuclear omnipotence was challenged in another way—by the October 1964 Chinese nuclear test, which represented a plate shift in the geopolitical sphere. The government had known it was coming, and since at least 1962 had debated an appropriate response. The parameters of this debate, ranging from psy-ops to preemptive strike proposals, reflected the relative powerlessness of a nuclear state when confronted with a "new entrant."

To begin with, the State Department enlisted the CIA to prepare articles for overseas publication, without attribution to U.S. sources, to discourage the Chinese from thinking that by becoming a nuclear power the U.S. would be more accommodating of Chinese demands. At the same time, there were discussions in Washington about preemptive strikes, just as there have been recently regarding the Iranian nuclear program. Another idea was to use Soviet influence to pressure the Chinese into backing down, because the full extent of the Sino-Soviet split was not well enough understood. But during the fall of 1963, a State Department policy planning council staffer named Robert Johnson turned around thinking about the Chinese nuclear problem. Johnson warned against preemptive strikes, saying they would result in "long-lasting political costs." And he suggested that for a variety of reasons, a nuclear China would not be as ominous or act as recklessly as some had feared. To counter the prospect of India going nuclear in response to a Chinese bomb, Johnson floated ideas about broad U.S.-Soviet defense guarantees, guarantees applicable only to India, and an Asian nuclear-free zone. But for a variety of reasons these were deemed unworkable.

By late September 1964, the State Department had adopted a posture of outward equanimity toward the pending event, even though the range of possible reactions still being mulled included covert action and preemptive strikes. When CBS ran a report that a Chinese test was imminent, the State Department responded with measured calm during a background briefing September 29, 1964. Spokesman Robert McCloskey noted that the "United States has fully anticipated the possibility of Peiping's entry into the nuclear weapons field and has taken it into full account in determining our military posture."[15] Anne Marks, the former secretary to Groves and Oppenheimer, had moved on to the State Department by then and was working for McCloskey. She remembered the weeks surrounding the Chinese test with a sense of great achievement because of the way in which the department's press office had handled the event. The main thing, she said, was that "we preempted the Chinese. I think it can be said that we were the best news managers in the world."[16]

On that front, the Chinese apparently had not done too badly themselves. The Chinese wanted to make things up with the Soviets after a split with Khrushchev four years earlier. They intentionally let news of the test slip out ahead of the actual event, evidently in part to further undermine the now embattled Soviet leader. Khrushchev was ousted less than twelve hours *before* the mushroom cloud appeared over the Lop Nur test site in the western desert province of Sinkiang, near the Sino-Soviet border. In the aftermath of their first nuclear success, Mao Zedong, chairman of the Chinese Communist Party, extended "warm greetings" to the new Soviet party leader, Leonid Brezhnev. Having been subjected to nuclear threats by the United States during the 1950s—twice in Korea, once in Vietnam, and during two crises over the Taiwan Strait—the Chinese were attempting to level the playing field.[17] After Lop Nur, Mao issued a communiqué stating that the purpose of developing nuclear weapons was to protect the Chinese people "from the danger of the United States launching a nuclear war."[18] He was basically saying he did not want to be subjected to further American nuclear taunts.

The Chinese still had a lot of catching up to do. Between 1955 and 1960, the Soviets had nurtured their bomb program with assistance on everything from uranium prospecting to nuclear weapons designs. But the countries had different assumptions about the nature of their relationship. The Soviets saw China as a sphere of influence, in somewhat the same way the United States viewed Europe. The Chinese were not interested in subservience, and so the relationship broke apart in 1960. Although the split signaled China's determination to remain independent, the Soviet withdrawal prevented any chance of quickly matching the superpower arsenals in size and scale, and the Chinese were still without adequate delivery systems. But the test marked a watershed moment in the international political order. Now all five permanent members of the UN Security Council, originally drawn from the victorious powers of World War II, formed a permanent club of "haves"—those that had nuclear weapons as opposed to those that did not. The Chinese test propelled the United States to push hard for a non-proliferation treaty; when one was signed four years later, the legitimacy of the "haves" was established in international law, making any other country that acquired nuclear weapons an "illegitimate" nuclear state. "There is not much doubt that last week's events, taken in total, spell a turning point in the atomic age and in the history of the Twentieth Century, but where the new road will take us, no man knows," wrote Hanson W. Baldwin in the Sunday *New York Times* two days after the Chinese test.[19]

The political pendulum was shifting to the left. Britain had just elected Harold Wilson prime minister, and the Labour leader favored closer ties with the Chinese. The United States could do little to stop further atmospheric testing by either the French or the Chinese. Twenty-two further tests were conducted at Lop Nur through 1980, including at least seven thermonuclear weapons. The French continued testing in the Pacific, in the Mururoa and Fangataufa atolls, carrying out forty-four atmospheric explosions, five of them thermonuclear. French testing provoked a wave of local and international protests and boycotts of French goods and airlines, until finally the governments of Australia and New Zealand brought proceedings against the government of France in the International Court of Justice at The Hague. The court ordered a halt to the testing in 1974, and a new president, Valéry Giscard d'Estaing, had it moved underground.

KENNEDY WAS SHOT in Dallas a month after the test ban treaty took effect, on Friday, November 22, 1963. By coincidence, Seaborg heard the news while at Lawrence Livermore in Berkeley hosting a group of Soviet scientists. He happened to be in the same room where he had been three years earlier when Kennedy called to offer him the AEC chairmanship. The Soviet scientists were as stunned by the event as he was and offered to end the tour and fly back to Moscow. Instead, Seaborg arranged for them to travel to the Idaho National Reactor Testing Station, so he could fly to Washington to attend the state funeral the following Monday. The Idaho site was nearly deserted when the visitors arrived because a day of commemoration had been declared so staff could watch the service at home. When the Soviets asked if they too could watch, a television set was placed in a cafeteria. On the tour's final day, the leader of the Soviet delegation, Andronik M. Petrosyants, made another unexpected request. Could he and his colleagues lay a wreath on President Kennedy's grave?

Petrosyants was chairman of the State Committee for the Utilization of Atomic Energy. He was essentially Seaborg's counterpart in Moscow, except that Petrosyants controlled only the civilian side of nuclear development, while Seaborg had charge of both military and civilian aspects, according to Seaborg. Petrosyants's wish was granted. The small band of scientists traveled to Washington and, without any fanfare, carried out a private act of détente ten years before the two superpowers would declare a formal period of mutual respect and partial reconciliation. These sympathetic gestures, while undoubtedly genuine and keenly felt, also underscored the symbiotic relationship between the nuclear establishments in both countries. Each had a vested interest in seeing the momentum maintained, whether they were involved in military or civilian nuclear activities. Petrosyants might not have been directly involved in nuclear weapons production, but the research and development money effectively flowed both ways, just as it did in the United States.

All over the world there was lasting grief at Kennedy's death. Chester Bowles, then American ambassador to India, later reported seeing pictures of the president in remote villages—alongside Gandhi's. Seaborg and many others believed the outpouring of affection for the slain president was greatly influenced by his handling of the Cuban crisis and the subsequent signing of the partial test ban treaty. The American president had shown finesse and restraint during a period when most of the world felt threatened by nuclear holocaust, and then he had reached out to Khrushchev to hammer out an agreement that offered the best hope the world then had for a curb on the arms race.

But the treaty and the momentous events that led to it were in fact the beginning of a new phase in the arms race between the two countries, as the Soviets tried to make good on their previous claims of nuclear superiority, misguidedly promoted in the West as a "missile gap" and since debunked. As a handful of Soviet scientists laid their wreaths at the gravesite where an eternal flame burned, the earnest hopes so many had for a total test ban seemed to die with the young president.

ONE OTHER SEEMINGLY positive consequence of the Cuban crisis also did not turn out the way it was supposed to. McNamara, the defense secretary in both the Kennedy and Johnson administrations, thought he had decreased the possibility of an accidental nuclear war by ordering the installation of the safety systems to prevent an unauthorized launch. But McNamara was misled, according to Bruce Blair, a former Minuteman launch officer who now heads the World Security Institute. In 2004, Blair wrote a column on his Web site explaining that he had recently told McNamara that "the locks had been installed, but everyone knew the combination. The Strategic Air Command (SAC) in Omaha quietly decided to set the 'locks' to all zeros in order to circumvent this safeguard." Blair left the air force in 1974, and until at least that point, he maintained, the firing crew were under instructions to double-check the digits had not been inadvertently changed to something other than zero. "SAC remained far less concerned about unauthorized launches than about the potential of these safeguards to interfere with the implementation of wartime launch orders. And so the 'secret unlock code' during the height of the nuclear crises of the Cold War remained constant at 00000000."[20] McNamara, according to Blair, was dumbfounded. "I am shocked, absolutely shocked and outraged," he quoted him as saying. "Who the hell authorized that?"[21]

The locks were properly activated in 1977, at least partially in response to an article Blair wrote that same year. One of the reasons for skewing control over the launch site in favor of the military, according to General George Lee Butler, was that the policy of deterrence was unrealistically based on the premise of being able to accept the first wave of attack. "We never said publicly that we were committed to launch on warning or launch under attack," said Butler. But that proved impractical at an operational level, he said. "The consequence was a move in practice to a system structured to drive the president invariably toward a decision to launch under attack."[22]

According to Blair, even now this means that the briefings U.S. presidents receive on the nuclear command structure wrongly convey the impression that in the event of an enemy missile attack, real or apparent, they are in charge. Instead, he argues, the system "is so greased for the rapid release of U.S. missile forces by the thousands upon the receipt of attack indications from early warning satellites and ground radar that the president's options are not all created equal . . . The option to 'ride out' the onslaught and then take stock of the proper course of action exists only on paper. That is what presidents never learn during their tenures. Their real control is illusory."[23]

If, as these experts assert, the safeguards on American nuclear weapons are deficient, the possibilities for either nuclear terrorism or accidental nuclear war are more likely. And what about the control systems in other nuclear states? Increasingly, the United States would find itself at cross-purposes: on the one hand it would try to prevent other countries acquiring nuclear weapons; on the other it would be forced to look for ways to accommodate those countries once they did, if for no other reason than to quietly find ways of keeping their arsenals safe. Ultimately, though, the United States had no control over other countries' weapons. Neither could it force them to sign test ban or disarmament treaties.

THE YEAR AFTER Kennedy's assassination, Bob Dylan produced "A Hard Rain's A-Gonna Fall," one of his earliest and longest lyrical songs, graphically painting a world the way he imagined it after a nuclear war.

> Oh, what'll you do now, my blue-eyed son?
> Oh, what'll you do now, my darling young one?
> I'm a-goin' back out 'fore the rain starts a-fallin',
> I'll walk to the depths of the deepest black forest,
> Where the people are many and their hands are all empty,
> Where the pellets of poison are flooding their waters,
> Where the home in the valley meets the damp dirty prison,
> Where the executioner's face is always well hidden,
> Where hunger is ugly, where souls are forgotten,
> Where black is the color, where none is the number,
> And I'll tell it and think it and speak it and breathe it . . .
> It's a hard rain's a-gonna fall.

In America, the tableau was changing. The memories of the crisis in Cuba gradually faded, and people once again tried to put aside any fears they had about prospects for nuclear war. Kennedy's national security adviser, McGeorge Bundy, regretted that the administration's big civil defense push never took off. Why not, he asked, when similar efforts in countries like Sweden and Switzerland were more successful? His explanation was intriguing. Bundy believed the failure reflected not only a general lack of trust in the government but an intriguing form of collective denial about, and responsibility for, American nuclear statehood. "The meaning of civil defense may not be the same for us as for the Swiss and the Swedes because their governments are guarding against what their people know can never be the product of a Swiss or Swedish choice. But when our leaders talk of shelter, are they telling us that we are going to need them? What do they have up their sleeves, then?"[24]

The soul of the songwriter was heard only by those willing to listen, which evidently remained a minority. Dylan's voice could pound the airwaves with great effect, but for many it was not enough to drown out warnings, like one from Kissinger, that giving up nuclear weapons "would amount to giving the Soviets a blank check."[25] People in the nuclear states had become, unwittingly, weapons-dependent. A person dwelling in that metaphorical forest of Dylan's ballad might, if he stayed there too long, lose his soul, if not his entire way of life. So it was best to check out and go about life as if everything were normal. You could forget about the weapons, unless you were an activist, because sometimes it seemed like they weren't really there—except in the newspapers—unless you were unlucky enough to live in a place like Palomares.

But the angst associated with them never quite disappeared. It dwelt beneath the surface, and, in big and small ways, America and the world shifted gears. As psychedelic rock groups like the Grateful Dead attempted to replicate the mind-altering experiences of hallucinogenic drugs, race riots broke out in Detroit and Newark and London's Notting Hill. In the spring of 1968, people twice turned on their radios or televisions to hear reports of other assassinations: April 4—Martin Luther King Jr.; June 6—Robert F. Kennedy. Kennedy, by then a senator, was shot in the early morning hours of June 5, moments after claiming victory in the California Democratic primary election for president. He died the following day. That fall, Richard Milhous Nixon was elected thirty-seventh president.

The world is paying a price for the fear that sat quietly and pervasively in most of us over the cold war years. It would be difficult to draw a straight line between then and now, but if it exists it is along a taut seam of anger that grew among nations and people who resented the reckless behavior of the superpowers. This manifested itself not only in the intractable threat of nuclear war but in events suggesting the mighty powers had lost control over their nuclear weapons. To the masters of this supremacy, one mistake was only that, and somehow it could always be fixed. Certainly it was no cause for undue alarm. Even a disastrous accident was, as Voltaire's eternal optimist Pangloss repeatedly said, as it should be.

To keep the juggernaut going, decorated men could not afford to think too much about the dark consequences of their mistakes. But for a young Spanish girl, the meaning of nuclear power was fixed forever in a memory of the sky aflame and shards of metal falling to earth, and of being warned to touch nothing.

CHAPTER 12

The Grand Bargain

SEPTEMBERS IN VIENNA ARE WARM and pleasant enough to enjoy the outdoor cafés in the Stadtpark. Visitors pass by statues of the composers while strolling violinists play the music that evokes their memories. Certainly Vienna is far from the front line of suspicious nuclear activity. So it might seem strange that the sleepy European backwater is headquarters to the International Atomic Energy Agency—an organization that provides relatively high-paying jobs for its twenty-three hundred employees and maintains an elegant, curved skyscraper headquarters just outside Vienna's center, a plush swimming pool and sports complex, two laboratories, and offices in four other cities. On the other hand, the location is entirely fitting. For most of its existence, the IAEA has administered nuclear safeguards with the civility and unobtrusiveness of a Viennese waiter. Americans in a hurry run up against the old-world gentility soon enough. Ask for the bill just after being served, as I once did, and the waiter smiles gently and says, "What's your hurry?"

After World War II, Vienna was a city of spies and bootleggers, a no-man's-land between east and west, eerily portrayed in Graham Greene's novel *The Third Man*. And it was in this Vienna, in the crucible of the cold war conflict, that the stage was set for the Grand Bargain. According to the famous legend, Faust traded his soul to the devil in exchange for knowledge. The deal was made in the nuclear context, and by the time it was formalized in 1968 the negotiators could only hope that not too much harm would come from it. That year the

Nuclear Non-Proliferation Treaty (NPT) was signed. By then nuclear knowledge and technology were already widespread and the number of covert bomb programs was growing. Israel had assembled several nuclear weapons the previous year, though it would not make that fact public, and over the next several decades a third wave of proliferation threatened to engulf the Middle East and the Indian subcontinent in nuclear wars of their own. That left everyone wondering: why hadn't the IAEA stopped it?

Critics charged that the agency's inspectors had not been effective in preventing the technology from proliferating. That criticism was perfectly valid. The IAEA had a built-in conflict of interest because it spent roughly as much of its budget promoting nuclear energy as it did policing it. Its members had little interest in overly zealous inspectors, and the agency took the cue accordingly. But the argument overlooked the complicity of IAEA member states, not only in the agency's overall priorities but in the fact that they encouraged and sometimes sanctioned the flow of dangerous nuclear traffic.

Most of the bomb programs that surfaced between then and now— in Israel, India, South Africa, Pakistan, Iraq, North Korea, Libya, and Iran—were either known about or suspected long before they had reached the point where stopping them presented serious obstacles. The IAEA's overseers were content to allow the agency to go about its business in a nonconfrontational manner because governments had more pressing geostrategic and commercial priorities. Sometimes the values they assigned those other issues directly conflicted with nonproliferation aims. When that happened, nuclear exporters, contravening the spirit, if not the letter, of their own laws, willingly allowed nuclear equipment, fuel, and even bomb components to be shipped to countries believed to be harboring secret weapons programs. Government officials who tried to stop the flow became like wallflowers at a dance, totally ignored—and, if they were unlucky enough, were shifted out of their jobs to less sensitive positions. Or as one official put it, "During the cold war non-proliferation was for sissies."[1]

WITHIN THE NUCLEAR world, the weapons crowd was hard to compete with. When an Irish foreign minister, worried about a nuclear arms race in Europe, first proposed a nonproliferation treaty in 1958, the superpowers professed to support the idea. But they never allowed it to get in the way of their first priority, which was to design, build, and deploy thousands of nuclear weapons.[2] When the Chinese tested their first nuclear bomb in 1964, the problem of proliferation took on a greater sense of urgency. That helped propel negotiations toward a nonproliferation treaty four years later. But the basic cold war framework was still in place, and that meant that other concerns would be more pressing during the 1970s and 1980s. As weapons expert Stan Norris puts it, "The race is on and it's pretty frantic because the MIRV missiles are coming."[3] These "multiple independently targeted reentry vehicles" carried as many as ten warheads on a single strategic ballistic missile. They could be fired from a silo or a submarine. That made the scope of their destructive power positively breathtaking. "What any of this had to do with the NPT?" Norris asked rhetorically. "Nothing. I mean, the Russians are coming. Don't bother me!"[4]

At IAEA conferences, people don't talk about MIRVs or ICBMs. They talk about "haves" and "have-nots." Their status is defined primarily by whether the countries they represent have nuclear weapons, and most of them do not, and secondarily according to whether they have nuclear equipment or fuel to sell. Every five years when they meet to review the NPT, the have-nots complain about being ignored by the haves, basically the kind of people Stan Norris was talking about. Over the years, countries once defined as have-nots, like India, whose first atomic leader Homi Bhabha invented the term, have to some extent moved into the other category, although not entirely. India has nuclear weapons, for example, but it still relies on the outside world for nuclear fuel and equipment. Well before the review conferences take place, the have-nots send out dire warnings of the treaty's imminent collapse. But these are really vain pleas for more attention by the superpowers. The have-nots want further progress on disarmament and easier access to nuclear technology. More recently some have complained about a special deal the United States made with India allowing it access to the fuel and technology it needs, even though it is considered an "illegitimate" nuclear weapons state and never signed the treaty. Why had they signed the treaty, asked other countries, when India could get all the benefits without bothering?

In truth, though, the treaty has always been weak, and on the verge of collapse, because it tried to satisfy too many competing interests and legitimized a permanent "elite" club of five nuclear weapons states. All other countries were relegated to inferior status as non-nuclear-weapons states. At the time the treaty was negotiated, the five "declared" weapons states—the U.S., the USSR, China, France, and Britain—had no intention of relinquishing their arsenals. Many other countries were still weighing their options. For these countries, the primary concern was to prevent any agreement from impeding commercial nuclear trade. Big business was at stake, so naturally the weapons states had no desire to do that either. A deal was struck: the weapons states agreed not to transfer nuclear weapons to countries that did not already have them; those countries would in turn forswear developing nuclear weapons and promise to open their nuclear facilities to inspectors. Tossed into the bargain were promises of "the fullest possible exchange" of "peaceful" nuclear technology. That was the reward for relinquishing claims to first-class seats at the international negotiating tables.

But the treaty, with its lopsided, inherently controversial features, did not erase the presumption that non-nuclear-weapons states had the right to have nuclear weapons. It only said that right would not be exercised. Nor, more immediately, did it stop the United States continuing its nuclear deployments in Europe. That was taken care of under a separate deal with the Soviet Union.[5]

THE JOB OF enforcing the treaty fell to the agency in Vienna. That was good news for the IAEA. For years the United States and its allies had tried to convince countries to agree to IAEA inspections as a condition of receiving nuclear exports, but the effort met with only moderate success. Under the NPT, safeguards agreements with the IAEA became mandatory. But putting the IAEA in charge of inspections immediately raised questions. Was the agency a promoter or a policeman, or both?

When it was founded in 1957, the IAEA was little more than an organization of scientists from different countries who wanted to advance nuclear energy and exchange ideas and information, and the agency never lost that function. As its involvement in administering safeguards grew, its mission was split between promotional and safeguards activities, which meant it had conflicting interests. Delegates to IAEA meetings found this ambiguity convenient, particularly if they were secretly running bomb programs under the guise of peaceful nuclear activities. Just by attending an IAEA conference they signaled to the world their country's nuclear bona fides, no matter what else was suspected about their activities back home. Saddam Hussein's minions showed up at IAEA meetings for years.

The agency also provided fertile ground for future bomb-makers employed to run its programs. For example, in 1958, just after the IAEA came into existence, a prominent Pakistani scientist, Munir Ahmad Khan, was put in charge of the nuclear power and fuel cycle programs, arguably the most sensitive part of the agency's work. When Homi Bhabha, head of India's Atomic Energy Commission, signed a contract for two General Electric reactors in the early 1960s, he insisted on American inspectors instead of chancing it with the agency. "They [the Indians] knew that while we would be reasonable and objective, this crowd of [then] seventy-four countries with all sorts of bizarre agendas could be a real pain in the neck," recalled Kratzer, who negotiated the U.S. safeguards agreement with India.[6]

What Kratzer was really saying was that Bhabha had no desire to have a Pakistani nuclear scientist, or someone who worked for him, snooping around India's nuclear facilities. Who, with the possible exception of Bhabha, could have suspected then that Khan would return to his country more than a decade later to head up a secret nuclear weapons program? Educated on a Fulbright scholarship in the United States, Khan himself might not have realized it then. As Kratzer remembered: "He [Khan] was an extremely personable fellow, seemingly very pro-American with an attractive, pleasant European wife—Dutch, I believe. He was genuinely committed to nuclear power and was very active in IAEA nuclear power promotional activities."[7]

Over the next several decades, the IAEA's promotional activities would directly or indirectly contribute to illicit bomb programs in countries such as Iraq, and North Korea, while a small legion of inspectors tried to keep up with the expanding activity. Millions were spent on research reactors and uranium exploration and mining programs, and this allowed countries to get the basics they needed to begin developing nuclear weapons. In one egregious case of abuse, in the late 1980s and early 1990s, the agency funded a program to help North Korea develop a uranium mining industry. It paid off, too, although in unintended ways. As tensions mounted over North Korea's suspected nuclear weapons program in the late 1990s, experts estimated uranium output in the hermit kingdom at two thousand metric tons per year, roughly on a par with U.S. uranium production.[8] Without its own uranium, North Korea would have found it more difficult to produce the fissile material it needed for the bombs it eventually tested. Moreover, assuming those figures are correct, North Korea had a valuable commodity to trade with other proliferators.

The IAEA knew about North Korea's nuclear fuel cycle activities because the North Koreans never hid them. Nothing was done about it because the agency's inspectors did not even go to North Korea until *seven years* after the government in Pyongyang signed the NPT. In other words, while the agency was extending North Korea assistance in uranium mining, its inspectors were off somewhere else. When the IAEA finally came under pressure to take action in the early 1990s, North Korea's government not surprisingly proved recalcitrant. North Korea was labeled a "rogue state," and the might of the industrialized world was brought to bear upon it. But the clamor over North Korea disguised a discomfitting fact. As Peter Hayes, executive director and cofounder of the Asia-focused Nautilus Institute, points out, "The IAEA and Western companies have played a significant role in developing the early DPRK [Democratic People's Republic of Korea] uranium program."9

EVEN WHEN IT was adhered to, though, the NPT helped to reinforce the IAEA's inbuilt conflict of interest by legitimizing inherently dangerous commercial nuclear trade. This in turn encouraged the nuclear industry's propensity for institutionalized secrecy and deception. The definition of a "peaceful activity" was so vague that it was easy for governments to approve questionable exports when it suited their purposes. That the treaty was crafted in this manner is no surprise: its primary architects were nuclear promoters with questionable, if not skewed, priorities, and the governments that supported them at the time (and to this day) viewed the bargain as useful to achieving other geopolitical objectives.

In the 1960s, when the treaty was being negotiated, for example, nuclear enthusiasts like the American AEC chairman, Glenn Seaborg, still believed they could use the power of the atom to rebuild the world. One of Seaborg's pet projects was known as Project Ploughshare. Its aim was to encourage the use of "peaceful nuclear explosives" (PNEs) to mine canals, divert rivers, and build tunnels. Seaborg had a great many admirers (as well as detractors), and enthusiasm for his project was still strong when the NPT was being negotiated. "It was the excavation applications that most stirred the world's imagination," Seaborg later wrote. "The list of contemplated projects was a long one. Aside from the canal across Israel, a partial list, as it emerged in the late 1950s, included a new sea-level canal across the Isthmus of Panama; shortening and straightening the Santa Fe Railroad in the Mojave Desert; connecting the Mediterranean with the Qattara Depression, a below sea-level area in western Egypt, to produce hydro electric power . . ."[10] The list went on.

There was just one problem. PNEs were virtually identical to nuclear weapons—and their advocacy by the United States would only encourage other countries to build nuclear weapons under the guise of "peaceful uses." Moreover, Ploughshare had advanced to the point in the United States where, according to Seaborg, "it absolutely required thermonuclear devices of very advanced design."[11] Not surprisingly, India and other countries insisted that they too had a right to have PNE programs. So a provision was drafted into the treaty allowing them to "lease" PNEs (basically from the United States) under "international observation." It was essentially a rent-a-nuke policy, but it never amounted to much because the PNE program in the United States soon fizzled out. Nevertheless, India was able to use its own PNE program as legitimate cover for a nuclear weapons program, and then claim its first explosion in 1974 was peaceful.

Safeguards, meanwhile, were continually being eroded by commercial competition, a situation that existed both before and after the NPT was agreed in 1968. For example, by 1962, officials from Canada's Atomic Energy Control Board (AECB) were getting nervous about the absence of safeguards at the early CIRUS (or CIR) reactor they had supplied to India. Work had started on a reprocessing plant in India that could turn the CIRUS fuel into plutonium for a bomb—and eventually did. The Canadians hoped to rectify the situation by using negotiations for a second reactor, called RAPP, as a bargaining chip to obtain safeguards on both reactors. John McManus, who became the AECB's assistant director of material and equipment, explained later: "One side said, 'Look, we can use RAPP as a lever; we can say we won't go ahead unless the Indians agree to safeguard CIR. We know CIR was naked, here was a chance to do something about it.' But the commercial people kept saying that 'if we don't give the Indians what they want, they'll buy it elsewhere, they'll get it from the French or the Americans.' That was the telling argument. Eventually, it went to [the prime minister's] Cabinet, and you know who won."[12]

The Canadians supplied a second reactor without safeguards, but the United States was not much better. It allowed an American company, Vitro International, to provide design work for the reprocessing plant at Trombay with few strings attached.[13] And in 1963, the AEC approved the General Electric contract for two boiling-water reactors at Tarapur. The reactors, which genuinely were intended for civilian use, would fall under a safeguards agreement; but there was no demand for inspections at the other facilities clearly designated for India's military nuclear activities.

AFTER THE CHINESE test, the United States began paying more attention to the problem of nuclear proliferation. In the aftermath of the test, President Lyndon B. Johnson appointed a panel to study the problem, chaired by Roswell L. Gilpatric, a deputy defense secretary in the Kennedy administration. The committee unanimously agreed that the prospect of proliferating nuclear weapons was indeed a serious problem, and it concluded that action was needed on three fronts: negotiation of formal multilateral agreements, applying "influence" on other countries considering the acquisition of nuclear weapons, and setting an example by "our own policies and actions."[14] Also vital to getting the treaty talks under way was a Soviet agreement to back off demands for the total elimination of NATO warheads in Europe.[15]

Mired in the Vietnam War, Johnson could not attend the opening session in Geneva on July 27, 1965, but he sent a message that recalled the Fourth Horseman of the Apocalypse—described as Death in the Bible, he said. This was no longer just a "parable" but a "possibility," Johnson said. He urged members of the Eighteen-Nation Disarmament Committee to "bring the weapons of war under increasing control." The talks would mark the last time disarmament diplomats would concern themselves with nuclear proliferation issues not related to the superpower arms race. After the NPT was signed, the issue of "horizontal" proliferation basically came under the IAEA umbrella. The job of negotiating warhead cuts was left to the arms controllers. The day after the opening session, the American president ordered a massive increase in troop levels in Vietnam. "We did not choose to be the guardians at the gate," Johnson said in an emotionally charged televised speech, "but there is no one else."[16]

The Soviets were never fooled by the American enthusiasm for safeguards. So it is not surprising that in 1966, a year after the NPT talks officially began in Geneva, Seaborg's Soviet counterpart, Igor D. Morokhov, complained to the AEC chairman about what he viewed as safeguards hypocrisy. Morokhov pointed out that the United States had furnished tons of plutonium to Euratom, the European Community's nuclear agency, without requiring IAEA safeguards. Then, according to Seaborg, he "went on to say that the prevention of proliferation would require much stronger safeguards" than the IAEA had at the time and "seemed to doubt that the IAEA framework would ever be sufficient."[17]

But the Soviets had an interest in the treaty negotiations because of their concerns that West Germany would acquire the expertise to one day build its own nuclear arsenal. "There was no fear more deeply rooted in the Russian psyche at this time than that of a revanchist Germany with nuclear weapons," Seaborg wrote.[18] West Germany, precluded from developing nuclear weapons by the post–World War II agreements, was equally anxious about the Soviets. As the former chancellor Ludwig Erhard put it: "Soviet medium range rockets on the boundaries of this country are a reality. We have never demanded control over nuclear weapons, but we desire to be defended with the same weapons as threatened us."[19]

In 1967, a year before the NPT was agreed on, German leaders spoke out against the treaty in operatic fashion, arguing that it would reduce Germany's standing in the world economy to second class status. It was "a Morgenthau plan raised to the second power," argued Erhard's predecessor, Konrad Adenauer, in February 1967, referring to a postwar settlement plan put forward by former U.S. treasury secretary Henry Morgenthau Jr. that would have done away with most of German heavy industry.[20]

President Johnson was mindful of German concerns. Two years earlier, he was reported to have said during a White House meeting, "The Germans have gone off the reservation twice in our lifetime, and we've got to be sure that doesn't happen again, that they don't go beserk."[21] The president instructed the American negotiators in Geneva "to exercise the greatest care that the treaty not hinder the nonnuclear powers in the development of nuclear energy for peaceful purposes." He went on to say that this should include access to "the full benefits of peaceful nuclear technology—including any benefits that are the by-product of weapons research."[22] But because of ever louder demands by developing countries, what began as a concession to the

Fanning Flames of Proliferation—now ironically Germany is pushing nuke out?

West Germans ended up as a promise to pay special attention to them. Within this large body of countries were budding "rogue states." *further* The irony was that West Germany then possessed the most advanced uranium enrichment technology in the world, although that was not yet widely recognized. Moreover, West Germany had been developing an extensive network of nuclear contacts in other countries, most intriguingly in South Africa, Brazil, and Argentina. That raised the possibility that not only was its level of nuclear expertise growing, but that the government might be contemplating an outsourcing arrangement to develop nuclear fuel cycle facilities for a German bomb, since it was politically impossible within West Germany.[23]

The Americans and the Soviets found themselves in an unusual position. Instead of being adversaries as they were on the military front, they became partners in fending off complaints about their nuclear weapons. This they did by offering greater scope for technical assistance, not only from them but from other advanced industrialized countries as well. By enlarging the pool of supplier countries, they hoped to dissipate complaints about the imbalance between the haves and the have-nots. Thus in January 1968, the two superpowers submitted identical drafts containing one-half of the Grand Bargain—Article IV of the proposed treaty: potential exporters were no longer simply countries with nuclear weapons but those "in a position to do so"—which meant West Germany and Canada, and a number of other potential suppliers without nuclear weapons such as the Netherlands, Sweden, and Japan.

As the language was clarified, the developing countries asserted their numerical weight within the negotiating committee, and when the final draft appeared on May 31, 1968, the onus was on all countries with nuclear know-how and manufacturing facilities to give "due consideration for the needs of the developing nations of the world." In other words, a measure originally intended to assuage West German concerns about being left out of the technological loop provided a legitimate means of proliferating. Henceforth, supplier nations were encouraged, if not obliged, by the treaty to provide nuclear exports to developing countries.[24]

The nonaligned states had not given up advancing the cause of disarmament either. For India's ambassador V. C. Trivedi, disarmament was meant not just "as a pious preambular platitude, not just as an insubstantial incantation to be repeated occasionally as a simple magic charm, but as envisaging a concrete programme of specific action."[25]

Accordingly, a promise by the weapons states to work toward disarmament was moved from the treaty's preamble to a new section, Article VI. It did not include a timetable, as Trivedi proposed, but instead contained a single sentence obligating the superpowers to "pursue negotiations in good faith on effective measures relating to cessation of the nuclear arms race at an early date and to nuclear disarmament." American negotiators never took it very seriously. "I don't want to belittle the significance of Article VI," said Alan Labowitz, the former AEC official who had over the course of two decades moved from the shop floor at Oak Ridge to negotiating nuclear technology exchanges. "I guess people thought, okay, that's way in the future. We'll get to that eventually. But we don't have to worry about that right now."[26]

THE TREATY WAS adopted on June 12, 1968, and signed by the United States, Britain, the Soviet Union, and fifty-nine other countries on July 1. It entered into force on March 5, 1970. China and France refused to sign until 1992, although the official French position was that it would always behave as if it had. From the viewpoint of the Americans and British, and to some extent the Soviets, the NPT was a remarkable achievement. A number of countries that might have developed nuclear weapons were now committed to giving up any remaining aspirations. The five declared weapons states could keep their stockpiles, and there was nothing in the treaty that specifically prevented enlarging them. The United States also could retain its existing nuclear NATO arrangements.[27] Noticeably absent from the list of signatories, however, were Israel, India, and Pakistan, all of whom are today nuclear weapons states.

By 1976, when suspect nuclear programs were reported to be under way in Iran, Argentina, Brazil, Pakistan, Spain, South Africa, Taiwan, and Egypt, fewer than fifty IAEA inspectors were traveling the world to keep tabs on some four hundred nuclear plants.[28] During this time the challenge of preventing unwanted nuclear weapons grew as shipments of plutonium continued in anticipation of a new generation of breeder reactors. The hijacking of plutonium was not just a theoretical possibility. After attending an AEC meeting on the topic in 1968, Sam Edlow, whose nuclear transport company shipped tons of plutonium between facilities in the United States and Europe, reported to clients that the regulators had "developed a unanimous opinion" that "under present conditions, the Mafia or Cosa Nostra has so thoroughly infiltrated the transportation industry in the United States that it is capable of organizing and committing a theft of any consignment or cargo which it may choose to steal."[29]

There were slipups, too. In July 1969, AEC officials at the Hanford plutonium plant failed to put the required number of safeguards seals on three plutonium shipments destined for a West German government nuclear installation at Karlsruhe. These were important because if a seal was broken or in any way tampered with it might indicate theft. In a telex to his West German client, Edlow, who was handling the shipment, described it as a "fiasco and crisis." In a subsequent telex to AEC officials, he complained, "We are astounded at the failure of staff at Hanford to apply even minimal and rudimentary safeguards measures."[30]

These and other mishaps only underscored the dangers associated with commercial nuclear trade. All that stood between that commerce and potential nuclear chaos were export officials susceptible to political and commercial influence, and a small team of inspectors competing for funding in an agency whose priorities were still largely promotional. In 1974, the Nuclear Suppliers Group (NSG) was formed by officials from nuclear exporting countries. They agreed to voluntarily restrict nuclear trade in sensitive technologies, but their rules were lax, and in any case compliance was not mandatory. Meanwhile, as late as 2006, after the discovery of illicit bomb programs in Iraq, North Korea, and Libya and the near certainty of one in Iran, the IAEA still devoted only slightly more than a third of its $270 million budget to nuclear verification, or safeguards, activities. Nearly the same amount, $90 million, was earmarked for programs directly related to nuclear promotion, and another $50 million for administrative functions. About 8 percent, or $22 million, was devoted to nuclear safety and security, including radioactive waste management.

The treaty set up a more or less permanent forum for the struggle between haves and have-nots, while offering no respite from the arms race because there was no timetable for disarmament. The split between arms controllers and nonproliferators meant that at NPT review conferences, delegates from the weapons states were not necessarily in a position to offer progress on disarmament as an inducement for stronger safeguards because they had no voice on it within their own governments. As a State Department official with long experience in nonproliferation explained: "Arms controllers have their own world, and their world is 'what can we do in terms of negotiations with our enemy to make our own security safer?' That's sort of disconnected from the people who worry about nonproliferation. They don't turn to us for our views on how big the stockpile should be or whether we should have bunker busters."

Meanwhile, the people who talked about MIRVs and ICBMs did so within the closed framework of the superpower rivalry and the aftermath of the cold war. Possibly there was no other way. On the other hand, had the arms controllers remained more engaged with the nonproliferators, they might have been better able to leverage stockpile cuts when they finally came up against demands for greater access to technology by countries seeking to build their own stockpiles. Trivedi had made his timetable proposal, but he had been ignored. And life went on in Vienna, where it was easy to cross the thin line between the civilian and military sides of nuclear and not be noticed.

CHAPTER 13

Golda's Visit
to the White House

B Y GOLDA MEIR'S ACCOUNT, the summer of 1969 had been a hellish one. Her enemies had banded together and were attacking from across the Jordanian border—she counted ninety-eight shelling incidents in July alone. Not only were Iraqi and Saudi Arabian forces inside Jordan, the Syrians had moved in with long-range guns. The Israeli leader reckoned that Jordan's King Hussein had lost control of his borders. Making matters worse for the Israeli leader, Soviet leader Leonid Brezhnev had sent a message to Egypt's Gamal Abdel Nasser promising him whatever military equipment he needed to fight the Israelis.

So why, asked Golda Meir, was the United States government asking for another inspection of the Dimona nuclear plant? "The U.S. ought to have more things to do at such a time than search Israel for atomic bombs," the sturdily built Israeli leader said in so many words to the American ambassador, Walworth Barbour, who paraphrased the July 31 conversation in a telex back to Washington.[1]

But it was precisely the combination of escalating regional tensions and the near-certain knowledge that Israel had crossed the nuclear threshold that had led to Barbour's request. In a memorandum to President Richard M. Nixon July 19, 1969, two weeks before Barbour's meeting with Meir, Henry Kissinger warned, "The Israelis, who are one of the few peoples whose survival is genuinely threatened, are probably more likely than almost any other country to actually use their nuclear weapons." Moreover, the national security adviser noted, "there is cir-

cumstantial evidence that some fissionable material available for Israel's weapons development was illegally obtained from the United
States in about 1965 . . . This is one program on which the Israelis have
persistently deceived us and may even have stolen from us."[2]

Confronted by evidence that Israel had nuclear weapons and that
the United States might have been an unwitting accomplice to the
effort, Kissinger had in April launched a highly secret policy debate
among a small group of senior officials. Their mission was to determine whether it was feasible, or even possible, for the U.S. government
to try to prevent Israel from becoming what it had already effectively
become—a state in possession of nuclear weapons. Alternatively, and
more realistically as far as both Nixon and Kissinger were concerned,
these officials were to consider ways in which the United States could
live with a nuclear-armed Israel. This second option was immensely
complex. How could the United States promote the Non-Proliferation
Treaty while appearing to sanction Israeli nuclear weapons? And how
could it avoid the appearance of U.S. complicity in the Israeli nuclear
program?

The thorny issues facing the Nixon administration, and the manner
in which they would be resolved, were the culmination of more than
two decades of international tolerance, and enabling, of the Israeli nuclear project. They came to a head just as the United States was embarked on an effort to convince the rest of the world to sign the NPT.
While Nixon and Kissinger were lukewarm on the treaty, they were not
willing to publicly abandon it, and yet they faced this vexing problem
over Israel. In a broader sense, the Israeli situation demonstrated the
enormous stakes of the nuclear game each time they were raised.
Governments had to weigh the consequences of emerging weapons
states against their own relationships with the countries in question as
well as their other political and commercial aims. Part of the calculation involved assessing the likelihood of being able to stop a weapons
program once it had gained traction, and what it would take to do it. De
Gaulle tried and failed to prevent Israel making nuclear weapons, because the promises he secured were ignored. He thought he had stopped
French participation at Dimona in 1960, but French contractors remained on site, at least until the nuclear fuel was delivered and the reactor went critical in 1964.[3]   *Accd*

American U-2 planes had been capturing images of activity in the
Negev since 1958, the year that hundreds of workers began laying the

foundations of Ben-Gurion's most prized desert project. To questions
about the effort, the Israelis gave various explanations. Dimona was
described as a textile plant, an agricultural station, and a metallurgical research facility. Finally, in December 1960, Ben-Gurion stated
that Dimona was a nuclear research center. But he said it would be
used for peaceful purposes, which was another way of saying he would
abide by the rules.[4]

In truth, Israel had been embarked on a mission to develop nuclear
weapons. When the NPT was agreed in 1968, Israel, like every other
country embarked on clandestine weapons development, had choices
in the way it could go about it. A country could sign the treaty and
cheat on it, as Iraq would do. Or it could opt out of the treaty, like India, adhere to the rules that existed prior to the treaty, and achieve its
aim. Or it could remain on the periphery of the system as a member of
the IAEA, but little else, and engage in subterfuge and possibly even
criminal behavior to accomplish its purpose. That choice was Israel's.
The full story of how Israel played the game is still not known, in part
because its government to this day does not officially admit to the existence of its nuclear weapons, but also because the people who assisted the Israeli effort had much to lose—possibly even their lives—if
their roles were fully revealed.

Israel is in a situation like no other country in the world. Surrounded by enemies in its immediate neighborhood, it could nevertheless reach out for help to a strong network of political and financial
backers in Europe and the United States. These connections were immensely important to the nuclear weapons effort. Israel also is the
only country in which the question of collective guilt for the crimes
of the Holocaust played a role in the decision by other countries to
lend nuclear assistance, dating back to the French, British, and Norwegian efforts in the late 1950s and early 1960s. Otherwise, the story
of how Israel acquired nuclear weapons is a case study of the means by
which countries can exploit weaknesses in the "safeguards" system,
poor monitoring, existing supply lines, access to wealth and power,
and geopolitical relations, to get what they want.

Israel was a founding member of the IAEA, and that was useful for
keeping up contacts and an outward appearance of respectability in
the nuclear world. But to achieve its aims, Israel faced enormous challenges. It needed fissile material, and that initially required uranium,
which Israel lacked. It had a reprocessing plant but that may have had

technical problems. Enriching uranium was another potential route to securing bomb-grade material, and while Israel had the know-how, it needed to find suppliers to build a plant. Finally, if Israeli scientists and engineers succeeded in building a nuclear weapon, how could they test it without being found out? Opacity, as Avner Cohen notes in his book on the Israeli bomb program, was crucial to the effort. By refusing to admit it had a bomb program, Israel hoped to discourage other states in the region from developing their own nuclear weapons.

Nothing would stop Israel's own pursuit of that objective, however. In the 1960s, that effort extended to abducting a nuclear engineer in West Germany in order to obtain more information about uranium enrichment and equipment supplier names. It also may have included the theft of American bomb-grade nuclear fuel as mentioned by Kissinger, and did involve an elaborate undercover operation to obtain uranium from Europe. Finally, most experts agree that the Israelis joined with the South Africans to test its weapons off the South Atlantic in 1979, in violation of the Limited Test Ban Treaty, which Israel had signed in 1964. These illustrate major weaknesses in the nonproliferation system that, in theory, any country or terrorist group with the means could exploit, to do just what Israel did.

While all this went on, the United States adjusted, and readjusted, its sights. How, after all, should it respond to what it knew was happening? Each new entrant to the nuclear weapons club would over time pose the same conundrum. Could they be stopped? Should they be stopped? And if so, how? In Israel's case, accommodation became the easiest way out, but there would be a price to pay for that, in Iraq, then in Libya, and more recently in Iran. But it also added to reasons for restraint against India, and hence Pakistan, after those countries joined the club, because any other response would have raised questions about the treatment of Israel.

CONCERNS ABOUT AN Israeli bomb program date back to the final years of the Eisenhower administration. A British newspaper broke the story in December 1960 and shortly afterward, the AEC chairman, John McCone, leaked a story to the *New York Times* revealing that U.S. officials were "studying with mounting concern recent evidence indicating that Israel, with assistance from France, may be developing the capacity to produce nuclear weapons."[5]

On January 6, 1961, Dimona was the subject of discussion at a closed session of the Senate Foreign Relations Committee, where Eisenhower's secretary of state, Christian Herter, was giving his final briefing. According to a transcript of the meeting, declassified in 1984, Bourke B. Hickenlooper, who also was chairman of the Joint Committee on Atomic Energy, used the occasion to vent a considerable amount of anger over the subject. "I think the Israelis have just lied to us like horse thieves on this thing," the conservative Iowa Republican said. "They have completely distorted, misrepresented, and falsified the facts in the past. I think it is very serious . . . to have them perform in this manner in connection with this very definite production reactor facility which they have been secretly building, and which they have consistently, and with a completely straight face, denied to us they were building."[6]

All of that was basically true, but Herter, probably wanting to leave his watch with the situation under some semblance of control, had been pressing Ben-Gurion, Israel's prime minister, to allow in American inspectors. This seemed a good way out of the problem. If everything was as innocent as the Israeli leader claimed, the inspectors could verify that and thus put at ease both the public and Israel's increasingly nervous neighbors—in particular, Egypt—who might have nuclear ambitions of their own.

On January 19, 1961, the day of the Eisenhower administration briefing with the president-elect, Herter sent a secret report to the joint committee. It said that the United States had been assured at the "highest level of the Israeli government that Israel has no plans for the production of nuclear weapons." Furthermore, the report said, "we have been assured that Israel will be glad to receive visits by scientists from friendly countries at the Dimona reactor."[7]

It is doubtful that Herter believed Israel's claim. Not only had he advised Kennedy and his closest advisers to keep a close eye on both Israel and India, he had also urged the new president to make Israel follow through on its promise of allowing in inspectors. But the ambiguity of the Israeli program at that early stage made it relatively easy for the outgoing administration to accept Israel's claims of innocence. Ben-Gurion reluctantly granted Herter his wish, but the question was whether the inspectors would really be able to see anything. The answer, in a nutshell, was no. Inspections would be carried out on Israeli terms, under conditions of strictest secrecy, and for the next several years the American inspectors would find no evidence of a bomb program. In part this was because the Israelis went to great lengths to hide it—for example, installing false control room panels and bricking over elevators and hallways that led to areas they did not want the inspectors to see. But the other reason was that the American government really did not want to know what was going on. By 1969, when the last inspection took place, the team had "drawn the inference that the U.S. government is not prepared to support a real 'inspection' effort in which the team members can feel authorized to ask directly pertinent questions and/or insist on being allowed to look at records, logs, materials and the like," according to a State Department memorandum written in August of that year.[8]

IN THE INTERVENING period, Israel's secret service, Mossad, had stepped in to assist the scientists at Dimona to obtain the material and information they needed to achieve their objectives. The tactics, judging by what is known about them, were worthy of Hollywood. Israeli agents began tracking an Austrian-born engineer named Gernot Zippe, who was developing state-of-the-art centrifuges—electrically driven cylinders spinning at high speeds—for enriching uranium. Zippe, who had been a glider pilot and a member of the Luftwaffe, had been a leader of the team of war prisoners in the Soviet Union that invented early models of these machines. Although uranium enrichment, one route to the bomb, was evidently not as important to the Israelis as plutonium production—the path favored by the French—the attention directed toward Zippe demonstrated interest and supports other evidence of an active uranium enrichment program within the Israeli nuclear establishment.[9] It also is not surprising since most, if not all, weapons programs, particularly in their early stages, follow this dual course to obtain fissile material.

I reached Zippe, now mostly deaf, at his home near Munich. He had for years kept the story about what happened to him secret, possibly fearing for his life if he said anything. But word of his coerced meetings with the Israelis had quietly circulated in recent years, and he decided to respond to my questions in writing by facsimile: "I was tricked into a meeting with Israeli agents and scientists by an Austrian agent who approached me as an expert on glider flying but actually wanted me to

come to Egypt on gas centrifuges, what [sic] I refused to do. The same
agent later changed sides and organized my first meeting with the Israelis in a hotel in Brussels."[10]

Mossad agents and Israeli scientists were present at the meetings,
according to Zippe. They took place in late 1964 or early 1965—Zippe
could not remember the exact dates. The agent who initially approached Zippe, although identifying himself as a representative of
the Egyptian government, may in fact have been working for Mossad
all along, Zippe believes. Zippe was forced to assure the Israelis that
he would never provide his centrifuge knowledge to the Egyptians. He
wrote that he was also pressured into providing the names of centrifuge equipment suppliers, ostensibly so the Israelis could keep an
eye on the companies and prevent any equipment getting to Egypt.
However, over the course of several meetings, Zippe realized the Israelis wanted the information for their own program. He developed an
impression, he wrote, that they knew "how to build centrifuges and
how to handle the theory of mechanics and separation."

With demands for further meetings, Zippe became increasingly uncomfortable and looked for a way out. Fortunately for him, Germany
and Israel were moving to establish diplomatic relations, and when
they were formalized May 12, 1965, he had the protection he needed
because he was employed by the German government. Henceforth, the
Mossad agents could not question him without going through proper
government channels. "I requested to stop our meetings and [for them
to] seek further information through official diplomatic channels," he
wrote. "The Israelis agreed and I promised not to report about our [ear-
lier] meetings."[11]

BUT WHAT IS known in the spy trade as the "soft" approach, which
Zippe described, evidently was only the beginning. As tensions in the
Middle East escalated, the bomb program in the Negev went into high
gear, and efforts to secure fissile material evidently became more aggressive. In two well-reported incidents, the Israelis allegedly arranged
for the "disappearance" of more than two hundred pounds of bomb-
grade uranium from a nuclear fuel plant in Pennsylvania, and a few
years later the hijacking of natural uranium from Europe. The case involving the Nuclear Materials and Equipment Corporation (NUMEC)
plant in Pennsylvania has never been proved, but at the time the alle-

gations first surfaced in 1966, the Central Intelligence Agency took
them very seriously. A report by the CIA's deputy director for science
and technology, Carl Duckett, in 1968 argued the NUMEC affair was
one strand of evidence supporting his judgment, which later proved
correct, that Israel already had nuclear weapons.

When CIA director Richard Helms brought Duckett's report to
Johnson that same year, the president exploded and reportedly told
him not to tell anyone, not even Dean Rusk, the secretary of state, or
Defense Secretary Robert McNamara.[12] Johnson wanted to hide what
Helms had told him about the probable existence of Israeli weapons
because if it had been revealed, the information could have undermined or even derailed the Non-Proliferation Treaty, then nearly
ready for signing. "A public revelation would have shown that previous U.S. 'visits' to Israeli nuclear facilities—to make sure they were
not supporting bomb work—were a farce, and that U.S. assurances on
this point to Arab countries were false," said Victor Gilinsky, a former Nuclear Regulatory Commission member who studied the affair
in detail during a lengthy agency probe in 1976.[13]

Gilinsky, who was a rising star at RAND when the incident was
first reported, believes that the "real reason for the hyper-secrecy"
was Duckett's information about missing material in Pennsylvania,
enough, he had said, for four nuclear weapons of crude design. Had the
allegations ever been proven, not only would NUMEC's owner, Zal-
man Shapiro, and possibly other NUMEC officials have faced severe
penalties, the repercussions for the American government, let alone
Israel, would have been enormous. "In the Israeli case, American officials started by wishing away the obvious and progressed to hiding
deep inside the government what they knew was politically explosive," Gilinsky wrote.[14]

Only recently, a 1976 memorandum to President Gerald R. Ford by
Attorney General Edward H. Levi surfaced, suggesting the possibility
of criminal violations in the NUMEC affair.[15] Levi, who was preparing
to give congressional testimony on government oversight of nuclear
materials, requested a Federal Bureau of Investigation report on NU-
MEC. He attached the FBI document, dated April 22, 1976, to his
memo to President Ford of the same day, in which he wrote that the
FBI did not conduct an investigation into the alleged discrepancy at
NUMEC at the time "because it was advised by the AEC that any loss
likely was attributable to inadequate accounting procedures and that

there was no evidence or suspicion of a violation of law. Since no investigation was undertaken, the Department of Justice cannot state that there is no evidence which would support a criminal charge."

Levi then proceeded to state a list of ten possible violations of the Atomic Energy Act and criminal statutes that might have been committed. Two involved unauthorized dealing in special nuclear material and transportation of dangerous articles. Three others suggested the involvement of one or more government officials, listing as possible violations accessory after the fact, misprision of felony (which means concealing knowledge of a felony, usually by an official), and conspiracy. Such a suspect would almost certainly have been in the AEC.

Levi called for an investigation on the basis that the statute of limitations might not have run out on those against whom charges might be brought, noting that section 2271 of the Atomic Energy Act provides that "the Federal Bureau of Investigation of the Department of Justice shall investigate all alleged or suspected criminal violations" of the act.

Gilinsky, apparently the first to discuss Levi's memorandum in print, wrote: "The attorney general was telling the president there might at that time still have been persons employed by the federal government that may have earlier 'participated in or concealed' offenses related to the misappropriation of nuclear material from Numec."[16] If an investigation ever took place, the results were not publicly revealed. Moreover, several key documents related to the NUMEC case remain classified. Gilinsky has requested their declassification, but the answer so far, he says, has been "Items denied in full."[17]

THE NUMEC BOMB-GRADE uranium is believed to have disappeared in 1963 or 1964, when the Israelis were uncertain about their ability to produce fissile material fast enough for the bombs they so desperately wanted. Almost certainly the Dimona reprocessing plant was not yet operating in any reliable fashion either. That seems to have occurred in 1966, although the facility's output at that time is not publicly known. If there was any enrichment capability, it was probably only in the form of a pilot facility.

By May 1967, with the Egyptian and Israeli armies poised to strike at each other, the situation was far more tense than usual. Egyptian fighter planes had been flying over Dimona since 1961, a sure sign Israel's enemy knew what was going on in the desert; once again on

May 17 two Russian-built Egyptian high-altitude reconnaissance MiG jets made the pass without being intercepted.[18]

In Washington, CIA director Helms assured a National Security Council meeting on May 24 that he "was quite positive in stating there were no nuclear weapons in the area." In fact, Israel was only days away from proving him wrong.[19]

Five days later, on May 29, just prior to the outbreak of the Six Day War, Israel assembled its first nuclear weapon. Cohen records the chilling scene in his book, quoting from a diary entry of one of the key scientists:

> The time was after midnight. Engineers and technicians, mostly young, were concentrating on their actions. Their facial expression[s] [were] solemn, inward, as if they fully recognized the enormous, perhaps fateful, value of the weapons system that they [had] brought to operational alert. It was evident that the people of the project were under tension, the utmost tension, physical and spiritual alike.[20]

Cohen, an Israeli with unusually good access to people involved with the program, wrote originally that two bombs were assembled and made operational that night, suggesting they contained plutonium rather than highly enriched uranium; however, he later learned there may have been as many as five or six and did not know for certain whether they were all made of plutonium.[21] On the question of whether NUMEC material ever made its way into the basement that night Cohen is conspicuously silent, as he also is about the theft of natural uranium from Europe and the 1979 tests off the coast of South Africa.[22]

On June 5, 1967, the Israeli air force launched an attack on Egypt's poorly defended airfields and destroyed its air force. By the end of the conflict, Israel had gained control of the Sinai Peninsula, the Gaza Strip, the West Bank, and the Golan Heights. Afterward, according to Cohen's account, the Israelis discovered that Egypt had put Dimona and another nuclear research facility at Hachal Soreq on its high-priority target list.[23] Nuclear weapons were never used, but the nuclear element played a role in the war, he points out.

While officials in Washington publicly denied knowledge of Israeli nuclear weapons, Nasser was not fooled; nor, evidently, was the average

Arab citizen. "It was common knowledge in the Arab world that Israel had a bomb, especially after the 1967 war," says George Hishmeh, a Washington-based columnist for *Gulf News* and the *Jordan Times*. "The feeling was the [Israeli] government would be unlikely to use one because of the proximity of Arab capitals like Beirut, Damascus, Cairo, and Amman to its own major cities—they would be showered with fallout as well."[24]

BY 1968, THE Israeli scientists needed more uranium to use as fuel in their plutonium production reactor at Dimona. To get it, Mossad would conduct one of its most daring nuclear operations to date, hijacking two hundred tons of natural uranium—enough to make plutonium for roughly twenty bombs—from Europe. The operation, code-named Plumbat (*plumbum* means lead in Latin), was designed to exploit Europe's weak safeguards system and secure uranium without leaving any footprints. Already facing difficult negotiations over the NPT, the Israeli government knew discovery of the transaction would raise suspicions. Among other things, it would have signaled to experts that the Dimona reactor was running many times over its claimed twenty-four megawatt capacity to secure more plutonium.

Obtaining the material by stealth was Israel's only option. This was accomplished by arranging for its purchase through a German front company, which plausibly claimed it was needed as a catalyst to accelerate chemical reactions for planned petrochemical production. First, though, the uranium needed to be shipped from the Belgian port of Antwerp to Genoa, Italy, and taken to a plant near Milan for processing. Having secured Euratom's approval for the transaction relatively easily, Mossad made arrangements for the uranium-laden ship that left Antwerp in November 1968 to rendezvous with an Israeli freighter in the eastern Mediterranean. There, somewhere between Cyprus and the coast of Turkey, with two gunboats providing protection, the uranium was transferred to the other vessel. One day later, on December 3, 1968, the Israelis had their uranium.[25]

Euratom soon realized that the uranium had disappeared, but it took another five years to confirm suspicions that Israel had been its final destination. In many people's minds, the disappearance of the uranium in Europe echoed the alleged shipment of bomb-grade uranium from the NUMEC plant in Pennsylvania. Barring a confession or some other evidence, the earlier diversion, if it occurred, may never be proven. But with its taint of possible criminality, it revealed not only shoddy monitoring practices but the lengths to which the U.S. government would go to protect Israel. Meanwhile, the poor bookkeeping could have also been intentional, making it difficult to prove or disprove allegations of an illegal diversion.

IN WASHINGTON THE guessing game over Israel's nuclear intentions had by 1969 reached a point of hand-wringing absurdity—no one wanted to admit the obvious. Policy-makers convinced themselves that the Israelis would stop short of assembling weapons, instead retaining a nuclear "option"—meaning they had the capability to assemble a weapon within six months if necessary. Gilinsky, still at RAND, said he told National Security Council senior staffer Morton H. Halperin that it was "inconceivable" the Israelis would opt for this course because they would never know for certain they could do it. But for U.S. policy makers believing in the "option" was another way of avoiding the uncomfortable truth. As Gilinsky put it, "We really wanted to be deluded because the consequences were so horrible [and] they didn't know what to do."[26]

Yet by the time this exchange took place, the evidence the Israelis had weapons was so overwhelming that Kissinger, for one, recognized something had to be done about it. The Israelis had been moving aggressively to advance their delivery capability, with aerial exercises and missile deployments that could only be related to nuclear weaponry.[27]

In April, Kissinger launched a highly secret policy debate, known as NSSM 40 (the acronym is for National Security Study Memorandum), into how the United States should respond to the situation. Officials debated the pros and cons of withholding a delivery of F-4 Phantom jet fighters that could be adjusted to fit nuclear weapons, hoping that would result in Israel's signature on the NPT, although that was not regarded as a realistic option. For one thing, the same threat had been tried in the waning days of the Johnson administration, and when it did not work, Johnson had insisted on the contract going through anyway.

By July 1969, Nixon had signaled he was "leery" of using it again. Nixon and Kissinger were not big fans of the NPT and were extremely cynical about the chances of Israel signing it. In Kissinger's hardball view of the world, the NPT was both ineffectual and undesirable. He told two of his staff in the early days of the administration that any country with major security issues would try to get the bomb and the United States should not interfere. Kissinger wanted a bilateral understanding on Israel's nuclear intentions because he did not regard the NPT as precise enough and because the Phantom aircraft were potential nuclear weapons carriers.[28]

Kissinger's push for a "bilateral understanding" became absolutely critical in the weeks leading up to Meir's state visit. Three topics were on the table: the meaning of Israel's long-standing pledge not to "introduce" weapons to the Middle East, its status with respect to the NPT, and its plans for Jericho missiles that had been ordered from the French firm Daussalt and test-fired on French sites.

Only in 2006 were the first documents related to these secret discussions finally released.[29] More came into the public domain the following year. Yet the most important papers, related to a meeting that took place on September 26, 1969, between Meir and Nixon—at which not even Kissinger was present—are still missing from the official files; possibly there are none, because the meeting and whatever was decided apparently was not recorded. But it was at this summit that some kind of understanding almost certainly was reached.[30]

On the eve of Meir's visit, the State Department prepared a background paper, concluding that Israel might very well now have a nuclear bomb and drawing up a wish list: Nixon should press the Israeli leader for assurances that "Israel would not possess nuclear weapons, would sign the NPT, and would not deploy missiles."[31]

The day of the summit, Nixon welcomed the Israeli leader at a small ceremony on the White House lawn. While the president spoke into a microphone, the short, wrinkled seventy-year-old grandmother stood to one side, her ample figure corseted in a light-colored suit with short sleeves and cloth-covered buttons. Regarded then as a stopgap leader who would be pushed aside when the right man came along, Golda Meir was only beginning to assert her authority. Her wiry hair pulled back into a braided arrangement, Meir would defend her country's right to its "secret" stash of nuclear weapons as if she were protecting her offspring.

Nixon, with his near-diabolically complex mind, admired her; her relations with Kissinger were more prickly, but he would not be there to interfere during the private meeting in the Oval Office. And it was during this exchange that the State Department advice was quietly put to one side, subsequent documents indicate, and the Israeli leader pretty much got what she had come for—delivery of the Phantoms and no commitment on the NPT. She agreed to hold off deploying the missiles for three years. Finally, the haranguing and the inspections would end.

In return, the Israelis would promise restraint in the nuclear area. That meant keeping its national survival program under wraps—no testing, no declaration, and no visibility. The two leaders apparently also reached some kind of understanding over issues of procedure and communication, possibly setting up direct channels between their offices to bypass their foreign policy establishments.[32]

under Golda, not Menachem

BY THE TIME the summit took place, it had become plain to U.S. policy-makers that the Israelis interpreted "nonintroduction" to mean they could possess nuclear weapons as long as they did not test them, deploy them, or make them public. The United States, on the other hand, had long made it clear to the Israelis that mere possession constituted introduction, and that it would be cause to cancel the F-4 contract.[33] But that had been earlier, before Nixon decided he would let the Phantom deal go forward and made his secret deal with Meir.

When Yitzhak Rabin, then Israel's foreign minister, visited Kissinger in his office the following February to talk about the NPT, he couched what he knew would be bad news in light of the Nixon-Meir "understanding," of which neither man evidently could be absolutely certain. "Israel has no intention to sign the NPT," Kissinger wrote to Nixon after the meeting. Rabin, he said, "wanted also to make sure there was no misapprehension at the White House about Israel's current intentions." Rabin seemed to be telegraphing Israel's intentions of keeping its nuclear program clothed in ambiguity while seeking American assurances that arms sales to Israel would continue.

That February exchange, even more than the September meeting, is now considered the end point of a decade-long effort to curb the Israeli nuclear program. It could also be viewed as the moment in which de facto tolerance for Israeli nuclear weapons finally became policy. Subsequently, the White House decided to end the annual "inspections" at Dimona.

In Congress, America's willingness to tolerate Israel's nuclear weapons—by 1976 the CIA was estimating there were ten—crossed party lines, which helped ensure that legislation was written in a way that protected the Jewish state. For example, when lawmakers approved punitive measures for nuclear testing by other countries in 1977 in response to the 1974 Indian nuclear explosion, they included a provision specifically intended to protect Israel in the event she decided to follow India's example. This came in the form of a provision for a presidential waiver of the requirement for a cutoff in U.S. military and financial assistance. "When that amendment was written and being discussed at the staff level I recall expressions of concern as to whether a cutoff for exploding a nuclear weapon should be taken out in order to maintain Israel's option without a threat of losing U.S. support," said Leonard Weiss, who drafted the amendment while working for Senator John Glenn, the Republican astronaut from Ohio, as the staff director of both the Senate Subcommittee on Energy and Nuclear Proliferation and the Committee on Governmental Affairs. "It was left in because I explained that there was a presidential waiver of the cutoff, and everyone assumed that the waiver would be granted for Israel."[34]

When Israel reportedly conducted a series of nuclear tests, with the help of the South Africans, two years later, U.S. protectiveness continued. The test team, believed to have consisted of both Israeli and South African officials, had been unlucky. On the morning of September 22, 1979, the cloud cover they had counted on to hide one of the tests suddenly broke, and two bright flashes went through to the upper atmosphere, where an American Vela satellite picked up the evidence and relayed it back to the United States. It had been ten years since Nixon's secret deal with Meir. Now, a new president, Jimmy Carter, was in a serious bind. If Israel was conclusively determined to have been behind the event, it would be liable for a cutoff under the recently passed legislation; moreover, it would be in violation of the 1963 Limited Test Ban Treaty, which it had signed and ratified, requiring action in the United Nations.

Carter appointed a panel of experts to investigate the possibility that the flashes were caused by some other atmospheric disturbance. Ten months later the group, headed by an MIT professor named Jack P. Ruina, presented conclusions in line with what the administration would have wanted. A nuclear test could not be ruled out, the report said, but "the panel considers it more likely that the signal was one of the zoo events [a signal of unknown cause], possibly a consequence of the impact of a small meteoroid on the satellite."[35]

Within the administration, members of the Nuclear Intelligence Panel, consisting of nuclear scientists and professional bomb-makers, did their own study and concluded just the opposite, that it was a nuclear explosion, but they were ordered by the White House not to discuss their findings. Carter's line on the event was that the alleged test was "unconfirmed" and that the South Africans denied involvement. To the extent possible, Israel was kept out of the discussions. Today, opinion among nuclear experts is almost universally that Israeli nuclear weapons were the cause of the bright flashes.

AFTER THREE DECADES of obfuscation, secret meetings, and separate rooms, irrefutable evidence of the Israeli bomb program was splashed across the front pages of the London *Sunday Times* on October 5, 1986. The paper obtained it from a Moroccan-born Jew (who converted to Christianity the same year) named Mordechai Vanunu. He had worked as a technician for nearly ten years in Machon 2, a top secret underground bunker built to provide the components necessary for weapons production at Dimona. In November 1985, he was made redundant along with 180 other workers as part of a cost-cutting drive, although security officials had long been concerned about Vanunu's political contacts with West Bank Arab students at Beersheba University, where he was taking a philosophy course.

After he lost his job, Vanunu left Israel with a cache of negatives and documents he had obtained while he was employed that would stun the world. He eventually ended up in Australia, where he first met *Sunday Times* reporter Peter Hounam, who would break the story. Vanunu's next stop was London. There he was debriefed by experts the paper had contacted in order to verify the information. They calculated that at least one hundred and as many as two hundred nuclear weapons of varying destructive capability had been assembled—many times the previously estimated amounts. Moreover, the Israelis were producing deuterium and lithium, evidence they had been at work on thermonuclear, or boosted fission weapons.

"There should no longer be any doubt that Israel is, and for at least a decade has been, a fully-fledged nuclear weapons state," the former American weapons designer Theodore Taylor told the paper after looking at the evidence. "The Israeli nuclear weapons programme is considerably more advanced than indicated by any previous report or conjectures of which I am aware." In Britain, Frank Barnaby, who like Taylor had turned away from weapons work and was focused on proliferation, said, "As a nuclear physicist it was clear to me that details he gave me were scientifically accurate and clearly showed that he had not only worked on these processes but knew the details of the techniques. Also the flow rates through the [reprocessing] plant, which he quotes exactly confirm the quantities of plutonium that were being made."[36]

Vanunu disappeared on September 30, five days before the story appeared. Lured to Rome by a Mossad agent named "Cindy," he was then bundled into a car, sped to the coast, and taken on a fishing boat back to Israel. He was charged with espionage and other crimes and barred from testifying in his own defense, evidently for fear he would reveal more state secrets. He spent the next eighteen years in prison, at least twelve of them in solitary, where the lights were kept on twenty-four hours a day. Before he made the decision to go public, Vanunu told an interviewer that he had asked himself whether he was ready to sacrifice his freedom and possibly his life to do it. In the end, he said, he felt "glad and happy" he had because "my mission was accomplished." Nevertheless, for eighteen years he lived "like a man in a train station, waiting for a train to take me."[37]

While he languished in prison, the mainstream media in the United States tended to ignore or marginalize Vanunu and the issue of Israeli nuclear weapons. However, a number of peace groups rallied to his cause, and the European Parliament on numerous occasions called for his release. Joseph Rotblat, who himself left a bomb project to save the world from a nuclear holocaust, repeatedly proposed Vanunu for the Nobel Peace Prize.[38] He was supported in that effort by other members of Pugwash and by the Norwegian Peace Bureau.

Upon his release in 2004, Vanunu was granted sanctuary in an Anglican cathedral complex in Jerusalem and received a letter of support from Rowan Williams, the archbishop of Canterbury. But he was under house arrest, barred from leaving Israel, banned from talking to journalists, and subjected to further investigations and charges—despite numerous pleas to allow him to leave the country. In 2007, he was sentenced to a further six months in jail for violating the terms of his parole. A justice minister told the BBC that Vanunu is a "born traitor," someone who "even betrayed his synagogue" and is "hell bent to harm this country. He hates this country."

Vanunu does not look at it that way. "It's not about betraying, it is about reporting, about saving Israel from a new holocaust," he told the BBC in 2004. "I am a symbol of the human spirit. You cannot destroy the human spirit."[39]

Israel has remained largely unmoved by these arguments, and in the two decades since the story appeared there has been little change in its official position. Like much else about the nuclear story, the problem of Israeli nuclear weapons has been left to fester, while other countries in the Middle East sought to equalize the situation by acquiring their own nuclear weapons. As the Bush era drew to a close in 2008 and the Iranians boldly continued a uranium enrichment program in defiance of international sanctions and threats of military action by the United States or Israel, the rest of the world awaited a denouement. Would an Iranian bomb be next, or another war in the Middle East, this time a nuclear war? Is this the way the world ends?

CHAPTER 14

That's the Way
We Play the Game

FIVE YEARS AFTER GOLDA MEIR's meeting with Nixon, when India exploded its first nuclear weapon in May 1974, the Washington press corps naturally turned its attention to the White House for comment. But the real action was a few blocks away in the offices of Edlow International. A year earlier, Sam Edlow's son Jack had flown to Tennessee for what was no ordinary meeting. Two men from India's Atomic Energy Commission had wanted to talk to him about shipping nuclear fuel from the United States to India. "They were living in a rooming house with one bedroom that had two beds," the younger Edlow, then twenty-five, recalled. "They cooked on an electric plate. I don't know what I expected. I sat in their room while they ate their food and struck a deal to ship fuel to India."[1]

By coincidence, on the day Indians conducted their test, the Edlows' first Indian fuel consignment was on a truck somewhere between Tennessee and the port of New York. Its ultimate destination was the site of the General Electric nuclear plant at the industrial town of Tarapur in northwest India near Bombay, birthplace of Homi Bhabha, the father of the Indian nuclear program, who had died eight years earlier in a plane crash.

Aware of the shipment, AEC officials were quietly wringing their hands. They knew that by allowing it to go through they risked undermining the Non-Proliferation Treaty, which they were still trying to persuade other nations to sign. How could the United States justify continuing its nuclear trade with India when the treaty's very purpose—to stop other nations acquiring nuclear weapons—had just been so flagrantly ignored? Yet as time went on and these same officials found themselves embroiled in an enormous political controversy over nuclear trade with India, the argument was turned on its head: U.S. influence in India would be completely lost, they would maintain, if export approvals were terminated. This was a spurious contention in one way, because it was precisely the kind of thinking that had led to the problem in the first place. Nevertheless it highlighted the conundrum—could nuclear energy be developed and at the same time effectively controlled?

For India, the Tarapur shipments were critical because the country did not have the capability at the time to enrich uranium; nor did it have much in the way of indigenous natural uranium. Realizing all this, an AEC official called Sam Edlow after learning about the explosion and told him he should have the truck turned around and returned to Tennessee with the Indian fuel. Edlow refused, saying that he had an export license and that in order for him to comply with the request the AEC would have to rescind the licence.

"I was blunt," Edlow wrote in an unpublished memoir. "No cancel the export license, out it goes . . . After all, that's the way we play the game."[2]

THE AEC LICENSE was not rescinded, but for the next eight years, the issue of nuclear fuel shipments to Tarapur would become the focal point of a hugely contentious debate over India's nuclear program and America's role in it, and a much wider debate about the dangers of nuclear proliferation. It resulted in a congressional effort to strengthen the nonproliferation regime by passing the 1978 Nuclear Nonproliferation Act (NNPA). At the core of the controversy was the interplay between the civilian and military sides of nuclear, an ambiguity that India had clearly exploited to her advantage.

As Kissinger had noted in his discussions about Israel, the Non-Proliferation Treaty lacked precision, which meant that countries like India, if they had chosen to join, could have used its membership like a good conduct pass for securing the technology, equipment, and material they needed to secretly develop nuclear weapons. But India chose to play the game a different way. If Israel, also a nonsignatory, behaved like a gangster to achieve its aims, India was something of a coy mistress. Her leaders were seductive, their arguments compelling, and they presented endless opportunities for making (and spending) money. India's debate over nuclear weapons had largely been with itself and its long pacifist tradition, but when it conducted its first nuclear test the whole world had something to say.

Reaction to the event was mixed. Government leaders in many countries viewed it as a flagrant challenge to the treaty; Indian officials would counter that they could not violate something they had not agreed to. Moreover, they propounded the wily explanation that the test was no more than the culmination of a peaceful program of the kind Seaborg had advanced with proposals for blasting tunnels and river channels using nuclear explosives. To India's nuclear people and those in other developing countries, the 1974 explosion was a real achievement, a milestone in the developing world's race to catch up with the West.

Two months after the test, in July, Jack Edlow traveled to India for discussions about future fuel shipments to Tarapur. In Bombay, Edlow met India's new atomic leader, Homi Sethna. Sethna explained the rationale behind the test. "He impressed me because the one thing I remember him saying was they were a sovereign nation with eight hundred million people with a right to protect themselves, with China and Pakistan on their borders," Edlow recalled. "I felt they were right because after all we wanted it [the bomb] to protect ourselves from the Germans. He was saying the Americans didn't want the Indians to have it because they were people of a different color. I was impressed by that comment that they deserved it as much as we did."

The argument that India "deserved" weapons of mass destruction was in reality self-serving. India's military had been largely absent from the formative stages of nuclear decision-making, and influential members of its ruling class, including government leaders, had opposed nuclear weapons on both moral and strategic grounds. Instead, the push for nuclear weapons came from an elite atomic establishment desperate for the prestige associated with a successful outcome. While these scientists prevailed and even flourished, the country's real "have-nots" endured famine and poverty. This was evident less than three miles from the first atomic test site in the village of Lokhari, where there was no running water or electricity, and maize farming, the main source of income, kept the inhabitants occupied for just four months of the year. On a broader scale, the absence of a decent infrastructure affected the nuclear program, which was beset with technical troubles:

leaking valves and pipes, corrosion, and equipment contaminated with radioactivity. Workers at Tarapur's two reactors had tried for months to repair leaking fuel elements, but a "high level of radioactivity throughout the plant" slowed their effort.[3]

On the streets of Bombay, the tall, blue-eyed Edlow saw a world in jarring contrast to what he had known growing up in Ohio. "People were living inside concrete pipes that were being laid for sewers. There was a man with a rat who let it run up and down a string that was tied to a tooth and a toe. He wore only a loincloth and hat. There were monkeys" and "a guy with a bag of snakes—a snake charmer." In Delhi it was much the same. The AEC headquarters were just across the street from Edlow's hotel, but to keep beggars away from him, a car whisked Edlow safely to the AEC every day, although that car had one door missing.[4]

Was India really ready for nuclear energy?

INDIA'S NUCLEAR ORGANIZATION, for all its technical challenges, had always existed in a sphere of its own, well apart from snake charmers and people living in sewers. It was a dynastic group, rooted early on in Bhabha's close relationship with Jawaharlal Nehru, India's aristocratic and nominally pacifist leader. Bhabha was a member of the Parsi group, an elite minority of Indians descended from Persians who had left what is now Iran when it was overrun by Islamic forces in AD 600–800. He impressed American visitors from more ordinary backgrounds. Bhabha genuinely wanted to develop nuclear power for civilian purposes, but he taught Nehru the hedged meaning of "peaceful" in the nuclear context. And Nehru's own ambivalence about nuclear weapons fit comfortably into the Janus-like paradigm. Nehru could build on Mahatma Gandhi's pacifistic legend, proclaiming nuclear's innocent intent, while leaving the weapons option open.

From this close relationship, a program grew, and after Nehru's and Bhabha's deaths it overcame many obstacles, including changing political tides and fierce public debate over nuclear weapons, economic hardship, and mounting international pressure. More amazingly, the atomic establishment was able to persevere in the face of two firmly committed pacifists, one who succeeded Nehru as India's leader, and the other who followed Bhabha as head of the atomic program. The "organic necessity" of developing nuclear weapons, as Oppenheimer had described the early American efforts, took precedence over all else.

China's nuclear test in October 1964, five months after Nehru's death, put the pacifistic convictions of his successor, Lal Bahadur Shastri, to the test and unleashed fierce debate within India about the wisdom of developing nuclear weapons.[5] Bhabha waited patiently on the sidelines. And when the hard-liners proposed a motion in the Indian Parliament explicitly calling for nuclear weapons production, he wisely discouraged it, knowing that such an extreme measure would invite pressure from the West and jeopardize his access to nuclear technology and equipment. Instead, he took a leaf out of Seaborg's book and, working with Shastri, persuaded the lawmakers to approve a compromise measure, namely development—and use—of peaceful nuclear explosives. They might be needed, he successively convinced lawmakers, to make tunnels, or "to wipe out mountains for development parks." With his funding secured, Bhabha had just what he needed, reasonably respectable cover for a bomb program.[6]

Two years later, in 1966, India's nuclear progress was once again threatened. Shastri died of a sudden heart attack on January 11; then, thirteen days later, Bhabha's plane crashed into Mont Blanc en route to Europe. Nehru's daughter, Indira Gandhi, succeeded Shastri, and she eventually named Vikram Sarabhai, a wealthy, Cambridge-educated physicist, as Bhabha's successor. A committed pacifist who had previously headed a fledgling space program, Sarabhai ordered a halt to the PNE program, but he was basically ignored. "Sarabhai could not keep scientists from doing their work. He couldn't look over our shoulders," Raja Ramanna, who headed the PNE program, reportedly said. "You could keep doing what you could if it was on resources you already had, but you couldn't go to him for help on anything new involving explosives."[7]

A heart attack claimed Sarabhai's life on December 30, 1971, and that is when Sethna took over as chairman of India's AEC. By then it appears that support at least in principle for fabricating a device had been given.[8] The test took place successfully May 18, 1974, in the desert at Lokhari near Pokhran in the western Indian state of Rajasthan. Immediately following the explosion, Indian scientists sent their superiors in New Dehli the now famous message "The Buddha is smiling." In Paris, both the French government and Goldschmidt personally sent Sethna congratulatory messages.[9] A young Indian man delivering newspapers on his bicycle told a *Washington Post* reporter: "Now we're the same as America and Russia and China. We have the atomic bomb."[10]

Although most of the nonaligned world applauded the exercise, other governments, including Sweden and Japan, criticized the Indian government for undermining nonproliferation efforts. Canada briefly cut off further nuclear assistance because plutonium from the CIRUS fuel had been used in the bomb. Pakistani leader Zulfikar Ali Bhutto predictably reacted furiously. But the Nixon administration's public response was muted. Bogged down by the Watergate affair, Kissinger advised his underlings against a "public scolding."[11]

THE UNITED STATES had been trying for a number of years to head off an Indian bomb, even to the extent of toying with the idea of providing the Indian military with nuclear warheads as a deterrent to the Chinese.[12] In 1970, ten years after his first visit to India, Myron Kratzer and his assistant in the AEC's international division, Harold Bengelsdorf, decided to send India a warning against a peaceful nuclear explosion, saying it would violate the terms under which India had received heavy water for the CIRUS reactor back in the mid-1950s. Instead of a direct missive to the government in New Dehli, the message was cabled to the U.S. consul general's office in Bombay for transmission to the Indian AEC, whose headquarters were in Bombay. In diplomatic terms, it was viewed by its readers in India as no more than "advice," and treated accordingly. The Indians basically ignored it.[13]

At the time of the explosion, Kratzer had been replaced by Abe Friedman as head of the AEC's international division, having himself transferred to Tokyo with the State Department. Friedman had just arrived in London with an AEC commissioner named Gerald Tape. Friedman was awakened in the middle of the night with the news. "My thought was 'wow!' Let me put it this way. It didn't surprise me because those were the days when people were talking about plowshares, peaceful uses of nuclear energy, and nuclear explosions, and the Indians latched onto that."[14]

Also in England at the time, but outside London, was Daniel Patrick Moynihan, then U.S. ambassador to New Delhi. Friedman was asked to find him to deliver the news. "Tape and I met Moynihan at a railroad station in London. He had been either at Oxford or Cambridge and he came down just to meet us. And we told him as much as we knew about the fact there was this nuclear explosion in India because we figured the ambassador should know."[15]

In Washington, Bengelsdorf was rattled by the news. He expected State Department officials to come down hard on the government in New Delhi, which is in fact what they were preparing to do, and he may have been the official who called Edlow to try to stop the fuel shipment.[16] But Kissinger, in the Middle East, scotched the stern rebuke his staff had drafted on the theory that it "would not undo the event, but only add to U.S.-Indian bilateral problems and reduce the influence Washington might have on India's future nuclear policy."[17]

The government's official message, delivered by Moynihan (later senator from New York) direct to Indira Gandhi, dealt only with the likely strategic repercussions. "India has made a huge mistake. Here you were the No. 1 hegemonic power in South Asia. Nobody was No. 2 and call Pakistan No. 3. Now in a decade's time, some Pakistani general will call you up and say I have four nuclear weapons and I want Kashmir. If not, we will drop them on you and we will all meet in heaven. And then what will you do?" Talks aimed at normalizing relations between the two countries, scheduled for June 10, were canceled.[18]

In fact, Pakistan had already started its own nuclear weapons program two years earlier. And India was not in much trouble insofar as the United States was concerned, at least at that point, because the fuel shipments to Tarapur were continued. "We would have had a reasonably strong case to say to the Indians, after the 1974 explosion, that having broken the CIR(US) peaceful use pledge, they were no longer eligible to receive nuclear fuel from us under even the Tarapur agreement, since the subject matter was closely related," Kratzer wrote me in an e-mail. "However, we didn't say this in 1974, and instead in effect reconfirmed our obligation under the Tarapur agreement." Bengelsdorf was said to be "shocked" by the light treatment.

Yet both Kratzer and Bengelsdorf would become staunch defenders of India's right to receive nuclear fuel when the fuel shipments were legally contested in the United States two years later and Kratzer was back in Washington working for State. Kratzer said he took that position because after the Indian explosion the AEC secured an additional pledge that Tarapur fuel would not be turned into bomb material. Kissinger did what he could to mend relations as well. In October 1974, he traveled to New Dehli hoping to convince India's leaders to at least hold off on another test until after an NPT review conference scheduled for May 1975. Far from criticizing Mrs. Ghandi when he met her, the secretary of state congratulated her. He also requested further joint efforts aimed at preventing regional nuclear catastrophe and pressed her to refrain from exporting nuclear technology, material, or equipment. India turned down the offer of dialogue but showed restraint in its nuclear export policies—and, significantly, chose not to embark on a series of tests.[19]

Kissinger had basically recognized India's de facto status as a nuclear power, even though the explosion occurred well after the NPT's January 1967 cutoff date for being a "legitimate" nuclear power. In the civilian nuclear industry, it was business more or less as usual. According to official records, the first nuclear fuel export license in Edlow's name was issued May 16, 1974, two days before the nuclear test, and the enriched uranium left the United States a day after the test. An amendment to Edlow's export license was granted a month later, and the following year a new shipment was approved. India was almost entirely dependent on external sources for nuclear fuel. Without it, the country would have been hard-pressed to continue its nuclear program.

BUT THE STATUS quo was under threat. In 1974, Washington was rife with change. Americans were still reeling from the first Arab oil embargo a year earlier, Watergate was coming to a head, and a consumer and environmental protest movement was gaining ground. After Congress drove Nixon from power in August over the illegal break-in and bugging of the Democratic campaign headquarters and the subsequent cover-up, the year rolled to a close in what New York Times political correspondent Hedrick Smith described as a "political earthquake." In November, a new class of House Democrats swept into power. "As if that were not upheaval enough," Smith writes in his book The Power Game, "the House of Representatives also assaulted the citadel of the old congressional power system—seniority—and then balkanized its own power: it created scores of 'subcommittee governments,' each taking charge of a slice of federal policy."[20]

Public opposition to nuclear energy still lagged well behind its mounting dangers, but that too was changing. The AEC was under attack. "Public confidence in the safety of nuclear power plants and in the determination of the AEC to enforce adequate safety standards is at a low ebb," the *Washington Post* said in an October 1971 editorial. Paul Leventhal, a staff aide for the Senate Government Operations Committee, started looking into the situation. "I pursued it like it was a new beat," said Leventhal, a jaunty, confident, bow-tied New Yorker; a former journalist, he came out with sentences like slingshots. "I immediately discovered how rotten the nuclear industry was."[21]

The AEC had become an oligarchy controlling all facets of the military and civilian sides of nuclear energy, promoting them and at the same time attempting to regulate them, and it had fallen down on the regulatory side. Leventhal and a growing legion of critics saw too many inbuilt conflicts of interest. Another target was the congressional Joint Committee on Atomic Energy, which had become wedded to the establishment it was set up to oversee.[22]

The crowd of nuclear critics—some hesitated to call themselves outright opponents—included a mix of liberal environmentalists, right-leaning conservatives, and nuclear scientists. They tended to focus on different areas of concern such as proliferation or safety, although virtually all agreed that the AEC needed breaking up. The idea was also gaining traction with fiscal conservatives who wanted more financial accountability from the nuclear front. In 1973, the Nixon administration submitted the first legislative proposal aimed at shaking the AEC loose from its moorings. It created the Energy Research and Development Administration (ERDA) to take over all of the AEC's nonregulatory functions, including the weapons complex. *Business Week* wrote in June 1973, "The break-up of the AEC is long overdue. Nuclear power is under attack as never before, and even nuclear proponents contend that the AEC is largely to blame."[23]

But that measure was not enough for Leventhal and his boss, Senator Abraham Ribicoff, a Democrat from Connecticut. They wanted to abolish the AEC and eventually the JCAE, and they got their way. President Ford signed the Energy Reorganization Act of 1974 into law on October 11, and the AEC was formally disbanded at the end of the year. The bill split the AEC into two new organizations, ERDA, which became the Department of Energy two years later, and the Nuclear Regulatory Commission, which would carry out the AEC's civilian nuclear regulatory functions.

THE AEC'S DEMOLITION acted like lighter fluid on an already burning fire of nuclear activism, which had a direct impact on the situation in India. Opponents of breeders and reprocessing immediately cited India's use of a "peaceful" reactor to produce plutonium for its bomb. Fuel inside the nation's growing number of civilian reactors also contained plutonium that once separated could be used for weapons. Since the intention then was to reprocess the fuel for advanced reactors, critics sounded the alarm—hundreds of tons of plutonium would be in general circulation, and vulnerable to diversion for illicit weapons programs. The fuel destined for Tarapur from the American enrichment plants became a kind of poster child of that campaign.

As the energy reorganization bill wound its way through the legislative process, the *New Yorker* published a series of articles by John McPhee pointing out how relatively simple it would be for a terrorist to steal nuclear material and build a homemade nuclear bomb. The articles were based on a detailed study coauthored by Mason Willrich, a University of Virginia law professor, and Theodore Taylor, a leading weapons designer at Los Alamos.

Among a number of outstanding intellectuals and scientists who took up the proliferation cause in the 1970s, Taylor stood out. Taylor not only repudiated the field in which he excelled but opposed commercial nuclear development, unlike many other nuclear scientists who had come to oppose nuclear weapons but still supported nuclear power. Taylor's misgivings began in 1950 when he became a father. He would later tell his daughter that at the time of her birth he was working at the Pentagon on plans to annihilate Moscow. The life and death juxtaposition led him to reorient his scientific work. "Many of the people in the bomb business got to where they wanted nothing to do with it," Taylor's Princeton colleague Freeman Dyson said after Taylor's death in 2004. But "generally speaking, those working with reactors still believed in nuclear. Ted was unusual in that he became opposed to nuclear energy in general as too risky, too dangerous."[24]

The Willrich-Taylor report inspired a separate report commissioned by the Arms Control and Disarmament Agency entitled *Moving Toward Life in a Nuclear Armed Crowd?* It concluded that the IAEA safeguards system was not up to the task of detecting the diversion of plutonium for nuclear weapons because it could take place over a matter of a few weeks. The chief author of the report was not a left-wing environmentalist, as one might imagine, but Albert Wohlstetter, the former RAND

analyst and academic who later gained prominence as a prime mover behind the neoconservative movement. Wohlstetter never disavowed
nuclear weapons (as long as they were American), but he became a leading voice for preventing their spread. Inspired by Wohlstetter's report,
ACDA released its own in July 1976. It too pointed to the problem of
"timely warning" and focused on plutonium recycling as the biggest potential hazard in the effort to stop the spread of nuclear weapons. It was
the first time a U.S. government publication described breeder reactors
as a proliferation danger with questionable economic value.

These were serious issues highlighted by India's exploitation of weak
safeguards to produce nuclear weapons. But there were others. The
intellectuals probably had not read Sam Edlow's 1968 report about
mobsters infiltrating the U.S. transport system; nor would they have
experienced the lapses that had occasionally frayed the transport executive's nerves. But in the everyday world of nuclear commerce any number of unexpected things could happen that highlighted the dangers of
putting nuclear fuel into widespread circulation—like the time a truck
trailer carrying five cylindrical containers of uranium fuel, each weighing eight thousand pounds, collapsed under the strain along the New
Jersey Turnpike. Soon state police, an official from the Oak Ridge na-
tionwide nuclear response network, and various other authorities surrounded the eighteen-wheeler. Someone spotted a pool of liquid under
the truck and started yelling, "Radioactive! Radioactive!" An Oak Ridge
official had started measuring for radioactivity when a state trooper
confessed, "I peed there." It was ridiculous, the elder Edlow said, because the enriched uranium in the truck was solid—although the
truck's capacity had evidently been tested to its limits.[25]

Ridiculous or not, if leaking containers, missing seals, and other
mishaps caused occasional panics in the world's most advanced, highly
regulated country, what might go wrong when nuclear fuel was shipped
to a country where government drivers turned up in cars lacking a door?

ON MARCH 2, 1976, fifteen months after the Indian nuclear test, three
environmental and public interest groups—the Natural Resources
Defense Council, the Sierra Club, and the Union of Concerned
Scientists—filed a petition with the NRC to block further exports of
U.S. nuclear fuel to India. The aim was to discourage further bomb de-
velopment in a country that had refused to sign the NPT, detonated a

nuclear explosive apparently in violation of safeguards understandings with the United States and Canada, and existed in a region fraught with frictions and rivalries, chiefly with Pakistan and China. But the petitioners also cited lax safety at Tarapur, persistent problems with fuel rods leaking fission products, the lack of suitable infrastructure to support the reactor, untrained staff, and the absence of a permanent waste storage facility. *oh, like in U.S. — Do H!*

The intervention sent a shock wave through the nuclear community worldwide. Under the old AEC, the United States had signed more than thirty agreements for cooperation, issued ninety-eight licenses to export nuclear power and research reactors, and approved approximately two hundred and twenty nuclear fuel exports.[26] Not one of these had been challenged. Now, not only were the interveners calling the nuclear establishment to account for its apparent lax approach to nuclear exports, they were also questioning the entire system of international safeguards. "The roof was caving in," admitted the short, stocky Bengelsdorf, whose wiry hair seemed a natural extension of his frequently agitated, though basically warm, personality. "It was a groundswell—Willrich, Ted Taylor, Leventhal, even Wohlstetter . . . Kratzer and I were seen as pro-nuke and we were getting it from all sides."

The new generation of activists did not realize the United States had supplied the heavy water to CIRUS, whose fuel had been used to produce the plutonium for India's bomb. But it did not take long for them to find out. Recently appointed NRC commissioner Victor Gilinsky happened upon the information at an industry conference in Florida. He was talking to a member of the old guard, a Swiss official named Rudolph Rometsch, when the topic came up.

Gilinsky was irate. He had asked a State Department official why the United States had not followed Canada's example and stopped providing nuclear assistance to the Indians after the explosion. The official told him that no U.S. equipment had been involved, failing to tell him about the heavy water, which Gilinsky regarded as a lie "because it was intended to deceive, to shield the heavy water."[27]

Gilinsky was by both background and temperament a fighter and a survivor, qualities probably fostered by a boyhood escape with his family from Nazi-occupied Warsaw and subsequent flight from the Soviet Union across Siberia. With a PhD in theoretical physics from Caltech, Gilinsky focused on nonproliferation while still at RAND.

Very early in January 1975, before the NRC had officially opened for business, Kissinger instructed the five newly appointed commissioners, Gilinsky included, to exercise their export authority, which had been transferred to the NRC by mistake, as instructed by the State Department. Four of them agreed to sign a letter asking Congress to change the law to take their authority away and give it back to the executive branch. Gilinsky refused, and the letter did not go out because it was not unanimous. "I said I wouldn't sign it and if they [the other commissioners] did it I would attack it. They pulled it back."[28]

In June 1976, the issue of the heavy water came to a head during Senate hearings over proposed legislation to reform nuclear export law. Gilinsky told Leventhal about his conversation with Rometsch. Leventhal said he had already found out about the heavy water because of "a chance slip of the tongue by a State Department briefer on the Hill."[29] The effect was explosive. The State Department, now on the defensive, advanced the spurious argument that India had since produced its own heavy water, in excess of what it needed for the CIRUS plant. Thus, it was claimed, U.S. heavy water was "not essential to the production of plutonium for India's 1974 nuclear test." But this was splitting hairs, and in any case based on a gross miscalculation of the rate at which heavy water had to be replaced at CIRUS, which Kissinger's staff eventually had to concede.

Senators Ribicoff, John Glenn, and Charles Percy, an Illinois Republican, issued a joint statement on June 29: "The Indian explosion illustrates what can happen when some nuclear activities in a non-NPT nation are safeguarded by the IAEA and some are not. It also illustrates the inability of the IAEA to prevent the use of some safeguarded material for nuclear explosions in non-NPT nations." The senators criticized the government for failing to "verify or acknowledge the probable use of our heavy water in the development of India's version of an atomic bomb."

Leventhal put it more bluntly: "The stuff [heavy water] was sent via Canada, and the AEC and State had said it was all Canadian. We caught them in a lie. That helped turn things around."[30]

THE STATE DEPARTMENT became a defendant in the NRC export licensing proceedings. Kratzer spent five hours responding to questions and answered a further one hundred questions in writing. When he stated in his affidavit that the threat to the shipments "strike[s] at the heart of long-standing U.S. nuclear foreign policy," he was arguing for everything he stood for—not just the system of international safeguards that he had been instrumental in developing, but the decision to send nuclear exports to countries he, and those around him, knew might very well be applied toward military programs. Kratzer fought to defend the notion that the United States had to maintain its reputation as a "reliable supplier" in order to further its nonproliferation policy. Without exports, he maintained, the United States would have little to no say over whether other countries would accept IAEA inspections at their nuclear facilities.

Yet Kratzer's arguments were beginning to sound hollow. And what of the NPT? The "reliable supplier" was crashing head-on into the chief promoter of the safeguards system. What good were safeguards at only some facilities, when the others could be used to make bombs? Moreover, when Kratzer attempted to influence India's behavior with the 1970 warning, putting his own "leverage" theory to the test, Indian officials had not even bothered to reply.

A number of high-level interveners stood Kratzer's arguments on their head. George W. Ball, undersecretary of state in the Kennedy and Johnson administrations, castigated the United States for allowing "an unthinking enthusiasm for nuclear power to lead to the spending of hundreds of millions of dollars to spread nuclear equipment and technology around the world." Government policy on nuclear transfers after the NPT "can only be judged improvident," he said, because exports were still allowed to countries that had not signed the treaty. Ball said, "Our policy thus gave non-nuclear nations an incentive not to join the Treaty. A non-signatory nation might be able to build up unsafeguarded stockpiles of uranium; a signatory nation could not."[31]

Adrian Fisher, ACDA's deputy director between 1961 and 1969, offered that allowing further nuclear fuel exports to India would be viewed as "tacit approval" by the United States of India's nuclear explosives program. Other nations would be encouraged to think that the United States would not take any action that would "adversely affect their atomic energy programs" even if they developed nuclear bombs. It also undermined the NPT. If a nonsignatory country such as India could continue to receive U.S. material after it had been used in an explosives program, why would any country bother to sign a pact that obligated it to accept safeguards? Fisher pointed out that the treaty's preamble obligated the United States to adopt an export policy "in such a way as to obtain the widest possible adherence to the Treaty." Under the circumstances, he said, sending nuclear fuel to India hardly lived up to the promise.[32]

Kratzer's broader point was the old rationale that the United States had to keep on giving in order to ensure it maintained control, albeit limited, over India's nuclear program. But he was also advancing the interests of the international nuclear bureaucracy in which his career and those of his friends and colleagues had flourished. The interveners were saying that by providing fuel the United States would undermine the existing safeguards regime by appearing to ignore it, while enabling the further development of nuclear weapons. These were the two uninviting paths on a slippery slope, and the denouement of Oppenheimer's contention in 1946 "that if you don't try to develop atomic energy, you can't control it." Tarapur brought into sharp relief the basic dilemma of attempting to develop nuclear energy for "peaceful purposes" while assuming that its beneficiaries could be prevented from diverting the technology, hardware, and fuel to military uses.

THE INDUSTRY WAS being torn wide open by arguments that were hard to ignore, and the atmosphere was getting uglier. In May 1976, as he campaigned for the U.S. presidency, Jimmy Carter made nuclear proliferation a major theme. Carter had credibility on the subject because he had been a nuclear engineer in Rickover's nuclear navy. The Georgia Democrat had also seen dangers from the safety side; he had assisted in disassembling a damaged reactor core after one of several early accidents at the Chalk River complex near Ottawa. "I am acutely aware of its potential—and its dangers," Carter told a UN conference on nuclear energy in May 1976. Power reactors could "malfunction and cause widespread radiological damage, unless stringent safety requirements are met. Radioactive wastes may be a menace to future generations and civilizations, unless they are effectively isolated within the biosphere forever. And terrorists or other criminals may steal plutonium and make weapons to threaten society or its political leaders with nuclear violence." As far as Carter was concerned, "U.S. dependence on nuclear power should be kept to the minimum necessary to meet our needs."[33]

Ford, seeking to gain the offensive in what had become one of the hottest issues of the race, responded on October 28 by announcing a halt to reprocessing "unless there is sound reason to conclude that the world community can effectively overcome the associated risks of proliferation." Furthermore, the president said, the United States would pursue strong export controls, safeguards, and other measures to minimize proliferation risks.[34]

After Carter was elected, the breeder and reprocessing programs in the United States faced an uphill battle for survival, as Carter consistently opposed funding for the Clinch River breeder demonstration reactor at a Tennessee Valley Authority site in Tennessee. Meanwhile, Congress moved to tighten export laws, which made life more difficult for American nuclear manufacturers. Determined to avoid losing valuable business overseas, they tried hard to derail the legislation spearheaded by Senator Glenn and his chief scientific adviser Leonard Weiss. In the spring or summer of 1977, Weiss alleged that he was approached by Westinghouse's chief nuclear lobbyist, Dwight Porter. "He shook his finger at me," recalled Weiss, "and said, 'You know you're not going to get this bill passed. So unless you play ball with us, you're not going to get anything out of this.'"

The NRC in theory should have been neutral about the legislation since it no longer was legally bound to promote nuclear energy. But that did not stop one commissioner, Richard Kennedy, from adding his weight to Porter's warning. Weiss said: "Dick Kennedy invited me to lunch and said, 'You know, Len, there is something you ought to know. This bill is being referred to as the Len Weiss bill, and that isn't going to be good for your career.' This was all new to me. I had been lobbied before but no one had explicitly threatened me."[35]

Congress passed the Nuclear Nonproliferation Act March 10, 1978. It prohibited U.S. nuclear cooperation with any country not recognized as a nuclear weapons state in the NPT that conducted a nuclear explosion, or that had not agreed to subject all its nuclear facilities to IAEA "full-scope" inspections. The aim was to stop the Tarapur shipments since India did not meet the requirements, although the legislation provided an eighteen-month grace period to allow some flexibility in the NRC decision-making process. In essence, though, the law's provisions virtually required any country doing nuclear business with the United States to join the Non-Proliferation Treaty, under which they would renounce possession of nuclear weapons. In practice, ways were continually found to circumvent either the spirit or the letter of the law, in U.S. relations not only with Israel but also with Pakistan, Iraq, and even North Korea.

Carter, meanwhile, partially reversed his earlier strong nonprolif-eration stance, proving a huge disappointment to activists. With the president's mother visiting India, but also encouraged by the pacifist, antiweapons stance of India's new prime minister, Morarji Desai, the Carter White House wanted a nuclear license for India. So the presi-dent overrode all subsequent NRC objections to the shipments. Most notably, in June 1980, when the grace period was over and four of the five commissioners voted against approving an export license (the fifth commissioner, Richard Kennedy, was absent but said he would have dissented from the opinion), Carter overruled the decision.

Congress had sixty days to rescind the order, so Carter and his deputy secretary of state, Warren Christopher, embarked on an aggres-sive campaign to persuade the lawmakers against that. It was a close call. The foreign affairs committees of both bodies opposed Carter's po-sition, and the House of Representatives overwhelmingly supported their views. The Senate seemed primed to follow suit, but when the vote was cast on September 24, it was 48–46 in favor of the shipments. Carter had been phoning the senators from Air Force One right up un-til the roll call was started, Gilinsky later told me.

Not until 1982, after Carter had left office, did the United States fi-nally stop shipping nuclear fuel to India. Over the next several years India was able to get some fuel from the French, but international pres-sure finally put an end to those exports too. Over time India found itself facing such dire shortages of fresh nuclear fuel that it was confronted with a choice: it could throttle back its reactors and use its remaining nuclear fuel for the weapons program or vice versa. Not surprisingly, it opted for the former course. By 2008, India's power reactors were run-ning on average at approximately half their nameplate capacity, while its stockpile of nuclear weapons had expanded to include anywhere from fifty to one hundred warheads.[36]

In July 2005, President George W. Bush overturned more than two decades of U.S. policy by signing a groundbreaking nuclear deal with In-dian prime minister Manmohan Singh. The pact, approved by Congress three years later, allows India access to desperately needed uranium and nuclear technology, without onerous safeguards. That in turn provides India significant scope for increasing its production of fissile material for nuclear weapons, as well as for ramping up its civilian reactor output. India's neighbors in Pakistan are not sitting still. They too are increasing fissile material production. The agreement with India, which required a special safeguards agreement with the IAEA and a unanimous exemption from the now more stringent rules of the Nuclear Suppliers Group (NSG), is understandably causing an outcry among people who believe the government should abide by its nonproliferation commitments. Once again that plea is being ignored in the interests of geostrategic priorities whose "logic lies in the containment of China and a U.S.-dominated strategic matrix in Asia, including West Asia, with India, Japan and Israel as its pillars," in the view of Indian commentator Praful Bidwai. But there were other commercial reasons too, as Bidwai points out—intense lobbying by the U.S.-India Business Council in Washington and major corporations all anxious to get a slice of the "emerging India" market, including the energy technology and nuclear power sectors. One final inducement may have been the fact that more than ten billion dollars was at stake in India's plans to buy hundreds of U.S. military aircraft.[37] The irony is that by paving the way for similar nuclear agreements between India and France and Russia, the United States is unlikely to get as much business as it had hoped for.

And what of India and its energy needs, the supposed basis for the U.S. policy turnaround? Bidwai is far from sanguine that nuclear energy will bring "energy security" to India, with or without U.S. assistance. "India was projected to generate 43,500 megawatts of nuclear electricity by 2000. Today, India produces less than 1/10 that amount," writes Bidwai.[38] Even if the nuclear sector grows according to the government's own plans, he reckons, nuclear energy's contribution to India's total electricity generation in 2030 will be only 6 percent. India traded megawatts for bombs, and the United States, for short-term political and commercial gain, decided to ignore that and sacrificed policies aimed at preventing the further proliferation of nuclear weapons.

CHAPTER 15

A Snatched Pen

T HE CITY OF MULTAN, almost exactly in the middle of Pakistan, has known war and peace like few cities on earth. In the wash of its five-thousand-year history, it endured legions of conquerors—Greeks, Huns, Muslims, Mughals, among others—and great cycles of devastation, rebuilding, and reinvention. But Multan is other things, its admirers say. They describe a city of saints, Sufis, writers, poets, and calligraphers and point to mosques, shrines, and ancient city gates among a concrete jungle of haphazardly placed buildings and roads. In 1972, Multan achieved another distinction: the birthplace of Pakistan's nuclear weapons program. That event would seed a loose coalition of nuclear alliances among a crescent of ancient kingdoms, stretching from China to Egypt, potentially rivaling anything dreamed of by Alexander or the Mughal conqueror Alamgir. But this was a disparate and dangerous group of countries. They had fallen behind and wanted desperately to catch up. Most of all, they sought some kind of parity with India, and through India with the great powers that lay well outside their once mighty sphere.

Pakistan began its effort to balance the regional power on January 20, 1972. That day its new leader, Zulfikar Ali Bhutto, held a rally of the nation's leading scientists on the manicured lawn of a colonial mansion in Multan. Many of those who watched and listened as Bhutto told them he wanted a nuclear weapon had been summoned back from posts in Europe and the United States. Munir Khan, who had been at the IAEA in Vienna since 1958, was among them. Bhutto had long wanted Pakistan to have a bomb, but he had not been able to overcome political resistance to the idea. Now he was in charge and his country was reeling from defeat a month earlier at Dhaka in East Pakistan. India had crushed Pakistan's army in just thirteen days. The defeat followed an unsuccessful attempt by the Pakistanis to quash an uprising by East Pakistanis who had long felt ignored by their rulers in Islamabad. Just as the epaulets were summarily stripped from a humiliated Pakistani lieutenant general's uniform, Islamabad was voided of control over its poor eastern province, and East Pakistan became the independent country of Bangladesh. The loss of its eastern half, so quickly carried out by the stronger Indian army, highlighted Pakistan's vulnerability to total dismemberment. Four days after the defeat, the charismatic Bhutto assumed power as the first civilian head of government of a truncated Pakistan, itself formed by the British partition of India in 1947.[1]

Bhutto, like the civilian leaders who followed, constantly vied for power with the military. The country's generals had been "on steroids," as one American-based Pakistani-born expert put it, ever since 1954, when Pakistan became a U.S. client state in the cold war conflict. The flow of American military and financial assistance to Pakistan over several decades is key to understanding why relatively little was done to prevent it becoming a nuclear power: Successive U.S. administrations basically ignored their obligations under the Non-Proliferation Treaty as well as several important pieces of nuclear export legislation, to prop up a military viewed as vital to thwarting Soviet expansionism. The theft of centrifuge enrichment designs from Europe facilitated the program's success; nationalism, greed, and hubris greased the wheels; but without American accommodation and financial assistance a Pakistani nuclear arsenal almost certainly would not exist today.

The indulgence toward Pakistan was hardly exceptional. To the contrary, it followed a pattern that began with early assistance to the Indian nuclear program, tolerance of the Israeli project, and in the 1980s a "tilt" toward Iraq that allowed Saddam Hussein to acquire the components needed for his secret nuclear weapons program. In all three instances, too many other immediate issues were at stake to be overly concerned about the longer-term dangers posed by the proliferation of nuclear weapons.

Despite this, the emergence of a Pakistani nuclear weapon, in the late 1980s, unnerved the West. For the first time, the power balances in an unstable region were tipped by two rivals frequently at war with each other but with both having nuclear weapons. The Pakistani bomb signaled the possibility that in the post-cold-war world developing nations would jockey for position and power, and nuclear weapons would be essential to their strategy. Outside the well-understood norms of the cold war rivalry, this regional nuclear contest was still in the making with its own dynamic. No one knew how it would turn out. Moreover, these new nuclear states could generate a domino effect as nuclear technology proliferated and countries in the Middle East, possibly in northern Africa, and in Asia fell under the spell of nuclear power. After 1989, the cold war rivals were ramping down, but in the Indian subcontinent and the Middle East the action was only beginning.

Bhutto believed nuclear weapons were the only realistic response to the Indian threat. In 1965, as foreign minister, he famously declared, "If India builds the bomb, we will eat grass or leaves, even go hungry. But we will get one of our own." As part of a political elite of landowning aristocrats with his own forty-thousand-acre family estate, Bhutto hardly had to worry about starving; nor would the scientists who worked with him go without food. Pakistan's survival, in his view, depended on them. It was hard not to be somewhat sympathetic to this point of view. What was Bhutto's option now that India had the bomb? In 1966, a former senior Indian military official, Major General Som Dutt, the first director of India's Institute for Defense Studies and Analyses, had warned of this eventuality. But Dutt was ignored in part, writes George Perkovich in his book on the Indian bomb program, because the leading scientists in the Indian nuclear establishment and a large number of politicians wanted "to prove the prowess and mettle of postcolonial India to Indians themselves."[2] The drive for technological supremacy, seen in the ability to deliver nuclear weapons into the hands of political leaders, had been a driving force behind atomic bomb development since the very start of the Manhattan Project. Pakistan had not even been a country when the first bomb exploded over Hiroshima. Now it would be a nuclear power.

As Bhutto spoke to this select group gathered on the lawn, there were doubters, mainly wizened elders, including the head of the Pakistan Atomic Energy Commission (PAEC), I. H. Usmani. During the 1960s, Usmani sent six hundred scientists abroad to study physics and nuclear engineering. He pushed hard to develop Pakistan's nuclear fuel cycle capabilities, but he had been part of a government coalition that opposed Bhutto's earlier, less successful lobbying for nuclear weapons. Toward the end of the gathering, Bhutto reportedly dismissed Usmani as PAEC chairman, replacing him with the more compliant Munir Khan, the internationally trusted longtime IAEA official.[3]

This raised a few eyebrows in the West. "I remember being somewhat surprised when he became chairman of the PAEC," admitted Kratzer, "since it never occurred to me that he had retained whatever political connections getting that job required, after so many years in Vienna."[4] Although his employment with the agency ended, Khan continued to attend IAEA meetings while focusing on the effort to make fissile material for Pakistan's first nuclear weapon. Following the path laid out by France, Israel, and India, Khan naturally emphasized the plutonium route, and with everyone in Europe talking up breeder reactors, it was an ideal time to acquire the necessary know-how for reprocessing. Usmani had already started fuel cycle activities in Pakistan; Khan would just be continuing them.

So it was under this pretext that in 1973 three Pakistani nuclear scientists went to the Mol reprocessing plant in Belgium to learn firsthand how to produce plutonium. The Mol facility was a product of Atoms for Peace: it had started as a joint European undertaking to train nuclear scientists and engineers, with assistance from the United States. Bengelsdorf had been a key promoter of the project as principal negotiator on the U.S. agreement for nuclear cooperation with Belgium, a highlight of which had been personally meeting with the Belgian ambassador Baron Silvercruys—"one of the senior glittering figures," Bengelsdorf recalled, and both he and Kratzer attended the plant's dedication ceremony.[5] Since reprocessing was becoming big business in the commercial sector, the Pakistani presence at Mol seemed a perfectly legitimate arrangement.

Bhutto, meanwhile, had gone on a fund-raising tour shortly after the Multan convocation, cultivating relationships in the Middle East and China. In the Middle East, awash with petro dollars, the Pakistani leader reportedly secured financial assistance from Saudi Arabia and other Gulf States, whose desire for a "Muslim bomb" became even greater after the Yom Kippur War in 1973. He opened up a dialogue with Libya's dynamic new leader, Colonel Moammar Gadhafi, just twenty-seven when he and Bhutto first met in 1972.[6] But Bhutto's biggest coup was China.

Besides sending Pakistan tanks, planes, and other conventional military equipment, China became a silent ally in Pakistan's early bomb effort, somewhat in the way France had teamed up with Israel, part of an international buddy system among unequal underdogs. Bhutto described the access he had gained in Beijing as "my greatest achievement and contribution to the survival of our people and our nation."[7]

As these events took place, another player moved into place. He was in Europe living the inconspicuous life of a Dutch burgher, married with two children. His name was Abdul Qadeer Khan. He would turn the Pakistani program upside down, showing Bhutto that the other route to acquiring bomb-grade material—enriching uranium—was possible after all. Khan was not related to Munir; moreover, he became his chief rival. Khan not only completely circumvented the international nuclear safeguards regime to deliver his country the technology and eventually the material for nuclear weapons, he also upset the PAEC by producing highly enriched uranium faster than they could manufacture plutonium. A. Q. Khan was lucky in one important respect: the people who worried about nuclear safeguards at that time were focused almost exclusively on the threat posed by breeders and reprocessing plants. And just as reprocessing was becoming big business in Europe, so too was commercial enrichment. That meant that nobody was looking when Khan commited his crime.

A. Q. KHAN WAS BORN in 1936 in the Indian village of Bhopal, now remembered for the 1984 disaster at a Union Carbide insecticide plant that has over time claimed an estimated twenty thousand lives. He was one of seven children. His schoolteacher father was a Muslim League partisan who evidently believed the league's propaganda that Mahatma Gandhi was out to annihilate Muslims. The league agitated for a separate state, although Khan's parents remained in India after 1947. His siblings left for the new country, and Khan, aged sixteen, followed in 1952.[8]

More than ten million people fled across the new frontiers during that period, and the train rides became famous for their wrenching violence. Khan watched as Hindu railroad officials and police stole jewelry and money from fellow passengers. Khan himself escaped relatively unscathed. A border guard snatched a pen from his pocket, a minor offense under the circumstances, but it had been a gift from his brothers when Khan passed his secondary school exams. "The pen had almost no monetary value, but the guard's behavior hurt me, and it was something I'll never forget," he told an interviewer many years later.[9] As if to reinforce the point, a picture of what was reportedly the last train out of India before the borders were closed, hangs in the Pakistani's Islamabad study. The train is engulfed in flames.[10]

Khan lived in Karachi with a brother and in the early 1960s went to Europe for university, first studying in Germany, then later in Holland and Belgium. In The Hague, he met his future wife, Hendrina, nicknamed Henny, born of Dutch parents in South Africa. The couple married in 1963, and Khan studied metallurgy at the Delft University of Technology for four years. After that, he and Henny moved to Leuven in Belgium so Khan could study for a doctorate at Catholic University. In 1972, with a Ph.D., Khan was thirty-six and ready for a job.

WITH REACTORS BEING built all over the world—most needing enriched uranium—West Germany faced the prospect of being left out of a major business opportunity if it could not build an industrial enrichment plant. Yet because bomb-grade material could be acquired from such a facility, it was still politically impossible in the late 1960s to build one on German soil. So in 1967, the Germans asked the Dutch to collaborate on a commercial venture, and the British were asked to join the following year. On March 4, 1970, officials from all three countries arrived at the headquarters of an old water management company in the Dutch textile town of Almelo and signed a treaty to establish the Uranium Enrichment Company, or Urenco. The three partners—British Nuclear Fuels Ltd. (BNFL), Holland's UltraCentrifuge Nederland (UCN), and Germany's Uranit—held equal shares in the management company and equivalent cross-shareholdings in the national companies.[11]

To begin with, Urenco planned to build two plants, one in Britain and the other at Almelo. There was a design competition to see which of the companies would secure the contract to build the centrifuges, all of which were based on modified versions of the designs developed by the German and Austrian war prisoners at Sukhumi under Gernot Zippe, the engineer the Israelis had inveigled into providing information.[12]

A. Q. Khan secured a job in May 1972 with a subsidiary of Urenco's

Dutch arm known as FDO. Khan was not only a well-regarded metallurgist, he was also fluent in languages, enabling him to translate
documents from the partner firms. Settled into family life in Zwa-
nenburg, a suburb of Almelo, Khan hardly appeared suspicious. He had
many European references, a clean record, and no connections with the
Pakistani government, and there is no evidence he began the job intent
on stealing the intensely coveted technology. He was cleared by Dutch
security services for the classified work without a problem.

The timing was extraordinary. Khan arrived during a mélange of
design competition, plant development, and organizational teething
problems, and when the German technology finally won out for the
plant at Almelo, he was there to translate the sensitive documents as
they flowed over the border in early 1974.

By all accounts, Khan was a likable man, but when India exploded
its first nuclear bomb in May 1974, a worm turned inside the seemingly easygoing fellow. A few months later, on September 17, he delivered a letter through Pakistan's embassy in Belgium offering Bhutto
his assistance on the country's bomb project, which was widely
known about at the time, even if the United States and other governments feigned ignorance. Khan explained that he could provide an alternative to the plutonium-production route that Munir Khan was
pursuing. Bhutto was delighted. How better to achieve his goal than
to have two people competing with each other to produce the material
for Pakistan's first atomic bomb?

At Almelo, Khan disguised the anger and ambition underlying his
breathtaking move beneath a veneer of goodwill and charm. But in
1975 a close friend and colleague, Frits Veerman, began picking up signs
that something had changed. During social visits to the Khan home, for
example, Veerman saw stacks of classified documents. Pakistanis were
coming and going too, with no explanation. Possibly one of them was a
scientist named S. A. Butt, who was assigned to the Pakistani embassy
in the Netherlands in July 1975. Butt had been at the Multan meeting
and was now engaged as Bhutto's chief purchasing agent in Europe for
sensitive nuclear supplies. Butt reportedly became Khan's chief conduit
for passing centrifuge-related technical literature, blueprints, and lists
of equipment and material suppliers to the PAEC, although enough material had been sent the previous year for the authors of a PAEC feasibility study to recommend in November 1974 that Pakistan should
build its own enrichment plant.[13]

At first, Veerman believed Khan's explanation for the stacks of sensitive papers—that his wife was helping him with the translations. But Khan tripped up in October 1975 when he asked Veerman, who was also a staff photographer at FDO, to take pictures of centrifuge drawings he had at home.[14] Then Khan suggested that Veerman accompany him on a holiday to Pakistan. When Veerman demurred, Khan offered to pay for the trip. Insulted by what he regarded as a patronizing offer, Veerman slowly began putting it all together—the documents, the unnamed visitors, the proposed vacation.

Veerman tried to alert Urenco and FDO's senior management but was initially met with skepticism and even scolding; one manager warned against making accusations without substantial proof. Khan did not realize that his friend had turned on him. Dutch government officials learned about Butt's attempts to buy centrifuge equipment and realized that the level of knowledge required for his transactions could only have come from Khan. FDO was informed, and in October, the same month Veerman's suspicions were first reported, Khan was quietly promoted to a less sensitive job. Khan realized the game was up. Two months later, in December, he left with his family for Pakistan, claiming he was going on vacation. He never returned to his job in Holland, but he continued traveling to Europe on business in the 1980s. Butt shifted his operation to Paris. Three decades later, Ruud Lubbers, who had been the economic affairs minister at the time, blamed the Americans for the failure to arrest Khan, saying that Dutch authorities were considering that step but were stopped by the CIA because they wanted him followed. A U.S. official involved at the time reportedly denied this, faulting Dutch authorities for failing to realize he would flee.[15]

IN PAKISTAN, A. Q. KHAN was quickly bumped up the organizational ladder. By July the following year, he had his own program to develop a uranium enrichment plant. His new base was at a town called Kahuta, near Islamabad, where the rolling, wooded terrain would at least partially screen a new Engineering Research Laboratory (ERL). Here was where the metallurgist would have to prove himself, designing and building the centrifuge enrichment plants to turn uranium into material for bombs.

A race was on between the people at Kahuta and the PAEC to see who would deliver the goods first. Unfortunately for the PAEC and its leader, the other Khan, the proliferation activists were getting in the way of the effort to produce plutonium. Early in 1976, press coverage focused on a meeting between Canadian prime minister Pierre Trudeau and Bhutto at which Bhutto kept stubbornly refusing to accept safeguards on a proposed Canadian reactor at Karachi. But the real headline-grabber was the French sale of a reprocessing plant to Pakistan in March that year.

Kissinger had not been overly concerned about the Indian explosion two years earlier, but the reprocessing contract alarmed him, according to Kratzer, then an acting assistant secretary of state.[16] In August, Kratzer accompanied Kissinger on a trip to Islamabad. During a tense private meeting with Bhutto, the secretary of state threatened to block the sale of 110 A-7 Corsair long-range fighter-bombers unless Bhutto agreed to put the French plant under safeguards and use its output for peaceful purposes.[17] There was no deal. After a lavish dinner, attended also by Benazir Bhutto, a university student at that time, America's leading diplomat flew to Paris to press the French to relinquish the sale. The effort was unsuccessful.[18]

The rebuffs prompted Kissinger to lobby for an agreement among nuclear suppliers to withhold sensitive nuclear items from countries, like Pakistan, that refused to agree to safeguards. So Kratzer went to London later that same year and, together with representatives from Canada, West Germany, France, Japan, the Soviet Union, and the United Kingdom, persuaded the recently established Nuclear Suppliers Group to refrain from exporting reprocessing and enrichment plants. The agreement left a lot of wriggle room for countries intent on developing their own bomb material. Other items, such as uranium or conversion plants, both necessary for enrichment, were not on the original list. And it was this wide berth that allowed Khan to access the European supply chain to get what he needed for Kahuta.

I asked Kratzer why the list hadn't included more items.

"If you try to make the lists too long," he rationalized, "the system breaks down and nothing gets controlled. It is important to identify the things that really are hard to get and concentrate on them."[19]

Pakistan's continued refusal to give up attempts to acquire the French-built reprocessing plant led President Carter to announce in June 1977 that he would withhold the Corsairs, and in August he succeeded in pressuring the French into canceling their nuclear sale. But by then A. Q. Khan's minions had quietly lined up a host of deals to ensure Kahuta's success—none of which violated the terms of the new suppliers group. The British firm Emerson Electric Industrial Controls sent to Pakistan thirty-one complete inverter systems that could be used to regulate a large number of centrifuge machines. Around the same time, a Swiss firm, CORA Engineering, fabricated a uranium conversion plant for the Kahuta facility. The entire facility was airlifted to Pakistan on a C-130 Hercules transport plane, and CORA sent engineers and other technicians to help with postsales servicing.[20] This facility would produce the gas feed material for the enrichment plant.

These are only two examples of dozens of exports from Europe that contributed to the successful completion of an enrichment operation at Kahuta, not to mention what U.S. suppliers brought to the party. While some, like the Emerson deal, raised a few eyebrows, they went ahead without much fuss. Some of Emerson's scientists were pretty certain what the inverters were for, but they joked that they would rust away in their crates before the Pakistanis could figure out how to use them.[21] Apparently, none of these exports came close to violating the NSG agreement, revealing how the international nuclear bureaucracy relied upon the absolute minimum to prevent the spread of nuclear weapons. Even CORA's uranium conversion plant, said Kratzer, "would not have been viewed with much alarm by us or the NSG, since, as far as we were concerned, the reactor in which the fuel would be used could be and was being effectively safeguarded."[22]

There were other attempts to shore up the system. For example, Congress in 1976 passed the Symington Amendment to the Foreign Assistance Act, named after Senator Stuart Symington, a Missouri Democrat. The amendment prohibited U.S. military and economic assistance to any country that imported nuclear technology not covered by IAEA safeguards; it was specifically targeted at Pakistan. Simultaneously, work was under way on the Nuclear Nonproliferation Act that would be enacted two years later, upping the ante even further by requiring blanket safeguards on every nuclear facility within a country in order to secure approval for nuclear exports from the United States. But these measures were like building a dike when the dam had already burst—and in many ways it was a weak dike too. The new export control laws contained presidential veto provisions for Israel, but that opened a loophole for every country, which meant that waivers could be granted to allow the goods to go through. And, as Kratzer pointed out, the NSG list was intentionally less than comprehensive. By the mid-1970s, an extensive network of nuclear suppliers was eager for business, A. Q. Khan was their perfect customer, and there was not much that could get in anyone's way.

PAKISTAN ITSELF WAS going through one of its periodic upheavals. On July 5, 1977, General Muhammad Zia ul-Haq, army chief of staff, overthrew Bhutto in a largely bloodless military coup, becoming the nation's third ruler to impose martial law. Bhutto was thrown into prison. From his jail cell, he tried to reassert his primacy by claiming that Pakistan was near to attaining "full nuclear capability" prior to his overthrow. "All we [Pakistanis] needed was the nuclear reprocessing plant," he wrote in a lengthy document smuggled out of his cell.[23]

But continued pressure from the United States finally led France, under Valéry Giscard d'Estaing, to cancel the contract in late 1978. French technicians reportedly continued to work at the site in Chashma, but eventually stopped and the plant was never completed.[24] Giscard d'Estaing's move was evidence that even in France, the champion of breeders, the government was no longer blind to the proliferation threat posed by reprocessing the fuel for them, or agreeable to selling the technology to any willing buyer.

U.S. policy toward Pakistan vacillated during that period between cooperation and condemnation. But the administration was getting more evidence of the activities at Kahuta and was not pleased about Pakistan's human rights record. There were more threats about cutting off military and economic aid if construction continued. Bhutto was subjected to a show trial and hanged in the early hours of April 4, 1979. Two days later, citing fresh intelligence reports on the Pakistani enrichment effort, Carter finally severed U.S. military and financial assistance to Pakistan, insisting that Bhutto's execution had nothing to do with the decision.

The downturn in U.S.-Pakistani relations was short-lived. After the Soviets invaded Afghanistan in December 1979, the administration reverted to the old pattern of shoring up the generals. In a flash, nonproliferation, as a political issue, turned back into a pumpkin. "People joked about it—'good-bye nonproliferation,'" Gilinsky recalled.[25] Once again Pakistan was lavishly courted, Symington and the Nuclear Nonproliferation Act were ignored, and for the next decade, millions of dollars in financial and military aid flowed into Pakistan, with much of it going to rebel mujahideen waging war against the Soviets in Afghanistan. Apart from emboldening the fighters who would one day be America's enemy in the "war on terror," successive administrations signed off on restricted, high-tech American exports to Pakistan's nuclear program, helping to ensure the successful emergence of another nuclear weapons state. This, said Senator John Glenn, amounted to "a nuclear non-proliferation policy bordering on lawlessness."[26]

INSIDE PAKISTAN, A. Q. KHAN, a mere engineer who had once lived a quiet life in Europe, was on his way to achieving almost mythical status. Zia renamed the Kahuta plant the Khan Research Laboratories (KRL) in May 1981. Khan was now the undisputed king of the third-world nuclear city. A superb self-promoter, he tried to take credit for actually assembling the country's first nuclear weapon, although the work was done by the PAEC, according to several authoritative sources. In a video he later used to sell Pakistani nuclear technology to other countries, Khan says: "On the 10th of December, 1984, I wrote a letter to the then President, General Zia ul-Haq, and informed him that we were now in a position to detonate a device—a nuclear device—on a week's notice."[27] But Khan's main contribution to the effort was building a successful enrichment enterprise; without a reprocessing facility, the Pakistanis were totally dependent on him to produce their bomb material, highly-enriched uranium. His role in actually designing and assembling a nuclear weapon, on the other hand, was minimal. "The bomb design stuff was done at the PAEC in Islamabad," says Zia Mian, a research scientist with Princeton University's Program on Science and Global Security. "He just took credit for it."[28]

As Kahuta rose in importance, Chinese officials began showing up at the guesthouse next door to Khan's own home. And Khan began traveling to China, a practice he would continue to the end of his career. Information about these activities came through a variety of sources, including a procurement trail left by Khan and his underlings in Europe and a bit of luck on the part of U.S. intelligence agents. In one noteworthy case, American operatives in the early 1980s managed to get into Khan's European hotel room and riffle through his suitcase. Inside the bag, they reportedly found a drawing of a workable nuclear bomb design and a list of the steps needed to make it. It bore China's imprimatur.[29]

Two decades later, the same design would be found in Libya, in a shopping bag imprinted with the name of Khan's favorite high-end tailor. Pakistan's foreign minister, Sahabzada Yakub Khan, reportedly was present at the Lop Nur site for a May 1983 Chinese nuclear test, and there was speculation that the Chinese actually tested a Pakistani weapon. In return for assistance on reactors, weapons design, missile technology, and even uranium feed material that allowed Khan to test his centrifuges in the start-up phases, the Chinese are believed to have received Pakistan's valuable centrifuge enrichment drawings, which they needed because they lagged in that technology.

The American intelligence community was not only well aware of the affinity between China and Pakistan but knew of suspect or illegal Pakistani nuclear-related purchases made in the United States and Europe throughout the 1970s and '80s. As early as 1983, a State Department memo stated: "We now believe [Sino-Pakistani] cooperation has taken place in the areas of fissile material production and possibly also nuclear device design."

Then, the following year, a group of Pakistanis was arrested in Texas attempting to export fifty electronic triggering switches, known as krytons, for nuclear weapons. Two of the men admitted that the Pakistan Atomic Energy Commission had ordered the parts. Another case around that time involved the export of dozens of high-speed cathode-ray oscilloscopes and special cameras from a California couple to a Pakistani purchaser in Hong Kong. These were apparently needed to check the symmetry of compression on the core of a nuclear bomb, to ensure that the implosion triggers the nuclear explosion.[30]

Evidence, to say the least, was mounting. Yet throughout this period the Pakistani government continually denied the existence of a nuclear weapons program, and American leaders, intent on their struggle against the Soviets in Afghanistan, strained to believe them. Congressman Stephen J. Solarz, a New York Democrat, tried to break the dysfunctional relationship with a 1985 amendment requiring a cessation of aid to any country trying to buy sensitive nuclear items from the United States. That year, another amendment, drafted by Senator Larry Pressler, a South Dakota Republican, specifically required the administration to certify at the start of each fiscal year that Pakistan did not possess a nuclear device. But these well-intended laws would not work the way their authors intended. (In 1998, Solarz became a lobbyist for India, as senior counsel to the public relations firm APCO Worldwide, which was hired by the Indian embassy in Washington to deal with the aftermath of India's nuclear test explosions that year.)

In 1986, a National Intelligence Estimate (NIE) finally concluded that Kahuta had enriched enough uranium for a bomb and that assembly could take place within a matter of two weeks. Pakistan, said the NIE, was "two screwdriver turns" from assembling a weapon.[31] There were more warnings—and more aid—and in July 1987 the high-profile arrest of a Pakistani-born Canadian named Arshad Pervez (known as "Archie") for attempting to buy maraging steel manufactured in Pennsylvania, which is used in centrifuges. The ultimate buyer was a retired Pakistani Army brigadier, Inam ul-Haq, who ran a front company for purchasing components for Pakistan's nuclear program. An attempt to arrest ul-Haq failed.

Caught in the crosshairs of the constant dissembling by the American and Pakistani governments was a CIA analyst named Richard Barlow. Barlow had worked with nonproliferation officials in the State Department to ensnare both Pervez and ul-Haq in an undercover sting operation. But this plan came at an inconvenient moment: the administration was putting through a $480 million aid package, and a high-profile arrest could jeopardize approval. Congressional supporters of the anti-Soviet crusade commenced a huge lobbying effort to get the aid approved, urged on by former national security adviser Zbigniew Brzezinski, architect of the pro-Pakistani position under Carter as well as the covert aid to Muslim extremists aimed at drawing the Soviets into the December 1979 invasion of Afghanistan.

Solarz fought back, asking Barlow to testify about Pakistan's nuclear activities, which he did in a classified briefing. But it was to no avail. Solarz watched with growing anger as the aid package passed in December 1987. The White House was obligated to invoke the Solarz Amendment in January but immediately issued a waiver, and Pakistan got what it wanted. Indeed, in three successive years, 1987, 1988, 1989, the Reagan and Bush administrations certified Pakistan as having no nuclear weapons, although Richard J. Kerr, the CIA deputy director for intelligence all that time, told a journalist in 1993, "There is no question that we had an intelligence basis for not certifying from 1987 on."[32]

Barlow's testimony put him on a collision course with the CIA and the State Department's regional policy officials. He was taken off the

Pakistan case and shortly thereafter quit. He later became an analyst at the Pentagon Office of Non-Proliferation Policy but ran into more trouble over Pakistan. In 1989, with the government poised to sell $1.4 billion worth of new F-16 fighter planes to Pakistan to further the cause in Afghanistan, Barlow once again tried to get in the way, telling Congress that the F-16s could be used to deliver nuclear bombs. A colleague argued precisely the opposite, maintaining that Barlow's supposition "far exceeded the state of art in Pakistan."

Within days, Barlow was fired. Squeezed between the promoters of a regional policy and his own view that the truth, however inconvenient, should be told when U.S. laws were being violated, Barlow became a classic victim of whistle-blowing. He was stripped of his classified clearances and secretly accused of being a national security risk, a charge of which he was eventually cleared. Federal investigations found that Barlow had been unfairly fired.[33] In July 2007, a reporter from the *Washington Post* found Barlow living in a trailer at a campground in Montana, still battling Washington. His intelligence career destroyed, a marriage collapsed, Barlow, aged fifty-two, had been fighting for seventeen years, so far unsuccessfully, to gain a federal pension, the newspaper reported.[34]

IN THE SPRING of 1990, with civil unrest in Kashmir leading India and Pakistan toward another military confrontation, the Washington intelligence community received information regarded as "one hundred percent reliable" that Pakistan's army chief, General Aslam Beg, had ordered technicians at Kahuta to assemble a small number of nuclear weapons—and that Beg was willing to use them to prevent India's army from crossing the border. Tensions between the two sides had been escalating since the end of 1986 when India conducted a huge military exercise near Pakistan's border and was believed by some to have integrated tactical nuclear bombs into the day-to-day field maneuvers.[35]

Zia had died in a plane crash two years earlier. With Benazir Bhutto as prime minister, Washington analysts believed that control over the nuclear button lay with General Beg and the country's president, Ghulam Ishaq Khan, both enthusiastic political and financial supporters of A. Q. Khan's operation at Kahuta. Having tacitly, if not openly, encouraged Pakistan to build nuclear weapons, the American government was confronted with a frightening prospect: a nuclear exchange between India and Pakistan. After studying reams of satellite photos and other evidence, nervous officials in Washington concluded that the U.S.-supplied F-16s were "locked and loaded" on an airfield with nuclear weapons, according to a 1993 article in the *New Yorker*.[36] Richard J. Kerr, who as deputy director of the CIA coordinated the intelligence report during the May 1990 crisis, called it "more frightening than the Cuban missile crisis" and said it was "possibly as close as the world had ever come to nuclear war."[37]

Robert M. Gates, a longtime CIA official then serving the White House as deputy national security adviser, was sent to Islamabad and New Delhi to negotiate a settlement. "The analogy we kept making was to the summer of 1914," he told the article's author, Seymour Hersh, referring to the mishaps that led to the outbreak of World War I. "Pakistan and India seemed to be caught in a cycle that they couldn't break out of. I was convinced that if a war started, it would be nuclear."[38] When he arrived in Islamabad, Gates told Hersh, "I looked straight at Beg and said, 'General, our military has war-gamed every conceivable scenario between you and the Indians, and there isn't a single way you win.'"

The confrontation ended without a war, but that was not the end of tensions or the threat of nuclear war between the two countries.[39] In 1997, Pakistani prime minister Nawaz Sharif made it official that his country had nuclear weapons. The following spring, on May 28, 1998, the PAEC carried out five nuclear weapons tests in response to the same number of nuclear explosions by India, on May 11 and 13. Pakistan tested one more nuclear device May 30. The tit-for-tat exchange of tests prompted Pakistan-based militants, with the support of the military, to invade Indian-controlled Kashmir. Sharif met in Washington with President William J. Clinton, who convinced him to withdraw, and the confrontation ended. General Pervez Musharraf, who backed the operation and later overthrew Sharif in a coup, claimed that if a single Indian soldier had stepped into Pakistan, the response would have been nuclear. Indian officials maintained they had the capability to survive a first strike and then destroy Pakistan.

In December 2001, India again mobilized forces near the border and said it was considering military strikes on terrorist camps in Kashmir, after terrorists killed fourteen people in the Indian Parliament. More terrorist strikes followed in 2002, and tensions remained high. Then an Indian general exceeded his authority by moving armored vehicles close to the Pakistani border. He was dismissed, but the event rattled

nerves in Washington, New Delhi, and undoubtedly Islamabad. It bore a
striking parallel to the provocation caused by a Soviet official in Cuba
who ordered the shooting down of the U-2 plane at the height of the
Cuban Missile Crisis—without permission from Moscow. Both incidents, one in 1962 and the other forty years later, demonstrated the risk
of inadvertent nuclear war stemming from misunderstood or unauthorized behavior, or misperceptions. As U.S. diplomatic pressure to avert
war intensified, Secretary of Defense Donald Rumsfeld went to India
and Pakistan to discuss with his South Asian counterparts the results of
a classified Pentagon study. It concluded that nuclear war between the
two countries could result in twelve million deaths.[40]

While his own country three times stood poised for nuclear war, A.
Q. Khan was busy operating an underground nuclear suppliers network,
selling to other countries—Libya, Iran, Iraq, and probably North Korea—
the centrifuge designs he had stolen from Europe, as well as blueprints
for manufacturing nuclear weapons and access to his supply line.

The Indian-Pakistani rivalry has since lain mainly dormant, and
both sides have taken confidence-building measures to reduce the
threat of nuclear war. But theirs is an uneasy truce, as demonstrated by
the outrage that followed the terrorist attack in Mumbai in late 2008,
and the nuclear establishments in both countries are pursuing ambitious plans to increase their capacity for manufacturing fissile material. Presently, they are estimated to have enough for approximately
one hundred warheads in India's case and sixty-five in Pakistan's.[41] But
much is still unknown about both programs. Even more frightening is
the extent to which this arms race, chiefly through Khan's proliferation activities, may have sparked others in the Middle East, possibly
northern Africa, and conceivably even farther afield in Asia or Latin
America. Multan, city of war and peace and birthplace of the Pakistani
nuclear weapons program, may yet endure another cycle of destruction
and devastation, though this time it would be like nothing ever before
witnessed in its venerable, ancient history.

CHAPTER 16

First They Drive You Crazy

I T IS A LONG WAY FROM MULTAN to Cincinnati, and people selling bombs seem a world away from construction workers building nuclear plants. Yet in June 1980, when a private detective named Thomas Applegate started poking around the construction site of the William H. Zimmer plant for a client involved in a divorce case, he unraveled a tale as replete with secrecy and deception as anything A. Q. Khan could conceive at Kahuta, even if the consequences were not the same.

Applegate discovered that contract employees were falsifying their time cards. When the utility subsequently hired him to find out more, he uncovered something potentially far worse—records of pipe welds also were being doctored. The utility, Cincinnati Gas and Electric, had not banked on that discovery and was attempting to bury the information without repairing the welds. So Applegate informed the Government Accountability Project, a nonprofit public interest group in Washington, which in turn alerted the U.S. Office of Special Counsel— and Henry Myers, the chief scientific adviser to the House Committee on Interior and Insular Affairs, chaired by Representative Morris Udall, a Democrat from Arizona.[1] That was the beginning of the end for the Zimmer nuclear project.

Myers was part of the "political earthquake" unfolding on Capitol Hill. He worked in "a different part of the forest," as he put it, highlighting nuclear safety issues the way Leventhal and others called attention to proliferation dangers. In Myers's woods, people lied about

x conscientiously

what they had or had not done to make plants safer, they let problems fester until it was too late, and they used psychological forms of avoidance—even to the extent of inviting criminal legal investigations—to convince themselves, and they hoped the public, that nuclear reactors were safe. The reactors themselves were enormously complex machines with an incalculable number of things that could go wrong. When that happened at Three Mile Island in 1979, another fault line in the nuclear world was exposed. One malfunction led to another, and then to a series of others, until the core of the reactor itself began to melt, and even the world's most highly trained nuclear engineers did not know how to respond. The accident revealed serious deficiencies in a system that was meant to protect public health and safety. There were shortcomings not only in the design of the plant but in the underlying approach the Nuclear Regulatory Commission took to licensing Three Mile Island—and every other reactor operating in the United States.

The failure to adequately address the complexity of reactor operating systems in order to prevent nuclear accidents is analogous to the inability of governments and industry to prevent nuclear proliferation. The systems that were put in place to address both risks were minimalist. They sought to reduce the chances of theft or accident, but they did not begin to address the scope of the challenges they faced. The people who wrote the rules were smart enough to realize they could not guarantee the outcome. Thus the NRC's basic job as mandated by Congress was, and still is, to ensure only that the plants it licenses and regulates will provide "adequate protection" to public health and safety. The NRC was left to decide what "adequate" meant, and later interpretation of the word made it clear that it did not mean absolute protection. After all, how could it?[2]

People who genuinely worried about safety, like those who concerned themselves with proliferation, also faced formidable political and commercial obstacles. Utilities in a hurry to build reactors, and then maximize profits once they were operating, brought pressure to bear on the regulators, and that meant that safety concerns were shunted to the side. This put a large segment of the population at risk. Most reactors are situated near large urban areas to reduce electricity transmission costs. This means that a massive accidental release of radioactivity from just one unit could bring unquantifiable harm to millions of people. When Chernobyl exploded seven years after the Three Mile Island accident, it was compared by some to a nuclear bomb explosion. This was understandably awkward for an industry that has always been at pains to disassociate itself from the military side of nuclear. After all, reactors are meant to produce electricity, not nuclear devastation. But the fact is that a reactor explosion, such as occurred at Chernobyl, is potentially even more harmful to long-term human health and the environment than an atmospheric nuclear weapons blast. The issues associated with nuclear plant safety are therefore just as important to understand as those associated with proliferation. Each demonstrates a different way in which systemic failures and human fallibility make nuclear energy so risky.

MYERS MOVED TO the Hill in January 1976, with a Ph.D. in nuclear physics from the California Institute of Technology. Udall hired him as the chief scientific adviser for the House Interior Committee, which had charge of monitoring the Nuclear Regulatory Commission after the breakup of the AEC and the demise of the JCAE. The oversight function was turned over to the panel's Subcommittee on Energy and the Environment. Henry would be the subcommittee's expertly tuned eyes and ears.

Myers and his small staff spent the better part of a year investigating Applegate's allegations. The NRC began two separate probes and in November 1981 fined Cincinnati Gas and Electric two hundred thousand dollars—the largest fine in the agency's history—for a faulty quality assurance program. But a series of subcommittee hearings organized by Myers, beginning in 1982, revealed so many other serious misdeeds that the NRC, under pressure, eventually issued an order to halt work on the reactor in the autumn of 1982. The utility was forced to abandon the project and convert the facility into a coal-burning plant after spending $1.6 billion constructing a reactor.

Myers arrived on the Hill somewhere between an agnostic and a believer in nuclear power. Basically he thought smart people could build reactors, but he had a few lingering doubts about operational safety. In Congress, Myers found himself dealing with human weaknesses far beyond what he had thought likely, or what his education and experience had prepared him for. Based on the subcommittee's investigations,

Myers estimated that as many as three-quarters of the more than one hundred reactors then operating or under construction had "serious problems" that should have entailed costly repairs or closure.

Henry could hold forth on many of these cases—and did—for hours, guiding his listeners on a virtual tour of a nuclear Hell's Kitchen, where cracks, leaks, faulty welds, false records, and human vice made an unsettling portrait of reactor sites in the United States. Describing the Zimmer investigation, for example, he wrote in an e-mail: "This is the one where there was an overabundance of workers and purportedly three trailers on site, one for drinking, one for gambling and one for prostitution. It is also the place that led an NRC official to tell his guy to take documents (related to the weld cheating) home so they would not have to be released per a Freedom of Information request. When this became known, the official was removed from his job and sent on a sabbatical to the U of VA [University of Virginia] for an MBA."

In another instance, the Diablo Canyon plant near Los Angeles, located near an earthquake fault line, went through three years of costly modifications after it was discovered that the drawings for the two units had been inadvertently swapped while the plants were being built.

Henry worked long hours in a cramped office in the Longworth Building, surrounded by stacks of documents. His hair was almost white, and he wore wire-rimmed glasses that appeared to be a permanent feature on his harried face. People who valued their serenity would run like mad from Henry because they might not like to hear what he had to say. On the other hand, if they wanted to know about nuclear safety in those critical years when many plants were still being built, running away was not an option. His foes, of which there were many, variously referred to Myers as a "whacko" or a "Commie." Henry would say about them: "First they drive you crazy, then they call you crazy."[3]

ANIMOSITY BETWEEN THE industry and its critics grew during the oil-hungry 1970s and early 1980s when activists, many of whom had protested the Vietnam War, turned their venom on a smug, overly confident nuclear establishment. Industry officials pitched nuclear power as the answer to both the energy crisis and the air pollution caused by fossil fuel plants, just as they now portray it as the solution to the energy crisis and global warming. In 1973, the year of the first Arab oil embargo, Nixon launched an energy plan called Project Independence, an effort to wean Americans off imported energy.

That year, the AEC predicted that by the turn of the century one thousand reactors would be producing electricity for homes and businesses across the nation. The nuclear industry seemed to be booming. Compared to 22 reactor orders in the decade up to 1965, 68 units were booked in only two years between 1966 and 1968. After a slowdown, orders picked up again between 1971 and 1973 when utilities signed up for a total of 106 reactors, including 44 in 1973, a record year.[4]

After 1973, orders declined sharply as forecasts of electricity demand fell and construction costs rose. The 7 percent annual electricity demand growth typical of the previous two decades fell to about 3 percent, while utilities were forced to borrow heavily at rates above 15 percent to finance lengthening construction delays. And no one really knew whether nuclear power was safe. People either had forgotten or never heard about the accidents that had occurred in the 1950s and early 1960s.

Most industry experts would admit, if pressed very hard, that a nuclear plant had so many variables there was no telling what might go wrong. Yet in judging the reliability of a reactor design, the NRC by and large weighed the potential for large-scale, single failures, assuming that if a design could handle a big accident, it would naturally be able to handle a variety of smaller ones—all of which were regarded as being "within the design envelope," in the regulators' jargon. This approach had long been criticized both within the NRC itself and by industry critics.[5]

In 1973, the year of Project Independence, the consumer advocate Ralph Nader said, "If the country knew what the facts were and if they had to choose between nuclear reactors and candles, they would choose candles."[6] What even Nader apparently did not know was that at the Tennessee Valley Authority's (TVA) Browns Ferry nuclear station in northern Alabama, technicians actually used candles routinely to check for air leaks. This activity took place in a large room containing hundreds of electrical wires and cables for monitoring and powering the station's two operating reactors; a third was under construction. Workers would move around the edges holding the lighted candles near the openings where the cables penetrated the thick walls containing the two adjacent reactors. Highly flammable polyurethane foam had been applied as a sealant around the openings, precisely where the crew looked for leaks. Small fires occasionally broke out, but they had always been extinguished without a problem, so the practice continued.

On March 22, 1975, the workers were not so lucky. As they made their rounds with lighted candles, a rush of air sucked the open flame into the foam, and the fire spread too quickly to snuff. It burned for seven hours, engulfing some two thousand electrical cables in the process. Without power, many of the plant's valves, pumps, and other electrical equipment simply shut down. The emergency system for cooling the reactor core was destroyed completely in one reactor and partially in the other. The TVA was embarrassed by the negative publicity the fire attracted, but it got off lightly considering what might have happened. The operators managed to "scram" the reactors, one automatically and one manually—meaning they were able to lower enough of the control rods to stop the fissioning process—and there was enough water in the primary cooling systems to prevent damage to the cores. No measurable quantities of radiation were released, and plant personnel emerged without serious injury. But the accident left basically unresolved a key question: could a reactor's safety system adequately protect it from a core melt in the event of a more serious accident?

NUCLEAR PLANTS ARE on one level nothing more than giant furnaces whose heat is used to generate electricity. Utilities like them because they supply base load capacity, which is the minimum amount of electric power that a utility can deliver over time at a steady rate. But because of the dangers associated with the heat source, radioactive nuclear fuel, reactors are costly to build and consume a lot of energy in the process, requiring vast quantities of cement, steel, and electrical wiring. The consequences of a mistake are potentially catastrophic, and that is leaving aside the question of where to put the nuclear fuel once it has been discharged from the core, a process that takes place once every eighteen months during a reactor's forty-year initial lifespan (many utilities are now extending that to sixty years). A nuclear accident can result in a large loss of life, expose huge populations to cancer risk, and render great swathes of land essentially uninhabitable. What reactors lack in elegance, they make up for in magnitude, scale, and complexity. For these reasons, nuclear power plants can be said to exist in an industrial category of their own.

Reactor stations seem to swallow people who work inside them. Technicians work like Lilliputians next to steam-carrying pipes as big around as manhole covers and machinery the length of city blocks. They might be alone or in small teams at lonely outposts in a turbine hall, or on top of the reactor core, exposed to humming, hissing machines, loud beeping noises, and the crackle of a paging system that "has the tonal quality of a bad bronchial cough."[7] There are few people under the four-acre roof of a nuclear plant because it mostly runs itself; most of the human activity is inside the control room from which engineers monitor and occasionally inspect systems inside the plant. Unlike a plumber who can look inside a boiler to check, say, the pilot light, reactor operators cannot visually inspect the reactor core, where the biggest danger lies. Even after the accident at Three Mile Island, it took the better part of a decade to determine the full extent of damage to its core—radioactivity prevented the crew from getting too near.

Because of their dependence on the control room panel, however, reactor operators are really less like plumbers and more like airline pilots flying permanently on instruments. Yet control rooms offer minimal comfort during a crisis and sometimes even during routine operations. Skilled operators with engineering backgrounds, years of experience and training, and logical, linear thinking patterns can find themselves feeling more like tea leaf readers than commanders of advanced technological citadels. Confronted by panels of lights, gauges, and other monitors and alarms, their job becomes essentially interpretive. If they read the instruments incorrectly, as happened at Three Mile Island, the rest can go horribly awry. In such an environment, it is entirely possible that mental acuity, the ability to ask the right questions, and the facility for acting on instinct are reduced or even disappear.

A REACTOR'S DEFENSE, or safety, system is not unlike the multiple barriers—towers, moats, drawbridge, portcullis—in a castle. The difference is that the potential enemy is within, rather than over the next hill. Hence, defense-in-depth—a term used by the industry to describe multiple safety systems—starts with cladding around the fuel rods inside the reactor core. This first barrier is made of a zirconium alloy called Zircaloy, which has a high melting point. The next main layer of protection is the pressure vessel containing the core, with its fuel assemblies and control rods and associated piping. Then there are engineered safety features such as the emergency core cooling system (ECCS) to remove heat in the event the primary cooling system fails. There are also filters, vents, scrubbers, and air circulators to collect radioactive gases and particles in an accidental release. Finally, there is the containment building, which can be as high as twenty stories and often is shaped like a dome. Its walls are approximately three to four feet thick. Despite the impressive amount of cement, the architect-engineers who designed the first generation of American reactors regarded the containment as the last line of defense. This is a crucial point; in the aftermath of the Chernobyl accident, the question of whether the Soviets had an adequate containment, or one at all, became a big issue—all the other defense systems had been obliterated in the explosions that took place.

One key concern early on, as opposed to containments, was the viability of the ECCS. It became essential to safety because it was intended to provide backup cooling if the primary cooling system unexpectedly shut down. Experiments in the early 1970s provided little comfort that these systems would kick in and behave as they were supposed to when the time came. In one test series at the Idaho laboratory, 90 percent of the water from a scaled-down model flowed out of the same break that had caused the loss of coolant in the first place and never reached the core.[8] In a real-life event—the Browns Ferry fire—the ECCS also failed, according to Hal Ornstein, an NRC official who investigated it. "What happened was the nonsafety equipment bailed them out—the control rod drive pump . . . it gave them the water they needed," Ornstein said. "The ECCS didn't work. It was compromised by the fire."[9]

Uncertainty over such an important safety system should have given regulators pause. Yet all through the 1970s, they continued to license new reactors, without having resolved key questions about backup cooling in reactors already under construction. Moreover, they were discouraged from looking too deeply into the matter. Milton Shaw, director of the AEC's Division of Reactor Development and Technology, even went so far as to forbid researchers on the ECCS experiments in Idaho to talk with regulatory officials, according to the agency's own historian.[10]

BUT AS THE times grew more turbulent during the late 1960s and the 1970s, a growing opposition organized large demonstrations at reactor sites, and an increasingly knowledgeable, articulate, and media-savvy group of people began challenging the industry inside congressional and NRC hearing rooms and on television. At a series of AEC hearings on the ECCS, Daniel Ford, of the Union of Concerned Scientists, proved a smart, challenging David against an unsuspecting Goliath, forcing Shaw to admit that there was little solid evidence that the ECCS would function properly in an emergency. A Harvard-trained economist, Ford had schooled himself enough in core physics and heat transfer dynamics to formulate mind benders like "Mr. Shaw, what, if any, experiments demonstrate the conservatism of applying steady state heat transfer correlations to blowdown analysis?" Shaw was "verbally floored," reported *Nucleonics Week*, and could not provide the answer Ford was looking for. In late 1972, three years after starting the Union of Concerned Scientists as an MIT faculty organization, Ford and a colleague joined forces with Nader, and Nader went on the nationally televised *Dick Cavett Show* afterward and told three million viewers that "the risks of something going wrong with these nuclear power plants are so catastrophic that they are not worth the benefit."[11]

Then, in early 1976, three midlevel engineers with General Electric's nuclear power division in California—Gregory C. Minor, Richard B. Hubbard, and Dale G. Bridenbaugh—resigned with a damning statement that "nuclear power is a technological monster that threatens all future generations." They had families to support and no immediate job prospects but, with fifty-four years of experience at GE between them, a lot of credibility. Just a few days later, on February 8, 1976, *60 minutes* aired an interview with an NRC staff member named Robert D. Pollard, filmed on January 13, the day he resigned. He contended that the NRC was failing in its duty to ensure reactor safety, and had ignored concerns he raised about the Indian Point plant twenty-four miles north of New York. "It will be just a matter of luck if Indian Point doesn't sometime during its life have a major accident," he told CBS's Mike Wallace. Pollard joined the Union of

Fukashima - oops - 1950-2010 = 60
288   & I think the est was   IN MORTAL HANDS
              far off - or no accid for long time]

Concerned Scientists and became an important, lasting critic of the
industry for many years.

In June that year, Myers organized hearings on nuclear accident
risk. The focus was the latest multimillion-dollar, taxpayer-funded report, known as WASH-1400 in support of an extension of the Price-
Anderson nuclear insurance scheme. Written by a panel of more than
sixty experts headed by an MIT nuclear engineering professor named
Norman C. Rasmussen, the report concluded that in a single reactor,
the chances of a severe accident, in which part, or all, of the nuclear
core melted, were one in twenty thousand years.

A stream of critics attacked the report, once again opening a window
on the arcane world of probability analysis—and, as had happened back
in the late 1950s, demonstrating the difficulty of accurately gauging nuclear risk. Princeton physicist Frank von Hippel, who had urged Udall
to hold the hearing, argued the report overlooked "enormous uncertainties" in its calculations. "While categories of accident initiating events
such as earthquakes and fires were dismissed with hand waving arguments, sabotage was explicitly not considered; it was assumed without
substantial analysis that the performance of emergency systems would
not be degraded by accident conditions when the reactor building
would be filled with superheated steam and water . . . and, when crucial numbers were not available, they were simply guessed—although
different investigators might have guessed values 10 to 100 times larger
or smaller."[12]

The hearing had no effect on the Price-Anderson bill because Congress, against Udall's wishes, already had extended the legislation, but
it raised public consciousness about nuclear risk. And in 1978, a new
review group appointed by the NRC and led by Professor Harold Lewis
of the University of California at Santa Barbara concluded that the uncertainties in WASH-1400's estimates of the probabilities of severe accidents were "in general, greatly understated."[13]

1978

BY COINCIDENCE THAT same year, on March 28, the second of two
units at the Three Mile Island (TMI) nuclear plant in Pennsylvania
went online. One day later the reactor tripped, meaning something
had happened to cause the control rods to automatically reinsert themselves into the core to stop fission. Another eighteen trips, or "scrams,"
occurred during the subsequent twelve months, until precisely one

year to the day after the reactor went online, a scram occurred that would lead to what was then billed as the world's worst nuclear reactor accident, and the unit's permanent closure. If a home heating system failed that many times, the homeowner would probably have the heating contractor in court. But by the NRC's standards, having eighteen reactor scrams in one year was not considered out of the ordinary. Based on the number of reportable "events"—those considered serious enough to warrant notification to the NRC—TMI-2 was ranked "average."[14]

Despite numerous plant inspections, NRC reports on TMI during that period were scanty. They provided accident investigators with few clues about the plant's operating history, and the information was "of such a general, cursory nature that it frequently is inscrutable," a report on the accident would later observe.[15] Yet had even these inspection findings been aggressively followed up, the utility might have taken steps that would have prevented the accident. And that would have saved the operator, Metropolitan Edison (Met Ed), from losing a unit that cost seven hundred million dollars to build and produced power for the equivalent of less than six months before the disaster that would cripple it forever.

By an amazing coincidence, less than two weeks prior to the event, *The China Syndrome* opened in more than six hundred movie theaters across the country. Starring Jack Lemmon, Jane Fonda, and Michael Douglas, the movie is about a venal utility executive attempting to cover up the severity of a nuclear accident until it is discovered that a meltdown is in progress. The hugely entertaining thriller became even more popular after the events at TMI, helping to lift stock prices for Columbia Pictures.[16] To journalists covering the real event, the accident at TMI seemed even more frightening. "I do remember thinking at the time that reality had proved to be much more disturbing and dramatic than the fiction—that the event effectively upstaged the film," said Sarah Miller, then a reporter for *Nucleonics Week*.

THE REAL ACCIDENT began in an eerie predawn silence. Three technicians were in the cavernous turbine hall trying to clear a pipe blockage when suddenly they heard "loud thunderous noises, like a couple of freight trains." It was 4:00 A.M., March 28, 1979. The shift supervisor, William Zewe, was sitting in the control room with two other operators, Craig Faust and Edward Frederick, sorting through papers when an alarm like a loud horn sounded and the control panel lit up with more than one hundred warning lights. Zewe's strained voice could barely be heard over a faulty paging system. "Turbine trip— reactor trip!"[17]

The problem started in a part of the plant where steam is produced, known as the secondary loop, a water circulating system separate from the primary loop around the reactor core. Water circulates through these loops at high speed, under tremendous pressure to prevent it boiling, moved along by four coolant pumps, each the size of a small truck. In simple terms, the job of the primary is to transfer heat from the reactor core to the secondary, where a generator turns it into steam that drives the turbine to produce electricity. The separate loops are necessary to keep the mildly radioactive water in the primary from getting into the secondary.

Once steam is produced, it is condensed back into water for a return trip to the generator. Its route includes a detour through "condensate polishers"—there were eight in all—like multiple car washes designed to clean the water by removing impurities. One of the polishers was blocked, and for reasons that have never been determined, the system's pumps shut down—a bypass valve that would have allowed the water to continue flowing failed to open. That set in motion a series of events that occurred with orchestral complexity and blinding speed and left the reactor without an operating turbine or working feedwater pumps. Eight seconds after the polisher pumps tripped, the effect was felt in the primary loop, and no water moved to the secondary. This meant that the steam generator could no longer remove heat from the water coming from the core, so heat and pressure rose. That triggered the scram. But that only ended the production of more heat; it did nothing about its recent rapid buildup, or the urgent need for its removal.

For the next two hours, Zewe and his crew made a lot of mistakes. Much would be said later about a supposed lack of operator experience and training at TMI. That seemed to ignore the fact that Zewe, Faust, and Frederick were veterans of Rickover's elite navy nuclear corps, as were approximately half the other nuclear plant operators in the United States at that time. Rickover trainees were the most highly prized nuclear engineers in the country. Nevertheless, their training seemed to count for little as the three men faced the bank of lights, each flickering signal competing with the others for their attention. They were not able to decipher their meaning. "I would have liked to have thrown away the alarm panel. It wasn't giving us any useful information," Faust later said.[18]

The situation only worsened. Unbeknownst to the operators, a mechanism known as the pilot-operated relief valve (PORV) was stuck open. The PORV sits above the pressurizer, a large tank half filled with coolant water. Under normal conditions, a cushion of steam sits on top of the water in the tank to keep the pressure in the primary loop at the correct level so water does not boil on its way to the generator. If the pressure suddenly increases, the PORV is supposed to automatically open to release steam so the pressure returns to normal—and then it should close.

At TMI-2 that morning, the PORV had opened in response to the pressure buildup, but it never closed—and neither Zewe nor the crew working with him realized that. Babcock & Wilcox, which built the plant, well knew about the problem with stuck PORVs. A similar sequence of events had occurred at Toledo Edison's Davis-Besse reactor in 1977, but the operators had recognized that the valve was open and blocked it before the situation spiraled out of control. A warning guidance was drafted for other B&W reactors, but it was never sent out, apparently because B&W's senior management did not think it important enough.[19]

Because of the open valve, the pressurizer no longer performed the job for which it was intended. The steam bubble soon disappeared, and the pressurizer itself became a conduit for the rapid loss of coolant water, effectively turning itself into a depressurizer. Now instead of circulating around the core, the coolant water began emptying out of the primary loop, through the PORV, and into a waste tank on the containment floor. Soon the tank was filled. Then it burst open, spilling contaminated water over the floor. A sump pump kicked into action and began sending radioactive water into the auxiliary building next door. Zewe realized this at 4:38 A.M. He quickly shut off the sump pump, but by then the emergency core cooling pumps had turned themselves on, pushing more water into the system to compensate for the water that was going out through the pressurizer. Zewe and his colleagues still did not realize the PORV was open.

Several instruments screamed for attention, some of them going off-scale, others well outside their normal range. Individually, they signaled trouble; viewed collectively, they were telling Zewe that disaster was at hand. Zewe and his crew were in the midst of a loss-of-coolant accident, which became more serious as each minute ticked by, but they failed to realize this and therefore did nothing to stop it. Amazingly, there was nothing that gave the operators a direct reading of the amount of coolant in the primary system. (Imagine driving a car without a fuel-tank gauge.) Zewe saw all the indicators that should have told him what was happening, but he and the other operators would later tell investigators that they pretty much ignored them because they did not think they were reliable.

Instead, thinking that water still was circulating more or less normally, Zewe focused on keeping the water pressure under control, and that led another operator to shut down one of four emergency cooling pumps and throttle back another to about half its original flow. Shutting down the emergency coolant pumps was precisely the wrong thing to do. It got worse. When the two operating pumps began violently vibrating, they too were shut down. With the water flow reduced to a trickle, the overheated core turned into a teakettle, boiling water, making steam, and gradually dropping the water level until the twelve-foot-high fuel bundles were more than half uncovered.

When Brian Mehler arrived around 6:00 A.M. to relieve Zewe as shift supervisor, he looked at all the indicators Zewe had basically decided to ignore and ordered a block valve shut that stopped coolant hemorrhaging out of the PORV. But it was too late. By then, two hours and twenty minutes after the initial scram, about thirty-two thousand gallons of water had escaped the primary loop, more than one-third its total volume. Over the next several hours, approximately half the core turned into a molten mass. That created yet another crisis. As steam passed over the fuel bundles, the zirconium in the cladding oxidized, creating zirconium dioxide and hydrogen, and the fuel inside began melting. Hydrogen in combination with oxygen could lead to a massive explosion.

WHY ZEWE AND his crew failed to realize they were dealing with a loss-of-coolant accident remains essentially a mystery despite the numerous legal, regulatory, and congressional investigations that took place after the accident. One clue that emerged afterward, pointing to shoddy management practices and poor regulatory oversight, offers only a partial explanation. The utility had been experiencing abnormally high leak rates in its coolant system for several weeks before the accident but failed to report these to the NRC. Met Ed later would be indicted for the violation. Although the PORV itself apparently functioned the way it was supposed to during these previous events, the leakages had caused the outlet temperature readings to rise. So Zewe might have thought that the high readings that particular morning were related to the earlier problem, rather than a major loss-of-coolant accident. But it does not explain why he misread all the other indicators that Mehler seems to have instantly understood.

Mehler had other problems. He and his crew had to try to understand the extent of the accident, and its precise nature. They declared a site emergency shortly before 7:00 A.M., contacted the Pennsylvania Emergency Management Agency, and one hour later sent several foremen and instrument technicians to take temperature readings of the core. These varied to such a degree, from two hundred degrees Fahrenheit to upwards of four thousand degrees, that they were apparently disregarded—no one wanted to think the worst, that a core melt was in progress. But several of the crew who had actually taken the readings were in no doubt about what was happening. One of them, identified only as Instrument Man B in a later NRC transcript because he did not want his name revealed, said that "it was the general consensus of the instrument people that the core was definitely uncovered . . . no one really knew what was actually happening, some had an inkling and didn't want to believe what was going on. Once you start seeing a temperature of 3000 to 4000 degrees in a core, well . . . the first thing that starts coming to mind, you've got a meltdown coming. The core is uncovered."[20]

Around the same time, technicians collected water samples from the reactor coolant system, a procedure that involved opening a valve to allow a small amount of highly radioactive fluid into the container. "The people taking that sample got a significant dose," said Myers. "That was proof of a melted core. That this was not reported to the NRC in a timely manner was a significant contributor to the forty-eight-hour delay in recognition by the Commission that the accident ranked near the top on the NRC's severity scale."[21]

In Harrisburg, the state capital, a staff member of the state Bureau of Radiation Protection, William E. Dornsife, the state's only trained nuclear engineer, heard the news and immediately called the TMI control room. When one of the crew answered the phone, Dornsife

heard an announcement in the background telling employees to evacuate the fuel-handling building adjacent to the containment. "It didn't
hit me until I heard that," he later said. "And I said to myself, 'This is
the biggie.' "[22]

By midmorning, fifty-five minutes after high radiation readings in
the control room forced TMI's operators to put on respirators, making
communication between them difficult, Lieutenant Governor William
Scranton told a press conference in Harrisburg that "everything is under control" and that "there is and was no danger to public health and
safety." Harrisburg is about an hour's drive from TMI.

If ever there was a time for evacuation it was then, when plant conditions were at their most dangerous, but the public had no way of
knowing that. Those in charge seemed determined to downplay the
enveloping crisis. For example, Met Ed's first statement said the plant
would be "out of service for about a week." Then it disclosed a "malfunction" but said it was not that serious. There were conflicting and
confusing statements about radiation releases. General Public Utilities, Met Ed's parent, evidently concerned about the veracity of the
utility's early statements, issued its own release later that morning
announcing that a "low level release of radioactive gas beyond the site
boundary" had occurred, but that it did "not believe that the level
constitutes a danger to the health and safety of the public."[23]

While these assurances were put out, operators struggled for most
of the day to get the coolant pumps working. Finally, just before four
in the afternoon, they got one of them running. Temperatures in the
core began to come down for the first time in twelve hours.

As the disaster unfolded, NRC officials, whose offices were spread
out between different locations in Washington, D.C., and suburban
Maryland, responded clumsily and halfheartedly to the news from
Pennsylvania. It was not until Friday, two days after the scram, that
senior commission officials finally were dispatched to the site. In the
meantime, a decision by TMI operators to vent radioactive gas through
the exhaust stack led to confusion about the extent of the threat to
public health, with the NRC itself incorrectly concluding that the
plant was emitting extremely high radiation levels to the ground.[24]
The situation was potentially so serious, in the regulators' view, that
NRC staff contacted civil defense officials in Pennsylvania on Friday

and advised them to begin an evacuation. When Governor Richard Thornburgh got wind of what was going on, he was furious.

Thornburgh had final authority to order an evacuation, but he was not yet prepared to give it. It was his worst nightmare. Within a twenty-mile radius of the plant, there were six hundred thousand people, thirteen hospitals, a prison, and presumably at least a few retirement homes.[25] "No matter how well they are planned, massive evacuations can kill and injure people," he would later say.[26]

But people were already packing up to leave because a county emergency official had tipped off a radio station about a possible evacuation order, and they heard it on the radio. Increasingly exasperated, Thornburgh called the White House on Friday and asked President Carter for "one good man" from the NRC who could evaluate the plant situation and "advise us as to the crucial problems." Carter tapped Harold R. Denton, the NRC's director of nuclear reactor regulation, for the job and sent him to Pennsylvania as his personal representative. A southerner like Carter, Denton, from North Carolina, was a calm man, highly respected by the NRC staff. He had supported the ill-advised NRC evacuation advisory that morning. But neither Carter nor Thornburgh knew that.

While arrangements were being made for Denton's departure later that afternoon, NRC chairman Joseph Hendrie told Thornburgh: "We really don't know what is going on . . . The plant is not under control and it is not performing the way it should."[27] Although the radiation readings were now known to be less of a threat, a bigger potential problem loomed—the possibility of an explosion caused by a buildup of hydrogen from the melting fuel rods.[28] That could set off a chain of events leading to a cataclysmic containment breach. Hendrie told Thornburgh later on Friday afternoon that chances of a hydrogen explosion in the pressure vessel were "pretty close to zero" because of the lack of "any oxygen in there."[29] But the hydrogen issue was extremely complex, and no one knew for certain how the situation would evolve.

After conferring with Hendrie, Thornburgh decided to issue an evacuation advisory after all, but only for pregnant women and small children within a five-mile radius around the plant (mainly because existing evacuation plans only covered that much ground), and also to close all twenty-three schools within the area. As thousands hastily prepared to leave their homes, phone lines jammed, lines formed at gas stations, and traffic backed up. Kids were picked up from schools.

A mother later recounted how her children warned her not to breathe outside. They asked her why "the electric company put all of that radiation in our air."[30]

THAT NIGHT ON the *CBS Evening News* Walter Cronkite told sixteen million viewers: "The world has never known a day quite like today. It faced the considerable uncertainties and dangers of the worst nuclear power plant accident of the atomic age." Three Mile Island had at least claimed no lives as had the accident in Idaho many years earlier; nor had it resulted in a major radioactive release as did the fire at Windscale and the explosion at Kyshtym. These disasters, though, were generally not known about.

Denton had set up operations at a house near the plant that belonged to a Met Ed employee. He had a red phone that connected him directly to the White House and seventy-four NRC staff members working with him on the site. In Washington, Denton's key safety expert, Roger Mattson, worked all day Saturday to determine the extent of the threat posed by the hydrogen bubble, placing calls to experts across the country. That morning, Mattson told the commissioners: "Let me say, as frankly as I know how, bringing this plant down is risky. No plant has ever been in this condition, no plant has ever been tested in this condition, no plant has ever been analyzed in this condition."[31] And nothing heard from the various experts, all of whom came up with different answers, changed the view of the man who ran NRC's safety systems division. By early afternoon, Mattson had concluded there was enough free oxygen to present a potential problem. Hendrie, who had a nuclear engineering background, also was worried.

But at the TMI site itself, Victor Stello, who ran NRC's division of operating reactors and had also consulted with experts, was convinced that the hydrogen bubble was not a problem and that any oxygen that formed would simply recombine with hydrogen to create water. Even if some oxygen remained, its rate of generation would be so low, he reasoned, that it would take many weeks to create a flammable mix.[32]

Most of the people who had already left their homes went to stay with friends and relatives. But a hundred or so remained behind at a temporary shelter in the sports arena at Hershey, home to a popular amusement park. On Saturday, while scientists and engineers across the country puzzled over the hydrogen problem, those stranded got free passes to the local zoo and the Hershey's Chocolate World museum and confectionary.

By Saturday night, Associated Press reporters had fleshed out the basic story. "Federal officials said tonight that the gas bubble inside the crippled reactor at Three Mile Island is showing signs of becoming potentially explosive," the AP's lead story said. The article cited an anonymous NRC source suggesting that the "critical point could be reached within two days." Radio and television stations immediately picked up the story. Many of those living within the vicinity of the unfolding disaster who had not already left home did so then. In all, 144,000 people within a fifteen-mile radius of the plant evacuated at some point during the crisis.

Stello could not believe what he was witnessing. A big, burly, dark-haired, and sometimes emotional man, Stello was the son of a coal miner from central Pennsylvania, where mining accidents and black lung disease were common. Stello's sense of desperation only increased after he attended mass in nearby Middletown on Sunday morning and the priest offered general absolution to a sparse congregation, a rite given in rare instances where either large-scale loss of life seems imminent or individuals are not able to make confession. Afterward, he would recount, "Everybody started crying, and I started crying." He returned from the church service extremely upset and exclaimed to Joseph Fouchard, the chief NRC spokesman, "Look what we have done to these fine people!"[33]

President Carter had also gone to church that morning. Afterward, accompanied by his wife, Rosalynn, and a small group of advisers, he boarded a helicopter and arrived at the stricken plant that afternoon, still not certain about the wisdom of a general evacuation. Stello and Mattson, both now on the scene, continued arguing over the hydrogen problem, as they had while Carter's helicopter was landing at the Harrisburg airport. Stello's view proved correct. By late afternoon there were indications the problem was not getting any worse. "It was clear that we had been chasing a myth . . . You weren't getting any net oxygen and never had," Hendrie said later.[34] More frightening in retrospect was the fact that in a country where the depth of nuclear expertise was unsurpassed, no one knew for certain how the situation would play out until the problem disappeared.

BY MONDAY MORNING, NRC officials concluded that the "acute" phase of the accident was over, although Hendrie warned that a "reduced—but still serious—risk" loomed. However, as regulators and utility officials kept a close watch on the plant, the threat of a large radiation released gradually diminished.[35]

The next step was to try to determine what had happened. In June 1979 the NRC commissioned two lawyers, Mitchell Rogovin and George T. Frampton Jr., of the Washington law firm Rogovin, Stern, and Huge, to head a special inquiry into the accident, assisted by a large team of experts. Their report, released in January 1980, was highly critical of the NRC's "single criterion failure" approach to regulation, pointing out that numerous "*small* loss-of-coolant accidents and relatively routine *transients* [italics in original] compounded by multiple failure or human error" had been "all but ignored by the NRC in the regulatory review process." The accident at Three Mile Island involved all four elements: "a routine loss-of-feedwater transient, which should have been easily handled by plant safety systems; a stuck-open valve, causing a small loss-of-coolant accident at a confusing time and in an unexpected place, the top of the pressurizer; misleading instrumentation; and operator error in cutting down the effectiveness of the emergency core cooling system." Moreover, "virtually the entire feedwater system, including the condensate polishers, was regarded as 'nonsafety related.' " That meant it had been given no scrutiny by the regulators to identify potential safety problems.[36]

The failure of the plant's operators to communicate the dangers to both regulators and the public while the accident was in progress was blamed on a number of factors. These included "the inability to recognize and comprehend the full significance of the information, and certain psychological factors: the difficulty of accepting a completely unexpected situation, the fear of believing that the situation was as bad as the instruments suggested, and a strong desire to focus on getting the reactor stable again rather than dwelling on the severity of the accident."[37] But many questions remained unanswered. Myers believes the reasons for that are less than innocent, and he blames the information gap in part on the fact that the utility's law firm also represented its employees. In his view, that was one way of ensuring that everybody kept to a similar story line. But it also means that there is still a less than complete understanding of why the many alarm signals during the first few hours of the accident were not correctly read.

Even after the accident, Met Ed officials did not realize how badly the core had been damaged; they planned to return the unit to service. At the same time, they quickly applied to the NRC to get TMI-1 back online, since it had been out for a refueling when the accident began. But opposition to the plant quickly grew, and it soon became clear that neither reactor would be producing electricity anytime soon. A court case against TMI-1 would last five years.

There was more disturbing news. Evidence surfaced that a number of TMI shift supervisors had cheated on their senior reactor operator examinations as far back as August 1979. Most serious of all, a federal indictment that year charged that prior to the accident the utility had provided false test results of leaking coolant pipes from the TMI-2 pressurizer, the focal point of the critical misreadings during the early phases of the accident. The utility pleaded guilty to one count and no contest to six other counts of criminal misconduct for willfully misrepresenting the results of the tests.[38] Finally, after numerous federal court injunctions, the Supreme Court declined to order any further stays of TMI-1, and in October 1985 the undamaged reactor was allowed to return to service. TMI-2 never did.

In the late 1980s, Stello became the target of Justice Department investigations into his role in the alleged cover-ups at TMI. There were also accusations that he altered commission regulations, to the detriment of safety, in order to assist utilities with operating nuclear reactors, and that he authorized cash payments to an informer as part of a vendetta within the agency. These allegations were never proven.[39] But as the probe continued, a Justice Department investigator named Julian Greenspun was dumbfounded by the insular world unfolding before him. Testifying before the Senate Committee on Governmental Affairs in 1987, Greenspun said, "I know of no other regulatory or investigative agency where senior agency officials have taken as many bizarre and seemingly deliberate actions intended to hamper the investigation and prosecution of individuals and companies in the industry the agency regulates."[40] When the first Bush administration tapped Stello to head up the nation's nuclear weapons program as assistant energy secretary for defense programs, President George H. W. Bush was pressured to withdraw the nomination, because of Stello's alleged "record of circumventing health and safety regulations and obstructing investigations while at the Nuclear Regulatory Commission." At Stello's request, Bush complied with the requests. As a consolation prize, Stello was made the Department of Energy's principal deputy assistant secretary for safety and quality, a job that did not require Senate confirmation. That meant his primary duty was to ferret out potentially unsafe practices in the department's nuclear weapons facilities, which were considered far worse than in the civilian sector.

Stello died of cancer at his home in Potomac, Maryland, in January 1999. He was sixty-four. I asked Greenspun why he thought Stello seemed so intent on protecting the nuclear industry. He said, "It was an ideological thing. He felt nuclear power was crucial. He thought it would be bad for the industry to have aggressive enforcement and what he viewed as nitpicking over certain issues."[41]

But Myers believes that overprotecting the industry actually helped ensure its demise: "You have an obligation to hold people accountable to these things . . . While the nukes would probably have something negative to say about the whistle-blowers and interveners like 'Sure they had an impact but it was negative and had a debilitating effect'— I believe their effect has been positive and their actions may well have prevented an accident in the United States worse than Three Mile Island. The problem wasn't that the nukes weren't intelligent people but that what they were dealing with was something much more complex than what most of them had believed prior to having dived in."

AFTER THE ACCIDENT at Three Mile Island, steps were taken to make nuclear reactors safer. For example, in June 1979, four industry groups announced plans for a national institute to establish benchmarks for good safety practices, and to conduct independent evaluations to determine whether they were being met.[42] The industry was essentially saying that its new Institute for Nuclear Power Operations (INPO) would act as a backstop to the NRC, but its reports have not been made public, so there is no way of independently assessing its effectiveness. Improvements were made in the regulatory system, but the underlying "single failure criterion" approach to achieving "adequate" safety assurances remained. Instead, the regulators tackled the numerous safety challenges through a series of reactor backfitting requirements, carefully weighed against costs and only necessary if they lead to "a substantial increase in the overall protection of the public health and safety."[43] In other words, the regulators gave the industry ample room for maneuver.

Myers retired to Maine in the early 1990s. In 1995, Pollard, still at the Union of Concerned Scientists in Washington, received a tip-off from a worker at the Maine Yankee nuclear plant, alleging safety calculations had been falsified. That led to a lengthy NRC investigation revealing a number of other issues. In spite of the NRC's generally accommodating attitude toward utilities, the staff had identified so many problems that the expense of repairing them became untenable. "In the end, they [Maine Yankee Atomic Power Co.] decided it would be too costly to correct these deficiencies to the extent required by the NRC and [decided] to shut the plant down," Myers said.

I asked Myers if he had anything to do with it. "I sent thirty letters to the NRC," he replied.

Thanks, Myers!

CHAPTER 17

Vesuvius

MOST OF EUROPE LAY SLEEPING on the night of April 25–26, 1986, when at twenty-three minutes, forty seconds past one in the morning Leonid Toptunov is reported to have pushed the panic button at the Chernobyl nuclear station. Spring was on its way, and if farmers in the fertile rural regions that surround the facility had not yet turned out their livestock for summer grazing, they soon would. The barns were nearing the end of their wintertime stocks of hay, and people were getting ready for the large planting season ahead. Lyudmilla and Vasily Ignatenko, recently married, were due to leave their apartment in Pripyat, the town nearest the reactor, after breakfast that morning to plant potatoes at his parents' house in a village thirty minutes away. They would never make it.

Two minutes after the button was pushed, a steam explosion lifted the fourteen-hundred-metric-ton upper plate off the core of reactor number four, blowing a hole in the roof above it, according to official accounts. Two or three seconds later, a second more powerful explosion occurred, a so-called power excursion, and overheated graphite blocks and fuel rod material swept out from the core and the reactor hall and into the atmosphere. The tanks containing water for emergency cooling broke open, spilling their contents onto the floor, and air rushed in from above, eventually fanning a graphite fire in the core that burned for days and may have taken two weeks to fully extinguish. Flames raced across the bitumen-covered reactor roof, licking the oil-based tar as if it were lighter fluid.

Lyudmilla, known as Lyusa, could see the flames from the couple's bedroom window. Her husband, a firefighter, had left the apartment in his shirtsleeves as he usually did when he went to fight a fire, assuring her he would be back in a few hours. On the burning roof, molten lava and blazing tar surrounded the firefighters. As they tried to beat down flames, the men kicked pieces of burning, highly radioactive graphite in their path, exposing themselves to lethal levels of radiation. The intense heat sent a radioactive plume more than four miles into the atmosphere that first night.

The Soviet government did not admit to the accident until three days after it happened, and then only in the most cursory terms. While those in the reactor's immediate vicinity and the rest of the world struggled to understand what had happened, the graphite fire discharged a steady stream of volatile radionuclides, like spray rising from a geyser—and it lasted ten days. This was when the real harm was done. Great quantities of toxins fell to earth on an area known as the Soviet's breadbasket, covering Ukraine, Belarus, and adjacent sections of Russia. But shifting winds scattered significant amounts across many parts of Europe and the northern hemisphere during that period, too. Relatively high concentrations were even measured in Hiroshima, over five thousand miles from the stricken reactor.[1]

Six days after the cataclysm, when the plume hovered directly over their city, Kiev's residents poured into the streets for the traditional May Day celebrations, apparently oblivious to the dangers. Women in brightly colored costumes performed traditional dances, beaming radiant smiles under the watchful eyes of Vladimir Shcherbitsky, Ukraine's hard-line Communist Party leader. But the top party officials had been conveniently forewarned. They were spotted a day or two before the festivities lined up at a pharmacy, waiting patiently for iodine tablets that would block their body's absorption of radioactive iodine. Some of them desperately wanted to flee the city, but Shcherbitsky would not allow it. "Shcherbitsky callously ordered us on to the streets," complained Vitaly Korotich, the deputy leader of the Ukraine Supreme Soviet. "Shcherbitsky had his own grandson join the parade."[2]

CHERNOBYL WAS THE largest core meltdown ever and widely considered the worst industrial accident in history. Thousands lost their homes and their health, and millions more felt the effects in other

ways—seven million, according to UN Secretary-General Kofi Annan.[3] Children's lives were ravaged and their futures made less certain. Even those who have so far escaped health consequences but
lived in the path of the fallout will always live in Chernobyl's shadow,
never knowing when a latent cancer whose roots were planted that
night—in the air they breathed, the ground they walked on, or the
food they ate—might stake its claim. It is small wonder that a general
breakdown in mental health is the biggest health problem that must
yet be overcome by Chernobyl's victims, according to the World
Health Organization (WHO).

None of the nuclear industry's previous risk assumptions judged
such an event credible. Two years after the accident, scientists peered
into the core shaft of the crippled reactor for the first time. Incredibly,
it was almost empty. Three levels below, they discovered prehistoric-
looking shapes, like stalactites, made of a material for which they had
no name. It looked like cooled lava. How had this happened? The answer was unsettling: heat generated from the graphite fire was so intense, at twenty-five hundred degrees centigrade, it had melted the
reactor's lower biological shield, allowing what remained of the molten
fuel to flow into the subterranean chambers below, where it turned
into the cavelike formations. The scientists called this odd-looking
material corium.

Chernobyl demonstrated much about what no longer worked in the
Soviet Union, including poor quality of materials, rigid bureaucracy,
and a "don't ask, don't tell" system that rewarded industrial progress
over human health and safety. Details about the accident also revealed
the fault lines within the Soviet nuclear industry. An autocratic, secretive culture had proved ideal for fostering the weapons establishment but made it all the more dangerous when it came to managing
nuclear power because there was so little transparency and accountability. In the face of disaster, the tendency toward obsessive secrecy,
denial, or even outright lying, and insufficient understanding of the
complexities of producing electricity from a nuclear reactor, only made
things worse. There were cover-ups, unexplained events immediately
preceding the event, and a colossal failure by the Soviet government
to level with officials from other countries—let alone its own
people—about the event's significance.

Once the initial shock was over, Western officials, as if hiding behind the Kremlin's veil, also denied the dangers and tightened their

hold over the flow of information. Industry publicists in the United States and Europe made misleading comparisons between Western reactors and the Chernobyl unit in order to convince the public their own were safe. Health officials discounted evidence of high radiation readings. A kind of holy order was at work. It existed largely to protect its own existence and ensure its future, and its concern for the rest of the human race was markedly absent. This was a dark hour for the Soviet people, but it also highlighted the congenital defects of a global enterprise born in closed, secret cities—and in people working from an ancient code that counted secrecy and unstinting faith in their endeavor above all else.

BIG AND UNGAINLY, the Chernobyl reactor was known as an RBMK—reaktor bolshoi moshchnosty kanalny, or high-powered channel reactor. The RBMK's progenitor lay in the early plutonium-producing reactors at Hanford, but the Soviet version was designed with safety features the Hanford reactors did not have. At the time of the accident, the RBMKs were the workhorse of the Soviet fleet, with a dozen units supplying roughly 60 percent of the country's nuclear-generated electricity. At least that many operate in Russia, Lithuania, and Ukraine today, although they have been retrofitted with added safety features based on lessons learned from the accident.

Unlike Western pressurized-water reactors with a single cooling system around the core and a separate steam-generating loop, the so-called channel reactors circulate heat and steam within individual fuel channels—1,660 in all—separated by graphite columns acting as neutron moderators. There are pros and cons to the design from a safety standpoint. But the RBMK's main attraction was that it could be recharged with fresh fuel without going offline. That meant that when the Soviets still needed plutonium for weapons, the old fuel could be taken away for reprocessing while the reactor continued supplying electricity to the grid. Similar systems were used in France and Britain in their early programs.

The RBMK's enormity and its compartmentalized design make it potentially difficult to control, with the chain reaction in one part only loosely coupled with that in distant parts. A relatively minor shift in "reactivity," or fission, in one section could lead to a disproportionately large redistribution of power in the whole, making the reactor unstable. Thus an operator trying to achieve stable, overall power distribution was like the conductor of a dysfunctional orchestra trying to perform a complex symphony. During the accident, these fission fiefdoms produced an extraordinary decoupling effect—the chain reactions in the upper and lower halves of the core proceeded almost independently of one another. Meanwhile, a buildup of xenon, a gas that gobbles up neutrons, led to lower power levels in the middle part, thereby exacerbating the reactor's growing unreliability.

There was one notable defect—and that lay, paradoxically, in the functioning of the control rods. Normally, the reactor's chain reaction should stop once the scram signal is received and the control rods are lowered. In the RBMK at that time, however, this process could actually cause a dramatic power increase. The Soviets had detected this anomaly in another reactor in 1983 but done nothing to correct it, and when the unthinkable occured on April 26, the so-called positive scram effect kicked in, with devastating consequences. In essence, the graphite on the end of the rods displaced the water and served to locally accelerate the nuclear chain reaction even though other parts of the core were being shut down. The high power, in turn, caused localized overheating and ruptured the pressure tubes containing fuel.

The Soviets waited until 1987—after an IAEA experts committee known as INSAG (International Nuclear Safety Advisory Group) had written its first report of the catastrophe—to tell their scientific peers in Vienna about the defect. It was, to say the least, embarrassing. The disclosure revealed a fundamental flaw in the Soviet industry's way of doing things, and a basic disregard for safety, because earlier promises to rectify the flaw had never been carried out. Once INSAG began receiving information on the defects in the control rod mechanism, it came to a startling hypothesis about the accident's causes. "The scram, which preceded by seconds the sharp rise in power that destroyed the reactor, may well have been the decisive contributory factor," INSAG later concluded.[4]

Ironic Evidently, when Leonid Toptunov pushed the button to save the reactor, he was dropping the torch that lit the bonfire.

AS THE OPERATORS at TMI discovered, there is a point during accident sequences when all predicted scenarios become guesswork. Toptunov was less than an hour into his shift when he apparently reached that

point. According to official reports, the accident occurred during a
safety test that had been delayed more than ten hours because of an
area grid manager's request for more power. The aim of the exercise
was to verify whether, during a sudden power outage, the turbogener-
ator would provide enough "rundown" current to keep the feedwater
pumps working in the brief interval before backup diesel generators
could kick in. It was a test that should have been carried out successfully before the reactor was ever licensed to operate. When Toptunov
came on duty around midnight, the test was under way but the power
level was dropping far faster than it was meant to. In an attempt to
stabilize the reactor, he did something he should not have done: he
raised more than the authorized number of control rods.

   The unit was out of sync with itself, and the operators and engineers could not read vital signals—a "diagnostic parameter recording
program," known by the Dickensian acronym DREG, kept breaking
down. To make matters worse, if that was at all possible, sections of
the test instruction manual had been crossed out, further confusing
the men in the control room. Valery Legasov, who supervised the
postaccident reporting for the IAEA, held in his safe a transcript of a
telephone conversation that took place sometime during this critical
period. The transcript made "one's flesh creep," Legasov admitted.
"One operator rings another and asks: 'What shall I do? In the program
there are instructions of what to do, and then a lot of things are crossed
out.' His interlocutor thought for a while and then replied: 'Follow the
crossed out instructions.'"

Just past one o'clock, Toptunov had stabilized the reactor, but he
was still short of the power level prescribed for the test. The rundown
test should have long since been aborted. But it went ahead, on orders
from above, Soviet experts later said, most probably by the person in
overall charge that night, Anatoly Dyatlov, deputy chief engineer of
the station. Dyatlov was later sentenced to ten years in prison.[5]

   At twenty-two minutes past one, only eight control rods were still
down—just under half the authorized minimum. One minute later, an
order was given to start the rundown. At twenty-three minutes, forty
seconds past one, Toptunov pushed the EPS-5 button to scram the reactor. At twenty-four minutes past one, the operating log recorded severe shocks. It was then that an explosion reportedly lifted the cover
shield plate off the reactor core and tore a hole through the roof.

The Kurchatov Institute of Atomic Energy in Moscow, where the

RBMK had been designed and developed under Legasov's supervision, ruled out all but one of the explanations put forth by Soviet experts. It blamed the deadly consequences on the positive scram effect of the control rod displacers, and its conclusions influenced a revised IN-SAG report in 1992.

In a memoir, Legasov compared the events of that night to the eruption of Mount Vesuvius, which buried Pompeii in A.D. 79. Chernobyl had become a radioactive volcano that, like Vesuvius, would be remembered for many thousands of years. Legasov committed suicide on April 27, 1988, a day after the disaster's second anniversary.

So Sad...

MANY QUESTIONS ABOUT the accident have not yet been satisfactorily answered, which has naturally led to doubts about the official IAEA version of events. One mystery is why the scram order was given (and who gave it) since the reactor, although still in trouble, was "closer to being stable than at any other time," according to a later Soviet report.[6] Another puzzle is why the important safety test had been delayed ten hours. The official explanation—that the Kiev grid controller requested more power—seems odd since the unit was running at lower power anyway and would have contributed very little. Whatever the reasons, the delay meant that the test would be conducted in the middle of the night with less experienced personnel in the control room.[7]

A trial of six senior Chernobyl administrators for criminal negligence took place in July and August 1987 in the nearby city of Chernobyl, but it was out of the public eye, except for the opening and closing days. At least three operators and engineers present at the court proceedings who had worked earlier shifts on April 25 and were involved in setting up the preparations for the rundown test later expressed strong reservations about the official attempt then to blame the accident on the incompetence of the operators—a view that IN-SAG more or less came around to in 1992, based on revisions in the Soviet account.[8]

Some blamed the event on the authorities' failure to successfully complete the safety tests prior to licensing the unit. In particular, the station's director, Viktor Bryukhanov, was under pressure to certify the reactor by the end of 1983 so thousands of workers, engineers, and officials in various ministries would get their bonuses and other awards, often amounting to as much as two or three times a monthly salary. He gave his approval, according to published extracts of trial transcripts, even though the tests had been "unsuccessful and incomplete."[9]

Another theory is that the reactor was deliberately sabotaged. Articles began to appear in the Russian press in the early 1990s suggesting that the accident was staged by "foreign secret service agents" and that Soviet technicians involved in disconnecting safety mechanisms were now living "comfortably abroad."[10] It is true that in the early years of the Reagan administration, the National Security Council orchestrated a covert subterfuge program deliberately designed to wreak havoc on Soviet industrial operations, but it has not been publicly linked to Chernobyl.[11] One American expert on the accident said he does not believe the NSC exercise, which resulted in a major gas pipeline explosion, would have extended to the nuclear field because the technology differences were so great. "There were two nuclear systems—ours and theirs. A lot of this stuff that was developed internally was not easy to match up with outside technology . . . They had their own software and computers . . . My guess is it probably isn't credible."

Despite numerous studies by experts in other countries, INSAG ultimately depended on what the Russians told them, and some of the panel's members and virtually all its advisers were from former Soviet nuclear institutions or government agencies. Yet by 1992, the Russians seemed overall to be unsparing in their criticism of what now could be safely blamed on Soviet-era mismanagement and persons other themselves. One scientist complained of "a lack of understanding, primarily on the part of the scientific managers," of many of the reactor's operating characteristics and "a false confidence in the effectiveness of the RCPS [control rod system]."[12] A second charged that because of the failure to follow up on problems with the emergency power protection system, "we are bound to conclude that an accident such as that at Chernobyl was inevitable."[13]

SADLY, THE EMERGENCY response was as flawed as the reactor operating system. Within hours of the explosions, more than one hundred and eighty firemen were at the scene. Few, if any, of these early responders had respirators, apparently because there weren't any. Those who got closest to the blaze soon would be delirious, hardly able to stand, and sped to hospital beds where they would fight for their lives.

A thousand policemen spread out over the plant site and began setting up roadblocks in Pripyat on orders of local party officials. The idea was to prevent cars from entering the town. That made leaving difficult too.

Valentin Belokon, reportedly the first doctor on the scene, admitted later: "I was afraid. But when people see someone in a white coat nearby, it calms them. Like everyone else, I had no respirator, no protective clothing . . . I telephoned the medical station in town: 'Do we have any [respirators]?' 'No, we don't.' So that was that."[14]

By early morning, Belokon began to feel the telltale signs—a tickling in the throat, headache, nausea. The doctor finally gave himself up to the ambulance and returned to the town clinic, too sick to drink a glass of spirits offered by one of his colleagues. He was released from a hospital that autumn and later became a surgeon in a children's hospital. Belokon was lucky to survive, but he sustained lasting lung damage, which resulted in permanent breathing problems.[15]

During the height of the emergency, while Belokon and other doctors and paramedics in Pripyat struggled to save lives, station director Bryukhanov called Moscow at 3:00 A.M. From that moment on, the Soviet Union was on a war footing, although no one in the Kremlin yet understood the extent of the threat. Only a year into Mikhail Gorbachev's radical overhaul of the nation's economic system, a project known as perestroika, the Soviet leadership faced an unprecedented enemy, the peaceful atom.

Gorbachev's determination to make the government more open and accountable—the policy called glasnost—would also be put to the test. The slow official response to the accident, widely criticized by governments all over the world, bore hallmarks of what had happened at Three Mile Island, from the failure of responsible officials to grasp where the real dangers lay, to the "business as usual" pose adopted by those in positions of authority, and finally to the lies told to the public. There was one major difference in the Soviet case: the military was involved from the outset, and it seems to have proved far more adept than civilian nuclear officials in responding to the crisis.

Twelve minutes after Bryukhanov's call, Colonel General Vladimir Pikalov, commander of the Soviet army's chemical service, used an emergency alarm system to alert his specially trained troops in the central and western parts of the eleven-time-zone nation. Unlike the firefighters and the police, the army men came prepared with protective clothing and masks. Meanwhile, the Politburo, the chief political and executive committee of the Soviets' Communist Party, put an obscure, relatively low-level deputy prime minister, Boris Shcherbina, in charge of a commission to find out what had happened, but he was five thousand kilometers away in Siberia when he got the call.

PRIPYAT'S FORTY-FIVE THOUSAND residents awoke on Saturday morning to a city under siege: blockaded streets, roads covered in white foam, and policemen everywhere, at the post office and other public buildings, with nothing much to do but wait for their next orders. Military convoys moved in, and older people started remembering what it was like during World War II when they hid from invading Germans in the nearby forest. Many trees were red with radioactive dust and later died. Huge areas were contaminated with invisible radioactive fallout.

A decision to evacuate didn't come until Sunday because of a brief drop in gamma radiation. But these readings provided no information on the potentially more dangerous alpha and beta radiation from radionuclides such as plutonium-239, iodine-131, strontium-90, and carbon-14. These nuclides were in the hot particles and aerosols from the reactor fire. The threat they posed was terrifying to consider because these invisible particles emit radiation inside the body when they are breathed in, or consumed in food or water. By the time residents boarded the buses, radiation levels had reached what later turned out to be their peak. The delay meant that for thirty-six hours Pripyat's residents were exposed to approximately one roentgen per hour, equating to roughly ten times the internationally recommended annual dose limit. [16]

During this time, lives went on more or less as usual. People walked their dogs, planted gardens, and took their little ones to playgrounds. A Ferris wheel had been set up for the upcoming May Day celebrations. Older children were in school because they had a six-day week. People standing in the central square could see the still-smoldering reactor, but information was scarce, and no one really knew what it meant, or what lay ahead.

Lyubov Kovalevskaya, a journalist who had written about the poor quality of construction at Chernobyl, woke up late that morning. Kovalevskaya's daughter, Anya, was already in school. Kovalevskaya went down to the square, and after she saw what was happening she knew Anya should be kept indoors. Anya told her mother later, "Mama, we had physical exercise outside for almost a whole hour."[17]

One woman's husband came back from the barber and told her to turn on the radio. Announcers were warning listeners to prepare for evacuation, advising people to pack enough clothing—for just three days—and to wash everything. Children were instructed to take their school books. The husband packed the family's important documents and his wedding photos in his briefcase. His wife would take a gauze kerchief in case it rained. But still there were no orders to leave.[18]

Legasov, Shcherbina, and other officials arrived at Chernobyl in a cavalcade of black government cars Saturday night. Underscoring the general lack of comprehension, not to mention confusion, that prevailed, Legasov said later that "it did not even enter my head that we were driving towards an event of global magnitude."[19] One of the reasons that the men from Moscow did not appreciate the disaster's full extent during the first twenty-four hours was that senior station officials apparently did not want them to know.

These officials ignored or chose not to believe what their own crews were telling them; in the process at least two workers, in order to determine the extent of damage, exposed themselves to lethal doses of radiation.[20] (This was similar to what happened at TMI when the operators concealed information about core samples, also taken at great risk, indicating a meltdown.) Fearing panic, Bryukhanov, the station director, reportedly even went so far as to cut the telephone lines that would have allowed the local civil defense chief to report the high radiation levels to Moscow. Bryukhanov also was put on trial the following year. Besides Bryukhanov and Dyatlov, the others who stood trial were chief engineer Nikolai Fomin, shift manager Boris Rogozhkin, Alexandr Kovalenko, manager of unit two, and Yuri Laushkin, inspector of the committee for reactor safety.[21]

It was Pikalov, the army man, who, late Saturday, first came to realize that a graphite fire was in progress, posing the threat of a complete meltdown and further explosions. The information was passed to the Kremlin at seven the following morning, Sunday. This was the first time Soviet leaders understood the scope of the disaster and its possible consequences. A few days later, a new, higher-level commission was set up under Nikolai Ryzhkov, Gorbachev's trusted reform-minded economist. Ryzhkov was chairman of the council of ministers and a Politburo member. Chernobyl had been bounced up on the Kremlin's priority list.[22]

Sunday morning, before dawn, the Pripyat firefighters, Vasily among them, were flown to Moscow. Pripyat's residents would leave their town later that day.

Incredibly, two of the four reactors at the Chernobyl station continued to operate. These were taken out of operation within an hour of each other at about the time people boarded the buses Sunday afternoon. The woman whose husband had just had his hair cut, Nadezhda Petrovna Vygovskaya, climbed onto the bus with her kerchief in hand. She later recalled how all the passengers were crying, except for one man toward the front, who was yelling at his wife for leaving personal items behind but bringing empty pickling bottles for her mother who lived along the way.[23]

Within the space of a few hours Pripyat became a ghost town.

Around Chernobyl, the pattern of delaying evacuation decisions was repeated again and again over the next several weeks as the cloud moved in different directions. Within two weeks, an estimated one hundred thousand people had been forced to leave their homes. In the intervening period, they were exposed to high external and internal doses that might have been avoided had they been ordered to leave earlier. Another sixteen thousand were reportedly evacuated before the autumn of 1986.[24]

Most of Pripyat's evacuees were taken west and south of Chernobyl to villages little more than thirty miles from the nuclear station, and some were transported to Kiev. But large pockets of heavy radiation spread much farther afield. According to a report commissioned for the European Parliament, some 40 percent of Europe's landmass was contaminated with above noticeable levels of Caesium-137. Of the total fallout, less than half fell on the European part of Russia. Elsewhere, in terms of total land surface area, Belarus was worst affected, with 22 percent contaminated with high levels of radioactivity.[25] Austria was second, with 13 percent, while more than 5 percent each of the whole of Ukraine, Finland, and Sweden had high readings. The situation in Belarus was so bad that at the beginning of 1989, twenty villages in two regions closest to the disaster—Gomel and Mogilev—were evacuated. Similarly, in March 1989, the residents of twelve more villages in districts close to the Ukrainian exclusion zone were instructed to leave their homes.[26]

WHILE TWELVE HUNDRED buses rolled out of Pripyat, Lyusa discovered what it meant to love a dying, radioactive man. She followed him to Moscow and schemed for ways to see him at Moscow Hospital No. 6, where he was isolated in a special biochamber like the other victims of acute radiation sickness. Lyusa repeatedly ignored warnings not to get near her husband. She talked or bribed her way past guards and doctors. She even lied about how many children she had, reassuring doctors that she already had two and had no plans for more. But the truth was she was pregnant with her first child. When she had a dizzy spell and nearly fainted in the Moscow facility, the doctors found out. Yet Lyusa kept finding ways to get in. One method was to wait until night when most of the doctors had left. Then she would plead with more pliant nurses, although they begged her to stop coming. "You're young," they would tell her. "Why are you doing this? That's not a person anymore, that's a nuclear reactor. You'll just burn together."

The news at No. 6 was predictably bad. The doctors told her Vasily's central nervous system was completely "compromised." So was his skull. Vasily had received sixteen hundred roentgens, four times the lethal dose. He was one of thirteen to receive a bone marrow transplant from the American specialist Dr. Robert Gale, whose well-publicized trip to Moscow was underwritten by the wealthy benefactor Armand Hammer. Gale tried to comfort Lyusa before the operation, telling her there was a "tiny ray of hope . . . not much, but a little."

Lyusa would hear about the "boys" from the Pripyat fire brigade in the other biochambers and, one by one, about their deaths. Lying in his bed behind a transparent curtain, her own husband produced stools with blood and mucus twenty-five to thirty times a day. His skin began to crack. Boils soon appeared over most of his body. Clumps of hair fell off his head each time he turned on the pillow. During the final two days of his life, his arm dangled as if disconnected from the trunk of his body. Pieces of his lung and of his liver came out of his mouth as Lyusa watched. "He was choking on his internal organs. I'd wrap my hand in a bandage and put it in his mouth, take out all that stuff. It's impossible to talk about. It's impossible to write about. And even to live through. It was all mine. My love. They couldn't get a single pair of shoes to fit him. They buried him barefoot."[27]

In all, about six hundred emergency workers were involved during the first day of the accident. Of these, more than a third were eventually diagnosed with acute radiation sickness, and twenty-eight died in 1986, including Lyusa's husband. The bodies of Vasily and his fellow firefighters were wrapped in cellophane bags and then placed in wooden coffins. The coffins were put in another bag, and finally into a second coffin made of zinc. The sealed coffins were buried in a Moscow cemetery under concrete tiles. The families were told there was no way their loved ones could be buried near their homes. This was a twentieth-century form of mummification and entombment, as the embalmers in Idaho had realized more than twenty years earlier after the SL-1 reactor disaster. The idea was not to protect souls for the afterlife, but the living from the radioactive dead.

THE OUTSIDE WORLD did not officially learn of the accident until the Soviet state news agency Tass issued a brief report on Monday, April 28, three days after it occured. By then high readings had already been picked up in Scandinavia and elsewhere, and U.S. intelligence agencies were receiving satellite photos of the damaged reactor. While the Soviets appeared mute to the outside world, the Politburo actually was engaged in a roiling debate over how much information to release. The day before the announcement, Gorbachev called a meeting on short notice to discuss the situation. "He called us in because we had released no information," said Geidar Aliev, a Politburo member who attended the meeting. "But Sweden, Poland and Germany were reporting high radiation . . . The whole world knew, so we had to come to a decision."[28] Aliev argued in favor of an immediate forthright statement, but Gorbachev, apparently influenced by his conservative deputy, Yegor Ligachev, was either unwilling or unable to overcome the old-style manner of managing information. The government released only a brief announcement that day.[29]

The next day, Tuesday, Tass reported two deaths and admitted only that the accident had "resulted in the destruction of part of the structural elements of the building housing the reactor . . . and a certain leak of radioactive substances." The bulletin said the radiation level at the station and its environs "has now been stabilized, and the necessary medical aid is being given to those affected."[30] It mentioned that Pripyat and nearby towns had been evacuated. Apart from that, the rest of the statement was almost entirely false. The reactor, with its smoldering graphite fire, was a ticking time bomb; potassium iodide pills had not been widely distributed; contaminated milk and food were being sold; and the "leak of radioactive substances" was a large radioactive plume circumnavigating the northern hemisphere and creating hot spots as far away as the highlands of Scotland, Wales, and Cumbria.[31]

As the graphite fire burned, more than five thousand metric tons of sand, clay, and other heat-resistant materials such as boron carbide, lead, and dolomite were dropped on the reactor to damp down the fire. Much of it missed the target; the rest pushed the core hard against the concrete foundations, causing the basement to flood with water, which in turn threatened a steam explosion. The helicopter sorties were halted on May 2 as scientists and engineers searched for better solutions.

Ultimately, the water was drained and liquid nitrogen was pumped under the reactor to freeze the earth and prevent the reactor melting any further. These were mammoth operations involving divers and trucking in nitrogen from every available source in Ukraine. On May 5, the plant belched its last significant quantity of radioactive toxins into the air—eight to twelve million curies—almost as much as on the first day of the accident. No one will ever know precisely how much in total was ejected into the skies, but most experts agree that after the cumulative fallout from atmospheric testing, Chernobyl's was the greatest release of long-lived radioactivity into the environment caused by humans.

The fire gradually subsided because all the graphite had burned. Nevertheless, with 190 tons of melted nuclear fuel still remaining, neutron and gamma radiation would continue indefinitely, and there was little anyone could do about this radiation but cover it over. Eventually Chernobyl would be shrouded in a concrete and steel sarcophagus, wired up with sensors so operators could keep tabs on the levels. This was a dragon that could at any moment breathe fire again.[32]

VLADIMIR GUBAREV, PRAVDA's science editor, left Moscow for Kiev on May 2 with just six other journalists selected by the government to report on the accident. They sat in a vast empty train—no one was headed for the Ukrainian capital. "The first thing we saw there was massive panic," Gubarev told a television documentary maker. "People were storming the trains leaving Kiev. It was terrible. You can't imagine it if you haven't seen it yourself. Everything was in bloom. Birds singing, spring in the Ukraine. Yet you know that all around is death." Gubarev and his colleagues wrote the first stories and took the first pictures.

Summoned to a meeting with Gorbachev and the Politburo's propaganda secretary, Alexander Yakovlev, Gubarev poured out his anger at what he had seen. "I was furious. I'd seen so much incompetence. I'd seen so much stupidity. It was such a disgrace." Gubarev was asked to write a brief by morning. In it he blamed the panic on lack of information. "Nothing about what had happened, not even on radiation in the city . . . Not one Ukrainian leader has appeared on television to explain," his report said.

On May 14, Gorbachev appeared on television to talk about the accident for the first time, but despite Gubarev's complaints his speech was defensive and provided little hard information. Glasnost had been a dismal failure.[33]

With much of their farming land now contaminated, the Soviet authorities found themselves facing the prospect of widespread food shortages, and a nightmarish choice between risking general starvation and long-term excess radiation exposure. Basically they opted for the latter and began relaxing permissible dose levels in order to avoid further evacuations. Control over dosimeters became vital to the strategy since knowledgeable health experts armed with the instruments might begin issuing their own health warnings. More than two years after the accident, the unauthorized possession of an individual dosimeter was considered a crime. Even laboratory dosimeters were banned if they had not been approved for special use.[34]

Glasnost, Gorbachev's new policy of openness, had no place in an event of this magnitude, because there were too many people in the system accustomed to doing things the old way. But it was more than that, as British radiation specialist Ian Fairlie, coauthor of the European Parliament study on Chernobyl's effects, explained: "Nuclear power was a sacred cow in the USSR and faith in its supremacy ran deep and wide in Soviet hierarchies: indeed the nuclear hierarchy was by far the most prestigious in the U.S.S.R. When the accident occurred, all Soviet officials were in deepest denial. And because of the psychic shocks delivered daily to their values and beliefs from the unfolding disaster at Chernobyl, many officials were completely disoriented—how could something so sacred in their lives turn into such a dangerous monster in front of their very eyes? Not a few committed suicide, and a number of scholars consider that the accident delivered such a psychic blow it resulted in the break-up of the Soviet Union three years later."[35]

In the West, the accident seemed only to strengthen the instinct for secrecy. Upon learning of the event, the U.S. Department of Energy (DOE) and the Nuclear Regulatory Commission issued gag orders to their staffs. "It goes without saying that no one should volunteer separate or independent speculation to the press," said a May 2 note from Delbert F. Bunch, DOE's acting deputy assistant secretary for reactor deployment. NRC staff were instructed to channel all media queries about Chernobyl to the agency's public affairs office, while other government officials were directed to one of two NRC staff members. "There is a strong determination on the part of the US government to speak with one voice on all matters that relate to this issue," said an April 30 internal memo from Victor Stello, the NRC's top staff official, then under investigation for alleged cover-ups at TMI.[36]

The NRC and the DOE defended their orders, saying they simply wanted to avoid confusion, which, while understandable, disguised other less innocent reasons. For journalists, the implications were clear. Suddenly, hundreds of experts in virtually all areas of nuclear energy, living in the country that likes to think of itself as the most open in the world, were not supposed to express opinions or answer technical questions about the world's worst industrial accident. The government's position was even more curious since officials involved in the review complained they were getting very little solid information about what had happened anyway.

There were many possible reasons for the clampdown other than those cited. The DOE understood immediately that Chernobyl would—and indeed did—raise embarrassing questions about the state of its aging military plutonium reactors, similar in design to the Soviet RBMKs. But another concern was that a runaway chain reaction—the key process involved in a nuclear bomb explosion—had been involved. The connection in the public's mind between nuclear reactors and nuclear weapons could further damage acceptability of nuclear power, already seriously undermined by TMI. "The rationale for public protection rests on the idea that accidents will develop slowly," former NRC commissioner Victor Gilinsky told me at the time. "Nowhere is there an assumption that the whole thing can blow up."[37]

Getting anyone to admit that was another matter. I had my chance when Morris Rosen, the IAEA's nuclear safety division director, agreed to talk by phone immediately after returning May 8 to Vienna from a helicopter tour of the stricken reactor. Rosen, an American, had accompanied the IAEA's Swedish director general, Hans Blix, along with the Soviet Leonard Konstantinov, the IAEA's deputy director general for nuclear energy. Blix and Rosen were the first officials from outside the Soviet Union to see the actual site, albeit from a helicopter. Because Rosen was an enthusiastic supporter of nuclear energy, I knew he would be loath to admit what Gilinsky already had guessed. Yet after a number of questions, Rosen finally conceded "there were several explosions within a short period of time" in what he termed "a somewhat spontaneous event."

A DOE scientist who discounted various "slow burn" theories told the U.S.-based *Science Magazine* that he believed the explosions were caused by a runaway chain reaction—just what no one else in government or industry wanted to hear. According to the magazine's editors, the scientist made his comments before the federal clampdown and requested anonymity afterward. "This scientist, an expert in reactor fuel, has been directed by the Energy Department not to discuss the Soviet accident with the press," the editors pointedly stated in their May 16, 1986, issue.[38]

There were evidently other ways in which the long arm of the nuclear state reached out to suppress information in the United States. Much to my surprise, in 2005, while researching this book's chapter on the Crossroads bomb tests, I noticed at least a dozen documents missing from a National Archives file, dating from the 1940s and 1950s, on the health effects of the earlier bomb test fallout. The withdrawal notices were dated between June 6 and June 23, 1986—about two months after Chernobyl. This may have been purely coincidental, or related to the Reagan government's nuclear military buildup in Europe. But the timing struck me as possibly part of the Chernobyl clampdown.

On February 22, 2005, I placed a request for the documents under the Freedom of Information Act. Only one has been sent so far, by chance as I began writing this chapter. Dated February 7, 1955, it was a National Security Council memorandum on a "Proposed Public Announcement of the Effects, Particularly Fallout, of Thermonuclear Explosions." It read a little like the gag orders issued after Chernobyl. Officials from various agencies had agreed on a carefully timed release of an AEC statement about thermonuclear weapons, but cautioned that even after the release "other governmental departments and agencies should defer any public announcements" until the NSC could consider a report "on the psychological reactions to the AEC announcement within approximately two weeks following its release." This was presumably an extension of Operation Candor, Eisenhower's attempt to make both fear and acceptance of nuclear weapons, as manipulated by the former president's psy-ops team, a part of modern life.

Hypocracy- Hyp-ops

OTHER GOVERNMENTS, NOTABLY France and Britain, went to great lengths to reassure the public they faced no health risks, when radiation readings were beginning to tell them that just the opposite might be true. The French also refused to cooperate fully with American authorities trying to evaluate the extent of contamination in Europe. "They made one or two submissions and that was it. And the levels we got we didn't believe," an Environmental Protection Agency (EPA) official told me on background, meaning I would not reveal his name. The readings sent by French authorities were at least a third, and perhaps as much as a half, too low, based on readings obtained from bordering areas in neighboring countries, he said. The apparent suppression of information in France eventually resulted in legal proceedings. In December 2005, the investigating magistrate, Maîtresse Marie-Odile Bertella-Geffroy, released a report she had commissioned stating that the government's Central Service for Protection Against Ionizing Radiation, or SCPRI, had known of high levels of contamination in Corsica and southeastern France but had concealed that information.[39]

Nor were British officials entirely open. On May 1, the UK Department of Health issued a press release that said: "There is no need for anyone resident in the UK to take any special precautions in relation to the radioactivity released from the Chernobyl power station accident since there is no risk to health. So far no raised levels of radioactivity have been detected in any tests." But within days, the Ministry of Agriculture, Fisheries, and Food (MAFF) started picking up high readings in lamb, fruit, and vegetables in the country's northwest. Some of the readings were above the government's trigger levels at which action is deemed necessary. This was not disclosed until mid-June, and it took MAFF until June 20 to announce a ban on the slaughter of lamb and sheep in the affected areas, which included Cumbria, Snowdonia in Wales, and parts of Scotland.

Hundreds of farms, mainly in upland areas, were eventually included in the quarantine. Farmers received compensation for sheep they could not sell. They were told the bans would last a matter of weeks. Instead they lasted many years; as of 2007, a total of 374 farms with almost two hundred thousand sheep remainded under the UK's special control scheme.[40] The UK environmental officials had incorrectly assumed that the earth would soon swallow the long-lived radionuclides like cesium-137. Instead, in the peaty soil of the upland fells, the radionuclides were continually churned over; rather than sinking, they kept rising to the surface, like nuts or raisins in a frothy batter.[41]

WITHIN WEEKS OF the accident, after the initial furor over the Soviet government's behavior died down, it seemed as if East and West were making a concerted, if not coordinated, effort to limit the public relations damage to nuclear energy. Western nuclear organizations loudly proclaimed that the RBMK reactor bore little relationship to their own designs and that it had fewer safety features. Nuclear promoters focused on the RBMK's supposed lack of containment, meaning a thick concrete barrier strong enough to withstand a sudden release of radioactivity. They argued that the Western pressurized-water reactor design prevented significant amounts of radioactive release during the TMI accident. But the statements were misleading because they ignored the question of whether any containment could withstand the force of Chernobyl-like explosions. Within INSAG, senior industry officials and safety experts hotly debated this issue, finally concluding that "ultimate protection may not be technically feasible in every case, and it is not clear that such a containment could have been designed to protect against the consequences of the reactivity excursion which occurred at Chernobyl."[42]

At the same time, both the Soviet and American governments were striving to keep their nuclear programs alive. On May 5, 1986, at an economic summit meeting in Tokyo, the leaders of seven major industrial nations, President Ronald Reagan among them, and the European Community declared that "properly managed" nuclear power would continue to produce an increasing share of the world's electricity. But for the next two decades nuclear programs in Europe and North America basically ground to a halt.

Industry spokesmen to this day do their best to downplay the repercussions of Chernobyl. For example, they will say that "only twenty-eight died," referring to the number of emergency workers who lost their lives in the months following the accident—a further nineteen perished between 1987 and 2004. But the truth is less convenient. The time interval between exposure to ionizing radiation and a diagnosis of cancer can be fifty to sixty years. A key longer-lived radionuclide like cesium-137 will not lose all its radioactivity for three hundred years, which means that food pathways in certain areas might continue harming people well after we are all dead.

The World Health Organization in conjunction with the International Atomic Energy Agency conservatively estimates that over the next seventy years there will be four thousand "excess" cancer deaths—meaning more than would normally be expected—caused by lingering radiation in the ground and contaminated food. However, this projection covers only Ukraine, Belarus, and the area of Russia most severely affected, where a total of some seven million live.

About two-thirds of Chernobyl's collective dose was deposited on populations elsewhere, especially in Western Europe, home to some six hundred million. When these other regions, with their large populations, are factored in, the potential death toll significantly rises, according to the study coauthored by Fairlie and fellow British scientist David Sumner, commissioned by the European Parliament's Green Party. They calculate the final figure of excess cancer deaths at somewhere between seven and fifteen times the WHO's estimate, meaning that thirty thousand to sixty thousand lives are potentially at risk.[43]

The final death tally will never be known for many reasons, including the lack of reliable dosimetric data and the fact that these deaths will occur over an extended period of time in different countries, with different methods of tabulating health statistics. But perhaps the biggest reason for the lack of conclusive casualty figures is that scientists have so far been unable to discover genetic markers for radiation-induced cancers. "We just might not be able to ever say, after fifty to seventy years when we've observed the life span of everybody, we may not be able to say whether the risks of diseases were increased or not," said Kenneth J. Kopecky, of the Fred Hutchinson Cancer Research Center in Washington State. He worked on the 2006 WHO report on Chernobyl's health impact. "If we found a way to distinguish radiation-caused leukemias from all the other leukemias, then we could give an answer."[44]

WHO and other health organizations have not been able to definitively connect increases in breast cancer, leukemia, and other types of cancers to the fallout, although some of the people who worked on the WHO study think there probably is one. "My sense is that the evidence for detrimental health effects is much, much stronger [than indicated by the report]," said Kopecky. "It's virtually overwhelming."

Based on existing studies, WHO has concluded that a significant rise in thyroid cancers, particularly among children, is related to the Chernobyl fallout: the number of cases among children under eighteen at the time of the accident stands at five thousand so far and is rising. Children were put at risk in other ways too. Doctors started noticing many more cases of cataracts and, among all age groups, increases in cardiovascular and immunological disease and mental, psychological, and central nervous system effects.

The biggest visible impact was on mental health. "Chernobyl unleashed a complex web of events and long-term difficulties, such as massive relocation, loss of economic stability, and long-term threats to health in current and, possibly, future generations, that resulted in an increased sense of anomie and diminished sense of physical and emotional balance," said the WHO study, adding that "the high levels of anxiety and medically unexplained physical symptoms continue to this day."[45]

CHERNOBYL IS AN epic story of mythical dimensions. Man lost control of his invention; it turned against him for reasons not yet fully understood. Modern technology inflicted disaster that, short of all-out nuclear war, was as violent as almost any imaginable natural event.

Chernobyl was important not only because of the numbers who died but because of the way tens of thousands had to live afterward.

ere moved to communities where they had no roots. They
stigmatized as Chernobyl victims, rather than survivors. Their
children went to new schools where their classmates taunted them
for being "radioactive." People feared for their own lives and those of
their children, not knowing how much radiation they had absorbed.
They agonized over their daily bread, wondering whether it was safe
to eat. These were sturdy people; some had lived through the battle of
Stalingrad or war in Ukraine. But now this new invisible enemy, the
atom, was everywhere, it seemed—"in the bread, in the salt," as one
evacuee put it. "We breathe radiation, we eat it." They were gripped
by what some have cynically termed "radiophobia," not ever knowing
the extent of the threat they faced.[46]

Ultimately, it is the stories of the children and their anguished parents that make what happened so heartbreaking. "You can imagine the
state of a mother who takes her child to the dosimetrist," said the journalist Kovalevskaya, referring to a new category of medic responsible
for checking contamination levels. "He measures the child's shoes.
'contaminated.' Trousers—'contaminated.' Hair—'contaminated' . . .
When I had sent my mother to Siberia with the children, I began to feel
better."[47]

The number of children with Down syndrome in Belarus almost
tripled in January 1987—they were conceived during the period of high
radiation exposure. Parents of babies born with deformities struggled to
establish eligibility for Chernobyl relief funds. The mother of a baby
girl born with aplasia of the anus, vagina, and kidney—failure of those
organs to develop—reportedly took four years to get a paper from doctors confirming the connection between her daughter's condition and
radiation. The woman later recalled the doctors saying: "We have instructions. We are supposed to call incidences of this type general sick-
nesses." A bureaucrat yelled at the young mother, accusing her of
wanting Chernobyl victim funds. She said, "How I didn't lose consciousness in his office, I'll never know."[48]

Yet the industry and its government backers were determined to persevere. Only four months after the accident, in August 1986, Rosen, the
IAEA's most senior safety official, made this remarkable declaration:
"Even if there was a Chernobyl type accident every year, I would still
consider nuclear power an interesting type of energy production."[49]

Two months after her husband's burial, Lyusa went back to Moscow to visit the cemetery and to have her child. She went into labor sitting by her husband's tombstone and talking to him. The baby girl was born at the hospital where her father died. Two weeks premature, she looked healthy. But radiation exposure had taken its toll: she had cirrhosis of the liver and congenital heart disease. Four hours after her birth, the baby died, one of the first victims of the next generation claimed by the fire-breathing dragon at Chernobyl.

OVER TIME, PEOPLE went back to Pripyat and the other abandoned towns for brief visits. One couple buried their son, a fireman, in Moscow and then returned to their former home to bag their tomatoes and cucumbers and fill their canning jars as they had always done. Others went back to dig potatoes. They spent time at cemeteries with their loved ones. They collected Chernobyl earth in urns and put them on mantels. They tried to forget about radioactivity.

One old woman returned to her house in Pripyat and stayed, alone. Her sons and daughters were away in a city. Her husband was buried nearby. The flowers and plants were growing again. A few stray cats and dogs ran around. Wolves visited her at night and tried to stare her down with eyes that beamed like lasers. Policemen, her only human contact, occasionally dropped by with a loaf of bread. She looked everywhere for the cat she had left behind, named Vaska, but could not find him. One day she saw a cat crouched under a store. She talked to him and invited him home, but he sat, meowing. "The wolves will eat you," she warned. "They'll tear you apart. Let's go. I have eggs, I have some lard." Of course, she realized the cat did not understand, but somehow he did. She called him Vaska, and they have been living together ever since.[50]

The city of Chernobyl was emptied of its fifty thousand inhabitants. Six thousand people now live there again, near a plant shrouded in heavy concrete that could collapse from the inside, bringing down the entire edifice, and raising yet another radioactive dust plume over this land of the living and the dead. The need for jobs is so great that people opt to work at the plant and risk the dangers rather than go without money, and radiation levels are gradually coming down. Tania D'Avignon, a photographer and translator from Kiev who now lives in the United States, described Pripyat after a recent visit: "Everything is overgrown, falling apart, graffiti in many places, the Ferris wheel has been repainted in bright yellow! It's different," she said. "I'd like to visit the villages again, but not Chornobyl,"[51] she added, using the accepted Ukrainian spelling for the city and the associated plant.

The larger meaning of Chernobyl is sometimes difficult to grasp. On one level it is the story of Soviet-era politics, unexplained events, and the suppression of truth. On another it is about the heroism of police, firefighters, and soldiers, about uprooted communities, children with cancer, anxious parents, and the fear of early death. As the Ukrainian journalist Svetlana Alexievich coaxed the stories out of her compatriots in her truly remarkable oral history, *The Voices of Chernobyl*, another bigger and ultimately more revealing picture emerged—a story that transcends its own tragic consequences by demonstrating the human capacity for overcoming fear and even anger with both love and courage.

Chernobyl broke the public trust. Its ultimate lesson, though, is that people find their own meanings amid the rubble. No one can take that from them, even if their fates are tragic. Lyusa eventually remarried and had a son. She lives in Kiev in a two-room apartment, spacious by local standards, but worries she will lose her boy. So she grabs on to him tight sometimes when they walk out of the house. "He's also sick," she explained, "two weeks in school, two weeks at home with a doctor. That's how we live."[52]

One man who left Pripyat agonized over whether to take the front door of the family's apartment. The door, by tradition, was special, almost sacred. For generations in Nikolai Kalugin's family, the dead would be laid out on it. Nikolai's father had, all night until the coffin came. The door had etch-marks on it showing Nikolai growing up—first grade, second grade, seventh, and so forth—then the height marks for his son and daughter. "My whole life is written down on this door. How am I supposed to leave it?" he wrote.

Two years after the evacuation, Kalugin returned for his door. He hauled it away on a motorcycle at night, through the woods, chased by police who thought he was looting his already looted apartment. Later he took his wife and daughter to the hospital. They had black spots all over their bodies that would appear and disappear. His daughter was six. She shared a room with six other girls who had lost their hair. Kalugin put his girl to bed one night and she whispered in his ear, "Daddy, I want to live, I'm still little."

She did not live. His wife returned from the hospital. They laid their daughter on the door until a small coffin was brought in. Kalugin did not want to record this event for Alexievich's book because he thought it might tarnish his daughter's memory. But then he changed his mind. "I want to bear witness: my daughter died from Chernobyl," he said. "And they want us to forget about it."[53]

CHAPTER 18

Our Lady of the Fields

I F YOU FOUND YOURSELF BARRELING along Interstate 40 past Amarillo, Texas, sometime during the past fifty years, you might have been surprised to learn that hidden nearby in the middle of wheat fields stood a plant that today is the nation's only remaining one manufacturing and disassembling nuclear weapons.[1] A little yellow brick church near the facility provides comfort to parishioners as it did through the cold war years, and before that to their elders during the hard times of the Dust Bowl. Outside the church, a shrine to Our Lady of the Fields features a statue of the Virgin with outspread hands amid wheat sheaves stretching almost as high as her waist. A prayer inscribed below asks plaintively for "fertile and abundant" harvests and for help in understanding "the dignity of our toil."

St. Francis Church has been the center of a small German American Catholic community since 1909 when a group of German American farming families settled several miles outside Amarillo and built their first house of worship. They carved and planted fields on the treeless expanse of the Texas high prairie that earlier pioneers passed by in their rush to get to the West. In the harsh landscape, there is little sense of permanence outside the community they formed. After losing years of crops and thousands of cattle in the black dusters of the Depression, nineteen families were ordered to move off their land in 1942 so the government could build a conventional bomb factory, the Pantex plant, during World War II. Six of those families were St. Francis parishioners. They had two weeks to pack up all their belongings and leave, and they received only a pittance for their crops.[2]

People were disheartened by the partial dismemberment of their close-knit community. Nevertheless, they kept their feelings to themselves because, as German Americans, they feared they might be interned if they spoke out. But the land grab was seen as the "single greatest tragedy that visited St. Francis because of World War II," according to a commemorative book published in 1983 for the church's seventy-fifth anniversary. "Things would have been different for the parish if this 16,000 acres of fertile farmland could have been left to make a more economically healthy farming area to support the parish. At the very least, it would have prevented considerable hardship to the dispossessed farmers and the lingering antipathy against the facility by area residents would not exist."[3]

Instead, beginning in 1951, the land was used as the site of a new plant to churn out nuclear weapons like loaves of bread at a grist mill, and the costs, both direct and indirect, began to mount. Pantex, just seventeen miles northeast of Amarillo, became one of seven facilities in the United States with the ability to assemble nuclear and nonnuclear components into completed nuclear explosive devices, a process known as "final assembly."[4] As the largest of these—the others have since been shut down—it became the hub of a wheel whose spokes included hundreds of other plants supplying nuclear fuel and components for the weapons, and the aircraft, missiles, submarines, and battlefield weapons for delivering them. What happened at Pantex and the surrounding area over the next several decades was a microcosm of events unfolding elsewhere in the vast complex, and the way they affected the economic, social, and political fabric of the country as a whole.

Eisenhower saw it coming, even if he felt unable to stop it. In his January 1961 farewell address, the president famously warned "against the acquisition of unwarranted influence, whether sought or unsought, by the military-industrial complex." He said its "total influence—economic, political, even spiritual—is felt in every city, every State house, every office of the Federal government . . . Our toil, resources and livelihood are all involved; so is the very structure of our society."[5]

More than four decades later, in 1996, the financial cost to the nation of the nuclear weapons program since 1940 was estimated at almost $5.5 trillion. Only nonnuclear defense spending, at roughly $13 trillion, and Social Security, at nearly $8 trillion, were higher. As a percentage of

total government spending in that period, programs involving nuclear weapons soaked up roughly 11 percent, compared to just 3 percent
each for health, education, and transport—and less than 1 percent for
energy. There were many indirect costs that could not be adequately
measured: the long-term consequences of land and groundwater contamination, the mounting health toll from excess exposure to radioactivity, the brainpower and capital investment that might have been used
more productively elsewhere, and the vast cleanup and monitoring operations that are now under way and will be for generations to come.[6]

THE PEOPLE WHO live near the Pantex plant are politically and socially
conservative, and for many years they had no more than a shoulder-
shrugging attitude about their proximity to a nuclear weapons plant.
From time to time they'd hear explosions and make a few inquiries, and
they would get answers like "it was a soap bubble that blew up or what
not," said Phil Smith, who lives on a ranch across the road from one
side of the vast complex. "They would not come out and actually tell
us what they were doing. Over a period of time, we put two and two together."[7]

Smith was actually raised on the Pantex site, because his father ran
an experimental cattle-feeding program for Texas Technological College in Lubbock, which had purchased the land after the war (for one
dollar) and was allowed to retain some of it when the government exercised a reclamation clause to build the nuclear weapons facility.[8] As
a teenager, Smith rode around chasing hogs and cattle and saw government security agents, also on horseback, with rifles slung across
their midriffs, looking for intruders.[9] He watched as strange white
domes appeared, stretching more than thirty feet across their inside
diameter, with thick concrete walls, and a roof overlaid with seventeen feet of sand and gravel.[10]

Beneath the domes, thirteen in all, were cells where men performed
one of the final acts of nuclear bomb-making, mating high explosive
components with bomb cores. These technicians always knew that in
the event of a chemical explosion, the roof was designed to collapse in
on them, limiting the scattering of radioactive material and snuffing
out their lives. No such accidents ever were reported.[11] The cells were
not, of course, designed to withstand the impact of a nuclear explosion. Like other landmarks of the nuclear age, such as Little Boy

and Fat Man, the dome-covered cells acquired an innocuous-sounding nickname—Gravel Gerties—that helped neutralize their meaning. The name came about because the gravel and sand mix on the dome's roof reminded someone of Gravel Gertie, a 1940s *Dick Tracy* comic strip character with curly gray hair.[12]

Procter & Gamble, otherwise known for its soap products, won the first five-year contract to manage and operate Pantex. Nuclear weapons made odd bedfellows with the company's other products, so in 1956 it opted out of the business and turned the job over to Mason & Hanger–Silas Mason Co., Inc., an engineering and construction company that built the Grand Coulee Dam and the Lincoln Tunnel, among other landmark projects. It runs the plant to this day.

In May 1962, the same month Khrushchev dreamed up his missile gambit in Cuba, Phil Smith married a tall, slender woman with an effusive smile, and personality to match, named Doris Berg. Her father lost some of his land to Pantex during the war but still retained several hundred acres, enough to give the young couple to set up a ranch. They would have been married at St. Francis, but because there were so many guests invited to their wedding the ceremony took place at a cathedral in Amarillo. As they settled down to married life on their ranch, the Smiths adopted a certain kind of fatalism about their proximity to Pantex, knowing that if there was nuclear war with the Soviets, as Doris Smith said, "we would be the first to go and we would not have to suffer." In the meantime, she explained, "we did Pantex some favors; they did us some favors. They had the best law enforcement and fire protection in the area, so we could benefit. It was live and let live. We got lots of friends working there too."

But the explosions continued, and considerable amounts of contaminated material were burned in the open air for years. "No one ever gave it a second thought," said Jim Giles, a big, lumbering man who worked at Pantex when it opened and remained there his entire working life. "Bending the rules was permissible. It was acceptable." Production took precedence over everything else. "We'd turn out twelve to fourteen weapons a shift, twenty to twenty-five weapons in a twenty-four-hour shift. I was working twelve-hour days, seven days a week."[13]

Giles became one of the plant's top managers, in charge of program planning. That meant he and his staff were like air traffic controllers, overseeing a vast network of connections that brought nuclear material, as plutonium, highly enriched uranium, and tritium, as well as a array of electronic equipment—arming, fusing, and firing switches, neutron generators, and testing devices—to Pantex from factories all over the country. By the mid-1950s, Pantex was part of an enterprise that had soaked up nearly nine billion dollars of federal-taxpayer-funded capital investment, exceeding the combined capital investment of General Motors, U.S. Steel, DuPont, Bethlehem Steel, Alcoa, and Goodyear.[14]

Two decades later, in the 1980s, antinuclear activists and peace groups began tracking the movement of nuclear warheads out of Pantex to various military bases on "White Trains"—so called because of their distinctive white, unmarked cars—and set up trackside vigils in various states to call attention to their cause. The trains were eventually stopped because of the protests, and Pantex relied on heavily armored, fire-resistant tractor-trailers, called safe secure transporters (SSTs). Despite their inbuilt security features, the trucks were not immune to accidents. In one incident, on November 16, 1996, for example, an SST transferring two warheads from the Ellsworth Air Force Base in South Dakota to Pantex, apparently for routine maintenance, skidded on an icy two-lane highway in Nebraska and tipped over into a ditch. The truck was eventually righted, but the bombs were transferred to another SST and returned to Ellsworth.[15]

During these years protestors and journalists learned more about what went on inside Pantex than Giles's wife, Bernice. As I interviewed Giles at the couple's home near the north end of the plant site in May 1994, she told me happily the pair would be celebrating their eighteenth wedding anniversary that September. In all that time, she said, she had never asked her husband what he did and he never told her. His first allegiance, before the cold war ended and he retired, was to the plant and its strict rules of secrecy. "I knew he was over in program planning and met the people he worked for. But what he did—I felt like it was none of my business."[16]

FOR MANY YEARS, the pastor of St. Francis, Monsignor Leroy T. Matthiesen, felt the same way. He avoided making moral judgments about nuclear weapons, in part because he believed that was the responsibility of bishops, but also because, much like the rest of the parish, he was conservative and not prone to stirring up trouble, and some of his parishioners worked at Pantex. Born in 1921 to a family of eight children, Matthiesen grew up on a cotton farm near Olfen, Texas, another small rural Catholic community. After nine years at St. Francis, he was ordained bishop of Amarillo in May 1980. Only then did his thoughts begin to change. An activist nun urged him to make a statement against nuclear weapons. Then a woman who worked at Pantex told him she was angry about the working conditions, convinced she had cancer. She wanted desperately to find another job, although that would be a tough move. The pay at Pantex was about a third higher than anywhere else in the area, and she did not have a college education. "You have to understand we are not ordinary people because of what we're doing," she told the bishop.

In February 1981, six people scaled the plant's outer security fence; it took the guards thirty minutes to find them, and then the protestors were arrested. One was a Catholic priest. Matthiesen said he was "kind of astonished and almost offended" that a priest would be breaking the law. He went to visit him in jail, expecting a radical firebrand, and instead found a gentle, deeply spiritual man. Then, in June 1981, Archbishop Raymond Hunthausen of Seattle, Washington, suggested Americans withhold income tax to protest the stockpiling of nuclear weapons; he himself withheld half his income tax, prompting the Internal Revenue Service to garnish his wages. "That got my attention," said Matthiesen. There was more pressure when a permanent deacon at his church, who also worked at Pantex, sought Matthiesen's opinion about whether he should continue working at the plant. "I said off the top of my head 'no' because clerics should not be involved in the making of bombs."[17]

Matthiesen decided to speak out in August 1981 after Reagan announced his decision to proceed with the neutron bomb, a thermonuclear weapon designed to kill enemy personnel by using neutron radiation to penetrate tanks and other heavy armor while theoretically leaving the surrounding infrastructure in place. Matthiesen viewed the neutron bomb as particularly venal because its purpose "was to destroy biological life while preserving buildings and armaments." In a statement to the *West Texas Catholic*, the diocesan newspaper, he called the decision the "latest in a series of tragic anti-life positions taken by our government." He urged the administration to reverse its decision and stop accelerating the arms race. Most controversially, though, he urged workers "involved in the production and stockpiling of nuclear bombs to consider what they are doing, to resign from such activities, and to seek employment in peaceful pursuits."

Pantex had always striven to be a model citizen. With an annual operating budget at the time of more than ninety million dollars, it contributed to about 25 percent of the local economy through its payroll, taxes, and purchases. It also was a major donor to charitable organizations, including United Way, the Amarillo Chamber of Commerce, and various educational programs. And it sponsored an "Atomic Energy Merit Badge Program" for local Boy Scouts. Matthiesen was now confronting that corporate citizen and its management head-on. The Associated Press picked up Matthiesen's statement, and the *New York Times* turned it into a front-page story. The BBC and reporters from the German and Japanese press interviewed him. The Reverend William Sloane Coffin, a longtime peace activist with international standing, asked Matthiesen to "pinch-hit" for Hunthausen at New York's Riverside Church. Matthiesen received a standing ovation.

A lay missionary group in Nebraska, seeking to support Matthiesen's call, donated ten thousand dollars for a worker relief fund so people could quit their jobs making weapons and be supported while they found new work. The only taker, a father of seven, was Eloy Ramos. At Pantex, Ramos was a truck mechanic, but he had grown up on a farm and liked being outside. "He loved the feel of warm sand between his toes, animals, the sun. He just loved life," said Matthiesen. Ramos made the decision to leave about the time Matthiesen issued his statement, although it was made independently, according to the bishop. "Eloy figured out that the trucks were part of the whole process. He worked out this [the weapons] was something that could destroy the trees, the grass, the life he loved." And for a while he had no job. "It was an act of faith." Ramos later developed a fence business. One other employee, a young nuclear engineering student who rode a bike along the assembly line, quietly thought about the hundreds of thousands of people that might be killed by a nuclear weapon. He decided to pursue another career.

Amarillo's city fathers greeted Matthiesen with months of stunned silence or vehement insults. "All hell broke loose. I was told to go to Siberia and stay there," said Matthiesen. His appeal to conscience was viewed by a lot of people as posing a threat not just to the Pantex workforce and Amarillo's economic fortunes but to the nation's security. Ramos had described weekly pep rallies at Pantex where employ-

ees were told, "Don't listen to those pinkos. Don't worry about what
you're doing," Matthiesen recalled, paraphrasing. "It was 'patriotic.'
People carried on normal conversations in the cafeteria, about newly
arrived babies and parties, as if you wouldn't know from the conversation what they were actually doing."

United Way was an important contributor to the Catholic Family
Service (CFS), which provided aid to abused children and runaways
and counseling and care for pregnant teenagers and troubled families. Charles Poole, then plant manager at Pantex, was a member of
the local United Way governing board. He asked the charity for a
"quick response" to the question of whether the United Way should
continue supporting the CFS. Concerned it would lose financial support from Pantex, then its single largest corporate contributor, United
Way terminated funding to the Catholic charity on April 1, 1982.[18]

SOMETHING WAS BEGINNING to crumble inside America's nuclear
fortress, but it would take another decade for the weaknesses to be exposed. Before that could happen, defense spending in the United States
would skyrocket, the Soviet Union would collapse, and the rot inside
the military-industrial complexes of both countries finally would be revealed. While Soviet military spending remained more or less constant,
Reagan's military expansion, much of it nuclear-related, cost taxpayers
$2.8 trillion between 1982 and 1989. Never before had so much money
been doled out for defense when the country was not at war.[19] Publicly
advertised as necessary to combat an increasingly menacing Soviet military, it has since been widely viewed as part of a sustained effort to
bankrupt America's cold war foe.[20]

Reagan's fixation on the Star Wars program, or SDI (Strategic Defense Initiative), scuttled two attempts, at Geneva and at Reykjavik, to
achieve groundbreaking arms reduction agreements with the Soviets.
The plutonium people also were back in the big tent. Reactors at
Hanford and Savannah River were reconfigured and restarted to fill a
supposed "plutonium gap"—which meant churning out enough new
material to fill as many as seventeen thousand new warheads.[21] On the
civilian side, Reagan lifted the Carter ban on reprocessing and breeders,
and everyone involved with nuclear energy, whether at Pantex or some
other government-run facility, seemed assured a secure future.

Like Reagan, Soviet leader Mikhail Gorbachev wanted to find a way out of the arms race, but in SDI, he saw only the prospect of another colossal and expensive arms race, just as his country was embarked on a difficult political and economic transition. "We can't go on living like this. There has to be change," he told his wife, Raisa, as he came to power in March 1985.[22]

Although the two sides failed to conclude an arms reduction treaty during their key October 1986 meeting in Iceland, the Reykjavik summit represented a breakthrough. An agreement was reached on the substance of a deal, based on the Soviet leader's initial three-part offer of a 50 percent cut in each of the three main weapons categories.[23] The following year, they finalized an Intermediate Nuclear Forces (INF) Treaty, completely eliminating all medium-range ballistic missiles worldwide and containing the most comprehensive verification regime ever agreed. Things moved quickly after that. By May 1991, all intermediate-range and shorter-range missiles, launchers, and related support equipment and support structures had been eliminated.[24]

The Soviet Union itself was changing dramatically. By the end of 1986, Gorbachev's first full year as leader, government censors had allowed a film critical of Stalin to be released, marking the start of a campaign to discredit the former dictator. The dissident physicist Andrei Sakharov was freed from exile. In February 1988, Gorbachev announced that Soviet forces would begin to withdraw from Afghanistan that May and would be out within a year. During a walk with the Soviet leader in Red Square during a May summit that same year, Reagan was asked by a reporter what had happened to the "evil empire" he had denounced at the beginning of his presidency when Leonid Brezhnev was still in power. Reagan said, "I was talking about another time, another era."[25]

The Soviet Union, and the cold war with it, was collapsing like a house of cards. On May 25, 1989, a new legislative body called the Congress of People's Deputies of the USSR held its first session, with more than two thousand elected deputies from all over the Soviet Union. That November the world watched in amazement as images of the Berlin Wall coming down flashed across their television screens. The wall was all gone by the end of 1990. Then, on June 12, 1991, Boris Yeltsin became the first popularly elected president of the Russian Republic in Soviet history, promising to transform the socialist economy to one based on market principles. Only six weeks later, on July 31, the two sides finally agreed for the first time to reduce strategic arms—missiles, bombers, subs, and warheads—that can deliver nuclear destruction to each other's cities. As suggested by its acronym, START-1 (Strategic Arms Reduction Treaty) was only a beginning, but it held great promise.[26]

In December that year, Yeltsin called President George H. W. Bush from a hunting lodge near Brest, in Belarus. "Today a very important event took place in our country," Yeltsin told the American president. "I wanted to inform you myself before you learned about it from the press."[27] Yeltsin told Bush that he had been meeting with the presidents of Belarus and Ukraine and that the three leaders had decided to dissolve the Soviet Union. Two weeks later, Bush disclosed, "a second call confirmed that the former Soviet Union would disappear. Mikhail Gorbachev contacted me at Camp David on Christmas morning of 1991. He wished Barbara and me a Merry Christmas, and then he went on to sum up what had happened in his country; the Soviet Union had ceased to exist. He had just been on national TV to confirm the fact, and he had transferred control of Soviet nuclear weapons to the President of Russia. 'You can have a very quiet Christmas evening,' he said." Reflecting upon that emotional moment, Bush added, "And so it was over. It was a very quiet and civilized ending to a tumultuous time in our history."[28]

A second START agreement was signed two years later, in January 1993, calling for an overall reduction in deployed strategic weapons to between 3,000 and 3,500 warheads, and steps were taken by both sides to rid themselves of thousands of tactical nuclear weapons. But disarmament efforts hit numerous obstacles over the next decade and in 2002 the United States withdrew from the Anti-Ballistic Missile (ABM) Treaty, prompting Russia to walk away from START II. More cuts were made under Bush but without the strict verification measures mandated by START. It would take a new U.S. administration to revive the talks and finally agree in March 2010 to further lower the numbers— to 1,550 deployed warheads on each side—but that agreement still left enough nuclear firepower in each country's arsenal for planetary disaster.

As THE COLD war came to an end, distant rumblings could be heard from one end of the nuclear state to the other. Dirty, dark secrets— discomfiting truths—began spilling out. In the United States, the ghosts of the AEC's past came back to haunt. The contaminated waste piles AEC officials like Alan Labowitz had confronted back in the 1950s had grown bigger, and some sites were so hot there was talk of roping them off and setting up "national sacrifice zones." Edlow's lead had not shielded (nor, of course, had it been intended to) even a fraction of the people suffering the effects of radiation exposure, whether they were the sons and daughters of uranium miners, people who worked in nuclear fuel factories, soldiers, sailors, and pilots exposed to radiation during the testing, or members of the public exposed to fallout either from testing or the catastrophic accidents. The Atoms for Peace banners had long since been torn down, fragments of an era that promised far more than it could deliver.

Upshot   Instead, in the United States, just over one hundred reactors, as opposed to the one thousand once forecast, were more prosaically delivering approximately 20 percent of the nation's electricity (while the gaseous diffusion uranium enrichment plants from which they obtained their fuel continued consuming a hefty number of kilowatt hours),[30] and radioactive spent fuel accumulated on the ground, with no place to bury it. Today, reactor operating costs are decreasing, but the units are not providing too-cheap-to-meter electricity. Meanwhile, decommissioning and waste disposal have created enormous tabs for $ the future. For example, the costs of building and maintaining the Yucca Mountain facility designated by Congress for permanent disposal of all the nation's spent civilian nuclear fuel (from existing reactors) plus a fraction of its military waste has now reached Star Wars proportions: in August 2008, the Department of Energy put the cost at ninety-six billion dollars.[31]

The energy department has been the focus of intense public and even industry criticism for as long as most people can remember, but its real problems started after Chernobyl, which drew attention to safety deficiencies at its aging Hanford reactors. "Chernobyl was like sprinkling lighter fluid on something already smoldering," explained former DOE senior adviser Robert Alvarez, who was then at the Environmental Policy Institute in Washington, D.C. After the Soviet accident, Alvarez organized a press conference to call attention to the dangers at the department's plants. "They [DOE] were locked in time, out of step with nuclear safety."[32]

The immediate effect was to hasten the closure of the plutonium production reactors, but that was just the beginning. Alvarez left the Environmental Policy Institute to work for Senator Glenn, and then or-

ganized hearings "on the whole DOE mess." The Senate probe began a
lengthy national self-examination that raised the basic question: what
price had Americans paid for being the world's leading nuclear power?
Investigators, auditors, researchers, and the media probed the inner re-
cesses of an enterprise that had run amok. A lot of the effort focused on
the weapons establishment, but that included fuel plants that served
both the civilian and military sides, and contractors that worked both
sides of the fence. "It was carpet bombing on DOE," said Alvarez."[33]

There were some surprising discoveries.

Among other things, the General Accounting Office (GAO) found
out that Gorbachev had been right to question Reagan's motives for
advancing SDI. It turned out that in order to deceive the Soviets, SDI
tests had been rigged, and test data fabricated, to make the system appear as if it worked. The GAO also said that over a period of three
years, the Defense Department misled Congress about the need for
new weapons, as well as their effectiveness and cost, and exaggerated
the vulnerability of bombers and intercontinental ballistic missiles to
Soviet attack. In carrying out the tests, the department's plan "was
seen as a means of impacting arms control negotiations and influencing Soviet spending," the report said.[34]

When President Clinton appointed Hazel O'Leary energy secretary
in 1993, she upset the entitlement culture that had grown up and
wrapped itself around the weapons establishment like bindweed. Lab
directors expecting a more or less automatic sign-off on proposed underground nuclear tests were challenged to explain why the tests were
needed. "Everyone was stunned. I like to say she's the only secretary
of energy we've ever had with balls," said Frank von Hippel, professor
of public and international affairs at Princeton University's Program on
Science and Global Security.

O'Leary presided over a vast, arcane, and secretive domain that was
forced to open up. She began making records available so people could
see in more detail what went on inside, and what it meant for the future. Her most startling revelation was that for the better part of three
decades, beginning in the 1940s, the government subjected more than
twenty-three thousand people to radiation experiments, many without their informed consent. The DOE was only one of several agencies
implicated; others included the defunct AEC, the Department of Defense, the National Aeronautical and Space Administration, and the

Department of Veterans Affairs. National laboratories and prominent universities also played a role, including the University of Chicago, New York University, the University of Rochester, Vanderbilt, MIT, and Harvard. In one particularly grim program, overseen by MIT, oatmeal laced with radioactive trace elements was fed to more than one hundred boys between the ages of twelve and seventeen at a Massachusetts school for children with mental retardation. Prisoners in Oregon and Washington were used in testicular irradiation trials, while another test involved giving pregnant women small doses of radioactive iron. In late 1993, after learning about a trial involving plutonium and uranium injections into unknowing subjects, O'Leary said, "The only thing I could think of was Nazi Germany."[35]

A similar pattern of national self-examination began in the former Soviet Union. Officials in Moscow admitted the huge devastation caused by the Mayak nuclear weapons plant at Kyshtym, where some ten thousand square miles remained contaminated. Soldiers no longer bound by their oaths of secrecy told journalists and filmmakers about their roles in the atmospheric tests, and the government opened its once top secret archives so people could read the records and see footage of the tests. "These tests shouldn't be called tests," Russian health minister Andrei Vorobyev told the makers of *Nuclear Tango*. "How can you experiment with poison? Only stupid people allow these kind of things on their own people. I have no urge to defend this . . . We knew the risks. Did we know this [radiation risks] before Hiroshima and Nagasaki? We knew this before Hiroshima and Nagasaki."[36] Like many others who had taken charge, Vorobyev would have been a child when the tests started.

With more information, environmentalists and health officials could begin to assess the extent of the damage, even worse than in the United States, stretching across the vastness of Semipalatinsk, Novaya Zemlya, and dozens of nuclear fuel processing and weapons production sites in the Soviet atomic cities. The realizations and the admissions that something had gone vastly awry did little to comfort those who had lost a place they could only revisit in their memories. One woman forced to leave Novaya Zemlya told the filmmakers in a voice that swayed with rhythm: "And still today I have dreams of Novaya Zemlya because it was so beautiful, flowers of all kinds— daisies, red carnations, forget-me-nots . . . poppies . . . it remains my dreamland full of flowers." She smiled as she explained how lush it had been.

In the early 1990s, Congress enacted legislation to help the Soviets dismantle their weapons program and secure fissile material, but there were many problems to deal with in America's own nuclear waste-land. The United States had not collapsed, but it was not exempt from the long-term implications of spending trillions of taxpayer dollars on products (warheads and missiles) that had no economic value and moreover cost money for upkeep, or dismantlement and waste burial. This was hardly an example of good capitalism: a "monopsony," as some have termed it, was created, meaning the government had become both a monopoly producer and monopoly consumer. The private contractors that supped off the bounty in order to keep it going generally found it easier to attract more capital, because theirs was never really at risk, and this meant others had to wait further back in the line and probably pay more for their borrowings. What this cost the country in lost opportunities is impossible to gauge.[37]

After tabulating the $5.5 trillion tab that the weapons extravaganza had already cost the nation, William J. Weida, one of the authors of *Atomic Audit*, made this sobering assessment: "To the extent that demand for investment in nuclear defense has crowded out other, valid investment requirements in the economy in general, the share of the gross domestic product (GDP) allocated to nuclear weapons has potentially lowered both the productivity and competitiveness of the U.S. economy (the same situation attains [sic] in Russia, although deeper structural problems exacerbate the problem there)."[38]

Alvarez and others had already begun describing certain areas within the costly expanse as "national sacrifice zones" because there was no obvious way they could be decontaminated. Among the most likely candidates were the facilities at Oak Ridge, Hanford, and Savannah River, but hundreds of other sites were contaminated. At Oak Ridge, thousands of containers containing highly enriched uranium stood in deteriorating buildings, posing the risk of fire, theft, unplanned chain reaction incidents, and further worker exposure to radiation.[39]

Across the country at Hanford, there were 177 underground tanks containing a complex brew of hot bubbling radioactive toxins and chemicals; roughly a third had leaked more than one million gallons of waste, some of which has migrated into groundwater that eventually enters the Columbia River. Even worse, over two decades beginning in 1946, the Hanford people, after stripping out most of the cesium and strontium by adding chemicals, intentionally dumped more than 120 million gallons of liquid wastes directly into the ground. "They were using the environment they occupied as a storage and disposal media," said Alvarez, "so you know the Columbia River was like their flush toilet." A belief among GE's engineers that they could reduce waste volumes by adding other chemicals has probably made the job of getting rid of the wastes "the most expensive, complex, and risky environmental project in the United States," he added.[40]

DuPont's chemical engineers, overseeing the Savannah River complex, knew better. They tried to maintain chemical "homogeneity" and began encasing the liquids in glass "logs," a process called vitrification, which Hanford is only now attempting. Even then, Alvarez says, they have been able to process less than 5 percent of the radioactivity in the waste—after some twenty-five years and billions of dollars spent.[41] And DuPont was hardly a model citizen. It routinely burned solvent in the open air and stored liquid wastes in drums that are now old and leaky, sitting atop a series of aquifers in a stratified groundwater system, in a seismically active zone.

Perhaps the biggest headache is getting rid of tritium, which travels quickly in air and water and takes a century to lose most of its radioactivity. Scientists at Savannah River hit upon a plan to use trees as waste processing "machines," a process known as phytoremediation. "Because we can't treat this tritium—there's no process we can run it through to remove it—we finally arrived at a solution which was we should irrigate some of these pine forests we have a lot of with the tritiated water and evaporate it to the atmosphere," Gerald Blount, a senior environmental official at the plant, told a local reporter in 2000. Plans called for creating whole plantations specifically for this purpose, harvesting the trees and selling them for timber after they are more or less flushed of tritium.[42] What to do if the trees catch fire, or decay and die while tritium is still churning around in their branches? "It becomes organically bound tritium which increases the absorption in the human environment," says Alvarez.[43] Local environmentalists are concerned because the scientists apparently have no answer to that problem.

As scientists grope for answers, workers seek new language [to de]scribe the situations they find themselves in. At the Rocky Flats plant in Colorado that once fabricated plutonium bomb cores, employees came up with a label for areas they could no longer access because radiation monitors would go off-scale the minute they stepped inside. They called them "infinity rooms"—and sealed them off.[44]

IN THE OPTIMISM that followed the major disarmament agreements, O'Leary also decided to let journalists, even from overseas, tour Pantex. In May 1994, on assignment with Britain's *GQ* magazine, I flew from London, where I was then living, to Texas. Inside the compound, the employees were predictably incredulous at the sight of reporters. "Five years ago, we wouldn't have dreamed this could happen. This amazes many of us who have been here for very long," said one. "It takes some of the fun out of it because we were top secret and now it's more open."

The plant was shut down the day of our tour on orders from the Defense Nuclear Facilities Safety Board, which was set up in 1988 to confront the vast array of safety problems throughout the DOE complex. At Pantex one warhead had nearly exploded in 1992 while a bomb was being taken apart and the surface of the core cracked. Workers were forced to evacuate the underground cell. The sloppy safety practices extended to poor security too. Plutonium pits from disassembled weapons were stowed in aboveground World War II bunkers underneath the flight path to the Amarillo airport, clearly visible from the air. There were no antiaircraft guns.

At Pantex, as at most other government-owned large nuclear sites, workers were exposed over years to excess radioactivity. They paid for it with their health and sometimes with their lives. One worker at Pantex, John Bell, was poisoned with radioactivity after being ordered to drill part of a bomb component containing radioactive material. His supervisors, who watched from a more protected area, warned Bell afterward, as he recalled, "to wash up real well."[45] Bell suffered permanent damage to his nervous system, fibrosis in one lung, and bladder problems, and eventually he contracted cancer. He won a worker's compensation award of eighty-seven thousand dollars, although the plant operators, Mason & Hanger, fought the decision. Describing the management's attitude toward worker exposure, Bell told a DOE hearing later: "You'll come back and they'll tell you you didn't get a significant amount to hurt you . . . They don't tell you about the latent part of it. The latent part of it is the roughest part of it. You slowly go down, and you don't know what it is that's doing it."[46]

During the tour, we walked through vast underground tunnels bathed in hallucinogenic green-yellow light, past emergency vats of eyewash and traffic-light-size alarm lights, as workers rode by on bicycles like aliens from some other world. Finally we were taken through interlocking safety doors and a staging area to the cell of a Gravel Gertie, like the one where the warhead almost exploded. In 1993, a GAO investigator described Pantex as "probably one of the worst, in terms of occupational safety and health of any of the facilities."[47] Alvarez agreed: "Pantex is one of the huge bottlenecks for disarmament. It was never meant for dismantlement. The United States and the Soviet Union never envisioned stopping [weapons manufacturing] and they had no contingencies for stopping, but it stopped. All these sites were operating on a production flow sheet, not a disarmament flow sheet."[48]

Some Pantex workers were troubled by disarmament because their highly paid jobs no longer seemed secure. "The trust the government has in Russia isn't shared here," Ronnie Payne, head of the local Metal Trades Council, assured me. "Most of us think we'll be back building them [warheads] in a few years. I think it's just been instilled in us not to trust them. One guy summed it up for all of us: 'Russia was a reliable enemy. As soon as we get another reliable enemy, we will go back to work.' "[49]

PAYNE WAS NOT the only one worrying. The disarmament treaties sent a shock wave throughout the DOE weapons complex. In May 1993, the directors of Los Alamos, Sandia National Laboratory, and Lawrence Livermore decided to do something about it. They arranged a top secret meeting with O'Leary and other officials to press for more weapons testing, although their real purpose may have been to prevent layoffs, in the opinion of Frank von Hippel, who attended the meeting. The Comprehensive Test Ban Treaty still was three years away.

The meeting took place over the course of two afternoons inside a vault at the bottom of the Forrestal Building. Along with O'Leary and her top aides, long-serving government advisers on nuclear weapons also were present, including James Schlesinger, former defense secretary under Nixon and Ford, and a longtime advocate of higher defense spending and modernization of strategic and conventional forces. He attended only the first session and, according to von Hippel, argued for continued testing on the basis that the British still wanted to test and had only the American test sites to use, although the United States had ended the program for its own "parochial" reasons. In order to impress everyone with the importance of more testing, the lab officials had brought in a full-scale warhead model. Von Hippel still recalls the event with amazement. "It was a cross-section of a bomb about this big," he said, spreading his arms wide. It was the first time the Princeton scientist had ever seen the inside of a bomb. As he leaned over it to give it a close inspection, one of the lab officials said: "Now we've got you, Frank."[50]

But the "wow effect" did not achieve the desired results. Von Hippel argued that apart from the configuration of the material in the core, all the rest of the bomb parts could be tested without explosions. Surprisingly, he said, the lab directors did not argue with him very much. According to von Hippel, one of them said: "Well, you know, if you give us as much money for not testing as for testing we might see it your way."[51] That, said von Hippel, was the beginning of the Stockpile Stewardship Program.

With congressional support, Stockpile Stewardship was formally launched in 1994 with a mandate to ensure the safety and reliability of the nation's remaining nuclear arsenal. It sounded very worthy, and the early funding levels were relatively modest. But the lab directors wanted to go back to the kind of budgets they had grown used to during the Reagan and Bush years, and they had the support of the National Security Council. "The number was four billion. If the administration would guarantee them four billion [dollars] in perpetuity they could assure the safety and reliability of the stockpile. That's what the national security director signed onto," said Robert Civiak, a program and budget examiner in the White House Office of Management and Budget in 1988–99. Added von Hippel: "The NSC said, 'We don't care about the details, but we're committed to this level of funding.'"[52]

By 1997, the laboratories had all but achieved their aim. With support from loyal followers in Congress, such as Senator Pete Domenici, a Republican from New Mexico, known as "St. Pete" on both the

civilian and military sides of the nuclear industry, they were only one
hundred million dollars shy of four billion.

WITH DISMANTLEMENT UNDER way, the DOE drew up plans to consolidate its operation, shutting some facilities and expanding others.
Pantex was marked for expansion, and the DOE decided it needed
more land around the Texas facility to accomplish the task. Amarillo's mayor came up with a list of suitable properties for condemnation. Doris and Phil Smith and a few of their neighbors found out
about the plans. A meeting was called at St. Francis Church in February 1991.

"It was the big city folks ready to slay the hicks," said Doris, who
was a vivacious woman in her fifties when I met her three years after
that meeting. "They [the Amarillo officials] came struttin' in and the
hicks started asking questions. They started talking about the land
they needed outside the FM [farm-to-market] roads. I said, 'Well,
Mayor, we live there!' He said, 'That's nontillable farmland and no
one lives there.' He told me this three times," she said as if she still
could not believe the man's ignorance. "Anyway, the hick slayers went
out with their heads between their knees."[53]

This time no land was taken. But the meeting led to the formation
of a new anti-nuclear-weapons group, Panhandle Area Neighbors and
Landowners (PANAL). At first the new organization was meant to address the property concerns, but then it took up issues related to the
environment, health and safety, and the long-term plutonium storage
problem. These were not left-leaning liberals typically associated with
antinuclear activities. One of the new PANAL members, Jeri Osborne,
was chairwoman of the Republican Party in Carson County and president of her local gun club. She had converted her grown daughter's
bedroom into a makeshift office where she kept a local map marked
with pins for each recent death from cancer. There were leukemia
clusters forming a line from inside the plant to several miles to the
northeast. Jeri admitted her map was an amateur's attempt to catalog
the possible effects of the Pantex operation on local health. But what
angered her was that state and federal officials had historically shown
so little concern.[54]

Over time, the Smiths discovered tritium in a well on their ranch.
The government denied there was a problem. "What happens really is

that you get a high reading in any of the wells and then the government comes back and says it was a lab error or it was false," explained Doris in a phone conversation in 2003. "Very few people that don't work at Pantex believe the government much anymore." Phil Smith had contracted prostate cancer.[55]

The Smiths had grown even more politically active than when I first met them in 1994. They hooked up with the Alliance for Nuclear Accountability, an umbrella group founded in 1987 to highlight concerns of people living near DOE weapons facilities. Through the alliance, the conservative Texans made contact with Russian citizens in situations similar to their own and hosted them in Texas. In the spring of 1997, Doris Smith flew to Washington and gave a national press conference to protest plans for a national plutonium research center at Pantex. On April 29, the day she spoke, someone started a fire at St. Francis Church and it burned to the ground. The arsonists were never found.

"There are members in our church community that actually work at Pantex. We don't think those families were involved in this," said Doris, "but we think that it could have been some of the workers that were not happy with the stand that we were taking, and thinking that we were actually trying to shut Pantex down."[56]

Groundbreaking on a new church began in January 1999. The statue of Our Lady of the Fields, spared from the flames, continues to watch over a divided flock, with her prayer for understanding.

CHAPTER 19

Maggie's Blue-Eyed Boys

Margaret Thatcher had a weakness for scientists, especially the nuclear kind. Two of her favorites, Brian Flowers and Walter Marshall, were both leading figures in Britain's nuclear establishment when Thatcher was a rising star in Britain's Conservative Party. Their standing with her became a weathervane for her changing views about nuclear energy during a period of fierce debate over the issue before and after she became prime minister in 1979. "She had an instinct for scientific quality," said Flowers, who years earlier had taught Marshall physics at Birmingham.[1]

But Thatcher did not always get it right. In 1976, Flowers chaired a study that made two warnings, and they were heretical as far as the nuclear industry was concerned. One advised against new reactors until the waste problem was solved; the other said breeder reactors and reprocessing were bad ideas.[2] Leading industry figures, Marshall in particular, were predictably upset, but Thatcher was not sure who to side with. Marshall "lobbied her hard," said Flowers, and she made up her mind. "I was her blue-eyed boy before Walter Marshall. She read that report and thought she'd have to think hard about it. But Walter persuaded her that it was wrong, and she chose to take Walter's side. With her, you were either one hundred percent or zero."

It was the wrong choice, and it would come back to haunt her. More than a decade later, when Thatcher was prime minister, her Conservative government tried to sell off the state-owned nuclear industry to private investors. London's savvy financial types told her it would not wash with investors, and she had to publicly abort the sale. This caused the government much embarrassment and ended Marshall's career. More than that, the canceled sale finally exposed what economists like Britain's Eric Price, who worked on the nuclear privatization attempt, had known since the early 1950s: that nuclear could not compete on economic grounds with other energy sources because there were so many hidden costs and unknown liabilities. It also brought to the fore the volatile issue of nuclear's "back end"—including waste, reprocessing, reactor decommissioning, and their costs.

The report's contributors were a cross-section of experts on soil, oceans, and the atmosphere who at the behest of the Royal Commission on Environmental Pollution studied the pros and cons of nuclear energy for two years. They concluded that there should be no further large-scale nuclear development without a solution to the issue of "how radioactive waste could be permanently, safely stored."[3] And they warned against breeders because they would be expensive, crowd out other energy options, and present a proliferation risk. Their advice challenged a prevailing attitude that nuclear energy would be the answer to dependence on oil.

"The basic belief of the [UK] Department of Energy and the [UK] AEA is that nuclear fission using the fast breeder reactor is the only real option for meeting our future energy needs," the report said. "We fear that on this premise there may be a gradual, step-by-step progression to overriding dependence on nuclear power through tacit acceptance of its inevitability, and a gradual foreclosing of other options that might have been available had they been exercised in time."[4]

Echoing many of the same themes proliferation activists in Washington were raising, the Flowers report said that "the construction of a crude nuclear weapon by an illicit group is credible." For that reason the report concluded: "The dangers of the creation of plutonium in large quantities in conditions of increasing world unrest are genuine and serious. We should not rely for energy supply on a process that produces such a hazardous substance as plutonium unless there is no reasonable alternative."[5]

To a casual observer, the commission's advice seemed like common sense. But the panel's recommendations threatened to further brake the industry's growth and undermine its most cherished assumptions. The idea of "closing the fuel cycle"—sending spent reactor fuel for reprocessing and eventual use in breeders—had become an obsession by

then, even though it was proving extremely costly, dangerous, and ultimately futile. (There were no breeders in Britain to send the reprocessed fuel to, and experimental breeders elsewhere were plagued with
technical problems.) But nuclear men clung to the vision—literally to
their deaths. Lord Hinton, who presided over design and construction
of the Sellafield complex, requested in his will that his ashes be scattered around the site—and when he died in 1983 his wishes were carried out, according to a driver named John who picked me up at the
train station during a visit I made to the plant in 2004. "It was his [Hinton's] place. He was so engrossed in it," the driver said.

Even Flowers had a conflicted reaction to the report. "I grew up in
the forties, and I believed in the complete fuel cycle, the whole idea of
producing plutonium and having an infinite supply. The idea that you
start off with uranium and you make more fuel than you can burn—
the whole industry was based on it. It was a long time before I came to
accept that there was enough uranium in the world that you didn't
need it [plutonium]. It took me a long time before I was emotionally
able to declare plutonium a waste."

BY THE MID-1970S, when the report appeared, Marshall exerted enormous influence over the direction of the country's energy policy, as
both deputy director of the UK Atomic Energy Authority and chief
science adviser at the Department of Energy. Tall and heavyset, with
blue-gray eyes that appeared expressionless and cold, Marshall had developed a reputation for arrogance, accentuated by an odd, haughty
manner of speaking. During a period when Britain was awash with
North Sea oil and gas, the Welsh-born Marshall steered the government toward more nuclear. The same year as Flowers's report, Marshall too oversaw the drafting of a study. It not only advocated further
nuclear energy development but said priority should be given to fast
breeders—already costing British taxpayers close to one hundred million pounds per year and the largest single absorber of government energy research funds, with little to show for it.[6]

"Walter Marshall thought he was God," said a former senior official
at Rio Tinto–Zinc, the major uranium supplier to Britain's state-owned
Central Electricity Generating Board (CEGB), where Marshall was later
made chairman. "Walter thought that Mrs. Thatcher would support
nuclear energy to the hilt. He thought when the CEGB was formed he

would naturally be the head of it. He was a magician, like the Wizard of Oz. That was Walter . . . They [the nuclear industry] believed the public should know nothing . . . The whole industry was arrogant. They believed they were scientists with special information that nobody would understand."

And that establishment is what Flowers, who was part of it, had challenged. Despite mixed feelings, he was proud of his panel's effort. "We were the first ones [in Britain] to point out that it wasn't a question of *whether* but *when* nuclear material would fall into the hands of evil-doers," Flowers said. "What really brought it home was how very little had been done about the problem of nuclear waste . . . There we were creating radioactive wastes by the yard and doing almost nothing about how to deal with it. It did not make me antinuclear. I still want nuclear power. They [the nuclear industry] only behaved like any other industry." *Precisely, industry is Inherently*

The question was, would they do anything about it? *unsustainable*

— wrong turn! —

AT THE TIME of the Flowers report, Britain's minister responsible for nuclear energy, the Rt. Hon. Anthony Wedgwood Benn, had become disillusioned with nuclear energy. He also was hearing reports that Marshall, his scientific adviser, was moonlighting as nuclear adviser to the shah of Iran. Marshall had become cheerleader in chief for American light-water reactors by this stage, but Benn was still backing the British advanced gas-cooled reactor (AGR), so in 1978 there was an inevitable parting of ways. Marshall returned to Harwell to head up research.[7] *how we complain?*

But the ignominious retreat was only temporary. After Thatcher's election in 1979, he was made chairman of the Central Electricity Generating Board and became one of the prime minister's chief allies in her brutal and legendary fight against the powerful National Union of Mineworkers and its militant leader, Arthur Scargill. Thatcher's struggle with the coal miners was part of a long-term plan to extricate Britain from a left-wing ideology that she and her party blamed for the country's descent into economic calamity and second-rate status. Her aim was to sell off state-owned industries, including the National Coal Board, then headed by American industrialist Ian McGregor, and eventually the monopoly electricity board headed by Marshall.[8]

She took aim at Scargill through the coal board, which in early 1984 announced the closure of twenty coal mines, with the loss of twenty thousand jobs, on the grounds they were uneconomical. Well before the announcement, Thatcher quietly ordered Marshall to stockpile coal, which he did by lining up contracts from cheaper overseas suppliers. When Scargill called a national strike on March 12, the CEGB had enough coal in the pipeline to keep the lights on for what promised to be a lengthy action. The strike lasted almost a year, and resulted in violent clashes with police and at least ten strike-related fatalities.[9]

While miners stood in the cold, Marshall and his wife spent weekends being entertained at Chequers, the prime minister's weekend residence south of London. He was awarded a life peerage. Thatcher "thought the world of Marshall," said Eric Price, chief economic adviser at the UK Department of Energy from 1980 to 1992.[10] Thatcher's plan succeeded—the National Coal Board was sold to private investors in 1994 after she had left office and all but seventeen of some 170 mines left in Britain were shut down.[11] "The miners chose the wrong time to go on strike," said Price. "Lord Marshall delivered the goods. He kept the nuclear stations working and he kept coal going and they won. They annihilated the miners. She [Thatcher] had a lot to thank him for."

But stockpiling coal was a relatively simple matter compared to running nuclear stations. And when the government made plans to sell off the electricity industry in 1988, Marshall would discover what it was like to be on the "Iron Lady's" wrong side. Energy Department economists like Price were skeptical that nuclear privatization would work the way the government had organized it. But Marshall persuaded Thatcher to proceed, convinced that the numbers-crunchers were wrong. Then, as a detailed prospectus was drawn up, the government's outside financial advisers came to the same conclusion already reached by the energy economists.

They discovered, among other things, that the CEGB had grossly exaggerated the supposedly low costs of nuclear-generated electricity—their own figure of 6.25 pence per kilowatt hour was roughly double that of the CEGB's 3.2 pence, a number that could only be arrived at by assuming an unrealistically low rate of return on capital over a forty-year period, as opposed to a more realistic fifteen- or twenty-year time frame.[12] The nine Magnox reactors were nearing the ends of their lives, and their closure charges would be extremely high. The CEGB had been grossly understating these costs too. "They had been able to get away with this," according to Nigel Lawson, Thatcher's chancellor of the exchequer, "because no nuclear power station has so far been decommis-

[handwritten annotation: X That's why it has always been a cost to the tax payer]

sioned, and it was only the intense scrutiny required for the privatization prospectus that brought it starkly to light years later."[13]

Prospective investors were hardly swayed by the government's offer of a hefty subsidy to sweeten the deal, and they were right not to be. By 1990, decommissioning costs were put at fifteen billion pounds, versus the CEGB's figure of just over three billion, and even that higher number would prove far too low.[14] The bigger problem was that no one actually knew what the final costs would be, and they still don't more than fifteen years later. And no one could be certain how long the subsidies would last, or how much they would amount to. Private investors were not about to be saddled with apparently unquantifiable risk. Another factor was the requirement for the private company to build four new reactors. "What the market didn't want was the risk of building and operating a whole new fleet of plants, because they would have been responsible for them," said Steve Thomas, professor of energy policy at Greenwich University in London.[15]

The energy secretary, Cecil Parkinson, was "taken aback" when Lawson told him the sale could not go through, the former chancellor asserted in a memoir. "Moreover," Lawson added, "Margaret, with her deep commitment to nuclear power, would never wear [accept] it." But Lawson persuaded Parkinson they would have to tell her. "I pointed out that the situation had changed completely, and that it was now clear from the new figures that privatization would be impossible with the Magnox reactors included in the package. Not only did they give the enterprise a negative net worth, but the uncertainties alone would frighten off investors." Thatcher found it "distinctly unpalatable," in his words, but "she recognized that—to coin a phrase—there was no alternative." Parkinson announced the withdrawal of the Magnox reactors from the sale on July 24, 1989. The remaining reactors, including a planned new pressurized-water reactor plant, were withdrawn in November.

Marshall resigned from the CEGB. Seemingly oblivious to the realities, he declared on November 30, 1989, that "the broad story of nuclear power in this country is the most powerful argument in favour of privatization that I have ever seen. Over the last forty years, governments have interfered with this business so continuously, and with such appalling effects, that I am thoroughly convinced that it must be best to do everything that can be done in the private sector."[16]

Although Marshall got a job as head of a nuclear organization in Paris, his career in Britain was effectively over. Thatcher was said to be

She was! see p. 348

"furious" and felt that she had been misled, or even deceived, by him, and the invitations to Chequers ceased. For Lawson the affair provided valuable lessons: "First, that ministers can always be led astray by scientific experts. Second, that the dangers of state ownership are greater than even the Thatcher government realized. Had it not been for privatization, who knows how much longer the country would have been paying the price of the phoney economics of nuclear power."[17]

THE CEGB FIASCO was only a scene setter for a far bigger disaster: the reprocessing venture at Sellafield. Its primary purpose originally was to provide fuel for plants that existed mainly in the imaginations of their die-hard promoters. As the breeder mirage continually receded into the distant future, Sellafield and the French reprocessing plants at Cap de la Hague (and to a lesser extent Marcoule) churned out ton after ton of plutonium, for which there was no use. That effort in turn produced huge quantities of toxic radioactive wastes described in the Flowers report "as the most intractable of all those produced in the nuclear fuel cycle." Nuclear operators in Britain basically viewed Sellafield as an interim storage facility for their spent fuel, while breeder thumpers saw it as a necessary stage toward the magic day when existing reactors would be replaced by breeders.

In the spring of 2004, I visited Sellafield. The plant was probably less than a mile away from a guesthouse, visible behind lush green borders so tall I could barely see the high wire security fence surrounding it. The guesthouse, owned by British Nuclear Fuels, then the plant operator, looked like the setting for an eighteenth-century English novel. Cowslips and bluebells were blooming. Cattle grazed on a field, and a river down a short slope behind the guesthouse ran clean and clear on its way toward the grounds of the facility and the Irish Sea. It was an odd, jarring mix, a John Constable landscape beside a grim Max Ernst.

Roger Howsley, a quiet, modest man of middling years with dark hair and a retiring manner, the head of plant security, explained his overall approach to the job over dinner that evening in a wood-paneled private room at the guesthouse. "Security is as much about people managing it as it is about fences and guards," he said. "Are threats being properly assessed and communicated? Fences are fences."[18] When Greenpeace protestors easily scaled the plant's perimeter fence on Easter Monday 1995, the headlines read: "The Fence That Is No Defense."

Most experts agree with Howsley that even if terrorists got into the facility they would be hard-pressed to get inside the two buildings that contain a total of about one hundred tons of plutonium (enough for twenty thousand bombs), because the buildings are reinforced with thick concrete walls and wired with sophisticated security systems.[19] A potentially bigger risk is that terrorists would blow up building B215. Inside it are eighteen enormous tanks of high-level radioactive liquid waste from the reprocessing operations. "There is a thousand times more activity inside my plant than released by Chernobyl," said Paul Robson, who was in overall charge of B215. "If you divided Sellafield into one hundred blocks, ninety of them would be my plant in terms of risk. I dominate the site's risk barometer."[20]

The interior of THORP, the main "thermal oxide reprocessing plant" at Sellafield, is a factory-scape of yellow rails, girded staircases, catwalks, overhead cranes, and spaces filled with dark, deep ponds, and thickly shielded cells where the chemical separation takes place. "Master slave manipulators" with long metallic claws operate the machinery that chops, mixes, and otherwise handles the hot fuel, adding to the plant's surreal quality. In the "shearing caves" where huge blades sever the fuel rods, the radiation is so intense that a person standing inside would in a matter of minutes be exposed to levels at least twenty-eight times above normally lethal amounts. Every piece of equipment in the process, not to mention the floors, walls, ceilings, and lightbulbs of the plant itself, is tomorrow's nuclear junk. The financial liabilities are enormous. So far, the site's decommissioning costs are estimated at more than forty billion pounds, roughly half the total (as of mid-2008) for mothballing eighteen other nuclear facilities in the country, and once the plant shuts down the process is expected to take more than a hundred years.[21] wow — — —

After the plant tour, Janine Allis-Smith, a Dutch woman, met me for an "alternative tour" with a Geiger counter. She and her English husband, Martin Forwood, run an activist group called Cumbrians Opposed to a Radioactive Environment, or CORE. Before inviting me into her beat-up old car, Allis-Smith took a reading—a little above normal background. As we drove around the plant's periphery, along the road that separates the site from the Irish Sea, she pointed out a huge pipeline that discharges effluent. Then we headed to a nearby beach, and the Geiger counter dial went higher than it had at the visitor center, to about ten counts per second, about twice background levels. "This is a beach where I used to take my son," Allis-Smith explained. "He used to pick up mud and put it over his head. At the time, plutonium discharges were so high. My son got leukemia."

Her boy, Lee, was born in 1972 and contracted the cancer when he was twelve. When she took him to the hospital, she remembers a nurse said, "God, another one from Cumbria." Allis-Smith's son survived, though she does not know whether he will ever be able to have children.

"He was lucky," she admitted. "But I blamed Sellafield."

Then she drove me to a house in the nearby village of Seascale overlooking the sea. Two eccentric sisters who once lived in it had taken to collecting pigeons by keeping them constantly fed, and there were so many that the neighbors finally complained. The Ministry of Agriculture, Food, and Fisheries was called in, and investigators discovered the pigeons were "so hot" they issued a warning not to touch or eat them. "They were literally flying nuclear waste," said Allis-Smith.

oh shit...

THE BRITISH GOVERNMENT has been at pains over the years to play down attempts to correlate cancers with Sellafield radioactivity, particularly when it involves individuals living near the plant but not working at it. For example, when a 1997 Ministry of Health report revealed that children living close to Sellafield had twice as much plutonium in their teeth as children living more than one hundred miles away, Health Minister Melanie Johnson said the quantities were minute and presented "no risk to public health."[22] Dundee University's Professor Eric Wright, a leading expert on blood disorders, challenged her claim, saying that even microscopic amounts of the man-made element might cause cancer. Other experts pointed out that while there was little risk from plutonium in the dead tissue of tooth enamel, its presence during the formation of the enamel would indicate a parallel inclusion in bones, where the potential for harm is much greater.[23]

BNFL employees who develop cancer are now compensated on as little as 20 percent probability of a link to work-related radiation. Yet no individual or group outside the plant has ever successfully prosecuted a health or property claim against BNFL.[24] The closest official admission of a possible connection between cancers and Sellafield is suggested in a series of reports by a government committee of medical experts, known as COMARE, or the Committee on Medical Aspects of Radiation in the Environment. Yet the panel, which has been reporting since

1986, has been at pains to avoid any definite conclusions and continually suggests only that further study "might" be warranted.

Glasgow University's David Sanderson, who organized a radiation sample-mapping exercise across the UK and Europe after Chernobyl, believes that "the likelihood is there have been radiation-produced cancers both within the plant and from without." While tracking Chernobyl fallout, he and a colleague stumbled on a Sellafield footprint larger than he or anyone else could at first believe. Walking on a lush salt marsh near Ravenglass, a village just a few miles south of the plant, they picked up a reading of some three hundred thousand becquerels per square meter.[25] "I was shocked at this," he said. "I had never seen a signal like that in the environment before." The reading was so high Sanderson was almost certain it must be from a piece of radioactive metal. He and his colleague returned to investigate early the following morning. "We walked across the field and discovered it wasn't an object. It was the whole field."[26]

My final stop with Allis-Smith was at the end of a rural road, just past a farm. "If you were a tourist and discovered this road you'd think you were in heaven. It's ideal for a picnic," said Allis-Smith. Those were my thoughts exactly. We parked where a public bridleway beckoned in one direction and a footpath in another. In the distance, a narrow river cut a sluice through grassy marshes. Cows chomped away and swatted their tails in a nearby meadow. We walked a short distance down the footpath. Allis-Smith turned on the counter. It registered one hundred counts per second, or twenty times background. "These marshes have higher levels than they'd allow inside Sellafield—and there are several square miles and lots of areas we haven't explored . . . We all think this area should be closed off and evacuated. In some of these riverbanks, we've found readings of six hundred." But that would put local farmers out of business and attract more negative publicity about Sellafield, the future of which currently hangs in the balance.

DURING THE 1990s, the British government continued efforts to sell off the nuclear industry with only superficial success. The aging Magnox reactors were dumped like excess baggage into a separate government-owned company and eventually transferred to the beleaguered British Nuclear Fuels Ltd., and the newer reactors were transferred to a company called Nuclear Electric.[27] In 1996, Nuclear Electric was renamed British Energy and sold off to private investors. The price, slightly less than two billion pounds, was embarrassing. It equated to roughly half the cost of just one recently built American-style reactor in Britain, and well under a tenth of the estimated replacement cost of all eight nuclear plants owned by the company. By the end of 2002, British Energy was near to collapse and was only allowed to continue trading through a highly controversial loan at a cost to future taxpayers estimated then to be in excess of ten billion pounds.[28]

Meanwhile, BNFL limped along under the weight of liabilities stretching into the future for as far as anyone could imagine—decommissioning was envisioned as a process that could take 135 years. After a number of complex corporate maneuverings—including at one point BNFL's acquisition of Westinghouse, which itself had gone bankrupt in the 1990s—what remained of the UK's nuclear fuel company was an entity called British Nuclear Group. Westinghouse, flagship of the U.S. nuclear industry, was sold to Japan's industrial giant Toshiba in 2006 as the industry regrouped in an effort to stay alive.

In 2005, Sellafield's THORP was forced to close after eighty-three thousand liters of highly radioactive liquid, enough to fill half an Olympic-size swimming pool, leaked from a ruptured container into a huge stainless steel chamber too radioactive to enter.[29] The cleanup and repair were estimated at some fifty million pounds. That same year, the British government passed responsibility for waste and decommissioning of most of the country's existing nuclear sites to a new National Decommissioning Authority (NDA). The NDA has "conservatively" estimated its total decommissioning costs at more than seventy billion pounds, but the figure is likely to be considerably higher because of the technical, environmental, and managerial challenges. That figure does not include decommissioning the eight British Energy advanced gas-cooled reactors; nor does it include a repository for reactor spent fuel disposal. The NDA's annual budget is slightly more than two billion pounds, and like every other government agency, it will have to compete for future funds each year.

FOR YEARS, BRITAIN'S nuclear establishment looked wistfully across the English Channel to the seemingly successful French program, convinced that had it taken France's stylish centralized approach, and adopted the American PWR long before the 1980s, it would have more to show for its efforts. Today, with the carbon crisis at the forefront of the news, much of the rest of the world also has turned its attention to France, looking to follow its example and build more "clean" nuclear power plants.

But France has its own problems. By relying so heavily on nuclear energy—it provides just under 80 percent of the country's total electricity output—France may have painted itself into a proverbial corner. The economic argument for nuclear power rests on the assumption that reactors will provide a continuous supply of electricity, meeting base load demand. But most of France's reactors are employed in load-following mode, making it the only country in the world forced to shut down reactors on weekends because it cannot find a market, at almost any price, for its surfeit of electricity. The flip side is that during periods of high demand, Electricité de France for years has been routinely forced into the relatively expensive spot and short-term power markets because it lacks adequate peak load generating capacity.[30]

By saturating its grid with nuclear power instead of diversifying its power sources, EDF—Europe's biggest electricity generator by volume—deprived itself of the flexibility a broader energy mix would deliver, almost certainly at less cost. From this perspective, France, with its heavy dependence on nuclear, can hardly be called a model of energy efficiency. Moreover, the French have deliberately underpriced their electricity in order to attract investment and win electricity export business.

The rationale underlying France's low-profit electricity operation is that centralized planning ultimately benefits the economy as a whole. But just the opposite seems to have happened. Over the past quarter century, France's economy has been in a state of decline, moving from seventh to seventeenth place in the world in per capita gross domestic product. It has the fastest-growing public sector debt in Europe, along with high unemployment, entrenched protectionism, and a bloated public sector.[31] Moreover, France's fleet of fifty-nine operating reactors has not reduced the country's dependence on oil as the hype about its nuclear program often suggests. Seventy percent of the total energy consumed in France during 2006 was provided by fossil fuels.[32]

Meanwhile, EDF's pricing policies appear to have encouraged greater overall electricity consumption. Between 1978 and 2006, the period during which all EDF's reactors were connected to the grid, load demand more than doubled, while the gap between total requirements during peak and off-peak hours rose nearly 50 percent. The result is that France now imports the equivalent of a third of the amount of electricity it exports in order to meet peak demand during winter months. Demand is so heavy during those periods that EDF is investing in new fossil fuel capacity and taking old coal plants out of mothballs.[33]

BESIDES BRITAIN, FRANCE is the only other country in the world with a commercial reprocessing operation, and that too is causing problems. Although France's plant at Cap de la Hague in northern Brittany developed a reputation for being better managed and cleaner than Sellafield, it may no longer deserve its reputation, according to Paris-based consultant Mycle Schneider, who closely monitors the discharge levels from both plants. While improved removal technology and waste-stream management led to significant reductions of radioactivity from some sources, such as plutonium and cesium-137, other changes in effluent management shifted releases that formerly went into the atmosphere into the ocean—in particular iodine-129. Basically, he says, that move appears to be intended to reduce doses to the local population while increasing the long-term global collective dose.[34]

Although much anger from other countries has been directed at Sellafield, contamination from both plants travels by different routes around the North Sea, affecting coastlines in Ireland and Norway. Gradually national governments and the international community are taking steps to deal with the issue of cross-border contamination, but what is already there will continue to pose a threat of unknown extent and duration. Estimates about future cancer rates from the discharges are highly dependent on the time period used, and in the end they are only guesses. "The ethical question," said Schneider, "is, do you count people who will die twenty thousand years from now?"

Meanwhile, the world's largest owners of separated "civil" plutonium, British Energy (the nuclear rump of the CEGB, after it was finally sold) and EDF, have allocated a zero value in their accounts to their plutonium stocks. However, utilities with reprocessing contracts are legally bound to take it back—along with the reprocessing waste—which has become politically and economically embarrassing. So instead of accepting it "neat," some are feeding the plutonium into a special facility where it is mixed with uranium and fabricated into mixed oxide (MOX) fuel. Only certain reactors can use MOX fuel, and the units have to be modified to accept it, which is partly why so much plutonium is still sitting in storage. No reactors have been modified or licensed for MOX use in Britain, so it is all manufactured for export. If the plutonium didn't constitute a disposal problem, it is doubtful any utility would go the MOX route. All of this is far more costly than using and disposing of conventional fuel. And, as Schneider notes, "with the liberalization of the electricity sector, the economic burden of reprocessing is increasingly weighing on the French utility EDF."[35]

THE NUCLEAR SCENE today seems a far cry from what it was just after World War II, when, as André Finkelstein admitted, everyone was having so much fun. The radioactive mess that started then will still be around for many future generations to deal with and pay for, and some sites may never be returned to "green fields." France, Britain, and other countries follow a "polluter pays" principle, but because of the time scales involved and the lack of adequate past provisioning, the reality is that future taxpayers—not the nuclear developers—will bear much of the cost. No country with a nuclear program has yet built a repository for its high-level radioactive waste, and none are under construction. Geological characterization studies are under way at potential sites in some countries, including the United States, France, Sweden, and Finland, but these must still surmount safety and regulatory hurdles and continued public opposition before actual building can begin. Likewise there is little experience with reactor decommissioning. Essentially all countries with nuclear programs must estimate future "back end" costs with very little to go on.

The future of both the Sellafield and La Hague operations are uncertain. After its accidental discharge in 2005 the THORP plant eventually reopened in 2008 but its existing contracts end in 2014, after which the complex may gradually be turned into a more or less permanent waste site.[36] In France, La Hague's operator, Areva, is almost totally dependent now on EDF, which has enough spent fuel on site to keep the plant running for another decade.[37] But if that happens, the French nuclear industry's overall back-end costs will be much higher than if direct disposal was chosen instead.[38]

Making matters even more complicated, the U.S. Department of Energy stunned the nuclear community in 2006 with a proposal to revive reprocessing in the United States after officially abandoning it in 1982 for nonproliferation and cost reasons. The DOE move was in part a response to congressional pressure to start moving spent fuel off

U.S. power reactor sites because of protracted delays over the proposed permanent repository at Yucca Mountain in Nevada, but it was put forward by people who never lost the "breeder" bug either. The DOE pitch was part of the Global Nuclear Energy Partnership (GNEP) announced by President George W. Bush in 2005 and formally launched by the DOE in February 2006. Besides reprocessing, it would develop a new generation of advanced reactors and link up with existing programs in France, Japan, and Britain, and possibly even Russia. The DOE argued its new fuel cycle technologies would be "proliferation resistant" by containing, rather than separating out, the plutonium. No one knew whether this could be achieved, and many experts were skeptical, pointing out that the United States was unwilling to deploy the technology (assuming it is developed) in countries that are a proliferation concern.[39]

Under President Barack Obama the plan may be doomed or significantly scaled back. Nevertheless, the Bush initiative sent a confusing message to nuclear officials in other countries, who were beginning to look for a way out of the morass created by existing reprocessing and breeder programs.

PEOPLE LIVING NEAR Sellafield generally shun locally caught fish, and most of it ends up elsewhere in Europe. The plant at La Hague sits on a peninsula jutting into the English Channel. Tourist brochures in nearby Beaumont-Hague advertise the region's fresh mussels, tart cider, and creamy butter, but the region's name is generally not used on the products, in contrast to most locally produced French goods, because of its association with the reprocessing plant. Nuclear energy is not a source of pride to everyone in France. A tourism official in Beaumont-Hague told a *Wall Street Journal* reporter that when she was handing out copies of a brochure in Nantes one man refused to touch it. "He thought it was radioactive," she said.[40]

The Flowers report warned of the dangers of creating plutonium in large quantities, in part because of the eventual threat to the food chain. Plutonium never was needed to produce electricity. "The U.S., France, Japan, United Kingdom, Germany, Italy, and the Soviet Union spent several tens of billions of dollars trying to develop fast reactors for breeding plutonium. These programs were universal failures," said Thomas B. Cochran of the Washington, D.C.-based Natural Resources Defense Council, who also warned against breeder development in the 1970s. But the nuclear industry, rarely short of government funding for such projects, could not kick the habit. Marshall died in 1996, from bone cancer, not long after the privatization debacle forced him to retire from the CEGB. He had not yet turned sixty-four. People who knew him said he was dispirited. ⊕ *Poisoned, idiot!*

Flowers and Thatcher made up in 1985 when Flowers was rector (i.e., president) of Imperial College London and she arrived on campus to open a new building. Flowers was recuperating from a heart attack, so he couldn't attend the ceremony. Afterward, the prime minister, accompanied by her aides, went to visit her old friend. "They all came upstairs to the sitting room," Flowers recalled. "Maggie said, 'Now, a little whiskey would do me good, and it wouldn't do you any harm either,' so we sat around sipping whiskey and playing with my grandchildren for quite a long time while her secretaries went wild trying to rearrange all her appointments for the day."[41]

Flowers never lost his devotion to nuclear energy either. In January 2005, less than a year after I first interviewed him, he stood in the House of Lords and repudiated one crucial part of the environment commission's 1976 report—the one that recommended there should be no more reactors until the waste problem had been shown to be manageable. He maintained that a solution to the waste problem in other countries, especially in Finland, "has been demonstrated beyond reasonable doubt," and that even "reprocessed waste is nowadays being vitrified in containers that protect it from the environment for decades to come." He also said that new reactors are being designed to produce less waste. His remarks received little notice. One expert opponent noted that the vitrification process he cited has encountered numerous problems (one of three lines had broken down when I visited Sellafield) and that the new reactors, while producing less waste by volume, will in fact produce more when measured by radioactivity. Finland's progress appears impressive, but basically, he said, "they've dug a hole in the ground" and still face numerous licensing hurdles. More importantly, as Flowers himself stated, "it can never be possible to prove experimentally the safety of any method of disposal of substances that remain dangerously radioactive for tens of thousands of years, short of waiting for that period to see what happens."

Those grandchildren are now grown up. Their grandchildren and their grandchildren's grandchildren will be paying for the nuclear legacy that Flowers and his committee warned about before any of them ever was born.

CHAPTER 20

The "Five Who Control the World"— How Much Longer?

WHEN HE FIRST HEADED INTO Iraq in June 1991, David Kay and his team of inspectors knew something few experts would ever have guessed. At the heart of Saddam Hussein's secret nuclear weapons effort was an outdated World War II technology long since discarded by other countries—a process for enriching uranium that relied upon calutrons, giant disclike pieces of equipment that it was Kay's job to find. "The thing that scares me," the former chief UN inspector told me a year later, "is that if Saddam had waited a year or two longer to attack Kuwait, we would have been dealing with a nuclear power." Perhaps. But one thing was true: Saddam had been hiding a lot.

This, of course, was not the case in 2002 when the second Bush administration tried to make the supposed existence of mass-destruction weapons a case for going to war in Iraq again. But it was true in 1991 after the First Gulf War, when the UN Special Commission, or UN-SCOM, was set up to find all the parts of the dictator's secret kingdom, nuclear, chemical, and biological installations and missiles. "Indeed, what we found was a program that had employed over 20,000 people," Kay told a House Armed Services Committee during hearings on Iraq on September 11, 2002. "It cost well over $10 billion, had gone on for longer than a decade, had 24 major sites, most of which were not known prior to the war, nor were they bombed during the course of the war. It was unknown."[1] And that was just the nuclear part.

By 1995, if not earlier, Iraq's nuclear program had pretty much been torn apart. The calutrons were discovered on the very first mission that Kay had headed, four years earlier. Invented during the Manhattan Project, these machines were used to make bomb-grade uranium using a process called electromagnetic separation, but the technique was abandoned after World War II and the technology associated with it later declassified. Electromagnetic separation was considered so antiquated that no one had thought about it as a possibility for use in a covert nuclear weapons effort.

UNSCOM only learned about the calutrons because of a defector. And they only proved it by setting up an operation that risked inspectors' lives. On June 29, 1991, after tricking the Iraqis into letting them into a base suspected of harboring the machines, three members of Kay's team climbed on a water tower to have a better look, "and almost ninety seconds after they are on top, the base erupts," Kay recalled. "It looked like dinosaurs in heat. There were over a hundred trucks with calutrons on them, flat-bed transporter trucks with giant iron Frisbees on them. They had been ordered to move so quickly that the ramps on some of the trucks hadn't been put up." UN inspectors gave chase; they stopped at a lay-by to take photographs—and that was when shots were fired. "The last picture on the roll," said Kay, "is of a foot, because that's where the photographer was falling to the floor as he clicked the camera." The film was flown out, and one of the photographs was later enlarged to measure six feet across. It was first unveiled in Whitehall at a British cabinet meeting.[2]

It was not the IAEA's finest hour. Agency officials had repeatedly held up Iraq's cooperation under the Non-Proliferation Treaty as a model of good behavior. A year before the calutron discovery, Hans Blix, then the IAEA general secretary, had gone even further, telling an audience in Europe that the safeguards system was working because the agency had never discovered any diversion of fissionable material or misuse of installations for military purposes.[3] "I am convinced it is because none has occurred," he said. The new inspection techniques were revealing an altogether different reality. After the calutron episode, Blix and his deputy, Mohammed ElBaradei, flew to Baghdad to find out more. When they were shown the photos, they didn't believe them, according to both Kay and Rolf Ekeus, who was then UNSCOM's director.[4]

Kay was dismayed, and Ekeus could see it. "I saw something breaking down in Kay," Ekeus told me later. Ekeus argued with Blix, saying it was "clear there is something here." He had to convince him because the IAEA director general "had repeatedly said that Iraq was an exemplary member of the NPT," recalled Ekeus. "It was a setback or even the collapse of the IAEA . . . A couple of days later Blix saw them [the calutrons] physically. He had to give in."[5]

The strained relations between the two Swedes, Ekeus and Blix, was only a microcosm of the anger and frustration that had been building for years over the agency's seeming incompetence when it came to preventing proliferation. Blix's attitude toward the inspections in Iraq was symptomatic of the apparent faith held by governments in the safeguards system over which he presided. *Faith* here is used pejoratively; what the IAEA offered governments and exporters was convenience. It was so wedded to an underlying belief in the value of nuclear energy that it could not be viewed as either objective or entirely rational.

The failure in Iraq was not solely the IAEA's fault. In a way the agency had become a convenient whipping boy for the refusal of its members to take proliferation seriously. For years prior to the Gulf War, the United States and other countries had not only tolerated suspect nuclear exports headed for Iraq but tacitly encouraged them. Donald Rumsfeld, who with Dick Cheney played a key role in drumming up support for the Iraq War, was famously photographed shaking hands with Saddam in 1983, when he was Reagan's special envoy.[6] And for the next several years, the blind-eye syndrome extended to overlooking, and even suppressing, evidence of questionable dual-use exports and blatant misuse of five billion dollars in U.S. agricultural loan credits to Iraq, some of which reportedly flowed toward Iraq's nuclear program. Whistle-blowers who sounded warnings about the loan abuse and other suspect activities were fired from their jobs or shunted off to less interesting posts.[7]

As Gilinsky had noted, the U.S. attitude during the cold war years was basically that nonproliferation was for "sissies." As a policy priority, it was not allowed ever to get in the way of strategic interests, particularly in the areas where it counted most: the Middle East and the Indian subcontinent. That left less important officials to deal with proliferation, and they were part of the circuit that drafted rules, attended conferences, supported nuclear energy, and defended the safeguards system against critics who continually pointed out how relatively easy it was to circumvent. Only when the threat involved "rogue states," such as with North Korea, Libya, and now Iran, or served other priorities, such as toppling Saddam Hussein, was proliferation bumped up the priority list. *Hello! ~ Bomb, Bomb, Bomb Iran*

The devaluation of proliferation in favor of more immediate concerns—a pattern that arguably started as early as the Roosevelt-Churchill rejection of Bohr's push to talk to the Soviets—created a more dangerous world. Today, there are nine nuclear weapons states that between them possess at least twenty-seven thousand intact nuclear warheads.[8] Of those, roughly 97 percent are in U.S. and Russian stockpiles, but the remaining 3 percent are in the world's most volatile regions, making quantities less an indicator of potential trouble than existing geopolitical tensions. At the same time, there are some three thousand metric tons of fissile material, of which roughly a third comes from civil operations.

While the warhead stockpile numbers are significantly lower than the cold war high of seventy thousand weapons in 1986, plutonium stockpiles continue to grow as a result of both civilian reprocessing in Europe and Japan and military production in India, Pakistan, and Israel.[9] Moreover, there are more than a thousand metric tons of plutonium in the spent fuel produced by power reactors worldwide, and that amount grows each year by some seventy-five tons.[10] That poses a long-term proliferation threat because of the possibility it could be reprocessed. It is along this seam between the commercial and military uses of nuclear fuel that ambiguity, secrecy, power, and greed have permitted covert nuclear weapons programs to flourish, in spite of IAEA cameras, seals, inspections, and accounting procedures. And there is nothing that science can do to remove the two sides of this Janus, one monstrous and the other apparently benevolent, because they are a fact of nature. *—major point*

IN 1981, A decade before the discoveries in Iraq, an American IAEA inspector named Roger Richter warned Congress that the Vienna agency could not be counted on to discover illicit diversions of weapons-grade material from nuclear facilities in countries where the agency routinely conducted inspections. The timing of Richter's testimony probably was not coincidental. It followed by only a couple of weeks the Israeli bombing of Iraq's Osirak reactor, still under construction by French contractors, at least one of whom died in the raid along with several Iraqi soldiers. Nevertheless, Richter raised legitimate concerns.

Addressing the Senate Foreign Relations Committee on June 19, 1981, Richter listed among the system's many deficiencies the fact that countries could choose when and where the inspections would take place and specify which countries they wanted their inspectors from. Furthermore, inspectors were dependent on what governments told them. Iraq was within its rights to withhold information about facilities that could be used to produce plutonium, as long as the Iraqis maintained that they were not actually using the facilities for that purpose. Writing later in the *Washington Post* to amplify his Senate testimony, Richter explained: "You have no authority to look for undeclared material. Your job is to verify that the declared material accountancy balance is correct. The IAEA does not look for clandestine operations. The IAEA, in effect, conducts an accounting operation."[11]

That provided no guarantees that diversion would be spotted, Richter said, because only three IAEA inspections took place each year, usually at four-month intervals, leaving enough time for illicit irradiation and fuel withdrawal to take place without the inspectors ever knowing. In that way, over time, said Richter, "Iraq could acquire a stockpile of plutonium sufficient to make several atomic bombs."[12]

Other experts have said, and indeed since pointed out to the agency, that Blix had more scope for intrusiveness had he chosen to use it. While there were no formalized intelligence-sharing arrangements with the IAEA, the agency at the very least could have paid more attention to mainstream media reports of suspect nuclear activities. And inspectors could have followed up their hunches based on what they believed a country might be hiding. Also, the agency was hardly aggressive in getting recalcitrant members to sign safeguards agreements. For example, only in 1993, when North Korea threatened to unleash "the dark clouds of nuclear war," did the agency finally insist on conducting inspections there. And it had been more than seven years since North Korea signed the NPT; a safeguards agreement should have been concluded within eighteen months of that.[13] The agency also was conflicted: it had been assisting North Korea with uranium development over those years; how could it turn around and accuse it of developing nuclear weapons?

Oppenheimer always knew that a nonproliferation system based on inspections would not be enough, and that was reflected in the language of the 1946 Acheson-Lilienthal report, which stated "that a system of inspection superimposed on *an otherwise uncontrolled exploitation of atomic energy by national governments* will not be an adequate safeguard" (italics in original).[14] The experience over the past sixty years has proved that warning prescient, to say the least. Oppenheimer's solution to the conundrum was to place nuclear fuel cycle facilities in various countries under an international authority, with the idea that one miscreant could be checked by all the others. But the emphasis on international institution-building, while laudable and necessary, overlooks the fact that nations, commercial organizations, and individuals are motivated by interests that often clash with the higher purpose of preventing nuclear war.

THE FAULT LINES in the international nuclear safeguards system have over several decades manifested themselves in ways that never attracted headlines or have long since been forgotten. For example, Iran would not be running its highly publicized enrichment plant today without uranium. The story of how it acquired that material underscores the ease with which commercial transactions ostensibly undertaken within the "peaceful uses" context, and in another political era, might eventually be used to produce nuclear weapons. It also demonstrates a loophole in the safeguards system—uranium mining is not covered by the IAEA inspections. Thus, a year or two before the mullahs took over in 1979, few eyebrows were raised when the shah contracted for a hefty supply of uranium from one of the largest producing mines in the world, an open cast pit in Namibia, majority-owned by the London mining giant Rio Tinto–Zinc.

Good fortune and timing—and a short, wily Scotsman from Glasgow named Ronnie Walker—were on the shah's side. Shortly after Walker took over running the Rössing mine in 1976, a disastrous fire broke out, destroying half the plant. He needed capital to rebuild. After soliciting as much as he could from his parent company and the mine's other European partners, Walker offered shares in the project to the Iranians in return for uranium. He also borrowed money from the Iranian government. By the time of the 1979 revolution, said Walker, the Iranians "had paid a lot of money up front. We owed them quite a lot of money; we also owed them a lot of uranium."

Like almost everyone else operating in southern Africa at the time,

Walker was skilled at "sanctions busting"—finding ways to get around UN sanctions against the South African and Rhodesian apartheid regimes, in order to get products to overseas markets without the public finding out.[15] That meant shipping uranium would be a relatively easy matter too. However, to get his uranium safely out of Windhoek, Namibia's capital, he needed landing rights somewhere else in Africa, because of the distances involved, and a plant in Europe that would accept the uranium for further upgrading before the final leg of its journey to a nuclear power station in Iran, although none yet had been built. The Shah had plans for at least twenty reactors, which never bore fruit.

The landing rights difficulty was resolved by "getting someone to talk to President [Omar] Bongo of Gabon who would do anything for anyone and he agreed on the basis that the [airplane] tails were painted white," Walker said. After that, "it was great fun. I went to South African Airways and said, 'You can have half of this contract, provided you paint your tails white instead of orange.'" The second challenge was a bit thornier since only the Americans, British, and French operated the conversion and enrichment plants. "The French were the only people with the facilities who didn't ask questions," he said. So the uranium would be shipped to France. Pilots nervous about Windhoek's high-altitude takeoff were calmed with "a supply of first-class claret." And, said Walker, "We had no accidents during the whole time."[16]

Things went quiet for a while after the political upheaval in Iran, and Walker heard nothing from his new partner. In Iran, the scientists, some of whom had trained at MIT under a program organized by the shah, were treading carefully, mindful of the Ayatollah Khomeini's aversion to nuclear weapons on religious and moral grounds. Some fled, although at least three of the MIT-trained students remained and worked on the Iranian nuclear program.[17] And within a couple of years there was movement again. Walker was called to meet an Iranian delegation in Geneva. The message from the Iranians was simple: it was time to deliver the goods. "We found we still owed them uranium so we sent it to them and paid back the money we owed," said Walker.

Walker would not reveal how much was delivered; nor was it clear how much of the consignment arrived in Iran via France. The IAEA only learned in 1991 that a transaction had taken place. According to agency documents, Iran acquired 531 tons of uranium in 1982.[18] No further details were revealed. And that material—enough for about a hundred bombs—is what is almost certainly being fed through Iran's enrichment plants today.[19] Flush with Iranian capital, Walker rebuilt the mine, and Iranian representatives are still on the Rössing board, although a Rio source assured me they no longer receive uranium from the mine.

IN THE EARLY 1980s, South Africa's secret bomb program also was helped by seemingly innocent assistance from people operating within the commercial nuclear sector. At that time, U.S. intelligence analysts had been writing reports about a weapons effort that they believed, correctly as it turned out, centered around a highly secret pilot enrichment plant, supplied by West Germany, near the South African administrative capital Pretoria. Its name was Valindaba, a conjunction of two words common to many of the area's indigenous languages meaning "the council is closed," and by extension, "no talking about this."

Valindaba was off-limits to IAEA inspectors, and because of that, the United States could not legally export nuclear fuel to the country after the 1978 U.S. Nuclear Non-Proliferation Act was passed. That presented enormous problems for the South African state-owned utility Eskom, which needed the fuel for two reactors under construction at a site called Koeberg. Once again, as they had with India, the Edlows came to the rescue. By then, Sam Edlow had a small Bermuda-based uranium brokering operation specializing in unusual foreign deals requiring anonymity. For these "other than routine transactions," Edlow wrote in his self-published memoir, "we were able to charge some magnificent fees."[20]

The South Africans had plenty of natural uranium but had contracted to have it enriched in the United States prior to the NNPA. They faced huge penalties if they failed to deliver the feed material to a U.S. Department of Energy enrichment plant. Meanwhile, in 1979, the year of the mysterious flashes over the Indian Ocean, the CIA estimated in a top secret report that, if necessary, Valindaba's design capacity was enough to provide the requisite quantity of enriched fuel for an initial core load at Koeberg, in time for the scheduled start-up of the first reactor at the end of 1982. The report speculated that the South Africans wanted foreign-origin fuel in order to take pressure off the Valindaba operation, which had been plagued with technical problems and was proving expensive to operate. If forced to rely upon Valindaba's output for Koeberg, the suspected bomb program could have been set back by three to five years, the analysts estimated.[21]

Like anyone else attuned to what was going on in the nuclear sphere in those days, Sam Edlow would have known the South African government was suspected of having a covert nuclear weapons program. But he operated in the civilian area and did not overly concern himself with such matters; thus to him helping out Eskom was simply playing the game the way he played it, as he had in 1974 when he refused the AEC official's request to turn back the Tarapur nuclear fuel shipment.

But in reality, Edlow, like anyone else in the nuclear fuel business, could find himself straddling the divide between the commercial and military applications of nuclear energy. And understanding the enormity of what was at stake in the South African situation, he understood too that there were handsome profits to be made. Eskom wanted the foreign-origin fuel, and it stood to lose a lot of money if it could not somehow find a way out of its contract with the DOE. The only way around the problem was to find someone to take over its contract in the United States, and to find utilities in other countries willing to sell it replacement material.

Edlow teamed up with a man named Walt Wolf, who ran a company called SWUCO in suburban Maryland, which specialized in trading enrichment contracts. Together they arranged a complex series of swaps, and Eskom got the material it needed, while assigning its DOE obligations to another utility. The pathway for this tricky circumvention of U.S. law was smoothed by officials within the government itself, including Bengelsdorf, Kratzer's former assistant, then in charge of fuel export approvals for the Energy Department, and officials at the State Department sympathetic to Eskom's plight. This process even extended to quiet nods by the American officials to their counterparts in Europe worried they would be hammered by the United States for allowing the substitute fuel exports.[22]

Proud of their accomplishment, Edlow and Wolf many years later boasted of it. Wolf called it his "biggest caper" and said he personally pocketed $1.5 million for his effort.[23] Edlow did not reveal his profits but wrote: "To celebrate the Koeberg deal we took the family to a beautiful resort for the annual meeting of ERL [Edlow Resources Limited], and spent a few days together in Bermuda in the lap of luxury."[24]

works the same foo other Industry/
regulatory Relationships.

At the time, the deal was carried out so secretly that it took several weeks before anyone even learned about it and longer still to find out who was behind it. When the story came out, there was a lot of anger. Len Weiss, one of the authors of the NNPA, described it as "feeding the South African nuclear machine" and said it amounted to an end-run around the law. "The feeling was it wasn't illegal, but it was immoral," he said. "What does it say about our government and the individuals involved that it got resolved in favor of helping the nuclear industry and lining the pockets of some people in it?"[25]

In March 1993, almost two years after signing the NPT, South Africa's last white president, Frederik Willem de Klerk, announced that his government had manufactured and dismantled six gun-type nuclear weapons. A seventh weapon had been under development but was never assembled. When the IAEA inspectors went in, they found that the South Africans had produced a substantial reserve of highly enriched uranium, in addition to the material used in the bomb cores. They believed it might have been for contingency use at Koeberg (after down blending to the correct level of enrichment for the reactors) in the event Eskom had not succeeded in obtaining material from abroad. Since they had their reactor fuel, the apartheid government, had it remained in power, could have used the excess material to make more nuclear weapons. This was the thin line between military and civilian uses of nuclear fuel that could be exploited through nominally commercial transactions when government officials were willing to overlook the intent, if not the letter, of existing nonproliferation law.

IF PEOPLE WITHIN the safeguards system could bend the rules so easily, it is relatively easy to imagine what might go on in countries at the margins. Along the old Silk Route, leaders of the ancient kingdoms simply ignored the edicts of a club from which they were effectively excluded. Struggling through the 1990s to reclaim some portion of their long-lost power, and believing that nuclear warheads and missile delivery systems held the key, they formed separate alliances, while A. Q. Khan's agents oiled the machinery of nuclear trade between them. "Pakistan firmly holds the view that nuclear non-proliferation should not be made a pretext for preventing states from exercising fully their right to acquire and develop nuclear technology for peaceful purposes," Benazir

Bhutto declared to an agreeing audience in Pyongyang in December 1993, shortly before leaving with a planeload of either parts or blueprints for a Nodong (short-range) missile.[26]

Only five years earlier, when she was first elected Pakistan's prime minister, *People* magazine listed Bhutto among the world's fifty most beautiful people, and her government was still in Washington's good graces because the Soviets had not yet departed Afghanistan. But all that had changed, and Pakistan was cut adrift.

A natural symbiosis existed between North Korea and Pakistan on the nuclear front, and although Bhutto would deny it, U.S. intelligence analysts strongly believed the two governments used it to their mutual advantage, with the North Koreans swapping their missile designs for Khan's centrifuge expertise. But a greater immediate fear was that the North Koreans had already started manufacturing plutonium at a nuclear complex some sixty miles north of the capital, in Yongbyon. This plutonium was produced from uranium dug out of the ground with IAEA assistance. Rather than yield to the IAEA demands to see the suspect facilities, however, North Korea announced on March 12, 1993, that it was withdrawing from the Non-Proliferation Treaty.

The following year, the deified Kim Il-sung died, after presiding over the hermit kingdom since its founding in 1948. His son, Kim Jong-il, emerged as his successor, a playboy who wore lifts in his shoes, sported a bouffant hairstyle, and drank expensive cognac while much of the rest of the country grew hungrier because of worsening food shortages. During that year of transition, the North Koreans agreed to a "framework" deal with the United States under which North Korea shut down, but nevertheless maintained, the Yongbyon plutonium production facility in exchange for two large reactors, worth at least five billion dollars then, as well as fuel oil.

The deal never worked, in that North Korea, while apparently halting its plutonium production, did not give up its nuclear weapons activities, and relations between North Korea and Pakistan evidently continued.[27] In May 1998, the Pakistanis conducted their first nuclear tests, and some experts believe one of them was a North Korean warhead.[28] Marching in lockstep with their friends, the North Koreans, just two months after the Pakistani tests, stunned the world by sending a long-range ballistic missile, the Taepodong-1, streaking across the sky, threatening Japan. There also were reports of a Taepodong-2 under development that could conceivably threaten even the United States. During this five-year period of intense progress on the nuclear front, from 1994 to 1998, an estimated two to three million North Koreans died of starvation and hunger-related illnesses.[29]

IN IRAN, THE death of Ayatollah Khomeini in 1989 proved good news for the country's nuclear promoters. Iranian scientists and engineers could move quickly to match their skills with those of their colleagues in Pakistan, India, and even China. As if in an intramural competition, success to them was a matter of national prestige, and if that would result in a strategic balance with Israel, then so much the better.

By then A.Q. Khan had moved further afield to sell his expertise and supplier contacts to clients outside Pakistan. The reasons for this can only be surmised, and insofar as he wanted to make money, Khan's motivations were not much different than those of nuclear exporters who had for the past thirty years traded among themselves, reaching out to developing nations (uranium here, a reprocessing plant there) when it suited them. The difference was that Khan was advertising his merchandise as weapons-related.

Khan turned his network into a global operation, with suppliers in Malaysia, China, South Africa, the United States, and Europe. His prospective clients, with the exception of North Korea and China, seem to have been mainly in the Middle East and northern Africa.[30] Iran was apparently among the earliest. In 1987, Khan offered the Iranians everything from a few sample centrifuges to a complete package, including designs and equipment to build an industrial-scale enrichment plant, as well as important technical data for assembling a nuclear weapon. Prices ranged from millions to hundreds of millions of dollars, depending on the order. The Iranians bought the designs, but they had their own network of front companies out shopping for many of the components, and the Chinese were providing assistance on other fronts.[31]

The Libyans had been an enthusiastic customer. By 1997, they had ordered ten thousand advanced centrifuges—enough to produce fissile material for up to ten bombs a year—designs for an enrichment plant, twenty tons of converted uranium, and almost all of the associated equipment. But while Libya's leader, Colonel Moammar Gadhafi, pursued a fast track to the bomb, he also opened back-channel negotiations with the United States and Britain to extricate his country from crippling sanctions imposed in the aftermath of the shooting of a London policewoman and the bombing of a Pan Am jet over Lockerbie, Scotland. And it was this trade-off—nuclear weapons or access to the international community—that Gadhafi was forced to consider.

In 2003, a joint Anglo-American investigating team, acting on a tip, stopped a Libya-bound ship called the *BBC China* and discovered crates of nuclear components linked to Khan's network. On December 19, Gadhafi, unsettled by the capture of Saddam Hussein a few days earlier, announced he was giving up his nuclear, chemical, and missile programs. A month later, on January 20, 2004, in a formal ceremony at the Libyan National Board of Scientific Research, the main front for the nuclear program, the blueprints for the weapons were officially handed over to American and British officials. They were in a white plastic bag that bore the name of the Good Looks Fabrics and Tailors—Khan's high-end tailor in Islamabad. The tailor reportedly heard about this later and removed his customer's photograph from the wall of his shop.

Khan was cornered. The metallurgist-turned-merchant is said to have collapsed, then begged for mercy, as President Pervez Musharraf confronted him with the evidence that the United States had on him on February 1, 2004. Khan was asked to sign a twelve-page confession, the details of which were never made public, and then he went on television and made a public admission of guilt.[32]

But this display of personal remorse left open a question that has never been satisfactorily answered, namely, how much support did the Pakistan government and its military provide Khan? The evidence points to complicity, particularly among Pakistan's army and Inter-Services Intelligence Agency, many of whose members are believed to have close ties to al-Qaeda. As one observer commented, "The Pakistanis wanted to spread the bomb because it gave them cover; it would be harder to roll them back."

Several men involved in the supply chain ended up in custody and went on trial, but none received harsh sentences. Khan remained under house arrest. In the spring of 2008, he was allowed to give his first media interviews since his arrest. He expressed no regret for what he had done, only for his confession, and said that he had been made a scapegoat for others in the Pakistani government. On being asked if he was willing to speak to officials of U.S. intelligence agencies and the International Atomic Energy Agency, he said, "Why should we? We are an independent country, we have not violated any international law, we are not signatory to the NPT, I am a free man, we have no obligation, then why should I agree to that?"[33] And U.S. officials apparently did not press the Pakistani government on the matter.

AS THE UNITED States and its allies struggled to contain the fallout from the increasingly alarming revelations about the extent of Khan's activities—about which much is still not known—there was more trouble in the Middle East. In August 2002, an Iranian opposition group announced what analysts already suspected: that an enrichment plant was under construction at Natanz, south of Tehran. Six months later, in February 2003, IAEA inspectors headed to Iran, accompanied by ElBaradei, who had replaced Blix as the IAEA's director general. Beginning with that trip and over the next several months and years, layers of Iranian deception were gradually revealed. The Iranians had not been living up to their safeguards agreement for more than two decades, having failed to report a number of their nuclear activities. Among other things, in 1991 Iran had kept quiet about the import of a substantial quantity of "converted" uranium, apparently from China, which could quickly be fed into an enrichment plant.[34] And it emerged the centrifuges were based on the Pakistani designs previously stolen from Europe.[35] After intense diplomatic pressure, work on the Natanz facilities was suspended in 2004, but the plant was restarted two years later after talks broke down.

Stranger things were happening in Washington. With the intelligence community roiling from the intense publicity over its bungled assessments in Iraq, a National Intelligence Estimate released in December 2007 concluded that Iran was no longer pursuing nuclear weapons. Newspapers jumped on the story, even though the report had not said the threat had disappeared altogether.[36] "Intel officers are human too," said one observer. "What we might be seeing here is the price to be paid for the vilification of the [intelligence] community on the Iraq issue."[37] Nevertheless, the atmosphere had relaxed enough that work on the first of two Russian-supplied reactors at Bushehr was completed, and by early 2008 the Russians, over mild U.S. objections, had delivered nuclear fuel for the plant.

Less than three months after the NIE, in February 2008, in a board-room high above the Danube, IAEA officials presented new evidence, including information contained on a laptop obtained in Iran during a 2004 intelligence operation, that demonstrated an effort "not consistent with any application other than the development of a nuclear weapon." The presentation included documents related to key nuclear weapons components such as "high-tension firing systems" and "multiple EBW detonators fired simultaneously."[38] By then, the authors of the National Intelligence Estimate report were backtracking from their original assessment, admitting they had downplayed the significance of the continuing enrichment activity. Basically, they did not want to be used to rationalize another war, as they had been over Iraq.

While the world's attention was focused on Iran, in April 2004 a dispute broke out in Brazil after IAEA inspectors were prevented from viewing centrifuge components at the country's uranium enrichment facility near Rio de Janeiro.[39] The plant, originally built by the military in Resende, had just become operational. Since its centrifuges were possibly like those being used in Iran, the IAEA was naturally interested to learn more. Brazilian officials maintained their technology was "100 percent Brazilian," but there were suspicions that they were attempting to hide technology secured covertly in the past, possibly from Germany, and later even Pakistan, all based on the work Gernot Zippe had originally done as a war prisoner in the Soviet Union.

Brazilian diplomats were still chafing from a proposal made a year earlier by President George W. Bush that would prevent countries that did not already possess enrichment technology from acquiring it. And Brazil was refusing calls by the IAEA to sign on to stricter safeguards drawn up in the aftermath of the earlier discoveries in Iraq.[40] A Brazilian diplomat told the *Washington Post*, "We don't like treaties that are discriminatory in their intent." He said that Bush's proposal was "unacceptable to Brazil, precisely because we see ourselves as so strictly committed to nonproliferation, to disarmament, to the peaceful uses of nuclear energy."[41] The IAEA eventually came to an agreement over the enrichment plant inspections. Inspectors would be allowed back but only because, according to a Brazilian official, the agency was no longer requiring "total and unrestricted access." The agency refused to divulge details.[42]

The problem of "rogue" nuclear states intensified on October 9, 2006, when North Korea announced it had conducted an underground nuclear test. Although it was widely dismissed as a failure because of its low explosive impact, a few experts speculated it could have been a compact warhead for North Korea's ballistic missiles. While others disputed that idea, the test nevertheless demonstrated a determination to pursue nuclear weapons. The North Koreans have since agreed to disable their main nuclear facility at Yongbyon, but the pace has slowed, and the road to total denuclearization, if ever successfully negotiated, promises to be long and hard.

The same can be said for the Middle East, where Israel still refuses to publicly admit its status as a nuclear weapons state, while seeking to discourage its neighbors' ambitions in that direction. On September 6, 2007, the Israelis bombed a suspected Syrian nuclear site. The IAEA responded by sending in its inspectors, but the visit was predictably inconclusive. There was speculation the Syrians were building a plutonium production reactor with North Korean assistance, but further investigation was needed.

In November 2008 the IAEA itself was again the center of controversy. After inspectors determined the site bore hallmarks of a reactor and criticized Syria for denying access to three other suspect locations, the agency's board approved a $350,000 assistance package for building a reactor in Syria, a decision termed "wholly inappropriate" by a U.S. State Department spokesman.

MORE THAN SIXTY years ago, on July 29, 1947, David Lilienthal returned home and wrote in his diary that he had "quite a blow" that day. The General Advisory Committee, the panel of scientific advisers whose members then included Oppenheimer, Rabi, and Seaborg, among others, had drafted a statement that "not only discouraged hope of atomic power in any substantial way for decades, but put it in such a way as to question whether it would ever be of consequence." There were political reasons for the statement, but Lilienthal was worried that when it finally appeared it would be "interpreted to mean that atomic energy is actually just a matter of military weapons and little more."[43]

At that stage, that is pretty much all nuclear energy amounted to, despite Lilienthal's wishes for it to be otherwise. The same is true today for countries trying to catch up, like Iran, Pakistan, and India, irrespective of the fact they each have civilian nuclear programs. Their priority evidently is to increase fissile material production, first for nuclear weapons and only secondarily for power reactors. This in essence is the failure of Atoms for Peace, and in a broader sense of science itself. "Science has always promised two things not necessarily related," wrote author Joseph Wood Krutch in 1929, well before the atomic bomb was invented, "—an increase first in our powers, second in our happiness or wisdom, and we have come to realize that it is the first and less important of the two promises which it has kept most abundantly."[44]

The safeguards system is not working in part because it is structured around the way the United States, and to a lesser degree the other weapons states, wanted the world to remain, in contrast to the way it became. When he was still Egypt's ambassador to Washington, Nabil Fahmy summed up the attitude of the five permanent Security Council members this way: "We're the five who control the world; why give it up?"

The Bush administration's push to bring India in from the cold—a process that involves tearing a hole in what is left of the NPT and the existing nuclear export regime—may indicate a gradual shift away from the five-power lock-in, but if so, that involves other problems. If India, why not Pakistan, or Iran, or even Brazil? "The NPT was the lowest common denominator achievable in 1968," said Fahmy. "It was meant to be a good start. We had a static NPT [instead]. It didn't grow with the challenges."[45]

The more important point is that the treaty embraces nuclear weapons as a legitimate form of national defense—for only five countries. The numbers don't add up when India, Pakistan, Israel, and North Korea are counted. There are undoubtedly more nuclear weapons states on the horizon. That leaves us with a world where the dangers are far greater than they were during the cold war years. It is absurd to think the current situation will hold, particularly now with the big push on for more nuclear energy.

Holding the situation in at least some form of check now are treaties focused on disarmament and test bans as well as nonproliferation. And there are a number of other efforts to ban fissile material production, reduce existing fissile material stockpiles, and keep weapons and the facilities that store them safe. There are plans to build regional nuclear fuel cycle facilities along the lines Oppenheimer suggested, and in many parts of the world there are nuclear-weapons-free zones. But it is easy to get lost in the acronyms, and there are serious questions as to

whether international institution-building can be fast and effecti͟
enough to stop the proliferators, and ultimately accidental or intentional nuclear war.

Ultimately, institutions and treaties can only provide a semblance
of security. They are as strong as their weakest links, whether that
means a recalcitrant member or expediency in the geopolitical and
commercial sphere. The IAEA is further hampered, though, by its obligations to dole out nuclear largesse while also attempting to play
tough in the countries it inspects. Given its original mandate, its behavior toward Syria is no more surprising or inappropriate than its
previous activities in North Korea. But if governments are serious
about controlling nuclear energy, the agency's dual role must surely
be called into question.

Yet even the best safeguards system in the world cannot guarantee
100 percent protection from a determined country or group pursuing
and achieving its objectives, because people cheat, money talks, and the
technology is now widely available. That leaves three options for response: diplomacy that may or may not succeed while the state in
question continues its illicit program; a military response—combat
proliferation—such as the United States carried out in Iraq (even
though the government apparently knew the nuclear threat no longer
existed); or accepting the prospect of further nuclear weapons states and
even nuclear-armed terrorists. None of these is a welcome prospect.
Once it acquires nuclear weapons, no nation, apart from an apartheid
regime on the verge of handing over power to its black population,
would willingly give them up. And there's the difficulty. The UNSCOM
inspectors found that out in Iraq—under gunfire.

CHAPTER 21

A Broken Promise

A S MY LAST INTERVIEW WITH Joseph Rotblat ended, walking toward his front door, I asked if he felt despondent about the future. The answer surprised me: "I'm optimistic. We're going forward. It will never be smooth, but we're going forward."

I asked why he felt this way. His eyes brightened; he lifted his arms, palms facing upward, and replied, "Because we're still here."

There was one dark cloud on Rotblat's horizon: news of a secret American policy to act preemptively if necessary to forestall or prevent hostile acts by an adversary. Preemption was nothing new, nor was the idea of using nuclear weapons against smaller countries, like Iran or North Korea, irrespective of whether they had them. The difference was in the way the policy had been enlarged in scope and broadcast, not only through a "posture review" but numerous speeches, policy papers, and military strategy documents.

For the duration of the cold war there had been secret plans for using nuclear weapons preemptively, or to end other wars, but this time it was out in the open. Defense Secretary Donald Rumsfeld talked of transforming the cold-war-era offensive nuclear triad (of intercontinental and submarine-launched ballistic missiles and bomber weapons) into "a New Triad designed for the decades to come." There were plans for low-yield "bunker busters," rapid production of replacement warheads, and making a "responsive infrastructure" with the "capability to resume underground testing."[1] This worried people like Rotblat who were frightened that with an apparently more reckless team in charge in Washington, a nuclear attack might actually be carried out. And it was just the beginning of a series of steps by an administration that seemed intent on regressing in the nuclear arena, rather than moving toward a better, safer future. It had been a hundred years since Curie struggled to separate radium and Soddy made his famous prediction that whoever got there first would control the world.[2] George W. Bush and many others still believed in that idea.

But the history of the human engagement with nuclear energy turned out to be more complex. In the excitement of the early discoveries, we had contemplated the two extremes that they appeared to promise: military supremacy on the one hand and energy security on the other. After consummating our courtship with the bomb in 1945, we declared our allegiance to peaceful applications, the other side. Nuclear energy would deliver prosperity, and no one, we assumed, would ever actually again use the bomb. But between 1945 and 1990, the U.S. government built about seventy thousand warheads, and we never let go of our commitment to their power.[3]

Other players had different objectives, and as they weighed the choices, the human motivators—pride, greed, and the lust for absolute power—led some to be two-faced, using the cover of peaceful programs to disguise military nuclear activities. More countries acquired nuclear weapons. The tableau shifted, the dangers grew, and the industry and its overseers continually deceived themselves into thinking they could keep the dark side in check while reaping rewards through the peaceful uses of nuclear energy. "I am sure," wrote Lilienthal in 1946, "that if we have some wisdom and patience, and divine guidance, we will find, we mortals, that the cloud has indeed a lining of silver."[4]

That kind of thinking led to sixty years of "what if" and "almost" nuclear wars, and foolhardy men were prepared to wage them. Others were willing to draw up the plans—for striking the Soviet Union and later China before they struck first, "twenty Hiroshimas" in Germany, or dropping bombs on North Vietnam. Missile deployments upped the ante, in Europe and Turkey, then Cuba. There were mistakes and accidents. B-52s crashed and burned and dropped their thermonuclear payloads from forty thousand feet on other countries. In 2007, six nuclear missiles were accidentally flown across America, and it took thirty-six hours before anyone noticed.[5] The peaceful atom delivered a relatively minor amount of electricity globally compared to what it cost to build the plants—on the order of eighty-five billion dollars in the United

States alone—and paid us back in other ways with Three Mile Island, Chernobyl, and mountains of waste we do not know where to put.[6]

More than that, an old world disappeared. In its place, a secret empire grew, spawning an immense network of personal and professional relationships, and a scientific-technological elite within the national laboratories, government agencies, nuclear manufacturing firms, utilities, lobbying groups, and the military. This "peculiar sovereignty" has outposts in little towns and big cities, lonely steppes, barren deserts, and Arctic climes. In the early days, human and animal life—in fact, all biological life in the affected areas—was sacrificed as the mushroom clouds went up so scientists could study the fallout and the strategists could plan wars. An island paradise disappeared. When Admiral Blandy neared the countdown for Baker during Crossroads, he sent the Joint Chiefs a plea for advice on how to respond to an awkward request from an island chief:

"Understand 'King' Judah formerly of Bikini now of Rongerik may seek to witness Test 'B.'"[7]

For Judah's people, a world was borrowed and never returned.

The question always was framed this way: did we control it, or did it control us? The truth was, it tempted us and then it swallowed us, and now we have to ask if we will ever get out safely.

In recent years, growing panic over rising oil and natural gas prices and global warming has made fertile ground for promoters of a "nuclear renaissance," enthusiastically backed by the Bush administration and some leading Democrats. In response, Congress in December 2007 approved more than twenty billion dollars in long guarantees to encourage the building of reactors and fuel plants—about twice as much as they gave to alternative energy programs. Spending on nuclear weapons is rising in real terms, which, besides the obvious dangers that poses, makes urgent the question of what to do about the vast number of remaining warheads, stockpiles of fissile material, and military waste.

It might seem unfair to lump a resurgence in nuclear energy with spending on nuclear weapons, but an undeniable relationship between the two still exists. The Department of Energy oversees both military and civilian nuclear activities in key areas such as fuel cycle technologies, nonproliferation efforts, and reactor technology, and the Nuclear Regulatory Commission, which used to review naval reactors, has also licensed some Department of Defense activities.[8] The entire safeguards system is predicated on the notion that military and civilian nuclear ac-

tivities are neatly divided, so that countries can have the benefit of
nuclear power without the risk they will acquire nuclear weapons. Yet
in those countries that have nuclear weapons, the line is administratively blurred within the responsible government agencies.

That said, there are taboos against mixing certain military and civilian nuclear activities in order to avoid tarnishing the civilian industry's
"peaceful" image. However, those lines, too, are crossed for the sake of
expediency and cost. For example, in 2002 the NRC, after four years of
testing by the DOE, approved licenses to allow tritium production for
nuclear weapons at two Tennessee Valley Authority reactors, Watts Bar
and Sequoyah.[9] That means that the same electricity that lets people
watch television, play computer games, or read at night in Tennessee
also is being used to produce a gas that enhances the explosive power of
nuclear weapons, particularly thermonuclear weapons.

After September 11, whether it was global warming or the threat of
nuclear-armed "rogue states," the purported need for nuclear weapons
and new reactors seemed more pressing, not just in the United States
but in Britain, while the call for a "nuclear renaissance" was echoed
by government and industry officials all over the world. "I am bewildered," admitted UK energy expert Steve Thomas, explaining that he
could not understand why Britain, a country saddled with upwards of
two hundred billion dollars in nuclear decommissioning liabilities,
would build more nuclear stations. "It's lunacy."[10]

Indeed it is bewildering. Using nuclear energy to create weapons or to
generate electricity never was as simple as making gunpowder or burning coal. It was "disturbing the universe," as Freeman Dyson suggests in
his book with that title. It required a "peculiar sovereignty," or as Jungk
called it, a "nuclear state." And it is that sovereignty, swollen to its present size, together with the radioactive entrails of the cold war years it left
behind, with which we are lumbered today. It is bloated but powerful,
flush with money, and it feeds off a complex network of dynamic, inces-
tuous relationships within the military-industrial complex that Eisenhower warned about a half century ago. Nuclear weapons have not made
the world safer; nor has nuclear energy weaned us from oil. Yet we are
pouring significantly more money, brainpower, and resources into both.

I first heard the phrase "nuclear renaissance" at a nuclear industry
conference in London in September 2002 before either global warming

or rising oil prices was a major concern of the Bush administration. Earlier that year, in February, the DOE announced a joint government-industry cost-sharing effort to build and deploy new nuclear power plants "in the 2010 time frame."[11] There was other good news for the beleaguered industry. Finally, after twenty years, it looked as if the waste problem in the United States had been solved. In July 2002, Congress approved a DOE plan to make Yucca Mountain in Nevada ready for seventy thousand tons of civilian nuclear waste—the total amount arising from existing operations at 104 reactor sites. A major impediment to building new reactors was lifted, it seemed. "We've removed the psychological and emotional issues with Yucca Mountain," declared Joe Colvin to the audience in London. Colvin was then president of the Nuclear Energy Institute (NEI), the industry's main lobbying organization in Washington. And Colvin repeated a mantra from long ago: "Nuclear energy is the cheapest, most competitive energy source we have."

Also, Russians were joining hands with the Americans. After a long post-Chernobyl pause, America's new energy policy "practically coincided" with Russia's own nuclear energy plans, said Andrei Gagarinskii, the Kurchatov Institute's director of research and development. That made it possible to rapidly intensify cooperation between the two "pioneers in the nuclear era." Gagarinskii's speech in London even employed the industry's English-language buzzwords "nuclear renaissance" in its title. Although the Russians were willing to consider private capital for financing new nuclear ventures, Gagarinskii said the main burden would be borne by the state. "Only governments can formulate policies and invest in the technologies necessary to manage these risks over the long term," he said.[12]

In the United States, the Bush administration agreed that government support was necessary to bring the industry back to life. So it persuaded Congress to grant more than ten billion dollars in new subsidies, in the form of production tax credits, loan guarantees, federal "cost-sharing," and "regulatory risk insurance," as part of the 2005 Energy Policy Act.[13] That was a pittance compared to what the NEI wanted, so it lobbied harder, and in December 2007 its efforts were rewarded: Congress approved $18.5 billion in loan guarantees to underwrite new reactor construction. Another $2 billion was allocated for nuclear fuel plants, ostensibly to help a failing, now privately owned U. S. uranium enrichment industry. Renewables got $10 billion, less than half of what went to nuclear.

The deal was done so quietly that it took nuclear critics by surprise. They were shocked by its sheer magnitude. "What's going on is the taxpayer is taking on the ultimate liability for these projects so Wall Street will feel comfortable pouring billions into these new projects," said Natural Resources Defense Council nuclear expert Christopher Paine.[14]

That was only for openers. The lobbyists and the Energy Department were thinking big—planning for as many as three hundred new reactors over the next several decades.[15] The money Congress had just authorized would provide enough backing for only a handful of new projects, if that. In other words, the industry would be marching back for billions more in the coming years. "Obviously that's ambitious, but it reflects the consensus that's emerged about providing baseload electricity for a rapidly expanding population," said a confident NEI spokesman, John Keeley. "Everyone is concerned with greenhouse gases and gaining energy independence, and nuclear is the elephant in the room for that."[16] *Nuke ≠ independance*

Utilities are naturally cautious about entertaining elephants again, and virtually all have said they will not do it without government loan guarantees. Their hesitancy is understandable. The risks are enormous and the price of building new reactors extremely high. There are bottlenecks at factories that produce reactor pressure vessels and other equipment, and there is a dire shortage of qualified personnel to build and operate reactors. Only a few years ago, industry officials were guessing "new build" at three to four billion dollars per reactor. Then a 2008 public filing with the Florida Public Service Commission revealed those estimates to be only wishful thinking. The true cost *Per reactor* would be almost double that, or seven billion dollars, plus, for a two-unit station, three billion dollars for necessary transmission upgrades. This "sticker shock" jolted the industry. As one industry report noted, these figures "were not for the faint of heart" and "dashed the hopes of nuclear industry boosters that the next wave of new nuclear plants would be an economic slam dunk."[17] Utilities began filing applications for new reactors, but numerous challenges meant that the 2010 time frame for one new reactor in the United States was, putting it mildly, optimistic.[18]

Nevertheless, none of this could have even been imagined a few years earlier. American utilities had not ordered a nuclear reactor since 1978, the year before Three Mile Island, and more than one hundred other projects had been canceled. In Europe the impact of TMI and Chernobyl led one country after another to impose moratoriums on nuclear power, which in some cases extended to shutting down operating reactors. But with worldwide demand for electricity expected to double over the next quarter century, and a search on for alternatives to coal-burning plants, nuclear was back in fashion.[19]

Is the world really ready for more nuclear power?

Leaving aside the issue of proliferation, I asked Colvin, a naval nuclear officer until 1980, if the industry was safer than it had been two decades earlier. He said, "When I came out of the navy, the nuclear industry wasn't operating with a proper safety culture. It didn't respect the technology. Today, the industry has demonstrated that it is light-years from what it was."[20]

He correctly pointed out that after TMI and Chernobyl the industry took steps to improve safety. Regulators required better plant operating procedures, and control room operators were supposed to get more training. Utilities were asked to retrofit and modify existing plants, and databases were set up for reporting "incidents"—meaning unexpected events, or accidents—so reactor operators could learn from others' mistakes.

Had these measures made a difference? *Fukashima, 4/11!*

As fate would have it, the World Nuclear Association, which sponsored the London conference, had chosen that year to bestow a prestigious award on Tokio Kanoh, a leading Japanese politician and former executive of the Tokyo Electric Power Company, or TEPCO—the world's largest privately owned electricity utility. But Kanoh could not be there to receive it because five days before the meeting started, on August 29, 2002, Japan's Nuclear Industrial Safety Agency (NISA), stunned the nation by announcing that for at least a decade TEPCO had been falsifying records of safety violations and cracks at its nuclear power plants. All seventeen of its boiling-water reactors were shut down for inspection and repair as a result. TEPCO's president, Nobuya Minami, was later forced to resign, and the utility eventually admitted to two hundred occasions over more than two decades between 1977 and 2002, involving the submission of false technical data to authorities.[21]

2002? The American nuclear industry had its own share of woes. In February, seven months before Colvin's reassuring assessment, a workman at the Davis-Besse reactor near Toledo, Ohio, discovered a rust hole the size of a pineapple in the top of the reactor pressure vessel, where control rods enter the vessel. Corrosion had turned seventy pounds of carbon steel, half a foot thick, to rust. Luckily the plant was down for refueling and maintenance, which also happened to be why the hole was discovered. Safety experts were plagued with a recurring nightmare: what if the reactor had been operating and the hole had unleashed a jet of steam and water out of the vessel, damaging the control rod drives above, and triggering a runaway chain reaction? The only thing preventing that happening was a thin stainless steel liner on the head that was never intended to serve as a barrier. "You wouldn't know it from the bland pronouncements of the Nuclear Regulatory Commission, but the U.S. nuclear industry just had its closest brush with disaster since the 1979 Three Mile Island accident," wrote former NRC commissioner Victor Gilinsky in an op-ed piece for the *Washington Post*.[22]

The plant itself was shut down for two years and cost the utility more than $600 million, plus a $33.5 million penalty for its role in an alleged cover-up. The discovery led to two federal criminal trials centering on charges that utility employees knowingly covered up the problem, but activists charged that at least one of the accused was a scapegoat and that the real culprits were higher up the chain of command within the utility, FirstEnergy, or possibly even within the NRC itself.[23]

Meanwhile, more than thirty years after the Browns Ferry fire, the Government Accountability Office issued a report in 2008 criticizing the NRC for failing to adequately address fire safety. Between January 1995 and December 2007, the report said, there had been a total of 125 reactor blazes. These broke out at all but eleven of the country's sixty-five reactor sites and were of "limited safety significance." Nevertheless, the congressional oversight agency said, "NRC has not resolved several long-standing issues that affect the nuclear industry's compliance with existing NRC fire regulations, and NRC lacks a comprehensive database on the status of compliance."[24]

HARNESSING THE POWER of the atom, even after half a century, is still an immensely complex and even mysterious business. Each year operators around the world report hundreds of "events" that require intuitive

responses when the manuals and control panels fail to act as a guide.
The list of what can go wrong is lengthy: primary coolant leaks, fuel
degradation, fires and explosions, blackouts, hurricanes, tornadoes,
floods, and breaches of security. Depending on the sequence of events,
these can lead to an unwanted "power excursion"—a massive release
of radioactivity—as happened at Chernobyl. The public usually hears
nothing about such incidents, in part because most are not worth reporting about. On the other hand, serious accidents that should be
known about also go unreported. The world almost immediately
learned of a near catastrophe at Sweden's Forsmark nuclear plant in
July 2006, caused by a station blackout, but few people were aware
that five years earlier there had been another accident—and fire—also
involving a blackout, at the Maanshan reactor in Taiwan. A hydrogen
explosion in December 2001 at the Brunsbüttel nuclear plant in Germany received only regional attention.[25]

The public has few ways of knowing what really goes on inside nuclear reactors because official reporting channels are mostly off-limits
to it, and that was even more true after September 11. What is made
available is generally scant and difficult for laypeople to understand.
But Chernobyl taught governments a lesson: an accident in one country could have devastating consequences in another. In Europe, with
its numerous national borders, this concern following the Forsmark
blackout drove the European Parliament's Green Party to study what
was going unreported—and why. The findings, released in May 2007,
were alarming. Countless incidents had been insufficiently documented or not documented at all. In one little-known cover-up, for example, officials at Japan's Hokuriku Electric admitted to a criticality
crisis in which operators essentially lost control of the Shika-1 boiling-
water reactor for a quarter hour. The disclosure was made only a
month before the European report was issued, but the accident had occurred almost *eight years* earlier.[26]

Another worrying tendency, the report revealed, is that the same
kinds of failures, such as primary coolant leaks, tend to be repeated,
indicating that reactor operators are not learning from each other, or
putting a high enough priority on maintenance. In France, the Civaux-
1 unit was shut down for five days after a pipe cracked open, sending a
torrent of cooling water—three hundred cubic meters—into the reactor
building. It took nine hours to isolate the leak, an eighteen-centimeter-

long crack on a weld, and to stabilize the reactor. The unit had been operating for only six months. Yet similar events involving primary coolant leaks also had occurred at reactors in Belgium and Japan. "It shows how fragile the whole thing is," said Mycle Schneider, one of the report's authors.[27]

Reactor operators, already at the mercy of extraordinarily complex machinery, also are vulnerable to natural disasters. The most costly so far was the July 2007 earthquake in Japan that forced TEPCO to shut down a massive seven-unit nuclear station at Kashiwazaki-Kariwa, the world's largest nuclear plant in terms of combined electricity generating capacity. The closure was expected to last at least two years and led to a massive drop in nuclear output, forcing the utility to purchase costly replacement fossil fuel. By November, with the plant still undergoing repairs, TEPCO was reporting an 88 percent drop in its first half earnings. There were environmental costs too. The utility initially said there had been no radiation release, only to admit later that more than three hundred gallons of radioactive water had spilled into the Sea of Japan. "It's clear that this earthquake, as Tepco, the operating company, indicated, was stronger than what the reactor was designed for," noted IAEA director general Mohamed ElBaradei.[28]

Fukashima – 2 yrs After watbys

THE INDUSTRY KNOWS it is on trial. "We cannot afford another accident," ElBaradei, whose agency still promotes nuclear energy, has said.[29] Yet the flow of information is so carefully controlled that the public has little by which to judge the chances of another big one. The IAEA ranks accidents on a scale of one to seven—Chernobyl was seven, and TMI was five—but deletes any rated accident from its Web site that is more than six months old.[30] Industry censorship is bad for the public and even worse for operators and safety officials. It leaves emergency planning officials and first responders, particularly at the local level, mostly ignorant of the dangers and ill-prepared for a disaster.

It also hurts efforts by operators and design and safety engineers genuinely trying to make reactors safer. As the industry moves toward more standardized reactor designs, shared reporting will become more critical. Yet the number of reports to the IAEA has steadily decreased from more than two hundred in 1985 to only eighty-nine in 2006. And no one seriously believes the number of reportable incidents fell over that period. "We know about many more events that we think should be reported," said Christer Viktorsson, who monitored the reporting for the IAEA's nuclear installation safety division.[31]

Hajimu Maeda, chairman of the World Association of Nuclear Operators in London, warned against the "loss of motivation to learn from others," "overconfidence," and the "negligence in cultivating a safety culture due to severe pressure to reduce costs following the deregulation of the power market."[32] These are particularly serious issues in Europe, where nuclear-generated electricity is concentrated in eight countries that generate more than 30 percent of the region's electricity, and other countries, like Ireland and Austria, still oppose nuclear energy.

Nuclear regulators need closer scrutiny too. Over the past few years, U.S. utilities have applied for and received permission to extend the operating lives of aging reactors from some forty years to sixty years. These extensions are intended not only to reduce the lifetime nuclear generating costs and provide more electricity, they also enable the operators and the NRC to put off complicated decisions about where to put the waste. As former NRC chairman Dale E. Klein recently admitted, "life extensions just kick the can down the road. Even with another round of license renewals, giving plants life extensions beyond 60 years, we would still have to confront the immense challenge of decommissioning waste when these plants eventually cease operations."[33]

The NRC has been handing out life extension approvals like good conduct passes, according to the NRC's own Office of Inspector General (OIG). It reported in the fall of 2007 that, in most cases, the NRC staff failed to verify the authenticity of technical safety information submitted by the utilities and "cut and pasted" sections of the actual applications into their own safety reviews, rather than writing their own evaluations.[34] "The NRC is not doing a great job regulating this particular issue," said Richard Webster, a lawyer with the Eastern Environmental Law Center, a nonprofit organization in New Jersey that fought to stop the relicensing of the Oyster Creek plant.

Gilinsky was more critical. "The NRC is a wholly owned subsidiary of the NEI," he said, referring to the industry lobbying group in Washington. Hal Ornstein, a former NRC safety official who investigated the Browns Ferry fire, believes shoddy utility practices and a lack of oversight will eventually lead to another disaster. "It's not a question of if another bad accident is going to occur," he said, "it's a question of when."[35]

The NRC struggles to keep up with the demands of a very tough job, and it has highly skilled technical people working for it. But the reality is it can only do so much. Each of the 104 reactors subject to its scrutiny is susceptible to technical malfunctions, corrosion, and other effects of poor maintenance and aging. They also are vulnerable to unpredictable human behavior and malfeasance. Finally, they are inviting targets for terrorists.

In February 1993, a thirty-one-year-old man driving his mother's Plymouth station wagon about forty miles an hour flew past a guard booth at the Three Mile Island nuclear plant, then smashed through an entry gate into the so-called protected area. The car kept going, crashing through a corrugated metal door until it entered the turbine building of the Unit 1 reactor, operating at full power. The car finally came to a halt inside the turbine building, after striking and damaging the insulation of an auxiliary steam line. The intruder, who had only recently been released from the mental ward of a local hospital, hid in the darkness of the condenser building and was not apprehended until four hours after he entered the site. NRC investigators concluded the event had "no actual adverse reactor safety consequences and was of minimal safety significance."[36]

What if he or she had been armed with a car bomb?

Something like that happened in November 2007 when a worker at the Palo Verde nuclear plant in Arizona was stopped with a pipe bomb in the back of his truck. Authorities described the device as a six-inch capped explosive, probably homemade; it was galvanized pipe. Tom Mangan, a spokesman for the Bureau of Alcohol, Tobacco, Firearms, and Explosives, told a reporter, "If this thing went off in the back of the truck, it certainly would put a hole in it. It was rather crude in construction, but it could certainly injure somebody." The worker told authorities he did not know how the device ended up in his truck, and after being detained for a few hours he was released.[37]

In a real attack, terrorists are more likely to use snipers, grenade launchers, and automatic weapons, and to move in from several directions. However, at most plants security guards are armed only with pistols, rifles, and other handheld weapons, and trained to fend off a few attackers from one direction. Sentries are not protected, said the European study, against "multiple vehicle bombs (in which the first bomb is used to breach a vehicle barrier, enabling a second vehicle to enter the protected area), even though such tactics are being increasingly used by paramilitary groups around the world."[38]

The NRC tried to address the weakness in a series of drills during the 1990s, evidently with little success, and after that effort and the events of September 11, the agency still did not appear to take security too seriously. It took the regulators almost a year to follow up on allegations in early 2007 that security guards employed by Wackenhut at Exelon's Peach Bottom reactor in Pennsylvania were falling asleep on the job. The agency initially investigated but took the utility's word that there were no problems. Only when the security guard who reported the problem took a video of the dozing guards to a New York City television station were the regulators forced to take the charges more seriously. At the time, Wackenhut provided guards for about half the nation's nuclear reactor stations as well as DOE nuclear weapons facilities. "Let me say up front that I am not going to make excuses for what happened here. The NRC missed it," said NRC chairman Klein during a visit to Peach Bottom in February 2008. "The plant missed it."[39]

The incident at Peach Bottom was symptomatic of a bigger challenge: how can the government and utilities adequately protect nuclear plants from sabotage, intruders, or terrorists? After the DOE's inspector general, Gregory Friedman, cited Wackenhut for numerous other deficiencies at the nation's most sensitive nuclear weapons sites, including the National Nuclear Security Administration's Nevada Test Site and Oak Ridge, a spokeswoman for the IG reportedly said the Energy Department "is considering doing a feasibility study of federalizing the guard force."[40]

That may be fine for the military nuclear plants. But the prospect of transforming privately owned reactor stations into state-of-the-art military installations, possibly even with antiaircraft guns, is strongly resisted by utilities and their regulators because it would detract from the image of "peaceful" nuclear energy; moreover, utilities are in the business of producing electricity, not running defense establishments.

I doubt most people like the idea either.

AND WHAT OF Colvin's optimistic outlook for America's nuclear waste? When Colvin claimed the problem was solved in 2002, four years had passed since the date when the DOE was legally obligated to accept spent nuclear fuel from the nation's reactors for permanent disposal at Yucca Mountain. As a result, dozens of utilities are paying for the upkeep and monitoring of spent fuel piling up at their reactor sites, currently amounting to some fifty thousand tons. They also are suing the Energy Department for its failed promise. All this is costing utility ratepayers and taxpayers more money in legal fees.

On the face of it, the presence of thick concrete steel-lined casks does not seem a bad trade-off for years of electricity production. But in the town of Rowe, Masschusetts, which hosts sixteen of them, the residents know better. Spent fuel contains hundreds of radionuclides that lose their radioactivity over varying amounts of time and, in the process, generate enormous amounts of heat.[41] Scientists have calculated that after a thousand years a lot of the radioactivity will disappear, and that after ten thousand years the total activity will be roughly 0.01 percent of what existed a month after the assemblies' removal. However, three isotopes (plutonium-241, americium-241, and neptunium-237), linked through the decay process, take between one hundred thousand and one million years to lose their radioactivity.[42]

Right now, only a citizens' advisory board plus the utility managers at Rowe monitor that hot waste, with supervision by the NRC. Former DOE official Robert Alvarez thinks that, at the very least, all of the nation's spent fuel—what he terms "orphaned material"—should be put under DOE control because the level of safeguards and security would be higher. He also points out that more than 95 percent of the spent fuel is currently stored in densely compacted spent fuel pools. If someone drained just one of those pools, he says, "you could render an area the size of Connecticut uninhabitable from cesium exposure."[43] But experts have told Rowe's citizens that even their "dry storage" casks are not safe from the threat of fire, sabotage, or direct attack.[44]

The NRC under Bush expressed confidence that within the first quarter of the twenty-first century there "is reasonable assurance that at least one mined geologic repository will be available" and that "spent fuel generated in any reactor can be stored safely and without significant environmental impacts for at least 30 years beyond the license life for operation (which may include the term of a revised or renewed license)."[45] That would mean in practice that utilities would be "allowed" to keep their fuel for fifty years or more, which is probably what they will end up doing, because in 2007 Deputy Secretary of Energy Clay Sell said it could be "decades" before Yucca Mountain ever opens.[46]

What caused the delay? The simple truth is that geologists and engineers had not been able to prove that either geological or man-made barriers at Yucca, or the two combined, would prevent the waste leaking out over the next million years—which is the Environmental Protection Agency's court-mandated revised time frame. Their task had no precedent. Geologists were being asked to turn their traditional discipline on its head. Instead of studying historical earth movements as they had been trained to do, they were attempting to determine how the site might change over thousands of years. Two geologists connected with the project, Jane Long and Rodney Ewing, pointed out in an academic paper that Congress effectively prejudged the outcome when it amended the original Waste Policy Act in 1987, eliminating four other sites from consideration and leaving geologists to put their scientific imprimatur on what was basically a political decision—to store the waste at Yucca.[47] Meanwhile, miracle metals that would supposedly keep the waste safe in containers turned out to be corrosion-prone in Yucca's underground environment.[48]

With costs of the Yucca project heading toward one hundred billion dollars and strong public opposition in Nevada, the DOE under the Bush administration looked for another solution, anxious that its "nuclear renaissance" not be derailed. The administration was not giving up on Yucca, but DOE officials knew that even if the site ever got licensed, it would not have enough room to store waste from all the new reactors being planned—meaning a second repository would be necessary. As an interim measure, the DOE drew up plans for a large storage site next to Yucca to handle about twenty-five thousand tons of fuel. This is in part to relieve some of the congestion at reactor storage sites, but evidently also to create a legal precedent that could pave the way for a license to build a permanent repository.[49] "The Nuclear Waste Policy Act forbids such a storage site in Nevada," contends Gilinsky, a consultant to the state of Nevada, because it was "part of the compromise that put the repository in Nevada—but DOE claims—an outright lie—that such a large storage site is integral to the repository. This will be a big legal issue before NRC and the courts. What they are trying to do is to collect the fuel whether or not a repository gets built or they have the capacity—to create 'facts on the ground.' "[50]

× Still Stuck In the 1950's

THESE PRESSURES ALSO prompted the DOE to announce its intention to put plutonium recycle and advanced reactors at the core of its sweeping nuclear revival plan, the Global Nuclear Energy Partnership (GNEP), in February 2006. The plan's authors envisioned a new American-dominated global nuclear order in which the United States and other fuel supplier nations, such as Britain, France, and Japan, would operate a cradle-to-grave nuclear fuel-leasing program, similar to what the AEC tried in the 1950s. The broad vision was to prevent other countries acquiring the sensitive fuel cycle technologies, while at the same time providing a means of reducing the heat content of waste for a repository by keeping the really hot isotopes, like plutonium, aboveground. Over time, spent nuclear fuel would be returned to the suppliers for reprocessing, and the resulting plutonium-based fuel would be used in advanced reactors.

In an attempt to head off critics, the administration tried an old public relations ploy—relabeling. Reprocessing was changed to a pet word of this environmentally conscious generation, "recycling," and breeders were called "burners." The discarded terms were associated with plutonium *creation*, but the mavericks at DOE wanted to make it appear they were finding a way to get rid of it. There was one real change: the technology they were talking about was far more complicated than the old one, it had not been developed, and developing it would cost the earth. Claims were made that the technology would simultaneously solve the waste and proliferation problems, all in one go. But the primary focus was on waste. "Their attitude is basically that if you can't ship it someplace [for permanent burial], then just keep it in circulation," said Princeton physicist Frank von Hippel.

It sounded positively magical, if only the science could really be proven. Like wizards attempting to reverse-engineer nature, the program's backers moved forward with plans to create a vast complex of expensive recycling facilities, fast reactors, and waste plants that depended on their claims that an uncertain alchemy would actually work. This would take anywhere from twenty to sixty years and cost at least one hundred billion dollars, possibly two, while no one, not even at the Argonne National Laboratory, where much of the work is being done, is sure the stated objectives can be achieved.[51] In fact, one of the laboratory's chief lobbyists has privately admitted the venture will never succeed because the chemistry is simply too complex.

GNEP satisfied long-pent-up frustration among people at DOE who never lost faith in breeders. Moreover, by placing greater emphasis on transmutation research and development—part of the advanced nuclear fuel cycle program—DOE hoped it could downplay the importance of final storage. Nevertheless, a final repository such as Yucca Mountain remained a critical part of the Bush administration's overall "renaissance" since GNEP would not deliver results anytime soon, or eliminate all nuclear waste. However, Bush's successor, Barack Obama, moved quickly to kill the project, arguing there were better solutions than burying spent fuel under a desert mountain that some geologists had argued was unsuitable to the task. In January 2010, the administration appointed a blue-ribbon panel to seek "all alternatives for the storage, processing, and disposal" of spent fuel—and report back in 2012.

In his first year in office, President Obama canceled the GNEP program but crucially retained funding for fuel "recycling" research—an option viewed favorably by several blue-ribbon panel members when they convened for the first time in March 2010. Just a few weeks before that meeting, Obama, vying for Republican votes on energy and climate change legislation, tripled loan guarantee funding for new reactors to $54.5 billion, an astounding move given the almost total absence of support on Wall Street for financing reactors, not to mention the continuing dilemma over waste. As the DOE formally withdrew its Yucca license application from the NRC that same month, the NRC's new chairman, Gregory B. Jaczko, said his agency would seek solutions allowing high-level waste to sit aboveground for centuries rather than decades.

THE QUESTION STILL remains: how will we meet future electricity demand and at the same time reduce carbon emissions? By 2030, current official estimates say, electricity demand will double in some parts of the world and grow by 30 percent in the United States. Given that scenario, supporters argue that nuclear must play an even bigger role than it currently does. "Significant investment and expansion is needed just to maintain the current 20% share of electricity production that nuclear power currently represents in the U.S.," said DOE assistant secretary for nuclear energy Dennis Spurgeon in May 2008. "We will need approximately 30 GWe [gigawatts] of new nuclear power on line by 2030 to maintain that 20% share, and it is projected that we will need at least 300 GWe of new capacity by 2050 to start turning the corner on carbon emissions, using nuclear power to generate 30% of our electricity."[52] Roughly speaking, three hundred gigawatts equates to a little less than three hundred reactors.

Leaving aside the prospect of an ever larger "radioactive footprint," can those targets be achieved? Can nuclear energy make a significant contribution to reducing the carbon footprint? The answer is almost certainly no. Two Princeton University scientists, Stephen Pacala and Robert Socolow, identified fifteen existing technologies that could, by 2054, each prevent one billion tons a year of carbon emissions. From that they created a graph divided into seven wedges, each representing one of those technologies that they said would help halt the rise in greenhouse gas emissions for five decades and then stabilize the concentration of carbon dioxide in the atmosphere.

One of those wedges was nuclear energy.

Filling that wedge would require seven hundred new reactors worldwide by 2054, in addition to the 435 operating units that would require replacing or operating extensions in that time frame. Just completing the new plants would mean building, on average, two units per month over the next fifty years. Given the logistical, financial, and political hurdles, that is a practical impossibility. Such a growth rate represents more than twice the industry growth forecast by the Energy Information Administration for the United States, the world's most advanced country, over the next thirty years.[53]

Even the industry does not believe it will happen. The World Nuclear Association's 2009 market report—more bullish than its forecast two years earlier—predicted a net increase in the number of new units to 145 reactors by 2030, representing roughly 30 percent of the units the Princeton scientists say would be necessary by then to make an impact on climate change. Meanwhile, most of the new construction is happening in China, although infrastructure issues, shortages of trained personnel, and safety concerns are leading to delays. The same is true at other sites, most notably in Finland and France, where two projects are not only behind schedule but also well over budget.[54]

Pacala thinks nuclear power is "a non-starter . . . I cannot imagine that in this era of concerns about terrorism that we are going to start the production of fissionable material all over the world," he stated. "If you try to solve even one wedge of this problem with nuclear, it would require a doubling in the amount of nuclear power deployed. Solving the problem entirely with nuclear means increasing deployment by a factor of ten, and if you calculate how many of these plants would have to be in countries like Sudan and Afghanistan, you are just not going to do it."[55]

IN THE RACE against time, expecting nuclear energy to compete with other more versatile methods of non-carbon-emitting energy production is like pitting an elephant against a gazelle. The accepted wisdom, traditionally advanced by the oil and nuclear industries, is that solar, wind, and tidal power technologies are immature, uncertain, and futuristic. But that is where the smart money is right now. The Natural Resources Defense Council, which is critical of nuclear energy but not explicitly against building more reactors, argues that "windpower is already growing at twice the potential growth rate of nuclear over the next decade, and the outlook for wind is for even faster growth. In a similar vein, recent dramatic improvements in the processes for mass-producing solar photovoltaic cells suggest that by the time these subsidized new nuclear plants are connected to the grid, distributed solar power will be a formidable, and likely superior competitor."[56]

At present, however, the government's energy spending priorities are skewed in precisely the opposite direction. Consider the following: Between 1948 and 2003, the U.S. government spent a mere $131 billion on energy research and development, according to the Congressional Research Service. More than half, or $74 billion, went to nuclear, while a quarter went to fossil energy. Meanwhile, research funding for renewables and energy efficiency, which only began in 1973 with the first oil crisis, received far less—less than $15 billion (11 percent) and under $12 billion (9 percent), respectively.[57]

Alternatives need government support, but Congress has not been as generous in allocating financial assistance to these industries compared to what it has doled out for the nuclear lobby. At the same time, it has followed an "on-again, off-again" pattern in approving production tax credits that help both. Three times between 1999 and 2006, the tax credits were not extended, and wind power capacity additions plummeted. In the years the credits were in place, the increases were impressive. In

2005 and 2006, for example, more than two thousand megawatts of capacity, roughly equivalent to two reactors, were added each year.[58] By comparison, the first of some thirty-two planned reactors in the United States is not expected online for another eight to fifteen years. And because of financial and other uncertainties most utilities planning new reactors have not yet committed to actually building.

Global nuclear power capacity grew by less than two thousand megawatts in 2007, a figure equivalent to just one-tenth of the new wind power installed worldwide last year, according to the Washington, D.C.-based Worldwatch Institute.[59] Nuclear power capacity outside the United States is increasing steadily but not dramatically, with thirty-five reactors under construction in twelve countries, mostly in China, India, and other parts of Asia.[60]

A national cap on carbon emissions will help reduce the current huge cost differential between nuclear and large coal- and gas-fired power plants but will not go far in helping nuclear energy compete with smaller, cleaner, and more flexible sources of energy. Any comparison, to be sure, has to consider that nuclear energy is intended to provide a steady supply of baseload electricity, while solar and wind are not constant. But a growing movement to decentralize electricity distribution by turning consumers into producers, with, for example, solar electric panels and small wind turbines installed in homes and offices, may start to provide a solution to this dilemma. Pacala argues that improved energy efficiency, where the government has historically spent the *least* amount of money, is one of the wedges on which he would place a high priority. "This is because there is a market incentive that once the efficiency improvements exist, they will stay in place forever . . . It is amazing how much of a wedge you get just out of replacing the remaining incandescent light bulbs with compact fluorescents," he wrote.[61]

Since 1997, an organization based in Washington, D.C., called the World Alliance for Decentralized Energy, or WADE, has been working to accelerate worldwide deployment of decentralized energy systems and to increase their market share in the global power mix. These include high-efficiency cogeneration (the simultaneous production of both electricity and useful heat), on-site renewable energy, and industrial energy recycling and on-site power.

Amory B. Lovins, a longtime advocate of alternatives, calls the legion of small, fast, and simple newer projects "mighty mice," and he says they are gradually overcoming the nuclear and carbon-based behemoths in economic competitiveness and overall contribution to electricity generation. To support his argument, he cited recent WADE data: in 2004 decentralized sources supplied 52 percent of Denmark's electricity, 39 percent in the Netherlands, 37 percent in Finland, 31 percent in Russia, 18 percent in Germany, 16 percent each in Japan and Poland, 15 percent in China, 14 percent in Portugal, and 11 percent in Canada. Even with new nuclear build in countries such as China, Lovins argued, "micropower will continue to pull ahead."[62]

MICROPOWER IS THE antithesis of traditional big government and big business, and it needs to be backed by public policy and a determination by lawmakers not only to increase funding for energy research and development but to allocate a greater proportion of it to alternatives. Effecting change will be difficult because of entrenched interests that use their power and deep pockets to promote more nuclear energy. The situation is even further complicated by interlinking military and civilian nuclear programs within the bureaucracy, particularly within the Energy Department, which spends two-thirds of its budget on weapons-related activities and only 17 percent on programs directly tied to energy, according to the former DOE adviser Robert Alvarez.

During the later Bush years, a DOE official named Victor Reis and a few colleagues worked in a section they jokingly referred to as "the pig pen."[63] I don't remember the basis of the joke, but the nickname served as an apt metaphor for what these men were doing. Reis was the Bush administration's chief GNEP promoter as senior adviser to Energy Secretary Samuel Bodman; prior to that, in the late 1990s as a former assistant secretary for defense programs, Reis was the DOE's chief salesman for the Stockpile Stewardship Program. In both cases, Reiss's real job was to satisfy demands from the national nuclear laboratories, whose directors were looking for ways to justify budget requests without a cold war on.

Reis proved adept at administering and advancing the cause of the nuclear pork barrel. More than six billion dollars is currently funneled into the DOE's weapons complex each year to support a vast research and manufacturing enterprise focused on upgrading existing U.S. nuclear weapons and designing new ones. "Beyond being an appalling waste of federal funds, this massive nuclear weapons development effort belies commitments the United States has under the nuclear Non-

Proliferation Treaty (NPT) to work toward the elimination of nuclear weapons," wrote Robert Civiak, the former Office of Management and Budget official who monitored spending on national security programs during the 1990s.[64]

American leaders have always professed to want to eliminate nuclear weapons, even well before the NPT was signed, and sometimes very convincingly. "It is not enough to take this weapon out of the hands of soldiers," said Eisenhower in his Atoms for Peace speech. "It must be put into the hands of those who will know how to strip its military casing and adapt it to the arts of peace."[65] But that desire has been in continual conflict with the view that nuclear weapons are necessary to the national defense and the projection of power on the world stage. Hence, when the idea of a nonproliferation treaty was first proposed in 1958, the United States supported it in principle while artfully dodging any agreement that would thwart its missile emplacements in Europe. Later, after China became a nuclear power, U.S. support for the treaty became genuine, but not for that part of the bargain that obligated the government to do away with its nuclear arsenal.

Some argue that as symbols of power nuclear weapons are a good thing—that by promising wholesale destruction they actually prevent it. Yet the line between their psychological value and the real threat they pose is thin. The fact that planners still incorporate nuclear weapons into their defense strategies means there is a possibility they could be used: under the Bush administration, the emphasis was on increasing the range of scenarios in which nuclear weapons could conceivably be employed. Defense strategy was no longer centered on the number and explosive power of warheads, but rather on the ability to adapt nuclear technology to shifts in the nature of military conflicts, and, if necessary, to consider nuclear strike options against countries such as Iran or North Korea. Meanwhile, the deployment of ballistic missile interceptors in Poland threatened to rekindle the cold war. Russian president Vladimir Putin warned he would aim some of his country's nuclear missiles at any country that agreed to accept the American interceptors.[66] He also began what could become strategic nuclear partnerships in Latin America.

Obama has moved to improve relations by scaling back the missile shield plan and successfully concluding a major arms control agreement. Assuming it is ratified by lawmakers in both countries, the treaty would trim by about 30 percent the number of deployed strategic weapons (to the 1,550 count mentioned earlier), with the number of launchers, including land and sea-based missiles as well as bombers, coming down to 800 on both sides.[67]

These shifts, while welcome, do not suggest the superpowers are any nearer to contemplating the total elimination of nuclear weapons, which is one reason other countries feel justified in seeking to acquire their own. The Bush administration's decision to resume nuclear commerce with India picks up where the relationship was left in the 1970s, except that in the intervening period India acquired an estimated fifty to one hundred nuclear warheads. India remains one of three nuclear weapons states never to have signed the NPT, along with Pakistan and Israel, which means it is not legally obligated to achieve nuclear disarmament. In the meantime, unlike 179 other countries, India has not signed the Comprehensive Test Ban Treaty. It remains to be seen whether subsequent U.S. administrations will enforce the provisions of the 2006 Henry J. Hyde Act, which stipulates, among other things, that if India resumes nuclear testing, all U.S. nuclear trade with it will again cease.

Pakistan and Israel are positioning themselves to get the same deal, which raises a number of questions. "If or when they do, what then becomes the purpose of the Nuclear Suppliers Group?" asks Sharon Squassoni, previously with the Carnegie Endowment for International Peace and now of the Center for Strategic and International Studies. Indeed, as was the case with India, each "deal" would require the NSG to waive its rules prohibiting the export of sensitive technologies to non-NPT countries—and thus call into question its raison d'être. "Who are the bad guys? The states that don't have the technology yet? Terrorists? Nobody has thought this through," says Squassoni. A potentially significant segment of nuclear growth over the next half-century could occur in other developing countries where big increases in electricity demand are forecast. They include Indonesia, Nigeria, Egypt, Saudi Arabia, Iran, and Turkey, which have little or no nuclear power today. The resources to build reactors will pose obstacles, but as Princeton scientist Harold Feiveson argues, "Let's not kid ourselves. If, as we are positing here, nuclear power comes to play a substantial role in the world energy economy, it will have to be located in many of these countries . . . Today, we have to be realistic in admitting that in many countries the nuclear technology genie is well out of the bottle; but this does not in itself justify letting genies everywhere out of the bottle."[68]

The more nukes, the more bad

After the bargain with India was announced, there were dire warnings of the NPT's imminent collapse. After all, if a nonsigner could gain access to the commercial nuclear market with few strings attached, what purpose was there in remaining a signatory? Meanwhile, Iran's determination to proceed with uranium enrichment, purportedly for civilian purposes, has spawned a wave of new nuclear programs in the Middle East. In just eleven months between February 2006 and January 2007, some thirteen countries in the region announced new or revived plans to pursue or explore civilian nuclear energy.[69] Egypt's Fahmy hinted at the ultimate reason: "The idea was you'd get technology quicker within the system—but those outside got it easier than those inside."[70] These countries are playing by the rules right now, but their leaders know that if they decide to pursue the weapons option, the civilian platform will serve as their base.

In a broader sense, the NPT suffers from a conversation that has long since gone stale. The treaty is the product of another era, with little relevance to the situation that exists today. Its central bargain is based on the supposition that nuclear energy is not only beneficial, but something every country is *entitled* to, a message promoted by supplier countries ever since Atoms for Peace and by the IAEA. The treaty predates Three Mile Island and Chernobyl. It overlooks the steady stream of reactor "incidents" that in total spell complexity and danger. And it has nothing to say about the vexing issue of nuclear waste. If to continue adding to the earth's carbon footprint is morally wrong, it stands to reason that it is equally unconscionable to leave radioactive spent fuel around, whether aboveground or in a geologic repository whose movements over the next one thousand years are impossible to predict. People in every country understand the risks, in spite of the "clean nuclear energy" message touted by the industry and many governments. Praful Bidwai, a noted Indian commentator, writes: "Nuclear power is a dubious route to security because it is fraught with grave problems of operational safety, accident-proneness, routine radioactivity releases and above all, high-level wastes that remain radioactive for centuries."[71]

It seems impossible to imagine the problem of nuclear proliferation disappearing as long as nuclear commerce flourishes—particularly when supplier countries openly embrace trading with countries like India that have no legal obligation to disarm. The two—commerce and proliferation—are inescapably related. As the superpower warhead counts come down and the number of countries with nuclear weapons grows, disarmament and nonproliferation efforts will inevitably come together again, or certainly should. "Disarmament," says Sergio Duarte, the UN's High Representative for Disarmament Affairs, "represents the fusion of idealism and realism—it is the right thing to do, and it works. As for nuclear non-proliferation, it gains its own collective legitimacy from its intimate connection with disarmament."[72] The core dangers of the nuclear age remain: as long as nuclear commerce continues, more countries will have nuclear weapons, and the existence of weapons means there is a risk of nuclear war. The other nuclear dangers and their lingering long-term effects are, as Bidwai noted, with us right now.

TO THE EARLY believers, the atomic path looked as if it would bring about endless wealth—even to the point of eradicating poverty—and reasonably quickly too. Today, nuclear energy contributes between 19 and 34 percent of total electricity supply in the United States and Europe, respectively. Globally its contribution is declining, with IAEA figures suggesting it slipped to just 13 percent of electricity supply in 2008. Around the world, spent fuel is piling up at reactors, increasing the risk of radioactive release in the event of an attack or sabotage at these facilities—and governments seem hell-bent on creating more. A proliferation system is on the verge of collapse, and the IAEA's safeguards' budget, at roughly one hundred million dollars, is comparable to the payroll of the Washington Redskins football team.[73]

It is easy to be lulled into seeing the containment dome as a symbol of clean, safe energy, and nuclear weapons as the ultimate form of security. But reactors and the fuel plants that support them are not clean or safe, and twenty thousand warheads, the rough count on September 11, 2001, did not stop terrorists from hijacking four airplanes. Since then, Americans have developed a creeping sense that the country is more vulnerable than ever before, and that our democratic way of life is fast eroding.

The fragile balance is apparent in many other parts of the world. In early April 2003, around the time Saddam Hussein's statue was toppled in central Baghdad, Jafar dia Jafar, the man understood to have headed Iraq's secret nuclear weapons effort, quietly slipped over the Iraqi border into Abu Dhabi. He has since emerged as the head of an engineering firm helping to rebuild Iraq. At a conference in London, I asked him if he had run the bomb program under duress. He shook his head and said, "It was the Israeli bombing of Osirak," referring to the reactor that was destroyed in 1981. The anger and quest for nuclear parity that fed the Iraqi program is little different from the motivations that drove the scientists during and after World War II, and in the Iraqi case, the enemy actually has nuclear weapons.

These sentiments have not disappeared in the Middle East, and the existence of an Iranian nuclear program makes the temptation and, as some would see it, justification to pursue nuclear weapons even stronger. Jafar's adopted country, the United Arab Emirates, is moving so quickly toward "peaceful" nuclear capability that IAEA officials fear the reactors they build will not be run safely. One way or another, governments pushing for more nuclear energy are tempting fate, particularly in the Middle East and on the Indian subcontinent. For in a very literal sense, there is no such thing as peaceful nuclear energy. It is based upon one of the most violent, though invisible, forces of nature known to man, and it is this power that nations seek. Nuclear weapons cannot be disinvented. But mind-sets can be changed, even in the Middle East. And nuclear energy, for electricity or other purposes, can be used more wisely, which must mean minimally, until we wean ourselves from it entirely. The question, again, is whether that happens before or after a nuclear war.

Security is no longer purely a national affair. When rival countries threaten each other with nuclear war, or an accident sends radioactivity across many borders, people have to think about safety, stability, and confidence in their future in broader terms. As Rotblat and his co-writer, Robert Hinde, point out in their book *War No More*, "Surrender of sovereign rights is going on all the time . . . Each international treaty we sign, every agreement on tariffs, or other economic measures is a surrender of sovereignty in the general interests of the world community. To this equation we must now add the protection of humankind."[74]

The problem we face with nuclear energy ultimately is not about global warming or even nuclear weapons. It is about our relationship to the atom and the extraordinary hold it has had over us for the past century, and the power structures that have evolved to support it. President Eisenhower warned against not only "unwarranted influence" by the military-industrial complex but the "danger that public policy could itself become the captive of a scientific-technological elite."[75] That warning has largely been ignored, allowing a huge, secretive, self-rationalizing system to take on a life of its own, backed by

history, money, power, and a default conviction in its own inevitability. It is this world and the fissures that run through it that I have shed
light on. Seeing and understanding are only first steps toward what
must happen, which is taking apart an edifice that sustains and promotes a planet-threatening enterprise. This has to happen because we
want to survive, and for that we need a safe and habitable place to live.

In the United States that process should begin with a critical look
at the Energy Department, a legacy bureaucracy steeped in the country's nuclear past. The burden of maintaining nuclear weapons and
the associated cleanup costs constrains the agency from delivering
what is really needed, which is an aggressive, solution-seeking program to meet future energy demand. Such a program must be as dynamic as the brilliant, though tragically fateful one that led to the
first atomic bomb, and as spirited as the other that landed a man on
the moon. At a more practical level, it will require identifying and
truly separating the DOE's military and energy functions, even if that
means splintering the agency, a step proposed by the Office of Management and Budget early in the Obama administration but quietly
dropped. Instead of pushing for more nuclear energy, Obama should
instead discourage it and explore with other countries truly sustain-
able and economically viable energy alternatives. If Obama truly
seeks a world free of nuclear weapons, as he famously declared he did
in Prague in April 2009, he and his successors must prove a willingness to cut, rather than increase, and finally end U.S. spending on
weapons at home. The symbolic value of such steps would be immense, and ultimately there would be no turning back. As stockpile
numbers decreased and nuclear commerce around the world died
down, proliferators would have a harder time achieving their aims.

Prometheus was chained to the rocks, he thought for all eternity.
Each day a vulture, or in some accounts an eagle, ate his liver, and each
day it was restored. His crime was stealing, or reclaiming, fire from the
gods. Thirteen generations later Prometheus was freed by Heracles.

Right now we are in chains. If we recycle plutonium and build more
weapons, we are inviting our own endless punishment, and both types
of activity look set to continue for the foreseeable future. The question
is, who will save us from this fate?

The answer, as we know, does not lie with the gods. It lies in our
mortal hands.

A Final Note

When I began writing this book in London, I used to see a sprightly older lady walk past my house most mornings. I knew she was a nun from a convent around the corner, but I had never talked to her. One day she introduced herself as Sister Margaret, and we struck up a conversation, mostly about the shrubs and flowers in my front garden. She had bright blue eyes, a kindly smile, and short, wavy gray hair. In her light southern Irish accent, she asked what it was that I did "up there in the window, all day long."

I told her I was writing a book about nuclear energy and how it had developed from bombs into reactors, and the challenges that posed.

"It'll pass," she said.

I asked her what she meant.

"The Dark Ages. They passed."

I did not have the heart to ask her how soon we would emerge from the darkness, but I knew that before we could find our way out, the journey would be long and treacherous.

We switched back to talking about an overgrown sky-blue ceanothus and a yellow waxy flowering plant called a fremontodendron that had grown so big it was in the way of the front door. But when Sister Margaret was ready to walk on, she told me she would say a prayer each time she looked up to my window. So now I pass it on.

A prayer for us all.

Acknowledgments

This book took shape with the help and support of a wonderful community of people on both sides of the Atlantic during the more than eight years it took to produce. My gratitude goes to Jim Thackara in London for suggesting the idea and to Lucy Sullivan in Connecticut for seconding it. Thanks also to Lucy for acting as a sounding board and reader in the very early stages and, over many years, to both her and Jim for imparting belief, courage, and confidence in what I was trying to achieve. Lucy's husband, Chris Sullivan, deserves special thanks for organizational advice and a steady flow of news, information, and moral support. Also thanks to Ed Fox in London, who always said I should write a book and helped me to get this one launched through his introduction to my literary agent.

The moral, political, and technical issues that surround nuclear energy are deeply complex, which made the task of reading and advising unusually challenging for readers with only a general knowledge of the topic. For precisely that reason I am profoundly grateful to Maureen Connolly and Tom Allen, who read the book as it was being written and ensured it remained accessible to readers outside the industry. Maureen especially gave up many precious hours applying her writing and editing skills to help me steer the project through to completion. Sarah Miller, my longtime colleague, was an equally important reader because she, like me, had covered the nuclear industry as a journalist. She raised questions and provided helpful analytical comments. Maureen, Sarah, Tom, and Tom's wife, Scottie, provided unwavering support and encouragement throughout.

I am indebted to a number of other readers who came in at later stages, sacrificed valuable time to ensure the book's political and technical accuracy, and provided valuable criticisms. In particular, physicists Frank von Hippel and Frank Barnaby offered not only their personal stories in the nuclear field but read through the entire manuscript and made many helpful comments, corrections, and suggestions. Randy Rydell lent his special expertise in nonproliferation and general knowledge of the topic to the entire book. Others to whom I am grateful are Len Weiss, Stan Norris, Victor Gilinsky, Henry Myers, James Joosten, Samuel Walker, and Jonathan Weisgall. Mycle Schneider in Paris, David Lowry, Steve Thomas, Martin Forwood, and Janine Allis-Smith in the UK all contributed much to this project. Thank you to Mike Edwards for advice on the Chernobyl chapter and to Jennifer Urquhart for helpful comments on the entire manuscript prior to publication. I am also grateful for advice and assistance from George Hishmeh, Matt Severn, Eric Lewis, Kerry Thompson, Patty Frakes, Elisa Torres, and Mary Corrigan.

Many thanks to Ana Lucic at Dalkey Archive Press for permission to use material from Svetlana Alexievich's *Voices from Chernobyl*, to Mary Flowers for use of material from her diary, and to Terry Price for excerpts from his memoir. Also thanks to Matthew Stephen for permission to use material from the uravan.com Web site and for putting me in touch with some of the people on it. Much appreciation to Norma Percy in London and Masha Oleneva in Moscow for providing Russia-related television documentaries, and to Masha for translating. Thanks also to Meirion Jones in Britain and David Stout of the *New York Times* for valuable documents and insight.

The nuclear industry is not known for its openness, particularly to writers with a critical perspective. Hence, I am grateful to those who were willing to talk to me and help in other ways. Big thanks to Jack Edlow for opening his company files and for reintroducing me to people in the industry after a long absence. I am also grateful to Myron Kratzer for spending countless hours clarifying complicated issues. Others who gave their time were Alan Labowitz, Walt Wolf, and three men who have since passed away, Harold Bengelsdorf, Sam Edlow, and Paul Leventhal. Thanks to Frances Edlow for her hospitality and good cheer. My appreciation extends to many, many others, but I would like to mention in particular Bob Gallucci, Bob Alvarez, Tom Cochran, Richard Stratford, Nabil Fahmy, Henry Sokolski, Avner Cohen, Norm Ornstein, Norm Palmer, and the late Anne Marks. In Europe, my deep thanks go to Lord and Lady Flowers, the late Sir Joseph Rotblat, Rolf Ekeus, Terry Price, Ian Fairlie, Roger Howsley, and David Cope. In Paris, my former colleague Ann MacLachlan and her husband, Pierre Zaleski, were extremely helpful. I appreciate their introductions to people in the French nuclear industry who, along with Pierre, helped to illuminate its long history. Thanks especially to André Finkelstein for his innumerable stories and two very nice lunches, and to George Vendryes and Rémy Carle.

Thanks too to Tom Wallin at Energy Intelligence Group for his support, and to my colleague at *Uranium Intelligence Weekly*, Phil Chaffee. The views expressed in this book are my own and in no way reflect those of my colleagues or *UIW*.

Embarking on this project involved moving back to the United States from London. That move, and writing this book, would have been a lot more difficult without the support of great friends and family on both sides, especially Marcus and Susie Bicknell, Albert and Diana Voorthuis, Jennifer Urquhart, and Lili Hishmeh, and, for her gift of yoga, Giulia Mainieri. Much gratitude goes to my sisters, Allison Gradwell and Catharine Cooke, and their husbands, Dave Gradwell and Ian Gribble, and their families for their hospitality when we needed it. Their thoughts, comments, support, and especially patience were always deeply appreciated.

I am grateful to my parents, the late John and Valien Cooke, who taught me to think critically, gave me courage and confidence, and showed me the importance of understanding life's innumerable shades of gray. Many thanks also to Lucy Sullivan's mother, the late Lucy Emerson, who cheered me on, and especially to her father, Bill Emerson, who lit a fire a long time ago.

My first agent in London, Maggie Noach, believed in this project from the start and I am grateful for her efforts on my behalf. Sadly and very unexpectedly, she died before it was completed. The book would not have been possible without the constant support of Cynthia Cannell, my agent in New York, and the willingness of my editor, Anton Mueller, to take it on. Anton's comments and suggestions were defining, and his encouragement at the eleventh hour, a lifeline. I thank them both for their patience. Also much appreciation to India Cooper for her fine copyediting and to Greg Villepique and the rest of the team at Bloomsbury.

My deepest thanks, and a big hug, go to my son, James, who was only two when this journey began. Perhaps when he is older the world will be safer and saner, and this effort will not have been in vain.

Notes

Introduction

1. Rhodes, *Making of the Atomic Bomb*, 703.
2. Diary entry, courtesy of Mary Flowers.
3. Rhodes, *Making of the Atomic Bomb*, 722.
4. Frank Barnaby, pers. comm., April 1, 2008.
5. Diary entry, courtesy of Mary Flowers.
6. In his diary, David Lilienthal wrote: "I recall now Chester Barnard's comment when he first heard of the drop at Hiroshima: 'This is the end of our democracy.'" Lilienthal, *Journals*, 533.
7. This refers to the fact that all nuclear information was deemed "born classified," meaning it was classified from inception.
8. Rhodes, *Dark Sun*, 384.
9. Seaborg, *Stemming the Tide*, 310.
10. Patterson, *Plutonium Business*, 3.
11. International Panel on Fissile Materials, Res. Rpt. 3, von Hippel, *Managing Spent Fuel in the United States*, 7–10.
12. R. S. Norris of the Natural Resources Defense Council recalled this statement.
13. Cooke and Thackara, "Ekeus vs. Saddam."
14. Royal Commission, *Nuclear Power and the Environment*.
15. Jones, "Sir Joseph Rotblat."
16. Cooke, "Boom and Bust," 107–13.
17. The comment was made by John E. Gray, who at the time was chairman and chief executive officer of International Energy Associates Limited (IEAL), a consulting firm based in Washington, D.C.
18. Jürgen Schieber, *Earth: Our Habitable Planet* course notes, week 3, "The Earth: Differentiation & Plate Tectonics," Indiana University, http://www.indiana.edu/~geol105/1425chap3.htm (accessed October 11, 2008).
19. Frank von Hippel, pers. comm., April 5, 2008.
20. Quinn, *Marie Curie*, 159.
21. Ibid., 169.
22. Easlea, "Conflict, Science and the Garden of Eden."
23. Heisenberg, *Physics and Philosophy*, 12.

24. Reid, *Marie Curie*, 108–9, 272–84; Quinn, *Marie Curie*, 184.
25. Mogren, *Warm Sands*, 25–29.
26. U.S. Department of State, *A Report on the International Control of Atomic Energy*, 4.
27. International Panel on Fissile Materials, Res. Rpt. 3, von Hippel, *Managing Spent Fuel in the United States*, 4.
28. Ibid., 10.
29. Jeremy Bransten, "Radio Free Europe—Rogue Nuclear Programs Threaten New Arms Race," Prague, October 19, 2006 (RFE/RL), International Institute of Strategic Studies, http://www.iiss.org/whats-new/iiss-in-the-press/press-coverage-2006/october-2006/rogue-nuclear-programs-threaten-new-arms-race (accessed October 11, 2008).
30. Easlea, "Conflict, Science and the Garden of Eden."
31. World Nuclear Association, "World Nuclear Power Reactors 2007–08 and Uranium Requirements," October 1, 2008, http://www.world-nuclear.org/info/reactors.html (accessed November 1, 2008).

Chapter 1: A Voice in the Wilderness

1. "White House Press Release on Hiroshima, Statement by the President of the United States," n.d., http://www.atomicarchive.com/Docs/Hiroshima/PRHiroshima.shtml (accessed October 11, 2008).
2. Polmar and Allen, *Why Truman Dropped the Atomic Bomb*, 270–71; Bundy, *Danger and Survival*, 133.
3. Jungk, *Brighter than a Thousand Suns*, 221, 226.
4. Ibid., 74–75, 81.
5. Ibid., 81.
6. Joseph Rotblat in discusion with the author, London, June 25, 2004, and January 25, 2005.
7. Hinde and Rotblat, *War No More*, 5.
8. Rotblat, "Leaving the Bomb Project."
9. Jungk, *Brighter than a Thousand Suns*, 48.
10. Rotblat, "The Spy Who Never Was."
11. Groves, *Now It Can Be Told*, 222.
12. Rhodes, *Making of the Atomic Bomb*, 571.
13. Rotblat, "The Spy Who Never Was."
14. Ibid.
15. Polmar and Allen, *Why Truman Dropped the Atomic Bomb*, 121.
16. Rhodes, *Making of the Atomic Bomb*, 617–18.
17. Herken, *Winning Weapon*, 19.
18. Rhodes, *Making of the Atomic Bomb*, 692.
19. Ibid., 690–91.
20. Polmar and Allen, *Why Truman Dropped the Atomic Bomb*, 270; Rhodes, *Making of the Atomic Bomb*, 691. The actual order went up the chain of command on July 24 via Groves in Washington and Gen. George C. Marshall and Stimson in Potsdam.
21. Bundy, *Danger and Survival*, 133.
22. Ibid., 133.
23. Bok, *Secrets*, 199.

24. Ibid., 200.
25. Krutch, *Modern Temper*, 39–40.
26. Spencer Weart, pers. comm., August 19, 2008.
27. Jungk, *Brighter than a Thousand Suns*, 222–23.
28. Ibid., 223.
29. Bundy, *Danger and Survival*, 131.
30. Bok, *Secrets*, 200–201.
31. Ibid., 201.
32. Schell, "Genesis in Reverse."
33. John Pilger, "The real nuclear threat," Mail & Guardian online, September 10, 2008, http://www.mg.co.za/article/2008-09-10-the-real-nuclear-threat (accessed November 1, 2008).

Chapter 2: Rites of Passage

1. Reid, *Marie Curie*, 118.
2. Rhodes, *Making of the Atomic Bomb*, 308.
3. Bundy, *Danger and Survival*, 115–17.
4. Ibid., 70–71.
5. Macmillan, *Ruin of J. Robert Oppenheimer*, 10, 60.
6. Herken, *Winning Weapon*, 123.
7. Ibid., 83–85.
8. Groves was on the panel along with other influential figures in the bomb effort, including James B. Conant, Vannevar Bush, and John J. McCloy, a former aide to War Secretary Henry Stimson.
9. Anne Marks in discussion with the author, Washington, D.C., April 14, 2005.
10. Lilienthal, *Journals*, 10.
11. Rotblat, "The Spy Who Never Was," 3–4.
12. Smyth, *Atomic Energy for Military Purposes*, foreword.
13. Herken, *Winning Weapon*, 112, 157.
14. Groves, *Now It Can Be Told*, 411.
15. Lilienthal, *Journals*, 14.
16. Ibid.
17. Ibid.
18. Rhodes, *Making of the Atomic Bomb*, 277.
19. U.S. Department of State, *Report on the International Control of Atomic Energy*, 47.
20. Lilienthal, *Journals*, 27.
21. Ibid., 30.
22. Lilienthal, *Journals*, 42.
23. Herken, *Winning Weapon*, 170; Anne Marks in discussion with the author, Washington, D.C., April 14, 2005.
24. "*The Baruch Plan (Presented to the United Nations Atomic Energy Commission, June 14, 1946)*," http://www.atomicarchive.com/Docs/Deterrence/BaruchPlan.shtml (accessed October 11, 2008).
25. Lilienthal, *Journals*, 60; Herken, *Winning Weapon*, 173.
26. Coit, *Mr. Baruch*, 587.
27. Herken, *Winning Weapon*, 190.
28. Ibid.

29. Oppenheimer, "Failure of International Control."
30. Lilienthal, *Journals*, 127.

Chapter 3: Crossroads

1. Goldschmidt, *Atomic Rivals*, 303.
2. Weisgall, *Operations Crossroads*, 90.
3. National Archives, Photo #80G627486; also see http://www.de220.com/
   Strange%20Stuff/Crossroads/Operation%20Crossroads.htm (accessed August
   2008).
4. Rabbi Yitzchok Breitowitz in discussion with the author, Woodside Synagogue,
   Silver Spring, Maryland, November 19, 2004.
5. Weisgall, *Operation Crossroads*, 90.
6. Herken, *Winning Weapon*, 176.
7. Ibid., 199.
8. Letter to Leahy from Compton, December 18, 1947; Forrestal letter to Truman, April 6, 1948; press clippings, October 14, 1947; all in U.S. Joint Chiefs of
   Staff, Records of Operations Crossroads, National Archives.
9. Weisgall, *Operation Crossroads*, 45–52.
10. "Proposed Plan for Atomic Bomb Test," U.S. Joint Chiefs of Staff, Records of
    Operation Crossroads, National Archives; *Operation Crossroads*, 32.
11. Weisgall, *Operation Crossroads*, 119.
12. "Proposed Plan."
13. "Proposed Plan"; Weisgall, *Operation Crossroads*, 32.
14. CIA Approved for Release 2003/02/27: CIA-RDP78-01617A005800020024-7,
    CIA Database, National Archives; Weisgall, *Operation Crossroads*, 143–44.
15. Lloyd J. Graybar and Ruth Flint Graybar, "America Faces the Atomic Age:
    1946," *Air University Review*, January–February 1984, http://www.airpower
    .maxwell.af.mil/airchronicles/aureview/1984/jan-feb/graybar.html (accessed
    October 11, 2008).
16. Makhijani, I. Schwartz, and J. Weida, "Nuclear Waste Management and Envi-
    ronmental Remediation," 379.
17. Goldschmidt, *Atomic Rivals*, 154–59, 196–201.
18. Goldschmidt, *Atomic Complex*, 45–46.
19. Goldschmidt, *Atomic Rivals*, 101–7, 149–59.
20. Ibid., 160–72, 177.
21. B. Flowers, pers. comm., August 20, 2008.
22. Goldschmidt, *Atomic Rivals*, 215.
23. Ibid., 215–16.
24. Ibid., 283.
25. Ibid., 175.
26. Ibid., 63–64, 300.
27. Weisgall, *Operation Crossroads*, 31–32.
28. Goldschmidt, *Atomic Rivals*, 300.
29. "Chuck Hansen's uscoldwar.com About *The Swords of Armageddon: History
    of the U.S. Development of Nuclear Weapons*," http://www.uscoldwar.com/
    histry_testing.htm (accessed October 11, 2008).
30. Goldschmidt, *Atomic Rivals*, 304.
31. Weisgall, *Operation Crossroads*, 120–21, 175, 190–91.

32. Goldschmidt, *Atomic Rivals*, 306.

33. Ibid.

34. Ibid., 304.

35. Ibid., 305.

36. Memorandum to Joint Chiefs, July 29, 1946 (from President's Evaluation Committee to President Truman), U.S. Joint Chiefs of Staff, Records of Operations Crossroads, National Archives; Goldschmidt, *Atomic Rivals*, 306–7.

37. Video clips available at http://www.cfo.doe.gov/me70/manhattan/crossroads.html.

38. Goldschmidt, *Atomic Rivals*, 307; Weisgall, *Operation Crossroads*, 225–26.

39. Goldschmidt, *Atomic Rivals*, 306–7.

40. Jose Goldemberg, pers. comm., June 26, 2007.

41. Memorandum to Joint Chiefs, July 29, 1946 (from President's Evaluation Committee to President Truman), U.S. Joint Chiefs of Staff, Records of Operations Crossroads, National Archives.

42. Weisgall, *Operation Crossroads*, 230.

43. Ibid., 231.

44. Ibid., 234.

45. Ibid., 261.

46. Ibid., 233.

47. Dewey letter to Joint Chiefs, August 9, 1946; letter to Joint Chiefs from Karl T. Compton, August 16, 1946, both in U.S. Joint Chiefs of Staff, Records of Operations Crossroads, National Archives; Weisgall, *Operation Crossroads*, 90, 294–95.

48. Weisgall, *Operation Crossroads*, 296-7.

49. U.S. Joint Chiefs of Staff Evaluation Board, "The Evaluation of the Atomic Bomb as a Military Weapon," June 30, 1947; Weisgall, *Operation Crossroads*, 291–92.

50. Ibid., 293.

51. Norman, "Startling Atom Report Quashed by White House"; Weisgall, *Operation Crossroads*, 294.

52. Compton and Dewey correspondence, U.S. Joint Chiefs of Staff, Records of Operations Crossroads, National Archives.

53. U.S. Joint Chiefs of Staff, "Report by the Chief, Armed Forces Special Weapons Project to the Joint Chiefs of Staff on Final Report of the Joint Chiefs of Staff Evaluation Board for Operation Crossroads," Dec. 14, 1955 (Letter from Dewey to Major Howard D. Elliott, August 1, 1955), in U.S. Joint Chiefs of Staff, Records of Operation Crossroads, National Archives.

54. Ibid.

55. Herken, *The Winning Weapon*, 226–29.

56. U.S. Joint Chiefs of Staff, "Report by the Chief, Armed Forces Special Weapons Project to the Joint Chiefs of Staff on Final Report of the Joint Chiefs of Staff Evaluation Board for Operation Crossroads," Dec. 14, 1955, in U.S. Joint Chiefs of Staff, Records of Operation Crossroads, National Archives.

57. "Memorandum by the Secretary, Joint Chiefs of Staff, Enclosure 'A'-Report," Declassified June 13, 1986, U.S. Joint Chiefs of Staff, Records of Operations Crossroads, National Archives.

58. Goldschmidt, *Atomic Rivals*, 303.

59. Makhijani, Schwartz, and Weida, "Nuclear Waste Management and Environmental Remediation," 379.

60. Goldschmidt, *Atomic Rivals*, 307.
61. Ibid., 64.

Chapter 4: The *Hausfreund*

1. Diary entry, courtesy of Mary Flowers.
2. Eventually, the leftist influence in France's scientific community would become less pronounced; that shift began with Joliot-Curie's dismissal in 1950 for public statements in support of Soviet Communism.
3. Goldschmidt, *Atomic Rivals*, 325–29.
4. Price, *Political Physicist* (unpublished version).
5. Goldschmidt, *Atomic Rivals*, 326.
6. Holloway, *Stalin and the Bomb*, 222.
7. Holloway, "Soviet Nuclear History: Sources for *Stalin and the Bomb*."
8. Rhodes, *Dark Sun*, 332.
9. Polmar and Allen, *Spy Book*, 252.
10. Ibid., 251–53.
11. Ibid.
12. Rhodes, *Dark Sun*, 259.
13. Norris, Barrows, and Fieldhouse, *Nuclear Weapons Databook*, vol. 5, 18–23.
14. Records of the Security Service, The Security Service: Personal (PF Series) Files KV 2/2082, National Archives (UK), http://www.nationalarchives.gov.uk. (accessed November 1, 2008).
15. Diary entry, courtesy of Mary Flowers.
16. "Soviet Intelligence Agents and Suspected Agents: Klaus Fuchs," National Archives (UK), http://www.nationalarchives.gov.uk/releases/2003/may22/fuchs.htm (accessed October 11, 2008).
17. Terry Price, pers. comm., March 27, 2008.
18. Price, *Political Physicist* (unpublished version).
19. Ibid. According to other accounts, the Pontecorvos flew to Stockholm on September 1, 1950 and left immediately after that for Helsinki, after which they are presumed to have traveled to the Soviet Union.
20. Ibid.
21. Jungk, *Nuclear State*, 54, citing *Nucleonic News*, April 29, 1976.
22. Brian and Mary Flowers, pers. comm.
23. Ibid.; diary entry, courtesy of Mary Flowers.
24. Jungk, *Nuclear State*, viii.
25. Brian and Mary Flowers, pers. comm.; newspaper cuttings, courtesy of Mary Flowers.
26. "Oscar Buneman, Pioneer of Computer Simulation of Space, Dies at 79," Stanford University News Service, January 26, 1993.

Chapter 5: Two Scorpions

1. Holloway, *Stalin and the Bomb*, 128–29.
2. Ibid. Holloway guesses that is when it may have occurred but says that in any case the exchange occurred around that time.
3. Ibid., 128–29.

4. Ibid., 133.
5. Physics Ethics Education Project, "Robert Oppenheimer," University of Bristol, Institute of Physics, www.peep.ac.uk/content/877.0.html (accessed October 11, 2008).
6. Holloway, *Stalin and the Bomb*, 134. The description "evil genius" is attributed to Stalin's daughter, Svetlana Alliluyeva.
7. Bukharin, Cochran, and Norris, *New Perspectives on Russia's Ten Secret Cities*, 23.
8. Holloway, *Stalin and the Bomb*, 87.
9. Kaufman, *Citizen Kurchatov*.
10. Holloway, *Stalin and the Bomb*, 102–3.
11. Ibid., 115.
12. Ibid., 148.
13. Ibid., 132.
14. Ibid., 211.
15. Ibid., 182; Rhodes, *Dark Sun*, 275.
16. Rhodes, *Dark Sun*, 275.
17. Bukharin, Cochran, and Norris, *New Perspectives on Russia's Ten Secret Cities*, 2.
18. Berlin, *Scientific Supervisor*.
19. "*Russia Before the Second Advent*, Holy Trinity St. Sergius Monastery," Voice of Russia, October 2, 2005, www.vor.ru/English/homeland/home_025.html (accessed October 11, 2008).
20. Associated Press, "Putin Participates in Pilgrimage at Closed Russian City," July 31, 2003.
21. Berlin, *Scientific Supervisor*.
22. Bukharin, Cochran, and Norris, *New Perspectives on Russia's Ten Secret Cities*, 1–2, 10.
23. Berlin, *Scientific Supervisor*; Holloway, *Stalin and the Bomb*, 197.
24. Holloway, *Stalin and the Bomb*, 137.
25. Ibid., 175–77; Rhodes, *Making of the Atomic Bomb*, 119. Oppenheimer traveled to the area as a boy with his grandfather, who encouraged him to collect rocks, and again as a young man. It was through these visits that he developed a fascination with the structure of crystals.
26. Holloway, *Stalin and the Bomb*, 186.
27. Smyth, *Atomic Energy*, 146.
28. Holloway, *Stalin and the Bomb*, 187.
29. Ibid., 189.
30. Ibid., 213–19.
31. *Scientific Supervisor*, documentary.
32. Ibid.
33. Holloway, *Stalin and the Bomb*, 213–19.
34. Frank Barnaby in discussion with the author, Chilbolton, Stockbridge, Hampshire, England, June 14, 2004.
35. Ibid., 216–17.
36. Holloway, *Stalin and the Bomb*, 216.
37. Rhodes, *Dark Sun*, 367.
38. Lilienthal, *Journals*, 569.
39. Rabinowitch, *Atomic Age*, 134, 138.
40. Lilienthal, *Journals*, 572.

41. Ibid., 573.

42. Rhodes, *Dark Sun*, 378.

43. Ibid., 233–63.

44. Ibid., 400, 402n.

45. Tritium is an artificial element that is produced, like plutonium, in reactors. Deuterium occurs naturally—one of every ten thousand hydrogen atoms—and so must be enriched, a process that is far easier than enriching uranium because it weighs twice as much as ordinary hydrogen. (Uranium-235, by contrast, weighs only 1 percent more than the abundant uranium isotope uranium-238.)

46. Rhodes, *Dark Sun*, 253.

47. McMillan, *Ruin of J. Robert Oppenheimer*, 32.

48. Rhodes, *Dark Sun*, 382.

49. Bundy, *Danger and Survival*, 201.

50. Accounts of this meeting vary. McMillan (*Ruin*, 24–25) says the memo was read at the meeting, whereas Rhodes (*Dark Sun*, 380–81) says that Lilienthal prevented Strauss from reading the memo and that it was distributed immediately afterward.

51. Rhodes, *Dark Sun*, 381.

52. Ibid.

53. Ibid.

54. Lilienthal, *Journals*, 230.

55. Rhodes, *Dark Sun*, 384.

56. Ibid., 394.

57. Rhodes, *Dark Sun*, 395, 397, 401.

58. McMillan, *Ruin of J. Robert Oppenheimer*, 36–40. Seaborg was away in Sweden and not voting, although he had been inclined to vote in favor. The main report argued that the nation's resources would be better spent building the stockpile of conventional atomic bombs instead of going forward with the Super. A majority annex said that "a super bomb should never be produced" and warned against the "possible global effects of the radioactivity" from such a bomb and the prospect that it would become "a weapon of genocide." Rabi and Fermi dissented from the majority opinion, proposing a delay in development to allow time to secure a worldwide ban on thermonuclear weapons. Only in the absence of such an agreement would they sanction a U.S. program. The thermonuclear "goes far beyond any military objective and enters the range of very great natural catastrophes," they wrote. "By its very nature it cannot be confined to a military objective but becomes a weapon which in practical effect is almost one of genocide."

59. Ibid., 51.

60. Ibid.; Rhodes, *Dark Sun*, 405.

61. Bok, *Secrets*, 111.

62. McMillan, *Ruin of J. Robert Oppenheimer*, 53.

63. Ibid., 51.

64. Herken, *Winning Weapon*, 319.

65. Carlson, Bengt, "How Ulam Set the Stage."

66. Rhodes, *Dark Sun*, 509–10.

67. Ibid.

68. Becky Miller, "Honoring U.S. Atomic Veteran Capt. Jimmy P. Robinson," Atomic Veterans History Project, December 12, 2001, http://www.aracnet.com/~pdxavets/becky.html (accessed October 11, 2008).

69. Norman Polmar, pers. comm. The full story of his death was not revealed for another fifty years, after Robinson's daughter pressed for an explanation, according to a family Web posting. On April 4, 2002, the couple's wedding anniversary, Robinson's family attended a memorial service at Arlington National Cemetery, where the former pilot was given full military honors; www.aracnet.com/~pdxavets/becky.html (accessed October 11, 2008).
70. Rhodes, *Dark Sun*, 332–33.
71. Ibid., 524.
72. Holloway, *Stalin and the Bomb*, 306–8; Rhodes, *Dark Sun*, 334, 524–25.
73. Rhodes, *Dark Sun*, 333.
74. Ibid., 333–34.

Chapter 6: A Certain Wildness

1. Sam Edlow in discussion with author, Frances and Jack Edlow present, Bethesda, Maryland, July 20, 2003.
2. Chernus, *Eisenhower's Atoms for Peace*, 17.
3. Ibid., 16–24.
4. Ibid., 47–52; Sokolski, *Best of Intentions*, 25–28.
5. C. D. Jackson Papers, 1931–1967, Scope and Content Note, Dwight D. Eisenhower Library, http://64.233.169.104/search?q=cache:uspy7NbDG9MJ:www.eisenhower.archives.gov/listofholdingshtml/listofholdingsJ/JACKSONCD Records195354.pdf+C.D.+Jackson&hl=en&ct=clnk&cd=3&gl=us&client=firefox-a (accessed November 7, 2008).
6. Chernus, *Eisenhower's Atoms for Peace*, 48.
7. Bundy, *Danger and Survival*, 246.
8. The text of the "Atoms for Peace" speech is in Chernus, *Eisenhower's Atoms for Peace*, xi–xix.
9. Bundy, *Danger and Survival*, 294–95.
10. Sokolski, *Best of Intentions*, 3.
11. Holloway, *Stalin and the Bomb*, 350.
12. Ibid.
13. Fischer, *History of the International Atomic Energy Agency*, 30.
14. Ibid. 32.
15. Ibid.
16. Price, *Political Physicist* (unpublished version).
17. Patterson, *Plutonium Business*, 83–85.
18. Price, *Political Physicist* (unpublished version).
19. Ibid.
20. Mazuzan and Walker, *Controlling the Atom*, 31.
21. Samuel Walker in discussion with the author, October 10, 2008.
22. Myron Kratzer in discussion with the author, December 3, 2003, and January 30, 2004.
23. Ibid.
24. Harold Bengelsdorf in discussion with the author, July 22, 2003.
25. Glaser and von Hippel, "Global Cleanout: Reducing the Threat of HEU-Fueled Nuclear Terrorism."
26. Harold Bengelsdorf in discussion with the author, July 22, 2003.
27. E-mails from Kratzer, July 1 and July 30, 2006.

28. Myron Kratzer in discussions with the author, July 2006. In the end, the AEC effort led to only three U.S.-style demonstration reactors in Europe, but they helped convince European utilities to forgo the British and French natural uranium reactors in favor of the American technology. Significantly, one of the earlier purchasers was the French state-owned utility Electricité de France, which built a small pressurized-water reactor (PWR) at Chooz, effectively snubbing the powerful Commissariat à l'Energie Atomique (CEA), France's equivalent to the AEC. Over time, the CEA would lose a long-fought battle with the utility to advance the gas-graphite design (a design also favored by the British) in favor of a Westinghouse model. Siemens, the German manufacturer, also reversed its development priorities in favor of the Westinghouse technology, and apart from Britain, the American PWR eventually dominated the reactor market worldwide.

29. *Newsweek*, January 1955.

30. Haber, "Our Friend the Atom," 127–59.

31. Mazuzan and Walker, *Controlling the Atom*, 60.

32. Ibid., 77–78.

33. Ibid.,78–79

34. Ibid., 357.

35. Ibid.

36. Ibid. GE's lawyers proved prescient. Among the early GE sites was the plutonium production facility at Hanford, Washington, now one of the world's worst nuclear waste dumps, whose cleanup is largely being funded by taxpayers.

37. Mazuzan and Walker, *Controlling the Atom*, 94.

38. Fuller, *We Almost Lost Detroit*, 36–37.

39. Mazuzan and Walker, *Controlling the Atom*, 136–40.

40. Ibid., 97–98.

41. Ibid., 61.

42. Polmar and Allen, *Rickover*, 614–15. Designed and built by Westinghouse, Shippingport was jointly owned by the AEC and the Duquesne Light Company.

43. Ibid., 615.

44. Fuller, *We Almost Lost Detroit*, 14–18.

45. Ibid., 34.

46. Ibid., 38.

47. Mazuzan and Walker, *Controlling the Atom*, 103.

48. Ibid., 108.

49. Ibid., 112.

50. Ibid., 204.

51. Fuller, *We Almost Lost Detroit*, 153.

52. Mazuzan and Walker, *Controlling the Atom*, 208.

53. Ibid., 211.

54. McKeown, *Idaho Falls*, 183.

55. Fuller, *We Almost Lost Detroit*, 109–15; SL-1 Report Task Force, USAEC, report on the Nuclear Incident, 21–34; McKeown, *Idaho Falls*, 136, 140–45.

56. McKeown, "Idaho Falls," 230–36.

57. Ibid., 192–93.

58. Ibid., 227.

59. Ibid., 254.

60. U.S. Department of Energy, "History of Energy in the United States: 1635–

2000, Nuclear Energy," http://www.eia.doe.gov/emeu/aer/eh/nuclear.html (accessed October 22, 2008).

61. Fuller, *We Almost Lost Detroit*, 223.
62. U.S. Nuclear Regulatory Commission, Facility Info Finder, http://www.hrc.gov/info-finder/decommissioning/power-reactor/enrica-fermi-power-plant-unit-1.html (accessed October 24, 2008).
63. Fuller, *We Almost Lost Detroit*, 231.
64. Taylor and Yokell, *Yellowcake*, 26, 29.
65. Debra Munckers Borton comments, http://www.uravan.com (accessed August 2008).
66. Ibid., old Union Carbide ad.
67. Mazuzan and Walker, *Controlling the Atom*, 45. Scientists had partially understood radiation risks since at least the 1920s. By the 1930s, most experts had dismissed the notion that low levels of radiation (meaning those only slightly above background levels) were biologically harmless. In 1946, a reorganized National Committee on Radiation Protection (NCRP) changed its guidelines to reflect that view, with a new "maximum permissible dose." Within the AEC and later the JCAE, the question of where that level should be set was hotly debated. As more information accumulated, standards were gradually tightened.
68. O'Neill, "Building the Bomb," 64–69.
69. Alan Lobowitz in discussion with the author, July 25, 2003.
70. Ibid.
71. Makhijani and Schwartz, "Victims of the Bomb," 422–23.
72. Alan Lobowitz in discussion with the author, July 25, 2003.
73. Mogren, *Warm Sands*, 1.
74. Makhijani, Schwartz, and Weida, "Nuclear Waste Management and Environmental Remediation," 378.
75. Comments from people living in Uravan and the surrounding area, www.uravan.com (accessed August 2008).
76. Myron Kratzer in discussion with the author.
77. Alan Labowitz in discussion with the author, July 25, 2003.

Chapter 7: Caviar Electricity

1. The official Penny Inquiry report states the "diverge" process to trigger the Wigner energy release began at 7:25 P.M. on October 7. The report is included in Lorna Arnold's *Windscale 1957: Anatomy of a Nuclear Accident* as Appendix X1 (London: Palgrave Macmillan, 1992).
2. Wordsworth, preface to the second edition of *Lyrical Ballads* (1800); see www.enotes.com/nineteenth-century-criticism/industrial-revolution-literature (accessed October 2008).
3. Highfield, "Windscale Fire"; Ince, "History of Windscale's Trail of Disaster."
4. Price, *Political Physicist* (unpublished version).
5. UK Atomic Energy Office, *Accident at Windscale*, 13.
6. Cochran, Norris, and Bukharin, *Making the Russian Bomb*, 112.
7. Jungk, *Nuclear State*, 23.
8. Cochran, Norris, Bukharin, *Making the Russian Bomb*, 112.
9. Highfield, "Windscale Fire"; Ince, "History of Windscale's Trail of Disaster."

10. Cochran, Norris, and Bukharin, *Making the Russian Bomb*, 109–13.
11. Based on David Lowry's January 1983 recorded interview with Lord Hinton; David Lowry, pers. comm., September 12, 2007.
12. Hecht, *Radiance of France*, 88.
13. George Vendryes in discussion with the author, Paris, June 2, 2004.
14. Andié Finkelstein in discussions with the author, Paris, March 19 and June 3, 2004.
15. Pierre Zaleski in discussion with the author, Paris, March 20, 2004.
16. Hecht, *Radiance of France*, 230–31.
17. Patterson, *Plutonium Business*, xiii.
18. David Lowry, pers. comm., September 12, 2007.
19. International Panel on Fissile Materials, Res. Rpt. 3, von Hippel, *Managing Spent Fuel in the United States.*
20. International Panel on Fissile Materials, Res. Rpt. 4, Schneider and Marignac, *Spent Nuclear Fuel Reprocessing in France.*
21. Ibid.
22. Norris, Burrows, and Fieldhouse, *Nuclear Weapons Databook* 5:204.
23. Jungk, *Nuclear State*, 7–9.
24. International Panel on Fissile Materials, Res. Rpt. 4, Schneider and Marignac, *Spent Nuclear Fuel Reprocessing in France*, 6.
25. Jungk, *Nuclear State*, 18.
26. Norris, Burrows, and Fieldhouse, *Nuclear Weapons Databook* 5:23–27.
27. Hecht, *Radiance of France*, 93.
28. Hersh, *Samson Option*, 63.

Chapter 8: Parlor Games

1. Jones, "Britain's Dirty Secret"; Meirion Jones, pers. comm, February 12, 2007; see also Crick, "How Britain Helped Israel Get the Bomb."
2. Cohen, *Israel and the Bomb*, 61–62.
3. Foreign Office document (FO371/157284, 1961), courtesy M. Jones; Crick, "How Britain Helped Israel Get the Bomb."
4. Hersh, *Samson Option*, 31.
5. Ibid., 19–23, 30.
6. Goldschmidt, *Atomic Rivals*, 335.
7. Hersh, *Samson Option*, 31.
8. Ibid., 37.
9. Ibid., 67.
10. Ibid., 39.
11. Ibid., 39–40.
12. Hecht, "The Radiance of France," 23–24.
13. Rémy Carle in discussion with author, Paris, June 2, 2004.
14. It takes three megawatts of thermal power to produce one megawatt of electrical power. By comparison, the Hanford reactors each operated at about 250 megawatts.
15. Hersh, *Samson Option*, 45.
16. Norris, Burrows, and Fieldhouse, *Nuclear Weapons Databook* 5:326–27.
17. Ibid.
18. Ibid.

19. *Uranium Intelligence Weekly*, "China's Biggest Pu Complex May Have Been Hit by Earthquake."

20. Norris, Barrows, and Fieldhouse, *Nuclear Weapons Databook* 5:327.

21. Myron Kratzer, pers. comm.

22. Price, *Political Physicist* (unpublished version).

23. Perkovich, *India's Nuclear Bomb*, 29.

24. Hersh, *Samson Option*, 55.

25. Jones, "Britain's Dirty Secret"; Meirion Jones, pers. comm, February 12, 2007; see also Crick, "How Britain Helped Israel Get the Bomb."

26. Milhollin, "Heavy Water Cheaters."

27. Cohen, *Israel and the Bomb*, 101.

Chapter 9: Snow

1. Price, *Political Physicist* (unpublished version).

2. Jungk, *Nuclear State*, 40.

3. Ibid., 38.

4. Victor Gilinsky, pers. comm., August 2008.

5. *Nuclear Tango*, documentary.

6. Holloway, *Stalin and the Bomb*, 326.

7. Ibid.

8. *Nuclear Tango*, documentary.

9. Holloway, *Stalin and the Bomb*, 326–28.

10. Easlea, "Conflict, Science and the Garden of Eden."

11. Interview with Almira Matayoshi in April 1981 on Ebeye, conducted by Glenn Alcalay under the auspices of the Marshall Islands Atomic Testing Litigation Project (MIATLP), http://www.nuclear-free.de/english/almira.htm (accessed November 2, 2008). Almira died on June 5, 2005, in Honolulu.

12. "Radiation Exposure from Pacific Nuclear Tests," oversight hearing before the House Natural Resources Subcommittee on Oversight and Investigations, February 24, 1994, p. 61. Eisenbud served for 26 years as professor of environmental medicine and director of the Environmental Studies Laboratory at New York University Medical Center and before that as director of the AEC's Health and Safety Laboratory. (J. Weisgall, pers. comm., August 15, 2008.)

13. Wasserman, *Killing Our Own*, ch. 4 at n. 53, citing "A Report by the United States Atomic Energy Commission on the Effects of High Yield Nuclear Explosions," AEC release, February 15, 1955, http://www.ratical.org/radiation/KillingOurOwn/KOO4.html (accessed October 11, 2008).

14. Map, courtesy Physicians for Social Responsibility, Washington, D.C.

15. Wasserman, *Killing Our Own*, ch. 4 at n. 111, citing "Strontium Program Quarterly Report," AEC New York Operations Office, February 24, 1959, http://www.ratical.org/radiation/KillingOurOwn/KOO4.html (accessed August 2008).

16. Ibid., online, ch. 4 at n. 66, AEC Commissioners Meeting Minutes, March 14, 1955, 121, http://www.ratical.org/radiation/KillingOurOwn/KOO4.html (accessed October 11, 2008).

17. Joseph Rotblat in discussions with the author, London, June 25, 2004, and January 25, 2005.

18. "The Peace Symbol," http://www.designboom.com/contemporary/peace.html (accessed October 11, 2008).

19. Albert Schweitzer, "A Declaration of Conscience," April 24, 1957, Nuclear Age Peace Foundation, http://www.wagingpeace.org/articles/2004/04/19_schweitzer _declaration-conscience.htm.

20. SANE promoted a multilateral approach to disarmament, unlike CND, which wanted Britain to set an example by disarming on its own. However, the two groups on either side of the Atlantic worked closely together. SANE's membership grew to twenty-five thousand; CND's was four times as large.

21. Christopher Ross, review of *Over Twenty Years of the CND in Britain*, by Richard Taylor and Colin Pritchard, *Peace Magazine*, November 1985.

22. Seaborg, *Stemming the Tide*, 202.

23. Ibid., 203; O'Neill, "Building the Bomb," 78.

24. Cochran, Norris, and Bukharin, *Making the Russian Bomb*, 46–48.

25. Price, *Political Physicist* (unpublished version).

Chapter 10: Any Fool Can Start a War

1. Thrall and Wilkins, "Kennedy Talked, Khrushchev Triumphed."

2. Polmar and Gresham, *DEFCON*-2, 109–11, 178; Sorensen, *Kennedy*, 690–91.

3. M. Walker, *Cold War*, 170.

4. Crankshaw, *Khrushchev Remembers*; Bundy, *Danger and Survival*, 350–51.

5. Kissinger, *Nuclear Weapons and Foreign Policy*, 3.

6. Thrall and Wilkins, "Kennedy Talked, Khrushchev Triumphed."

7. Polmar and Gresham, *DEFCON*-2, 105; Norman Polmar, pers. comm.

8. Ibid., 51–68, 109.

9. Ibid.

10. Ibid.

11. Ibid., 51–68, 109.

12. Bundy, *Danger and Survival*, 396.

13. Polmar and Gresham, *DEFCON*-2, 30, 97 (maps), 101, 102; Bundy, *Danger and Survival*, 392, 394–96; Schlesinger, *Thousand Days*, 801–2.

14. Norris and Kristensen, "U.S. Nuclear Threats Then and Now," 69–71.

15. Ibid.

16. Kaplan, "JFK's First-Strike Plan."

17. Kissinger, *Nuclear Weapons and Foreign Policy*.

18. Zuckerman, *Monkeys, Men and Missiles*, 270–304.

19. Ibid.

20. Ibid., 288–89.

21. John Peyton, *Solly Zuckerman: A Scientist Out of the Ordinary* (London: John Murray Publishers, 2001), http://www.amazon.co.uk/Solly-Zuckerman-Scientist-Out-Ordinary/dp/product-description/071956283X.

22. Kaplan, "JFK's First-Strike Plan."

23. Bundy, *Danger and Survival*, 379.

24. Ibid, 375.

25. Ibid., 400.

26. Polmar and Gresham, *DEFCON*-2, 122; Crankshaw, *Khrushchev Remembers*, 550.

27. *Television History: The First 75 Years*, http://www.tvhistory.tv.

28. Polmar and Gresham, *DEFCON*-2, 129.

29. Ibid., 180.

30. NuclearFiles.org, Project of the Nuclear Age Peace Foundation, "Cuban Missile Crisis Timeline," http://www.nuclearfiles.org/menu/key-issues/nuclear-weapons/history/cold-war/cuban-missile-crisis/timeline.htm (accessed September 2008).

31. National Security Archive, George Washington University, Chang and Kornbluh, *Cuban Missile Crisis*, "A Chronology of Events," 367, http://www.gwu.edu/~nsarchiv/nsa/cuba_mis_cri/620928_621025%20Chronology%201.pdf (accessed November 2008).

32. Polmar and Gresham, *DEFCON-2*, 144; Kennedy, *Thirteen Days*, 67.

33. Bundy, *Danger and Survival*, 405.

34. Dobbs, "The Day Adlai Stevenson Showed 'Em at the U.N"; Polmar and Gresham, *DEFCON-2*, 201–2; American Rhetoric, Online Speech Bank, http://www.americanrhetoric.com/speeches/adlaistevensonunitednationscuba.html.

35. President Kennedy's Letter to Premier Khrushchev, October 10, 1962; Letter from U Thant to Khrushchev, October 10, 1962; The Air Force Response to the Cuban Crisis; all at "*The World on the Brink: John F. Kennedy and the Cuban Missile Crisis*," John F. Kennedy Presidential Library & Museum, http://www.jfklibrary.org/jfkl/cmc/cmc_intro.html.

36. Polmar and Gresham, *DEFCON-2*, 149–52, 189.

37. Ibid., 190.

38. Kennedy, *Thirteen Days*, 109.

39. Polmar and Gresham, *DEFCON-2*, 159–64.

40. Ibid., 163.

41. Bundy, *Danger and Survival*, 434.

42. Crankshaw, *Khrushchev Remembers*, 549.

Chapter 11: Fire in the Air

1. André Finkelstein in discussion with the author, Paris, March 19 and June 3, 2004.

2. Willard F. Libby, "Man's Place in the Physical Universe," *Physics Teacher* 4, no. 1 (January 1966): 29–33.

3. Blair, "Keeping Presidents in the Nuclear Dark."

4. Kenworthy, E. W., "Dirksen Dead in Capital at 73," *New York Times*, September 8, 1969.

5. Seaborg, *Stemming the Tide*, 205–6.

6. Civiak, *Still at It*.

7. O'Neill, "Building the Bomb," *Atomic Audit*, 78–79.

8. Seaborg, *Stemming the Tide*, 210–11.

9. Makhijani and Schwartz, "Victims of the Bomb," *Atomic Audit*, 408n.

10. Ibid., 409.

11. Ibid.

12. Ibid.

13. CNNinteractive, *Cold War*, episode 12: "MAD," http://www.cnn.com/SPECIALS/cold.war/episodes/12/script.html.

14. Makhijani and Schwartz, "Victims of the Bomb," 408–11.

15. Department of State, Transcript of Daily Press Conference, September 29, 1964, Source: RG 59, Records of Special Assistant to Under Secretary for Political Affairs, 1963-65, box 2, Psychological Preparation of Chinese Test 10/16/69, http://www.gwu.edu/~nsarchiv/NSAEBB/NSAEBB38.

16. Anne Marks in discussion with the author, Washington, D.C., April 14, 2005.
17. Norris, "Nuclear Threats Then and Now."
18. Norris, Burrows, and Fieldhouse, *Nuclear Weapons Databook* 5:327.
19. Baldwin, "China's Bomb."
20. Blair, "Keeping Presidents in the Nuclear Dark."
21. Ibid.
22. Ibid., citing Jonathan Schell, *The Gift of Time* (Metropolitan Books, 1998), 191–94.
23. Blair, "Keeping Presidents in the Nuclear Dark."
24. Bundy, *Danger and Survival*, 355–56.
25. Kissinger, *Nuclear Weapons and Foreign Policy*, 4.

Chapter 12: The Grand Bargain

1. Victor Gilinsky, pers. comm., August 2008.
2. Sokolski, *Best Intentions*, 39–56; Henry Sokolski, pers. comm.
3. Robert Norris, pers. comm.
4. Ibid.
5. Sokolski, *Best Intentions*, 39–56.
6. Myron Kratzer, pers. comm.
7. Ibid. Khan was no relation to Abdul Qadeer Khan, the Pakistani engineer who in 1974 fled Europe with a briefcase full of uranium centrifuge enrichment blueprints and became the other Khan's chief rival in the race to build Pakistan's first nuclear weapon.
8. Peter Hayes, "North Korea's Uranium Exports: Much Ado About Something," Nautilus Institute, Northeast Asia Peace and Security Network, Special Report, May 25, 2004, http://www.nautilus.org/archives/pub/ftp/napsnet/special_reports/Hayes-DPRKuranium.txt.
9. Ibid.
10. Seaborg, *Stemming the Tide*, 309–10.
11. Ibid., 315. Ploughshare may not have been as innocent as its name suggested. A former high-level government official, who requested anonymity, recounted a particularly chilling, and cynical, discussion on the subject by the director of the Lawrence Livermore Laboratory during that period: "I was an up and coming scientist; we had a briefing from Livermore on Ploughshare and he [the laboratory director] said . . . that the real reason [for the program] is to get people used to nuclear explosives so that the President will release them in wartime."
12. Nuclear Regulatory Commission: In the Matter of Edlow, Statement of Robert Anderson, Appendix 7 to July 8, 1976 submission.
13. Perkovich, *India's Nuclear Bomb*, 64.
14. Seaborg, *Stemming the Tide*, 140–41.
15. Ibid., 95–108. This was the MLF, or multilateral force, which originated in the concept of Britain and France turning over their independent deterrents to a European force, with the idea that American control, or even American participation, might not be necessary. It ended up being a proposal to allow Europeans to man NATO nuclear submarines and was seen as a way of binding Germany to NATO. But the proposal ran into opposition from many sides. By the end of 1964, many people thought it wouldn't work, but it was not for-

mally ended until two years later, and during that period it impeded progress on the nonproliferation treaty talks.

16. Ibid., 159–60.
17. Ibid., 282–83.
18. Ibid., 106.
19. Ibid., 104.
20. Ibid., 359.
21. Ibid., 104.
22. Ibid., 360.
23. Jungk, *Nuclear State*, 97–105.
24. Seaborg, *Stemming the Tide*, 363.
25. Ibid., 368.
26. Alan Labowitz in discussion with the author, Alexandria, Virginia, July 25, 2003.
27. Seaborg, *Stemming the Tide*, 190–96.
28. Jungk, *Nuclear State*, 99.
29. Edlow, *Quarterly Report: Trends in Traffic Management of Nuclear Materials*.
30. Telexes, July 1969, courtesy Edlow International.

Chapter 13: Golda's Visit to the White House

1. U.S. Department of State, AmEmbassy Tel Aviv to SecState WashDC, July 31, 1969, declassified January 4, 2002, courtesy David Stout, *New York Times*.
2. Kissinger, Memorandum for the President, Subject: Israeli Nuclear Program, July 19, 1969, declassified August 23, 2007, courtesy David Stout, *New York Times*.
3. "Nuclear Weapons—Israel, WMD Around the World," Federation of Atomic Scientists, http://www.fas.org/nuke/guide/israel/nuke/index.html (accessed November 28, 2007).
4. Ibid.
5. Cohen, *Israel and the Bomb*, 89; Myron Kratzer, pers.comm.
6. Hersh, *Samson Option*, 80–81.
7. Cohen, *Israel and the Bomb*, 95.
8. Ibid., 106–7; U.S. Department of State, Memorandum of Conversation, Subject: Dimona Visit, August 13, 1969, declassified January 24, 2006, courtesy David Stout, *New York Times*.
9. Author and Israeli nuclear weapons expert Avner Cohen told me the Israelis had an active uranium enrichment program at that time.
10. Gernot Zippe, facsimile transmission from Zippe in response to author's questions, March 29, 2007.
11. Ibid. Zippe apparently kept the promise for more than forty years. Although he told people about the episode privately, he said he did not want information about it to be made public until after his death. However, he agreed to answer my questions for publication, apparently realizing that word of his meetings had become more widely known.
12. Hersh, *Samson Option*, 188; Victor Gilinsky and Henry Myers, pers. comm.
13. Victor Gilinsky, pers. comm.
14. Gilinsky, "Israel's Bomb."

15. Gilinsky, "Time for More NUMEC Information."
16. Ibid.
17. Ibid. Several former government officials have downplayed the NUMEC affair, pointing out that the allegations were never proven. And there are claims that NRC officials "found" the missing material in heavily contaminated concrete flooring and piping when the plant was decommissioned in 1982. But given the sloppy record-keeping and the fact that decommissioning took place so many years after the alleged disappearance, it would be virtually impossible to prove the amount "found" was the same material that the AEC recorded as missing back in 1966. "The facts remain unclear after numerous half-hearted investigations and reinvestigations," says Gilinsky. "They [the Israelis] took tremendous risks and they never missed an opportunity to get their hands on stuff [for their bomb program]. So my conclusion is they did it."
18. Cohen, *Israel and the Bomb*, 269.
19. Ibid., 274.
20. Ibid., 273–74.
21. Avner Cohen in discussion with the author, Silver Spring, Maryland, February 6, 2007.
22. Gilinsky, "Israel's Bomb."
23. Cohen, *Israel and the Bomb*, 259–76.
24. George Hishmeh, pers. comm.
25. Davenport, Eddy, and Gillman, *Plumbat Affair*.
26. Victor Gilinsky, pers. comm.
27. Kissinger, Memorandum for the President, Subject: Israeli Nuclear Program, July 19, 1969, declassified August 23, 2007, courtesy David Stout, *New York Times*.
28. Cohen and Burr, "Israel Crosses the Threshold;" Cohen, *Israel and the Bomb*, 324–25; Hersh, *The Samson Option*, 209–11.
29. Stout, "Israel's Nuclear Arsenal Vexed Nixon."
30. Ibid.
31. Cohen and Burr, "Israel Crosses the Threshold."
32. Ibid.
33. Kissinger, Memorandum for the President, Subject: Israeli Nuclear Program, July 19, 1969, declassified August 23, 2007, courtesy David Stout, *New York Times*.
34. Leonard Weiss, pers. comm.
35. Hersh, *Samson Option*, 279–80.
36. *Sunday Times*'s Insight Team, "Revealed—The Secrets of Israel's Nuclear Arsenal/Atomic Technician Mordechai Vanunu Reveals Secret Weapons Production," October 5, 1986, http://www.timesonline.co.uk/tol/news/article830147.ece (accessed October 14, 2008).
37. BBC2, "Israel's Nuclear Whistleblower," interview with Mordecai Vanunu, May 30, 2004.
38. Yael Lotan, "The Vanunu Campaign and Its Lessons: Mordechai Vanunu—Imprisoned 1986–2004," Antiwar.com, April 24, 2004, www.antiwar.com/orig/lotan.php?articleid=2416 (accessed October 14, 2008).
39. BBC2, "Israel's Nuclear Whistleblower," interview with Mordecai Vanunu, May 30, 2004.

Chapter 14: That's the Way We Play the Game

1. Jack Edlow in discussion with the author, Kensington, Maryland, August 30, 2004.

2. Sam Edlow claimed in his self-published autobiography that the official's name was Abe Friedman, then head of the AEC's International Division; Friedman told the author that he was in London at the time and would not have phoned Edlow from there.

3. Nuclear Regulatory Commission: In the Matter of Edlow, Memorandum of conversation with J. C. Shah, chairman and chief executive, Indian Atomic Power Authority, March 8, 1973, Germantown, Exhibit 12 of testimony by Thomas B. Cochran, July 8, 1976, submission.

4. Jack Edlow in discussion with the author, Kensington, Maryland, August 30, 2004.

5. Perkovich, *India's Nuclear Bomb*, 68–73.

6. Ibid., 85.

7. Ibid., 123.

8. Ibid., 172.

9. André Finkelstein in discussion with the author, Paris, March 19, 2004; Bertrand Goldschmidt, pers. comm., circa 1990.

10. Perkovich, *India's Nuclear Bomb*, 179.

11. Ibid., 183.

12. Ibid., 115–16.

13. Myron Kratzer, pers. comm.

14. Abe Friedman, pers. comm., January 2, 2008.

15. Ibid.

16. Since Friedman says he was in London at the time and did not call Edlow, it is possible the call was placed by Harold Bengelsdorf, given his close professional association with Edlow, although that was not possible to confirm because both Edlow and Bengelsdorf had died by the time I became aware of it.

17. Perkovich, *India's Nuclear Bomb*, 183–84.

18. Ibid., 186.

19. Ibid., 185.

20. Smith, *Power Game*, 27.

21. Paul Leventhal, in discussion with the author, Washington, D.C., July 28, 2003.

22. Mazuzan and Walker, *Controlling the Atom*, 12.

23. Ibid., 32.

24. Joe Holley, "Theodore Taylor Dies; Tried to Redirect Nuclear Power," *Washington Post*, November 2, 2004, http://www.washingtonpost.com/wp-dyn/articles/A17358–2004Nov1.html (accessed October 14, 2008).

25. Edlow, *Reflections of a Lucky Man*.

26. Nuclear Regulatory Commission: In the Matter of Edlow, Brief for U.S. NRC on Petition to Review an Order of the U.S. NRC in the U.S. Court of Appeals, 1976.

27. Victor Gilinsky, pers. comm.

28. Ibid.

29. Paul Leventhal in discussion with the author, Washington, D.C., July 28, 2003.

30. Ibid.

31. Nuclear Regulatory Commission: In the Matter of Edlow, Statement of George W. Ball, July 13, 1976.

32. Nuclear Regulatory Commission: In the Matter of Edlow, Affidavit of Adrian Fisher, March 19, 1976.

33. Jimmy Carter, address to UN Conference on Nuclear Energy and World Order, May 13, 1976; reprinted in *Congressional Record* 122, no. 85, U.S. Senate, June 4, 1976.

34. Perkovich, "Nuclear Program Stalls"; Perkovich, *India's Nuclear Bomb*, 198–99.

35. Leonard Weiss in discussion with the author, Silver Spring, Maryland, July 14, 2006.

36. International Panel on Fissile Materials, Res. Rpt. 1, Mian et al., *Fissile Materials in South Asia*.

37. Bidwai, "N-deal and Beyond."

38. Ibid.

Chapter 15: A Snatched Pen

1. Corera, *Shopping for Bombs*, 8–10.

2. Perkovich, *India's Nuclear Bomb*, 130.

3. Corera, *Shopping for Bombs*, 10.

4. Myron Kratzer, pers. comm., December 2006.

5. Harold Bengelsdorf in discussion with the author, Bethesda, Maryland, July 22, 2003.

6. Corera, *Shopping for Bombs*, 12–13.

7. Ibid., 13.

8. Langewiesche, "Wrath of Khan," 64–67.

9. Corera, *Shopping for Bombs*, 5.

10. Ibid., 4.

11. Kehoe, *Enriching Troika*, http://www.urenco.com, About Urenco, history (accessed November 3, 2008).

12. Ibid., 56.

13. NTI, Pakistan Profile, source: Shahid-ur-Rehman, "Dr. A. Q. Khan: Nothing Succeeds Like Success," in *Long Road to Chagai* (Islamabad: Print Wise Publication, 1999) 51, http://www.nti.org/e_research/profiles/Pakistan/Nuclear/5593_5639 .html (accessed August 2008); NTI, Pakistan Profile, source: Steve Weissman and Herbert Krosney, "The Kindly Dr. Khan," in *The Islamic Bomb: The Nuclear Threat to Israel and the Middle East* (New York: Times Books, 1981), 180–82.

14. Corera, *Shopping for Bombs*, 14–16; NTI, Pakistan Profile, source: Steve Weissman and Herbert Krosney, "The Kindly Dr. Khan," in *The Islamic Bomb: The Nuclear Threat to Israel and the Middle East* (New York: Times Books, 1981), 180.

15. Corera, *Shopping for Bombs* 14–16.

16. Myron Kratzer, pers. comm., December 6, 2006.

17. NTI, Pakistan Profile, source: Bernard Gwertzman, Information Bank Abstracts, *New York Times*, August 10, 1976, in Lexis-Nexis Academic Universe, August 10, 1976, http://web.lexis-nexis.com; "U.S., Pakistan Discuss French A-Plant," Facts on File World News Digest, August 14, 1976, in Lexis-Nexis Academic Universe, August 14, 1976. Kratzer said that he was not in the meeting and that he remained outside the room talking with the PAEC chairman, Munir Khan, whom he had known since the late 1950s. Myron Kratzer, pers. comm., December 6, 2006.

18. NTI, Pakistan Profile, source: Information Bank Abstracts, *New York Times*, August 26, 1976; in Lexis-Nexis Academic Universe, October 13, 1976.

19. Myron Kratzer, pers. comm., December 6, 2006.

20. Corera, *Shopping for Bombs*, 23.

21. Ibid., 25.

22. Myron Kratzer, pers. comm., December 6, 2006. Kratzer also noted that "Switzerland was not in the London Suppliers Group during the Ford administration, which ended in Jan. '77. Moreover, the existence and the meetings of the group were classified and, while it is certainly possible that the Swiss knew of them from some other source, it is highly unlikely that they would have referenced the group in discussions with their companies."

23. NTI, Pakistan Profile, source: "Pakistan: A Clue to the Bomb Mystery," *Economist*, July 14, 1979, World Politics and Current Affairs, International, 60, in Lexis-Nexis Academic Universe, July 14, 1979, http://web.lexis-nexis.com.

24. NTI, Pakistan Profile, source: "Ban This Bomb-To-Be," *Economist*, April 14, 1979, World Politics and Current Affairs, International, 56, in Lexis-Nexis Academic Universe, April 14, 1979, http://web.lexis-nexis.com/; NTI, Pakistan Profile, source: Steve Weissman and Herbert Krosney, "More Bang for a Buck," *The Islamic Bomb: The Nuclear Threat to Israel and the Middle East* (New York: 1981, Times Books), 196.

25. Victor Gilinsky, pers. comm.

26. Corera, *Shopping for Bombs*, 48.

27. Coll, "Atomic Emporium."

28. Zia Mian, pers. comm.

29. Corera, *Shopping for Bombs*, 44.

30. Hersh, "On the Nuclear Edge."

31. Corera, *Shopping for Bombs*, 48.

32. Hersh, "On the Nuclear Edge."

33. Layton, "Whistle-Blower's Fight for Pension Drags On."

34. Ibid.

35. Hersh, "On the Nuclear Edge."

36. Ibid.

37. Ibid.

38. Ibid.

39. "Pakistan Nuclear Weapons: a Brief History of Pakistan's Nuclear Program," FAS WMD Around the World, Strategic Security Project, www.fas.org/nuke/guide/pakistan/nuke/index.html (accessed October 12, 2008).

40. "The Consequences of Nuclear Conflict Between India and Pakistan," Issues: Nuclear Weapons, Waste and Energy, Natural Resources Defense Council, last revised June 4, 2002, www.nrdc.org/nuclear/southasia.asp (accessed October 12, 2008).

41. International Panel on Fissile Materials, Res. Rpt. 1, Mian et al., *Fissile Materials in South Asia*.

Chapter 16: First They Drive You Crazy

1. Nusbaum, "Devine Intervention," Tom Devine, pers. comm., October 28, 2008.

2. Rogovin and Frampton, *Three Mile Island* 1:147.

3. Henry Myers, pers. comm.

4. Samuel Walker, pers. comm.
5. Rogovin and Frampton, *Three Mile Island* 1:147–48.
6. S. Walker, *Three Mile Island*, 27.
7. Rogovin and Frampton, *Three Mile Island* 1:9.
8. S. Walker, *Three Mile Island*, 54.
9. Hal Ornstein, pers. comm.
10. S. Walker, *Three Mile Island*, 58.
11. Ibid., 58–59, 141.
12. U.S. House, Subcommittee on Energy . . . , *Observations on the Reactor Safety Study*, 11.
13. U.S. House, Subcommittee on Energy . . . , *Reactor Safety Study Review*, 8.
14. Rogovin and Frampton, *Three Mile Island* 2, pt. 1, 110–11.
15. Ibid., 117–18.
16. S. Walker, *Three Mile Island*, 2, 121.
17. Rogovin and Frampton, *Three Mile Island* 1:9.
18. S. Walker, *Three Mile Island*, 74.
19. Ibid., 69.
20. U.S. House, Committee on Interior and Insular Affairs, *Reporting of Information Concerning the Accident at Three Mile Island*, citing interview by staff of the NRC Office of Inspection and Enforcement, Tape 315, pp. 17–19.
21. Henry Myers, pers. comm. August 10, 2008.
22. S. Walker, *Three Mile Island*, 80.
23. Ibid., 82–83.
24. Ibid., 124.
25. Ibid., 155.
26. Ibid., 129.
27. Ibid, 137.
28. This can occur as a result of the zirconium in the cladding reacting with water. When that happens it takes the oxygen, leaving only hydrogen.
29. S. Walker, *Three Mile Island*, 144.
30. Ibid., 138.
31. Ibid., 150–51.
32. Ibid., 176.
33. Ibid., 177.
34. Ibid., 184.
35. Ibid., 190.
36. Rogovin and Frampton, *Three Mile Island* 1:147–49. According to the report, "the 'single failure criterion' is a requirement that a system designed to carry out a specific safety function must be able to fulfill its mission in spite of the failure of any single component within the system, or failure in an associated system that supports its operation." In reviewing a reactor design, "the staff does not examine all of the systems and components in the plant, but only those deemed to be 'safety related.'"
37. Ibid., 160.
38. S. Walker, *Three Mile Island*, 233.
39. Associated Press, "Nominee for Energy Post Is Accused of Lying," December 20, 1989.
40. Wald, "Nuclear Agency Said to Lag in Seeking Out Crime."
41. Julian Greenspun, pers. comm.

42. Rogovin and Frampton, *Three Mile Island* 1:168.
43. Lyons, "Challenges Facing the NRC Administrative Judges."

Chapter 17: Vesuvius

1. Fairlie and Sumner, *Other Report on Chernobyl*, 8, 30.
2. *Second Russian Revolution*, documentary.
3. Fairlie and Sumner, *Other Report on Chernobyl*, foreword by Rebecca Harms, with statement excerpt by Kofi Annan, April 2000, 5.
4. International Nuclear Safety Advisory Group (INSAG), *Chernobyl Accident*.
5. Medvedev, *Legacy of Chernobyl*, 29.
6. INSAG, *The Chernobyl Accident*, Annex 1, 61.
7. Medvedev, *Legacy of Chernobyl*, 23–26.
8. INSAG, *Chernobyl Accident*.
9. Medvedev, *Legacy of Chernobyl*, 13.
10. David J. Krus, *Decline of the Age of Enlightenment*, chapter 11, "The Cold War," Cruise Scientific, 2008, http://www.visualstatistics.net/Catastrophe/Chernobyl/Chernobyl.htm.
11. Reed, *At the Abyss*, 267–71.
12. INSAG, *Chernobyl Accident*, Annex 1, 83.
13. Ibid., 84.
14. Medvedev, *Legacy of Chernobyl*, 132–34.
15. Ibid., 132–36.
16. Ibid., 144.
17. Ibid., 142–43.
18. Alexievich, *Voices from Chernobyl*, 156–57.
19. Medvedev, *Legacy of Chernobyl*, 50.
20. Ibid., 45, 47–48.
21. Ibid., 13.
22. *Second Russian Revolution*, documentary.
23. Alexievich, *Voices from Chernobyl*, 155–58.
24. Medvedev, *Legacy of Chernobyl*, 150–52, 186.
25. Fairlie and Sumner, *Other Report on Chernobyl*, 35.
26. Medvedev, *Legacy of Chernobyl*, 186.
27. Alexievich, *Voices from Chernobyl*, 19.
28. *Second Russian Revolution*, documentary.
29. Ibid.
30. Knapik, Ryan, and MacLachlan, "West Protests Soviet Secrecy as Radiation Spreads from Chernobyl Melt."
31. Medvedev, *Legacy of Chernobyl*, 59–60.
32. M. Edwards, "Chernobyl: Living with the Monster," 104.
33. *Second Russian Revolution*, documentary. *Izvestia* editor Ivan Laptev lamented later: "We can offer various excuses for the lack of information. But due to us, people didn't get out in time. Our excuses don't help them."
34. Medvedev, *Legacy of Chernobyl*, 149.
35. Ian Fairlie, pers. comm., September 13, 2007.
36. Cooke, "Official Reactions to Chernobyl." An April 29 memo from David Goldman, manager of the DOE's Argonne area office in Illinois, said that to "curtail

possible misinformation" department employees and contractors "are advised to avoid commenting on the situation in Russia" and "to avoid making comparison" between American reactors and Russian ones.

37. MacLachlan, "Western Scientists Wrestle with Chernobyl Meltdown Scenarios," 11.
38. Cooke, "Official Reactions to Chernobyl."
39. Fairlie and Sumner, *Other Report on Chernobyl*, 36.
40. Ibid., 9; Mycle Schneider, pers. comm., September 17, 2007.
41. Bell and Shaw, *Ecological Lessons from the Chernobyl Accident.*
42. INSAG, *Summary Report on the Post-Accident Review Meeting on the Chernobyl Accident.*
43. Fairlie and Sumner, *Other Report on Chernobyl*, 12–13; R. Edwards, "How Many More Lives Will Chernobyl Claim?"
44. Kenneth Kopecky, pers. comm., May 10, 2007.
45. World Health Organization, "Health Effects of the Chernobyl Accident and Special Health Care Programmes."
46. Alexievich, *Voices from Chernobyl*, 124.
47. Medvedev, *Legacy of Chernobyl*, 147.
48. Alexievich, *Voices from Chernobyl*, 85–88.
49. Fairlie and Sumner, *Other Report on Chernobyl*, foreword by Rebecca Harms, 5.
50. Alexievich, *Voices from Chernobyl*, 32.
51. Mike Edwards, e-mail from Tania D'Avignon, May 16, 2007, shared with author with D'Avignon's permission, May 20, 2007. D'Avignon acted as Edwards's interpreter during his reporting assignment to Chernobyl.
52. Alexievich, *Voices from Chernobyl*, 22–23.
53. Ibid., 34–36.

Chapter 18: Our Lady of the Fields

1. O'Neill, "Building the Bomb," 49.
2. St. Francis Historical Committee, *Harvest of Memories*, 34–36.
3. Ibid.
4. O'Neill, "Building the Bomb," 49; U.S. Department of Energy, *Pantex Plant.* The others included Lost Alamos; Sandia National Laboratories in Albuquerque, New Mexico; Buffalo Works in Buffalo, New York; the Burlington AEC Plant in Burlington, Iowa; the Clarksville Modification Center in Clarksville, Tennessee; and the Medina Modification Center near San Antonio, Texas. The Clarksville, Medina, and Burlington operations were closed, respectively, in 1965, 1966, and 1975, and their operations brought to Pantex.
5. Dwight D. Eisenhower, "Farewell Radio and Television Address to the American People, January 17, 1961."
6. Schwartz, introduction to *Atomic Audit*, 3–5; Makhijani, Schwartz, and Norris, "Dismantling the Bomb"; Makhijani and Schwartz, "Victims of the Bomb"; Weida, "Economic Implications of Nuclear Weapons and Nuclear Deterrence."
7. Phil Smith in discussion with the author, Panhandle, Texas, May 1994.
8. Texas Tech College, now Texas Tech University, was allowed to retain six thousand acres, but the land was gradually leased back from Texas Tech in 1984 and 1989, and the area now serves as a safety and security buffer zone south and west of the plant. U.S. Department of Energy, *Pantex Plant*, 2.

9. Phil Smith in discussion with the author, Panhandle, Texas, May 1994.
10. Photo caption from U.S. Department of Energy, *Pantex Plant*, 19.
11. O'Neill, "Building the Bomb," 49–50, n. 31.
12. Ibid.
13. Cooke, "Boom and Bust."
14. Makhijani, Schwartz, and Norris, "Dismantling the Bomb," 356–57.
15. Norris, Kosiak, and Schwartz, "Deploying the Bomb," 179, n. 176.
16. Cooke, "Boom and Bust."
17. Leroy T. Matthiesen in discussion with the author, Amarillo, Texas, May 1994.
18. Mojtabai, *Blessed Assurance*, 111–13.
19. Schwartz, "Congressional Oversight of the Bomb," 494–95.
20. Ibid., 494.
21. O'Neill, "Building the Bomb," 71.
22. *Second Russian Revolution*, documentary.
23. This covered intercontinental ballistic missiles (ICBMs), sea-launched ballistic missiles (SLBMs), and bombers, but the deal also called for the total elimination of medium-range nuclear missiles in Europe and an agreement on both sides to retain the ABM (Anti-Ballistic Missile) Treaty for ten years.
24. Federation of American Scientists (FAS), "Weapons of Mass Destruction: Intermediate-Range Nuclear Forces," www.fas.org/nuke/control/inf/index.html (accessed October 13, 2008).
25. *Second Russian Revolution*, documentary.
26. Ibid.
27. Reed, *At the Abyss*, introduction by George H. W. Bush, 1–2.
28. Ibid.
29. Robert Norris, pers. comm.; U.S. Department of State, Strategic Arms Reduction Treaties, 1991 and 1993, http://www.state.gov (accessed August 31, 2008). At the end of the cold war, the United States had approximately twenty-two thousand warheads, about a third less than the stockpile's historic high in 1967. The Soviet warhead count in 1991 was estimated at about thirty thousand against a total output of fifty-five thousand nuclear weapons since 1949. "Nuclear Notebook: "Global Nuclear Stockpiles, 1945–2006," July/August 2006, and "Nuclear Notebook: The U.S. Nuclear Stockpile, Today and Tomorrow," September/October 2007, *Bulletin of Atomic Scientists*, http://www.thebulletin.org.
30. Makhijani, Schwartz, and Weida, "Nuclear Waste Management and Environmental Remediation," 356.
31. *Uranium Intelligence Weekly*, "Yucca Mountain Total Cost Estimates Revised Upward—Way Upward."
32. Robert Alvarez in discussion with the author, Takoma Park, Maryland, June 28, 2007.
33. Ibid.
34. Schwartz, introduction to *Atomic Audit*, 17; Pike, Blair, and Schwartz, "Defending Against the Bomb," 293–95. In one case, an explosive that could be detonated from the ground was placed inside the intended target. That ensured the illusion of a direct hit when the missile was fired. In another test, the target vehicle was artificially heated to provide a better infrared signature for the interceptor. This was meant to boost the chances of a hit but proved unnecessary—the interceptor never came close enough to the target to make an explosion appear credible.
35. Makhijani and Schwartz, "Victims of the Bomb," 421–26.

36. *Nuclear Tango*, documentary.
37. Weida, "Economic Implications of Nuclear Weapons and Nuclear Deterrence," 528-29.
38. Ibid., 531.
39. Alvarez, "Reducing the Risks of High-level Radioactive Wastes at Hanford"; Robert Alvarez in discussion with the author, Takoma Park, Maryland, June 28, 2007.
40. Ibid.
41. Robert Alvarez, pers. comm., November 4, 2008.
42. Brian Neill, "From Tritium to 2x4s," *Columbia* (S.C.) *Free Press*, November 29–December 5, 2000.
43. Robert Alvarez, pers. comm., November 4, 2008.
44. Makhijani, Schwartz, and Weida, "Nuclear Waste Management and Environmental Remediation," 373.
45. Cooke, "Boom and Bust."
46. U.S. Department of Energy, Public Meeting, Workers' Compensation Initiative, June 29, 2000, http://www.defendingscience.org/upload/Hearing_Pantex.pdf (accessed August 2008).
47. Makhijani, Schwartz, and Norris, "Dismantling the Bomb," 331 n. 7.
48. Robert Alvarez in discussion with the author, Takoma Park, Maryland, June 28, 2007.
49. Cooke, "Boom and Bust."
50. Frank von Hippel in discussion with the author, Princeton, New Jersey, October 24, 2006.
51. Ibid.
52. Ibid.; Robert Civiak in discussion with the author, June 5, 2007.
53. Cooke, "Boom and Bust."
54. Ibid.
55. Doris Smith, pers. comm., 2003.
56. Ibid.

Chapter 19: Maggie's Blue-Eyed Boys

1. Brian Flowers in discussion with the author, London, February 26, 2004.
2. Royal Commission on Environmental Pollution, *Nuclear Power and the Environment*; Patterson, *Plutonium Business*, 100.
3. Royal Commission on Environmental Pollution, *Nuclear Power and the Environment*, par. 533.
4. Ibid, par. 512.
5. Ibid, pars. 532 and 535.
6. Patterson, *Plutonium Business*, 100.
7. David Lowry, pers. comm., September 12, 2007.
8. The Scottish generating boards and their distribution networks also were to be included in the sale. The CEGB was to be broken into two competing organizations of unequal size, with nuclear power going into the larger company, National Power, with a smaller company called PowerGen. The grid was to be split off as a separate entity and jointly owned by twelve regional distribution companies. Price, *Political Electricity*, 137.
9. Kjell Pettersson, "20th Anniversary of an Historic Battle: The British Miners

Strike," translated from April 8, 2004, issue of *Internationalen* by Socialist Action, http://www.geocities.com/mnsocialist/britishminers.html (accessed August 2008).

10. Eric Price in discussion with the author, London, November 20, 2002.

11. Pettersson, Kjell, "20th Anniversary," as in n. 9 above.

12. Lawson, *View from No. 11*, 168–70.

13. Ibid.

14. Today the figures for Magnox decommissioning are broadly estimated at two billion pounds per reactor, for a total of eighteen billion pounds, according to Britain's Nuclear Decommissioning Authority.

15. Steve Thomas in discussion with the author by phone, August 14, 2008.

16. Price, *Political Electricity*, 142.

17. Lawson, *View from No. 11*, 170.

18. Roger Howsley in discussion with the author, Sellafield, April 30, 2007.

19. Ibid.

20. Paul Robson in discussion with the author, Sellafield, April 31, 2007. Mycle Schneider, a Paris-based energy and nuclear consultant and founder of the energy information service WISE-Paris, calculates that the tanks contain about eighty times the amount of radioactive cesium-137 released by Chernobyl, as well as many other long-lived radionuclides. Critics of Sellafield believe a malevolent disruption of the plant—B215—by terrorists is more likely than a successful plutonium heist.

21. In 2007 the UK National Decommissioning Authority estimated that the undiscounted cost of decommissioning its nineteen sites over one hundred years was £61 billion, with an additional £12 billion needed to run operating sites to the end of their commercial lives. The £73 billion total was 18 percent higher than the 2005 estimate and does not cover the back-end costs associated with advanced gas-cooled reactors. Source, National Audit Office Press Notice, "The Nuclear Decommissioning Authority: Taking forward decommissioning," January 2008, http://www.nao.org.uk/pn/07-08/0708238.htm.

22. The research was undertaken by Dr. N. D. Priest, then of the Atomic Energy Authority's biomedical research department at Harwell. It was reported in *The Science of the Total Environment 201* (1997): 235–43 and also in the *News Scientist Journal*, August 2, 1997. CoreCumbria, http://www.corecumbria.co.uk (accessed October 14, 2008).

23. Ibid.

24. Martin Forwood and Janine Allis-Smith, pers. comm., April 30, 2007.

25. Sanderson identified the area in question as being near Muncaster Bridge in the Esk Valley.

26. David Sanderson in discussion with the author by phone, April 26, 3007.

27. Thomas, "UK Decommissioning Funds."

28. Thomas, "Collapse of British Energy."

29. Paul Brown, "Huge Radioactive Leak Closes Thorp Nuclear Plant," *Guardian*, May 9, 2005, http://www.guardian.co.uk/nuclear/article/0,2763,1479527,00 .html (accessed October 14, 2008).

30. Mycle Schneider in discussion with the author, May 31, 2004. Schneider, *Nuclear Power in France.*

31. Sciolino, "Voting Sets Up Left-Right Duel to Lead France."

32. Schneider, *Nuclear Power in France.*

33. Ibid.; Schneider, *Myths and Realities on Nuclear Power in the World.*

34. Based on the average routine discharges between 1999 and 2003, the global dose from annual discharges for the planned remaining life of the La Hague facilities implies a theoretical toll of more than three thousand fatal cancers, according to Schneider.

35. International Panel of Fissile Materials, Res. Rpt. 4, Schneider and Marignac, *Spent Fuel Reprocessing in France.*

36. *Uranium Intelligence Weekly,* "Sellafield's Future: To Call It Quits or Make More Plutonium?"

37. Schneider and Marignac estimate some twelve thousand metric tons, of which two thirds are stored at La Hague, the equivalent of of ten years' throughput at current reprocessing rates.

38. A report commissioned by the French prime minister in 2000 concluded that for the entire French nuclear program, the reprocessing option would lead to an average increase in generation costs of 5.5 percent, or an 85 percent rise in "back-end" costs. These are guesses, to say the least, since no one knows for certain what direct disposal will end up costing, but they do provide a general indication of what is at stake.

39. International Panel on Fissile Materials, Res. Rpt. 3, von Hippel, *Managing Spent Fuel in the United States.*

40. Ball, "France's Nuclear Push Transforms Energy Equation."

41. Brian Flowers, pers. comm., March 23, 2007.

Chapter 20: The "Five Who Control the World"— How Much Longer?

1. Vicki Silverman, "House Hears Iraq Could Construct a Nuclear Device in Six Months," Washington File, Office of International Information Programs, U.S. Department of State, September 12, 2002, http://www.usinfo.org/wf-archive/2002/020912/epf406.htm (accessed October 14, 2008).

2. Cooke, "Boom and Bust."

3. Cooke, "Time to Get Tough with Nuclear Villians."

4. Ibid.

5. Rolf Ekeus in discussion with the author, The Hague, February 19, 2003.

6. Wolf Blitzer, "Search for the Smoking Gun," CNN.com, January 10, 2003, http://www.cnn.com/2003/US/01/10/wbr.smoking.gun.

7. Broad, "U.S. Ignored Early Alert on Iraqi Nuclear Project"; Broad, "Energy Agency Opens Files on Iraq"; Safire, "What Was Iraq Supposed to Be Doing for America."

8. "Nuclear Notebook: Global Nuclear Stockpiles, 1945–2006," Norris acknowledges that this number may be on the low side, assuming Israel has more than the sixty to eighty-five warheads included in the estimate.

9. Ibid.; Albright and O'Neill, *Challenges of Fissile Material Control.*

10. Ibid.

11. Richter, "Suppose You Were a Reactor Inspector."

12. Ibid.

13. Cooke, "Time to Get Tough with Nuclear Villains."

14. U.S. Department of State, *Report on the International Control of Atomic Energy,* 5.

15. Namibia was still part of South Africa and known as South-West Africa.

16. Ronnie Walker in discussion with the author, King's Down near Box, England, October 13, 2003.

17. At least three of the students that attended the MIT program would spend their careers building the Iranian nuclear program, according to a 2007 *Boston Globe* investigation that tracked down twenty-eight of the program's thirty-five graduates. Stockman, "Iran's Nuclear Vision First Glimpsed at MIT."

18. *Uranium Intelligence Weekly*, "Russian Fuel Shipments to Bushehr Raise More Questions about Iranian Fuel Cycle."

19. Iran has only a small research reactor with minimal uranium requirements and a Russian-made reactor at Bushehr, but the fuel for that is supplied by Russia. Its own uranium producton is well under one hundred metric tons per year. *Uranium Intelligence Weekly*, December 17, 2007. The bomb calculation assumes 20 percent HEU per bomb and 90 percent final assay. In order to be fed into the enrichment plant, the natural uranium would have first been converted into gas. That may have taken place in France, since the Iranians only began operating their own conversion plant relatively recently.

20. Edlow, "Reflections of a Lucky Man."

21. "The South African Peaceful Nuclear Program: Its Dependence upon Foreign Assistance," National Foreign Assessment Center, CIA, November 1979, Top Secret, released September 2001.

22. Walt Wolf in discussion with the author, Bethesda, Maryland, July 22, 2003, August 11, 2005, and subsequent communication.

23. Ibid.

24. Edlow, *Reflections of a Lucky Man.*

25. Leonard Weiss, pers. comm., December 15, 2006.

26. Corera, *Shopping for Bombs*, 86–87.

27. Ibid., 93.

28. Ibid., 94.

29. Andrew Natsios, "The Politics of Famine in North Korea," Special Report No. 51, United States Institute of Peace, August 2, 1999, http://www.usip.org/pubs/specialreports/sr990802.html (accessed October 14, 2008).

30. Corera, *Shopping for Bombs*, 131–36. In the five years prior to his downfall in 2004, the list of countries he visited included Afghanistan, Egypt, Iran, Ivory Coast, Kazakhstan, Kenya, Mali, Mauritania, Morocco, Niger, Nigeria, North Korea, Saudi Arabia, Senegal, Sudan, Syria, Tunisia, the United Arab Emirates, and China.

31. Coll, "Atomic Emporium."

32. Corera, *Shopping for Bombs*, 208, 221.

33. Syed Irfan Raza, "A.Q. Khan Regrets 'Confession,'" *Dawn, the Internet Edition*, May 30, 2008, http://www.dawn.com/2008/05/30/top4.htm (accessed August 16, 2008).

34. "IAEA Presses Iran to Comply with Nuclear Safeguards," *Arms Control Today*, July/August 2003, http://www.armscontrol.org/act/2003_07-08/iran_julaug03 (accessed October 14, 2008). The China link was sourced to a State Department official.

35. "Implementation of the NPT Safeguards Agreement in the Islamic Republic of Iran," IAEA Board of Governors, November 10, 2003, http://www.iaea.org/Publications/Documents/Board/2003/gov2003-75.pdf (accessed October 14, 2008).

36. Institute for Science and International Security, "Briefing Notes from February 2008 IAEA Meeting Regarding Iran's Nuclear Program."

37. Broad and Sanger, "Vienna Meeting on Arms Data Reignites Dispute with Iran over Nuclear Program."

38. Institute for Science and International Security, "Briefing Notes from February 2008 IAEA Meeting Regarding Iran's Nuclear Program."

39. Dan Koik, "Brazil Denies IAEA Full Access to Enrichment Sites," *Arms Control Today*, May 2004, http://www.armscontrol.org/act/2004_11/Brazil (accessed October 14, 2008).

40. Sharon Squassoni and David Fite, "Brazil as Litmus Test: Resende and Restrictions on Uranium Enrichment," *Arms Control Today*, October 2005, http://www.armscontrol.org/act/2005_10/Oct-Brazil (accessed October 14, 2008).

41. Ibid.

42. Claire Applegarth, "Brazil Permits Greater IAEA Inspection," *Arms Control Today*, November 2004, www.armscontrol.org/act/2004_11/Brazil (accessed October 14, 2008).

43. Lilienthal, *Journals*, 229. The political reasons, he said, were to deflate criticism that the AEC wasn't moving fast enough on the civilian front and that the United States was preventing other countries from developing nuclear power.

44. Krutch, *Modern Temper*, 43.

45. Nabil Fahmy in discussion with the author, Embassy of Egypt, Washington, D.C., June 14, 2006.

Chapter 21: A Broken Promise

1. Norris and Kristensen, "What's Behind Bush's Nuclear Cuts?"

2. Easlea, "Conflict, Science and the Garden of Eden."

3. The stockpile reached its historic high in 1967 of more than 32,000 warheads of thirty different types. "Nuclear Notebook," Sept.-Oct. 2007.

4. Lilienthal, *Journals*, 127.

5. Warrick and Pincus, "Saga of a Bent Spear."

6. "Nuclear Facts: New nuclear power plants are unlikely . . ." Sixteen countries depend on nuclear power for at least a quarter of their electricity. France and Lithuania get around three-quarters of their power from nuclear energy, while Belgium, Bulgaria, Hungary, Slovakia, South Korea, Sweden, Switzerland, Slovenia, and Ukraine get one-third or more. Japan, Germany, and Finland get more than a quarter of their power from nuclear energy, while the USA gets almost one-fifth. World Nuclear Association, http://www.world-nuclear.org (accessed August 25, 2008).

7. Enclosure: From Commander, Joint Task Force One, To Joint Chiefs of Staff, NCR 4813, July 17, 1946, U.S. Joint Chiefs of Staff, Records of Operation Crossroads, National Archives, declassified January 28, 1975.

8. Victor Gilinsky, pers. comm.

9. "Tritium Production Licenses Granted to Civilian Power Plants," *Arms Control Today*, November 2002, www.armscontrol.org/act/2002_11/tritiumnov02 (accessed October 14, 2008).

10. Steve Thomas, pers. comm., September 2008.

11. U.S. Department of Energy, "Nuclear Power 2010," February 14, 2002.

12. Gagarinskii, "Nuclear Renaissance."

13. "Nuclear Facts: New nuclear power plants are unlikely . . ."

14. *Uranium Intelligence Weekly*, "A $25 Billion Preholiday Gift for Nuclear?"

15. U.S. Department of Energy, "16th Annual International Conference on Nuclear Engineering, Remarks as Prepared for Delivery for Assistant Secretary Dennis Spurgeon," May 12, 2008, http://www.doe.gov/6252.html (accessed August 25, 2008).

16. *Uranium Intelligence Weekly*, "Omnibus Spending Bill Retains $20.5 Billion for Nuclear."

17. NUKEM, "Nuclear Renaissance: USA—Coping with New NPP Sticker Shock."

18. *Uranium Intelligence Weekly*, "Year of the Renaissance for US?"

19. "Emerging Asia Drives World Energy Use in the International Energy Outlook 2004," Energy Information Administration, Official Energy Statistics from the U.S. Government, April 14, 2004, http://www.eia.doe.gov/neic/press/press235.html (accessed August 25, 2008).

20. Joe Colvin in discussion with the author, London WNA Conference, September 2002.

21. Schneider, *Residual Risk*.

22. Gilinsky, "Heard About the Near-Accident at the Ohio Nuclear Plant?"

23. Henry, "Davis-Besse 'Deception' Trial to Begin."

24. U.S. Government Accountability Office, *Nuclear Safety: NRC's Oversight of Fire Protection at U.S. Commercial Nuclear Reactor Units Could Be Strengthened.*

25. Schneider, *Residual Risk*.

26. Ibid.

27. Mycle Schneider, pers. comm.

28. "Japanese Nuclear Leak Bigger Than First Reported Says Power Company," CBC News, http://www.cbc.ca/world/story/2007/07/18/japan-nuclear.html (accessed October 14, 2009).

29. Schneider, *Residual Risk*, 11.

30. Stecklow, "Nuclear Safety Reports Called into Question."

31. Ibid.

32. Schneider, *Residual Risk*, 11.

33. "Waste Confidence and Waste Challenges: Managing Radioactive Materials," remarks prepared for NRC chairman Dale E. Klein, Waste Management Symposium, Phoenix, Arizona, February 25, 2008, http://www.nrc.gov/reading-rm/doc-collections/commission/speeches/2008/s-08-008.html (accessed August 2008).

34. *Uranium Intelligence Weekly*, "License Extensions Under Fire in the U.S."; U.S. NRC Inspector General Reports: FY 2007 Index, "Audit of NRC's License Renewal Program," September 6, 2007, http://www.nrc.gov/reading-rm/doc-collections/insp-gen/2007/ (accessed August 2008).

35. Hal Ornstein and Victor Gilinsky, pers. comm.

36. Schneider, *Residual Risk*; Mayo, "The Big Duck Shoot;" Wald, "Gate Crasher Shakes Up Nuclear Debate."

37. "Pipe Bomb Incident at Palo Verde Nuclear Power Station—Worker Identified,"

National Terror Alert Response Center, November 2, 2007, http://www
.nationalterroralert.com/updates/2007/11/02/pipe-bomb-incident-at-palo-
verde-nuclear-power-station-worker-identified (accessed October 14, 2008).

38. Schneider, *Residual Risk*, 86–87.

39. Statement of NRC Chairman Dale E. Klein at Peach Bottom Nuclear Power
Plant in Pennsylvania, February 8, 2008, NRC Office of Public Affairs, http://
www.nrc.gov/reading-rm/doc-collections/commission/speeches/2008/s-08-
004.html (accessed October 14, 2008).

40. Mufson, "Video of Sleeping Guards Shakes Nuclear Industry."

41. Spent fuel generates approximately 2 megawatts per metric ton immediately
after removal from the reactor, falling to 1,300 watts per metric ton after forty
years. Long and Ewing, *Yucca Mountain*.

42. Statement of Dr. Phillip J. Finck, Deputy Associate Laboratory Director for
Applied Science and Technology and National Security, Argonne National
Laboratory, before the House Committee on Science, Energy Subcommittee
Hearing on Nuclear Fuel Reprocessing, June 16, 2005.

43. Robert Alvarez, pers. comm., November 4, 2008.

44. Meeting Minutes, Yankee Rowe Community Advisory Board, September 24,
1998, http://www.yankeerowe.com/september_24_1998.html (accessed August
2008).

45. U.S. Nuclear Regulatory Commission, 10 CFR 51.23: Temporary storage of
spent fuel after cessation of reactor operation—generic determination of no
significant environmental impact. This confidence was apparently first expressed in 1984 but has since been reaffirmed in 2007; http://www.nrc.gov/
reading-rm/doc-collections/cfr/part051/part051-0023.html (accessed August
2008).

46. Whitney, "With Democrats in Control, Yucca Project May Be Doomed."

47. Long and Ewing, *Yucca Mountain*.

48. Gilinsky, " 'Miracle Metal' and Embarrassment for Yucca Backers."

49. Existing reactors are projected to create a total of seventy thousand metric
tons of waste over their lifetimes, but that does not include waste arising from
recent twenty-year extensions granted to about forty reactors, which would
significantly increase that amount.

50. Victor Gilinsky, pers. comm.

51. Estimate by Frank von Hippel.

52. U.S. Department of Energy, "16th Annual International Conference on Nuclear Engineering, Remarks as Prepared for Delivery for Assistant Secretary
Dennis Spurgeon," May 12, 2008, http://www.doe.gov/6252.html.

53. Charles Ferguson of the Council on Foreign Relations, remarks delivered at
Carnegie International Nonproliferation Conference, June 26, 2007; Keystone
Center, *Nuclear Power Joint Fact-Finding*; Pacala and Socolow, "Toward a Hy-
drogen Economy."

54. *Uranium Intelligence Weekly*, "Japan Steel Works: A Key to Nuclear Revival"; *Uranium Intelligence Weekly*, "TVO Announces Further Delays."

55. Stephen Pacala, pers. comm.; The Climate Group, October 15, 2004, http://
theclimategroup.org/index.php/viewpoint/stephen_pacala (accessed October
14, 2008).

56. This assumes a favorable case for nuclear in which "by 2021 nuclear tax credits stimulate 1.5 times the amount of subsidized capacity, and with an average

capacity utilization factor of 85 percent, the $0.85 \times 9,000$ MW $= 7,650$ MW/15 years $= 510$ MW/yr as the average annual expected growth for nuclear, but with none of it available for at least 10 years. Even though wind has a much lower capacity utilization factor, and even assuming no further acceleration in its rate of growth, then $0.35 \times 3,000$ MW $\times 15$ years $= 15,750$ MW for wind over the same period, or at least 1,050 MW/yr, with all of it available each year." "Nuclear Facts: New nuclear plants are unlikely . . ."

57. Congressional Research Service, CRS-IB10041, June 2005.
58. Union of Concerned Scientists, "Renewable Energy Tax Credit Extended Again, but Risk of Boom-Bust Cycles in World Industry Continues," February 14, 2007, http://www.ucsusa.org.
59. Worldwatch Institute, "Nuclear Prospects Unclear," *Environmental Valuation & Cost-Benefit News*, July 1, 2008, http://www.envirovaluation.org/index .php/2008/07/01/nuclear_prospects_unclear (accessed October 25, 2008).
60. World Nuclear Association, London, http://www.world-nuclear.org/info/inf17 .html (accessed August 2008).
61. Stephen Pacala, pers. comm.; The climate group, October 15, 2004, http:// www.theclimategroup.org/index/php/viewpoint/stephen_pacala (accessed October 14, 2008).
62. Lovins, "Mighty Mice."
63. The story was told to me by a DOE press secretary while we sat in Clay's office waiting for him to turn up for an interview.
64. Civiak, *Still at It.*
65. The text of the "Atoms for Peace" speech is in Chernus, *Eisenhower's Atoms for Peace*, xi–xix.
66. Finn, "Putin Threatens Ukraine on NATO"; Myers and Shanker, "Aides to Bush Say Russia Offensive Jeopardizes Ties."
67. Arms Control Association, "U.S.-Russian Nuclear Arms Control Agreements at a Glance," March 2010, http://www.armscontrol.org/factsheets/USRussia Nuclear AgreementsMarch2010 (accessed March 28, 2010).
68. H. A. Feiveson, "Nuclear Power, Nuclear Proliferation, and Global Warming."
69. International Institute for Strategic Studies, *Nuclear Programmes in the Middle East: In the Shadow of Iran.*
70. Nabil Fahmy in discussion with the author, Embassy of Egypt, Washington, D.C., June 14, 2006.
71. Bidwai, "N-deal and beyond."
72. Duarte, "Moral Leadership and Nuclear Weapons."
73. NFL Valuations, Washington Redskins, www.forbes.com/lists/2005/30/300925 .html (accessed October 14, 2008).
74. Hinde and Rotblat, *War No More*, 215.
75. Dwight D. Eisenhower, "Farewell Radio and Television Address to the American People, January 17, 1961."

Selected Bibliography

Books

Alexievich, Svetlana. *Voices from Chernobyl*. Trans. and preface by Keith Gessen. Normal, Ill., and London: Dalkey Archive Press, 2005.

Allen, Thomas B., and Norman Polmar. *Why Truman Dropped the Atomic Bomb on Japan, Code-Name Downfall: The Secret Plan to Invade Japan*. Washington: Ross and Perry, 2003.

Ben-Menashe, Ari. *Profits of War: Inside the Secret U.S.-Israeli Arms Network*. New York: Sheridan Square Press, 1992.

Bird, Kai, and Lawrence Lifschultz. *Hiroshima's Shadow*. Stony Creek, Ct.: Pamphleteer's Press, 1998.

Bok, Sissela. *Secrets: On the Ethics of Concealment and Revelation*. New York: Vintage Books, 1989.

Bothwell, Robert. *Eldorado: Canada's National Uranium Company*. Toronto, Buffalo, and London: University of Toronto Press, 1984.

Brenner, Michael J. *Nuclear Power and Non-Proliferation: The Remaking of U.S. Policy*. Cambridge: Cambridge University Press, 1981.

Bundy, McGeorge. *Danger and Survival: Choices About the Bomb in the First Fifty Years*. New York: Random House, 1988.

Bupp, Irvin C., and Jean-Claude Derian. *Light Water: How the Nuclear Dream Dissolved*. New York: Basic Books, 1978.

Burrows, William E., and Robert Windrem. *Critical Mass: The Dangerous Race for Superweapons in a Fragmenting World*. London: Simon and Schuster, 1994.

Caldicott, Helen. *The New Nuclear Danger: George W. Bush's Military-Industrial Complex*. New York: New Press, 2002.

Chang, Laurence, and Peter Kornbluh. *The Cuban Missile Crisis, 1962*. New York: The New Press, 1992, 1998.

Chernus, Ira. *Eisenhower's Atoms for Peace*. College Station: Texas A&M University Press, 2002.

Cochran, Thomas B., Robert S. Norris, and Oleg A. Bukharin. *Making the Russian Bomb from Stalin to Yeltsin*. Boulder, Colo.: Westview Press, 1995.

Cohen, Avner. *Israel and the Bomb*. New York: Columbia University Press, 1998.

Coit, Margaret L. *Mr. Baruch*. Boston: Houghton Mifflin, 1957.

Corera, Gordon. *Shopping for Bombs: Nuclear Proliferation, Global Insecurity, and the Rise and Fall of the A. Q. Khan Network.* Oxford and New York: Oxford University Press, 2006.

Crankshaw, Edward. *Khrushchev Remembers.* Boston: Bantam Books, 1971.

Curie, Eve. *Madame Curie: A Biography.* Trans. Vincent Sheean. New York: Literary Guild of America, 1937.

Daniel, Peter. *Against All Odds: A History of Namibia's Rossing.* Rössing, Namibia: 1995.

Davenport, Elaine, Paul Eddy, and Peter Gillman. *The Plumbat Affair.* Philadelphia and New York: J. B. Lippincott, 1978.

Dyson, Freeman. *Disturbing the Universe.* New York: Basic Books, 1979.

Eggleston, Wilfrid. *Canada's Nuclear Story.* London: Harrap Research Publications, 1966.

Einstein, Albert. *Einstein on Peace,* ed. Otto Nathan and Heinz Norden. New York: Avenel Books, 1981.

Fischer, David. *History of the International Atomic Energy Agency, the First Forty Years.* Vienna: IAEA, 1997.

Fuller, John G. *We Almost Lost Detroit.* New York: Reader's Digest Press, 1975.

Garbutt, Gordon C. *Uranium in Canada: Nuclear Progress in Canada.* Ottawa: Eldorado Mining and Refining, 1964.

Goldschmidt, Bertrand. *The Atomic Complex: A Worldwide Political History of Nuclear Energy.* La Grange Park, Ill.: American Nuclear Society, 1982.

———. *Atomic Rivals.* New Brunswick and London: Rutgers University Press, 1990.

Gray, Earle. *The Great Uranium Cartel.* Toronto: McClelland and Stewart, 1982.

Gray, Mike, and Ira Rosen. *The Warning: Accident at Three Mile Island—A Nuclear Omen for the Age of Terror.* New York and London: W. W. Norton, 1982.

Greene, Graham. *The Third Man.* 1950; London: Penguin Books, 1971.

Grodzins, Morton, and Eugene Rabinowitch, eds. *The Atomic Age: Scientists in National and World Affairs, Selections from the Bulletin of Atomic Scientists.* New York: Simon and Schuster, 1965.

Groves, Leslie M. *Now It Can Be Told: The Story of the Manhattan Project.* New York: Da Capo Press, 1962.

Haber, Heinz. *The Walt Disney Story of Our Friend the Atom.* New York: Simon and Schuster, 1956.

Hecht, Gabrielle. *The Radiance of France: Nuclear Power and National Identity After World War II.* Cambridge: Massachusetts Institute of Technology, 1998.

Heisenberg, Werner. *Physics and Philosophy.* 1958; London: Penguin Books, 2000.

Herken, Gregg. *The Winning Weapon: The Atomic Bomb in the Cold War, 1945–1950.* New York: Alfred A. Knopf, 1980.

Hersey, John. *Hiroshima.* New York: Alfred A. Knopf, 1946.

Hersh, Seymour M. *The Samson Option: Israel, America and the Bomb.* New York: Random House, 1991.

Hinde, Robert, and Joseph Rotblat. *War No More: Eliminating Conflict in the Nuclear Age.* London and Sterling, Va.: Pluto Press, 2003.

Holloway, David. *Stalin and the Bomb: The Soviet Union and Atomic Energy, 1939–1956.* New Haven and London: Yale University Press, 1994.

Hughes, Donald J. *The Neutron Story.* Garden City, N.Y.: Doubleday Anchor Books, 1959.

Hurley, Patrick M. *How Old Is the Earth?* Garden City: Doubleday Anchor Books, 1959.

International Atomic Energy Agency, Personal Reflections. Vienna: IAEA Division of Publications, 1997.

International Physicians for the Prevention of Nuclear War and the Institute for Energy and Environmental Research. *Plutonium: Deadly Gold of the Nuclear Age.* Cambridge, Mass.: International Physicians Press, 1992.

Isaacson, Walter, and Evan Thomas. *The Wise Men: Six Friends and the World They Made.* New York: Simon and Schuster, 1986.

Jungk, Robert. *Brighter than a Thousand Suns: A Personal History of the Atomic Scientists.* New York: Harcourt, Brace 1958.

———. *The Nuclear State.* London: John Calder, 1979.

Kampfner, John. *Blair's Wars.* London: Free Press, 2003.

Karpin, Michael. *The Bomb in the Basement: How Israel Went Nuclear and What That Means for the World.* New York, London, Toronto, and Sydney: Simon and Schuster Paperbacks, 2006.

Kehoe, R. B. *The Enriching Troika: A History of Urenco to the Year 2000.* Marlow, UK: Urenco Limited, 2002.

Kennan, George F. *Memoirs, 1925–1950.* Boston and Toronto: Atlantic Monthly Press/Little, Brown, 1967.

Kissinger, Henry A. *Nuclear Weapons and Foreign Policy.* New York: Doubleday, 1957.

Krutch, Joseph Wood. *The Modern Temper.* New York: Harcourt, Brace & World, 1929.

Lawson, Nigel. *The View from No. 11.* London: Corgi, 1993.

Laxalt, Robert. *A Private War: An American Code Officer in the Belgian Congo.* Reno: University of Nevada Press, 1998.

Lettow, Paul. *Ronald Reagan and His Quest to Abolish Nuclear Weapons.* New York: Random House, 2005.

Letwin, Oliver. *Privatising the World: A Study of International Privatisation in Theory and Practice.* London: Cassell, 1988.

Leventhal, Paul, Sharon Tanzer, and Steven Dolley. *Nuclear Power and the Spread of Nuclear Weapons: Can We Have One Without the Other?* Washington: Brassey's, 2002.

Lilienthal, David E. *The Journals of David E. Lilienthal,* vol. 2, *The Atomic Energy Years, 1945–1950.* New York: Harper and Row, 1964.

Mann, James. *Rise of the Vulcans: The History of Bush's War Cabinet.* New York: Viking Penguin, 2004.

Mazuzan, George T., and J. Samuel Walker. *Controlling the Atom: The Beginnings of Nuclear Regulation, 1946–1962.* Washington: U.S. Nuclear Regulatory Commission, 1997.

McKeown, William. *Idaho Falls: The Untold Story of America's First Nuclear Accident.* Toronto: ECW Press, 2003.

McMillan, Priscilla J. *The Ruin of J. Robert Oppenheimer and the Birth of the Modern Arms Race.* New York: Viking Penguin, 2005.

McPhee, John. *The Curve of Binding Energy.* New York: Farrar, Straus and Giroux, 1973.

McSorley, Jean. *Living in the Shadow: The Story of the People of Sellafield.* London and Sydney: Pan Books, 1990.

Medvedev, Zhores A. *The Legacy of Chernobyl*. New York and London: W. W. Norton, 1990.

Metzger, H. Peter. *The Atomic Establishment*. New York: Simon and Schuster, 1972.

Miller, Judith, and Laurie Mylroie. *Saddam Hussein and the Crisis in the Gulf*. New York: Times Books, 1990.

Mogren, Eric W. *Warm Sands: Uranium Mill Tailings Policy in the Atomic West*. Albuquerque: University of New Mexico Press, 2002.

Mojtabai, A. G. *Blessèd Assurance: At Home with the Bomb in Amarillo*. Boston: Houghton Mifflin, 1987.

Moleah, Alfred T. *Namibia: The Struggle for Liberation*. Wilmington, Del.: Disa Press, 1983.

Moss, Thomas H., and David L. Sills, eds. *The Three Mile Island Nuclear Accident: Lessons and Implications*. New York: New York Academy of Sciences, 1981.

Murray, Stuart. *Koeberg: Eskom's Nuclear Success Story*. Cape Town: Churchill Murray Publications, 1994.

Newby-Fraser, A. R. *Chain Reaction: Twenty Years of Nuclear Research and Development in South Africa*. Pretoria: South African Atomic Energy Board, 1979.

Norris, Robert S. *Racing for the Bomb: General Leslie R. Groves, the Manhattan Project's Indispensable Man*. South Royalton, Vt.: Steerforth Press, 2002.

Oudes, Bruce, ed. *From: The President—Richard Nixon's Secret Files*. London: Andre Deutsch, 1989.

Patterson, Walter C., for the Nuclear Control Institute. *The Plutonium Business and the Spread of the Bomb*. London: Paladin Books (Granada), 1984.

Perkovich, George. *India's Nuclear Bomb: The Impact on Global Proliferation*. Berkeley and Los Angeles: University of California Press, 2001.

Pollack, Kenneth M. *The Threatening Storm: The Case for Invading Iraq*. New York: Council on Foreign Relations, Random House, 2002.

Polmar, Norman, and John D. Gresham. *Defcon-2: Standing on the Brink of Nuclear War During the Cuban Missile Crisis*. Hoboken, N.J.: John Wiley & Sons, 2006.

Polmar, Norman, and Thomas B. Allen. *Rickover, Admiral of the Nuclear Fleet—Controversy and Genius: A Biography*. Washington: Ross and Perry, 2003.

———. *The Spy Book: The Encyclopedia of Espionage*. New York: Random House, 2004.

Price, Terence. *Political Electricity: What Future for Nuclear Energy?* Oxford: Oxford University Press, 1990.

———. *Political Physicist: A Memoir*. Unpublished version shared with author; since published in Sussex, England: The Book Guild, 2004.

Pringle, Peter, and James Spigelman. *The Nuclear Barons*. London: Sphere Books, 1983.

Quinn, Susan. *Marie Curie: A Life*. New York: Simon and Schuster, 1995.

Reed, Thomas C. *At the Abyss: An Insider's History of the Cold War*. New York: Random House, 2004.

Reid, Robert. *Marie Curie*. New York: Mentor-Times Mirror, 1974.

Reston, James. *Deadline: A Memoir*. New York: Random House, 1991.

Rhodes, Richard. *Dark Sun: The Making of the Hydrogen Bomb*. New York: Simon and Schuster, 1996.

————. *The Making of the Atomic Bomb.* New York: Simon and Schuster, 1986.

Richelson, Jeffrey T. *Spying on the Bomb: American Nuclear Intelligence from Nazi Germany to Iran and North Korea.* New York: W. W. Norton, 2006.

Ritter, Scott. *Endgame: Solving the Iraq Problem—Once and For All.* New York: Simon and Schuster, 1999.

Ritter, Scott, and William Rivers Pitt. *War on Iraq: What Team Bush Doesn't Want You to Know.* London: Profile Books, 2002.

Roberts, Paul. *The End of Oil: On the Edge of a Perilous New World.* Boston and New York: Houghton Mifflin, 2004.

Romerstein, Herbert, and Eric Breindel. *The Venona Secrets: Exposing Soviet Espionage and America's Traitors.* Washington: Regency Publishing, 2000.

Rubin, Trudy. *Willful Blindness: The Bush Administration and Iraq.* Philadelphia: Philadelphia Inquirer, 2004.

Sagdeev, Roald Z. *The Making of a Soviet Scientist: My Adventures in Nuclear Fusion and Space from Stalin to Star Wars.* New York: John Wiley & Sons, 1994.

St. Francis Historical Committee. *Harvest of Memories: The St. Francis Story.* Amarillo, Tex.: Southwestern Publications, 1983.

Sampson, Anthony. *The Arms Bazaar.* London: Coronet, 1978.

Schlesinger, Arthur M., Jr. *A Thousand Days: John F. Kennedy in the White House.* Cambridge, Mass.: Riverside Press, 1965.

Schwartz, Stephen I., ed. *Atomic Audit: The Costs and Consequences of U.S. Nuclear Weapons Since 1940.* Washington: Brookings Institution Press, 1998.

Seaborg, Glenn T. *Adventures in the Atomic Age.* New York: Farrar, Straus and Giroux, 2001.

Seaborg, Glenn T., and Benjamin S. Loeb. *Stemming the Tide: Arms Control in the Johnson Years.* Lexington, Mass., and Toronto: Lexington Books, 1987.

Shultz, George P. *Turmoil and Triumph: My Years as Secretary of State.* New York: Charles Scribner's Sons, 1993.

Smith, Hedrick. *The Power Game: How Washington Works.* Glasgow: Fontana, Collins, 1988.

Smyth, Henry D. *Atomic Energy for Military Purposes: The Official Report on the Development of the Atomic Bomb Under the Auspices of the United States Government, 1940–1945.* Princeton: Princeton University Press, 1945.

Sokolski, Henry D. *The Best of Intentions: America's Campaign Against Strategic Weapons Proliferation.* Westport, Conn., and London: Praeger Publishers, 2001.

Sorensen, Theodore C. *Kennedy.* New York: Harper and Row, 1965.

Stewart, James B. *The Partners: Inside America's Most Powerful Law Firms.* New York: Simon and Schuster, 1983.

Talbott, Strobe. *The Master of the Game: Paul Nitze and the Nuclear Peace.* New York: Alfred A. Knopf, 1988.

Taylor, June H., and Michael D. Yokell. *Yellowcake: The International Uranium Cartel.* New York: Pergamon Press, 1979.

Thackara, James. *America's Children.* London: Chatto and Windus/Hogarth Press, 1984.

Trevan, Tim. *Saddam's Secrets: The Hunt for Iraq's Hidden Weapons.* London: HarperCollins, 1999.

Walker, Martin. *The Cold War: A History.* London: Holt Paperbacks, 1995.

Walker, Samuel J. *Permissible Dose: A History of Radiation Protection in the Twentieth Century.* Berkeley and Los Angeles: University of California Press, 2000.

———. *A Short History of Nuclear Regulation, 1946–1999*. Washington: U.S. Nuclear Regulatory Commission, 2000.

———. *Three Mile Island: A Nuclear Crisis in Historical Perspective*. Berkeley and Los Angeles: University of California Press, 2004.

Wasserman, Harvey, and Norman Solomon. *Killing Our Own: The Disaster of America's Experience with Atomic Radiation*. New York: Delta, 1992.

Weart, Spencer R. *Scientists in Power*. Cambridge and London: Harvard University Press, 1979.

Weinberg, Alvin, Marcelo Alonso, and Jack N. Barkenbus, eds. *The Nuclear Connection: A Reassessment of Nuclear Power and Nuclear Proliferation*. New York: A Washington Institute Book, Paragon House Publishers, 1985.

Weisgall, Jonathan M. *Operation Crossroads: The Atomic Tests at Bikini Atoll*. Annapolis, Md.: Naval Institute Press, 1994.

Welsome, Eileen. *The Plutonium Files: America's Secret Medical Experiments in the Cold War*. New York: Dial Press, 1999.

Watson, Mary Ann. *The Expanding Vista: American Television in the Kennedy Years*. Durham: Duke University Press, 1994.

Wells, H. G. *The Time Machine*. 1895; New York: Bantam Books, 1968.

Wordsworth, William. *Selected Poems*, ed. George W. Meyer. New York: Appleton-Century-Crofts, 1950.

Wrong, Michela. *In the Footsteps of Mr. Kurtz: Living on the Brink of Disaster in Mobutu's Congo*. London: Fourth Estate, 2000.

York, Herbert. *The Advisors*. Stanford: Stanford University Press, 1989.

Zuckerman, Solly. *Monkeys, Men and Missiles: An Autobiography, 1946–88*. London: Collins, 1988.

———. *Six Men Out of the Ordinary*. London: Peter Owen, 1992.

Reports, Research Papers, Speeches, and Historical Documents

Ad Hoc Working Group on Non-Proliferation and Arms Control. *Non-Proliferation and Arms Control: Issues and Options for the Clinton Administration*. Washington, January 1993.

Albright, David, and Kevin O'Neill. *The Challenges of Fissile Material Control*. Washington: Institute for Science and International Security, 1999.

Alvarez, Robert. *The Risks of Making Nuclear Weapons*. Washington: Institute for Policy Studies. August 23, 2006.

"The Baruch Plan (Presented to the United Nations Atomic Energy Commission, June 14, 1946)," http://www.atomicarchive.com/Docs/Deterrence/BaruchPlan .shtml.

Bell, J. N. B., and G. Shaw. "Ecological Lessons from the Chernobyl Accident." Department of Biological Sciences/Environmental Science & Technology, Imperial College at Silwood Park, Ascot, Berkshire, UK. Undated, courtesy of authors.

Bukharin, Oleg, Thomas B. Cochran, and Robert S. Norris. *New Perspectives on Russia's Ten Secret Cities*. Washington: Natural Resources Defense Council. October 1999.

Burr, William, and Thomas S. Blanton. "The Submarines of October: U.S. and Soviet Naval Encounters During the Cuban Missile Crisis." National Security

Archive Electronic Briefing Book no. 75, October 31, 2002, http://www.gwu.edu/~nsarchiv/NSAEBB/NSAEBB75.

Canberra Commission on the Elimination of Nuclear Weapons. *Report of the Canberra Commission on the Elimination of Nuclear Weapons.* Canberra, August 1996.

Carnegie Commission on Preventing Deadly Conflict. *Preventing Deadly Conflict—Final Report.* Washington, December 1997.

Carter, Jimmy. Executive Order: Export of Special Nuclear Material and Components to India. June 19, 1980.

Christopher, Warren. "Testimony by. . . . deputy secretary of state before the Senate Foreign Relations Committee and Senate Governmental Affairs Committee." Washington, D.C., June 19, 1980.

Civiak, Robert. *Still at It: An Analysis of the Department of Energy's Fiscal Year 2007 Budget Request for Nuclear Weapons Activities.* Prepared for Tri-Valley CAREs, Livermore, Calif., http://www.trivalleycares.org/new/reports.html.

Cochran, Thomas B. "How Safe is Yucca Mountain? A Case Study." Presented at the symposium Uncertainty in Long Term Planning—Nuclear Waste Management, Vanderbilt University, Nashville, Tenn., January 7, 2008.

Dale, A. A. *Monitoring of Radioactivity in Air and Rainwater in the U.K.—Annual Results Report 2001.* Commissioned for UK Department for Environment, Food, and Rural Affairs, Radioactive Substances Division. London, November 2002.

Duarte, Sergio, "Moral Leadership and Nuclear Weapons," Keynote Lecture, 2008 Sarah Smith Memorial Conference on Moral Leadership, Yale Divinity School, September 19, 2008.

Easlea, Brian. "Conflict, Science and the Garden of Eden." The Second Keith Roby Memorial Lecture in Community Science, Murdoch University, August 15, 1984.

Edlow, Samuel. *Quarterly Report, Trends in Traffic Management of Nuclear Materials.* October 15, 1968, courtesy of Edlow International.

———. "Reflections of a Lucky Man." March 1991, self-published, courtesy Sam and Frances Edlow.

Eisenhower, Dwight D. "Farewell Radio and Television Address to the American People, January 17, 1961." Public Papers of the Presidents, Dwight D. Eisenhower, 1960, 1035–1040, http://coursesa.matrix.msu.edu/~hst306/documents/indust.html.

Fairlie, Ian, and David Sumner. *The Other Report on Chernobyl (TORCH): An Independent Scientific Evaluation of Health and Environmental Effects 20 Years After the Nuclear Disaster . . ."* Commissioned by Rebecca Harms, MEP, Greens/EFA in the European Parliament. Berlin, Brussels, Kiev: April 2006.

Feiveson, H. A. "Nuclear Power, Nuclear Proliferation, and Global Warming." Forum on Physics & Society of the American Physical Society, January 2003.

"Nuclear Facts: New nuclear power plants are unlikely to provide a significant fraction of future U.S. needs for low-carbon energy." Factsheet, Natural Resources Defense Council, February 2007, http://www.nrdc.org/nuclear/plants/plants/pdf.

Gagarinskii, Andrei. "Nuclear Renaissance: A View from Russia." World Nuclear Association Annual Meeting, London, September 2002.

Garland, J. A. *Environmental Radioactivity from Chernobyl*. Commissioned for UK Department of the Environment, Radioactive Substances Division. London, July 1992.

Glaser, Alexander, and Frank von Hippel. "Global Cleanout: Reducing the Threat of HEU-fueled Nuclear Terrorism." *Arms Control Today*, January/February 2006.

Glenn, John. "At a Crossroads: An Examination of U.S. Nuclear Non-Proliferation Policy." *Harvard International Review* 14, no. 4 (Spring 1992).

Hansen, James H. "Soviet Deception in the Cuban Missile Crisis: Learning from the Past," n.d., http://www.cia.gov/library/center-for-the-study-of-intelligence/csi-publications/csi-studies/studies/vol46no1/article06.html.

International Atomic Energy Agency. Board of Governors. "Technical Co-Operation: Project Schedules for 1992." Vienna, November 1991.

———. Director General. "The Agency's Technical Co-Operation Activities in 1991." Vienna, August 1992.

———. *Environmental Consequences of the Chernobyl Accident and Their Remediation: Twenty Years of Experience*. Vienna, 2006.

International Institute for Strategic Studies. *Nuclear Programmes in the Middle East: In the Shadow of Iran*. London, May 20, 2008.

———. *Measures to Strengthen International Co-operation in Nuclear Safety and Radiological Protection*. Report to the IAEA General Conference, First Special Session, Post-Accident Review Meeting. Vienna, September 24, 1986.

International Nuclear Safety Advisory Group. INSAG-1. "Summary Report on the Post-Accident Review Meeting on the Chernobyl Accident." Vienna, International Atomic Energy Agency, 1986.

———. INSAG-7. "The Chernobyl Accident: Updating of INSAG-1." Vienna, International Atomic Energy Agency, 1992.

International Panel on Fissile Materials. Program on Science and Global Security, Princeton University. Reports available online at http://www.fissilematerials.org.

  Global Fissile Material Report 2006.

  Global Fissile Material Report 2007.

  Research Report 1. *Fissile Materials in South Asia: The Implications of the U.S.-India Nuclear Deal*. Z. Mian, A. H. Nayyar, R. Rajaraman, and M. V. Ramana. September 2006.

  Research Report 2. *Japan's Spent Fuel and Plutonium Management Challenges*. Tadahiro Katsuta and Tatsujiro Suzuki. September 2006.

  Research Report 3. *Managing Spent Fuel in the United States: The Illogic of Reprocessing*. Frank von Hippel. January 2007.

  Research Report 4. *Spent Fuel Reprocessing in France*. Mycle Schneider and Yves Marignac. May 2008.

  Research Report 5. *The Legacy of Reprocessing in the United Kingdom*. Martin Forwood. July 2008.

Institute for Science and International Security. Washington, D.C. Reports available online at http:/www.isis-online.org.

  "Can Military Strikes Destroy Iran's Gas Centrifuge Program? Probably Not." David Albright, Paul Brannan, and Jacqueline Shire. August 7, 2008.

  "Swiss Smugglers Had Advanced Nuclear Weapons Designs." David Albright. June 16, 2008.

"May 26, 2008 IAEA Safeguards Report on Iran: Centrifuge Operation Improving and Cooperation Lacking on Weaponization Issues. Rev. 2." David Albright, Jacqueline Shire, and Paul Brannan. May 29, 2008.

"The Al Kibar Reactor: Extraordinary Camouflage, Troubling Implications." David Albright and Paul Brannan. May 12, 2008.

"Syria Update III: New Information About Al Kibar Reactor Site." David Albright and Paul Brannan. April 24, 2008.

"Briefing Notes from February 2008 IAEA Meeting Regarding Iran's Nuclear Program." April 11, 2008.

IAEA Iran Latest—A Balanced Safeguards Report. David Albright and Jacqueline Shire. February 22, 2008.

"Iran Installing More Advanced Centrifuges at Natanz Pilot Enrichment Plant: Factsheet on the P-2/IR-2 Centrifuge." David Albright and Jacqueline Shire. February 7, 2008.

"ISIS Statement Regarding 'A Strike in the Dark' in the February 11 Issue of the *New Yorker,* by Seymour Hersh." February 6, 2008.

"Slowly but Surely, Pyongyang Is Moving." David Albright and Jacqueline Shire. Op-ed in the *Washington Post.* January 24, 2008.

"North Korea's Plutonium Declaration: A Starting Point for an Initial Verification Process. Rev. 1." David Albright, Paul Brannan, and Jacqueline Shire. January 10, 2008.

"November IAEA Report: Centrifuge File Not Closed; Natanz Enrichment Expands." David Albright and Jacqueline Shire. November 15, 2007.

"A Witches Brew? Evaluating Iran's Uranium-Enrichment Progress." David Albright and Jacqueline Shire. *Arms Control Today,* November 2007.

"Syria Update II: Syria Buries Foundation of Suspect Reactor Site." ISIS Imagery Brief. October 26, 2007.

"Syria Update: Suspect Reactor Site Dismantled." ISIS Imagery Brief. David Albright, Paul Brannan, and Jacqueline Shire. October 25, 2007.

"Suspect Reactor Construction Site in Eastern Syria: The Site of the September 6 Israeli Raid?" ISIS Imagery Brief. David Albright and Paul Brannan. October 24, 2007.

"USIP Working Paper: Disabling DPRK Nuclear Facilities." David Albright and Paul Brannan. October 25, 2007.

"Team GmbH and Ernest Piffl: The Case of the Illegal Centrifuge Preforms Exports to Pakistan." 2003.

John F. Kennedy Presidential Library & Museum. "The World on the Brink: John F. Kennedy and the Cuban Missile Crisis," http://www.jfklibrary.org/jfkl/cmc.

Kennedy, John F. News Conference 42, August 29, 1962, http://www.jfklibrary.org/Historical+Resources/Archives/Reference+Desk/Press+Conferences/003POF05Pressconference42_08291962.htm, September 2008.

———. "Statement on Cuba, September 4, 1962," http://www.mtholyoke.edu/acad/intrel/jfkstate.htm.

Keystone Center. *Nuclear Power Joint Fact-Finding.* Keystone, Colo., June 2007.

Kissinger, Henry A. Memorandum for the President. Subject: Israeli Nuclear Program, with Summary of the Situation and Issues. July 19, 1969, declassified 2007. Courtesy of David Stout, *New York Times.*

———. Memorandum for the President. Subject: Israel's Nuclear Program. November 6, 1969, declassified 2002. Courtesy of David Stout, *New York Times.*

Kudrik, Igor, Charles Digges, Alexander Nikitin, Nils Bøhmer, Vladimir Kuznetsov, and Vladislav Larin. "The Russian Nuclear Industry: The Need for Reform." *Bellona Report* 4 (2004).

Latell, Brian. "Intelligence in Recent Public Literature: *The Castro Obsession,* by Don Bohning. Review," https://www.cia.gov/library/center-for-the-study -of-intelligence/csi-publications/csi-studies/studies/vol49no4/Castro _Obsession_10.htm.

Long, Jane C. S., and Rodney C. Ewing. "Yucca Mountain: Earth-Science Issues at a Geologic Repository for High-Level Nuclear Waste." Annual Review of Earth and Planetary *Science*, 2004.

Lyons, Peter B. "Challenges Facing the NRC Administrative Judges." Remarks by NRC Commissioner Lyons, Annual Meeting, NRC Administrative Judges, Washington, February 5, 2008.

McCone, John A. "Memorandum of Mongoose Meeting Held on Thursday." October 4, 1962. Avalon Project at Yale Law School, http://www.yale.edu/ lawweb/avalon/diplomacy/forrel/cuba/cuba008.htm.

National Security Archive, George Washington University. "The Cuban Missile Crisis, 1962: The 40th Anniversary," http://www.gwu.edu/~nsarchiv/nsa/ cuba_mis_cri/declass.htm.

Norris, Robert S., Andrew S. Burrows, and Richard W. Fieldhouse. *Nuclear Weapons Databook,* vol. 5, *British, French, and Chinese Nuclear Weapons.* Boulder, Colo.: Westview Press, 1994.

"Nuclear Facts: New nuclear power plants are unlikely to provide a significant fraction of future U.S. needs for low-carbon energy." Factsheet, Natural Resources Defense Council, February 2007, http://www.nrdc.org/nuclear/ plants/plants/pdf.

Nuclear Regulatory Commission: In the Matter of the Application of Edlow International Company, as Agent for the Government of India, to Export Special Nuclear Material. Before the U.S. Nuclear Regulatory Commission, Washington, D.C.

   Natural Resources Defense Council, Inc., the Sierra Club and the Union of Concerned Scientists. Petition . . . for Leave to Intervene. License No. XSNM-845. March 1, 1976.

   Affidavit of Dennis H. Kux. March 11, 1976.

   Affidavit of Myron B. Kratzer. Docket No. XSNM-805. March 12, 1976.

   Affidavit of Dixon B. Hoyle. Docket No. XSNM-805. March 12, 1976.

   Brief for U.S. NRC on Petition to Review an Order of the U.S. NRC in the U.S. Court of Appeals for the District of Columbia Circuit, No. 76-1525, 1976.

   Petitioners' Response to the Commission's Letter of Inquiry of March 5, 1976. Docket Nos. XSNM-805 and XSNM-845. March 12, 1976.

   NRC Staff's Combined Answers to Petitions for Leave to Intervene . . . to Commission's Directive Dated March 5, 1976. XSNM-805, Docket No. 70-2071. XSNM-845, Docket No. 70-2131. March 12, 1976.

   Natural Resources Defense Council, Inc., the Sierra Club and the Union of Concerned Scientists. Petitioners' Supplemental Memorandum on Timeliness and Standing Issues. March 19, 1976.

   Affidavit of Adrian Fisher. Docket Nos. 70-2071 and 70-2131. March 19, 1976.

   Natural Resources Defense Council, Inc., the Sierra Club and the Union of Concerned Scientists. Petitioners' Response to the State Department on the Question of Further Delay on XSNM-805. License No. XSNM-805 and XSNM-845. Docket No. 70-2071 and 70-2131. March 23, 1976.

NRC Staff Supplemental Views Regarding Hearing Procedures. License No. XSNM-805 and XSNM-845. March 26, 1976.

Memorandum and Order. License No. XSNM-805. Docket No. 70-2071. July 2, 1976.

Natural Resources Defense Council, Inc., the Sierra Club and the Union of Concerned Scientists. For the July 20, 1976, Hearing on the Proposed Export of Special Nuclear Material to India . . . and Appendices." Docket No. 70-2131. July 8, 1976.

Statement of George W. Ball. Docket No. 70-2131. July 13, 1976.

Order. License No. XSNM-845. Docket No. 70-2131. July 19, 1976.

Order. License No. XSNM-1060, XSNM-1222. Docket Nos. 70-2485 and 70-2738. March 6, 1978.

Order. License No. XSNM-1222. Docket No. 70-2738. December 8, 1978.

Petitioners' Written Comments in Response to the Commission's Order of December 8, 1978. License No. XSNM-1222. Docket No. 70-2738. January 11, 1979.

Order. License No. XSNM-1222. Docket No. 70-2738. March 23, 1979.

Memorandum and Order. License Nos. XSNM-1379, 1569. XCOM-0240, 0250, 0376, 0381, 0395. May 16, 1980.

NUKEM. "Nuclear Renaissance: USA—Coping with New NPP Sticker Shock." *NUKEM Market Report*, April 2008.

Parker, Larry, and Mark Holt. *Nuclear Power: Outlook for New U.S. Reactors*. Washington: Congressional Research Service. May 31, 2006.

Perkovich, George, Jessica T. Mathews, Joseph Cirincione, Rose Gottemoeller, and Jon B. Wolfsthal. *Universal Compliance: A Strategy for Nuclear Security*. Washington: Carnegie Endowment for International Peace. March 2005.

Reynolds, Capt. K. C. USN Ret. "Boarding MARUCLA: A Personal Account from the Executive Officer of USS *Joseph P. Kennedy, Jr.*," http://www .battleshipcove.org/news-boarding-marucla.htm.

Richardson, Elliot L. Memorandum for the President. Subject: Israel's Nuclear Program. October 17, 1969. Enclosure: Memorandum of Conversation. Department of State. Participants: Lt. General Yitzhak Rabin, Ambassador of Israel; Shlomo Argov, Minister, Embassy of Israel; Moshe Raviv, Counselor, Embassy of Israel; The Under Secretary, Alfred L. Atherton, Jr., Country Director, Israel and Arab-Israeli Affairs. October 15, 1969. Declassified 2002. Courtesy David Stout, *New York Times*.

Rogovin, Mitchell, and George T. Frampton Jr. *Three Mile Island: A Report to the Commissioners and to the Public*. Washington: U.S. Nuclear Regulatory Commission, 1980.

Rotblat, Joseph, ed. *Proceedings of the First Pugwash Conference on Science and World Affairs, Pugwash, Nova Scotia, 7–10 July*." London: Pugwash Council, 1982.

Royal Commission on Environmental Pollution. *Nuclear Power and the Environment*. London, September 1976.

Schneider, Mycle. *Myths and Realities on Nuclear Power in the World . . . and Case Studies France and Turkey*. Heinrich-Böll-Foundation, Istanbul, April 20–21, 2007.

———. *Nuclear Power in France: Systemic Issues Influencing Cost*, March 2008.

Schneider, Mycle, et al. *Residual Risk: An Account of Events in Nuclear Power Plants Since the Chernobyl Accident in 1986.*" Commissioned by Rebecca Harms, MEP, Greens/EFA in the European Parliament. May 2007.

SL-1 Report Task Force. *Report on the Nuclear Incident at the SL-1 Reactor on January 3, 1961, at the National Reactor Testing Station.* Idaho Falls: U.S. Atomic Energy Commission, Idaho Operations Office, January 1962.

Soran, Diane M., and Danny B. Stillman. *An Analysis of the Alleged Kyshtym Accident.* Los Alamos: Los Alamos National Laboratory, January 1982.

"Soviet Intelligence Agents and Suspected Agents: Klaus Fuchs." Kew, National Archives (UK), http://www.nationalarchives.gov.uk/releases/2003/may22/fuchs.htm.

Speier, Richard. *Plutonium Decision-Making in the U.S. Government.* Commissioned by the Pacific Asia Regional Energy Security (PARES) Project, February 1998.

UK Atomic Energy Office. *Accident at Windscale No. 1 Pile on 10th October, 1957.* Presented to Parliament by the Prime Minister by Command of Her Majesty. London, November 1957.

UK Food Standards Agency and Scottish Environment Protection Agency. *Radioactivity in Food and the Environment, 2001.* London, 2002.

UK House of Commons. Select Committee on Energy, Session 1980–81. *The Government's Statement on the New Nuclear Power Programme.* London, February 13, 1981.

U.S. Commander in Chief of the Atlantic Command (CINCLANT). Historical Account of Cuban Crisis. CINCLANT, April 29, 1963. Cuban Missile Document Set, National Security Archive, George Washington University, http://www.gwu.edu/~nsarchiv.

U.S. Comptroller General. *Evaluation of U.S. Efforts to Promote Nuclear Non-Proliferation Treaty.* Report to the U.S. Congress. Washington, July 31, 1980.

U.S. Congress. Office of Technology Assessment. *Dismantling the Bomb and Managing the Nuclear Materials.* Washington, 1993.

U.S. Department of Energy. *Pantex Plant.* GA93-0036/HB. DOE Amarillo Area Office, 1993.

———. "16th Annual International Conference on Nuclear Engineering, Remarks as Prepared for Delivery for Assistant Secretary Dennis Spurgeon," May 12, 2008, www.doe.gov/6252.htm.

U.S. Department of State. "A Report on the International Control of Atomic Energy." Committee on Atomic Energy, Washington, D.C.: March 16, 1946.

———. AmEmbassy Tel Aviv to SecState WashDC, telegram. Subject: Dimona Visit. July 31, 1969, declassified 2002. Courtesy David Stout, *New York Times.*

———. *Cuban Missile Crisis and Aftermath.* Briefing Paper, October 1, 1962. *Foreign Relations of the United States, 1961–1963, Volume XI,* http://www.state.gov/www/about_state/history/frusXI/01_25.html.

———. Memorandum of Conversation. Subject: 1969 Dimona Visit. August 13, 1969, declassified 2006. Courtesy David Stout, *New York Times.*

U.S. Department of the Navy. *Report on the Naval Quarantine of Cuba, 1962: Quarantine 22–26 October.*" Chief of Naval Operations, Operational Archives Branch, Post 46 Command File, Box 10. Washington, January 12, 2001.

U.S. General Accounting Office. "Department of Energy: Uncertainties and Management Problems Have Hindered Cleanup at Two Nuclear Waste Sites." Testimony before the Task Force on Natural Resources and the Environment, Committee on the Budget, U.S. House of Representatives. Washington, July 12, 2000.

———. *Nuclear Weapons: Safety, Technical, and Manpower Issues Slow DOE's Disassembly Efforts.*" Report to the Chairman, Committee on Governmental Affairs, U.S. Senate. Washington, October 1993.

———. *Uranium Mill Tailings: Cleanup Continues, but Future Costs Are Uncertain.* Washington, December 15, 1995.

U.S. Government Accountability Office. *Nuclear Safety: NRC's Oversight of Fire Protection at U.S. Commercial Nuclear Reactor Units Could Be Strengthened.*" Washington, June 2008.

U.S. House. Committee on Interior and Insular Affairs, Subcommittee on Energy and the Environment. *Observations on the Reactor Safety Study*, Washington, January 1977.

U.S. House. Committee on Interior and Insular Affairs, Majority Staff. *Reporting of Information Concerning the Accident at Three Mile Island.* Washington, March 1981.

U.S. House. Subcommittee on Energy and the Environment of the Committee on Interior and Insular Affairs, *Observations of the Reactor Safety Study.* Washington, January 1977.

———. *Quality Assurance at the Zimmer Nuclear Station.* Oversight Hearing. Washington, June 10, 1982.

———. *Quality Assurance at the Zimmer Nuclear Station, part II.* Oversight Hearing. Washington, September 14, 1982.

———. *Reactor Safety Study Review.* Oversight Hearing. Washington, February 26, 1979.

———. *Recycling of Plutonium.* Oversight Hearing. Washington, September 20, 21, 28, 1976.

U.S. Joint Chiefs of Staff Evaluation Board for Operations Crossroads. *The Evaluation of the Atomic Bomb as a Military Weapon. The Final Report . . . for Operations Crossroads, Enclosure D.* June 30, 1947. National Archives, College Park, Md.

U.S. Joint Chiefs of Staff. Records of Operation Crossroads. NND943011 FG218, Boxes 229–233. National Archives, College Park, Md.

UN Special Commission (UNSCOM). Reports on Iraq to the UN Securty Council. New York: S/1996/848 of 11/10/96; S/1997 of 11/4/97; S/1999/94 of 29/1/99; S/1996/356 of 30/3/99.

Union of Concerned Scientists. *Research Reactors Fueled by Highly Enriched Uranium.* http://www.ucsusa.org.

"Waste Confidence and Waste Challenges: Managing Radioactive Materials." Remarks prepared for NRC chairman Dale E. Klein, Waste Management Symposium, Phoenix, Arizona, February 25, 2008, http://www.nrc.gov/reading-rm/doc-collections/commission/speeches/2008/s<->08-008.html.

World Health Organization. *Health Effects of the Chernobyl Accident and Special Health Care Programmes.* Geneva, 2006; www.who.int/ionizing_radiation.

Worldwatch Institute. "Nuclear Prospects Unclear." *Environmental Valuation & Cost-Benefit News*, July 1, 2008.

Articles

"Atoms for All to See." *Newsweek*, c. January 1955. Courtesy Bill and Lucy Emerson.

Albright, David. "When Could Iran Get the Bomb?" *Bulletin of Atomic Scientists*, July/August 2007.

Albright, David, and Corey Gay. "A Flash from the Past." *Bulletin of Atomic Scientists*, November/December 1997.

Arbatov, Alexei, and Rose Gottemoeller. "New Presidents, New Agreements? Advancing US-Russian Strategic Arms Control." *Arms Control Today*, July/August 2008.

Allison, Graham. "Nuclear 9/11: The Ongoing Failure of Imagination." *Bulletin of Atomic Scientists*, September/October 2006.

Alvarez, Robert. "Reducing the Risks of High-Level Radioactive Wastes at Hanford." *Science & Global Security*, June 7, 2004.

Arkin, William M. "Nuclear 9/11: The Continuing Misuses of Fear." *Bulletin of Atomic Scientists*, September/October 2006.

Associated Press. "Nominee for Energy Post Is Accused of Lying." December 20, 1989.

Baldwin, Henry. "China's Bomb: Grave Problems Posed for West." *New York Times*, October 18, 1964.

Ball, Jeffrey. "France's Nuclear Push Transforms Energy Equation." *Wall Street Journal*, March 28, 2006.

Barry, John, and Carroll Bogert. "Special Report—Russia's Nuclear Secrets: Inside a Closed Atomic City." *Newsweek*, February 5, 1996.

Bidwai, Praful. "N-deal and Beyond." *Frontline*, July 29–August 10, 2007.

Blair, Bruce G. "Keeping Presidents in the Nuclear Dark." Episode 1: "The Case of the Missing 'Permissive Action Links,'" February 11, 2004. Episode 2: "The SIOP Option That Wasn't," February 16, 2004. Bruce Blair's Nuclear Column, Center for Defense Information, http://www.cdi.org/blair.

———. "Primed and Ready." *Bulletin of Atomic Scientists*, January/February 2007.

Blair, Bruce G., and Garry D. Brewer. "The Terrorist Threat to World Nuclear Programs." *Journal of Conflict Resolution* 31, no. 3 (September 1977): 379–403. Available online at http://www.cdi.org/blair/terrorist-threat.cfm.

Broad, William J. "Energy Agency Opens Files on Iraq." *International Herald Tribune*, April 24, 1992.

———. "U.S. Ignored Early Alert on Iraqi Nuclear Project." *International Herald Tribune*, April 21, 1992.

Broad, William J., and David E. Sanger. "Vienna Meeting on Arms Data Reignites Dispute with Iran over Nuclear Program." *New York Times*, March 3, 2008.

Cirincione, Joseph. "The Greatest Threat to Us All." *New York Review of Books*, March 6, 2008.

———. "Nuclear Cave In," *PacNet*, no. 8A. Pacific Forum CSIS, March 2, 2006.

Cohen, Avner. "Crossing the Threshold: The Untold Nuclear Dimension of the 1967 Arab-Israel War and Its Contemporary Lessons." *Arms Control Today*, June 2007.

Cohen, Avner, and William Burr. "Israel Crosses the Threshold." *Bulletin of Atomic Scientists*, May/June 2006.

Coll, Steve. "The Atomic Emporium." *New Yorker*, August 7, 14, 2006.

Cooke, Stephanie. "The Aftermath of the Accident at Three Mile Island." *Cycle*, Power Reactor and Development Corporation, Tokyo, October, 1982.

———. "Bomb Squad." *GQ, London*, October 1992.

———. "Boom and Bust." *GQ, London*, December 1994.

———. "The Great Nuke Chase." *GQ, London*, February 1995.

———. "Letters: Remembering Jo." *Bulletin of Atomic Scientists*, January/February 2006.

———. "Nuclear Inspections: Time for Hardball." *International Herald Tribune*, Op-Ed page, July 30, 1992.

———. "Official Reactions to Chernobyl." *Index on Censorship*, July 1987.

———. "Reprocessing: Just Within Reach?" *Bulletin of Atomic Scientists*, July/August 2006.

Cooke, Stephanie, and James Thackara. "Ekeus vs. Saddam: A Job Well Done, but There's More to Do." *International Herald Tribune*, Op-Ed page, June 25, 1997.

———. "Time to Get Tough with Nuclear Villains."*Reader's Digest*, March 1994.

Crick, Michael. "How Britain Helped Israel Get the Bomb." *BBCNewsnight*, August 3, 2005, http://news.bbc.co.uk/2/hi/programmes/newsnight/4743493.stm.

Dobbs, Michael. "The Day Adlai Stevenson Showed 'Em at the U.N." *Washington Post*, February 5, 2003.

Edwards, Mike. "Chernobyl: Living with the Monster." *National Geographic*, August 1994.

Edwards, Rob. "How Many More Lives Will Chernobyl Claim?" *New Scientist*, April 6, 2006.

Finn, Peter. "Putin Threatens Ukraine on NATO." *Washington Post*, February 13, 2008.

Gilinsky, Victor. "Heard About the Near-Accident at the Ohio Nuclear Plant? I'm Not Surprised." *Washington Post*, April 28, 2002.

———. "Israel's Bomb." *New York Review of Books*, May 13, 2004.

———. "'Miracle Metal' and Embarrassment for Yucca Backers." *Las Vegas Review-Journal*, November 25, 2003.

———. "Time for More NUMEC Information." *Arms Control Today*, June 2008.

Golovin, I. N., and Yuri N. Smirnov. *It Began in Zamoskvorechie*. Moscow: Kurchatov Institute, 1989.

Gusterson, Hugh. "Taking RRW Personally." *Bulletin of Atomic Scientists*, July/August 2007.

Harvey, John R. "Nonproliferation's New Soldier." *Bulletin of Atomic Scientists*, July/August 2007.

Henry, Tom. "Davis-Besse 'Deception' Trial to Begin." *Toledo Blade*, August 8, 2008.

Hersey, John. "From the Archives: The Day the Bomb Fell." *New Yorker*, July 31, 1995.

Hersh, Seymour. "On the Nuclear Edge." *New Yorker*, March 29, 1993.

———. "Watching the Warheads: Pakistan's Nuclear Weapons at Risk." *New Yorker*, November 5, 2001.

Hertzberg, Hendrik. "The Nuclear Jubilee." *New Yorker*, July 31, 1995.

Hibbs, Mark. "The Unmaking of a Nuclear Smuggler." *Bulletin of Atomic Scientists*, November/December 2006.

Highfield, Roger. "Windscale Five: 'We Were Too Busy to Panic.'" *Daily Telegraph*, October 9, 2007.

Holloway, David. "Soviet Nuclear History: Sources for *Stalin and the Bomb*." *Cold War International History Project Bulletin* 4 (Fall 1994).

———. "Soviet Scientists Speak Out." *Bulletin of Atomic Scientists*, May 1993.

Ince, Martin. "The History of Windscale's Trail of Disaster." Review of *Windscale 1957*, by Lorna Arnold. *New Scientist*, April 4, 1992, http://www.newscientist.com/article/mg13418155.500-reviews-the-history-of-windscales-trail-of-disaster-.html.

Jones, Meirion. "Britain's Dirty Secret." *New Statesman*, March 13, 2006.

———. "How Britain Helped Israel Get the Bomb" Unpublished, courtesy of the author.

Kaplan, Fred. "JFK's First-Strike Plan." *Atlantic Monthly*, October 2001.

Keen, Sam. "A Secular Apocalypse." *Bulletin of Atomic Scientists*, January/February 2007.

Kenworthy, E. W. "Dirksen Dead in Capital at 73." *New York Times*, September 8, 1969.

Khariton, Yuri, and Yuri Smirnov. "The Khariton Version." *Bulletin of Atomic Scientists*, May 1993.

Kimball, Daryl G. "Dangerous Deal with New Delhi." *Baltimore Sun*, March 9, 2006.

Knapik, Mike, Margaret Ryan, and Ann MacLachlan. "West Protests Soviet Secrecy as Radiation Spreads from Chernobyl Melt." *Nucleonics Week*, May 1, 1986.

Langewiesche, William. "The Wrath of Khan." *Atlantic Monthly*, November 2005.

Layton, Lyndsey. "Whistle-Blower's Fight for Pension Drags On." *Washington Post*, July 7, 2007.

Leake, Jonathan. "The Man Who Flipped a Nation." *Bulletin of Atomic Scientists*, March/April 2007.

Levine, Hannah. "Birth of a Notion." *Bulletin of Atomic Scientists*, July/August 2007.

Lovins, Amory. "Mighty Mice." Viewpoint, *Nuclear Engineering International*, December 21, 2005.

MacFarlane, Allison. "Stuck on a Solution." *Bulletin of Atomic Scientists*, May/June 2006.

MacLachlan, Ann. "Western Scientists Wrestle with Chernobyl Meltdown Scenarios." *Nucleonics Week*, May 15, 1986.

Makhijani, Arjun. "The Soviet Nuclear Waste Explosion America Helped Cover Up (And Other Crimes Against Public Health)." *Japan Focus*, September 26, 2005, at George Mason University History News Network, http://hnn.us/roundup/entries/16364.html.

Makhijani, Arjun, and Stephen Schwartz. "Victims of the Bomb." In Schwartz, *Atomic Audit*, 395–432.

Makhijani, Arjun, Stephen I. Schwartz, and Robert S. Norris. "Dismantling the Bomb." In Schwartz, *Atomic Audit*, 353–91.

Makhijani, Arjun, Stephen I. Schwartz, and William J. Weida. "Nuclear Waste Management and Environmental Remediation." In Schwartz, *Atomic Audit*, 353–94.

Mian, Zia, and M. V. Ramana. "Triumph of Fear." *Bulletin of Atomic Scientists*, July/August 2007.

Milhollin, Gary. "Heavy Water Cheaters." *Foreign Policy*, Winter 1987–88.

Mayo, Anna. "The Big Duck Shoot." *Texas Observer*, December 21, 2001.

Mufson, Steven. "Video of Sleeping Guards Shakes Nuclear Industry." washingtonpost.com, January 4, 2008.

Myers, Steven Lee, and Thom Shanker. "Aides to Bush Say Russia Offensive Jeopardizes Ties." *New York Times*, August 15, 2008.

Norman, Lloyd. "Startling Atom Report Quashed by White House." *New York Times Herald*, October 14, 1947.

Norris, Robert S., and Hans M. Kristensen. "What's Behind Bush's Nuclear Cuts?" *Arms Control Today*, October 2004.

Norris, Robert S., Steven M. Kosniak, and Stephen I. Schwartz. "Deploying the Bomb." In Schwartz, *Atomic Audit*, 105–96.

Norris, Robert S., William M. Arkin, and William Burr. "Where They Were." *Bulletin of Atomic Scientists*, November/December 1999.

Nuclear Notebook, *Bulletin of Atomic Scientists*, available online at http://www.thebulletin.org.

Nusbaum, Marci Alboher. "Devine Intervention." *Legal Affairs*, November/December 2002.

O'Neill, Kevin. "Building the Bomb." In Schwartz, *Atomic Audit*, 33–104.

Oppenheimer, J. Robert. "The Failure of International Control." *Bulletin of Atomic Scientists*, February 1948. In Grodzins and Rabinowitch, *The Atomic Age*.

———. "International Control of Atomic Energy." *Bulletin of Atomic Scientists*, June 1946. In Grodzins and Rabinowitch, *The Atomic Age*.

"Oscar Buneman, Pioneer of Computer Simulation of Space, Dies at 79." Stanford University News Service, Stanford, Calif., January 26, 1993.

Pacala, Stephen, and Robert Socolow. "Toward a Hydrogen Economy." *Science Magazine*, August 13, 2004.

Panofsky, Wolfgang K. H. "A Damaging Designation." *Bulletin of Atomic Scientists*, January/February 2007.

Perkovich, George. "The Nuclear Program Stalls," *India's Nuclear Bomb: The Impact on Global Proliferation*. Berkeley, CA: University of California Press, 1999.

Pikayev, Alexander A. "Unfair Advantage." *Bulletin of Atomic Scientists*, July/August 2007.

Pike, John E., Bruce G. Blair, and Stephen I. Schwartz. "Defending Against the Bomb." In Schwartz, *Atomic Audit*, 269–326.

Polidori, Robert, and David Remnick. "Showcase: Chernobyl, Pictures from a Dead City." *New Yorker*, August 4, 2003.

Rees, Martin. "Grounds for Optimism." *Bulletin of Atomic Scientists*, January/February 2007.

Richter, Roger. "Suppose You Were a Reactor Inspector." *Washington Post*, June 24, 1981.

Rotblat, Joseph. "Leaving the Bomb Project." Unpublished, courtesy of the author.

———. "The Spy Who Never Was." Unpublished, courtesy of the author.

Safire, William. "What Was Iraq Supposed to Be Doing for America." *New York Times*, June 23, 1992.

Salama, Sammy, and Heidi Weber. "Arab Nuclear Envy." *Bulletin of Atomic Scientists*, September/October 2007.

Sayle, Murray. "Letter from Hiroshima: Did the Bomb End the War?" *New Yorker*, July 31, 1995.

Schell, Jonathan. "Genesis in Reverse." *Bulletin of Atomic Scientists*, January/February 2007.

Schwartz, Stephen I. "Congressional Oversight of the Bomb." In Schwartz, *Atomic Audit*, 485–518.

———. "Warheads Aren't Forever." *Bulletin of Atomic Scientists*, September/October 2005.

Sciolino, Elaine. "Voting Sets Up Left-Right Duel to Lead France." *New York Times*, April 23, 2007.

Shen, Dingli. "Upsetting a Delicate Balance." *Bulletin of Atomic Scientists*, July/August 2007.

Stecklow, Steve. "Nuclear Safety Reports Called into Question." *Wall Street Journal*, August 3, 2007.

Stiglitz, Joseph E. "Nukes for Sale." *Forbes*, May 27, 2002.

Stockman, Farah. "Iran's Nuclear Vision First Glimpsed at MIT." *Boston Globe*, March 12, 2007.

Stout, David. "Israel's Nuclear Arsenal Vexed Nixon." *New York Times*, November 29, 2007.

"Successful Test: U.S. Fires Bomb at High Altitude." Associated Press, *Portsmouth Herald*, October 16, 1962.

"The Chernobyl Accident." *British Nuclear Forum Bulletin*, May 1986.

Thomas, Steve D. "The Collapse of British Energy: The True Cost of Nuclear Power or a British Failure." *Economia delle fonti di energia e dell' ambiente* 1–2 (2003): 61–78.

———. "UK Decommissioning Funds: A Cautionary Tale." *Platts Power in Europe Viewpoint*, issue 477, June 5, 2006.

Thrall, Nathan, and Jesse James Wilkins. "Kennedy Talked, Khrushchev Triumphed." *New York Times*, Op-Ed page, May 22, 2008.

Union of Concerned Scientists. "Renewable Energy Tax Credit Extended Again, but Risk of Boom-Bust Cycles in World Industry Continues." February 14, 2007, http://www.ucsusa.org.

Uranium Intelligence Weekly. "A $25 Billion Preholiday Gift for Nuclear?" December 10, 2007.

———. "China's Biggest Pu Complex May Have Been Hit by Earthquake." May 19, 2008.

———. "Earthquakes vs. Global Warming: Japan's Nuclear Dilemma," June 16, 2008.

———. "Japan Steel Works: A Key to Nuclear Revival," May 27, 2008.

———. "License Extensions Under Fire in the U.S." January 22, 2008.

———. "Omnibus Spending Bill Retains $20.5 Billion for Nuclear," December 17, 2007.

———. "Sellafield's Future: To Call It Quits or Make More Plutonium?" September 2, 2008.

———. "TVO Announces Further Delays—and Disputes with Areva-Siemens." October 20, 2008.

———. "Year of the Renaissance for US?" January 7, 2008.

———. "Yucca Mountain Total Cost Estimates Revised Upward—Way Upward." August 11, 2008.

Wald, Matthew L. "Gate Crasher Shakes Up Nuclear Debate." *New York Times*, February 11, 1993.

Wald, Matthew L. "Getting Power to the People." *Bulletin of Atomic Scientists*, September/October 2007.

Wald Matthew L. "Nuclear Agency Said to Lag in Seeking Out crime." *New York Times*, January 31, 1988.

Warrick, Joby, and Walter Pincus. "The Saga of a Bent Spear." *Washington Post*, September 23, 2007.

Wattenberg, Ben, Joseph Rotblat, and Kosta Tsipis. "Remembering Bernie (Bernard Feld)." *Bulletin of Atomic Scientists*, May 1993.

Weida, William J. "The Economic Implications of Nuclear Weapons and Nuclear Deterrence." In Schwartz, *Atomic Audit*, 519–41.

Weiss, Leonard. "Pakistan: It's Déjà Vu All Over Again." *Bulletin of Atomic Scientists*, May/June 2004.

———. "Testimony on the U.S.-India Nuclear Deal." Before the House International Relations Committee, May 11, 2006.

Whitney, David. "With Democrats in Control, Yucca Project May Be Doomed." McClatchy Newspapers, December 18, 2006.

Zuckerman, Lord. "The New Nuclear Menace." *New York Review of Books*, June 24, 1993.

Television Documentaries and Interviews

BBC2. "Israel's Nuclear Whistleblower." Interview with Mordecai Vanunu. May 30, 2004.

Brian Lapping Associates. *The Second Russian Revolution 1989–1991*, Episode 2: "The Battle for Glasnost." Norma Percy, Paul Mitchell, and Mark Anderson, producers. Released 1991.

Kaufman Vision Productions. *Citizen Kurchatov: Stalin's Bombmaker*. Brian Kaufman, producer-director. Released 1999.

The Stock Company (TOR). *Nuclear Tango*. Vyacheslav Larionov, producer; Victor Buturlin, director and author. Released 1993.

Index

A Note on the Author

STEPHANIE COOKE has covered the nuclear industry since the 1980s. She is currently an editor for the Energy Intelligence Group and a contributor to the *Bulletin of Atomic Scientists*. She has written for the UK editions of *GQ* and *Vogue*, the *Index on Censorship*, and many other publications. After living in London for twenty years, she returned to the United States and now lives with her son in Kensington, Maryland.